Check Map in back
of plastic folder

China

Hints for using the Guide

Following the tradition established by Karl Baedeker in 1844, buildings and works of art, places of natural beauty and sights of particular interest, as well as hotels and restaurants of especially high quality, are distinguished by one ★ or two ★★.

To make it easier to locate the various places listed in the "A to Z" section of the Guide, their co-ordinates are shown in red at the head of each entry: e.g., Beijing **K 3/4**.

Coloured lines down the right-hand side of the page are an aid to finding the main heading in the Guide: blue stands for the Introduction (Nature, Culture, History, etc.), red for the "A to Z" section, and yellow indicates Practical Information.

Only a selection of hotels, restaurants and shops can be given; no reflection is implied therefore on establishments not included.

In a time of rapid change it is difficult to ensure that all the information given is entirely accurate and up-to-date, and the possibility of error can never be entirely eliminated.

Although the publishers can accept no responsibility for inaccuracies and omissions, they are constantly endeavouring to improve the quality of their Guides and are therefore always grateful for criticisms, corrections and suggestions for improvement.

Preface

This guide to China is one of the new generation of Baedeker guides.

These guides, illustrated throughout in colour, are designed to meet the needs of the modern traveller. They are quick and easy to consult, with the principal places of interest described in alphabetical order, and the information is presented in a format that is both attractive and easy to follow.

The subject of this guide is China, principally the huge People's Republic together with Tibet, but also including the independent island of Taiwan, the British Crown Colony of Hong Kong, and the territory of Macau, at present under Portuguese administration. (The last two are dealt with in greater detail in a separate Baedeker guide, entitled "Hong Kong".)

The guide is in three parts. The first part gives a general account of the country, its landscape, climate, flora and fauna, conservation areas, population, language, education and science, religion and philosophy, government and administration, economy, history, famous people, art and culture. A brief selection of quotations and a number of suggested itineraries provide a transition to the second part, in which the country's places and features of tourist interest – towns, provinces and autonomous regions – are described. The third part contains a variety of practical information. Both the sights and the practical information are listed in alphabetical order.

The new Baedeker guides are noted for their concentration on essentials and their convenience of use. They contain numerous specially drawn plans and colour illustrations, and at the end of the book is a large map making it easy to locate the various places described in the "A to Z" section of the guide with the help of the co-ordinates given at the head of each entry.

Editorial Note:

In this guide topographical and other proper nouns are reproduced in the Latin transcription (Chinese "Hanyu Pinyin") which was officially introduced by the Chinese Republic in 1979. Basically this solves the problem of earlier varying transcriptions, but nevertheless it leads to unusual renderings of names which have been used by English-speakers for a very long time (e.g. Canton, Peking, Nanking, etc.) To avoid confusion the Chinese (Hanyu Pinyin) forms have been used throughout this guide, except for Canton, Hong Kong, Inner Mongolia, Macau and Tibet which have retained their more familiar forms. Cross-references facilitate the location of most well-known places.

Contents

Nature, Culture, History
Pages 9–118

Facts and Figures 9
General Information 9 · Topography 11 · Climate 22 · Flora and Fauna 30 · Environmental Problems 33 · Population 36 · Language 33 · Education and Science 40 · Religion and Philosophy 42 · State and Administration 49 · Economy 54

Sights from A to Z
Pages 120–499

Anhui 120 · Anshan 121 · Baotou 123 · Beijing 124 · Canton 159 · Changchun 167 · Changjiang 169 · Changsha 173 · Changzhou 176 · Chengde 179 · Chengdu 182 · Chongqing 191 · Dali 196 · Dalian 199 · Datong 204 · Dunhuang 209 · Foshan 214 · Fujian 215 · Fushun 216 · Fuzhou 218 · Gansu 221 · Great Wall 223 · Guangdong 225 · Guangxi 226 · Guilin 228 · Guiyang 233 · Guizhou 236 · Haikou 237 · Hainan 238 · Handan 239 · Hangzhou 240 · Harbin 249 · Hebei 253 · Hefei 254 · Heilongjiang 256 · Henan 257 · Hengyang 258 · Hohhot 259 · Hong Kong 263 · Huai'an 276 · Hubei 276 · Hunan 278 · Huzhou 279 · Inner Mongolia 279 · Jiangsu 282 · Jiangxi 283 · Jiaxing 284 · Jilin 285 · Ji'nan 290 · Jingdezhen 292 · Jinggangshan 293 · Jinghong 294 · Jinhua 295 · Jiujiang 296 · Jiuquan 300 · Kaifeng 301 · Kashgar 304 · Kunming 308 · Lanzhou 315 · Lhasa 317 · Lianyungang 320 · Liaoning 321 · Liuzhou 323 · Luoyang 324 · Ma'anshan 329 · Macau 330 · Maotai 336 · Nanchang 337 · Nanjing 340 · Nanning 346 · Nantong 347 · Ningbo 351 · Ningxia 353 · Qingdao 354 · Qinghai 359 · Qinhuangdao 360 · Quanzhou 362 ·

Practical Information from A to Z
Pages 500–570

Air Transport 500 · Antiques 501 · Bath Houses 501 · Beaches 504 · Bicycles 504 · Business Hours 504 · Buses 506 · Chemists 506 · Chinese Society and the Visitor 507 · Currency 508 · Customs Regulations 508 · Diplomatic Representation 510 · Electricity 511 · Emergency Services 511 · Events 511 · Food and Drink 515 · Getting to

Index 571

Principal Sights 575

Imprint 576

Principal Tourist Sights Map 514

Golden Rules 574

Large Map of China at end of book

History 61

Famous People 74

Art and Culture 84
Painting 84 · Calligraphy 89 · Pottery 90 ·
Architecture 93 · Literature 98 · Opera 102
· Celebrations 103 · Food 104

China in Quotations 108

Suggested Routes 110

Qufu 365 · Sanya 370 · Shaanxi 371 ·
Shandong 373 · Shanghai 374 ·
Shantou 383 · Shanxi 383 · Shaoxing 384
· Shashi 386 · Shenyang 387 ·
Shenzhen 392 · Shijiazhuang 393 ·
Sichuan 397 · Suzhou 398 · Tai'an 404 ·
Taiwan 408 · Taiyuan 423 · Tianjin 428 ·
Tibet 432 · Turpan 437 · Ürümqi 439 ·
Weifang 442 · Weihai 443 · Wenzhou 443 ·

Wuhan 444 · Wuhu 450 · Wuxi 454 ·
Xiamen 458 · Xi'an 461 · Xiangfan 473 ·
Xigaze 475 · Xining 478 · Xinjiang 480 ·
Xuzhou 482 · Yan'an 483 · Yangzhou 484 ·
Yantai 487 · Yichang 487 · Yinchuan 488 ·
Yixing 489 · Yueyang 490 · Yunnan 491 ·
Zhanjiang 493 · Zhaoqing 493 ·
Zhejiang 494 · Zhengzhou 495 ·
Zhenjiang 497 · Zhuhai 498 · Zibo 499

China 520 · Health Precautions 522 ·
Hotels 523 · Information 538 ·
Insurance 542 · Language 543 ·
Maps 548 · Medical Assistance 548 ·
Motoring 549 · Mountaineering and
Trekking 549 · Museums 550 ·
Newspapers and Periodicals 550 ·
Open Cities 551 · Post 551 · Public
Holidays and Festivals 552 · Public

Transport 553 · Radio and Television 556
· Railways 556 · Restaurants 557 ·
Rickshaws 561 · Shipping and River
Boats 562 · Shopping and Souvenirs 563
· Sport 566 · Taxis 567 · Telephone 568 ·
Time 568 · Tipping 568 · Travel
Documents 569 · When to Go 569 ·
Youth Accommodation 570

Baedeker Specials

Giant Panda	34
Table Etiquette	105

The Middle

Throughout the 700 years since Europeans first read with astonishment Marco Polo's account of a 20-year sojourn at the court of Kublai Khan, the West has regarded China as the embodiment of all that is strange and exotic. Even today the country has lost none of its fascination, its utterly different culture dating back more than 5000 years making each visit a quite special experience. Incomparable palaces such as the Forbidden City and Summer Palace in Beijing recall the days of China's rule by celestial emperors, concubines and eunuchs. The Great Wall – at its most impressive where it passes just a little to the north of Beijing – winds for 6700km/4000 miles westward from the Yellow Sea to Jiayuguan in Central Asia. Ancient temples such as the monastic temple of the Princess of the Azure Cloud on Mount Taishan or the Confucian Temple in Qufu exude the spirit of age-old Eastern religions and philosophies. The cities of the Middle Kingdom, more than 50 of which have populations of over a million, and the coastal provinces, are today enjoying a soaring economic boom. This vast Asian country, big as a continent, offers limitless scope for travel in landscapes as varied as the steamy jungles of south Yunnan, the mighty snow-clad mountains of the west, and the endless Central Asian deserts along the old Silk Road.

Imperial Palace
the most significant and larges Chinese building

Heavenly Temple
Symbol of Heaven and Earth

Terracotta Army
Buried in the Emperor's Tomb

Kingdom

Northern China presents tourists with a rich range of opportunities, from riding shaggy ponies through the huge expanse of the Inner Mongolian steppe, sleeping in a Mongolian yurt, visiting Kasak nomads in the Altai and participating in the ancient martial art of kung fu at the Shaolin Monastery, to exploring the impressive Buddhist caves at Datong and Luoyang and joining in the celebration of the Ice Festival in the crisp winter frost of Manchuria. The appeal of southern China lies not only in the glittering, shoppers' paradise of Hong Kong, where East meets West in unique

Lotus
a significant meaning in Buddhism

synthesis, nor in Portuguese Macao, but equally in the Guilin Mountains, a karst landscape of truly fairytale beauty unmatched anywhere in the world. Whether it be a luxury cruise through the picturesque Changjiang gorges, a visit to Jingdezhen to fathom the secrets of the famous Chinese porcelain makers, a stroll through the magical gardens at Suzhou, a gourmet excursion into the culinary capital Canton to sample the various styles of Chinese cooking, an ascent of the holy Mount Emeishan in Sichuan, a trip to Lesham to marvel at the world's largest buddha, or just sunbathing on palm-fringed beaches in Hainan, China has something for every taste and hence all the essential ingredients for an unforgettable holiday in a quite exceptionally absorbing country.

Panda
feeds only on bamboo

Suzhou
The beautiful garden of the Humble Administrator

Facts and Figures

Over thousands of years China evolved almost isolated from the western hemisphere and today's visitors will come face to face with an unusual and different world. They will ask themselves searching questions and seek explanations. China is a "Kingdom of Symbols" – symbols which need to be decoded: from the Chinese characters to the dialects, from the shan-shui silk painting to the limestone mountains of Guilin, from the seemingly incomprehensible concepts of its religion to the complicated nature of contemporary politics. Everything is different and it can be difficult to unravel the many mysteries of Chinese life. Allow plenty of time to examine and reflect on the people and their environment. There is probably no other country in the world where external reality and superficial impressions count for so little.

Please do not regard this travel guide as some sort of all-embracing encyclopaedia on China – an impossible undertaking anyway – but rather as a reference point and as a source of accurate information.

General Information

China occupies by far the major part of the mainland of eastern Asia. The People's Republic of China lies between latitudes 18° and 54°N and longitudes 71° and 135°E – extending from the Pamir Mountains in the west to the Pacific Ocean, or more precisely the Yellow Sea, East China Sea and the South China Sea, in the east.

This huge country is bordered in the west by Tadzhikistan, in the north-west by Kirgizstan, in the north by Mongolia and in the north-east by Russia. On the eastern coast lies the Korean peninsula and China shares a common border with North Korea. In the south-east, the country is bordered by Vietnam, Laos and Myanmar (Burma) and further west by India, Bhutan, Nepal, Pakistan and Afghanistan.

Neighbouring countries

The island of Hainan, situated off the mainland in the South China Sea, is a province of the People's Republic of China, while Taiwan (Formosa) – regarded as an integral part (the 23rd province) of the People's Republic – now very much Western-oriented calls itself the "Republic of China". On the south-east coast, off the Pearl river estuary, lie Hong Kong, a British Crown Colony, and Macau, a Chinese territory under Portuguese administration.

Territory

"Ten thousand rivers, a thousand mountains" was how Mao Zedong once described his country and these features do indeed dominate the Chinese landscape. They have played a significant role in shaping the history of Chinese civilisation, the economy, human relationships, trade and the country's culture. They define the many and varied regions of the Chinese sub-continent.

Land of rivers and mountains

With a total surface area of 9,627,343sq.km/3,716,154sq. miles, China's area is roughly equivalent to that of Europe and is only exceeded by that of Canada. At its widest point the greatest distance between the eastern and western borders equals 4400km/2725 miles, while from north to south it measures about 4100km/2500 miles.

Area and dimensions

◄ *Countryside near Guilin*

General Information

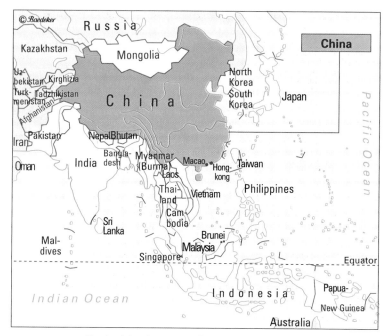

Borders	The land borders extend for 28,000km/17,300 miles and the coast covers more than 20,000km/12,400 miles. The current borders have evolved over thousands of years and countless wars.
Development	The beginnings of Chinese civilisation are to be seen around the middle reaches of the Yellow River (Huanghe) in the central eastern part of the country. Its territory gradually extended south, north and west and reached its present boundaries in the 18th c. under the Qing Dynasty.
Names and common terms	The "Mythical Land" or the "Middle Kingdom" as it was called in antiquity, became known by the Mongolian name of "Cathay" in the Middle Ages after the tales and written records of travellers such as Marco Polo. Following the demise of the Mongolian Yuan Dynasty, Europeans started to use the word "China" after Emperor Qin Shi Huangdi, the founder of the Qin Dynasty. In the last two centuries, after Qing Dynasty annexations, distinctions were drawn between the "China of the Eighteen Provinces" and "Outer China", the urban regions of the ancient Chinese civilisation and those regions which were colonised in later years. The terms "Inner China" and "Outer China" are still frequently heard and are used to describe the country in a geomorphological, economic and historical sense. Inner China refers to the flat, low-lying river regions, the main urban centres and the rural regions of intensive farming. Outer China stands for the mountain and desert regions, whose inhabitants live mainly from breeding livestock.
State and administration	The political history of China is covered on pages 49–53.

Topography

For a country which extends over 60 lines of longitude and 25 lines of latitude, all the geographical features typical of Asia can be found within its borders. The diverse and changing landscape exhibits many complex relief formations. The densely populated heartlands of the Pacific coastal plain and river basins, the agricultural settlements and industrial conurbations stand in stark contrast to the thinly populated, desolate semi-desert of outlying central Asia with its barren plateaux and steep high-mountain ranges. One third of China, a country sometimes described as the "Land of Mountains", consists of high-mountain ranges and high-surface plateaux, while one tenth comprises lower ranges and hilly lowlands. About 15% of the country is basin landscape and 10% is given over to intensively farmed lowland. This unfavourable topography goes some way towards explaining why only one eighth of the total surface area can be used for agricultural purposes.

Characteristics

The geology of East and Central Asia is determined by a complex structure of what are, in relation to the history of the earth, relatively stable, consolidated massifs. Around and between these Archaean mountain ranges, more recent evidence of earth movements can be found, demonstrating at the same time the continent's "growth ring".

Geology

The Sino-Siberian land mass represents the most important element in the geology of the Palaeozoic northern continent of Laurasia. This central region of the Eurasian plate is characterised by a mosaic of mountain ranges, composed of plates of varying degrees of rigidity, which during the various phases of mountain building gradually merged together. Only in recent times, in the course of Alpine-

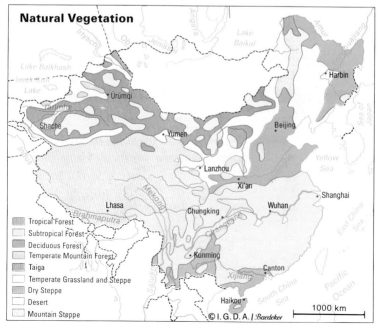

Natural Vegetation

Tropical Forest
Subtropical Forest
Deciduous Forest
Temperate Mountain Forest
Taiga
Temperate Grassland and Steppe
Dry Steppe
Desert
Mountain Steppe

1000 km

© I.G.D.A. / Baedeker

Himalayan fold movements, has the fault-block mountain range emerged. The craton of the east Siberian tableland (Angaria), which from the Pre-Cambrian Era has moved westward towards Europe linking with the east European platform (Fennosarmatia), came to form the heart of the Asian mainland and has subsequently been joined by further relatively stable plates, such as the Dsungarian, Tarim, Sinian (north Chinese/Korean), Tibetan and Vietnamese platform as well as the south Chinese and Indian plates. A huge belt of fold mountains serves as a dividing line and seam for these consolidated Pre-Cambrian primary rocks and the continental tables with their overlying rocks.

In East Asia there is evidence of four periods of tectonic activity, which have since the Pre-Cambrian repeatedly contributed to the upheavals. Between the Baikalic and the Sinian phase (the Assyntic Era), the Sayan Mountains and the mountains surrounding Lake Baikal of Angaria were raised, as well as the north Chinese platform in typical "Chinese strikes".

During the Palaeozoic in the several mountain formation phases of the Caledonian and Variscan Era, the Altaj massif and Kazakh rift were formed and in the Upper Palaeozoic Era the Pamirs, Kunlunshan, Nanshan, Quinlinshan and Tianshan were raised.

The two most recent phases, namely the Indo-Sinian (in the Upper Triassic Period) and the Yenshan orogeny, which is peculiar to China (between the Jurassic and Cretaceous periods), can be classified as Mesozoic (Cimmerian) forerunners of the modern Alpine-Himalayan era.

Even though a continuing consolidation of the Asiatic plate was identified in the Late Permian and Early Triassic, the force of the repeated movements was so great that massifs which were already consolidated and eroded broke up into separate mountain blocks.

Such relatively weak zones where continental mass breaks up are typical of East Asia and at every time of stress they were drawn into the cycle of emergence and peneplanation – a phenomenon known as "paraplatforms". Today's relief map of East and Central Asia is a result of these geological changes and the tectonic movements of relatively recent times.

With the impact of the Arabic-Iranian and Indian blocks (which had drifted away from Gondwana-land) against the Angarian buffer, to the south of the Eurasian plate at the collision point of the continents, a huge system of fold mountains emerged with overfolded nappe structures and considerable contractions in the earth's crust. The related translatory motion and pressure led to upfaults, wrench and stretching faults in the hinterland and generally to a reactivation of old mountain complexes. The huge upward movements of upthrown crust in the region of the most recently formed belt of fold mountains explains the emergence and formation of the greatest mountain range in the world.

This recent upheaval in the Central Asian mainland massif, linked with German-style fault tectonics, has led to a distinctive terraced land formation. The drop from the Asiatic mainland block to the Pacific Ocean takes place in a series of terraces, which lead down from west to east from the Tibetan Plateau to the Pacific Ocean floor like a giant staircase.

It is generally possible to discern four main terraces, in which the plateaux follow on from one another, falling off gently towards the west, but with the steep faces of the tilt block towards the east. The eastern edge of Tibetan terrace follows the course of the 104th meridian. To the north the high plateau is bordered by the Altunshan and the Nanshan. The Mongolian terrace runs along the Greater Xingan Shan, the Taihangshan and the Hukwang fault, marking the boundary between East and Upper Asia. The Manchurian terrace is formed by the Sikhote Alin Range, the Korean coastal mountains and the arc of the mountains. The boundary with the Mongolian basin is formed by the south Chinese coast. The Japanese terrace corresponds with the drop from the continental mainland to the Pacific plate with its island arcs and deep-sea trenches of the oceanic undercurrent zone.

These steps which as a rule follow a south-west to north-east track are crossed in various places by striking east-west fault lines, so that China's landscape is often characterised by basins and these can also be used to draw topographical distinctions between the various parts of the country, e.g. North Chinese Highlands, Changjiang lowland basin.

Topographical divisions

East Asia and Central Asia form two major regions of the Asian sub-continent and both include Chinese territory. They can be broken down into a total of seven distinct sub-regions. East Asia consists of Manchuria, North and South China, plus the intervening dividing line around the Central Chinese Mountain Belt, while Central Asia is formed from the Tibetan Plateau, the Mongolian Plateau and the basin area surrounded by a ring of mountains.

The extremes of temperature with cold, dry, almost polar winters and hot humid summers, typical of a continental climate, mark out this region which is bordered by the Lesser Xingan Range, the Amur river valley and the Russian frontier to the north, by Sinian mountain ranges which separate Manchuria from Korea in the east and from lowland China in the south-west.

East Asia
North-east China
(Manchuria)

Manchuria itself can be divided into three independent regions: the most important being lowland Manchuria with the Songhua plain and the thinly populated, barren sandy steppes of the Eastern Gobi to the north but in the south the lowlands have been transformed by man from wooded steppe to intensively farmed arable land. Typical features include loess and alluvial river deposits. Cereals such as soya, wheat, oats, barley and maize are grown intensively while further south sugar cane, cotton and groundnuts are cultivated.

On the western side of the lowland region, the Greater Xingan Range step fault dominates the landscape to the east of the Mongolian basin. The peaks on this mountain range reach 1500–2034m/4900–6650ft. The bedrock of ancient crystalline blocks is frequently superimposed by coverings of young basalt. The steep faces on the eastern side receive sufficient precipitation from the Pacific airflows to encourage the growth of dense deciduous vegetation – a forested mountain area which extends northward gradually becoming Siberian pine forest subject to extremes of cold in the winter.

The east Manchurian mountain woodlands are rich in minerals. Superimposed on the folded rock formations are horizontal, Palaeozoic layers of sediment and Tertiary igneous basalt, but it is the rich iron ore and non-ferrous deposits, as well as the coal in the Anshan/Fushun coalfields, which form the basis of the region's well-developed heavy industry.

North China consists of treeless steppe and is usually synonymous with the Huanghe River catchment area. It comprises the extensive tablelands between the Weihe and the Huanghe, the densely populated, agricultural Great Plain surrounded by Sinian mountains. "Yellow" China is characterised by hillsides with a smooth loess surface and the notorious unpredictability of the river. At the western extreme of this flood plain, the North Chinese Highlands consist of a sequence of narrow, folded mountain chains following the typical course of the Chinese strikes – from the south-west to the north-east – gradually sloping down to the northern Carboniferous tables and linking with the dry Gobi desert regions of Taihangshan, Wutaishan and the Jehol

North China

13

loess mountains of Shanxi and the barren Ordos Desert. One interesting feature of the landscape here are the "deflation basins" of the northern sandy steppes and the deposition since the Ice Age of windborne débris in the shape of huge 200m/650ft loess sand dunes.

Human intervention may well have damaged the already meagre vegetation on these steppes, but it has led to the formation of impressive eroded landscapes with gullying on the mountain slopes. The huge amounts of washed out top soil, which is carried away in particles by the Huanghe and its tributaries, then accumulate in the Great Plain as loess where they form the basis of the intensive farming.

The other important area with outcrops of Palaeozoic bedrock is the Shandong mountain region. The eroded fold complex of the Caledonian and Variscan periods broke into individual massifs, which in the west of the Shandong peninsula now create a landscape of sedimentary table and fault-block mountains. A steep coastal cliff-line is one unusual feature of the granite section to the east.

But the heart of northern China and one of the most intensively farmed and densely populated regions in the world is the Great or "Yellow" Plain. Geologically, this flood plain is simply a river basin that has only recently been wrested from the sea as a "present to China". The Great Plain is nothing more than a gently sloping but vast alluvial fan for the Huanghe, which has deposited huge quantities of sediment over thousands of years and has frequently changed its course.

A significant feature of the landscape and something which has influenced the local culture is the struggle of the north Chinese people with the level of the Huanghe which as an embanked river flows above the level of the plain. The threat of flooding preoccupies the local population and the construction of dykes and canals to protect this intensively farmed land involves considerable energy.

The Great Plain is bordered to the west by the Taihangshan, the Tongbaishan and the Dabieshan. Access to the loess highlands and the Ordos Desert is via the tightly constricted Tongguan gorge in the northern slopes of the Quinlinshan.

The Central Chinese Mountain Belt follows the course of a fault-line which is a continuation of the Kunlunshan. It forms a wall of peaks, some over 4000m/13,000ft high, and shelters the Great Plain from the Tangho basin and the South Chinese highlands to the south. It also forms a well defined barrier between north and south China. The individual elements of the belt merge together to form an east-west mountain belt interrupted by basins and lowland plains (Minshan, Quinlinshan, Tongguan gorge, Dabashan, Wushan, Dabieshan).

Central Chinese Mountain Belt

Clear differences are apparent in the topography, climate, hydrography and flora between the fertile, subtropical highlands of the moist south and colder northern China. The smooth, shrouded landscape of the north Chinese plains and loess plateaux stands in stark contrast to the south with its more uneven, rugged contours and less peaceful character. There are no appreciable accumulations of loess, as can be seen in the major lowland basins, to make the most of the soil, terracing and embankments have to be constructed and there is a wider range of cultivation methods in use.

South China

The rias or fjord-like inlets which run between the broadly parallel peaks create favourable locations for ports.

The South Chinese Highlands occupy the major part of southeastern China. The mountains and hills of this important region on the south Chinese table have evolved from Sinian folded/recently raised low-level mountain chains. Powerful tertiary tectonic forces produced the disintegration of the old structures into horsts, tilt blocks and depressions. The succession of longitudinal and transverse valleys, of

◄ *Mountain scenery in Sichuan*

Scenery in Guangxi

narrow watergaps and broad lowland basins creates a changing landscape. With a different climate, geological processes have worked more intensively; chemical weathering has had a serious effect on surface decomposition and formation.

Situated between the low-level mountain chains of southern highlands and with a broad seam stretching into the adjoining Great Plain to the north are the outlying plains, the second independent topographical region of southern China. By far the most important area is the mouth of the Changjiang, a flat alluvial delta criss-crossed with channels where the river emerges into the Gulf of Hangzou. Also significant is the alluvial basin of the Xijiang delta with its almost tropical vegetation. The outlying plains are among the most densely populated regions of China with rice cultivation a major occupation although urban centres and industrial complexes proliferate.

The lowland basins along the course of the Changjiang as it meanders its way between the mountains also form part of the south Chinese plains. Densely populated and with an important farming role, retention basins act as a natural barrier in the perennial fight against the summer flooding. Amid the vast amphibian maze of waterways of the central Chinese plain, the Dongtinghu and Poyanghu Lakes, for example, serve as important overflow reservoirs.

The basins of the upper reaches in the mountains occupy a special place among the south Chinese plains. The Red Basin of Sichuan (Sichuan Pendi) is an important example. It is a massive depression with huge red sandstone deposits over 1000m/3250ft high emerging from the valley floor.

To the south-west of the Red Basin, plateau-like Sinian highlands with huge limestone tables rise up in front of steep, folded peaks, the eastern end of the Alpine-Himalayan range and the point where southern China gives way to Central and South-east Asia. Climatic and formative processes in the Guizhou, Yunnan and Shan plateaux of the

South-west Chinese Highlands have led to carbonation, or chemical corrosion and it is here that the idyllic landscape often associated with China – the distinctive karst towers and cones set in broad plains – is found.

The island of Hainan, separated from the mainland peninsula of Leizhou by the Straits of Hainan, sits on an outcrop of continental shelf and marks China's most southerly point. The flatter northern section is covered with a layer of younger basalt pierced through by a number of volcanoes. Separated by a granite foreland, the southern peaks of the island's Sinian uplifted fold mountains reach up to 1867m/6123ft, but are subject to very severe decomposition as a result of what is known as "brick weathering". Tropical rainforest still covers about 40% of the island's surface.

Central Asia

The inner continental block of Central Asia with a surface area of about 11 million sq.km/7 million sq. miles is the other major Asiatic region within Chinese territory and has a clearly defined border with East Asia. High altitude, inland drainage of the plateaux, a continental climate with extreme temperature fluctuations, remoteness and sparse population, together with a leeward position sheltered on all sides by mountains and the associated low rainfall are the main features which distinguish Central from East Asia.

Climate and altitude are responsible for further differences such as the natural vegetation and limited amount of land which may be used for agricultural purposes. Generally speaking, Central Asia can be subdivided into the Turan lowlands between the Kazakh rift and the Hindu Kush – not within China territory – and the Asian highlands with vast basins (Tibetan Plateau, Mongolian Plateau, Dsungarian and Tarim Basin, Turpan Depression) separated by the intervening mountain ridges (Kunlunshan, Nanshan, Tianshan, Beishan, Altaj).

The depression between Ürümqi and Turpan

17

Topography

The Tibetan Plateau, Central Asia's great massif is subject to continuing movements from the Alpine-Himalayan mountain formation phases in the south. Positioned at an altitude of between 4000 and 4500m/13,000 and 14,750ft, it is bordered to the south by huge walls of mountains such as the Himalayas, Transhimalayas, Karakorams and Pamirs with summits of between 7000 and 8846m/23,000 and 29,020ft. It would be wrong to think of the Tibetan Plateau itself as flat terrain. It is in fact characterised by a changing relief pattern of parallel mountain ranges and intervening basins. The southern massifs drain down the deep, narrow gorges of the Sindh and the Indus or the Tsangpo/Brahmaputra system and thence into the Indian Ocean, while the large area on the north side of the Transhimalayas remains without an outlet. The higher ranges are generally snow-capped and subject more or less all the year round to the glaciation and nivation processes associated with high altitudes.

Frozen lakes without outlets occasionally form in sheltered depressions but they have water levels which fluctuate widely. In some protected locations the bleak climate permits the growth of meagre high steppe vegetation.

The Kunlunshan with peaks rising to between 6000 and 7723m/19,500 and 25,330ft forms the northern edge of the Tibetan Highlands. Further north lie the Tarim and Quaidam basins and the Mongolian Plateau.

Between the huge mountain ranges of Central Asia lie a number of important basins, which despite varying altitudes have some common features. As the surrounding peaks offer protection from rain-bearing air flows, these inland basins which have no water outlets, are inhospitably dry and are also exposed to very wide temperature fluctuations. Sandy deserts become broad salt clay plains or "takyr"; at the bottom of the mountains saline lakes alternate with huge piles of rock débris.

The most important Central Asian basins on Chinese soil are from west to east the Tarim Basin with the Turpan Depression, the Dsungarian and, a little further to the south-east, Quaidam Basin.

The Tarim Basin, a sunken plain sloping down to the east, is bordered on three sides by mountains. Altitude varies between 700 and 1400m/2300 and 4500ft and the basin covers an area close to 500,000sq.km/315,000sq.miles. Starting from the Pamir Knot in the west and extending across the heart of Turkestan, its east-west distance exceeds 1500km/950 miles and the distance from north to south measures 650km/400 miles. The Kunlunshan and the Altunshan separate the basin from the considerably higher regions of Tibet. In the north the Tianshan marks the limit of the Turpan Depression and the Dsungarian basin marks out the border with Kazakhstan. Access to the east and the Gobi Desert is blocked by the Beishan.

In the Tarim Basin, it is possible to observe an inland landscape without a water outlet produce a sequence of unusual topographical features. From the glacial outlying summits, the terrain falls steeply via scree-covered mountain sides down to rock débris strewn at the foot. The adjoining loess drift zone with a belt of oases is followed quickly by barren sandy desert. Beyond, the "takyr" landscape of salt clay plains and isolated lakes dominates the middle of the basin. The channels which drain water into the depression from the surrounding mountains come together in the Tarimhe, a river which skirts around the inhospitable Takla Makan desert at the middle of the basin. It finally reaches the saline Lop Nur lake via an underflow only re-activated in the 1930s.

Between the foothills of the Tianshan, 154m/500ft below sea-level to the north-east of the Tarim Basin, lies the Turpan Depression (Turpan Pendi).

The Dsungarian Basin (Junggar Pendi) at an altitude of between 200 and 750m/650 and 2500ft resembles an isosceles triangle. In the west and east there are openings into the expansive mountain ranges, while access to wooded North Asia and the Mongolian Basin involves crossing the Tarbagatai and the Altaj mountains. To the south the Tianshan separates the Dsungaria from the Tarim Basin and the Turpan Depression. Here too the basin which slopes gently to the west is largely given over to sandy desert. The northern part of the plain consists of extensive saline swamp.

Like the other basins of north-west China, a belt of oases have formed at the foot of the Tianshan and this zone is intensively irrigated and farmed.

The Quaidam basin, surrounded by the Nanshan and the Kunlunshan, lies between the Tibetan Plateau and the lower lying areas of the Tianshan. Covering an expanse of 120,000sq.km/46,500sq. miles, the basin lies at an altitude averaging 2700m/8850ft. The landscape in the west is largely sandy desert, while in the east, saline swamp is only passable when frozen.

The Mongolian Basin extends for about 2000km/1240 miles, stretching northwards beyond the Chinese border and the Autonomous Region of Inner Mongolia into Siberia. This broad, relatively flat basin at an altitude ranging between 1200 and 1500m/4000 and 5000ft is bordered to the north by the South Baikal Mountains, in the east by the Greater Xingan Range, in the south by the Nanshan and the Gobi Desert and in the west by the Altaj and Beishan.

Mongolian Basin

The climate of the whole region can be described as semi-arid and parts of the basin are subject to ridging. Huge mountain ranges including the Sayan Mountains, the Changaj, the Mongolian Altaj and the Gobi Altaj all serve to break up the level plain.

In the few places where productive rainfall occurs, sparse woodland vegetation has taken root, but on the leeward slopes of the mountains and in the basins, semi-desert or desert landscapes predominate.

The cold, northern steppes and mountain lands allow the native Mongols to lead a nomadic existence which involves moving between pastures. The distinctly hostile terrain of the dry and barren Gobi (Shamo) Desert has claimed many lives.

Lakes and rivers

While China divides into two in a topographical sense, the same is true in hydrographical terms. From the cold, dry central highlands with irregular internal drainage in the west, vast river systems flow east into the uplands and plains of East Asia. With modest amounts of precipitation on the high plateaux of Central Asia and year-round coverings of snow on the high peaks, there is little productive run-off.

Typical phenomena resulting from this type of drainage system are rivers which form from melted snows but which then seep through the never-ending desert and peter out or else shallow, saline lakes whose water level varies dramatically. Most notable for its "movements" is the Lop Nur lake in the Tarim Basin. With a surface area sometimes reaching 7000sq.km/2650sq. miles, it never exceeds 2m/6½ft in depth.

The irregular drainage flows and the large variations in the water level have made it difficult to use the lakes and rivers of Central Asia productively for such purposes as irrigation.

By contrast with the Asian interior, several mighty rivers cross the wetter, monsoonal East Asia in an west–east direction, irrigating land from the outer edges of the Asiatic highlands to the Pacific on their way. The change from cold, dry winters to damp, hot summers, plus the considerable monsoon rainfall leads to massive fluctuations in

Topography

River scenery on the Lijiang

water levels. To the already considerable dangers of flooding must be added the erratic changes in the course of the waters, which often coincide with the changes in wind direction as the rainy season starts accompanied by the monsoons and sometimes typhoons from the south-east. Topographical features in the upper reaches of the rivers can intensify the consequences, namely the changes from wide, open valleys to narrow gorges.

The East Asia region is dominated by three major river systems, which all flow roughly in a west–east direction, draining into the Pacific Ocean. From north to south, they are the Huanghe, the Changjiang and the Xijiang. Other tributaries of lesser importance exist, but there are no significant north–south flows.

Huanghe/
Hwangho
Yellow River

The Yellow River, named after the vast quantity of particles which give the river its characteristic colour, is the main river of northern China. The fertile Great Plain has been created from an immense amount of "yellow" silt and sands that has been carried down from the soft loess.

The Huanghe, 4800km/3020 miles in length, is the seventh longest river in the world. Its catchment basin extends over 772,000sq.km/ 300,000sq. miles, equivalent to the Danube's catchment area. The source of the Huanghe is to be found in the foothills of the Kunlunshan and the Nanshan and then with few tributaries, it passes through the Ordos Desert. Before turning to the east through the Tongguan gorge, the river cuts through the north Chinese loess region along narrow gorges and down steep gradients. It is here in the provinces of Gansu, Shaanxi and Shanxi that the river and its tributaries pick up over one billion tons of sediment, earning it a reputation as the "muddiest river on earth". 40% of the particles are deposited on the river bed or on the plains and 60% reaches the Yellow Sea.

The climate, in particular the seasonal variations in precipitation, has a serious effect on the Huanghe. During the dry season, the winter and spring, the Huanghe is regarded as the "creator of the plains", but during the high water months of the summer, it is known as "China's sorrow".

Time after time, the Huanghe has overflowed and caused catastrophic floods with the deaths of tens of thousands of people living alongside its densely populated banks. In 1867 more than a million people drowned and over 22,000sq.km/8360sq. miles of the Great Plain were inundated when the river broke its banks.

One problem which typifies the unpredictability of the Huanghe is the pendulum effect of its alluvial fan, which is constantly rising as a result of the ongoing silt deposits.

In the last four thousand years, despite tremendous efforts to contain the waters, there have been 430 incidents in which the dykes have been breached and at least eleven changes to the embanked watercourse. At the mouth of the Huanghe, the "swing of the pendulum", i.e. the various courses the river has taken as it approaches the sea, covers between 800 and 1000km/500 and 600 miles!

The Changjiang is of even greater proportions. Over 6000km/3720 miles in length, it irrigates a fifth of China. Originating in the Tibetan Plateau it links a number of basin landscapes (Red Basin, Tangho Basin, Wuhan and Anquing lake valleys), cutting through narrow gorges to finally flow through a delta out into the East China Sea near Shanghai just beyond the Jiangsu Plain. | Changjiang/ Yangtsekiang (Blue River)

On account of the larger catchment basin, greater precipitation and important tributaries which join from the south, the average outflow is in fact much greater then the Huanghe. The amount of water flowing from the Changjiang at its mouth (35,000 cubic metres/7½ million gallons per second) is only exceeded by the Amazon and the Congo!

Erosion-resisting vegetation within the catchment area and the greater strength of the flow reduces the extent of particle and sediment content to a relatively low level. By way of contrast with the Yellow River, the Changjiang is virtually free of silt and sand and is sometimes known as the "Blue River".

The Changjiang is not subject to the same risk of flooding as the Huanghe, for the simple reason that after the river has passed through steep, narrow valleys, it always opens out into wide lowland basins where flood plains can absorb increased flows. The amphibian landscape around the Tangho Basin near Wuhan is one of the most impressive examples of how the course of a river can become a maze of uncontrolled meanders when the speed of flow is suddenly reduced as it passes beyond the rapids and gorges of Wushan.

The Xijiang, the third longest of China's river systems, drains an area of 435,000sq.km/167,000sq. miles. Although it is only 2130km/1341 miles in length and has a catchment area half the size of that of the Huanghe, the outflow is nevertheless much higher, largely because of the considerable monsoon rainfall in the tropical south. | Xijiang West River

Despite the greater volumes of water, the risk of flooding is much less than for the northern rivers, thanks mainly to the more consistent rainfall levels and also the contours. The course of the river is determined by the South Chinese Highlands and the water is directed along tectonically-formed valleys to the South China Sea.

The differences between the rivers have had significant consequences on the development of the Chinese culture. In the north, there is considerable emphasis on communal strength in the battle with the river embankments and flood protection, while in the south, for thousands of years, the navigable southern rivers have had an important function within the Chinese economy as arteries for travel and trade. Furthermore, the huge volumes of water have provided magnificent opportunities for the development of irrigation schemes and also the cultivation of rice.

Climate

Lakes
There are in excess of 2000 larger lakes in China so only a few notable examples are included here to represent the very many different types which occur in such a vast country. The mainly saline lakes of the steppes and those between the mountain ranges in the Central Asian Highlands have already been mentioned.

The Lop Nur in the Tarim Basin is an example of a shallow lake only found in areas with no natural drainage. The shore line is constantly changing and the lake can sometimes dry up completely. But in the Quaidam Basin (Quinghai Nur) in the Tibetan Highlands (Nam Co, Tangra-yum Co) and also the Dsungaria (Ebi Nur), there are examples of extensive salt lakes and impassable swamps.

Of great importance in maintaining the water levels in East Asia are the vast amphibian landscapes of the lowland basins. The maze of rivers and freshwater lakes which have formed in these valleys serve as natural reservoirs and flood basins. They can have a regulatory effect on the water volumes of the lowland rivers. In addition, such lakes as the Dongtinghu, Poyanghu, Daguanhu, Chaohu, Hongzehu and Taihu fulfil a useful function where the agriculture requires intensive irrigation.

Water power
The major Chinese rivers have been put to good use as sources of electricity. Hydro-electric dams have at the same time helped to moderate the potentially destructive forces of these mighty watercourses. In recent decades many more dams and dykes have been built and sections of the Huanghe and the Huaihe have been modified to become reservoirs and flood basins.

The coast
China's 20,000km/12,500 mile coastline extends from Korea to Vietnam. It can be divided into two sections, mirroring the differences between the north and south of the country in both a topographical and cultural sense. The dividing line comes at the Bay of Hangzou where the foothills of the Quinlinshan and the Dabieshan reach the sea. To the north the coastline is generally flat and sandy, to the south it is rugged and indented with rias, or fjord-like inlets.

The flat, north Chinese coast is only interrupted by Sinian horsts, the Liadong and Shandong peninsulas. The remaining coast consists of late Quaternary river sediment. The mud and sand from the Huanghe and the Changjiang have created an inaccessible, shallow, shifting shoreline. There is a tendency to silting up and the beaches grow considerably every year.

Consequently, all important harbours in northern China are situated a little upstream in river estuaries such as at Shanghai and Tianjin or in the better protected bays of the previously mentioned peninsulas such as at Qingdao, Weihai, Yantai and Dalian.

The mountains of south China which extend as far as the sea are responsible for the creation of the steep and stable southern coastline. The mountain valleys lead down to inlets (rias), bays and countless offshore islands.

This type of coastline has of course always been much better suited for the siting of ports, which then provide a favourable environment for shipping, trade and fishing.

Climate

Monsoon climate
The differing climates of China are all influenced by the monsoon, but in a huge country with such great north–south and west–east distances plus the considerable variations in altitude, its effects are felt in diverse ways throughout the regions.

The seasonal change in the direction of the prevailing wind is typical of monsoon climates and it arises from the thermal contrast between the Asiatic continental mass and the Pacific Ocean.

During the winter the winds blow from the cold highlands in Central Asia and Siberia in the direction of the Pacific. The region between Lake Baikal and the upper reaches of the Huanghe is usually thought of as the source of these icy winds. The predominantly northerly air currents carry dry, cold air and consequently sunny but chilly weather. In the south the effect is less pronounced. The tropical heat subsides but there are no frosts.

In the summer predominantly southerly air-flows bring moist and warm air inland from the Pacific. These currents carry rainfall northwards across the country but amounts decline in the north. High temperatures and humidity create an almost unbearable sultriness and at night temperatures drop only slightly.

The change from winter to summer, marked by the arrival of the cyclonal monsoon season, occurs in what is known as the frontal zone. This zone is to be found in southern China in May and June but then shifts northwards, reaching northern China by July. During the later summer months rainfall subsides somewhat in the south. The frontal zone starts to retreat from the north towards the end of September. In September and October the cooler, drier air of winter begins to re-establish itself.

Autumn is the time of the violent cyclonic tropical storms, known in East Asia as typhoons (from the Chinese "tai fung" meaning "great wind"). They only occur in the southern latitudes above warm seas with temperatures between 26°–27°C/78°–80°F. These high temperatures combine with the warmth from the rising moist air to provide the impetus for the cyclone which can reach a height of 12km/7 miles and a diameter of 700km/450 miles. Southern China can expect at least three typhoons per year. They affect the southern Chinese coast, moving in from the south-east. Heavy winds, tidal waves and exceptionally heavy rain (150–300mm/6–12in. in the space of a few hours) regularly cause serious damage. They do, however, quickly lose their intensity as they meet land. | Typhoons

The further the region from the coast, the lower the monsoonal precipitation. Mountain ranges, which cause humidity to be precipitated as rain (relief rain), also reduce rainfall on the land beyond. Generally speaking, eastern China enjoys damp summers, while the west experiences dry weather throughout the whole year. | Climatic divisions

In the drier western half of China, it is necessary to differentiate between the cold Tibetan Highlands and the northern steppe and desert climate of Xinjiang. | The west

In the eastern half of the country the green of the south contrasts with the yellow, loess landscapes of the north. During the summer the temperatures in these two regions do not differ appreciably, but in winter the north is much colder than the south. The boundary between these two climates follows the Qinling Mountains (south of Xi'an) eastwards, meeting the east coast north of the Changjiang delta. To the south of this line the subtropical climate is ideal for rice cultivation. To the north of the line, only plants adapted to a temperate climate will grow. | The east

Climate diagrams (see pages 24/25)

The diagram gives details of the climate in the various regions of China. Temperature and rainfall for each month of the year is shown in the tables. The letters along the top of each table indicate the month (from left to right: J = January to D = December). | Temperature and rainfall

The temperatures are indicated in the orange band. The upper line shows the average maximum daytime temperature, while the lower

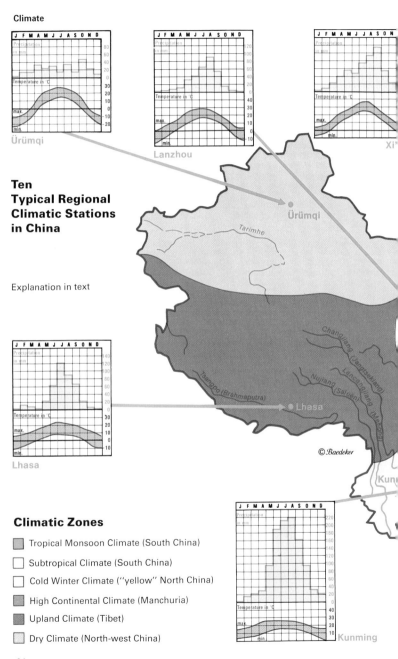

Climate

Ürümqi

Lanzhou

Xi'...

Ten Typical Regional Climatic Stations in China

Explanation in text

Lhasa

Tarimhe

● Ürümqi

Chang Jiang (Jangtsekiang)

Tsangpo (Brahmaputra)

Nujiang (Salween)

Lancangjiang (Mekong)

● Lhasa

© Baedeker

Kun...

Climatic Zones

- Tropical Monsoon Climate (South China)
- Subtropical Climate (South China)
- Cold Winter Climate (''yellow'' North China)
- High Continental Climate (Manchuria)
- Upland Climate (Tibet)
- Dry Climate (North-west China)

Kunming

24

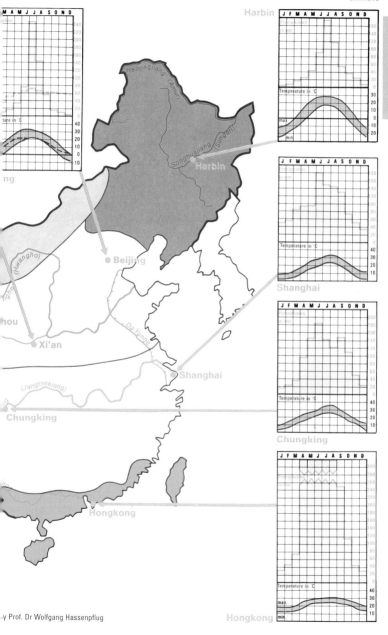

by Prof. Dr Wolfgang Hassenpflug

line shows the average minimum night-time temperature. Temperatures are shown on the red scale. The width of the band gives some indication of daily temperature fluctuations. The angle of the curve demonstrates the extent of annual temperature fluctuations.

The blue columns with the corresponding blue scale give average monthly precipitation (in mm).

Practical tips

The tables for the different cities of China can only give a general guide to the Chinese climate. Climate can of course vary within a region and the actual climate in any given place can vary from year to year. Appreciable deviations from the annual values are unlikely and infrequent.

As a general guide the following rules may be helpful:
• The higher the land, the lower the temperature.
• Rainfall is lower on the leeward side of the mountain ranges than on the sides exposed to the prevailing wind.
• Temperatures, rainfall and humidity generally lessen in a line from south-east to north-west.
• In the drier regions, daily and annual temperature fluctuations are greater than in the more humid zones.

Other factors

Daylight

Daylight hours depend on latitude and season. The far north of Manchuria lies on the same latitude as Paris, while Hong Kong lies just south of the Tropic of Cancer. The further south one goes – compared with the United Kingdom – the shorter the days are in summer and the nights are in winter. In the Tropics, day and night are practically the same length throughout the year.

Advice

The further south one goes, the hotter the sun is and the more hazardous the sun's rays are. Protection from the heat of the sun is vital both in the southern provinces and in all areas of high altitude, e.g. Tibet.

Air pollution

Many Chinese cities suffer from considerable air pollution. In a recent study by the World Health Organisation (WHO), Beijing was shown to be the second worst city in the world. In other conurbations the situation is not much better. The main cause, particularly in the north of the country, is the inefficient use of coal, the country's main source of energy. In certain weather conditions, smoke and exhaust gases can become so thick that satellite photographs have been unable to pick out the towns below.

Tropical Southern China

Hong Kong weather station (alt. 33m/108ft)

Tropical monsoon climate

A 100km/70 mile strip of land along the southern coast of China and the whole island of Taiwan are subject to a tropical monsoon climate, as they are furthest away from the cold air currents of continental Asia and are near to the warm South China Sea.

Temperatures and rainfall

From December to March, the average monthly temperature remains below 18°C/64°F, the normal limit for the Tropics. For Europeans such a climate at that time of year is quite tolerable, and much more acceptable than what is usually regarded as tropical weather. Certainly there is no risk of frost so close to the coast. A temperature of 0°C/32°F was once recorded in Hong Kong in January. In Canton temperatures have reached −0.3°C/31.5°F in December.

The winter months are also the driest time of the year. In November and December, there are on average two or three days of rain per month. Some years there is no rainfall at all during those months.

From February, cloud cover increases (145 hours of sun in January, 98 in February and 95 in March). From April, rainfall values rise and the number of rainy days increases (292mm/11½in. in eight days). This is nothing other than the period of heavy rain and storms which marks the onset of the summer monsoons. In May, almost 400mm/16in. of rain falls on thirteen rainy days. This amount roughly equals half the annual rainfall for central Europe. The highest recorded precipitation is 521mm/20½in. in 24 hours or 1240mm/49 in. in one month. In May 1992, 110mm/4in. of rain fell in one hour, the highest recorded amount in a hundred years. In June, although the monthly rainfall is slightly less, there are on average eighteen days of rainfall, the highest figure for any month. July brings the highest rainfall (394mm/15½in.) but also a good deal of sun (210 hours). Daily temperature variations are slight (see the diagram). Maximum temperatures reach 30°C/86°F with relatively high humidity.

While autumn temperatures start to fall slowly, rainfall values drop rapidly. In October, the hours of sunshine total reaches its peak (217 hours) and there are on average only eight rainy days.

Subtropical Southern China

Shanghai weather station (alt. 5m/16ft)
Chongqing weather station (alt. 261m/856ft) **and Kunming** (alt. 1893m/6209ft)

The boundary between the subtropical climate zone and the "yellow" north runs about 100–200km/60–1200 miles north of the Changjiang. Compared to tropical China, the winter influence of continental Asia is much more marked.
Subtropical climate

Although the winters are mild, temperatures generally remain below those of tropical China. In the lower reaches of the Changjiang, minimum temperatures stay just above freezing and from November to the end of March, frosts can occasionally occur, but temperatures do not fall below −10°C/14°F. On the other hand, summers are hot. Wuhan ranks alongside Nanjing and Chongqing as one of China's "hothouses". From June to July/August temperatures frequently exceed 30°C/86°F. In July and August they can on occasions reach 40°C/104°F. From June to September, relative humidity can exceed 80%, while in Nanjing this is only the case in July. Further away from the coast, humidity stays below this level.
Temperature and humidity

The climate in the Sichuan Basin (Chongqing weather station), by comparison with the lowlands in the lower reaches of the Changjiang, is somewhat different. Average annual temperature of 18.6°C/65.5°F exceeds that of Shanghai by 3.3°C/6°F. The Mingshan and Qinling Mountains keep the central Asian cold air currents at bay and winter minimum temperatures can be 5–6°C/8–10°F higher than further down the Changjiang. Frosts are rare. The lowest recorded temperature is −2.5°C/27.5°F in February. For months the Sichuan Basin lies under a constant cloud cover. The air is stuffy and sultry. From November to February the sunshine totals reach only 47, 54, 48 and 56 hours, only a third of the totals recorded in the eastern Changjiang regions.
Sichuan Basin

In summer, the heat in the Sichuan Basin can be oppressive. From June to August daily maximum values remain constantly 2–3°C/4–6°F above those in Shanghai. The best time to visit this region is undoubtedly during the spring or autumn.

The growing season in the best locations below 700m/2300ft lasts for eleven months and rice can be double-cropped.

Climate

South-west
China

In the higher altitudes (around 2000m/6500ft) of south-west China (Kunming weather station), the climate is more acceptable to Europeans. It is hot but never humid. Kunming is sometimes described as the "city of eternal springtime". Summer seems like an extended spring. The rainy season lasts from May to October and at the start can be very stormy.

Winter is more like an extended autumn: sunny and mild. Kunming has no equal in China – with its southern location, it is so mild and yet enjoys so many hours of winter sunshine. From December to April, monthly sunshine totals in hours average 203, 252, 234, 244, and 238. In Beijing, the corresponding figures are: 192, 206, 197, 237, 239.

"Yellow" Northern China

Beijing weather station (alt. 52m/170ft), **Xi'an** (alt. 412m/1351ft) **and Lanzhou** (alt. 1508m/4946ft).

Cold winters

The term "yellow" China usually refers to the loess-covered mountains and lowlands on either side of the Huanghe. There is no greater contrast in relation to climate and landscape than that between the subtropical Sichuan Basin with its red soil and luxuriant vegetation and – separated only by the Qinling Mountains – the yellow and dusty-dry countryside of northern China with its cold winters. The variations in aridity and winter cold can depend on such factors as latitude, distance from the coast and altitude. At the border between the subtropical south and northern China, average rainfall drops to below 1000mm/39in. at the north-western border of northern China these values fall to below 250mm/10in. Annual average precipitation in Beijing amounts to 619mm/24in., in Xi'an 578mm/22.5in. and in Lanzhou 338mm/13¼in. There are on average 250-frost-free days per year.

Beijing

In Beijing, representative of the lower reaches of the Huanghe, average temperatures can fluctuate by almost 30°C/54°F and the variation between night and day is just short of 10°C/18°F. For the three months from December to February, the average nightly temperature will be below freezing. Frost can occur as early as October and as late as April. By November the rivers and shores of the Yellow Sea will have iced up and will remain frozen for three to four months. Winter rainfall is low and relative humidity stands at around 50% or slightly below. Only 31mm/1¼in. of the total annual rainfall falls between November and March. Icy duststorms from the interior can leave blankets of sediment behind and can also cause the small amounts of snow to drift. The dust is deposited on surfaces in much the same way that loess formed in the Pleistocene period.

In the summer the currents of hot, moist monsoon air from the south can raise the temperature to 40°C/104°F. Humidity levels can be almost unbearable with relative humidity above 70%. From June to July, rainfall levels rise quickly and dramatically. In July and August, 384mm/15in. of rain falls on 24 of the annual 66 rainy days.

Loess mountains

In the loess mountains (Lanzhou weather station) rainfall levels of between 250 and 500mm/10 and 20in. are recorded each year, with the months of June to September being by far the wettest. These levels do vary greatly from year to year and there are sometimes long periods of drought and harvests can be badly affected.

Given the altitudes (Lanzhou is about 1500m/4920ft above sea level) the winters are very cold, but the summers are very pleasant, compared to the humidity and heat of the lowlands.

Tip

Visitors travelling to northern China from the tropical and subtropical provinces during autumn, winter and spring should be prepared for all weathers.

Manchuria

Harbin weather station (alt. 143m/420ft)

The climate in Manchuria can be characterised as upland continental. Annual fluctuations exceed 40°C/72°F and the shelter from the Pacific Ocean offered by the Manchurian mountains plays an important role.

Continental climate

While the January average in Beijing is −4.7°C/23.5°F, in southern Manchuria it is −9°C/15.8°F and in Harbin −20.1°C/−4°F, reaching −30°C/−22°F further north. By the Amur, on China's northern border, permafrost is not unusual. The rivers are frozen for three months in the south and four months in the north. In the depths of winter there is virtually no precipitation, after a thin covering of snow has fallen in October and November.

After a short spring, subtropical summers with considerable humidity begin. 80% of the annual rainfall occurs in the months between May and September. Ten times as much rain falls in the month with the highest rainfall as in the month with the lowest rainfall. Rainfall values are usually lower in the north. In general temperatures in the Manchurian Basin are moderate. Average maximum temperatures from June to September range between 26 and 30°C/78 and 86°F. Average annual temperatures vary between 20 and 25°C/68 and 77°F.

Tibet

Lhasa weather station (alt. 3685m/12,086ft)

Tibet's climate is determined by the considerable altitude and the all-round protection offered by the mountain ranges on the periphery. While the highlands occupy land at an average altitude of 4000m/13,000ft above sea level, the surrounding mountain ranges exceed this level by a further 3000–4000m/10,000–13,000ft. The mountain ranges on the Tibetan Plateau rise above the average altitude by a further 500–2000m/1600–6500ft.

Highland climate

The climate of Tibet is also defined by the changing air circulation patterns brought about by the monsoons. Winter brings bitter cold but in summer some monsoon rains are drawn in from the south, in particular those which have not fallen as relief rain on the windward side of the Himalayas or as snow on the summits.

The highland climate is characterised by major temperature fluctuations not just between summer and winter but between day and night. Cloud cover, rainfall and humidity are relatively low due to the protection offered by the mountains. On the other hand, with high altitude comes thin air and the sun's rays are very strong. Protection is absolutely essential.

The stormy winds which often start to blow around midday result from the high altitude and also solar radiation. Severe storms are fairly frequent occurrences in autumn and winter.

Using Lhasa as a weather station can be misleading as it only records climatic conditions in the more favoured locations of Tibet. A glance at the climate diagram will show that − despite an altitude of 3685m/ 12,086ft − Lhasa fares quite well. By comparison with Kassel in central Germany (see table for Beijing), average daily temperatures in June fluctuate between 9.4°C/49°F and 23.3°C/73°F (Kassel between 12.8°C/ 55°F and 23.3°C/73°F). By the end of February, winter is beginning to fade in Lhasa. Cherry blossom emerges here in April, earlier than in the lower reaches of the Changjiang.

Lhasa

Annual precipitation amounts to 410mm/16in. of which 211mm/8¼in. fall in July and August. Irrigation systems are in place to conserve water. Barley and even summer wheat are grown in southern Tibet at altitudes of nearly 4000m/13,000ft.

Flora and Fauna

North-west China

Ürümqi weather station (alt. 913m/2995ft)

Dry climate

The north-west of China consists of huge cold desert and steppe basin landscapes (Tarim Basin, Dsungaria, Mongolian Basin), surrounded by snow-capped mountain ranges. There is a succession of regular changes in altitude starting with the deserts in the lowland basins rising to a steppe and forest zone and leading to the year-round snow and ice in the mountains.

Temperatures drop the higher the altitude but rainfall and humidity increase. An increase in height of 1000m/3250ft results in a temperature drop of about 6°C/10°F. Woodland growth is possible at about 2000m/6500ft above sea-level and at 3700m/12,000ft glaciation can occur. The snow line can vary considerably from peak to peak – 3000m/10,000ft in the western Tienshan but 5600m/18,500ft in the Pamirs.

Melt water from the glaciers supplies the oases, often important watering places on the ancient Silk Road, and used in recent irrigation projects. The agriculture of Xinjiang province is not based on rain but on irrigation from the melted snow. The hotter the sun, the more snow melts. The local farmers are frequently heard to sigh: "We don't want rain (the clouds will block out the sun). We'll suffer from drought."

Xinjiang

The weather station at Ürümqi, Xinjiang's capital, lies on the northern edge of the Tienshan Mountains. Rainfall is spread over the whole year. In an average year, total precipitation reaches 273mm/11¾in., with the autumn months being the wettest. Daily and annual temperature fluctuations are considerable. In winter it is bitterly cold with daytime temperatures between November and March remaining below freezing. Sand and snow storms are not unusual.

Summers are hot and dry. Relative humidity between May and September falls below 50%.

Dsungaria

Conditions become hotter and drier as the mountain tops give way to lowland basins. The climate of the Dsungaria, north of Ürümqi, ranges from extremely cold steppe conditions in the west to the unmistakable desert climate of the east, on the edge of the Gobi. A desert climate also prevails in the Tarim Basin to the south of Ürümqi (Takla Makan), while in the Turpan Depression south of the Tienshan some 154m/500ft below sea level and one of the lowest dry points on the surface of the earth, temperatures can reach 47°C/116°F in summer with only occasional winter frosts. The extremely low levels of humidity in this area explain such phenomena as the Astana cemetery where bodies have mummified.

Flora and Fauna

General

China's many different geological formations, varied river catchment areas and regions with individual micro-climates have, not surprisingly, led to the evolution of a rich flora and fauna. This is particularly the case in the north-eastern forests, in the steppes of the north and north-west, the Tibetan Highlands and glaciers and also in the tropical and subtropical districts of the south-east.

The enormous range of flora and fauna to be found in China is extraordinary. Almost all species of plants and flowers grow here.

Forests

With its varied climatic conditions China is home to most main types of woodland. Pine forests and many examples of deciduous woodlands grow in the north and tropical rainforests flourish in the south. Over 2800 species of trees have been recorded and many are of commercial importance, such as the tung oil trees, cedars, rubber and cocoa trees. Woodland and forest accounts for about 13% of China's land surface.

In the north-east there are extensive forests of conifers (larches, firs and pines) and also deciduous woodland (maple, birch, linden and ash). Wildlife includes elks, deer, Siberian tigers and Amur leopards.

The ginseng (renshen), a small plant with red berries, is also a native to this part of China. Its roots are valued the world over and are in great demand. Sometimes described as the "elixir of youth" it is taken widely as a tonic but it is also used as a remedy for pulmonary complaints and hyperglycaemia, a complaint affecting blood sugar levels.

In Shandong province there are oak forests and further south along the lower and middle reaches of the Changjiang and in Sichuan, sub-tropical evergreens flourish.

In the tropical rainforests, which extend into Yunnan and Guangdong, bananas, lychees, mangoes, coffee and sugar cane are cultivated. This region is home to a wide range of animal species with numerous types of birds, monkeys, tree shrews, tigers, elephants, muntjac deer, Tibetan cats and leopards.

Steppes and deserts

The steppes extend across the north-eastern plain and the eastern part of Inner Mongolia. Camels, pheasants, hares, eagles, weasels, foxes, bears, lynx, deer, mountain goats and wolves are just a few of the species of game and predatory mammals which inhabit these barren wastes.

The provinces of Xinjiang, Gansu and the Quaidam Basin in Qinghai province contain sand and rock deserts, where only low-growing shrubs will grow. The desert regions of north-west Tibet at 5000m/16,000ft will also only sustain small shrubs and bushes.

Mountain regions

The West Chinese Highlands in north-west China reach a height of 5000m/16,000ft but creepers and climbing plants survive here. Tibet, the world's highest region, is subject to one of the harshest climates and huge seasonal variations in temperature. Mountain vegetation characterises the Tibetan Plateau and beyond into Yunnan and Sichuan province. This is the habitat of the yak, a shaggy-haired member of the ox family, which is used for milk, leather and as a beast of burden.

In the Himalaya region rare mammals include the Asiatic wild ass, wild yak and the Orongo antelope. The mountains of central China provide habitats for other typically Chinese creatures such as the giant panda, Himalayan black bear, lesser panda, serau (chamois), takin, snub-nosed langur and the clouded leopard.

Birds

China has a total of 1160 bird species, more species than any other country in the world. Many of these fall into the pheasant and chicken category of which the best known is the common pheasant. Other varieties include partridge, grouse, rock partridge, Franklin's gull, great bustard and little bustard and the hazel hen. Bamboo partridges and miniature quails are kept as cage birds.

A wide range of water fowl can also be seen. The colourful mandarin duck is one of the best known examples. Nearly all crane species are now protected. Some time ago, a bird measuring only 1cm/½in. was found in southern China. The Chinese nightingale, or sun bird as the Chinese call it, is the smallest bird in the world.

Rare species

Found only in the waters of the Changjiang, one of the rarest species in China is the Chinese dolphin. There are very few rivers in the world where freshwater dolphins can be found. Another protected species also found in the Changjiang is the Chinese alligator, which can grow to 2m/6½ft.

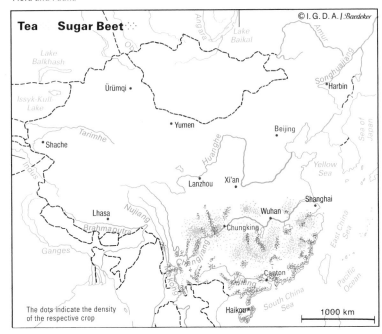

Tea   Sugar Beet   © I. G. D. A. / *Baedeker*

The dots indicate the density of the respective crop

1000 km

The white-lipped Thorold's deer was at one time under threat but now survives in a protected reserve. It lives on the Tibetan Plateau at altitudes of 3000 to 4000m/10,000 to 13,000ft.

Bamboo

Of the 520 recorded varieties of bamboo, 300 grow in tropical and subtropical China. The extent of the bamboo forests has declined in recent years, but they still occupy a total of 2% of the country's wooded terrain. Found almost as high up as the snow line, the bamboo is of immense importance as a commercial crop. Often a favourite subject in Chinese painting, it has become a symbol for this region of the country. It is used for building ships, houses, furniture and musical instruments. Even in the kitchen, shoots, seeds and pulp have their uses. It is also the main source of food for the giant panda (see Baedeker Special on page 34).

Traditional plants

A number of other plants have acquired a special symbolic value in Chinese culture, economy and tradition. For Buddhists the lotus flower has come to symbolise birth, life, fertility, justice and nirvana. It is edible and is used to make medicines and cosmetics.

The peach is another plant which acquired special status. It was cultivated throughout China and became a Taoist symbol. The peony, a favourite flower for the Chinese, features in ancient erotic literature and art and came to symbolise woman.

Tea

The tea plant, however, is of even greater importance to China, and its dried leaves have become the national drink of the Orient and beyond. Tea grows in the moist and misty climate of the tropical regions to the south and south-east and will thrive up to an altitude of 2000m/6500ft.

Rice

Rice, another vital crop for the Chinese, has been cultivated since the 3rd c. B.C. and rice paddy fields now occupy a high proportion of the flat

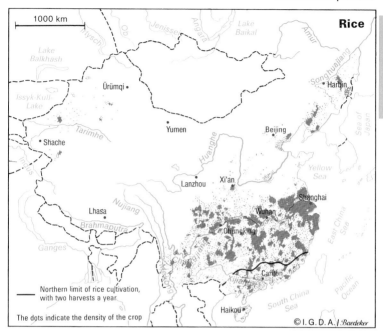

Rice

1000 km

Lake Balkhash

Issyk-Kul' Lake

Ürümqi

Shache

Tarimhe

Indus

Lhasa

Brahmaputra

Ganges

Nujiang

Yumen

Lanzhou

Xi'an

Huanghe

Wuhan

Chongqing

Beijing

Harbin

Songhuajiang

Amur

Sea of Japan

Yellow Sea

Shanghai

East China Sea

Canton

Xijiang

Haikou

South China Sea

Pacific Ocean

Northern limit of rice cultivation, with two harvests a year.

The dots indicate the density of the crop

© I. G. D. A. / *Baedeker*

land in "inner" China. In a warm, humid climate and with plenty of water at hand, sometimes three crops can be harvested each year. In the hillier regions, rice is cultivated in specially-dug terraces.

Environmental problems

A report issued in 1990 by the Ministry for Environmental Protection confirmed that the situation in China was a cause for concern, although there were some grounds for optimism. The increasing population, rapid economic growth and the demand for raw materials were causing considerable environmental damage.

General

With the economic reforms at the beginning of the 1980s, measures were introduced to alleviate the effect of increased industrialisation on the environment. These included the use of new energy sources, improvements in municipal refuse disposal and sewage treatment, curbs on air pollution and, in particular, commitment to a policy of planting new forests (deforestation being an especially serious consequence of population growth). More than 1000 committees were set up across the country to monitor these environmental initiatives

Environmental policy

The forests which cover about 13% of the country's land have been decimated by uncontrolled clearance (1.5 million ha/2.5 million acres). As the pace of modernisation has quickened and the population has continued to grow trees have been felled partly for building materials and fuel and partly to create more arable land. Soil erosion has taken

Excessive felling

Giant Panda

"**D**a Xiong Mao" (giant bear cat), as the Chinese describe the giant panda (*ailuropoda melanoleuca*), has been regarded for many hundreds of years as a bringer of good luck. A picture of the animal is painted on the front door of many houses and is thought to keep misfortune at bay.

At the beginning of the 1970s China started to donate pandas to zoos throughout the world. The animals delighted visitors with their appearance and playful behaviour. The latter seems to have resulted from their withdrawal into the mountain regions and their preference for vegetarian food, thereby reducing their need to compete for food or to fear other predators.

At the end of the 1970s it became clear that pandas, their numbers reduced to no more than 1000 in the wild, were likely to become further endangered by the destruction of the bamboo forests. So in 1981 the World Wildlife Fund (WWF), which had adopted the panda as its symbol, set up a research centre with the Chinese government in Sichuan province, where most pandas were found, with the aim of saving the panda from extinction. The Wolong reserve which covered an area of 2000sq.km/750sq.miles was dedicated to the preservation of the panda.

In addition punishment for poaching this rare species was to be the death sentence. There is a great demand for their distinctive fur in Taiwan, Japan and Hong Kong.

Pandas, known to have existed over 2 million years ago, are one of the oldest mammals on earth, but only in the last few thousand years did bamboo become their staple diet. With a panda weighing around 125kg/380lb, its daily bamboo requirements are in the region of 20kg/45lb. But bamboo is a poor source of protein and the animal's stomach rejects most of the stalk.

The bamboo, the panda's preferred food, flowers at very long intervals (sometimes as much as 100 years). After flowering, nearly all the plants in a forest die together. In 1975, all the plants within an area of 5000sq.km/1900sq.miles died and 140 pandas starved to death. In earlier times the animals would have moved on to new pastures, or new strains of bamboo would have spread into the affected area, but with the reduction in bamboo forests, this is no longer a possibility.

Their distinctive colouring of black ears, white neck and black body serves as an effective camouflage since the black-white contrast allows the outline of the body to merge with the background. A healthy panda has no natural enemies apart from man. Only young, old or sick pandas are likely to fall prey to leopards.

Although the animal feeds almost exclusively on bamboo, it is also a carnivore but it is too slow to catch other animals. The panda climbs well and in summer and autumn takes up residence at altitudes of 3000m/10,000ft or more. In the winter, however, it will look for lower-lying land. The panda is not a very sociable animal and has no fixed home. Males and females only come together during the annual mating season. The female panda nurtures the young in a hollow tree or some other shaded spot.

The panda's favourite occupation

place as a result of tree felling and this has been blamed for floods and the loss of agricultural and grazing land. The Changjiang alone carries away some 500 million tons of fertile soil a year – as much as the Nile, Amazon and Mississippi put together. And the Huanghe carries away three times that amount.

With the disappearance of the forests, valuable medicinal herbs, wild fruit and rare plants have also been lost. In addition many animal species have been threatened with extinction. The desert areas are expanding at a rate of 2300sq.km /880sq. miles a year. Since 1949 the area of land regarded as desert has increased by 6 million ha/15 million acres. Attempts to solve these problems have been made by using imported timber and by forestation programmes but more forest continues to be lost through over-exploitation than is gained by replanting.

Forestation schemes are planned mainly in northern China for the middle and upper reaches of the Changjiang and also for coastal regions. Under the Sanbei project a defensive strip of forest is planned which will begin in Helongjiang province and finish in Xinjiang province.

Many Chinese towns are suffering from high levels of air pollution caused predominantly by sulphur dioxide and coal smoke and dust from domestic fires and power stations. The situation is more serious in the north of the country where, unlike in the south, there is no ban on heating. Not only has rapid economic development caused coal consumption to soar, sharply increasing motorisation has brought even higher concentrations of carbon dioxide. Pollution levels were found to be ten times higher than those deemed to be acceptable by the World Health Organisation. Indeed the ten worst cities in the world from the point of view of air quality, five – Beijing, Shenyang, Xi'an, Shanghai and Canton – are in China. The nationalised industries are responsible for a high proportion of the air pollution. China is now second only to the USA in the emission of "greenhouse" gases.

Air pollution

In the 1980s a number of environmental laws were introduced to combat this pollution. Other areas of environmental concern such as refuse disposal and sewage treatment received more attention from the authorities as urban infrastructures were extended. Population growth posed particular problems as towns expanded. Plans to develop urban green belts and parkland were devised.

Industrial emissions of smoke and dust did indeed decline but in the smaller towns air pollution increased as more and more factories moved out of the major cities. Special emphasis was laid on environmental issues in recreational areas and tourist cities such as Guilin and Suzhou. Factories which polluted the atmosphere were moved elsewhere or closed.

Continuing economic development has also seen drastic intensification of the effects of acid rain, especially in the south of the country due to the particular combinations of soil and wind conditions. The industrial city of Chongqing is one of the most severely affected areas.

Acid rain

Water quality in China's rivers and lakes is adversely affected by the vast quantities of domestic and industrial effluent. Of 532 rivers tested 436 were classified as polluted, and about half of the larger lakes as very polluted. As a result fishing is in rapid decline. Illegal dumping of waste has caused contamination of ground-water.

Water pollution

Pollution further exacerbates the problem of water supply. In the 1950s in Beijing, for example, the ground-water level was some 5m/16½ft below the surface. Today water must be extracted from depths of 50m/165ft.

Population

The original
Chinese

What are nowadays known as the Chinese people or the Han, after the name of one of the dynasties, are not a pure race but a mixture of various ethnic groups and cultures. The earliest Chinese tribes, who settled on the banks of the Huanghe, had facial features which – as far as it is possible to reconstruct them – are found in the inhabitants of the central and eastern regions of the country: medium to small in height, sturdy build, white/yellow skin, black shiny silky textured hair, flat face with a small nose, prominent cheek bones and almond-shaped eyes.

Invasions

Repeated attacks by barbaric tribes from the north as well as periods of Mongol and Manchurian rule led, however, to a mixing of blood, which explains the bigger stature and narrower build of the typical north Chinese.

Of less significance was the contact between the northern Han tribes and the Turkic-Uigur and Persian peoples, who surged east along the Silk Roads to China. Their features are difficult to discern in Han Chinese today. At the beginning of Chinese civilisation the Han crossed the Changjiang and advanced south. In this way they avoided mixing with the northern tribes and it is assumed that they quickly became assimilated with the indigenous population.

Ethnic groups

Thanks to their isolated geographical location, the tribes of the south-west such as the Zhuang, Miao, Yi and Yao have survived. Although their numbers are greatly reduced they live on in the hilly regions. Unlike the Tibetans, Mongols, Kazakhs and Uigurs who developed their own culture and written language, these ethnic groups of south-

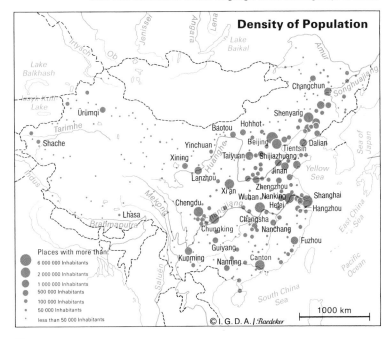

Density of Population

Places with more than:
- 6 000 000 Inhabitants
- 2 000 000 Inhabitants
- 1 000 000 Inhabitants
- 500 000 Inhabitants
- 100 000 Inhabitants
- 50 000 Inhabitants
- less than 50 000 Inhabitants

1000 km

© I. G. D. A. / Baedeker

western origin – on the border with Laos, Kampuchea, Myanmar (Burma) and Vietnam – did not develop a distinct culture of their own.

The Han Chinese, still a mixture of several different peoples, represent 93% of the total Chinese population. The remaining 7% belong to the 55 national minority groups which occupy land mainly in "Outer China" or on the southern border, areas which together make up some 60% of the country. In recent years a greater increase in population has been recorded among the minorities than among the Han, a situation that can be explained by the greater consideration now given to the interests of the minorities, the introduction of a degree of autonomy and the economic and cultural support of the Chinese government. They have also been given greater freedom in issues of family planning.

Of the 56 minorities, apart from the Han Chinese, eighteen exceed 1 million in population: the Mongols, Hui, Tibetans, Uigurs, Miao, Yi, Zhuang, Boutyei, Koreans, Manchurians, Dong, Yao, Bai, Tujia, Hani, Kazakhs, Dai and Li. Fifteen have populations exceeding 100,000: the Lisu, Wa, She, Lahu, Shui, Dongxiang, Naxi, Jingpo, Kirghiz, Tu, Dahuren, Mulao, Qiang, Gelo and Xibo. 22 nationalities have populations of less than 100,000: the Gaoshan, Blang, Sala, Maonan, Achang, Pumi, Tajiks, Nu, Uzbeks, Russians, Ewenki, Deang, Baoan, Yugurs, Jing, Tatars, Drung, Oroqen, Hezhe, Moinba, Lhoba and Jinao.

In 1993 China's population was reckoned to be 1,178,400,000, which made it the most heavily populated country in the world with a fifth of the world's population. The same set of statistics revealed that there were 123 Chinese per sq.km, a figure which had risen by 18 since 1982. *Population density and structure*

The proportion of males to females, which in the past had shown a surplus of males, had evened out somewhat to 52% males and 48% females.

The age structure of the Chinese population can be summarised as follows: 27% of the population are under 15, 66% between 15 and 64 and 7% 65 and above.

The population of China has risen dramatically in recent decades. In 1911, the population stood at a mere 374 million, in 1953, 582 million and 962 million in 1978. *Overpopulation*

Overpopulation is a historical phenomenon for China. On the one hand, it compensates for the shortage of productive capital resources, but on the other hand technical and industrial progress is held back and average income stays at very low levels. In the past, war and natural catastrophes have restricted population growth, but since 1949 living conditions have improved, mortality rates have dropped considerably and at the same time birth rates have risen.

The response of the Chinese government in the late 1950s to the alarming growth in population and its effect on the economy was to impose a birth control policy in which the legal age of marriage was raised to 25 for women and 28 for men. Various contraception methods were officially encouraged, abortion was legalised and voluntary sterilisation promoted. But a rural farming society such as the Chinese with low levels of education had difficulty accepting and applying the recommended measures. Taboos and long-standing customs were obstinately adhered to. Married couples did not stop having children and in the rural areas it was still regarded as a social and economic drawback not to have any sons. The higher proportion of men – an unusual contrast with most other countries – seems to have come about as the result of an ancient custom (still common in rural areas) of drowning girls at birth. Girls are regarded as unproductive and socially inferior. The government policy introduced at the beginning of the 1970s – and pursued with more vigour in the 1980s – allows one child per couple in the towns and two in the country. Married couples are *Population policy* advised about contraception, birth control and eugenics. The Chinese government provided contraceptives free of charge and also bore the costs of abortion and sterilisation. A number of social and economic sanctions were devised to deter couples from having more than two children. On the other hand, those Chinese who abided by the birth control guidelines became entitled to certain inducements and privileges (cash payments, favourable treatment in the allocation of apartments and schooling).

In the rural areas, home for about two-thirds of the Chinese population, many peasants did not comply with the "two child" policy and had to come to terms with the penalties that the state imposed.

Population growth rate

The imprecise Chinese government population statistics showed that the annual population growth rate, which stood at 2.6% in 1953, fell to 1.4% in 1982. But the ensuing years did not confirm this trend as by 1988 the rate had risen to 2.1%. The measures introduced by the government do not seem to have had the required results. Under the birth control scheme during the years from 1986 to 1990 an annual growth rate of between 0.7% and 0.8% was predicted. In 1993, the population grew by 1.3%.

Population distribution

Given the land surface area of China, there ought to be no cause for concern about population growth. The problems arise, however, when the nature of the Chinese landscape is taken into account: over 50% of China consists of mountains and deserts. The population is not distributed evenly across the country. The densely populated east contrasts sharply with the sparsely inhabited west. In the eastern province of Jiangsu 700 people are crammed into each square kilometre, while in Tibet the corresponding figure for a square kilometre is two! Furthermore, all the agricultural land – a vital source of food and income for the Chinese people – is already in use. The land available is hardly adequate for feeding the peasants as proved by the huge numbers of country-dwellers who have moved to the urban centres. While all the flat agricultural land is fully utilised and only productivity can be improved, in the peripheral regions it would still be possible to convert barren land into farmland and exploit mineral deposits. However, with the high costs of developing urban communities in the deserts, the low levels of education and also the hostility of the peasants to compulsory resettlement, it is proving difficult to implement what is already an unpopular policy.

Language

Chinese, the most important of the Sino-Tibetan languages, is characterised by monosyllabic word roots, intonation and isolation, i.e. grammatical relationships are shown only through word order. The very complicated ancient Chinese sound system has been simplified to create Putonghua, now regarded as standard Chinese. It derives from a northern Chinese dialect and has only about 1600 tonal differences, but it has become the most widely used form of spoken Chinese. The southern and south-eastern dialects (Cantonese, Hakka and Fukien) retain the older sound system with some highly complicated forms of intonation. As the limited number of sound combinations in standard Chinese did not do justice to the rich vocabulary and led to countless homophones (words similar in sound but different in meaning), words were juxtaposed to avoid confusion and the language became "multisyllabic".

Language groups

There are two language groups, corresponding with the two original tribal groups: Chinese as spoken by Han Chinese, i.e. 92% of the population (including the Moslem Hui minority) and the languages of the other national minorities. These can be divided into four language families: Tibetan, Hani, Tujia and Yi languages belong to the Tibeto-Burman group, Mongolian, Kazakh and Uigur to the Altaic group and the languages of the Zhuang, Dai, Bouyei and Dong to the Thai group. The Yao and Miao minorities from the southern mountain regions speak a language with idioms whose roots are unknown. For the minorities in the autonomous regions, their language is the official one.

Chinese is a difficult language to speak and understand. The main reason for the difficulty lies with the difference between the written and spoken language. There is no alphabet and there is no link between the sound uttered and the symbol which represents it. The meaning is shown by a symbol, originally it was a pictograph, to which a phonetic value has been assigned. Chinese is a monosyllabic language; each character has its own single- syllable pronunciation and its own meaning.

Chinese characters

The complicated relationship between the written and spoken language has had a lasting influence on Chinese culture and is rendered even more difficult by the limited number of monosyllabic phonemes (about 400). To differentiate between words and to help in the formation of new words, four different tonal levels are used. Conversely, in contrast with the small number of phonemes, there are many thousands of characters (about 45,000–50,000 but only 10,000 are in common use and only 4000 are used by the mass media). There are, for example, 37 characters which when spoken resemble the sound "pi". At the first tonal level alone, it can mean "splendid", "to hit" and "unfired clay". Consequently, readers of Chinese have to be able to recognise the character and its exact phonetic sound to understand the language completely – something that requires a considerable amount of memorisation.

Phonemes

Old and modern Chinese script

Homophones

The unequal relationship between phonemes and characters which has led to the evolution of countless homophones frequently causes misunderstandings. Close observation of Chinese people talking reveals that they often use the fingers of the right hand to draw a symbol on the palm of the left hand. They are simply writing the symbol of the word they have just uttered in order to facilitate understanding.

The difference between the written and spoken word was something which fascinated the philosopher Leibniz. He was enthralled by the potential of the Chinese language and thought it could become the best language of international communication.

Written language

Chinese writing is composed of ideograms which date back to a system devised in the 2nd millennium B.C. – some linguists believe it is even older. Emperor Qin Shi Huangdi who reigned from 221–210 B.C. combined the various dialects into one written language, so that each symbol had its own meaning but no link to pronunciation. This reform has remained the basis for the written language ever since.

The influence of foreign languages on the Chinese and related languages has been slight. The spread of Buddhism throughout China accentuated the division between the written language (a unifying factor among the variety of regional dialects) and the spoken language. The latter flourished during the campaigns to convert the people to Buddhism, leading to new and richer forms of self-expression. The period of Mongolian rule and the relocation of the capital in Beijing were important factors in ensuring that the northern dialect prevailed over other regional variations and it became the official language of the ruling classes (Baihua). Baihua found its way into popular literature, unlike the written language (Wenyan) of antiquity which only the upper strata of Mandarin society had mastered. The ability to write literary texts was tested in the famous state examinations. Precision in the use of grammar and syntax was an important feature of the written language, which could hardly be used in verbal form. It could be read but not spoken.

Spoken language

It was not until the beginning of the 20th c. – at the time of the first student movements and as a consequence of the writings of Lu Xun, modern China's greatest writer – that the classical language of academics was relinquished in favour of the spoken language.

Only after 1949 with help from newspapers, books, radio, television and language lessons did the common Putonghua language function successfully as a form of communication at all levels of society. The Chinese government introduced two measures which sought to make this language accessible to as many people as possible: the simplification of the written form and a phonetic transcription with letters from the Latin alphabet. This form of romanisation known as Pinyin is still only used in dictionaries, to help with the learning of foreign languages and as an aid to the international standardisation of proper names. Even Westerners have had difficulty adapting to this system as the principles of transcription devised in the 19th c. by the English (Wade), German (Lessing) and French (EFEO) are still retained by many.

Education and Science

Education policies

In 1977 after the cultural revolution when progress in education and science stagnated, new approaches to educational policy were considered appropriate. In 1985 a far-reaching reform of school and further education was adopted. Henceforth education was for developing political consciousness as well as acquiring knowledge, with the emphasis on specialist qualifications. Time at school was to be extended from six to nine years, but with no exemption from school

General compulsory school attendance lessens illiteracy

fees. Of the four elements of the modernisation programme – research, industry, agriculture and the army – research and science were granted the highest status. Academic achievement was to have priority over political consciousness and the re-introduction of marking and examinations underlined this point.

Children aged three to six are prepared for the primary school in kindergartens. Subjects studied include language, arithmetic, singing, painting and sport. However, it is estimated that as a result of a shortage of spaces only a quarter of all children receive pre-school education.

Kindergarten

Beyond the kindergartens, the education system consists of three stages: primary school, secondary school and university. Full-time primary education from the age of six comprises six school years. Mathematics, Chinese and one foreign language (English or Japanese) are the main subjects on the curriculum but biology, music, art, politics, history, physics, chemistry and geography are covered. Sport and productive work are also undertaken.

Primary school

Primary school is compulsory, but according to some estimates school attendance in the more remote areas is not always enforced. In 1991 97.9% of school-age children were attending school.

After passing an examination at the end of the first stage, pupils move into the secondary stage, which also comprises six years of study and is divided into middle and upper schools. About three quarters of primary school leavers continue their education into the secondary school.

The middle school stage lasts three years. At the end, more examinations are taken which allow entry into the final three-year upper school stage. Subject areas correspond with those of the primary school.

Secondary school

41

After the first three years at middle school, students can progress into vocational colleges where technical, teacher-training and agricultural courses are offered. Compared with a general education, this type of practical further education is gaining in importance. In 1990, nearly half of all upper middle school students were attending technical and vocational colleges. The final examination corresponds with A-levels and is an essential element in the demanding university entrance requirements.

University

The pinnacle of educational achievement is a place at university and such an opportunity is only available to a very small percentage of Chinese young people. In 1991, 2,044,000 students were attending university, roughly 2% of the population. From 10,000 students in any one academic year only eighteen will qualify for a place at university. As well as the universities, which are predominantly concerned with the humanities and science, there are many polytechnics, which offer courses in architecture and engineering. The period of study varies according to the subject and there are supplementary courses for the acquisition of certain specialist and professional skills. Gifted students or students from poor backgrounds receive assistance. Upon completion of their further education, the authorities decide where they will be employed after graduation.

Adult education

As the various educational establishments are unable to guarantee training to all Chinese, there has been increasing emphasis on adult education. The educational opportunities available include free-time, part-time and full-time courses in various types of college. The best known free-time colleges are in Beijing and Shanghai. In addition, radio and television provide vocational courses. Students are released from their work to study and fees are met by employers.

Illiteracy

Despite the efforts of the Chinese government to educate the masses, around 27% of the population, or 313 million people, are said to be illiterate. When the Chinese Republic was founded in 1949, the figure was 90% but it had been reduced to 38% by 1964.

There are a number of causes for illiteracy and the very poor record of school attendance in the early years. Poverty among the rural population is certainly a factor as for many, the payment of school fees represents a major problem. Burgeoning private enterprise discriminates against families with several children. The sanctions imposed by the state on couples who ignore family planning guidelines can cause hardship as does the absence of social security and pensions. Primary and middle schools in particular suffer from a shortage of teachers, who complain of poor pay and working conditions (inadequate teaching areas, few resources and large classes).

Religion and Philosophy

Religious thought

The Chinese are not familiar with the concept of religion in a Western sense. For them it has more to do with school and teaching. Throughout Chinese history it is not possible to discern any contradiction between worldly and religious power. There have been no crusades, no schisms or reforms, no beliefs have ever been met with intolerance, a phenomenon that Marco Polo observed. But most striking is the fact that in Chinese thought there has never been that contradiction or conflict between the natural world and the supernatural which has had such a far-reaching effect on Western history. In Chinese philosophy and religion, earthly matters and metaphysics are two complementary aspects of the same universe. Evidence for this can be found in the presence of historical figures in the divine world and the reverence for spirits or gods in the real world. In contrast to Christianity, there is no transcendental god and no creator.

The mind is focused on maintaining natural harmony, as chaos in nature brings catastrophes. Disturbing the natural equilibrium releases feelings of apprehension and anxiety, unlike Western religions where the threat of punishment in the after-life exists. Quite apart from the differences between the various Chinese philosophies, it is easy to understand how this way of thinking has developed in a world which is shaped by the land, which is exposed to unpredictable natural catastrophes and the whims of the seasons and water, but which at the same time seeks to bring these elements of nature under control.

Natural equilibrium

The foundations for this view of the world which sees the universe as a number of elements which have to be kept in equilibrium seems to have emerged during the Shang and Zhou Dynasties (16th c.–221 B.C.). It is thought that the myths and beliefs of Bronze Age hunters provided the fundamental ideas to which Chinese philosophical and religious schools later returned. These beliefs were expressed in the form of Taoism and the dualism of Yin and Yang. Tao means "The Way" and is concerned with the course of events and the principle of universal order.

Cosmology

Taoism comprises two major elements, the Yin and the Yang, which represent the contradictory but complementary and indivisible nature of all phenomena.

Yin and Yang

Yin represents woman, night, shadow, moon, death and earth. Yang symbolises man, day, life, light, sun and sky.

From this philosophical standpoint, it is easy to see how Chinese religions have eschewed metaphysical issues; on the other hand a principal concern has been the structure of society and the role of the individual within it.

Religious teachings

Common philosophical interests have influenced the great religions of China – Buddhism, Taoism and Confucianism. Those mutual influences have led to overlaps and to some extent there has been a merging of beliefs. For that reason it is never possible to state to which religion a particular tenet and its expression should be assigned.

In the 500 years before the birth of Christ, the cosmological philosophy and rites of classical antiquity did not present a view of an ordered world to society and the emerging classes. It was Confucius (see Famous People), an academic who lived between the 6th and 5th c. B.C., who provided the structure for a set of beliefs which later served as a standard of behaviour, philosophy, religion or more precisely a national code of ethics.

Confucianism

As Confucianism contains no mysticism, no gods or deities and does not seek to save souls, some may claim that it is not a true religion. Confucius' main concerns were the development of society and the exploration of the relationship between the individual and the community. He succeeded in creating legitimacy for the nobility and the ruling classes, but their existence was not to be based on any legal status or rights of inheritance, but on moral necessity.

Some of Confucius' basic tenets are outlined here: a just ruler is distinguished by his moral authority; society should be regulated by a system of relationships, based on personal and social virtues; the core element in society should be the family and the relationship between father and son, man and wife, young and old should be determined by a strict hierarchy; the state should be broken down into parts like a large family in which the master provides for his subjects.

Moral principles

Confucius

Laotse

Mencius (Meng Zi) and Zun Zi expanded Confucius' ethical teachings with some different emphases in the 3rd c. B.C. The most important of the four books which contain the teachings and ideas of Confucianism is entitled "Analects".

The Legalists

In opposition to the ethical standpoints of Confucian followers, a group known as the Legalists were convinced that self-interest motivated human actions and consequently to appeal to a sense of morality was pointless. To direct human behaviour and then to be in a position to control it did not require a system of moral guidelines but rather a system of laws which should be familiar to the people and which should be strictly applied.

These theoretical arguments between ethics and law were dismissed by Confucius in his writings. He declared: "If we govern with the support of laws and we then try to make things equal by punishment, the people will seek to avoid those sanctions and will feel no shame. If we govern with the support of virtue and then try to make things equal by applying norms of decency, the people will feel shame and behave well".

Development of the two approaches

After the Legalist school had provided the structure for the empire of Qin Shi Huangdi, China's first emperor, they were forced to yield to the superior force of Confucian thinking, which first in the 3rd c. B.C. under the Han Dynasty and later between A.D. 900 and 1200 under the Song Dynasty became the official national doctrine. The controversy between the Legalists and the Confucians became one of the thorniest and also one of the most interesting features of Chinese intellectual history, primarily because of the effects which Confucianism had, not just on the economic, social and political development of China but also on the evolution of an official class and imperial bureaucracy. Shortly before Mao's death a dispute over the same issue emerged within the Communist Party.

Furthermore, Confucianism had a greater influence than Buddhism or Taoism. It penetrated the whole structure of society and extended into all cultures. By appealing to virtue, wisdom and moral sensitivities, it succeeded in linking libertarianism with a strict, ritualised and hierarchical system.

Taoism which derives from the teachings of Laotse (see Famous People) evolved in the 6th and 5th c. B.C. at approximately the same time as Confucius was expounding his theories. It too owes its origins to the cosmological theories of classical philosophy, whose central concepts were the "tao", the eternal course of events as well as the Yin and Yang. The word Taoism or in Chinese taojia, i.e. the philosophy of things derives from the root word "tao", sometimes translated into English as "way".

Taoism, like Confucianism, seeks to examine human behaviour. Teachings stress the return to an original state, to a natural order. Preserving the equilibrium of this order is one of the purposes of life.

Man is just a tiny part of the universe but he has an important part to play in the general structure of the universe which must be maintained as it incorporates truth. This fundamental view often moves supporters of Taoism to withdraw from public life and to lead a life of solitude according to the principles of "effortless action".

What is understood by natural order is explained by the following words of Zhuang Zi (396–286 B.C.), one of Taoism's foremost philosophers: "The legs of the duck are short, but if we try to lengthen them the duck will suffer pain. The legs of the crane are long, but if we try to shorten them the crane will suffer pain. That is why we ought not to shorten anything that is by nature long and lengthen anything that is by nature short".

Taoism

Man and the universe

Buddha painted on a rock near Lhasa

45

Religion and Philosophy

Superstitions

Taoism tried to give theoretical depth to the fundamental concepts of the old philosophy (Tao, Yin and Yang) and all the empirical knowledge of the past (dietetics, geomancy and breathing techniques). But the re-examination of the conventional beliefs and traditions had the effect of transforming the movement into a type of religion and a doctrine based on superstitions. Almost in contradiction of Taoist philosophy (taojia), the religion (taojiao) gained ground among the people as it promised eternal salvation and immortality of the soul, just like Buddhism from where it had adopted the notion of heaven and rituals. Both such concepts were alien to the original teachings of Laotse (see Famous People) and Zhuang Zi.

Buddhism

Buddhism, the last of the great religions to reach China, arrived from India along the Silk Road and took root in the 1st c. A.D. under the Han Dynasty. As the Chinese were scarcely familiar with Indian culture, and the Sanskrit and Chinese languages had very little in common, Buddhism was originally falsely regarded as a form of Taoism. Although both religions started from the premise that life is a heavy load to bear when there is so much suffering and corruption in the world, the routes that the individual could follow to redemption were quite different.

Beliefs

While Taoists advocated a natural order, Buddhist monks preached salvation of the soul, but such an outcome was only achievable by renouncing all desire and earthly pleasures, thereby obtaining release from life and suffering – nirvana, a term which means eternal serenity or complete annihilation.

Unlike Taoism which regards itself as a doctrine for the individual with the hermit as its chosen symbolic figure, Buddhism possesses an organisational structure, an order of monks who withdraw into the monastery as novitiates, perform missionary work and lead a life of strict devotion.

Religious persecution

The possibility of salvation brought Buddhism many followers. In the 9th c. the movement grew to be a very strong economic force. The Tang Dynasty (618–907) which had until then treated all religious beliefs with tolerance, feared the loss of its economic and spiritual influence, ordered the closure of all Buddhist temples and banned the Buddhist religion – a severe blow to Chinese Buddhism. Only the Chan (Japanese Zen) school managed to survive the Tang Dynasty's campaign of persecution and to carry forward the religious and spiritual inheritance of Buddhism.

Religious Minorities

Other religious beliefs are widespread in China. While Nestorianism, Manichaeism and the teachings of Zarathustra – all hybrids in which Christian doctrine mingles with elements of Middle Eastern and Persian faiths – only enjoyed a short life under the Tang Dynasty (618–907) and Judaism won for itself small and isolated pockets of faithful adherents, it was Islam which won most support from the population of north-western China, where many people had Arab ancestors. Unlike Buddhism, the teachings of Islam never came close to the Chinese soul in a cultural sense.

Catholicism

Catholicism was never able to penetrate into the religious imagination of the Chinese. Attempts by Jesuit missionaries around 1600 had very little success and this was despite the intervention of the Italian Matteo Ricci who won the support of the Chinese court and became an official in the imperial bureaucracy.

Chinese Deities

The Eight Immortals are the deities of the Taoist paradise who enjoy eternal life. Three of the figures are identifiable historical personalities, but the remaining five are legendary characters. The various identities which they assumed in their earthly life (rich man and poor man, man and woman, soldier and official) symbolise not just the complementary Yin and Yang forces, but also the ordered society of the time. They can be seen sitting on a fluffy cloud on which they move from place to place, walking up steep cliff faces and seeking the truth or riding on the back of a crane, a mythical beast. In the most famous episode, the Eight Immortals cross the seas and engage in battle with adversity a thousand times, but then have to forego their cloud and continue their journey by other means – a fan, a sword and a bamboo cane.

Ba Xian, the Eight Immortals

The prince's son Siddhartha, who lived in India between the 6th and 5th c. B.C. became after many long years of contemplation the Buddha Sakyamuni. He is always represented sitting cross-legged on a lotus flower dressed only in a simple loin-cloth with no adornments or else lying on his side, resting his face on his hand. Apart from the existence of this historically authentic figure, five other cosmic or metaphysical buddhas, who never lived, led a supernatural existence. They are portrayed in various colours (white, red, black, green and yellow) on the back of an animal (lion, elephant, eagle, peacock and horse).

Buddha Sakyamuni

Statue of Buddha

Bodhisattva

Bodhisattva

Bodhisattvas are semi-earthly beings who temporarily relinquish their journey to nirvana in order to help sufferers. As they have not yet left this life, they are always shown wearing earthly clothing and in the same posture as Buddha Sakyamuni. They wear splendid clothes and their bodies are covered with jewellery and decorations, an allusion to the vanity of this life.

Of the many bodhisattvas who are revered for their closeness to the real world, four deserve special attention. Guanyin, the goddess of mercy and fertility is frequently portrayed in Chinese art and usually with a thousand arms encircling her body. An eye on the palm of each hand enables her to comprehend the endlessness of human suffering in this world.

Maitreya or Buddha of the Future, whose reincarnation is expected at the end of the next millennium, is shown seated on a throne as the god of contemplation with the wheel of truth or a flowering branch.

Wenshu is the master of the word and wisdom and Dizang the lord of hell who decides how souls are to be reincarnated.

Huangdi

The legendary Yellow Emperor who lived *c.* 2500 B.C. and is venerated as the god of architecture and roads, was originally associated with the cosmological teachings of antiquity but later found favour with Taoists. He is regarded as the inventor of the wheel and the boat and he helped develop early ceramic processes and also some advanced agricultural methods. He is also credited with advancing certain disciplines such as astronomy and mineralogy.

Heng and Ha

Heng and Ha are the two gods who guard the entrance to Buddhist heaven. According to legend these characters, who actually lived 1000 years before Christ, were granted special powers by Taoist magicians. With a deafening noise Heng would send deadly beams of white light from his nostrils, while Ha breathed an equally noxious yellow gas from his lungs. They fought each other in a duel but were killed by strange forces which knew their weaknesses. Both characters were later canonised and chosen to guard Buddhist temples. They will be seen staring angrily at each other at the entrance to Buddhist monasteries.

Comparable perhaps with Christ's followers, luohan are the apostles of Buddhism. After a lot of hard mental and physical work in this world, they have reached one stage on the route to nirvana. By meditation and suffering, their desires and emotions have been extinguished. They live in a state of grace and possess special privileges and powers. They can, for example, discover the thoughts of others and live past lives. Unlike the compassionate and helpful bodhisattvas, luohan are remote from humanity as they have already crossed the threshold of happiness. They usually form into groups of 9, 16, 18 or 500 with each one embodying a character who can be distinguished from the others by a gesture, an object or a physical feature. The best known luohan images are found in the Temple of the Azure Clouds in Beijing or in the Precious Light Monastery near Chengdu.

Luohan

Laotse (see Famous People) is often represented as Shoulao the god of old age, with a large bald skull, a broad prominent forehead as a symbol of deep meditation, long ear-lobes representing wisdom and a stick in his hand. He rides on a deer or a phoenix towards the world of immortality. As a philosopher or historical personality, Laotse usually appears in the form of an old man riding off to distant lands on the back of a buffalo.

Shoulao

State and Administration

The People's Republic of China or the Chinese People's Republic, transcribed in Pinyin as Zhonghua Renmin Gongheguo (pronounced Chung Hua Yen-Min Kung-He Kuo) was proclaimed by Mao Zedong (Tse-tung) on October 1st 1949. The (fourth) constitution of 1982 describes the nation as a "People's Republic" founded on the principles of socialism, the democratic dictatorship of the proletariat, Marxist-Leninist-Maoism and the absolute leadership of the Communist Party.

Form of government

The national flag, coat-of-arms and international code for vehicles are shown on page 50.

National emblems

The People's Republic of China maintains relations with most countries including the United Kingdom and all the members of the European Union.

Diplomatic relations

China was one of the founding members of the United Nations and from the beginning has sat as one of the five permanent members of the Security Council. It is also represented on many UN organisations. In 1971 the UN assembly voted to exclude the Republic of China (Nationalist Taiwan) and to replace it with the People's Republic of China.

Membership of international bodies

In 1975 a trading agreement was signed with the European Union (EU).

Organs of state

The 3,500 deputies to the National People's Congress (NPC), the highest organ of state, are elected for five years by the provinces, autonomous regions, directly-administered cities and military units. This

National People's Congress

People's Republic of China
Zhonghua Renmin Gongheguo

National Flag

International Vehicle Plate

TJ

State Arms

PROVINCES, AUTONOMOUS REGIONS

GD	Guangdong
GX	Guangxi
HEB	Hebei
HEN	Henan
JS	Jiangsu
NX	Ningxia
SD	Shandong
SX	Shanxi
TJ	Tianjin
ZJ	Zhejiang

RUSSIA

RUSSIA

Heilongjiang (Amur)

HEILONGJIANG

Songhuajiang (Sungari)

ER MONGOLIA)

NEIMENGGU
(INNER MONGOLIA)

OHarbin

Changchun

JILIN

Fushun O
Schenyang O

LIAONING

NORTH

Hohhot

Chengde

BEIJING
(PEKING)

ODatong

Beidaihe

TJ

Bohai

Lüda
(ehem. Port Arthur)

KOREA

SOUTH
KOREA

Yinchuan

Shijiazhuang

Huanghe (Hwangho)

Taiyuan

HEB

O

O Jinan

SD

Yellow
Sea

JX

SX

Yanan O

OQingdao

Qufu

Xi'an O

SHAANXI

Luoyang O

O Zhengzhou

HEN

Daiunbe

JS

ngdu

HUBEI

ANHUI

Hefei
O

Nanjing

OWuxi

Suzhou O O

SHANGHAI

Jangtsekiang

Wuhan O

Hangzhou O

O O Ningbo
Shaoxing

go O

East China
Sea

Guiyang
O

GUIZHOU

Changsha O

HUNAN

Nanchang

JIANGXI

ZJ

OFuzhou

TAIWAN
(REPUBLIK
CHINA)

Guilin

GX

GD

Conghua

FUJIAN

Formosa Strait

Xijiang

Nanning
O

Foshan
O

O Guangzhou (Canton)

HONGKONG

MACAO

AM

South China
Sea

HAINAN

⌐⌐⌐⌐ Great Wall

500 km

© Baedeker

51

body which can enact laws, adopt economic plans and decide if the country should go to war, meets once a year when it selects members for the Standing Committee of the National People's Congress. The president of the Standing Committee serves as Head of State. Between sittings of the NPC, the Standing Committee fulfils all legislative functions and convenes the State Council, (the central administrative body) and the executive organ of the NPC. The State Council appoints the Premier and its membership includes the Vice Premiers, General Secretary and a changing number of ministers with responsibility for the various departments of state. The government is accountable to the NPC.

Other important organs of state are the Supreme People's Court and the Supreme People's Procuratorates. There is universal suffrage.

Communist
Party of China

The ruling party of government is the Communist Party of China (with over 50 million members) and consists of the Central Committee (175 members), the Politburo (16 members) and the Military Commission. The highest decision-making body of the Communist Party is the Standing Committee of the Politburo with the General Secretary as its leader.

Administrative areas (see map on pages 50/51)

Local government

The People's Republic of China is divided into a complicated web of territorial units with regional autonomy.

Regions of Mainland China

Geographical
regions with
provinces,
autonomous
regions and
directly-
administered
towns

North-eastern China (*Dongbei*):
Heilongjiang · Jilin · Liaoning
Northern China (*Huabei*):
Hebei · Neimenggu · Beijing · Shanxi · Tianjin
Eastern China (*Huadong*):
Shandong . Jiangxi · Jiangsu · Shanghai · Anhui · Zhejiang · Fujian
Central and Southern China (*Zhongnan*):
Hainan · Henan · Hubei · Hunan · Guangdong · Guangxi
South-western China (*Xinan*):
Sichuan . Guizhou · Yunnan · Xizang (Tibet)
North-western China (*Xibei*):
Shaanxi · Gansu · Ningxia · Qinghai · Xinjiang

China's administrative areas (see map on pages 50/51)

People's Republic of China   Capital: Beijing (Peking)

Province	NAME	SURFACE AREA	POPULATION	ADMINISTRA-TIVE
Chu	(in alphabetical order)	(sq.km/ sq. miles)	(in millions; 1992)	CENTRE
	Anhui	139,000/52,800	57.61	Hefei
	Fujian	121,380/46,125	30.79	Fuzhou
	Gansu	451,000/171,380	22.85	Lanzhou
	Guangdong	198,500/75,430	64.39	Canton
	Guizhou	170,000/64,600	32.15	Guiyang
	Hainan	34,380/13,064	6.74	Haikou
	Hebei	190,000/72,200	62.2	Shijiazhuang

Province	NAME	SURFACE AREA	POPULATION	ADMINISTRA-TIVE
Chu	(in alphabetical order)	(sq.km/ sq. miles)	(in millions; 1992)	CENTRE
	Heilongjiang	469,000/178,220	35.75	Harbin
	Henan	167,000/63,460	87.63	Zhengzhou
	Hubei	180,000/68,400	55.12	Wuhan
	Hunan	210,000/79,800	62.09	Changsha
	Jiangsu	102,600/38,760	68.44	Nanjing
	Jiangxi	166,000/63,080	38.65	Nanchang
	Jilin	187,400/71,060	25.09	Changchun
	Liaoning	145,700/55,366	39.96	Shenyang
	Qinghai	720,000/273,600	4.54	Xining
	Shaanxi	195,000/74,100	33.63	Xi'an
	Shandong	153,300/58,254	85.7	Jinan
	Shanxi	156,000/59,280	28.42	Taiyuan
	Sichuan	567,000/215,460	108.97	Chengdu
	Yunnan	394,000/149,720	37.82	Kunming
	Zhejiang	101,800/38,684	42.02	Hangzhou
Autonomous regions	Guangxi	236,000/89,680	43.24	Nanning
	Neimenggu	1,200,000/456,000	21.84	Hohhot
	Ningxia	66,400/25,230	4.8	Yinchuan
	Xinjiang	1,650,000/627,000	15.55	Ürümqi
	Xizang (Tibet)	1,228,000/466,640	2.2	Lhasa
Directly-administered towns	Beijing	16,807/6,386	10.94	
	Shanghai	6200/2350	13.4	
	Tianjin	4276/1625	9.09	
Taiwan (Republic of China)		36,179/13,750	20.8	Taipei
Hong Kong (British Crown Colony)		1071/407	6.0	Victoria
Macau (Chinese territory under Portuguese administration)		18/7	0.5	Macau

The nation can be divided into 30 main administrative units: 22 (23 with Taiwan) provinces or chu, corresponding roughly with the eighteen provinces of imperial times, five autonomous regions with special status for the national minorities (Inner Mongolia, Ningxia, Xinjiang, Guangxi and Tibet) and three directly-administered towns (the capital Beijing, Shanghai and Tianjin, the country's main industrial areas). — Provinces / Autonomous regions / Directly-administered towns

The provinces and autonomous regions are divided into districts (diqu) and, including the autonomous districts with their ethnic minorities, total more than 150. — Districts

As well as the districts, autonomous prefectures exist predominantly for the ethnic minorities. — Prefectures
In addition, there are several Special Economic Zones (see page 56).

In rural areas there used to be an even lower administrative level, the People's Commune. As all property was owned by the collectives this was the basis of all administrative structures, but after recent economic and political developments which favour private ownership, the People's Communes have been almost abolished throughout China and replaced by communities or urban zones. — Communities

Economy

Economic history

The peasant culture

The Chinese civilisation, which developed along the muddy, fertile banks and in the wet lowlands of the Changjiang, was chiefly an agricultural culture. Recent excavations have revealed that even 3000 to 4000 years ago millet and rice were cultivated and advanced methods of land use and irrigation were already in use.

But it would be wrong to say that China was only an agrarian society, as it was producing hand-made consumer goods long before other cultures and also quarrying raw materials. Silk, porcelain, tea plantations, salt and coal mines are just a few examples of how China was able to diversify in the past.

Working methods

The progressive economic structure that Western visitors encountered in the 13th and 14th c. started to decay in the following centuries. This reversal in fortunes, in the view of several historians, had two causes. One was objective – an excess of manpower which discouraged the development of new, time-saving methods and one was subjective – the strict control of the imperial bureaucracy which suppressed individual freedom and personal initiative. Also important was the indisputable fact that farming had priority over every other productive occupation and for it to continue successfully, assistance from a strong political central source was essential as the hydraulic systems necessary to combat geological and climatic conditions had to be co-ordinated.

Foreign influence

Between the 14th and 18th c. China took a more prominent position on the world stage, but because of its economic and political weakness, it easily fell prey to the European powers who were mainly interested in its locally produced goods and raw materials. However, Western imperialist expansion also brought industrial technology to the country and the infrastructure was improved. The ports of Shanghai, Canton and Tianjin were created or enlarged. In 1876 the first railway line was built and steel plants, mechanical engineering and light industry developed.

Reconstruction after 1949

When the Chinese set about the reconstruction of their country after 1949, the economy lay in tatters. The role of industry was not significant as what little industrial plant existed was in a poor condition. All factories were mainly concentrated in the coastal regions around the four ports of Tianjin, Qingdao, Shanghai and Canton (where foreign companies were based) and in Manchuria, where the Japanese had developed a number of industrial projects during the civil war. In the interior, industrial development had been centred on Chongqing, Wuhan and Taiyuan. The situation in the rural areas was certainly not flourishing either. After the wars the hydraulic systems which were essential for irrigation and for the control of the rivers were no longer functioning properly.

Economic policy

The economic policies adopted after 1949 were based on a number of principles. Firstly it was vital to strengthen the key role of agriculture in the interior and secondly the industrial imbalance between the coastal regions and the interior had to be rectified. This involved building new plant and infrastructure in towns without any industry and close to the areas where the raw materials originated. Further improvements such as land drainage, forestation, river control, dam construction and extension of the road and rail network were to lay the foundations for opening up the desert areas and also achieving better returns on agricultural land.

After the death of Mao Zedong the 5th five-year plan of 1976 set about changing the direction of economic policy. Reforms were

Working in the fields

introduced from 1978, first in agriculture and then in 1984 under the 6th five-year plan for industry. The reforms, which brought about far-reaching changes to the economic system, were designed to encourage private, profit-oriented entrepreneurs in agriculture and light industry. Moves were also made to attract foreign companies in order to take advantage of new technologies. In 1980 a number of Special Economic Zones (Shenzhen, Zhuhai, Shantou, Xiamen and in 1988 Hainan) were set up with capitalist objectives.

Under the 7th five-year plan (1986–90), the economy was to be regulated with prices, taxation, credit, wages and exchange rates rather than with administrative measures. Several coastal regions and a number of towns were granted economic privileges including favourable working conditions and special fiscal and currency regulations. All these measures led not only to an enormous increase in gross national product, but also to higher levels of inflation and an increasing budget deficit. The aim of the 8th five-year plan (1991–95) is to continue the process of structural economic change by improving raw material production and processing and by extending the infrastructure more rapidly.

Economic situation

In 1994 China achieved an economic growth rate of about 12% with an inflation rate of more than 24%. Progress occurred predominantly in the Special Economic Zones on the coast and in the rural industrial developments of the richer provinces. State-controlled industry is continuing to decline in proportion to the private sector.

Economic data

Price inflation reached 26% and living costs rose as a result of deregulation of food costs and a reduction in state subsidies on rents.

T020694

Since the reform campaign foreign investors have shown more interest in China. The biggest investor is Hong Kong, followed by Taiwan, Japan and the USA. 90% of investment, however, goes to the coastal provinces. With an inadequate infrastructure and rigid bureaucracy, inland provinces are still unable to compete fairly.

Economic problems

Economic growth has brought with it a number of problems prompting government measures to counter signs of overheating in the economy (high inflation, large budget deficit) and structural weaknesses. Consequently most Special Economic Zones by the coast have been required to relinquish their special economic status. Furthermore, there is growing chasm between the prosperity of coastal provinces and the hinterland. The differences between income levels is widening. According to statistics supplied by the World Bank, 120 million Chinese live in poverty. A further problem is the inefficiency of the state-run industries 45% of which are loss-making and kept afloat only by subsidies. Their contribution to China's gross domestic product is negligible compared with that of the private sector (well above average). Many workers who have lost their jobs as a result of the reforms are now leaving their home towns and pouring into the coastal regions together with the impoverished peasants. These huge movements in population (150 million people) and the new "capitalist" way of thinking are threatening to destroy the social fabric in which solidarity and a sense of community are valued qualities. Corruption, violent crime and speculation have been the consequence of these latest developments.

Foreign trade

In 1994 China's foreign trade balance was in surplus, the country's principal exports being light engineering goods, clothing and textiles in which sectors highly competitive labour costs led to an increase in market share. Machinery and transport equipment are the main imports, accounting for more than half the total. Japan heads the list of China's trading partners as far as imports are concerned, followed by Taiwan and the US; in the case of exports the list is topped by Hong Kong, the US and Japan in that order. Trade with the EU continues to expand and in 1993 amounted to 13% of the import and export total.

Tourism

1988 was a record year for tourism, but the Tiananmen Square massacre in the spring of 1989 brought the tourist trade to an abrupt halt. However, by 1991 the tourists were starting to return. The number of travellers rose to 33 million, of which 3 million were foreigners. 1994 alone saw a 5% rise in the number of visitors, bringing the total to 44 million; 88% were from Taiwan, Hong Kong and Macao, the remainder from elsewhere.

China now has more than 1186 hotels with a rating of 1 Star or better and hence with the corresponding level of amenities.

Agriculture

Situation

Only 10% of China can be used for agricultural purposes. More than half of the population are employed on the land, which contributes 20% to the gross national product.

Peasants and farmers have had to cope with a range of difficulties ranging from floods, soil erosion, drainage and irrigation. 45% of the land has to be irrigated.

With such a relatively small amount of agricultural land it has proved difficult for agricultural productivity to keep pace with the population growth. The problem has been exacerbated as the needs of the population and industry plus the priority of private enterprise over the centrally directed planned economy have led to increased demands on available land. The result of this process is a continuing intensification of farming methods and increasing use of artificial fertilisers. Growers too are turning more and more to high-value produce, the returns on which are greater than on rice and wheat, which have to be sold at low prices fixed by the state. Another factor in the reduction of available farmland is the continuing growth of the desert.

The reform measures also increased incentives for peasants and farmers. A part of each plot could be used for private purposes once the quotas imposed by the government had been met. Two-figure growth rates in production were achieved and rural incomes improved.

In 1994, however, agriculture achieved a growth rate of only 1%, the poorest performance in the economy. The chief problems afflicting the sector are the low levels of investment in irrigation, drainage and soil improvement schemes and protection against floods and ground erosion. The situation is exacerbated by the inadequate commercial and transport infrastructure, as well as by a general shortage of fertilisers and seed. With national resources being channelled as a matter of priority into boosting industrial production, little is left over for investment in the countryside and rural incomes have fallen. The worsening financial predicament of agricultural workers is aggravated by rising prices, high taxation and levies. The result has been repeated protests to the government, which has recognised that a problem exists and intends to take steps to improve the situation.

Approximately three-quarters of agricultural land is used to grow cereals. In the south mainly rice is cultivated, while in the north wheat, maize, sorghum, millet and oats are the main cereals. Fruit is another important crop. Valuable products such as tea, tobacco, cotton, natural fibres, sugar cane and silk are either exported or sold to light industry; cultivation of these more profitable crops is increasing at the expense of staples such as wheat and rice.

Agricultural produce

The higher land of "Outer China" offers ideal pastures for cattle, horses and goats, but pigs, a vitally important ingredient in the Chinese diet, are reared in the central country regions, together with chickens and ducks.

Livestock

Woods and forests occupy only about 13% of Chinese land surface, as during the 1960s large areas of woodland were systematically cleared to meet not only the demand for fuel but also to create more farmland. The soil lost its natural capacity to absorb water with the result that floods became more common in the lower reaches of the main rivers. In recent years forestation schemes have been implemented to increase the proportion of woodland, while the number of tree clearance projects have been considerably reduced.

Forestry

Industry

Even by the Second World War the progress of Chinese industry had been very slow and in the subsequent decades it developed unevenly under a political system which was inconsistent in its support. There have, however, been some significant achievements considering all the complex social, economic and political difficulties with which the people have had to cope.

Development

After the first phase of modest investment in the steel industry and the development of new industrial centres in the more remote parts of the country, the second phase moved in the opposite direction with the construction of small factories in rural inland areas. This policy suffered from high costs, few technical resources, insufficient skilled manpower, was implemented at a time when the economy was in a poor state and close to crisis and it was soon adjudged to have failed. In the subsequent phase the emphasis shifted to light industry and the processing of raw materials such as cotton and silk. Heavy industry was subject to qualitative and quantitative improvements and was concentrated in certain key zones.

The political tensions engendered by the Cultural Revolution certainly had a detrimental effect on the realisation of economic projects. After Mao's death the Chinese economy took a new turn with liberalisation, the promotion of private initiatives, the encouragement of foreign capital, the development of international trade and the acquisition of advanced Western technology. Centralised planning also had a reduced role. However, the smaller enterprises, mostly in the coastal regions, were instrumental in raising industrial production. The suppression of the student movement in 1989 interrupted the economic upswing within the private sector, but fortunes quickly improved again.

Situation

Industry contributes the largest share to the gross domestic product (48%). With an annual growth rate of 18%, 1994 brought a continuation of the boom conditions of preceding years, the main stimulus for growth coming from private sector industries, particularly in the coastal provinces. Co-operatives in the consumer goods industry who had until then only been allowed to manufacture goods for export were now able to market their goods in China. Although state-run companies are subsidised, most of them make losses. Some change of ownership has indeed taken place, but radical restructuring remains unlikely for ideological reasons and for fear of the social instability likely to result from mass redundancies.

Mineral resources

Mining plays a key role in the industrialisation process. China, a country rich in raw materials, relies heavily on coal of which there are believed to be huge deposits. Chinese miners produce more coal than any other nation in the world, but aluminium, bauxite, gold, lithium, manganese, nickel and tin are also produced in large quantities. As well as the traditional heartlands of the coal mining industry in the north-east around Fushun and Tangshan, there are coal mines in the northern and central provinces of Shanxi, Shaanxi, Hebei and Anhui and the southern provinces of Sichuan and Jiangxi. Despite the plentiful reserves, new coalfields cannot be exploited quickly enough to meet the rapidly increasing demand.

Oil reserves are also substantial. In the west and south-west (Yumen/Gansu province) all the reserves were exhausted by the end of the 1930s. New oilfields have been discovered in the north-east near Harbin and also under the sea.

Meeting energy requirements

The most important source of energy is undoubtedly coal which supplies 73% of the nation's requirements with oil the second largest (17%). There are also major hydro-electric power stations on the Huanghe with Liujiaxia, Longyangxia and Sanmenxia as the most important. Other sites are located in the north-east on the Songhua (Sungari) and to the south in Guangxi and Guizhou.

Nevertheless shortages still occur as industry's energy needs continue to grow and new production methods rely on energy-intensive processes. In 1992 electricity production increased by 10%, while demand increased by 35%. Insufficient investment and the development of new reserves are the main reasons for the inadequate power supply network.

Sanxia dam

At Yichang on the Changjiang a huge dam which will serve as a source of power, prevent floods and aid irrigation has been opposed on ecological grounds. The biggest of its kind in the world – 185m/606ft high and 1983m/6504ft wide – the Sanxia dam will supply eight times as much power as the Aswan dam. However, 1 million people in over 20 towns and countless villages will be displaced and 28,700ha/70,890 acres flooded.

Traditional ceramic painting

Of all the light industries, textiles with its high production levels occupies the leading position. The cotton industry supplies two-thirds of total textile production.

Textiles

Silkworm cultivation and thread processing are traditional industries in the south of the country between the Changjiang and the Zhujiang and also in Shandong province, the home of tussore silk, and Sichuan.

Ceramics and porcelain production play a significant role in the Chinese economy. Although the industry does not deliver the high quality products of previous centuries, business is prospering and factories are turning out quality goods for the domestic market and for export. The south of the country is the traditional home of these skills and each province is noted for its special techniques or decorative style.

Ceramics and porcelain

Communications

Although the transport network has been extended in recent decades, it has not been able to keep pace with the economy's growth rate. The major problems continue to be the overloaded railway system and the inadequate roads.

The 1 million kilometres (650,000 miles) of roads are often of a poor standard. Only 23% of the main trunk roads are metalled. In recent years, the number of motor vehicles has increased dramatically to 5.5 million, of which 3.6 million are goods vehicles and 1.6 million private cars.

Road network, road transport

Only 1% of Chinese people own a car. Subject to high duties and taxes, imported vehicles are extremely expensive but even cars of Chinese manufacture are out of the reach of the average Chinese citizen. The bicycle is still the most popular form of transport.

A Chinese steam locomotive

Railways	Although it covers 54,000km/33,500 miles, the Chinese railway network is barely adequate with significant gaps in the north and southwest. About 16% is electrified. In the 70s and 80s there were extensions to the system but the programme has slowed down. Tracks and rolling stock are in poor condition. Railways are the most important form of freight transport, while passenger transport barely meets half its capacity. A new track is under construction from Beijing to Hong Kong. The 2400km/1490 mile project is the biggest in the history of Chinese railways and should be completed by 1996.
Rivers and canals	Over 120,000km/75,000 miles of river and canal are navigable, with the Changjiang and the Xijiang making up the biggest share. The waterways of northern China are either clogged with sand, have low water levels or are frozen. River traffic generally flows in a west-east direction and is responsible for roughly 5% of all freight and 3% of all passengers.
Air travel	Other airlines have been established apart from the Civil Aviation Administration of China (CAAC) or Air China. Airports have been expanded mainly in the Special Economic Zones and in the coastal cities. While Beijing and Shanghai remain the principal airports, those of other cities are steadily gaining in importance. Passenger traffic in 1994 totalled some 34 million.

History

Excavations have unearthed evidence of prehistoric settlement in China over a million years ago. Traces of settlements have been found throughout "Inner China" as well as in the north near Beijing and in the Changjiang and Huanghe river basins. Archaeologists have found firm evidence proving that some sort of organised society existed 500,000 years later. The human remains which were found in Beijing in 1921 prove that Peking man (*sinanthropus pekinensis*) had settled there 400,000 to 500,000 years earlier, had made his own tools to till the land and used fire.

Palaeolithic Era

It has been established that the first human societies, notably the Yangshao and Longshan civilisations, emerged at the beginning of the Neolithic Era about 6000–5000 years B.C. in the Huanghe basin near Xi'an and later expanded into the eastern and southern regions of China. The matriarchal Yangshao peoples formed themselves into small farming villages where they cultivated wheat and millet and bred pigs and cattle. Within the patriarchal Longshan civilisation some evidence of a class system has been found, but the most interesting finds are the examples of their pottery. As well as showing considerable skills in pottery manufacture and design, the Longshan settlements – villages with fortified walls – were relatively advanced.

Neolithic Era

The Xia, the first Chinese dynasty, established a system of inherited succession.

Xia Dynasty
21st–16th c. B.C.

The later Shang Dynasty took China into the Bronze Age. Engravings on metal and bone have provided considerable information, demonstrating that the people of that era had mastered the skill of producing bronze – utensils, weapons and tools from the Shang years are still of unsurpassed quality – and that an organised society could be established with rigid structures, based on the exploitation of slaves. Although the Shang were hunters and warriors, they were also skilled farmers. They cultivated mainly millet and wheat and bred silkworms which supplied the thread for their clothing.

Shang Dynasty
16th–11th c. B.C.

The Zhou Dynasty succeeded the Shang by developing more sophisticated methods of producing bronze and evolving a more advanced concept of society where slavery played no part. This society was organised around a patriarchal feudal system in which succession was based on inheritance by the first-born. The chief functioned as a feudal lord allocating land to princes on an hierarchical basis, while the rest of the community were subjected to a life of serfdom. Gradually a third layer of society emerged, the officials, who were of noble origins but possessed no estate. They earned their living as army officers or administrators in the services of the princes.

Zhou Dynasty
11th c. to 221 B.C.

Under the Eastern Zhou Dynasty, during the Spring and Autumn periods (the Hegemonic Empires) and the time of the Warring Kingdoms, further developments in the economic and social structure emerged. Iron brought such progress to the agricultural economy, trade and manual crafts (foundries, saltworks and workshops for the production of pottery and lacquer) that coins were introduced as a means of payment. Nevertheless, the dynasty had a number of problems to contend with: the sheer size of the empire, different racial groups and attacks from rivals. The Spring and Autumn periods and Warring Kingdoms period were times of transition marked not just by conflict and upheaval, but also by one of the most productive phases in

嗣王淫泆圖

紂王

妲己

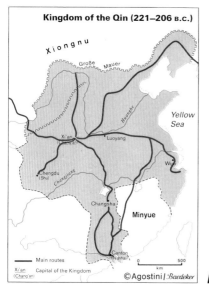

Kingdom of the Qin (221–206 B.C.)

Xiongnu

Große Mauer

Yellow Sea

Xi'an (Chang'an)
Luoyang

Wu

Chengdu (Shui)

Changsha

Minyue

Canton (Nanhai)

━━━ Main routes

Xi'an (Chang'an) Capital of the Kingdom

0   500
km

© Agostini / Baedeker

Emperor Qin Shi Huangdi

Chinese intellectual and spiritual history – the reason why this period is also known as that of the Hundred Schools. As well as the theoretical ethical philosophy of Confucius (see Famous People) which came to be opposed by the Legalist school, the thoughts of Laotse (see Famous People) and his pupil Zhuang Zi, founding partners of Taoism, were gaining acceptance.

A prince from western China united the individual autonomous empires into the first Chinese state. During the seventeen years from 238 to 221 B.C. and using a mixture of force and diplomacy he laid the foundations for his assumption of power. In 221 B.C. he was appointed Emperor Qin Shi Huangdi and founded the Qin Dynasty, after which China is named. During his reign from 221 to 210 B.C. the emperor succeeded in creating an economic, cultural and administrative structure. He was buried together with more than 7000 terracotta soldiers; his tomb was discovered in 1974 near Xi'an.

Qin Dynasty
221–206 B.C.

For the purposes of unification the borders between the smaller states were annulled, their defences destroyed and the first section of the Great Wall was built – it was intended not just as a defensive wall, but also as a border and a route for trade and transport. A network of roads was constructed to link all parts of the empire and the emperor also improved the country's waterways. The Silk Road was established to link China with the cities of the Middle East. Furthermore the emperor abolished the feudal system, replacing it with an administrative structure with prefectures and districts. Measures, weights, coins, the calendar, laws and Chinese script, an important factor in overcoming the language differences, were standardised.

The speed and the repressive nature with which the emperor carried out these changes lost him the sympathies of the landowners. The princes' weapons were confiscated, cultural heritage, including any scientific works, was destroyed and supporters of Confucianism

◄ *King Chou of the Shang Dynasty at his court*

63

persecuted. As a result, smaller, independent states were formed to resist centralised power. The dynasty's rulers incurred the hatred of the exploited masses, many of whom were forced to work on the construction projects. In 209 B.C. a peasants' uprising sealed the fate of the first imperial dynasty. It lasted only a short time but the basis for a constitutional state as laid down by the Legalists was to endure.

Han Dynasty
206 B.C. to A.D. 220

The Han Dynasty which followed had no choice but to adopt the institutions created by the Qin, but the Han rulers chose to take a less provocative stance and retained the existing social system. From an economic point of view great strides were made during the 400 years of Han rule, particularly in agriculture with the construction of hydraulic installations and the spread of iron tools. Socially the Han years led to the emergence of a land-owning class. Industry underwent a substantial qualitative improvement. Large state-run bronze foundries and salt refineries, textile and pottery workshops were established in both the north and the south. Industrial development resulted in a strengthening of trade relations. Assisted in part by military conquest commercial interests expanded mainly westwards into India, Persia and the Eastern Roman Empire and gave a boost to Chinese craftsmen. But the period of economic growth, coinciding with the defeat of the Huns, was followed by decline caused largely by the incompetence of the imperial court and a tough taxation policy. A series of peasant rebellions were triggered, but even after the Eastern Han Dynasty was re-established there was no improvement in the people's fortunes. A group known as the Yellow Turbans – supporters of Taoism and strongly opposed to the orthodox application of Confucianism by the imperial government – finally brought the Han Dynasty to an end.

220–581

Statuette from the Wei years (386–589)

A 300 year transitional phase followed the Han Dynasty and was accompanied by a fragmentation of power and the division of imperial territory. The period is known as the "Three Kingdoms" and the "Southern and Northern Dynasties".

The land was split into three economic and political regions: the central region along the Huanghe, the Changjiang lowland plain where five dynasties followed on from each other, and the province of Sichuan. A new source of manpower appeared in the form of northerners fleeing from foreign raiders and in the south agriculture, the manual crafts and trade received a tremendous boost. A further influx of settlers from the west and the political divisions within China gave a new impetus not just to Buddhism which had suffered setbacks on the western borders during the Han years but also to Taoism which was able to consolidate its position.

Sui Dynasty
581–618

The credit for the re-unification of the country towards the end of the 6th c. went to a military aristocrat who defeated the northern tribes, reconquered the south and founded the Sui Dynasty. But the repressive methods which were used to revive the flagging economy and to distribute the abandoned estates once again enraged the armed peasants who succeeded in deposing the Sui.

Tang Dynasty
618–907

The attempts by the Sui to retain a unified China were continued by the Tang, who sought to extend imperial territory in all directions. In the north-east Korea was occupied, they raided Yunnan in the south and in the west the Tarim Basin and the Takla Makan Desert were conquered.

Territorial gains gave trade a boost. The movement of goods and people along the Silk Road continued to grow and sea routes across the South China Sea gave access to the countries of the Indian Ocean. At the same time the demand for valuable products such as silk, tea, pottery and lacquer increased in both Eastern and Western markets, thereby boosting the confidence of the growers and manufacturers of these products. The continuing growth of the coal, copper and tin industries secured China's economic prosperity.

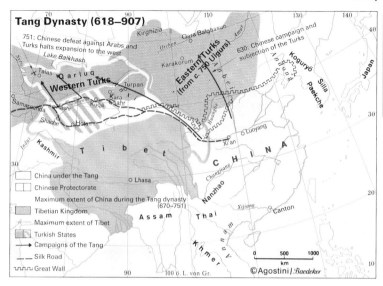

The 300-year Tang ascendancy brought advances in the world of the arts. Poetry of a quality rarely surpassed was written and the skilled pottery makers have bequeathed to posterity magnificent horse and camel figures – symbols of a trading culture which penetrated deep into the northern and north-eastern steppes. At the Chinese court, the theatre, fine arts, music, dancing and philosophy received imperial patronage. But meanwhile in the lower strata of society, areas of conflicts were emerging. The redistribution of land was intended to create larger farms and more efficient use of the land and also to equalise the balance of power among landowners, but it led instead to emigration into western regions and to armed resistance in the face of centralised power. Yet again peasant power sealed the fate of a once powerful dynasty. After the first rebellions in the west, which the imperial troops were able to put down, the dynasty's power waned. In the outlying regions, threatened by insurgents, control of the military protectorates was lost and nearer the capital the dynasty's forces were overcome by the peasants' revolts.

Fifty years of provisional government followed the Tang Dynasty, but the powerful economic and cultural movements which bore fruit during the Song Dynasty were advancing, leading to a climax in Chinese history with the clear superiority of the southern region over the north. Until then all Chinese dynasties had developed their power base and capital in the Huanghe valley with Xi'an or Chang'an in the west and Luoyang in the east alternating as seats of government. The Shang had also used Anyang and Zhengzhou on the Huanghe as capitals.

Song Dynasty
960–1279

When the Song came to power they initially chose the northern town of Kaifeng as their capital, but at the same time the southern industrial and agricultural centres of the Song culture were developing, safe from the incursions of the Kitan and Nuzhen tribes. While paying annual dues to foreign tribes and allowing them use of the land, the Song rulers gave the Chinese people not only many years of peace but also economic prosperity and cultural enrichment. Coal mining, salt refineries and foundries provided a firm basis for the manual crafts.

Imperial Dynasties and Capitals

Dynasty	Period of Rule	Capital
Xia	21–16th c. B.C.	Anyi
Shang	16–11th c. B.C.	Zhengzou
		Anyang
Western Zhou	11th c.–770 B.C.	Xi'an
Eastern Zhou	770–221 B.C.	Luoyang
Warring Kingdoms	475–221 B.C.	
Qin	221–206 B.C.	Xi'an
Western Han	206 B.C. to A.D. 24	Xi'an
Eastern Han	25–220	Luoyang
Three Kingdoms	220–280	
Western Jin	265–316	Luoyang
Eastern Jin	317–420	Nanjing
Sui	581–618	Xi'an, Yangzhou
Tang	618–907	Xi'an
Five Dynasties and Ten Kingdoms	907–960	
Song	960–1279	Hangzhou
Yuan	1271–1368	Beijing
Ming (Emperor Hongwu)	1368–1399	Nanjing
Ming	1402–1644	Beijing
Qing	1644–1911	Beijing

Certain discoveries gave the economy a powerful boost. Gunpowder, for example, proved to be a major advance for the arms industry and the discovery of the compass rendered sea navigation safer. New outlets and trading partners were established and movable print types created new ways of communication. China had become one of the richest and most advanced nations in the world.

The Mongols, used to the bleak steppes and deserts of the north, were attracted by the populous regions of China. Under the leadership of Genghis Khan, the nomadic warriors on horseback systematically encircled the western and southern outer regions and destroyed the Song army.

Yuan Dynasty
1271–1368

Genghis Khan's Mongols – the first non-Chinese people to hold sway over the Middle Kingdom – destroyed the basis of the agricultural economy in northern China. They settled in the north and established a new capital in Khanbaliq, modern Beijing. The conquerors transformed the farmland into pasture and confiscated the horses, which were used in the north as beasts of burden. Used to a nomadic existence and rearing livestock, the Mongols found it hard to abide by the rules of a long-established, peasant society, to settle down in one place and to come to terms with a subtle, sophisticated bureaucracy and the administration of an empire with centuries of tradition.

Under Mongol rule a four-class system soon emerged. The Mongols and to a lesser extent the peoples of the western regions demanded privileges and their own political rights, while the Han Chinese in the north and south had to endure a subordinate role, paying heavy taxes and deprived of their tools and arms. The repressive atmosphere and the withdrawal of rights from the indigenous population inevitably led to the demise of the Mongol Empire a hundred years later.

The Mongols strengthened the borders and frontier forces, not just because they were waging war with such countries as Burma and Japan, but also because they wanted to make the northern and western trade routes from Asia and the Mediterranean countries accessible again. Unlike the Han, the Mongols were more tolerant of peoples from different backgrounds, cultures and religion and wished to increase contact with the rest of the world.

The Mongols were undoubtedly aware of the enormous potential wealth to be derived from the southern agricultural and industrial regions, the source of much of the trade that they were promoting. They therefore took care not to destroy the agricultural systems in place there. In fact they sought to improve production and the hydraulic installations, provided more favourable trade links between north and south and safeguarded their craftsmen's markets. The Han's resistance to Mongol rule soon culminated in armed rebellion. After 20 years of struggle, the Yuan Dynasty was overthrown. China entered a new era, a period which historians describe as late feudalism.

After the new Ming emperors had pushed the Mongols back beyond the Great Wall – from where they repeatedly threatened China's borders – the emphasis was laid on restoring agricultural land in the north. Fallow land was cultivated, the Han were encouraged to settle in the peripheral regions, cotton plantations were extended, new hydraulic installations were constructed and taxes were reduced in order to accelerate production and as an incentive for the peasants and farmers.

*Ming Dynasty
1368–1644*

A number of political measures were taken, including the centralisation of administration – later to become a bureaucratic apparatus hostile to progress – the separation of military and political power, the division of land into "public" estates to which the imperial government had rights and "private" estates which were for the use of the people, the introduction of a ground rent as a form of tax and the setting up of a land register.

Contacts with abroad were established in particular through expeditions to the southern seas, East Africa (Somalia) and the Red Sea. Tales and legends of the Orient which were circulated by travellers who had visited China during the Mongol years aroused the interest of Europeans, some of whom made the long journey in person. Furthermore, it was during the 15th and 16th c. that the world was circumnavigated and the Voyages of Discovery took place. In 1516 the Portuguese landed in China, later settled in Macao and set overseas trade in motion. The Portuguese were followed by the Spanish, the Dutch and then in 1637 the English. The Italians, who thanks to the 13th c. journeys of Marco Polo had played an important part in familiarising Europeans with the Middle Kingdom, arrived with the Jesuits.

Once again China was facing harassment from all quarters: restless Mongols on the northern perimeter, bandits in the west and Japanese pirates whose fleets threatened the east coast. The political situation was also fraught. Corruption within the imperial court and the incompetence of the officials and eunuchs led to more peasant uprisings. The beneficiaries of this discontent were the Manchus who crushed the weak Ming nobility to found the Qing Dynasty.

In much the same way as the Mongols, the Qing first imposed a series of repressive measures on the Chinese population, such as the obligation to wear Manchurian dress and pigtail, the banning of mixed marriages and the creation of Chinese ghettoes in the towns. However, these policies were later moderated, the Manchus adapted to the Chinese way of life and even sought to expand into new territories with the aim of spreading Chinese culture. Emperor Kangxi annexed the Chinese state of Formosa, the provinces of Yunnan and Tibet, Mongolia and the central Asian regions – the extent of modern China's frontier. In addition, bordering states of Annam (Vietnam) and Korea became Chinese protectorates. After a long period of economic prosperity devastating natural catastrophes engulfed the country. The

*Qing Dynasty
1644–1911*

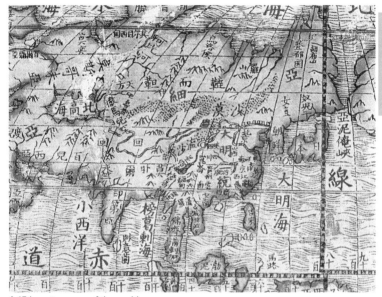

A 17th century map of the world

resulting famine hit the people, agriculture and trade badly. The ruling Manchus were in no position to impose a solution on the country. Meanwhile foreign powers sought to strengthen their position inside China.

The Opium War struck the first fateful blow to the Qing Dynasty. The British had imported opium from India into China in order to equalise the trade balance between the two main overseas markets. Attempts by the Qing Dynasty to bring a halt to the opium trade led to war with Britain. The Chinese were defeated, betrayed by their own officials. The rulers were forced to relinquish Hong Kong and to open up five new ports to trade with Europe. 1839–42

Exploited by their reckless rulers, stupefied by the opium of foreign powers and starving, the Chinese people rose up against the Qing in what was known as the Taiping revolt. They aimed to overthrow their current rulers and build a new and better society. Part of southern China was liberated, including Nanjing which was declared the capital. In a challenge to Confucian imperial thinking the rebels advocated the teachings of Taoism, introduced the right to own property and sought to create a society in which land was distributed evenly and men and women shared equal rights. 1851–64

The revolt was bloodily suppressed by the imperial army and foreign troops.

Meanwhile the Europeans took the opportunity to exploit a weakened Chinese government and unleashed another Opium War in order to win further concessions. By marching on Beijing and destroying the Summer Palaces, they unambiguously pressed their case. The Qing were forced to yield, handing over more territory. In the following years, the foreign states waged one war after another in the hope of

◄ *Imperial employees taking state examinations*

69

Original und Eigenthum No.9666. **Die Erſtürmung von Peking am 14. und 15. Auguſt 1900,** Neuruppin, zu haben bei Guſtav K

The Boxer Rebellion

incorporating a part of China into their own empire. The French claimed Vietnam and in 1895 Taiwan was handed over to the Japanese.

20th century
1900

In 1900 the "Boxer" movement (Yi He Tuan = Union for Justice and Freedom) opposed the persistent humiliation of China by foreign states. However, the emperor's widow Cixi used the rebellion for her own purposes. Initially she encouraged the uprising but then called upon foreign troops to butcher the rebels who had become an embarrassment. As a puppet in the hands of the imperialist powers, Empress Cixi survived for another eight years. In 1908 she died, whereupon the three-year-old Puyi became the last emperor of the Qing Dynasty.

1905–16

From the beginning of the 20th c. there had been much talk of a bourgeois revolution and in 1905 Sun Yat-sen (see Famous People) founded the Revolutionary Union (Tong Meng Hui) which sought to overthrow the Manchu Dynasty, restore Chinese nationhood and create a republic which would impose a fairer distribution of agricultural land on the people. The revolt began in Wuhan in 1911 and spread throughout the land. On January 1st 1912 a republic was proclaimed with Nanjing as its capital but it enjoyed a short life. To avoid civil war Sun Yat-sen was forced to resign in February 1912 in favour of Yuan Shikai, a supporter of the Constitutional Monarchists and a former member of the Qing court. The sudden death of Yuan Shikai in 1916 led to a series of civil wars between the various military factions, known as the Warlords.

First Republic

After the First World War the far-reaching changes on the international political scene, in particular the October Revolution in Russia, provided a favourable environment for the spread of socialist ideas in China. In 1912 Sun Yat-sen founded the nationalist Kuomintang which received support from the Communist Party of China. The latter developed from the May 4th Movement (1919), which sought democratic and cultural renewal. The two organisations opposed the Warlords and in 1927 proclaimed a new democratic republic with Nanjing as its capital.

The alliance between the Kuomintang and the Communist Party was short-lived. Chiang Kai-shek (see Famous People) who replaced Sun Yat-sen as leader of the Kuomintang began to suppress and persecute the Communists, who withdrew to southern China.

When the Japanese occupied Manchuria in 1931 and installed a puppet government led by Puyi (last emperor of the Qing Dynasty), the Kuomintang pushed southwards in order to eliminate the Communists led by Mao Zedong. Mao led his followers into the interior to prepare for the Long March north. They eventually reached safety in Yenan (Yan'an), but the brutality of the Japanese invaders, who caused the death of 20 million Chinese, forced Chiang Kai-shek and the Communists to re-unite and to fight alongside each other in the war against Japan, which lasted until 1945. | 1931–45

After victory over the Japanese the conflict between the Kuomintang and Communist People's Liberation Army rekindled, and the foundation by Mao Zedong of the People's Republic on October 1st 1949 was followed by Chiang Kai-shek's withdrawal to Taiwan (Formosa) where he established the Republic of China or Nationalist China. | **People's Republic** 1949

Between 1949 and 1952, the period of "Reconstruction", the Communists introduced agrarian reforms in which all land owners were dispossessed and the confiscated estates distributed among the peasants. Each peasant received three mu (about a fifth of hectare or half an acre). The government guaranteed price and currency stability, came to an agreement with the Soviet Union on economic co-operation to boost production, introduced a new law to outlaw arranged marriages and prepared the ground for the emancipation of women, who under Confucianism were condemned to a subordinate role within the family and society. | 1949–52

This period covered the 1st five-year plan. As well as the continuing land collectivisation programme, higher investment was planned for the war-damaged heavy industries.

In 1956 Mao introduced the "Hundred Flower" movement, a reference to the Hundred Schools of the Warring Kingdoms period, with the aim of promoting education, science and culture. | 1953–59

In 1958 the Communist Party applied the "Great Leap Forward" policy to create communes within the rural and urban communities in the hope of raising production levels. The purpose of the policy was also to even out the extreme differences between town and country, industry and agriculture, workers and peasants, but the experiment to develop heavy industry in rural areas failed because of the inadequate infrastructure. The failure of the experiment together with the natural catastrophes which befell China in 1960/61 resulted in famine and a serious economic crisis. | 1958

In 1960 an already dangerous situation came to a head with the breakdown of economic and political relations with the Soviet Union. There were several reasons for this situation: an inconsistency in Mao's thinking on the relationship between agriculture and industry and between heavy industry and light industry; the growing ideological gap between the two wings of the Communist Party after the death of Stalin; the role of the Soviet Union as an imperialist superpower; Soviet unwillingness to help the Third World; finally arguments over the border inflamed relationships between the two nations. | 1960

71

1966	An improvement in China's economic fortunes led in 1966 to the Cultural Revolution. Mao himself led the students in their protests against the bourgeois state and party apparatus. In outright opposition to Confucian tradition which demanded respect for society's norms and the prevailing hierarchy, Mao proclaimed that rebellion was a legitimate form of protest. The student movement demanded a fairer society, in which the people gained a greater share in political power, all citizens had greater access to culture and education and where the social, cultural and economic differences between the rural population, town dwellers and party cadres were less pronounced.

This struggle for political ideals quickly degenerated into political extremism and civil war. A least a million Chinese lost their lives in the upheaval and innumerable cultural treasures including temples, books and works of art were destroyed. |
1972–76	The Cultural Revolution cast a long shadow over Chinese politics. The death in 1971 of Mao's designated successor Lin Biao is still unexplained. In subsequent years ideological conflicts within the Communist Party intensified. Deng Xiaoping who was expelled from the party during the Cultural Revolution competed for power with the ideologists behind the Cultural Revolution, the Gang of Four or Shanghai Group, one of whose members was Mao's wife Jiang Qing.
1976	Prime Minister Zhou Enlai was successful in mediating between the two factions but he died in 1976. Later that year Mao Zedong also died after a serious illness, whereupon events moved quickly. The Shanghai Group or Gang of Four were arrested and the then Prime Minister Hua Guofeng took over the reins of power.
1977	Deng Xiaoping came to power again in 1977. He soon strengthened his position and promoted his policies as the party line. For him the most important concern was rebuilding China's industrial base.
1981	The Gang of Four under the leadership of Jiang Qing received death penalties, but these were later suspended and replaced by restrictions to freedom.
1989	The spring of 1989 saw rebellion at the heart of Beijing in the Square of Heavenly Peace (Tiananmen). Students demanded democratic reforms but the demonstration was brutally put down and thousands of protestors were killed.
1992	A White Paper published by the ruling council defended China's policy towards Tibet and reaffirmed Tibet's status as an integral part of China.

The Communist Party's Congress voted to dismantle the planned economy and to create a socialist market economy, but it opposed democratic reforms.

For the first time since the Second World War, a Japanese Emperor visited China.

In December China concluded agreements with Russia on political, economic, cultural and military co-operation; a joint declaration referred to the ties of friendship between the two countries. |
| 1993 | Separatist campaigns in Xinjiang intensified after the collapse of the Soviet Union at the beginning of the 1990s. The Tibetan campaign for independence from Chinese rule also gained momentum.

Many politically-motivated arrests and trials took place. Hundreds of people were detained for taking part in peaceful political and religious activities, among them many belonging to ethnic minorities. Torture was widespread, especially in Tibet. At the same time, other well-known dissidents were freed. |

At the first session of the People's National Congress held in March, Communist Party chief Jiang Zemin was elected to the presidency. The state constitution was amended, the phrase "socialist market economy" replacing references to a "planned economy".

A government White Paper emphatically re-iterated China's claims to sovereignty over Taiwan, mentioning, for the first time, the use of military force as a means of achieving re-unification. Nevertheless limited trade links were established with the island republic.

In a further clamp down on political opposition an increasing number of dissidents were arrested or banned from Beijing during sessions of the National Congress or important state visits. **1994**

Edward Balladur became the first French prime minister to visit China since 1978, both countries being eager to re-establish their traditionally good relationship.

An agreement concluded between China and Russia in July sought to defuse military tensions along their common border.

Having already carried out two atomic bomb tests in the previous year, China exploded two further bombs in tests at Lop Nor. **1995**

More than 60 dissidents were imprisoned or temporarily detained. Having returned to China, the civil rights campaigner Harry Wu, a US citizen, was sentenced to 15 years in jail for spying and deported.

In September the UN-sponsored World Women's Conference was held in Beijing, attended by some 7000 delegates. In the days preceding the conference delegates to the NGO Women's Forum in Huairou were subjected to heavy-handed treatment by the Chinese police.

Famous People

The following famous people listed in alphabetical order were all connected with China, whether they were born, lived, worked or died there.

Chiang Kai-shek (Jiang Jieshi; 1887–1975)

Chiang Kai-shek (Jiang Jieshi) was born into a merchant's family in southern China. He embarked on a military career and spent several years training in Japan. When the First Republic was proclaimed in 1911 he joined the Kuomintang, the party founded by the architect of the revolution Sun Yat-sen. In 1923 he was promoted to Chief of Staff of this militant democratic movement and later to leader of the Military Academy at Whampoa, where Zhou Enlai worked as a political commissar. On the death of Sun Yat-sen in 1925 Chiang Kai-shek – a close partner to whom he was in fact related as both had married daughters of the Soong family – was appointed as his successor. When he succeeded in ousting the Warlords he proclaimed a republic again in 1927, but he quickly turned away from the ideas and policies of Sun and broke off the alliance with the Communists. After his election to president he formed close links with the landowners and middle-class financiers and sought to brutally suppress the Communists. The latter, who had founded an autonomous republic in Jiangxi, were forced to retreat and prepare for the legendary Long March. It became apparent that Chiang Kai-shek and the Kuomintang were unable to win support from the people when the Japanese invaded Manchuria and installed a puppet administration under Puyi, the last emperor of the Qing Dynasty. Chiang sidestepped pressure from the people and democratic forces to organise resistance to the Japanese until he was finally arrested by some of his own generals (The Xi'an Incident) and forced to make a decision. Mao and Zhou Enlai intervened to save his life and he eventually agreed to join forces with the Communists against the Japanese. At the end of the long struggle against the Japanese (1937–45) Chiang's conflict with Mao's forces resumed. However he was forced to forego American assistance on mainland China and flee to Taiwan where their offer of help was willingly accepted. He founded the Republic of China (Nationalist China) as opposed to the People's Republic of China and he ruled the island as president until his death in 1975, bequeathing power to his son Chiang Ching-kuo.

Confucius (Kong Zi; 551–479 B.C.)

Very few details of the life of Confucius – his name was latinised from Kong Zi by Jesuits – can be established from "Analects" a collection of his writings and discussions which he conducted with his pupils. Confucius was a native of Shandong province where he spent a large part of his life as an official in the service of the state. The latter part of his life was spent roaming the country with a group of followers disseminating his views among the people.

At that point after the fall of the Western and Eastern Zhou Dynasty China was split into several states and was experiencing a time of large-scale economic, social and political changes, known as the Warring Kingdoms period. Confucius collected and studied classical scripts, which thanks to his work later became the basis of Chinese thinking. He linked the ancient concepts to a new kind of teaching which raised moral principles to an absolute yardstick against which human and social behaviour should be measured. Confucian philosophy which applies both to individuals and to rulers chiefly examines interpersonal relations; it views society as a large, hierarchically classified family and prescribes values and rituals, such as ancestor worship, love of parents, respect, kindness and integrity, which should apply in both public and private life. Although Confucius was not a preacher or an evangelist and his philosophies clearly concerned this life, temples were built in his honour all over China and the man and his teachings were greatly revered.

At the end of the 1920s Deng Xiaoping returned to China after stays in France and the Soviet Union and went underground in Shanghai adopting the name Xiaoping meaning little peace. He had studied in France, worked in a shoe factory and then worked with Zhou Enlai to develop the foreign section of the Chinese Communist Party. He completed his communist training in the Soviet Union. He took part in the Long March and when the People's Republic was founded in 1949 he soon emerged as one of the leading members of the party and government. In 1952 he was appointed as deputy prime minister and in 1954 became party secretary. He occupied this post until the beginning of the Cultural Revolution when with Prime Minister Liu Shaoqi he was accused of leading a capitalist counter-revolution and was stripped of his powers. He was, however, rehabilitated back into the party in 1973 with the help of his old friend from student days Zhou Enlai, whose more moderate political line was closer to Deng's pragmatism. He once again became deputy prime minister. In January 1976 Zhou Enlai died and Deng took over the office of prime minister but with the unrest in April on Tiananmen Square he was forced to resign. Mao died later that year and the Gang of Four's influence waned which enabled Deng's fortunes to rise within both the party and the government. In 1978 he succeeded in ousting Hua Guofeng who had confirmed Deng in all his previous posts and became army chief of staff and party secretary. Deng is seen as a man without fear, not afraid to speak his mind. "It doesn't matter whether the cat is black or white. Its job is to catch the mouse", is one of Deng's best known sayings. As a pragmatist he has sought to privatise parts of the economy to boost production, to open up the Chinese market to the West and to create administrative and political structures which prevent bureaucrats from impeding the work of managers. His reputation suffered badly when demonstrations in May and June of 1989 were brutally suppressed. Since 1992 Deng's reforming policies have gained ground and he is now the most powerful man in China.

The poet Du Fu and his contemporary Li Bai are the finest exponents of Chinese poetry.

After the peasants' revolt at An Lushan, Du, an official's son was, forced to leave the capital of Chang'an, withdrawing in 759 to Chengdu in Sichuan province, where he wrote more than 200 poems. His house on the banks of a small river in the middle of a bamboo forest can still be visited.

The works of Du Fu, a follower of Confucian teachings, are characterised by classical severity.

Poet, essayist and politician Guo Moruo was born in 1892 and studied medicine in Japan. As a student he wrote poems and short stories. After a short stay in China where he taught at Canton University, he fled back to Japan in the face of the Kuomintang persecution of Communists. In 1937 he returned to his homeland and took part in the resistance movement against the Japanese, being mainly involved with cultural matters. When the republic was proclaimed in 1949 he became president of the Chinese Academy of Science, the most elevated cultural institution in the country, and was also appointed vice-president of the People's Congress. Apart from a three-year break during the Cultural Revolution, he held the last post until his death.

Apart from poems and essays Guo published several plays and archaeological papers. In addition he translated literary and scientific works into Chinese from several languages.

Famous People

Han Kan
(8th c.)

Han Kan enjoys an almost legendary reputation in the history of Chinese painting and is the most influential Chinese horse painter. Little is known of his life other than that he worked in a wine shop in his youth. His talent was spotted by the famous painter Wang Wei, who then gave him lessons. Han Kan was a court painter from 742 to 756.

For the first time the close observation of nature was an important consideration for the painter. He studied horses and their movements very closely. Many horse paintings have been attributed to Han Kan, but only a few have been confirmed as authentic.

Jiang Qing
(b. 1914)

Jiang Qing was born in Zhucheng, Shandong province to a merchant family and later became an actress in Shanghai. She met Mao Zedong at his headquarters in Ya'an and in 1937 he left his wife for her, but the Politburo insisted that she should play no part in political activities. For almost 30 years she contested this condition and it was 1966 before she entered public life by involving herself in cultural work (reforming Beijing opera), although later she became a driving force in the Cultural Revolution. During the early 1970s Jiang Qing rapidly rose through the ranks to the highest level of the party hierarchy. With three other top party functionaries she was responsible for the dismissal and persecution of almost an entire generation of party officials. As an advocate of radical ideologies Jiang opposed the rehabilitation of the more pragmatic Deng Xiaoping. On the death of Mao in 1976, however, Deng was in no mood for tolerance and Jiang was expelled from the party. In 1981 as leader of the Gang of Four she was condemned to death for "counter-revolutionary crimes", attempting armed rebellion and torturing politicians during the Cultural Revolution. The death sentence was later suspended.

Lao She
(1898–1966)

The writer Lao She was born in Beijing in 1898 and went to university there. He subsequently became a reader in the Chinese language at Oxford University. During the war with Japan Lao became president of the Chinese Writers' Association. He was elected to the National People's Congress in 1949. During the Cultural Revolution he was accused of "petit bourgeois thinking" and disappeared without a trace. He was rehabilitated in 1978.

His works which are of world class enjoy great popularity in China. His best known novel "The Rickshaw Boy" (1937) was filmed and received great acclaim. Other works include "The Tea House" and "Four Generations under the Same Roof".

Laotse
(Lao Zi; c. 570
to ? B.C.)

Little is known of Laotse the founder of Taoism. It is recorded, however, that he lived at around the same time as Confucius and Buddha and that he was born in 570 B.C. He worked as an archivist for the Zhou Dynasty and a number of legends have grown up around his life. According to one tale he was born after a pregnancy lasting 81 years (hence his name Lao Zi meaning "old master"). Another story recounts how he wrote "Tao Te Ching", his most celebrated work and the principal inspiration for Taoism, in one day. This volume is divided into three parts which deal in turn with Tao, Yin and Yang. These are the fundamental elements of a philosophy which subordinates the life of the individual and society to a natural order. "Effortless action" is a guiding principle in life as the natural, harmonious order of things must not be disturbed. The wise man is advised to decline any opportunity to participate in public life and rulers are expected to show greater tolerance.

Li Bai
(701–762)

Also known as Li Tai-bai, this poet rivals Du Fu for the title of China's finest poet. An obstinate and unconventional man – he spent some time in exile as he was accused of dishonesty at the Chinese court – he was a follower of Taoism and led a dissolute existence. According to one legend Li Bai drowned when in a drunken stupor he tried to catch the moon's reflection in a lake.

Lu Xun   Mao Zedong   Zhou Enlai

His many poems are concerned with nature and the symbiotic relationship between man and nature. Literary historians regard him as one of the greatest poets of all time. The Chinese refer to him respectfully as the "immortal in exile".

Lu Xun, China's most celebrated modern writer, was said to be a lonely shy man and yet was inextricably linked with events in his country. He was born in 1881 the son of an intellectual family in the southern Chinese town of Shaoxing. At the age of sixteen Lu went to Japan to study natural science and medicine but his literary interests prevailed and he began to write. In Tokyo he joined the movement which opposed imperial rule in China, founded a literary newspaper and translated foreign authors. In 1909 he returned to his homeland and worked as a teacher. Initially he kept his distance from the cultural influences which held sway at that time throughout China, but in 1918 he attracted a lot of attention with a novel entitled "A Madman's Diary", which later came to be viewed as a seminal work of modern Chinese literature. Between 1920 and 1926 Lu lived in Beijing where he taught at a senior school. He then moved to Canton where he lectured at the Sun Yat-sen University. He was soon forced to move on when the Kuomintang started a witch-hunt against Communists. Shanghai became his home and he worked there until his death in 1936 as a writer, essayist and translator, joining in the cultural and political debates which raged during those years. In 1910 he formed the League of Leftist Writers and became its president.

Lu Xun (1881–1936)

Lu Xun has bequeathed a wide range of literary works which include speeches, aphorisms, dialogues as well as novels and letters on scientific and literary themes. The essays stand out as his most remarkable contribution to Chinese literature. Chinese readers can also thank him for translations of such foreign writers as Gogol. The best known of his novels are "The Story of Ah Q" (1921), "Medicine", "Home Village" and "Soap".

Mao Dun was born in 1896 and played a part in the May 4th Movement which was concerned with cultural and democratic issues. In 1930 he joined the literary circle founded by Lu Xun known as the League of Leftist Writers. During the war with Japan he lived in exile in Hong Kong but in 1949 he returned to his homeland and occupied the post of Minister of Culture until the Cultural Revolution when he became the object of fierce criticism. He re-appeared on the political stage towards the end of the 1970s. For many years he played a leading role in the magazine "People's Literature".

Mao Dun (1896–1981)

Mao Dun is the author of a series of novels dealing with the crisis in 20th c. Chinese society and many other stories.

Famous People

"Chairman" Mao was born in 1893 in the village of Shaoshan, Hunan province. The son of a peasant farmer, he went to school in Changsha and completed his studies at a teacher training college. He was both politically and culturally active in his student years and was instrumental, for example, in setting up a students' political society. In 1918 he moved to Beijing where he worked in the university library. It was here that he first met the professors Li Dazhao and Chen Duxiu, founding editors of a cultural magazine entitled "New Youth". Later Mao and the two academics were to found the Communist Party of China. During those years he also met and married Yang Kai-hui, the daughter of a university lecturer from his own home town. She gave birth to two sons, Mao Anying who lost his life in the Korean war and Mao Anqing.

After he founded the party in 1921 and during the struggle which he waged with the Kuomintang against the Warlords, Mao moved between Shanghai and Changsha, publishing the first of his writings on Chinese society and the economy. Unlike Marx and Lenin, Mao saw the peasant classes as a revolutionary force.

In 1927 the Kuomintang under Chiang Kai-shek began to persecute the Communists and Mao led the resistance in a number of southern towns. The party incurred serious losses during this period and Mao was excluded from the party leadership which held the view that the alliance with Kuomintang should be continued. Mao, however, set about forming armed units, withdrew into the mountains and founded the first "soviets" which he used as the basis for his guerilla campaign. It was during this period that Mao's wife, also a Communist Party activist, was taken prisoner by Chiang Kai-shek's soldiers and executed – a severe blow for Mao. With a weak, divided Communist Party matched against the Kuomintang's superior forces, Mao decided to refrain from frontal attacks and guerilla action. Instead he sought the active support of the people. In 1934 the Red Army of southern China set out on the legendary Long March, settled in the northern town of Yan'an and formed new collectives. By now Mao had been elected to the Communist Party's leadership and had set about formulating a social analysis which would provide a basis for the specifically Chinese route to Communism. In Yan'an he met Jiang Qing a Shanghai actress and in 1937 Mao married for the third time. His second wife He Zizhen whom Mao had married in 1931 is said to have lost her reason as a result of the hardships of the Long March. Both children from this marriage were entrusted to a peasant family but were later reported missing.

In the war against Japan, when the Kuomintang once again allied with the Communists, Mao's movement was able to drop its guard and win the support of the broad masses by demonstrating success. In 1949 the Communist forces celebrated a double victory over the Japanese insurgents and the Kuomintang before proclaiming the People's Republic. Mao occupied the position of Chairman of the Republic until 1958 when he delegated the administrative duties to others but remained party chairman. All other major political developments and events are closely linked with his name – from the Great Leap Forward to the Cultural Revolution. It was Mao's great charisma and gift for strategy which enabled him to hold his vast country together despite periods of profound crisis. Not only did he understand precisely the nature of the serious social conflicts and their causes, he was also able to anticipate them.

Within a month of his death on September 9th 1976, China had entered a new phase in its history with the arrest of Mao's wife Jiang Qing and the other members of the Gang of Four.

Ni Zan a poet, calligrapher and landscape artist was born in Wuxi, Jiangsu province, into a rich and aristocratic family. During the 1340s, however, he gave all his possessions away to relatives and friends and travelled the countryside staying mainly in Buddhist temples. Shortly before the end of the Yuan Dynasty (1368) he withdrew to a houseboat. He was offered a job by the Ming Dynasty but declined it, preferring to turn his back on worldly pleasures and to lead a simple life.

Ni Zan was one of the "Four Great Masters of the Yuan Period". His work is characterised by a chalky colour-wash effect. One of his own poems usually accompanies the landscape paintings to create a unifying impression. For Ni there is no place for the personality of the artist in a painting.

It is thought that Marco Polo was born in Venice in 1254. His father Niccolò and his brother Maffeo had already visited China as merchants (1260–69) and they took Marco with them on their second trip which passed through Palestine, Tabriz, Hormuz in the Persian Gulf, eastern Persia, Pakistan, over the Pamir and across the Takla Makan Desert to Cathay. It was here that they encountered the court of Kublai Khan, the Mongolian emperor, for whom Marco Polo worked between 1275 and 1292. In 1292 Marco received permission from the emperor for him and his family to return home. They sailed across the South China Sea to the coast of Vietnam, past the Straits of Malacca, Sumatra, Sri Lanka and southern India to Hormuz, where they took an overland route to Constantinople via Persia, Armenia and Trebizond. In 1295 they made the final part of the journey by boat to Venice.

Marco Polo (1254–1324)

Imprisoned by the Genoese at the end of the 13th c. Marco Polo dictated an account of his travels entitled "Livre de devisement du monde" to his fellow captive the Pisan novelist Rustichello. The original French version was soon translated into Italian and Latin and later into other languages. A large part of the book concerns Kublai Khan, his court and those areas of the empire that Marco Polo encountered on his travels. Many people doubted the descriptions he gave of the size and splendour of the towns and also the extent of Chinese wealth. He was called "Il milione", the boaster. It was not until the late 14th c. that credence was given to Marco Polo's descriptions and maps. Tales of the khan and his riches aroused considerable interest among European explorers.

Sun Yat-sen or Zhongshan is regarded by many as the founder of the Republic and the father of modern China. Born in 1866 in the south of the country, he studied medicine first in Honolulu, then in Hong Kong and later worked as a doctor. During his studies he became more and more interested in Western thought and acquired a deep aversion to the brutal approach to government adopted by the Manchurian Qing Dynasty. This slowly developed into political opposition, finally inspiring him to give up practising medicine in the colonies of Hong Kong and Macau and to devote his energies to political activity. He set off in pursuit of support and financial backing for his democratic beliefs, visiting a number of countries including Britain, the USA and Japan.

Sun Yat-sen (1866–1925)

In 1905 he founded the Republican Party, later to be known as Kuomintang. In accordance with his Western-style democratic and libertarian ideals the slogan he adopted was "Independence, Parliamentary Democracy and Agrarian Socialism". After the republic was proclaimed – having played a part in its emergence, although in exile – he returned to China in 1912 to become president. He was, however, forced to resign after just a few weeks in order to avoid civil war. He was succeeded by Yuan Shi-kai, a close associate of the Manchu Dynasty, landowners and an ally of foreign powers. Sun Yat-sen was obliged to return to exile. Once again he sought control over the democratic movement and with the help of the Chinese Communist Party and Russia he masterminded the rebellion against the Warlords. He managed to win control of parts of southern China and in 1923 Sun installed a revolutionary government in Canton. Chiang Kai-shek took control when Sun died two years later but he soon distanced himself

from Sun's political legacy and led China into a civil war. Sun Yat-sen's contributions to political thought are contained in two works "The Three Principles of the People" and "The International Development of China". His wife Soong Ching-Ling sought to advance his ideas, but moved towards the Communist Party and remained closely linked with it for the rest of her life.

The painter, poet, calligrapher and musician Wang Wei was born in Taiyuan. In 721 he passed the highest state examination as Chin-shih to become a senior government official. In 730 after his wife died he distanced himself from the imperial court, where he was highly respected, to lead a reclusive existence. When the emperor was deposed. In 756 he was invited by the leader of the rebels An Lu-shan to resume his duties in the service of the state. However he quickly found himself in prison when the capital was reconquered. Wang was soon pardoned, not just because of the intercession of his brother who had remained loyal to the emperor, but also because he had written a poem entitled "Frozen Pearls", in which he expressed his sadness at the fall of the imperial house. But the imprisonment had left him so physically and mentally scarred that he died two years later in Chang'an (now Xi'an).

Wang Wei (699–759)

Wang was the father of monochrome landscape painting and he remains the finest exponent of Chinese landscape painting. He is also regarded as the founder of what was known as the "Southern Tendency". The artist presents the landscape on a spiritual and yet realistic plane.

Only copies of his work remain. Wang's most celebrated work is a landscape scroll in which his country house at Wang-ch'uan near Chang'an is portrayed. On the death of his mother he converted the house into a Buddhist temple.

The painter/calligrapher Wang Xizhi is regarded as a master of this particular art form and responsible for present-day Chinese script. He used the "grass script" (kaoshu) in which several symbols are drawn linked together by one flowing line.

Wang Xizhi (c. 321–379)

Only copies of his 8th c. calligraphy exist and none of his paintings remains. The copies give a clear indication of the extraordinary beauty and expressive power of his script, which is characterised by an expressive, flowing elegance.

Born into a wealthy southern Chinese family in 1898, Zhou Enlai studied in Tianjin where he met his wife Deng Ying Chao, one of China's first female academics. He later went on to study in Japan, France and Germany where he was active in student politics. While in Europe he became a member of the overseas section of the Chinese Communist Party which was formed in Shanghai. In 1924 he returned to China and from then on played an important part in the party's hierarchy where he was able to demonstrate his immense organisational and diplomatic skills. While the Communist Party retained its links with the Kuomintang, he was the political leader of the Whampoa Military Academy, and during the Long March, political officer for the Red Army. He always maintained a close, friendly relationship with Mao even though the two men did not always share the same views, particularly in relation to the role which Zhou Enlai played in the late 30s as representative of the party at the Third International. Mao's position at that time was openly at odds with that of the Chinese Communist Party and the Soviet Union.

Zhou Enlai (1898–1976)

During the war with Japan and the subsequent civil war Zhou devoted himself to diplomacy. When the People's Republic was founded in 1949 Zhou became prime minister, an office he held until

◄ *Marco Polo in Tartar uniform*

his death. Between 1949 and 1958 he also served as foreign minister. He was a popular figure among the Chinese people on account of his balanced, sincere and always discreet personality.

Of all the Chinese political leadership he alone came through the purges and political campaigns untarnished and not once did he become a target for public criticism or accusations. He died of a tumour on January 6th 1976. Three months after Zhou's death on the occasion of Qingming, a festival to honour the dead, the Beijing people gathered on Tiananmen Square to show their respect for their deceased leader – the first sign of the simmering dissatisfaction which was to lead to unrest later on.

The poet Li Bai receives his friends in the pear-tree garden ▶

Art and Culture

Painting

The significance of the paintbrush

According to legend a certain Che Huang who lived c. 2500 B.C. invented the Chinese paintbrush. It consists of a tuft of soft animal hairs attached to the end of a bamboo cane. Unlike the Western version with its stiff bristles which follow the delicate movements of the finger, responding as it were consciously to a rational force, the Chinese paintbrush is so soft that it cannot be controlled quite so easily and thus reacts like a seismograph to the spiritual and physical impulses of the artist. The paintbrush records not just his rational will but also his moods and state of mind. "The brush stroke is the man" is an old Chinese saying. Throughout the history of Chinese art, the quality of the brushwork has been a central feature – its power, its lightness, its capacity to transform the world into fantasy.

Relationship between man and nature

Set against this background certain differences between Chinese and Western painting become easier to understand, e.g. little stress is laid on the study of the human body or the portrait. The Chinese painter is not concerned with rendering a likeness of a body or a face; much more important are the body's movements and its relationship with nature. In most Chinese painting the human figure is but a small detail within a much larger, all-embracing whole. Chinese painters also have little interest in perspective, often a starting-point for Western students of art. Chinese art tends more towards a psychological solution to this problem with vague distance and close-up effects which can create a thoroughly modern interpretation of landscapes.

A Chinese painter therefore will never paint a natural scene and never use a model and yet his relationship with nature is probably closer than his Western counterpart. When an artist has studied his theme for long enough and has absorbed the inherent qualities, he will reproduce it on rice paper or silk with a symbol that expresses his innermost feelings, his soul. The prominent features of his subject simply disappear into the background.

"Four Treasures"

The materials that a Chinese painter uses – the "Four Treasures" as they are traditionally known, i.e. brush, ink, rubbing stone and rice paper – do not permit any alterations or any time for contemplation. Quite the opposite, they demand spontaneous flowing expression, precise thought, a first-class technique and a spiritual and physical self-discipline which is to some extent comparable with religious meditation and the martial arts.

History of Painting

The Warring Kingdoms period (475–221 B.C.)

The bronze vessels and lacquer paintings of this period, in which Confucius and Taoism had flourished, were already displaying the different characteristics of Chinese art. Hunting scenes, symbols and animals are no longer the same as the ancient bronze examples and are not adorned with geometric symbols, but the image is expressed in a few flowing lines which give an impression of movement. The oldest Chinese painting in existence, a silk shroud which was discovered in the burial site of Mawangdui in the southern province of Hunan, dates from this period. It is now on display in the Changsha provincial museum. Unbelievably delicate brush strokes portray the journey of a princess into the underworld.

The Han Dynasty, the first major Chinese empire, corresponds with the "Greek" period in Chinese cultural history. Man and his deeds take precedence over magical rites and mythologies. The works of art which remain from this period are mainly wall paintings and casts of reliefs with themes taken from the teachings of Confucius or naturalist Taoist motifs. In some of the compositions it is possible to feel a sense of spaciousness and depth.

Han Dynasty (206 B.C. to A.D. 220)

Gu Kaizhi (334–c. 406) was working at a time when the empire appeared to be disintegrating following the demise of the Han Dynasty. He was the first painter to emerge from the anonymity of the schools and workshops. His best known work is "Admonitions of the Instructress to the Court Ladies", a horizontal scroll with a series of scenes which demonstrate the accepted norms of behaviour for the imperial court ladies. These scrolls appeared for the first time during this period and can be presented either in a vertical format known as hanging scrolls, kakemono in Japanese, or else in a horizontal scroll, known in Japanese as a makemono. The latter were designed to be unrolled from right to left and then rolled up at the other end so that only one scene at a time was visible. In this way the beholder was given time to reflect between each scene – an important factor in the appreciation of Chinese art and something which is no longer possible as museums display the complete, unrolled scrolls.

The Six Dynasties

The second major Chinese empire, the Tang Dynasty, was said to have been "more distinguished than the Han Dynasty and less manneristic than the Song Empire which followed". It was during this period that the landscape painter made his mark and the great artist Wu Daozi (b. c. 680) is generally accredited with inventing the genre. His landscape compositions of which only copies exist are characterised by quick, spontaneous brushwork with colour playing an insignificant part. This style was continued by his pupils.

Tang Dynasty (618–907)

Wang Wei (699–759; see Famous People) continued to develop in this direction and is regarded as the creator of the monochromatic landscape where everything is reduced to the barest essentials.

But the principal concern of Tang painters continued to be courtly and religious themes. Han Kan (8th c.; see Famous People) was a celebrated exponent of the former category and recognised as the finest "Horse Painter" in the history of Chinese art.

Dunhuang's extraordinary wall paintings are certainly the best examples of religious works. Rich symbolism and bright colours in the Indian tradition merge with the flowing lines so typical of Chinese art.

These years are often described as the classical period of Chinese painting, the years in which landscape painting reached its climax. The impressionistic use of ink with all the variations in shading represented an attempt by artists to "recreate the innermost essence of things". Attention was given to the minutest detail, from the bamboo shoot to the pine needle, from the rock to the bird. Emperor Huizong (1082–1135) himself was regarded as a talented painter of nature. The most famous painters of this Golden Age include Li Cheng (d. 967) and Xu Daoning (first half of the 11th c.) who developed the "pingyuan" technique where graduated depth creates an illusion of distance. Also important are Dong Yuan whose mountains seem to emerge from empty surfaces and Ma Yuan (b. c. 1150) who cleverly moved the focus of his composition to a peripheral detail. He came to represent the "one-corner style" as he portrayed only "one corner out of four".

The Five Dynasties (907–960) Song Dynasty (960–1279)

During this time one of the Far East's most distinctive philosophical movements emerged, that of Chan Buddhism or more commonly known by the Japanese variation "Zen". Its followers believe that

Painting

Rock paintings in Tibet

enlightenment is attained not just from spiritual insights but through intuition. Quite apart from the fact that Chan Buddhism with its notions of spontaneity and simplicity strongly influenced Chinese aesthetic notions, it encouraged a monks' school of painting where short brush strokes only hint vaguely at objects without really describing them. The finest exponents of Chan painting are Liang Kai (early 13th c.), who was able to portray the human form in just a few strokes as in his famous portrait of the poet Li Bai, and also Mu Chi (*c.* 1220–*c.* 1290) who painted small insignificant objects such as a leaf, a persimmon or an insect with great attention to detail.

Yuan Dynasty (1271–1368)

During the Mongolian occupation, painting suffered. Classical works were studied and copied. The "Four Grand Masters" of the Yuan years whose works exemplify the artistic tendencies of that era preferred to move south instead of accepting posts under the Mongolian rulers. On the other hand the famous horse painter Zhao Mengfu (1254–1322) and his wife Guan Daosheng, the most celebrated woman painter in the history of Chinese art, did accept such an offer.

The Yuan Masters certainly lived their lives in accordance with the Confucian ethic, since they remained faithful to the old Chinese dynasty. In their painting, however, they realised the Taoist ideal of a peaceful and serene landscape. The best known of the masters is Ni Zan (1310–1374; see Famous People) who used such a dry brush that it was said "he saved ink not gold". In his landscape paintings he reduced everything to its essence and there was no place for human forms. He used just a few light strokes of the brush, giving the blank spaces of white paper an important, constructive role.

"The Four Beauties" (painted on silk, 15th/16th c.) ▶

Painting

In a political and cultural sense China flourished under Ming rule, although there were some powerful conservative forces at work. Painting followed the motto "Back to the Past" and anything new and original was despised – the academic canon had to be retained. This was the first style of Chinese painting that the West encountered and wealthy Europeans certainly had ample opportunities to appreciate it. For one reason artists were simply more productive than the artists who worked in the preceding centuries. As more and more examples of Chinese art reached the West, however, the impression formed that it was affected and manneristic.

Dai Jin (1388–1462) ranks among the most influential artists of this period and he was the founder of the Zhejiang School. His works, which betray a gift for close observation, are full of movement and life. The painter did not seek to express emotion, merely fulfilment, not union with the infinite but peace in an idyllic setting. The Wu School in the south was more at odds with academic tradition and turned towards the landscapes of the Yuan painters. Works by Shen Zhou (1427–1509) and Wen Zheng-ming (1470–1559), the principal representatives of this movement, proved to be highly successful but they were little more than imitations.

Qing Dynasty
(1644–1911)

While the Manchu rulers were pushing the academic Ming style to its extreme with refined, if rather affected courtly paintings, between the 17th and 18th c. as a reaction to this kind of mannerism some highly "individualist" influences were at work, culminating in some of the most interesting examples of Chinese art. Zhu Da (1693–1775) a Buddhist monk also known as Bada Shanren was the leading light in this "Bohemian" movement. His aggressive brushwork suggested an inner torment. Distinctive features of his work include the grotesque exaggeration of figures and objects, the sarcastic humour of his characters and the belligerence of his animals. Clear "expressionist" traits were also in evidence in the School of the "Eight Eccentrics" of Yangzhou, where in the final years of the Qing era the influences of experimental Western painters encouraged the pursuit of new styles.

Another significant influence on Chinese art was the Italian Jesuit and painter Giuseppe Castiglione (Lang Shining in Chinese; 1698–1768) who spent some time at Emperor Qianlong's court. Castiglione was himself very happy to adopt the classical Chinese style, but was instrumental in introducing to China important new techniques such as perspective and the use of tempera and oil paints on silk, approaches which permitted a "more realistic" representation of the world. In addition, Castiglione familiarised the Chinese with the portrait. His portrayal of Emperor Qianlong is one of his best known works.

Modern painting

Unlike other spheres of the arts and culture, painting survived the disintegration of the empire and also the political events of recent decades, chiefly due to the extensive output of the few artists who have won international acclaim such as Qi Baishi (1863–1957), Xu Beihong (1895–1953) and Li Keran (b. 1907).

The new republic opened China up to fresh Western influences which provided the impetus for studies of nature, e.g. nude painting and pleinairism. The declared aim was to link traditional painting techniques with a realistic portrayal of man and his environment, plus the study of animals, plants and landscapes. Leaders of this movement during the 1930s and 40s included Huang Binhong (1864–1955), Qi Baishi who continued the poetic tradition of Chan Buddhism and the Taoists with his lively and expressive treatment of flowers, animals and domestic objects, Xu Beihong, the last horse painter, and Zhang Daqian (1899–1983). In the 50s and 60s Fu Baoshi (1904–1965) and the landscape artist Li Keran gave expression to a new realism, but without undermining the achievements of traditional Chinese painting.

Calligraphy

In China painting is inextricably linked with writing. The Chinese painter is always a calligrapher as well and learns the two skills together. Painting and calligraphy require a mastery of the brush and once a stroke has been executed it cannot be reconsidered or corrected. It is the "brush stroke which tells all about the personality of the artist and his technical ability".

Painting and calligraphy

Chinese writing, which started out as a series of pictograms, was first practised at the beginning of the 2nd millennium B.C. Over the centuries it has undergone a process of stylistic change in which the pictogram developed into an abstract symbol, an ideogram.

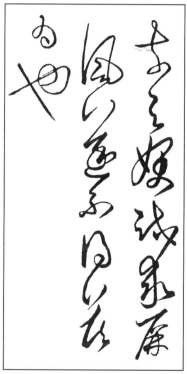

Grass writing (Kaoshu)

The court astrologers of the Shang Dynasty (16th–11th c. B.C.) who scratched their oracular inscriptions on tortoise shells or ox bones were already using a stylised script. During the Zhou Dynasty (11th c.–221 B.C.) inscriptions were usually marked on to bronze vessels. Towards the end of the 9th c. B.C. the symbols started to appear in parallel columns and also the lines became finer and rounder.

Various calligraphic styles have developed from these ancient scripts. The "dazhuan" (large seal script) and the "xiaozhuan" (small seal script), the oldest styles were in common use during the Zhou Dynasty (11th c.–221 B.C.) and at the beginning of the Qin Dynasty (221–206 B.C.). The pictographic origin of many of their symbols can still be recognised. The sun, for example, is shown as a small ring, mountains by a series of peaks and a horse as a silhouette with four legs. These symbols are difficult to create but are aesthetically very pleasing – some are still used by the Chinese on seals (hence seal script), as signatures, in calligraphy or as commercial hallmarks.

Calligraphic style

"Lishu", the style of officials and clerics, developed during the Qin era and is an angular, easily understood script. With its grand elegant lines it is often used on book titles, newspaper mastheads, signs and notices.

Gradually, around the time of Jesus Christ, "lishu" was transformed into "kaishu" or regular style which is now used throughout China as the standard script.

All the many thousands of symbols in a Chinese dictionary – a Chinese person with an average standard of education can recognise between 4000 and 5000 symbols – are actually formed from about 20 basic strokes. They should only be written according to very strict rules, but in fact there is flexibility and a calligrapher is granted some artistic freedom.

Cursive script

Under the Eastern Han Dynasty (24–220) efforts were made to devise a faster script and a more expressive brush stroke. "Xingshu", a cursive script, was the outcome from which then developed "kaoshu" or grass script – so-called because of its flowing straw-like lines. This script, later used by followers of Taoism and Chan Buddhists, became a form of artistry in its own right. The meaning of the symbols which were often linked together was of secondary importance and only the initiated were capable of deciphering them. The most famous calligrapher was probably Wang Xizhi (321–379) and it is said that his style can be recognised from a single dot.

In China every painter is also a calligrapher. A painting without one or more lines of verse written in a classical script is unthinkable.

Calligraphy and the intellectuals

Every politician and intellectual is also expected to be able to master calligraphy. In Mao Zedong's time a framed copy of one of the Chairman's own poems written in beautiful "xingshu" script hung in every public restaurant. The symbols in the title of the "Renmin Ribao" or "People's Daily", the official organ of the Chinese Communist Party, were written by Mao, while the inscription above his mausoleum came from the brush of his successor Hua Guofeng.

Pottery

Porcelain and trade

It was the Portuguese who were the first Europeans to arrive in Canton harbour at the beginning of the 16th century. Merchants from Lisbon were quick to realise the attraction of Chinese crockery with its lustre and lightness rather reminiscent of mussel shells. This unusual material, which came to be known as "porcelain", from the Italian "porcellana" (sometimes "porcella") meaning "cowrie shell", was soon in great demand at the European courts. The French king drank from cups edged with gold and silver and no European prince's display cabinet was complete without ostrich eggs, a philosopher's stone and a white and blue porcelain bowl. For a long time Westerners could only admire the technical perfection of the material and the exotic designs on Chinese pottery which found its way to every part of the civilised world. In Western aesthetic terms, pottery is simply a decorative craft. It amazes most Westerners that porcelain is valued so much in the Orient and also that it commands such high prices.

Porcelain as art

In China, where there is no differentiation between handicrafts and art in the Western sense, porcelain is something of cultural importance rather than merely a matter of taste. To know a piece of porcelain, its colour, its shape, its sound, to touch the surface, all these experiences are part of the education of a learned man, as the renowned poet Du Fu (see Famous People) testifies in his writings.

There are several reasons for this peculiar aesthetic sensitivity. Certainly the Taoist tradition places great emphasis on the mystical relationship between man and nature. Porcelain, a product of earth and fire, has much more to do with the warm, mysterious ways of nature than cold metal. To the Chinese it can be compared with flowers, water, snow and jade.

Another significant factor is the link between porcelain, painting and calligraphy. In porcelain's heyday the porcelain painter was an artist in the true sense. He would work in similar surroundings with the same brushes and apply the same brush strokes. As with silk or Chan painting, there is no place for mistakes. Success and quality cannot be fully judged until the work has been fired and to a large extent, there is little practical control over the outcome. This element of unpredictability which is not applicable to working with bronze or stone seems to conceal an elusive spiritual element. Decorative techniques

Finally porcelain is a part of the rural tradition. Collections are passed down the generations, representing security and continuity and a testimony to the superior skills of ancestors.

The History of Pottery

It is not clear when exactly porcelain was invented. Western art historians generally believe that its origins date from the Tang Dynasty (618–907) or the beginning of the Song Dynasty (960–1279). Artefacts have been discovered which date from this era and which have a glaze that has fused with the clay during the first firing. Thus the white crystalline solid now known as porcelain was formed. For the Chinese the concept of porcelain covers a variety of stoneware products all of which should be fired at high temperatures (1000–1300°C/1800–2400°F). The result is a material much harder than conventional clayware but not always with the glassy, smooth finish of what we would describe as porcelain. Stoneware, porcelain-style stoneware and porcelain are all known in Chinese as "ci" (pronounced "tsi"). Thus in the opinion of Chinese experts the date for the invention of "ci" must be brought forward to as early as the Wei or Jin Dynasty (4th c. A.D.). However, discoveries made in the 1970s of 16th c. B.C. fragments have led some archaeologists to conclude that porcelain dates from around that time. Special clay made from a combination of kaolin and feldspar was fired in the same kilns that produced the Shang and Zhou Dynasty bronzes. Invention

Whatever the truth, the discovery of a material which does not absorb liquid and is durable and easy to clean ranks as one of the finest achievements of antiquity – an achievement that could only have emerged from a settled culture with a long tradition of ceramics. While the Chinese were able to produce a wide range of clay products, the other Asiatic races, which still led a nomadic existence, showed no interest in making such delicate and fragile objects. In this respect the production of decorative pottery mirrors the national character of the Chinese and the stability of the society they had created.

Vessels for alcoholic drinks

In 6000 B.C., fine clay vessels were being produced by the Peiligang culture on the banks of the Huanghe. A little later the Yangshao culture introduced colour, while the Longshan culture was making shiny black bowls shaped on a potter's wheel. In the history of ceramics this type of thin-walled stoneware is still regarded by many as the perfect model. Neolithic Era

During the early days of recorded history in a society based on slavery large workshops were used to make bronze and pottery objects for the nobility. One type of white clayware made from fine kaolin and now referred to as "proto-porcelain" had to be fired at 1000°C/1800°F. Shang and Zhou Dynasties (16th c.– 221 B.C.)

With the unification of China the art of ceramics experienced an extraordinary boost. Funerary clayware replaced human sacrifice at burial rites, to which the celebrated terracotta army of Xi'an bears eloquent witness. During this period glazes were used for the first time, rendering the clay impermeable and conferring a new aesthetic value. In Zhejiang province, the centre of Chinese pottery production, the first "Yue celadons" appeared. Qin and Han Dynasties (221 B.C.–A.D. 220)

Pottery

Tang Dynasty
(618–907)

Tang Dynasty pottery is characterised by the "three colour" effect, which earned the Chinese craftsmen fame abroad. Warriors, ladies, scenes from daily life and the celebrated, unmistakable model horses are typical of this highly successful period.

Song Dynasty
(960–1279)

The Song years were the classical years of Chinese pottery with the establishment of those aesthetic qualities which would guide porcelain artists up to the present day. The emphasis moved from the Tang period's large ritualistic human and animal forms to smaller objects which were in daily use or those which occupied a place on the desk of the scholar, who was starting to replace the warrior as the key figure in Chinese society. Pottery manufacturers concentrated on improving the form and quality of the porcelain, while decoration was regarded as rather vulgar.

Yuan Dynasty
(1271–1368)

During their 100 year reign over China the Mongols created an enduring legacy in the art of ceramics. They introduced "Qinghua" ware, a white porcelain decorated with a cobalt blue underglaze. This technique originated in the Middle East, where it was used to finish Islamic pots and the geometric patterns typical of nomadic tribes predominated. The commonest items produced during Genghis Khan's rule were large vessels, often simply copies of metal objects such as wide plates and water bottles for the Mongol ruler's horsemen. Aesthetes initially viewed this style as incompatible with the Chinese ethos but some of the Yuan characteristics were gradually accepted.

Ming Dynasty
(1368–1644)

During the Ming period the elegant shapes and high quality of Song porcelain merged with the decorative style typical of the Yuan Dynasty to produce a product of unsurpassed perfection. Jingdezhen (Jiangxi province) became the national centre for the production of porcelain with about 300 workshops, the best of which produced porcelain for

Three-coloured ceramic plate of the Tang period

the imperial court in Beijing. Famous painters worked on the decorations and a supervisor appointed by the emperor checked the quality of their work. At the same time the export trade in porcelain was encouraged. Special workshops near the ports of Canton and Quanzhou concentrated on producing goods for exporting abroad.

Ming Dynasty teapot

Song Dynasty water bottle

Tang Dynasty tea cup

Interest in coloured porcelain intensified during the Manchu Dynasty. Lavishly decorated pieces became more readily available as new glaze colours were discovered. Different ranges of porcelain were classified according to their background glaze colour, e.g. "famille rose", "famille jaune", "famille verte" and "famille noire". Although the level of technical skill soared during this period and the workshops were producing wafer-thin porcelain, huge vases for the imperial court and an unbelievable range of shapes, the transition from manual to mass production methods – each piece required as many as 70 processes – signalled the end of creativity. European tastes came to demand cluttered decorative styles, Rococo gilt and adornments, which were alien to the classic Chinese tradition. From the middle of the 19th c. the political crisis came to adversely affect the ceramics industry. Products were increasingly manufactured to meet the requirements of the export market and the original creative vitality rapidly disappeared.

Qing Dynasty (1644–1911)

The kilns were destroyed in the course of the civil wars and the Japanese invasion of the 20th c., resulting in the dispersal of the skilled workforce. Maoist orthodoxy adopted a negative attitude to Chinese tradition and the ceramics industry finally succumbed to the prohibition on any kind of private initiative. Nevertheless, some elements of the industry have survived. In rural areas a few small workshops continue to manufacture naïvely decorated products and in nearby countries such as Japan a strong demand for master potters remains, while paradoxically the old artistic traditions are being perpetuated by a flourishing trade in the production of near perfect replicas which are flooding the market in Far Eastern countries.

Modern times

Architecture

North–south alignment, the square and high walls are the three elements which form the basis of the traditional Chinese town plan.
  According to the rules of geomancy (fengshui) which are based on the concepts of Yin and Yang – the contradictory and complementary constituents of all phenomena – every human dwelling must face away from the north representing cold and shadow (Yin) and face towards the south for light and the sun (Yang). The minor axis should run at right angles to the main north–south axis – an idea which would later accord with the principle of local and functional symmetry, an element of Confucian thinking.

The traditional town

The significance of the square originates in ancient Chinese thinking which visualised heaven as a sphere and the earth as a square. Living space could only be created in accordance with these geometric configurations. Houses, palaces, temples, even whole towns were built accordingly. In the Shang and Zhou Dynasties (16th c.–221 B.C.) country estates were planned using the "jintian" model, in which a square

The square

was divided into nine plots. The middle plot was common land and cultivated communally by the families living in the eight adjoining plots.

Town walls

Fortified walls are an inheritance of the first Chinese dynasty, the war-like Shang (16th–11th c. B.C.), who always built tall defensive walls around their settlements. The two concepts "cheng" (wall, enclosure) and "yi" (fortification) now combine to create the Chinese word for "town". Despite the flourishing economy and active trading links which several towns enjoyed between the 7th and 14th c. they were not able even in the course of their later historical development to grow out of their role as military garrison and administrative centre. They were also committed to this state function by Confucian teaching. He constructed the classical code (zhou li) by which Chinese society was expected to abide and which included a treatise on town planning known as "jian ren" (the builder). It clearly established the nature of the relationship that urban settlements were to maintain between each other and the imperial capital.

Town hierarchy

At an administrative level the "jian ren" created a hierarchical structure not unlike the hierarchy within the nobility. Every level within the feudal system had a corresponding type of town. The emperor's town was laid out as a square with each side split into nine units in a way similar to the old "jintian" pattern for dividing up agricultural land. The size of other towns corresponded with the position of the feudal lord within the hierarchy. The lower his rank, the smaller the town. This formalised ranking system was based on such criteria as size, height and numbers. No town could be larger than the emperor's and no building bigger than his palace.

Town plan

At the time that the "jian ren" was devised there was no firm guidance for the varied situations which existed in the real world. The walls of the Zhou Dynasty settlements often followed an irregular course allowing for the natural contours of the locality. Linzhe (near Zhengzhou) the Qi capital, for example, had an asymmetrical enclosure, Luoyang's outer walls had to accommodate a number of unusual salients, while in Shanghai the old town is elliptical in shape.

This gap between theory and practice closed over the centuries and the town-planning "jian ren" guidelines served as a binding model for later planners.

First Tang town

Chang'an (now Xi'an), capital of the Tang Dynasty, was the first town constructed in accordance with Confucian guidelines. It was built between A.D. 600 and 800 on the ruins of the earlier Han town.

A high, rectangular defensive wall – made originally out of straw and mud but from Mongol rule onwards out of stones and bricks – has since surrounded the town, protecting it from the gaze of outsiders. Depending on the size and importance of a town, each of the four walls would be reinforced by a number of towers.

Layout

The town was divided into districts, also enclosed. Straight roads constructed on a north–south or east–west axis crossed each other at right angles, forming the boundaries between the individual districts, but the roads surrounded a confusing maze of alleyways. In the centre of the town a second ring of walls enclosed the Forbidden City, comprising the emperor's residence and military garrison. Market stalls lined this second inner wall allowing the town's administrators to oversee all economic activity, while in the middle of the town, at the heart of the Forbidden City, stood the imperial palace, although hidden well away from the gaze of the court by another high wall.

Restrictions on urban development

This long and stubborn adherence to a town planning model incorporating old architectural theories bears witness to the imperial bureaucracy's inability to move beyond feudalism. Private initiatives were

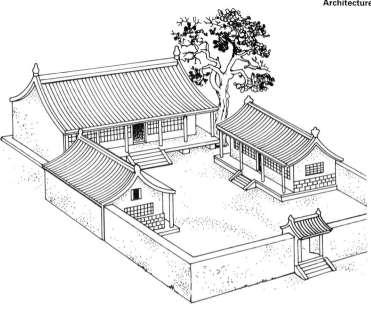

suppressed, boycotted or undermined by regulations. The merchant class occupied a very lowly position in the social hierarchy and were despised for their materialism. The state refused to offer any protection, privileges or even any written laws to this section of the community. Consequently Chinese towns never developed any real economic or political autonomy, the citizens enjoyed few civil rights and energies were devoted to unproductive, often purely administrative matters.

The unfavourable environment in the towns resulted in their commercial decline and to such an extent that the inhabitants were obliged to become consumers of goods produced elsewhere. By the beginning of the 20th c. Chinese towns had become stifled by bureaucracy and the unchanging commercial habits of the townsfolk. The sort of urban features and institutions that in Western countries make a town into a community, such as squares, markets and baths, private houses and public buildings, plus an extensive infrastructure, simply did not exist. Apart from the temples, which in terms of size and style were not particularly distinctive buildings, only two basic factors influenced Chinese society and its urban development, namely the emperor and his subjects or the imperial palace and the private dwelling.

Urban paralysis

The defensive walls which were once the unmistakable symbol of a Chinese town have had to make way almost everywhere for new wide ring roads lined by new residential tenement blocks. It is difficult now to imagine that these towns looked as they were portrayed in classical and modern Chinese literature or indeed some Western books. Gates with huge substructures but spanned by a light wooden construction are rarely seen these days; portals or "pailou" can occasionally be found, reminding inhabitants of glorious events of the past and still marking crossing points between distant, real or spiritual areas; pagodas, abstract monuments or concrete symbols, and even Buddhist,

Recent developments

Taoist or Confucian temples: these isolated landmarks are all evidence of a town's decaying past and then only to be seen within the confines of the historic town centres. After the Communist take-over, largely standardised housing blocks were constructed to make best use of the land. Complexes in which living, working and basic services are all assigned their own spaces, chequerboard or radial road construction and huge concrete edifices characterised urban development. In the ancient town centres, large expanses of land and many historic buildings were in many cases cleared to make way for new projects.

For about a decade, however, mainly in the coastal towns – unlike the cities in the interior – there have been attempts to move away from monotonous building designs. Thanks to economic progress some districts have emerged where international-style designs predominate. In suburban areas extensive housing estates and industrial zones have burgeoned.

Courtyard compound

While the square developed into the principal shape for urban divisions, the four-sided courtyard (si he yuan) remains the basic model for all forms of residential accommodation, ranging from the imperial palaces and temple, to the private town or country dwelling. Alongside the high, impenetrable walls which protect the courtyard of private houses from the gaze of the passer-by or residents of the adjacent house stand one- and two-storey buildings. The two or more buildings are usually rectangular in shape and serve as the living accommodation for each residence.

In northern China the traditional compound usually consists of three sections. The entrance faces a communal or outer hall in the middle between two other outbuildings at right angles. In the country the communal hall houses a kitchen with a stone fireplace, while the other

Hall of the Harvest Prayer in the Temple of Heaven in Beijing

two rooms are equipped with two raised platforms (kang), beneath which a fire burns and where during the day the residents gather round a table to eat, drink, play and talk. During the night the kang function as beds. Straw mats are laid on the stone surfaces and covered with soft, brightly coloured cotton-filled quilts.

The layout for the sacred palace and the spacious audience chambers in the emperor's palace was based on the model of the smallest living quarters. The official's fine town houses contained a greater number of rooms, sometimes several courtyards or one or two compounds. Temples and imperial palaces are basically just larger, more complex versions of the courtyard compound.

Temples and Imperial Palaces

The structure of a summer palace is quite simple. Resting on stone foundations a network of beams link supporting wooden columns, which bear the weight of a possible second floor or the roof. The surrounding walls usually made from wood have a protective rather than a supportive function.

Roofs are of special importance. A framework of sloping beams is covered with greyish terracotta tiles, coated with a gleaming majolica glaze – in yellow, green and blue, the colours of the Tang dynasty.

Roof

Apart from terracotta or majolica tiles and stone foundations, Chinese builders used mainly wood. Consequently many famous monuments from the past have not survived, falling victim to fire, dilapidation and wars. Wood was such a popular material because it was easy to repair, restore and replace. The fragile nature of buildings made from short-lived materials such as wood and clay is a source of fascination to many visitors. On the one hand, its use contrasts sharply with the opulence of Chinese history and culture as well as the rigidity of imperial administration. On the other hand wood allows the expression of a strong urge to replicate, to imitate at all levels.

Building materials

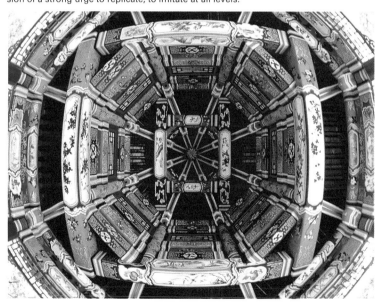

Wooden dome in the Beijing Summer Palace

97

The importance attributed to the roof as opposed to the subordinate role of the surrounding walls underlines how even Chinese architecture respects the duality of Yin and Yang, in this case the interior and exterior. The use of materials such as wood, glass and rice paper on the open sections serves to emphasise the secondary importance of the wall as merely a partition or protective panel.

Garden

Within the context of the town the courtyard represents the interior but in relation to the summer palace it stands for something external and empty. The palace is similarly subject to the dualism inherent in every phenomenon. It is a closed, or more accurately a protected, space but at the same time externally orientated towards the garden. In contrast to a building and to a town where criteria such as symmetry and right angles are important, the Chinese garden is laid out asymmetrically, with the aim of imitating nature, using curved lines to give form to the immediate environment and the structural features such as bridges, small pavilions and covered galleries. Its design cannot be perceived as a whole, but must be considered one section at a time, like the mystery that embraces the natural world. Hence it advances a tiny section at a time, each section alluding to the next scene or leading into it, by copying a small part. Like traditional Chinese landscape paintings, these miniature vistas always consist of mountains and water or what the Chinese regard as the two main features in nature, landscape and the factors which influence it.

Literature

Historiography

The existence of a written language with rules totally independent from the spoken language meant that literature and written culture were for very many years restricted to an exclusive segment of society and they became an instrument of power in the hands of the educated classes. The spread of Buddhism and missionary work based on an oral tradition led to the emergence of popular literature written in the vernacular language. Three principal literary categories can be established in Chinese cultural history: historical writings, poetry and the novel. Throughout the classical period, historical writing was an important literary genre. Writers not only sought to describe historical events objectively (natural catastrophes, loss of human life, eclipses of the sun and moon, conquests and peace accords), but also gave anecdotes from the lives of the people, little moral tales and the rites and traditions of earlier societies and eras.

"Historical Records" ("Shi Ji")

"Historical Records" or "Shi Ji" was the outstanding example of this literary category. It was written by Sima Qian (145–86 B.C.), a historical writer who lived during the Han Dynasty and who set out to record the history of China from its beginnings up to his own lifetime. Sima Qian, who is often compared with Thucydides and Tacitus, compiled the facts and then interpreted them, giving sources and quoting long extracts from the texts that he had consulted. He also produced comparative tables with contemporary methods of compilation and analysis. Sima Qian's work formed the basis for a series of official writings entitled "The History of 24 Dynasties" which were written by the archivists and officials at the imperial court. They describe the history of China from the Han period to the demise of the Ming Dynasty.

The significance and spread of these historical texts had an unfavourable effect on the epic tale. Given the unbridgeable gap between the written and spoken language, such narratives could only be passed on by word of mouth.

Poetry

While historical writing is the predominant literary genre of classical antiquity, the Tang and Song Dynasties (7–13th c.) are renowned as the golden age for Chinese poetry. The Chinese seem to excel at this form of self-expression. Poetry, surprisingly, serves as a catalyst, highlighting the differences and opposing elements within society and sharpening the individual and collective capacity for empathy. Poetry has always had a prominent part to play in the life of the Chinese people and continues to do so. It is read at public and private times, wars as well as weddings, and will be displayed inside people's homes and in temples. It will be found on porcelain vases, the plinths of statues, the gable ends of pavilions, at the entrances to gardens and in shop windows. The poem will very often just be a verse, perhaps only two lines, but will inform, describe, comment, narrate or imagine.

The simple syntax of the Chinese language and, in contrast, the fullness of meaning within the symbols and words open up a wealth of opportunities for such devices as allusion, ambiguity, assonance, as well as for tricks with sound and sense, and range is further widened by the four levels of tone. In fact, the melody of the spoken language helps to overcome the cultural divide between the written and spoken language without allowing the written version to lose any of its value. Indeed, the reverse is often true as the different impact of the poem on the eye and the ear enhances its appeal.

Chinese poetry has developed and refined over the centuries. The first collection of poems entitled "Book of Songs" dates from the Zhou Dynasty and the period of the Warring Kingdoms (11th c.–221 B.C.). These poems originated in the heart of the northern civilisation in the Huanghe valley. The "Chuzi", another collection of songs, comes from the south of China.

"Book of Songs" ("Shijing")

The finest exponents of Chinese poetry are the two Tang poets Du Fu (see Famous People) and Li Bai (see Famous People). Du Fu was born in the beautiful and prosperous town of Chengdu in the southern Sichuan province. He was a stout defender of Confucian ideas and portrayed the suffering of the Chinese people and the severe landscapes of the west, where the population was dying in wars between the tribes ("Home is in ruins:/mountains and rivers remain and in the towns it is spring/trees and thick grass . . .")

Du Fu (712–770)

Unlike his contemporary Du Fu, Li Bai fell under the influence of Taoism and was captivated by nature, its rhythms, sounds and colours ("and it is as if I can hear the pine trees breathing from a thousand mouths,/and a river flows by and washes the sorrow from my heart"). In a state of drunken euphoria he finds himself at one with the natural flow of life, the Tao, intoxicated by wine, passion and vice (". . . is it not said that pure wine makes man wise/and cloudy wine releases man from his ignorance?").

Li Bai (705–762)

That poetry was a genuinely popular form of expression is clear from the large number of poems that were written by courtesans. For them, poetic talent was a way of winning a man's admiration, of escaping from a lowly status, finding a husband or securing a position as a concubine. The Tang (618–907) courtesans Yu Xuanchi and Xue Tao who came from quite different social backgrounds write from the soul about their unhappiness, anxieties, the depth of their passion, their loneliness and their insecurity.

Courtesans' lyrical poems

It was during the 14th c. when the Mongols ruled China that the written story started to replace the oral tradition. The two most important works of this period are "The Romance of the Three Kingdoms" by Luo Guanzhong, recounting the heroic deeds and adventures of many of the figures who lived during the "Three Kingdoms" period and the "Water Margin" or "The Robbers of Liangshan Moor" by Shi Naian

The novel

Literature

Li Bai receives his friends (detail from a painting by Qiu Ying)

(1368), a tale in the popular Taoist tradition where a band of robbers seek to defend such ideals as justice and liberation. On the other hand in ''Record of a Journey West'' or ''Monkey'' written in the 16th c. during the Ming period, Wu Cheng'en (1510–1580) describes how Buddhism influences the journey of one man and his companions. ''The Plum Blossom in a Golden Vase'' (1610) by Jing Ping Mei is a famous erotic novel which describes in a lively manner the society, culture and customs of the Song era (960–1279). The last great novel of the imperial years is called ''Dream of the Red Chamber'' (''Honglou Meng'') by Cao Xueqin (1715–63) who describes the decay of imperial society and the fragility of social relationships expressed through the feelings and hopes of an adolescent.

Modern literature

Modern literature includes those works which appeared between the Opium Wars and the May 4th Movement of 1919. They made a significant contribution to the development and strengthening of a political and social conscience. In the first few years of the 20th c. a literary revolution occurred – students, writers, poets and journalists declined to use the written language, replacing it in their books and articles with the widely understood language of common use (beihua). In this way they forced the government to extend the use of this language variation to every school in the land. Of the many personalities of that era, Lu Xun (1881–1936; see Famous People) stands out as the father of this literary revolution. A Marxist writer, he translated many Russian works and helped to popularise the 19th c. novel including Gogol and Dostoyevsky. He also wrote a number of socio-critical stories such as ''A Madman's Diary'' (1918) and ''The Story of Ah Q'' (1921) both of which savagely denounced the deplorable state of Chinese society.

Contemporary literature

The following 20th c. men and women of letters have played an important role: Lao She (1898–1966; see Famous People) wrote the famous

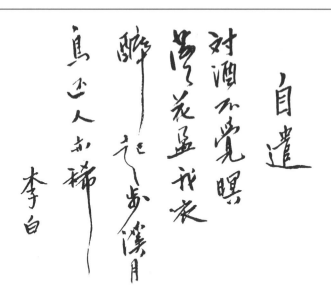

I drink, time flies.
I do not notice it.
The falling blossoms collect on my cloak.
I stagger about by the stream in the moonlight.
The birds fly home, the streets are empty.

Li Bai

novel entitled "The Rickshaw Boy" (1937) which recounts the fortunes of a rickshaw driver; Mao Dun (1896–1981; see Famous People) wrote his highly acclaimed "Midnight" (1932), which dealt with life in Shanghai at the beginning of the 1930s; Ba Jin (b. 1904) wrote the "Family", "Autumn", "Spring" and "Fog"; Ai Qing and the feminist writer Ding Ling (1904–86). Guo Moruo (1892–1978; see Famous People) was respected as a poet and scholar who also wrote novels. Cao Yu wrote several celebrated plays of which "Sunrise" and "Wilderness" are his best known.

Writers within the Communist Party were committed by Mao Zedong to the creation of class-based literature, which would, on the one hand, reflect the views and feelings of the proletariat, but on the other, fulfil a distinct educational function. When the Communists won power in 1949 most prominent writers were banned. Simple poetry in the vernacular language was encouraged as were reportage-type accounts of life among the peasants and workers and also a type of contemporary heroic novel which glorified the struggle against foreign and class enemies. During the Cultural Revolution literary output was reduced almost exclusively to the publication of works by Mao Zedong, but after his death in 1976 it was not long before writers soon re-emerged. Almost all of the proscribed modern writers were rehabilitated, sometimes posthumously. There was an intense interest in

China's classical literature and also in Western literature. Recent notable developments in prose include short stories by Wang Meng (b. 1934) and also the novella, which permits an unusual treatment of the hero and inner monologues.

A number of exiled writers are of world-wide renown. A. Cheng (b. 1949) who emigrated to the USA in 1987 is the author of "Chess King" (1985) and "Tree King". On the other hand, one of the most interesting young writers of Anglo-Saxon literature is Timothy Mo, a Hong Kong Chinese whose works include "Sweet and Sour" and "The Monkey King".

Opera

Traditional opera

Clanging cymbals, flutes and drums, acrobatic postures of the actors, high falsetto voices, abrupt geometrical movements of the warriors, dignified symbolic gestures, colourful mask-like make-up, shimmering, beautifully embroidered silk costumes – Chinese opera is the pinnacle of many varied disciplines which all unfold together on the stage.

Chinese theatre really has very little in common with Western theatre and seems – like the novel with which it originally identified – to have originated with the singing Buddhist monk who used a wide range of expressive forms to retell the story of Buddha. Theatre as an art form did not actually develop until the last phase of the Song Dynasty (1100–1200) and it was during the years of Mongol rule that it divested itself of its Buddhist associations to become independent, with the performance of such major works as "Romance of the Western Chamber" and "The Lute". As with later stage productions the main theme for both these examples is first and foremost a tender love story, but

Beijing opera

woven into the plot are robbers, courtly intrigue, myths legends and religious parables.

In the centuries that followed, Chinese opera pursued various directions. In the end, however, despite its emphasis on high stylistic standards, the southern school was pushed aside by the northern Beijing opera as it was known and this operatic style still dominates throughout China. The Cultural Revolution proscribed all earlier works, replacing them with contemporary works focusing on such themes as the Japanese war and the Long March, but now the Beijing opera is reviving original texts from the Yuan (1271–1368) and Ming (1368–1644) periods. The regional operas have retained their traditional style and are still performed.

Beijing opera

The differences between the traditions of local opera in the outlying areas and the Beijing opera manifest themselves mainly in the use of certain instruments and special types of enunciation.

The position of a hand, the movement of an arm, a raised eyebrow, colour variations in the make-up of a performer – all these can be significant elements in an intricate code where nuances – something which the Chinese are familiar with and fully understand – have their roots in the various ethnic and cultural backgrounds.

Gesture and symbolic language

There is no scenery. Place and action are only evoked by mime, another essential component in Chinese opera.

Celebrations

In the eyes of the Chinese, a new-born baby is already almost a year old as the months of pregnancy are included in the calculation of age. A birthday is therefore celebrated one month after the birth, when the baby's hair is cut for the first time. Far more generous celebrations are accorded to the first-born child than to subsequent siblings.

Birth

Traditionally, the bride moves in with the bridegroom's family, but she is only recognised as a full member of the family when she has produced a child. Although three-day wedding ceremonies are no longer normal in the urban areas, in the country such celebrations are common and they can also involve a number of complicated rituals. The bridegroom fetches the bride from her home and takes her to his, where a wedding room is prepared. No religious ceremony takes place in the true sense, but the marriage bond is confirmed by placing sacrificial offerings to the ancestors on the family altar.

Marriage

Respect for dead ancestors is a fundamental element in the cohesion of the family. The living and the dead have responsibilities to each other. The living must show reverence to the dead and the dead play their part from the afterlife to secure prosperity and a long earthly life for the living. As the young have a duty to respect the old, a son, should he die young, has no claim to such veneration. If he dies before his parents he is guilty of a misdemeanour. His descendants will pay him due respect, but not his parents or other living relatives. If someone dies without any descendants he or she becomes a "hungry spirit" who roams around restlessly in search of another who will pay the ritual honours. A ceremony is held in the autumn when offerings are made in the hope of satisfying these restless spirits.

Ancestor worship

Lengthy ceremonies and unusual costumes are the hallmark of Chinese funerals and the costs can often mean that families fall into financial difficulties. Seven days after burial (more recently replaced by cremation) the relatives of the dead person burn paper and bamboo models which can represent anything from food to cars. In this way the dead are provided with all that they need in the afterlife. On the seventh day a plaque is left on the family altar or in the temple.

Food

The philosophy of food

What has never failed to astonish Westerners are the strange ingredients that find their way on to the table in China: shark's fin, birds' nest soup, bamboo shoots and sea cucumber salad, not to mention mouse, snake, dog and cat meat. It is true that the Chinese are one of the few races that have no taboos with regard to food. The reality is, however, that something like 90 per cent of Chinese foods are readily available in the West. The significant difference between Chinese and Western cooking habits lies in the way certain flavours are combined or ingredients are seasoned with sauces and spices, how the food is cooked and served and the way it is eaten.

The fascination of Chinese food is due less to the interesting ingredients the cooks use, but more to the "philosophy", that mysterious, but complementary amalgamation of aromas, colours and essences, every single ingredient steeped in ancient tradition and with its own part to play. Those who wish to really understand and appreciate Chinese food must become familiar with the guiding principles of this "philosophy".

Food and medicine

In the course of their history the Chinese have never distinguished between food and medicine. Eating and looking after one's health amount to the same thing. Whatever does the body good is both medicine and food. Sun Simiao, a doctor who lived in the 6th c. B.C., put it this way: "A good doctor tries first and foremost to cure illness with food and only when that does not help, does he prescribe medicine." The science of nutrition has been practised in China for thousands of years and every doctor is advised to be something of a cook and every cook to be something of a doctor. While Western dieticians pay little attention to how food is prepared, concerning themselves more with recommending daily rations of meat, vegetables, etc., in China every good recipe must be planned to meet certain dietary guidelines. In classical Chinese cuisine (but not Sino-Moslem or Mongolian) pure meat dishes such as roasts or kebabs are rare. Animal fats and proteins are always compensated for by vegetable ingredients or purifying, digestion-aiding flavours such as onions in Peking Duck or aniseed in braised pork. Although the Chinese value mushrooms they would think it quite strange to eat sliced mushrooms. The principles of their medicine demand that every dish consists of a number of ingredients, never one single item, as otherwise the human body will lose its equilibrium. Equally, pure sweet desserts are alien to traditional Chinese culinary tradition. Something sweet should always be accompanied by a salty, neutral flavour. Too much sugar and honey "makes the stomach soft and lazy". Chinese chefs avoid not just harmful combinations, but also make a special effort to find easily digestible blends. For example, they like to process kidneys, brain, bone marrow, stomach and intestines, all ingredients which are rich in vitamins, nourishing and aids to digestion. It is, therefore, normal to feel pleasantly satisfied rather than full after a Chinese meal. Any reputable experienced chef will put together his own special menu which meets all the nutritional requirements of the human body.

Fresh food

Yue Zecai, an epicurean 17th c. poet, sang a song of praise to his chef who refused to cook a dish as the ingredients were not seasonal products.

Table Etiquette

The pleasure of a Chinese celebration meal lies not least in the accompanying rituals, the subtle interplay between the various courses, which may be served in a certain order to emphasise colour, aroma and taste, in the toasts and the conversation. Although even the Chinese no longer abide by it, there is a convention that dishes ought not to be ordered à la carte. In the best restaurants it is the custom to agree on a price and discuss in general terms what the meal will consist of, i.e. will it be based on duck, beef or vegetarian. It is then usually left to the chef's discretion to decide how he will create the different courses. In this way the guest is then relieved of the task of having to choose from hundreds of dishes. Tea is usually drunk before the meal to settle the stomach.

To help stimulate the circulation and freshen up, guests are offered a hot damp cloth with which to wipe their face and hands. During the meal, beer is often served – the best beer comes from Qingdao – or a few glasses of rice spirit (maotai) or Shaoxing rice wine but not sake. No Chinese would ever dream of drinking tea with a meal. Traditionally only strong spirits would be served at the table, but in recent years beer and lighter sweet liqueurs have become popular, while wine made from grapes is something of a rarity. Boiled or fried rice, bread and noodles are side dishes which should not be mixed with the other food.

The left-hand side of the table is more important than the right, apart from at official or diplomatic receptions. The host sits down last and always apologises for the inadequacy of the food. Lifting a glass with a "qing" (please) or "ganbei" (roughly equivalent to "let's empty our glasses") is the normal toast with which to start a celebration meal.

Diners at a Chinese meal either feed themselves or may help their neighbour. The food is taken from the dish with chopsticks, only as much as can be consumed should be taken and nothing should be left on the plate. Guests are invited to empty their glasses with a toast. To be correct a diner will eat a little of everything and will not indicate which was his or her favourite. After about two hours the oldest in the group will stand and the remaining guests follow suit.

Eating soup noisily or slurping tea, tangling noodles and belching are regarded as gestures of approval. In Western countries the chicken breast with its tender white flesh is regarded as the best part of the bird, while in China guests are honoured to receive a piece of wing or thigh. Fish is served intact with head and tail as these parts are the "royal mouthfuls".

The "kuaizi" or **chopsticks** are indispensable. Only when the soup arrives at the end of the meal is a spoon used.

The first chopstick is held motionless between ring finger and the groove between thumb and forefinger.

The second chopstick is held alongside the first one between the tips of the middle and forefinger. Keep the first chopstick still and manipulate the tip of the second one to grasp a morsel of food. The thumb acts as a sort of hinge.

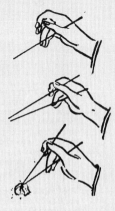

Spices

The Chinese have always appreciated fresh food. Hence tortoises are cooked alive or brain is eaten steaming hot. In the search for a life-prolonging elixir, Taoists waited out in the open for the sun to rise so that they could drink the early morning dew and eat the fresh shoots. Apart from soya paste, some vegetables pickled in vinegar or brine and a few dried fish, the Chinese have made little use of preserved foods. Even now they prefer seasonal products and fresh meat. "Better to use vegetables from your own garden," goes one proverb, "than the best cook in the empire."

Cooking as an art form

Apart from soups, braised meat and a few cold starters, Chinese dishes are not, as many people believe, prepared in advance but cooked just prior to eating. Most dishes need short cooking times over a high heat. Using this method, meat and vegetables stay crisp and juicy without losing their vitamins. A dish cooked in this way will glisten with colourful, nutritious ingredients all mixed together in a tasty sauce. This quick, but heat-intensive cooking method is a challenge to the cook, his skill, judgement and speed of reaction and requires movements akin to those of the Chan Buddhists. Preparation may well be lengthy and thorough, but the success of the dish depends on just a few moments which require large quantities of intuition and concentration. If something goes wrong, it cannot be corrected. To create a successful menu a Chinese chef needs meat and vegetables cut evenly. The ingredients are then all sautéed separately, first the firmer ingredients, then the softer ones and finally the various vegetables.

Co-ordinating the flavours

The Chinese recognise one taboo in their kitchens. Vegetables, fish and meat should never be eaten raw, but must be cooked thoroughly – this custom has its origins in the rules of hygiene laid down by Chinese pharmacists. There are few prejudices when cooks seek to match various tastes with each other and to create new flavour combinations.

Making noodles

The aim is not so much to bring out the natural flavour of any one ingredient, rather to combine it with others to make something new. The Chinese are particularly proud if their guest does not know precisely what he has just eaten, especially as the foods most valued by the local people can be rather tasteless and need to be seasoned with other ingredients. Birds' nest soup, shark's fin and sea cucumber come into this category. Chinese cooks can sometimes be rather daring with distinctively flavoured ingredients, creating colourful blends. They stuff fish with meat and noodles, eel with chrysanthemum leaves and lobster with bamboo shoots. Chicken flesh is cut into fish shapes and served with prawns. The webbed feet of the duck can also be transformed into little fish and garnished with pepper pods. The enormous range of ingredients that are available to the cook contrasts with the clearly defined cooking methods.

China in Quotations

Peter Mundy (16th century)	This Countrie may bee said to excell in these particulers: Antiquity, largeness, Ritchnesse, healthynesse, Plentifullnesse. For Arts and manner off governmentt I thinck noe Kingdome in the world Comparable to it, Considerd alltogether. *Travels in Europe and Asia,* 1637
Napoleon (1769–1821)	China? There lies a sleeping giant. Let him sleep! For when he wakes he will move the world. Attributed to Napoleon
R. W. Emerson (1803–82)	Why does the same dull current of ignoble blood creep through a thousand generations in China without any provision for its own purification, without the mixture of one drop from the fountains of wisdom & glory? . . . they worship crockery gods . . . the summit of their philosophy and science is how to make tea. *Notebooks,* 1824

The Chinese

Anthony the Armenian (12th century)	The inhabitants of those parts are exceeding wise and subtill, replenished with all kinds of skill and cunning, insomuch that they disdaine the endeavours of all other Nations, in all kind of Arts and Sciences: saying that they only see with two Eyes, the Latines with but one eye, and that all other Nations are blind. And albeit they are exceeding sharpe-sighted in the exercise of all bodily workes and labours; yet there is not amongst them any knowledge of spirituall things; the men of that Countrey are not bold, or couragious, but more fearfull of death then befitteth such as bearre Armes; yet are they very ingenious, and have oftener had victories of their enemies by Sea, then by Land. In *Purchas his Pilgrimes,* 1625
Father Ricii (*c.* 1579)	The Chinois are white (but neerer the South more browne) with thinne beards (some having none) with staring haires, and late growing; their haire wholly blacke; eyes narrow, of Egge forme, blacke and standing out: the nose very little, and scarcely standing forth; eares meane: in some Provinces they are square faced. many of Canton and Quamsi provinces on their little toes have two nailes, as they have generally in Cachin-china. Their women are all low, and account great beauty in little feet, for which cause from their infancy they bind them straight with clothes, that one would judge them stump-footed: this, as is thought, devised to make them housewives. In *Purchas his Pilgrimes,* 1625

The Great Wall

Joseph Addison (1672–1719)	An Account of it would have been throught Fabulous, were not the Wall itself still extant. *The Spectaator No. 415,* June 26th 1712
James Boswell (1740–1795)	I said I really believed I should go and see the wall of China had I not children, of whom it was my duty to take care. "Sir, (said he.) by doing so you would do what would be of importance in raising your children to eminence. There would be a lustre reflected on them from your spirit and curiosity. They would be at all times regarded as the children of a man who had gone to view the wall of China. I am serious, Sir." *Life of Johnson, (April 10th 1778),* 1791

Peking (Beijing)

To the South it is compassed with two walls high and strong, so broad that twelve Horses may easily runne abreast on the breadth without hindering one the other. They are made of Brickes, save that on the foot it stands on huge stones, the middle of the wall is filled with Earth: the height farre exceeds those in Europe. To the North is but one wall. On those walls by night is kept as vigilant watch as if it were time of warre . . .

Father Ricci
(c. 1595)

The Kings Palace riseth within the inner Southerne wall, neere the City gates and extends to the Northerne wall, seeming to take up the whole Citie: the rest of the Citie running forth on both sides: It is some-what narrower than the Palace of Nanquin, but more goodly and glorious; that seeming by the Kings absence, as a carkasse without soule. Few of the Streets are paved with Bricke or Stone, so that in Winter dirt, and dust in Summer, are very offensive: and because it raineth there seldome, the ground is all crumbled into dust, and if any wind blow it enters every Roome. To prevent which they have brought in a custom, that no man of whatever ranke goeth on foot or rideth without a Veile or Bonnet hanging to his brest, of that subtiltie that he may see, and yet the dust not annoy him: which also hath another commoditie that he may go any whither unseen, so freed from innumerable tedious salutations, and also he spares attendance and cost. In *Purchas his Pilgrimes,* 1625

Hong Kong

What is the secret of this sudden and enormous growth in population and trading importance, of a barren rock? This must be among the first questions of a stranger. Hong Kong itself, he sees at a glance, produces nothing but granite boulders and the thinnest scrub, – beneath the hottest of suns, and least healthy of climates. The city of Victoria, with its Cathedral and Episcopal palace, its Government House, and Supreme Court, with all its Merchants' palatial houses, is perhaps the very last spot, on all the coast of China, where a sensible man would have thought of placing house or home, if the choice had been left to himself. Victoria Peak rises 1200 feet above the level of the sea, and stretches its solid bulk across the whole line of the city, effectually shutting out the south-west breeze.– and all the cool air to be had during six months of a most oppressive summer when everyone gasps for want of that needful aliment. From this arid rock many go home sick every year, with spleens much larger than their fortunes; and not a few remain, to have their bones laid in six feet of Chinese earth, in the ''Happy Valley'', where an English cemetery has been located. *The Capital of the Tycoon,* 1863

Sir Rutherford
Alcock
(1809–95)

A borrowed place living on borrowed time
Quoted in ''The Times'', March 5th, 1981

Anon

Suggested Routes

Foreword

The following routes are suggested to give the visitor to China a comprehensive overview of the country, which includes all the main sights. The routes given here should not be taken as a fixed, unalterable programme and there are cross references within the book, mainly to connections between the most important towns, for those who wish to choose their itinerary to suit their own interests and to fit in with the time available. Although this section is intended for independent travellers, much of the information will be of interest to travellers on organised tours.

Beijing is taken as the starting point for this tour of the "Middle Kingdom" but for travellers setting out from Hong Kong, the routes can also begin in Canton.

Rail and plane are the best ways to get around, even though the railway network in China is not well developed. Hiring a car can be fraught with problems, although it is possible to hire vehicles in the bigger cities but only with a driver and then for limited distances.

Trains travel slowly and every journey takes a long time, but it is important to recognise that huge distances have to be covered to take in the whole country. When planning routes, journey times must be carefully calculated, but long train rides need never be thought of as monotonous – quite the opposite. There is no better way to get to know the people and the country. The visitor cannot fail to meet open and curious Chinese people keen to make contact. Before long many more of their countrymen will wish to join in the conversation.

The routes are chosen in such a way that the main tourist sights are included. Consult the main A–Z section of this book where each destination is described in detail but supplemented with countless other ideas for worthwhile visits in the immediate vicinity. The suggested routes can be traced on the enclosed map.

Classic
itineraries

Four classic itineraries are recommended here. Allow three to four weeks to cover the major sights of China.

a. Beijing – Xi'an – Shanghai – Nanjing – Hangzhou – Guilin – Canton – Hong Kong
b. Beijing – Ürümqi – Dunhuang – Lanzhou – Xi'an – Shanghai – Canton – Hong Kong
c. Beijing – Xi'an – Chengdu – Lhasa – Canton – Hong Kong
d. Beijing – Xi'an – Chengdu – Chongqing (cruise on the Changjiang) – Nanjing – Shanghai – Canton – Hong Kong

Tips

In the following descriptions, places and landscapes with their own entries in the A–Z section are shown in **bold**.

To enable users of the guide to find quickly the information they are seeking, most of the towns, villages, landscapes, mountains and rivers mentioned here, as well as many other individual tourist sights, are listed in the index at the end of the book.

1. From Beijing to Hohhot via Taiyuan and Datong

It is a 568km/325 mile overnight train journey from **Beijing** to **Taiyuan** the capital of the Shanxi province and home of the Chongshan Si Temple with its valuable collection of sutras. To visit the magnificent

Nanjing (Nanking) ▶

town of **Datong** another eight-hour journey (355km/223 miles) is necessary. No one should miss the Nine Dragon Screen and the world famous Yun Gang Shiku Caves which date back as far as the Northern Wei Dynasty (A.D. 460). They contain over 51,000 magnificent bas-reliefs and statues.

The capital of Inner Mongolia **Hohhot** is a five hour train journey (285km/176 miles) from Datong. The Five Pagoda Temple is certainly worth a visit as is the tomb of the princess Wang Zhaojun. The old town is also of interest.

Excursions into the grass steppelands can be made from Hohhot. The shortest trip (87km/53 miles) takes two hours by bus to a tourist village where visitors can spend the night in one of the 30 jurts (Mongolian tents).

2. From Beijing to Qufu via Tianjin, Jinan and Tai'an (Taishan)

Tianjin the city with northern China's biggest port is a good hour from Beijing. 357km/221 miles further on and seven hours by train on the same railway line lies **Jinan** the capital of Shandong province. It is situated close to the Huanghe and is famous for its many springs.

Tai'an is just over an hour by express train from Jinan. After a brief visit to the Dai Miao Temple a climb to the top of the Taishan, China's most famous holy mountain, is well worth the effort. If the four to seven hour ascent seems too demanding, then a bus service links Tai'an town centre with Zhongtianmen, where a cable car runs almost to the top. Adventurous visitors can stay the night on the summit of the Taishan and with luck enjoy a truly magnificent sunrise.

A few more hours by train from Tai'an lies Yanzhou and **Qufu**, Confucius's birth-place is a 20km/13 mile bus ride from there. A visit to the principal Temple of Confucius, the Kong Miao, is essential. Nearby lies the home of Confucius's descendants. Now converted into a hotel, the building retains all the typical features of a Chinese house including a series of pretty courtyards surrounded by single-storey buildings.

3. From Beijing to Xi'an via Anyang, Zhengzhou, Songshan, Kaifeng and Luoyang

To follow the course of the Huanghe is a journey to the roots of Chinese culture. A journey upstream is recommended, starting ideally from

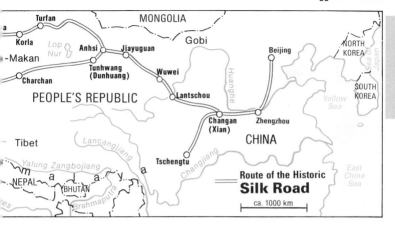

Route of the Historic
Silk Road

ca. 1000 km

Anyang, the cradle of this vast civilisation, where many important monuments and precious archaeological finds from the Shang Dynasty await the visitor. Anyang is situated some 600km/372 miles from Beijing on the line to Canton.

Zhengzhou is a further 200km/125 miles on the Canton line. Those with plenty of time to spare could make an excursion to ancient **Kaifeng** or to the top of Songshan to view the famous Shaolin Monastery. Kaifeng, a former capital, lies some way off the traditional tourist routes and parts of the city retain their original character. Of particular interest is the old Jewish quarter which housed the biggest Jewish community in China. Between Beitu Jie and Nanjioajing there remain a number of relics which testify to their presence here. In addition the Iron Pagoda and the Xiangguo Si Monastery are worth a visit. 100km/ 60 miles separate Zhengzhou from **Luoyang**, best known for the Long-men Shiku caves and one of China's most important historic sites.

Xi'an is a seven-hour train journey (400km/250 miles) from Luoyang. Such are the attractions of this beautiful city that a three-day stay is recommended. All the magnificent sights – and that does not just mean the amazing Terracotta Army – can then be admired at a rela-tively relaxed pace.

There are flights from Xi'an into most major Chinese cities (Beijing 1165km/722 miles; Shanghai 1500km/930 miles; Canton 2200km/1365 miles; Chengdu 850km/527 miles; Kunming 900km/558 miles), but for the Silk Road it is necessary to take the train to Lanzhou (676km/419 miles).

Another option is to take a two-day bus journey (return trip) to **Yan'an**.

The sandy landscape of rough, furrowed rock is typical of north-western China. The caves of Yan'an hollowed out of the rock now house a museum, but in the 30s and 40s the headquarters of China's Communist Party were located there.

4. From Chengdu to Wuhan via Emei (and the Emeishan) and Chongqing (through the Changjiang gorge)

Chengdu can be reached from all major Chinese cities either by train or plane (Beijing 2050km/1270 miles; Shanghai 2350km/1457 miles; Xi'an 842km/522 miles and Kunming 1100km/682 miles). There are a number of reasons for the undoubted charm and attraction of this city – the

113

lively atmosphere of the countless tea-houses, the narrow alleyways hemmed in by traditional low buildings, partly of wood and partly of stone, the colourful, well-stocked markets and not least the many small restaurants where visitors can sample one of China's most celebrated regional cuisines. Take care: the food served here is very spicy!

Take the train to the town of Emei on the Chengdu to Kunming railway line (130km/80 miles). Emei is the starting point for an ascent of Emeishan, the highest of China's holy mountains. At least two days should be allowed for such an expedition and climbers should be fully equipped, particularly for the second part of the climb. All the necessary equipment can be hired there. The Jinding Buddhist Temple stands at the summit and it is possible to stay overnight but be prepared to be woken at sunrise for morning prayers by the sound of gongs and cymbals.

After this visit to the holy mountain try to fit in a quick trip to Leshan, an old town founded about 1300 years ago. A short boat trip to the biggest Buddha sculpture in the world starts here.

An overland bus service operates from here to Neijiang (150km/93 miles), which is linked by rail with **Chongqing** (220km/136 miles). This important industrial centre stands on a hill at the confluence of the Changjiang and the Jianlingjiang. The city is noted for its wet climate and for most of the year it is covered by a thick mist.

Chongqing is a starting point for cruises on the **Changjiang** and every morning at 7am a boat sets off on a three-day journey downstream to **Wuhan**.

The cruise, which passes through a changing landscape (the Three Gorges, the Gezhou dam and Shashi), is a marvellous experience. The boat moors in Wuhan in the early afternoon of the third day so there is sufficient time for a stroll through the two interesting quarters of Hankou and Wuchang. Wuhan lies on the railway line approximately halfway between Beijing and Canton – eighteen hours to Beijing and seventeen hours to Canton. Regular flights link Wuhan airport with China's major cities.

Some of the cruise ships from Chongqing proceed to Nanjing (two days) or Shanghai (two and a half days).

5. From Nanjing to Shanghai via the Grand Canal, Wuxi, Suzhou and Hangzhou

Nanjing can be reached by plane, by boat from Shanghai or Wuhan or by rail on the Beijing–Shanghai– Fuzhou line. It is situated 1157km/ 717 miles from Beijing and 1466km/908 miles from Fuzhou. With its beautiful parks and wide boulevards, Nanjing is one of China's most beautiful cities.

After about 200km/125 miles along the Nanjing–Shanghai route the railway line from Nanjing to Suzhou follows the course of the Grand/ Imperial Canal, for many centuries a vital transport link and still used by freight barges.

Follow in the tracks of Marco Polo and visit **Yangzhou**, **Zhenjiang** and **Wuxi**, all towns on the banks of the Grand Canal. The Italian traveller was fascinated by this part of China.

In **Suzhou** countless bridges have been built to cross the canal linking the various districts of the town. It is consequently referred to sometimes as the "Venice of the Orient". This city, which was founded in antiquity, is certainly one of the most beautiful in China. For centuries the gardens have been reproduced in the grounds of many Chinese luxury residences.

It is possible to reach **Jiaxing** along the Grand Canal and a boat leaves Suzhou early every morning arriving in Jiaxing around midday. Trains run from here to **Hangzhou**, another of China's beautiful cities.

Hangzhou stretches along the banks of the West Lake, which has inspired many generations of artists. The pleasant peaceful atmosphere which prevails in and around the town has helped to create a relaxing holiday resort and it is the ideal place to take a few days off from travelling.

Hangzhou is about three hours by train from **Shanghai**. The charm of this famous city will become apparent after a stroll along the Bund, the impressive street which runs along the west bank of the Huangpu River and also through the city centre (Nanjing Lu, Huaihai Lu and Sichuan Lu).

With goods of an unrivalled range and quality on sale, many tastefully decorated shop windows and the exceptionally welcoming sales staff, the shops in these districts rank without doubt as the best in China.

The first impression of Shanghai is often misleading. The mass of humanity that throngs the city can seem threatening and oppressive, but once the visitor has become immersed in Shanghai life, it is clear that these millions of restless people are simply one essential element of the city of a thousand faces. A stroll in the inner city, where one should step inside one of the local confectioners and try one of the many cakes still made according to traditional recipes, should be followed without fail by a walk through the narrow alleyways of the old town.

Certainly the best place to spend the night and to capture something of Shanghai's atmosphere at the beginning of the 20th c. is Heping Fandian (Peace Hotel).

6. From Beijing to Qingdao via Shenyang (Mukden), Changchun, Harbin, Dalian (Port Arthur) and Yantai

Shenyang (Mukden) is situated north-east of Beijing and the 840km/520 mile journey takes about eleven hours by express train. Shenyang was the Manchu capital before the conquest of China (1640) and is not only an important industrial centre but also has much to offer the tourist including the Imperial Palace.

Continuing in a north-easterly direction into the Chinese steppe about 300km/185 miles beyond Shenyang lies the city of **Changchun**, capital of Jilin province. Changchun in Chinese means "Eternal Spring" but ironically winters in this part of northern China can be long and hard. During the Japanese occupation, it was the seat of Manzhouguo's government (1933–45). Today Changchun is a modern town and is home to one of China's biggest engineering factories.

Travellers who wish to continue further north will leave Jilin province and continue another 240km/150 miles to **Harbin**, the capital of China's northernmost province Heilongjiang, named after the river of the same name (Amur). Harbin is also a modern city with an important river port and many fine parks including Sun Island and Zhaolin Gongyuan Park where every year between January and February the famous Ice Lantern Show takes place when huge blocks of sculptured ice are displayed.

Beyond Harbin lies the far north of China, a steppe landscape extending 400km/250 miles to the border with Russia.

Returning by the same route south from Harbin, **Dalian** lies about six hours by train (397km/246 miles) due south of Shenyang. Built by the Russians in the 19th c. Dalian is a busy sea port situated on the northern cape of the Gulf of Bohai.

A boat crosses the Gulf of Bohai to **Yantai**, a small port on the north coast of the Shandong peninsula and renowned for its fine wine.

This route ends at **Qingdao** one of China's biggest tourist attractions and famed for its beaches, pleasant climate, picturesque setting and not least its brewery. A night train from Qingdao to Beijing will take about fifteen hours (400km/250 miles). There are two flights per week.

7. From Canton to Kunming via Guilin and beyond into the Autonomous Region of Xishuangbanna

This is the traditional route for visitors to southern China.

Direct flights connect **Canton** with a number of Chinese cities but boats and train links are also good. Hong Kong is situated only 183km/110 miles away and for many visitors to China, Canton is the gateway. Lying on the Zhujiang River it is famous for its cuisine, reputedly the best in China, for the cheerfulness of its people and for its parks and gardens. Important sights which should not be missed are the Conghua Wenquan springs and Baiyunshan.

By far the best way to get to **Guilin** is by plane and the flight lasts about two hours. Situated on the west bank of the Lijiang River, Guilin offers visitors the best scenery in China as it is surrounded by luxuriant vegetation and mountain landscape, eroded by water. Hills, caves and parks can be found throughout the town and in the surrounding area, but for the most spectacular sight a river cruise along the Lijiang is essential. Lasting between five and six hours the boat trip ends in Yangshuo. Solitary limestone mountains rise out of the green plain with their peaks sometimes hidden in mist.

A scheduled air service from Guilin serves **Kunming**, capital of Yunnan province. Although Kunming is located in a tropical climate it stands at an altitude of 1900m/6232ft and thus enjoys very pleasant weather, a picturesque environment and a broad ethnic mix. Yunnan province is home for 22 of China's different minorities. 126km/78 miles south-east of Kunming one of the most curious natural phenomena in China can be found. The Stone Forest is a typical karst formation where limestone has eroded limestone to create a fantastic landscape of rocks, columns, towers and many other shapes.

Those independent travellers who feel impelled to see more of South-east Asia can fly from Kunming to the Autonomous Region of Xishuangbanna, which borders Myanmar (Burma), Laos and Vietnam. The variety of ethnic groups, the delightful vegetation and rich fauna including tigers and elephants make Xishuangbanna a popular destination.

The beautiful dreamlike beaches and clear seas found mainly in the south of the tropical island of **Hainan** are only an hour's flight from Canton.

8. Tibet

The land route to Tibet is still a difficult undertaking. The only option is to take an overland bus from Katmandu which involves an exhausting journey lasting several days over one of the few Chinese-Nepalese border passes, which reaches first Xigaze and then Lhasa. It is therefore worth taking the plane either from Chengdu which offers frequent two-hour flights or else from Beijing, a good 4½ hour journey. The only airport is at Gonggar near Lhasa. It is some distance from the capital and the transfer bus takes a long time to reach the city centre.

Lhasa the capital of Tibet stands at an altitude of 3650m/11,972ft and is therefore unsuitable for travellers suffering from heart problems or breathing difficulties. **Xigaze** Tibet's second city is about 300km/185 miles from Lhasa and the journey takes a good six hours.

About halfway between the two towns lies the small settlement of Gyantse where the Kumbum, the biggest Nepalese-style stupa in Tibet, is worth a brief visit. This region with its mountains and lakes must surely rank as one of the most beautiful in the world. Excursions can be arranged.

Silk Road

The old overland caravan route that the merchants used to transport their goods between East and West Asia is known as the Silk Road (Sochou Zhilu). The discovery of the silkworm and the methods used to process the thread into silk probably date back thousands of years to well before recorded time and it was via the Silk Road that the prized fabric found its way to the West.

It is certain that this route existed over two millennia ago, perhaps even centuries before that. It started originally in the central Chinese town of Chang'an (Xi'an) – with connections to Beijing and Chengdu – and led westwards via Lanzhou, Anshi (Anxi) and Tunhwang (Dun-huang) dividing into a northern and southern route via the oases at the foot of the mountains to skirt the Tarim Basin and Takla-Makan Desert. The two routes met again in Kashgar and then followed a variety of paths through or around the Pamirs and on to Antioch (Antakya). Another route took a southerly course crossing the Karakorams towards India. It is thought that such a journey from Europe to China and back would have taken between six to eight years. The Silk Road which helped to create such Central Asian city-states as Turpan, Kho-tan and Yarkand was used mainly for transporting raw silk to the West but in return many plants and fruits found their way to the Middle Kingdom. Clover, peaches, almonds, spices and scented oils all began to appear but also glass, jewels and other luxury goods, not to mention Buddhism, Manichaeism, Nestorianism and Islam.

During the first thousand years after the birth of Christ, the Silk Road suffered badly from the violent disputes between the peoples of Cen-tral Asia, but during the years of Mongolian rule (13/14th c.), it reco-vered its importance as trade flourished. Marco Polo retraced sections of the Silk Road on his journey from Venice to China (1271–95), but shortly after, merchants began to prefer the sea routes between the Far East and the Old World. These routes proved both quicker and safer than the extremely long overland distances of the Silk Road.

History

Along the Silk Road from Lanzhou to Kashgar via Dunhuang, Turpan and Ürümqi

Following the old Silk Road involves taking exactly the same route – perhaps with a lighter load but still not without considerable effort – that travellers used over two thousand years ago as they established the first of what were to become important economic and cultural links between the Occident and the Orient.

Lanzhou is situated 676km/420 miles north-west of Xi'an (fifteen hours by train) between the Huanghe and a high, steep wall of rock. Beyond Lanzhou the railway follows the old caravan route through Gansu, a narrow strip of fertile land which separates the highlands of Qinghai from the Gobi Desert, and then crosses the Jiayuguan Pass. The remains of the last section of the Great Wall can be seen from the railway line. At Liuyuan, 24 hours (1800km/1120 miles) from Xi'an, a bus crosses the desert to **Dunhuang**, a journey of about 150km/90 miles. About 20km/12 miles south of the town lies the Mogao Caves, which are accessible by bus from the town centre or in jeeps which may be hired from the hotels. Dunhuang was once an important town on the Silk Road and between the 5th and 14th c. monks, painters, sculptors and other artists created a wealth of wall paintings and sculptures in the hundreds of caves. The expressive power of the outstanding work on display here was rarely surpassed in the periods that followed.

Returning to Liuyuan, the railway line continues westwards across the desert for a further twelve hours to **Turpan**, an extraordinarily beautiful and impressive oasis. Its climate and vegetation have much in common with Central Asia and visitors should take great care as Turpan is the hottest town in China and the sun's rays can sometimes be dangerously powerful.

Travellers who wish to continue into Xinjiang should take the bus to **Ürümqi** (6 hours). Although the city has little to offer in the way of tourist sights, excursions can be made into the surrounding region or else a four-day bus journey undertaken to **Kashgar**, the biggest and most distinctive of the Uigurian oases which are scattered throughout this desert region. For the monks, traders and pilgrims who plied the Silk Road Kashgar was the last town before the climb over the Pamirs.

Hall of Prayer for Good Harvests in Beijing ▶

China From A to Z

Amoy

See Xiamen

Anhui

Chinese
equivalent

安徽省

Province
Area: 139,000sq.km/53,670sq. miles
Population: 57,610,000. Capital: Hefei

Situation

The province of Anhui in eastern China lies between 114°43′ and 119°38′E
and 29°25′ and 34°39′N.

Topography

Two large rivers, the Huaihe and the Changjiang (Yangtse), flow through
Anhui from west to east. The province can be divided into three different
zones – the plain to the north of the Huaihe, the hilly region between the
Huaihe and the Changjiang, and the mountainous country south of the
Changjiang.

Climate

Summers in the province are hot and humid and the winters generally cool
but colder and drier in the north. Rainfall amounts are less in the north than
in the south.

China

Anhui Province

HEILONGJIANG

JILIN

INNER MONGOLIA
(NEIMENGGU)

LIAONING

XINJIANG

© Baedeker

GANSU

INNER MONGOLIA
(NEIMENGGU)

BEIJING
(PEKING)●

●TIANJIN

HEBEI

NINGXIA

SHANXI

SHANDONG

QINGHAI

GANSU

HENAN

SHAANXI

JIANGSU

XIZANG (TIBET)

ANHUI

SHANGHAI

HUBEI

ZHEJIANG

SICHUAN

JIANGXI

HUNAN

GUIZHOU

FUJIAN

YUNNAN

TAIWAN

GUANGXI

GUANGDONG

XIANG GANG
(HONGKONG)

AO MEN
(MACAO)

HAINAN

**The People's
Republic of China**
Zhonghua Renmin Gongheguo

Commencing with the Qin dynasty (221–206 B.C.), Anhui was the first region of southern China to be settled by the ethnic group known as the Hans. It suffered considerable hardship and distress when the Huanghe river changed its course in the mid-18th c. The province was occupied by the Japanese during the Second World War.

History

After 1949 the province's economy developed through the mining of coal and iron and copper ore, and it became a centre of heavy industry.
There are some 4·4 million ha/11 million acres of agricultural land, more than a half of which is irrigated; the main crops are rice, grain, soya beans, sweet potatoes, cotton and tea.

Economy

The provincial capital of Hefei, Ma'anshan and Wuhu (see entries), together with the famous Huangshan Mountains (see Wuhu), are all of interest.

Places to visit

Anshan

L 3

Chinese equivalent

Province: Liaoning. Area: 70sq.km/27sq. miles
Population: 1,210,000 (conurbation 2,510,000)

Anshan lies at 122°59′E and 41°08′N, in the centre of the north-eastern province of Liaoning, 90km/56 miles south of Shenyang and 300km/186 miles north of Dalian. It is linked to these two towns by rail and motorway.
Anshan, the "steel capital of China", still depends heavily on its iron and steel works, which form one of the largest centres of production anywhere in China. Other branches of industry include chemicals, textiles and electronics, as well as agricultural machinery and ceramics. Attempts have been made to improve the appearance of this typical industrial town by the growing of trees and flowers and by general landscaping.

Situation and Communications

Anshan can trace its history back to the 2nd century B.C. It is believed that the region's first local "iron industry" was formed here during the reign of Emperor Han Wudi (140–87 B.C.). Iron smelting flourished during the Tang period (A.D. 618–907). A postal station was set up nearby in 1395. After Anshan had been burned down during the Boxer Rebellion in 1900 and then suffered further serious damage during the Russo-Japanese War (1904–05), the new town was built 10km/6 miles to the north of the old. It developed economically following the discovery of fresh iron-ore deposits in the early 20th c. During the Civil War Anshan was occupied alternately by the Guomindang (Kuomintang) and the Communists, until the latter finally took control in 1948.

History

Surroundings

This famous mountain massif, 20km/12½ miles east of the town, is also known as Qianlianshan (Mountain of a Thousand Lotus Blossoms), because its peaks are shaped like lotus flowers. It comprises 999 hills, the highest of which, Xianren Tai (Terrace of the Immortals), is 708m/2324ft.

Thousand Hills
(Qianshan)

Above the mountain valleys are scattered dozens of Buddhist and Taoist temples, some of which are over 1300 years old, although most date from the Ming period (1368–1644). Some of the most beautiful examples from the Tang period (618–907) include the Temple of Great Peace (Da'an Si) and the Great Assembly Hall (Zhonghui Si), both of which lie near Xianren Tai (see above).
The monastery of Wuliang Guan in the north-eastern mountain region was founded by a Taoist monk in the second half of the 17th c.

Temples and monasteries

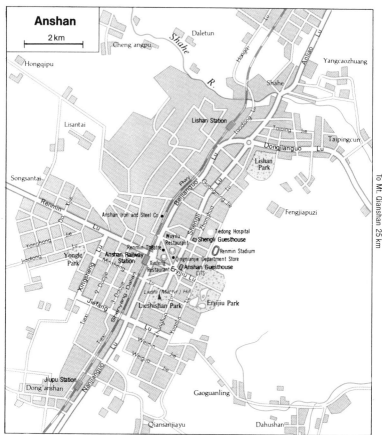

Anshan

2 km

Daletun

Cheng angpu

Shahe R.

Hongqipu

Lisantai

Lishan Station

Songsantai

Rennin Lu

Anshan Iron and Steel Co.

Wuyilu Restaurant

Renmin Theatre

Yongle Park

Anshan Railway Station

Xinfeng Restaurant

Yengle Park

Jiefang Lu

Jiupu Station

Dong'anshan

Qiansanjiayu

To Tanggangzi Hot Spring 15 km

Shahe

Yangcaozhuang

Taiping Jie

Taipingcun

Dongjianguo Lu

Lishan Park

Fengjiapuzi

To Mt. Qianshan 25 km

Tiedong Hospital

Shengli Guesthouse

Qianjianjie Department Store

Renmin Stadium

Anshan Guesthouse

CYTS

Lieshi (Martyr) Hill

Lieshishan Park

Eryijiu Park

Weimin Jie

Weiguo Jie

Gaoguanling

Dahushan

The Temple of the Spring of Dragons (Longquan Si), named after the spring which bubbles forth here, was – according to tradition – built in 1558, although some rooms appear older.

3km/2 miles west of this temple stands the highest monastery in the Qianshan Mountains, the Temple of Universal Peace (Pu'an Guan). From here the visitor can climb the peak of Wufo Ding (Peak of the Five Buddhas), from where there is a superb view.

Tanggangzi thermal baths (Tanggangzi Wenquan)

These popular baths, lying 10km/6 miles south of Anshan and accessible by train from there, date from the time of the Yin Emperor Taizong, who visited them in 1130. There is a park with eighteen springs in all, with water containing a number of minerals (including radium, potassium, calcium and phosphorus); the temperatures range from 55 to 70°C/130 to 158°F. The waters are used mainly for the treatment of rheumatism.

In the park will be found the villa in which Pu Yin resided in the 1930s; it is now a sanatorium for workers.

Baotou

包头市

Chinese
equivalent

Autonomous region of Inner Mongolia
Altitude: 1000m/3282ft
Area: 2152sq.km/831sq. miles. Population: 1,500,000

Baotou lies in the centre of Inner Mongolia at 109°49'E and 40°42'N, some 140km/87 miles west of Hohhot, the regional capital, on the north bank of the Huanghe river.
  Baotou is one and a half hours by air from Beijing and three and half hours by rail from Hohhot. It is an important rail station on the Beijing–Lanzhou line, which also passes through Hohhot.

Situation and
Communications

As a result of the growth of many branches of industry, including iron-smelting in particular, Baotou has become the economic centre of Inner Mongolia. Together with Anshan, Wushan, Shanghai and Beijing it is one of China's major producers of steel.

Importance

People lived in this region back in the Tang dynasty (618–907), but only in recent centuries did it develop into a trading centre. This development was accelerated by the construction of the rail link with Beijing in 1923, when it became the major trading hub of Mongolia and western China. Transport facilities were improved still further by the construction of the rail route to Lanzhou in the 1950s. Since then Baotou has become a centre of the steel industry, which utilises the rich iron-ore deposits found in Bayo Obo.

History

The famous Mongolian Nadamu Autumn Festival, which was celebrated originally to honour the gods of the hills and mountain paths, has become a popular festival with riding, wrestling and archery competitions as well as musical and theatrical performances.

Nadamu Festival

This temple, built in the Qing period (1644–1911) in a style reminiscent of that of Tibet, consists of flat-roofed buildings of two storeys. The complex also includes the White Pagoda (Bai Ta), surmounted by a stupa. The Awang Fu, a large "gateway of honour", is also worthy of note.

Sights

Kundulun Si

Surroundings

The "Willow Tree Monastery", a lamasery situated 70km/44 miles north-east of Baotou, is one of the best-preserved of any in Inner Mongolia. Built under the Kangxi Emperor Xuanye (reigned 1661–1722), it was restored in 1749. At one time more than 1000 monks lived here. The complex of 2500 rooms covers an area of 20ha/50 acres and embraces some twelve temple buildings containing statues of Shakyamuni and other Buddhist saints.

★Willow Tree
Monastery
(Wudang Zhao)

Covering an area of 5·5ha/13¾ acres this mausoleum, said to contain the remains of Genghis Khan, lies in beautiful surroundings 120km/75 miles south of Baotou and 15km/9 miles south-east of the town of Atengxilian. It was moved here in 1954 from Kumbum Monastery (Ta Er Si) near Xining. The mausoleum consists of three magnificent halls with roofs of gilt-glazed tiles. The great ruler and his three wives lie at rest in the main hall, where a statue of him also stands. The two side-halls contain Mongol costumes and weapons. In the south-eastern part of the complex stands the Palace of the Great Khan. The nearby museum village portrays the life led by the Mongols in the time of Genghis Khan.

Tomb of
Genghis Khan

Beijing · Peking   K 3–4

Chinese
equivalent

北京市

Capital of the People's Republic of China
Autonomous City
Altitude: 52m/170ft. Area: 16,807sq.km/6487sq. miles
Population: 7,450,000 (conurbation 10,940,000)

Situation and
Communications

Beijing lies at 116°20′E and 39°56′N, in the north-west of the North China Plain, not far from the western slopes of the mountains of Yanshan, and about 150km/93 miles from the Bo-Hai Sea.

A dense network of roads, railways and airways connects Beijing with China's other major cities.

Beijing, an autonomous city with the status of a province, is not only the political centre of the country, it also plays an outstanding part in the nation's cultural, economic, scientific and academic life. Many trading and industrial firms are situated here. The most important educational and cultural institution include: nine colleges for the various sciences, the Academica Sinica, several universities (including the University of Peking founded in 1898; the University of Qinghua founded in 1911, and the People's University founded in 1950), technological universities, numerous colleges and institutes (in particular the Central Institute for Nationalities and the Institute for Foreign Languages), and research establishments, as well as museums and libraries (including the Beijing University library with its ten million volumes and 22,000 periodicals), also the planetarium and the zoological and botanical gardens.

About 97% of Beijing's population belong to the Han race, but also included are Hui, Manchurians, Mongolians; other ethnic minorities also live here.

History

China's origins are lost in prehistoric times. The famous "Peking man" lived about 500,000 years ago in caves near Zhoukoudian, on the south-western outskirts of the present day city.

According to the oldest existing document Beijing was founded some 3000 years ago under the name of Ji. It gradually gained importance as a trading centre. At the time of the warring states, (475–221 B.C.) the ruler of the Yan empire choose the town as his capital, hence, at that time the city was also known as Yanjing (capital of the Yan). This name is sometimes still used today.

Under the Qin dynasty (221–206 B.C.) the seat of government was transferred to Xianyang (the present day Xi'an), and Ji became the military base and key traffic junction for the whole Chinese territory. Also under the Han (206 B.C.–A.D. 220), the city remained as a bastion against the northern Nomadic tribes, who ruled here from time to time.

Under Tang rule (618–907) the city was called Youzhou. Between 916 and 1125 under the Liao dynasty, Ji was upgraded to become the second most important city in the Empire, known at this time as Nanjing (southern capital). The Jin declared it their capital in 1153, and named it Zhongdu (middle capital). They employed hundreds of thousands of labourers to build fortifications and palaces. In 1215 the city was destroyed by the Mongols. Their ruler Kublai Khan, founder of the Yuan dynasty (1271–1368), chose the city as his seat of government, had it reconstructed and named it Dadu (great capital). Dadu then became the political centre of the Chinese Empire. Marco Polo, who stayed here at that time, preferred in his description of the "wonders of the city" the Mongolian name Cambaluc (a transliteration of Khanbaliq, which means "City of Khan" in Mongolian).

At the beginning of the Ming dynasty, (1368–1644) Nanking became the capital, and Dadu adopted the name of Beiping ("northern peace"). The Ming Emperor Yongle (1403–24), made Beiping the capital, giving it its present day name Beijing ("northern capital"). The majority of today's existing buildings and the layout of the city (see below) date from this dynasty.

In 1644 Li Zicheng, the leader of a peasant uprising occupied Beijing, but it was soon taken over by the Manchurians. From the middle of the 19th c. Beijing was the scene of conflict between the empire and foreign powers. English and French troops destroyed the old summer palace. The government was forced to grant the colonial powers their extra-territorial rights and allow them to establish permanent embassies. During the so-called Boxer uprising revolutionaries occupied the embassy quarter, but were soon forced to surrender to the foreign troops. Following the collapse of the Qing dynasty in 1911 Beijing became capital of the new republic. When the Treaty of Versailles stipulated that the former German possessions were to be given to Japan there were demonstrations here on May 4th 1919. As Nanking was the capital between 1928 and 1949 the name of the city was changed again; the nationalists decided to resurrect the old name of Beiping. From 1937 to 1945 the city was under Japanese occupation. On the October 1st 1949 Mao Zedong proclaimed the founding of the People's Republic of China and choose the city as capital again under the name of Beijing, which to this day represents the political centre of the republic. In June 1989 the People's Liberation Army violently suppressed a peaceful demonstration which was staged predominantly by students.

The historic city centre which dates from the Ming dynasty (14th–17th c.) has largely preserved its original appearance. Traces of the medieval city which was divided into two parts can still be seen. It joined the four points of the compass and consisted of the north city formerly known as the Tartar city which was laid out on a regular rectangular pattern. This section was defended by a 20km/12 mile long wall with nine gates (two in the east, three in the south, and two in the west and north sides). The south city was surrounded by a 14km/9 mile city wall with seven gates.

The City

The two city walls were completely destroyed, but two of the old gates are preserved – the "Qian Men" behind Mao's Mausoleum and the "Desheng Men" in the north of the forbidden city.

After 1949 a permanent change in the appearance of the city took place. Owing to a redevelopment programme the majority of the city walls and numerous old houses were demolished. Wide streets, various public buildings such as museums, sport centres, airports, etc. emerged in their place and the underground, which runs under the line of the former city wall, was built. Since the late 1970s an endless succession of unimaginative, monotonous skyscrapers have been built as well as tenement blocks to house the ever growing population, hotels, administrative buildings, etc.

From the mid-eighties the government has tried to carry out the redevelopment of the old city more cautiously; this plan also includes restoring cultural and historic relics. It is intended that usage of space will be reduced and that the ecological problems will be solved.

From the point of view of the tourist, Beijing is China's most interesting city. Among the city's historical and cultural monuments are the Imperial Palace, the Beihai Park, the Coal Hill Park and the Heavenly Temple.

On the city's outskirts there are many other sights, including the Summer Palace, the Fragrant Mountain, the Great Wall, and the Ming Tombs.

Industry, which has only developed to any great extent since 1949, consists predominantly of iron and steel production, engineering and the construction of heavy goods vehicles, locomotives and goods wagons, also petro-chemical industry (including an oil refinery with a pipeline from Daqing). Light industry includes electrotechnics and electronics, textiles (especially cotton-processing), printing and food industry. Besides this is a substantial cottage industry producing handmade wares including porcelain, ivory and jade carvings, lacquer ware, cloisonné, copper tableware, carpets, embroidery and lacemaking.

The Economy

To Yihehuan (Summer Palace) 5 km

To Badaling, 85 km, Sh

Beitaipingzhuang

Youyi (Friendship) Guesthouse

Baishiqiao

Xitucheng

Xinjiekouwai

Nanlu

Dajie

Xueyuan

Weigongcun

Xisanhuan

Guolangqiao

Lu

Beijing North Station

Deshengmen Xidajie

Xinjiekou

To Xiangshan Park 14 km

Zizhuyuan Park

Zizhuyuan

Lu

Beijing Zoo

Beijing
Exhibition Centre

Beijing

Shoudu (Capital) Gymnasium

Xizhimennei Dajie

Xizhimenwai Dajie

Dongjie

Beijia

Dajie

Baishiqiao

Beijing Planetarium

Xiyuan Hotel

Guanyuan

Ping an

Chegongzhuang

Xilu

Chegongzhuang Dajie

Ping'anli
Xidajie

Baitasi

Xisi Beidajie

Xihuangchengen

Fuchengmen

Beidajie

Baiwanzhuang

Dajie

Lu Xun Museum

Santihe

Zhanlanguan

Beidajie

White
Dagoba Temple

Guangji
Temple

Guangjimennei Dajie

Beiwaan

Fucheng

Ganjiakou

Lu

Fuchengmenwai Dajie

Fuchengmennei Dajie

Tongheju Restaurant

Nanlishi

Geological
Museum

Diaoyutai Guesthouse

Santihe

Yuetan Beijie

Fuchengmen

Long-Distance telephone Office

Dajie

Minzu (Nationalities')

Xidan

Jie

Yuyuantan Park

Xisanhuan

Cuiwei

Donglu

Yuetan Nanjie

Emei Restaurant

Cultural Palace of
the Nationalities

Dajie

Xidan Beidajie

Xidar
Marke

Military Museum of the Chinese
People's Revolution

Yanjing Hotel

Minzu (Nationalities') Hotel

Tele

Fuxing

Lu

Yangfangdian Lu

Beifengwo

Donglu

Fuxingmenwai Dajie

Fuxingmennei Dajie

X
Sichu

Zhonglu

Muxidi

Baiyun
Taoist Temple

Broadcasting
Building

Xinwenhua

Jie

Xuanwumen

Kaorouwan Restaurant

Lianhuachi

Lu

Lianhuachi Xilu

Donglu

Xibianmen

Xuanwumen Xidajie

Changchun Jie

Xuanwumennei Dajie

Xuar
Hote
Rong

Lianhua (Lotus) Pond

Tianning Temple

Huaibaishu Jie

Guang'anmen

Guang'anmenwai Dajie

Guang'anmennei Dajie

Baiguang

Niu Jie

Xuanwumenwai

Dajie

Luom
Qi

Mailiandao

Lianhua

Lu

Guang'anmen
Station

Binhelu

Niujie Mosque

Fayuan Temple

Caishikou
Qi

Jie

To Lugou Bridge 8 km, Zhoukoudian 43 km

Guang'an

Xisanhuan

Lu

Nanheng

Luomi

Baizhifang

You'anmen

Jie

T

Sanluju

Lu

You'anmen

You'anmen

) 37 km

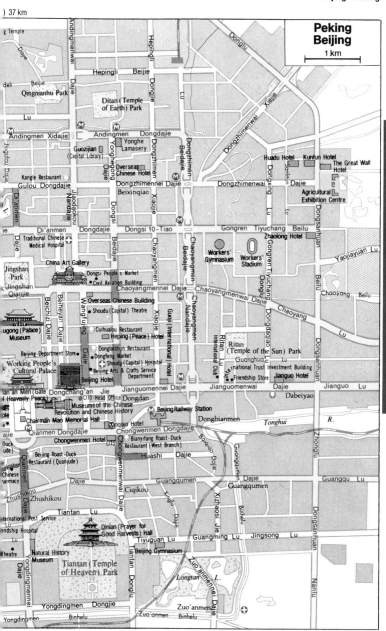

g Temple

Dajie

deli

Qingnianhu Park

Lu

Beijie

Hepingli Beijie

Hepingli

Andingmenwai Dajie

Jiugulou Dajie

Dongzhimenwai

Xieye

Donglu

Dongzhimen Beidajie

Dongzhimennei Dajie

Dongsi Beidajie

Ditan (Temple of Earth) Park

Andingmen Xidajie Andingmen Dongdajie

Guozijian
(Capital Library)

Yonghe
Lamasery

Longfugong Dajie

Kangle Restaurant

Overseas
Chinese Hotel

Dongzhimennei Dajie

Beixinqiao

Huadu Hotel Kunlun Hotel

The Great Wall
Hotel

Agricultural
Exhibition Centre

Dongsanhuan

Gulou Dongdajie

Jiaodaokou Nandajie

Di'anmen

Dongsi

Dongzhimenwai Dajie

Di'anmen Dongdajie Dongsi 10-Tiao

ie Traditional Chinese
Medical Hospital

China Art Gallery

Dongsi People's Market
Civil Aviation Building

Gongren Tiyuchang Beilu
Zhaolong Hotel

Jingshan
Park

Jingshan
Qianjie

Beichizi Dajie

Beiheyan Dajie

Wangfujing Dajie

Chaoyangmen Beidajie

Chaoyangmennei Dajie Chaoyangmenwai Dajie

Workers'
Gymnasium

Workers'
Stadium

Gongren Tiyuchang Beilu

Yaojiayuan Lu

Beilu

Chaoyang Beilu

ugong (Palace)
Museum

Overseas Chinese Building

Shoudu (Capital) Theatre

Cuihualou Restaurant

Heping (Peace) Hotel

Donglaishun Restaurant

Dongfeng Market

Shoudu (Capital) Hospital

Beijing Arts & Crafts Service
Department

Chaoyangmen
Nandajie

Guoji International Hotel

Xiaojie

Chaoyang Lu

Dongsanhuan

Beijing Department Store

Working People's
Cultural Palace

Beijing Hotel

Ritan
(Temple of the Sun) Park

Ritan International Club

Guanghua Lu

International Trust Investment Building

Friendship Store

Jianguo Hotel

k Dajie

an an Men (Gate
f Heavenly Peace)

ple

a

Dongchang'an Jie

Jianguomennei Dajie

Jianguomenwai Dajie

Jianguo Lu

CITS Head Office Dongdan

Museums of the Chinese
Revolution and Chinese History

Chairman Mao Memorial Hall

Dongan

Beijing Railway Station

Dongbianmen

Dabeiyao

Tonghui R.

Zhongl

ajie

Duck
ude)

Qianmen Dongdajie

Xinqiao Hotel

Chongwenmen Dongdajie

Chongwenmen Hotel CITS

Bianyifang Roast-Duck
Restaurant (West Branch)

Huashi Dajie

Haoqiao Dajie

Guangqumen

Guangqumen Dajie
Guangqumen

Guangqu Lu

ngtingchou
Chinese
harmacy

Beijing Roast-Duck
Restaurant (Quanjude)

Dajie

Guangqumen

Ciqikou

Kongu Lu

Dajie

Xizhaosi Jie

Binhelu

Dongsanhuan

Zhushikou Zhushikou

Tiantan Lu

International Post Service
endship Hospital

Dinian (Prayer for
Good Harvests) Hall

Tiyuguan Lu Guangming Lu Jingsong Lu

Theatre Natural History
Museum

Tiantan (Temple
of Heaven) Park

Dajie

Yongdingmenne

Yongdingmen Dongjie

Yongdingmen Binhelu

Tiantan Donglu

Beijing Gymnasium

Zuo'anmen Dajie

Longtan L.

Zuo'anmen Binhelu

Zuo'anmen

Nanlu

Square of Heavenly Peace

In the surrounding regions agricultural production includes vegetable and fruit growing, cotton and peanut farming, and breeding small animals (especially ducks).

As the capital, Beijing is also the main junction for the network of roads and railways, and has the largest international airport in the country. In 1996 the new West Station was opened which, with an area of some 500,000sq.m/ 5¼ million sq.ft, is the largest railway station in Asia. Tong Xian, east of the city, is the northern end of the Emperor Canal. There is an underground train service in the inner city, which serves all the main places of importance.

Beijing has an enormous traffic problem, the roads hardly being able cope with the volume of traffic.

Transport

Key sights in the City Centre

The Square of Heavenly Peace, situated in the city centre, measures about (500×800m/547×875yd). Up to a million people could fit into this square, making it probably the largest square in the world. It forms not only the geographical, but also the historical core of the city. The square was laid out in 1651, but was considerably enlarged in 1958. During the 20th c. important political events have taken place here. On May 4th 1919 students demonstrated against the Chinese provisions of the Versaille treaty. Following the memorial day of April 4th 1976 countless Beijing residents mourned their popular prime minister Zhou Enlai, and a demonstration against the Jiang Qing group ensued, which was forcefully suppressed. In the early summer of 1989 demonstrations for democracy and against press censorship took place here and these were also brutally suppressed. The

★★ Square of Heavenly Peace (Tian'an Men Guanchang)

◀ *The Hall of the Vault of Heaven in the Temple of Heaven*

129

west of the square is bordered by the colossal Great Hall of the People, the east by a further monumental building which houses the Museums of Chinese History and Chinese Revolution. The Chairman Mao Mausoleum lies to the south, and in the centre of the square is the Monument to the People's Republic.

★Gate of
Heavenly Peace
(Tian'An Men)

The Gate of Heavenly Peace (open: 9am–4.30pm), which was completed in 1417 and restored in 1651, once formed the main entrance to the Imperial Palace. The 34m/111ft high wooden building stands on a red brick sub-structure (over 10m/33ft high) which has a white marble base. The two-storey roof is covered with ceramic tiles. In front of the gate stand two stone lions, and two columns topped with the mythical creature Kong. A portrait of Chairman Mao hangs over the portal, to its left is the slogan "Long live the People's Republic of China", and to the right "Long live the unity of the people of the world".

The imperial decrees were once announced here and received by the dignitaries kneeling. Also from here Chairman Mao proclaimed the People's Republic on October 1st 1949.

Golden
Water Bridges
(Jinshui Qiao)

At the foot of the gate the seven Golden Water Bridges of white marble with sculptured sides cross the stream which bears the same name.

Great Hall
of the People
(Renmin
Dahuitang)

The west side of the Square of Heavenly Peace is dominated by the monumental Great Hall of the People (built 1959; open: 8.30am–3pm), which occupies a total area of 171,800sq.m/205,472sq.yd. The 76m/249ft wide, 60m/197ft long main hall can accommodate over ten thousand people. The building also has a large banquet hall with more than 5000 places and 30 rooms, one for each province, autonomous region and city, each laid out in the style of the region. Held here are the conferences of the national People's Congress, and other most important political conferences.

★Museum of
Chinese History
(Zhongguo Lishi
Bowuguan)

The Museum of Chinese History (open: 8.30am–5pm; no admittance after 3.30pm), was built in 1959 and occupies an area of 8000sq.m/9568sq.yd. It is housed in the right wing of the massive column embellished building (officially opened 1961). It forms the boundary for the east side of the square and was closed for many years. The 9000 exhibits illustrate matters concerning the Chinese Marxist historiography of the various stages of development of Chinese development, from prehistoric times through the slave age society (2100–475 B.C.), and the feudal society (475 B.C.–A.D. 1840) to the semi-colonial, quasi-feudaldal society. They include archeological finds and reproductions of discoveries such as that of papers. The museum serves predominantly didactic purposes.

★Museum of the
Chinese
Revolution
(Geming
Bowuguan)

The museum of the Chinese Revolution, also established in 1959, was closed during the cultural revolution and the subsequent years. It is housed in the left wing of the building and extends over two storeys, each with an area of 4000sq.m/43,056sq.ft. The exhibits in this museum illustrate the most important stages of the Chinese revolution from 1919, and the development of the Communist Party of China.

★Monument to
the Heroes
Republic
(Renmin
Yingxiong
Jinianbei)

The Monument to the Heroes Republic is a 38m/124ft high obelisk, the foundations of which were laid on the September 30th 1949. It was officially unveiled on the May 1st 1958. The monument rises from a two-tier platform and consists of 17,000 pieces of granite and marble. The north side is adorned with an inscription by Chairman Mao, which reads: "Eternal praise be to the heroes of the people". On the south side is a dedication by the deceased prime minister Zhou Enlai to martyrs of the revolution who gave their lives in the various wars after 1840.

On the base, the ten bas-reliefs with a total of 170 figures represent (from the east to the north side) the most important events of the Chinese revolution: the opium burning in Humen, the uprising in Jintian, the rebellion in Wuchang, the movement of May 4th 1919, the movement of May

Imperial Palace

30th 1925, the uprising in Nanchang, the guerrilla war against Japan, and the crossing of the Changjiang.

The rectangular Chairman Mao Mausoleum is 33m/108ft high and occupies an area of 20,000sq.m/23,920sq.yd. It is supported by 44 granite columns, dates from 1977, and lies in the south of Tian'An Men square. The inscription "Chairman Mao Mausoleum" above the entrance was calligraphed by Hua Guofeng.

★Chairman Mao Mausoleum (Mao Zhuxi Jiniantang)

In the entrance hall stands a marble statue of Chairman Mao, with a landscape background painting by the artist Huang Yongyu. In the central hall lies the body of Mao in a crystal sarcophagus. On the back wall can be seen an engraved homage to the "great chairman" which reads: "eternal praise be to chairman Mao, our great leader and master".

The Outer Gate was situated at the south end of Tian'An Men square. It was erected in 1421, and burned down in 1780 and again in 1849, and finally destroyed during the Boxer Rebellion. It was one of Beijing's nine city gates and the link between the north and south parts of the city. The structure consisted of two buildings one behind the other, connected by walls from which an inner courtyard came into being.

The Outer Gate (Qianmen)

★★Imperial Palace (Gugong)

The Imperial Palace, also known as the Forbidden City is China's largest and most significant building. Its origins date from the Yuan dynasty (1271–1368). Emperor Yongle of the Ming dynasty had the palace enlarged to its present day size between 1406 and 1420, after he had transferred the capital from Nanking to Beijing. The palace was the residence of 24 Ming and Qing emperors. Ordinary mortals were forbidden to enter the palace.

Open
8.30am–5pm, no admission after 4.30pm

The predominant colour of the building is crimson, which symbolises the polar star. The imperial palace reflects the cosmic order. The complex,

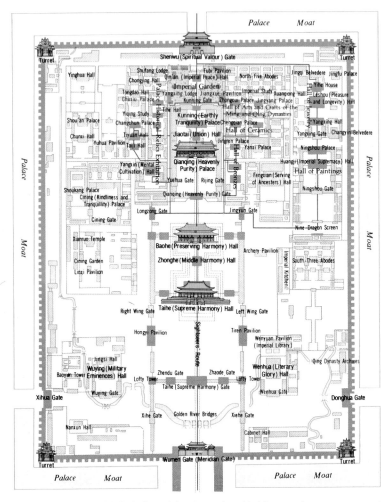

The following labels appear on the plan:

Palace Moat

Turret

Shenwu (Spiritual Valour) Gate

Turret

Yinghua Hall

Shufang Lodge
Chongling Hall
Qin'an (Imperial Peace) Hall
Fubi Pavilion
North-Five Abodes
Jingqi Belvedere   Jingfu Palace

Imperial Garden
Yangxing Lodge Jiangxue Pavilion Imperial Study
Xuangong Hall
Yihe House
Leshou (Pleasure and Longevity) Hall

Tongdao Hall
Chuxiu Palace
Kunning Gate
Zhongcui Palace   Jingyang Palace

Yiqing Study
Changchun Palace
Taihe Hall
Kunning (Earthly Tranquility) Palace
Chengqian Palace
Hall of Arts and Crafts of the Ming and Qing Dynasties
Hall of Ceramics
Yangxing Hall

Shou'an Palace

Chunxi Hall
Tiyuan Hall
Yuhua Pavilion Taiji Hall
Jiaotai (Union) Hall
Jingren Palace
Yanxi Palace
Yangxing Gate Changyin Belvedere

Ningshou Palace

Yangxin (Mental Cultivation) Hall
Qianqing (Heavenly Purity) Palace
Huangji (Imperial Supremacy) Hall
Hall of Paintings

Shoukang Palace
Cining (Kindliness and Tranquillity) Palace
Yuehua Gate   Rijing Gate
Fengxian (Serving of Ancestors) Hall
Ningshou Gate

Cining Gate
Qianqing (Heavenly Purity) Gate

Xianruo Temple
Longzong Gate
Jingyun Gate

Cining Garden
Linxi Pavilion
Nine-Dragon Screen

Baohe (Preserving Harmony) Hall
Archery Pavilion
South-Three Abodes

Zhonghe (Middle Harmony) Hall

Taihe (Supreme Harmony) Hall

Right Wing Gate   Left Wing Gate

Hongyi Pavilion
Tiren Pavilion
Wenyuan Pavilion (Imperial Library)

Jingsi Hall
Wuying (Military Eminences) Hall
Baoyun Tower
Zhendu Gate   Zhaode Gate
Lofty Tower
Wenhua (Literary Glory) Hall
Qing Dynasty Archives

Wuying Gate
Taihe (Supreme Harmony) Gate
Wenhua Gate

Xihua Gate
Xihe Gate   Golden River Bridges   Xiehe Gate
Donghua Gate

Nanxun Hall
Cabinet Hall

Turret
Wumen Gate (Meridian Gate)
Turret

Palace Moat

Palace Exhibition of Historical Relics
Hall of Bronzes
Imperial Kitchen
Sightseers' Route

which is built mainly of wood and brick, extends over an area of
720,000sq.m/861,120sq.yd. The palaces and pavilions together contain
over 9000 rooms, all of which have been very well preserved. The
complex is divided into two areas: an outer area, which was used for ceremonial
purposes, and an inner area, which is of a private nature. The whole place is
surrounded by a 10m/33ft high wall with four corner towers and a
50m/55yd wide moat. The main hall lies in the central north–south axis,
flanked by many other halls to the east and west.

Meridian Gate
(Wumen)

The forbidden city can be entered at four different points: in the south
through the Meridian Gate (Wumen), the main entrance behind the Gate of

Heavenly Peace, in the north through the Gate of Spiritual Valour (Shenwu Men), in the east through the Flowering Gate of the East (Donghua Men), and in the west through the Flowering Gate of the West (Xihua Men).

The Meridian Gate is also known as the Five-Phoenix-Gate, after its five pavilions. It was built in 1420 and has been restored several times. Every year the emperor would announce the New Year here, and decide on the fate of prisoners.

Passing through the Wumen, the visitor will see five white marble bridges richly decorated with sculptures, also known as the Golden River Bridges (Jin Shui Qiao).

Golden River Bridges (Jin Shui Qiao)

Three gates stand in the background. The middle gate (Gate of Supreme Harmony) is flanked by two bronze lions, symbols of imperial might.

In the enormous adjacent inner-courtyard 20,000 people assembled at great ceremonies. The imperial shops were previously housed in the side galleries, where furs, jewellery, tools and utensils, furniture, and fabric could be purchased.

The next three halls stand on a three-tiered marble terrace, which is surrounded by a marble balustrade. The middle hall was reserved exclusively for the emperor, where he would be carried in a sedan chair.

Gate of Supreme Harmony (Taihe Men)

The 35m/114ft high Hall of Supreme Harmony is also known as the Throne Hall (Jinluan Dian), as it contains the splendidly decorated guilded imperial throne. Important ceremonies took place here, such as the coronation, the imperial weddings, and the New Year celebrations. The emperors also gave audience to the imperial examination candidates here. The hall's total area; more than 2000sq.m/2392sq.yd make it without doubt China's largest wooden structure.

Many of the furnishings are of symbolic significance. The eighteen bronze incense burners on the terrace symbolise the eighteen provinces of

Hall of Supreme Harmony (Taihe Dian)

Bronze lion outside the Imperial Palace

133

the empire. The bronze tortoises and cranes represent long life; the pile of grain on the left of the hall, and the sundial on the right symbolise imperial justice. Inside are 24 pillars which correspond with the 24 hours of the day. These support a richly decorated coffered ceiling. The six pillars supporting the 2m/6ft high throne platform, are decorated with the gilded imperial dragon emblem.

Hall of Middle Harmony (Zhonghe Dian)	The Hall of Middle Harmony is situated behind the Hall of Supreme Harmony. This was where the emperor rested, and received homage from the officials and masters of ceremony before passing into the Hall of Supreme Harmony. Sometimes he came here to read his ministers' reports and speeches. Once a year in this hall the emperor inspected the seed in order to guarantee a good harvest.
Hall of Preserving Harmony (Baohe Dian)	The Hall of Preserving Harmony is situated behind the Hall of Complete Harmony. It functioned as the emperor's banquet hall. From the late 18th c. the imperial examinations were held here. Behind the hall the Dragon Pavement leads down from the terrace. Carved from a 250 tonne lump of marble, it forms the middle of three flights of steps.
Hall of Literary Glory (Wenhua Dian)	The Hall of Literary glory, to the south-east of the three main halls, was reserved for the prince who was heir to the throne during the Ming dynasty. From 1644 to 1911 it was used as a study for the emperors. The Imperial Library (Wenyuan Ge) is situated next to this hall.
Hall of Military Courage (Wuying Dian)	To the south-west of the main halls stands the Hall of Military Courage, which served the emperors as a permanent residence and private audience hall.

The three main halls together with the side buildings form the so-called outer courtyard, behind which are concealed the inner chambers consisting of three palaces and twelve courtyards (six to the left and six to the right). The private apartments of the imperial family were situated here.

Palace of Heavenly Purity (Qianqing Gong)	The Palace of Heavenly Purity is situated behind the gate of the same name (Qianqing Men); it separates the outer courtyard from the inner chambers. During the Ming period (1368–1644) this palace was the living quarters of the emperors, but after the 1730s it was used by them for studying.
Palace of Union between Heaven and Earth (Jiaotai Dian)	The Palace of Union between Heaven and Earth stands between the Palace of Heavenly Purity and the Palace of Earthly Tranquillity. During the Qing period, (1644–1911) the coronations and birthday celebrations of the empress took place here. In the building today are 25 imperial seals of China, a glockenspiel, and a bronze water clock.
Palace of Earthly Tranquillity (Kunning Gong)	The Palace of Earthly Tranquillity was the living and sleeping quarters of the empresses during the Ming period (1368–1644). Sacrificial rites were performed here under Qing rule (1644–1911). The emperor and empress spent their wedding night in the bridal chamber.
Imperial Garden (Yuhuayuan)	Behind the Gate of Earthly Tranquillity at the rear exit of the palace lies the garden (130m/142yd across, 90m/98yd long) which provide an excellent example of Chinese landscape architecture. Old pines, artificial slopes, lush bamboo plants, rare flowers, and charming pavilions dating from the Ming period, together form a harmonious garden landscape.
Hall of Imperial Peace (Qin'an Dian)	The Hall of Imperial Peace is situated in the centre of the gardens, its entrance being guarded by two unicorns.
Western Palaces (Xiliu Gong)	Around the six western courtyards are six palaces where the empresses, concubines, and princes resided. Officially the emperor was allowed three wives, six female favourites, and 72 concubines, although some kept up to 3000 women. These women mostly led a wretched existence.

The six palaces in the six eastern courtyards today function as museums. They house collections of great historical, archaeological, and cultural importance: paintings, ceramics, bronze vessels, handcrafted objets d'art, period clocks, and valuable gifts.

Eastern Palaces (Dongliu Gong)

At the easternmost end of the palace complex stands the Palace of Tranquillity and Longevity, which was inspired by the Palace of Earthly Tranquillity. It was the residential quarters of the widowed empress Cixi at the end of the 19th c.

This eastern section can be reached through the Xiping Men Gate, alongside which runs the 30m/33yd long Nine Dragon Wall.

Palace of Tranquillity and Longevity (Ningshou Gong)

Further City Centre Sights

The Park of the Beautiful View lies just a short distance north of the Imperial Palace. The hill in the centre of the park was named "coal hill" (Meisham), because under the Ming emperors (1368–1644) coal was stored at the foot of this hill. In 1416 during the construction of the Imperial Palace, the dumping of rubble from the old city wall and large quantities of soil from excavation of the moat surrounding the imperial palace, resulted in the naturally low-lying mound soaring in height. By the south gate is the Tower of the Beautiful View.

★ Park of the Beautiful View (Jingshan Gongyuan)

Under Emperor Qianlong who reigned from 1735 to 1796, pavilions were built on the five hilltops, and these still remain standing today. The middle and highest of them is called the Pavilion of Eternal Spring. From this pavilion a picturesque view of the city centre and the Imperial Palace can be enjoyed. To the Chinese it is therefore also known as the Hill of the Beautiful View.

At the south-eastern foot of the hill is the old acacia on which the last Ming emperor reportedly hanged himself on March 17th 1644.

Pavilion of Eternal Spring (Wanchung Ting)

In the north of the park complex is the Hall of Imperial Longevity, also built by the Emperor Qianlong.

Hall of Imperial Longevity (Shouhuang Dian)

The North Lake Park measures 680,000sq.m/813,280sq.yd (open: winter 6.30am–8.30pm, summer 6am–9pm). It lies to the north-west of the Imperial Palace and to the west of the Park of the Beautiful View. It is one of the oldest imperial gardens in Beijing. The park was laid out at the beginning of the 10th c. Its name is taken from Lake Beihai (north lake) which is situated here. The name north lake was adopted because it joins the lakes Zhonghai (middle lake), and Nanhai (south lake), in the south. On the south lake is the seat of the state council and its Central Committee of the Communist Party.

When the Jin rulers dug out the Xihua Tan Lake in the 12th c.the Island of Exquisite Jade was created, and the Guanghan Gong Palace was built on it. The Round City, which lies at the southern point of the lake was the centre of the capital Dadu in the Yuan period (1271–1368). Many of the buildings still standing today date from the time of Emperor Qianlong (reigned 1735–96).

The park, which is surrounded by a high wall, has become one of Beijing's favourite recreational venues. Access can be gained through the south, north, and east gates.

★★ North Lake Park (Beihai Gongyuan)

We arrive next at the 4500sq.m/5382sq.yd Round City, which dates from the Yuan period (1271–1368), and is situated near the south gate. It lies behind a 5m/16½ft wall built in the 15th c. Many of the present buildings were erected by Emperor Qianlong (1735–96).

★ Round City (Tuancheng)

The main attraction of the park is the Hall of Enlightenment (1690). A niche in the rear section of the palace conceals a splendid Buddha, standing 1.5m/5ft high, and carved from one single block of white jade. It was apparently brought from Burma to Beijing in the reign of Emperor

Hall of Enlightenment (Chengguang Dian)

Guangxu (1875–1908); the left arm was damaged by the allied troops in 1900.

At the front of the hall is a pavilion, which houses and protects a large black jade vase from the early 12th c. It stands 60cm/24in. above the ground, measures 1.5m/5ft in diameter, weighs 3500kg/7717lb and is decorated with representations of dragons and sea creatures. It was discovered in 1745 and four years later the Emperor Qianglong had the pavilion built for its safe keeping. According to archaeologists it is the largest jade vessel ever to be found in China. According to tradition Kublai Khan used it for storing wine.

Hall of Exquisite Jade (Qionghua Dao)	Crossing the Bridge of Eternal Peace (Yong'an Qiao) which dates from the Yuan period (1271–1368), we reach the Island of Exquisite Jade (Qionghua Dao), on which once stood the Palace of Guanghan Gong, built under the Mongol ruler Kublai Khan.
Temple of Eternal Peace (Yong'an Si)	In 1651 the Temple of Eternal Peace was built on the palace ruins, the buildings extending across the hill. On the way up is the Shanyin Dian Hall with its yellow and green glazed tiles and 455 niches housing Buddhas.
White Pagoda (Baita)	Behind the temple rises the 40m/131ft high Tibetan style White Pagoda, also built in 1651, on the occasion of the visit of the Dalai to Beijing. The pagoda was destroyed by an earthquake in 1651, was rebuilt a few years later and restored under the Emperor Qianlong. On its south side is a niche bearing a red emblem, which apparently served as a storing place for sacred objects.
Covered Walk (Yilan Tang)	Covered steps lead down the north slope to the covered Yilan Tang path which is richly decorated with paintings.
	Also situated here is the Fangshan restaurant which serves specialities of Imperial cuisine.
	In the south-west of the island it is worth visiting the Yuan Lou pavilion which houses a collection of manuscripts.
Five-Dragon Pavilions (Wulong Ting)	The north bank of the lake can be reached by ferry. Here can be seen the Five-Dragon Pavilions (1602), connected by stone bridges.
Iron Wall (Tieying Bi)	To the north of these is the Zhenguan Hall with the Iron Wall which dates back to the Yuan period. It is made from volcanic stone and stands almost 2m/6ft high and 3.5m/11ft long. Further to the west is the Pavilion of the Little Western Heaven (Xiaoxitian) of the Qianglong period and to the north of this the Botanical Gardens and the Tower of Ten-thousand Buddhas (Wanfo Lou)
The Nine Dragon Wall	The Nine Dragon Wall (1417) in the north is 5m/16ft high and 27m/29ft long. It is decorated in seven colours with representations of nine dragons.
	In the northern corner of the lake is the Silkworm Altar (Can Tan). Further south are the studio on a painted boat (Huafang Zhai) and the pavilion between the rivers Hao and Pu (Haopu Ting), both from the Qianlong period.
Sun-Yat-sen Park (Zhongshan Gongyuan)	This popular park, lying south-west of the Imperial Palace, was opened to the public in 1914. In 1928 it was renamed the Sun-Yat-sen Park. Emperor Yongle had the Sheji Tan altar built in the park grounds in 1421. From then onwards the emperors made sacrifices here twice-yearly, in the springtime to bring a good harvest and in the autumn for thanksgiving. The altar still stands and is situated in the centre of the park. The Xili Ting Pavilion in the south of park once housed the ceremonial chamber.
	The white gate was originally dedicated to the memory of Baron von Ketteler, who was assassinated in the Boxer Rebellion. However, following

In the Temple of Heaven

the German defeat in the First World War, the inscription was changed to "Justice Triumphs" and later to "Defend the Peace". This was written by Guo Moruo (See Famous People).

In the Stele Pavilion nearby can be seen an 18th c. stele which originally stood in the Garden of Perfection and Light (Yuanmin Yuan).

Stele Pavilion (Lanting Bei) Ting)

Also situated nearby is the Water Pavilion, once a meeting place for scholars and poets The Hall of Prayer (north of the altar), which was renamed Sun-Yat-sen Hall in 1928, is 550 years old and consequently Beijing's oldest well-preserved wooden building.

Water Pavilion (Shuixie)

The Culture Park of the Workers, which lies to the south-east of the Imperial Palace, was originally the Imperial Temple of Ancestors, constructed by order of Emperor Yongle in 1420. Today it is open to the public for leisure and cultural activities. Film and theatre performances, exhibitions, concerts and sporting activities all take place here.

Culture Park of the Workers (Laodong Renmin Wenhuagong)

From the south gate the actual temple compound is entered through a three-arched gate and through the Daji Men gate. Three halls are placed one in front of the other. In the First Hall (Taimiao) ceremonies of ancestor worship took place. In the Middle Hall (Zhongdian) were kept the rolls of honour of deceased emperors – the rolls were brought out only for ceremonies which took place in the First Hall – and the Rear Hall (Houdian) forms the conclusion of the temple area.

Sights outside the city centre

The Temple of Heaven, dating back to 1420 (open: 8am–6.30pm) in the south of the city, incorporates a group of sacred buildings surrounded by lush vegetation. With its southern rectangular section, and its northern semi-circular section, the complex symbolises heaven and earth.

★★Temple of Heaven (Tiantan)

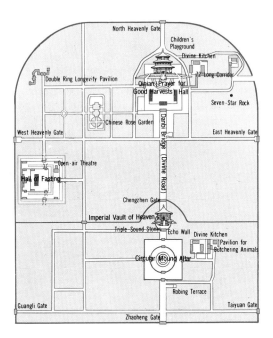

The following labels appear on the map:

North Heavenly Gate
Children's Playground
Divine Kitchen
Double Ring Longevity Pavilion
Qinian (Prayer for Good Harvests) Hall
72 Long Corridor
Seven-Star Rock
Chinese Rose Garden
Danbi Bridge (Divine Road)
West Heavenly Gate
East Heavenly Gate
Open-air Theatre
Hall of Fasting
Chengzhen Gate
Imperial Vault of Heaven
Triple-Sound Stones
Echo Wall
Divine Kitchen
Pavilion for Butchering Animals
Circular Mound Altar
Robing Terrace
Guangli Gate
Taiyuan Gate
Zhaoheng Gate

On the day of the winter solstice, having fasted and meditated for three days, the emperor would ascend the Heavenly Altar in solemn ceremony to pray for a good harvest and to offer sacrifices.

Hall of Prayer for Good Harvests (Qinian Dian)

The Hall of Prayer for Good Harvests was built over the Qinian Dian altar in 1420 and restored in 1545. In 1889 it was destroyed by a bolt of lightning and rebuilt a year later. Here the emperor prayed for a good harvest. The 38m/41yd high building with a diameter of 30m/33yd was, astonishingly enough, built without a using single nail. It towers up from a three-tiered, marble terrace with balustrades, and has a blue-glazed tiled roof (50,000 tiles), also three-tiered. The building is supported by 28 columns which have symbolic meanings, and are separated into three circles. The central four columns, (dragon fountain columns), represent the four seasons. The twelve smaller columns represent the twelve months of the year and, according to an old Chinese tradition, the twelve parts of the day.

On the floor in the centre of the hall is a marble flagstone, ornamented with depictions of phoenixes and dragons, the imperial symbols.

Hall of the Vault of Heaven (Huangqiongyu)

A raised pathway leads to the Hall of the Vault of Heaven (erected 1530, rebuilt 1752), with its blue tiled conical roof. The ceremonial plaques for the sacrificial rituals were stored here.

The temple's outer wall echoes to even the quietest of voices, hence its name Echo(i) Wall (Huiyin Bi).

In front of the hall are also three unusual echoing stones, and depending on which way they are facing, can throw back an echo up to three times.

Round Altar (Huanqiu Tan)

The Round Altar built in 1530, lies to the south of the Hall of the Vault of Heaven. It consists of three marble terraces built one over the other, and

**Temple of Heaven
Hall of the Vault
of Heaven**

symbolises "man-earth-heaven". The architectural structure is built around the figure nine, a celestial figure of great significance. So, the number of stones in the altar ring extend from: 9, 18, 27, and so on, up to 243.

Already in the 3rd c. B.C. there were human dwellings on this site, situated to the west of the Temple of the Vault of Heaven. A park was laid out here by the time of the Liao period (947–1125). During the Yuan period (1271–1368) the Monastery of Goodness and Pity (Cibei An) was built here, and in 1695 Jiang Zao, the civil servant, had the Taoran Ting Pavilion built next to it. This pavilion was named after a poem by Bai Juyi (772–846), as was the park. In the Qing period (1644–1911) the park was ready to be opened to the public and became a favourite meeting place for poets. It was extensively modernised in 1952.

Taoranting
Gongyuan Park

    The monastery and pavilion are situated between the two lakes in the park. Two Buddhist columns (1099 and 1131) can be seen in the inner courtyard of the monastery, also a Guanyin stele from the year 1663. To the south-west are two pavilions dating from the Qianlong period (ruled 1735–96) which were brought here in 1954.

The Niujie Qingzhen Si Mosque, (Beijing's oldest and largest), lies in an Islamic quarter in the south-west of the city, about 2km/1 mile to the west of the Temple of Heaven. It was built by two Arabs in 995. Throughout the three periods Yuan, Ming and Qing (13th–19th c.), it underwent several alterations. Since 1949 it has been repeatedly restored. On this site of at least 6000sq.m/7176sq.yd there are several buildings: the prayer hall, the Bangge Lou (minaret), a six-cornered moon observatory tower the Wan-gyue Lou, and two pavilions with numerous steles, where Chinese and Arabic inscriptions are engraved. The buildings of tiles and wood correspond externally to the classic Chinese style, whereas their interiors are Arab.

★Niujie Qingzhen
Si Mosque

★ Temple of the Source of Law (Fayuan Si)

The Temple of the Source of Law (open: Thur.–Tues. 8.30–11.30am and 1.30–4.30pm), lies about 500m/550yd to the east of the mosque, and dates originally from the year 645. It was not given its present-day name until 1734. The buildings consist of several halls, where many stone inscriptions are kept, the oldest of which dates back to the 7th c.

In the course of history the temple was the scene of important events. For a time the Emperor Huizong (1100–56) was held captive here; and in 1173 an imperial examination took place here for the award of the highest offices of state; in 1289 the temple was converted into a special prison to hold the former minister Xie Fang. Under Qing rule (1644–1911) the temple served as botanical gardens.

Today the temple is a place of worship although it is also the seat of the Buddhist academy, the most important educational establishment in China. The bell tower and the drum tower are situated in the first courtyard.

Hall of the Kings of Heaven (Tianwang Dian)

Displayed in the hall, are the four kings of heaven (Tianwang Dian), a Maitreya statue, and a Weituo statue.

Mahavira Hall (Daxiong Baodian)

The hall houses Buddhas of the present, past and future represented in eighteen Luohan figures.

Dabianjue Tang Hall

One of the most precious of objects belonging to the temple is a Han dynasty (25–220) ceramic statue in the Dabianjue Tang Hall.

Southern Cathedral (Nantang)

The Southern Cathedral is situated in the Xuannei Dajie. The present building was reconstructed in 1904 in the style of the church which was erected in 1650 (with financial support from the emperor) by the German Jesuit Johann Adam Schall von Bell. It stands on the site of the residences of the missionary Matteo Ricci. Regular church services, which many foreigners attend, are held here.

Temple of the White Clouds (Baiyun Guan)

The famous Daoist Temple of the White Clouds (open: 9am–4.30pm) lies only a short distance from the Yanjing Hotel. Although originally built in 739, the present buildings are only a few hundred years old.

The temple's interior decorations are Daoist; including mushrooms, storks, diagrams and portraits of the eight immortal Daoists.

Kept on the first floor of the Siyu hall is a copy of the sacred Daoist scriptures from the first half of the 15th c.

The main hall (not normally open to the public) is dedicated to Qiu Changchun (1148–1227), the spiritual head of the Daoists. Here a statue of the saint is worshipped, and below this can be seen his tomb. At the present time the temple is also the headquarters of the Daoist Association of China.

Temple of Universal Brotherly Love (Guangji Si)

The Temple of Universal Brotherly Love lies in the Fuchengmennei Dajie. The original building dates back to the 12th c. and was completed in 1457. In the 1930s it was destroyed by fire, and was gradually rebuilt.

Yuanton Baodian Hall

The Yuanton Baodian Hall is very noteworthy. Dedicated to Guanjin, the temple is now the headquarters of the Chinese Buddhist Society.

Temple of the White Pagoda Baita Si

To the west of the Temple of Universal Brotherly Love stands this temple with its 50m/164ft high white pagoda. It dates from the end of the 11th c., and was restored between 1270 and 1271 by Kublai Khan (advised by a Nepalese architect). It burned down several years later, however, and was not rebuilt until 1457. During its restoration in 1978 numerous religious artifacts and scrolls were found in the tip of the pagoda and these are now on display in the temple.

Lu Xun Bowuguan Museum

The Lu Xun Bowuguan Museum (open: Tues.–Sun. 8.30–11am and 1.30–3.30pm), lies not far from the Temple of the White Pagoda. On display are the diaries, letters, manuscripts and one of the only few examples of the complete works of the poet Lu Xun (See Famous People). The exhibition is divided into four sections which relate to different periods of the poet's life: childhood and education, e.g. the first translations (1909–27), travel and the early works (1909–27), the Shanghai period (1927–1936), and the influence of his work.

The house where Lu Xun resided from 1924–26 is situated next to the museum. It has been preserved in its original style, including the furniture.

The zoo (open: 7.30am–5.30pm) lies in the north-west of Beijing, it was a prince's estate during the Ming dynasty (1368–1644), and in the Qing period (1644–1911) the son of a minister had it transformed into private gardens. In 1906 the area temporarily became a public estate with cultivated fields and livestock. Since 1908 the zoo has been situated here and now has about 3000 animals of 400 species, including the giant panda, the Manchurian tiger and the snubnosed monkey.

★Beijing Zoo (Beijing Dongwuyuan)

This temple (north of the zoo; interior in poor condition) which dates back to the 15th c., was badly damaged in 1860, and was later pillaged. Only the structure with the five pagodas, after which the temple was named, remained standing.

Temple of the Five Pagodas (Wuta Si)

Already in Yuan times (1271–1368), water was taken from the three lakes here and channelled down the Changhe Canal to Beijing. This was of great importance to Beijing's water supply.

In 1577 the Wanshou Si temple estate was laid out in the north-west of the park, to which the small lamaist Purple Bamboo Temple belongs; only parts of this still remain standing today.

Purple Bamboo Park (Zizhu Yuan)

In the Temple of the Great Bell (open: 9am–4.30pm), which lies to the north of the zoo is a collection of old bells, including one of the largest in world. This bell is 6.75m/22ft tall, has a diameter of about 3.5m/11ft, and weighs 46.5 tonnes. It was moulded from bronze during the rule of Emperor Yongle (1402–24). Apparently its sound can be heard up to 50km/31 miles away. The bell was originally kept in the Temple of Longevity (Wanchou Si). As the temple came under threat of attack it was transported to the Juesheng Si Temple by means of a railway specially constructed for this purpose.

On the inside and outside of the bell Buddhist texts have been engraved amounting to 220,000 characters.

Temple of the Great Bell (Dazhong Si)

The Drum Tower which borders the city's north–south axis, dates from the year 1420. At night, drums were beaten here to announce the changing shifts of the night guards.

Drum Tower (Golou)

The Bell Tower looms north of the Golou tower. This bell tower also dates back to 1420 and its chimes informed the city's residents of the hour.

Bell Tower

The Lama Temple (open: 9am–4.30pm) in the north-east of Beijing is one of the city's most attractive and best preserved temples. It was originally built in 1694 as the residence of Prince Yong (later to become Emperor Yongzheng). When he came to the throne in 1723 parts of the complex were converted into a Lama temple in keeping with the old custom that the residence of an heir to the throne may only be used as a temple. In 1725 half the complex is burned to the ground. Around the five courtyards of the temple are numerous other buildings. The entrance to the temple grounds is the south gate. On the way through the gardens we reach a courtyard with a drum tower (Gu Lou) on the left, and on the right a bell tower and two stele pavilions.

★★Lama Temple (Yonghe Gong)

As the visitor proceeds through the grounds, he reaches the first of the five main halls. In the Hall of the Kings of Heaven stands a Maitreya statue surrounded by the four kings who are provided with symbolic objects: the eastern king with a toad, the southern king with a sword, the western king with a snake, and the northern king with a shield. Also noteworthy is the statue of Weituo, the protector of Buddhism, holding an iron staff.

Hall of the Kings of Heaven (Tianwang Dian)

Lama Temple

Pavilion of the Four-tongued Stele (Yubi Ting)	The Pavilion of the Four-tongued Stele stands in the centre of the next courtyard, it houses a stele dating back to the year 1792. The history of the Lama religion is written on it in Chinese, Manchurian, Tibetan and Mongolian. Nearby is a bronze representation of the mountain of paradise, Sumeru. In the adjoining halls the holy scripts were studied.
Yonghe Gong Dian	The adjacent building is the main hall, Yonghe Gong Dian. Inside are three Buddha sculptures: Shakyamuni the Buddha of the present, the Buddha of the past, and Maitreya the Buddha of the future. Also to be seen are representations of eighteen Luohan, together with Dizang, who releases people from the torments in hell and Guanyin, the goddess of mercy.
Medicine Hall	In the eastern side-hall, the Medicine Hall, are statues by Zongkaba (1357–1410), one of reformers of the Lama religion and founder of the Yellow Sect, and one of the Buddha of Medicine.
Hall of Mathematics (Shuxue Dian)	Natural sciences are studied in the Hall of Mathematics (Shuxue Dian), which is the western side-hall.
Yongyou Dian Hall	Further on is the Yongyou Dian Hall. Inside the Buddha Amitabja is displayed, to the right of that Yaoshi Fo, the Buddha of Medicine, and to the left Shihou Fo, the Buddha of the Lion's Roar.
Hall of the Buddhist Wheel (Falun Dian)	In the Hall of the Buddhist Wheel stands another statue by Zongkaba. Particularly noteworthy is a "hill" made from sandal-wood with 500 Louhan figures made of gold, silver, iron and tin. Some of the statues have been covered up as they are overtly sexual. Sacred manuscripts are kept on the walls to the left and right; on the east wall are 207 volumes, and 108 on the west wall.

The largest building, the Pavilion of Four Thousand Fortunes, is situated in the fifth and last courtyard. Here stands an enormous sandalwood statue in honour of the Buddha Maitreya; it measures some 18m/59ft high and has a diameter of 3m/10ft, although the 8m/26ft high base lies underground.

Pavilion of Four Thousand Fortunes (Wangfu Ge)

The Zhaofo Lou Hall is connected by two suspended galleries to the side halls. In the eastern side-hall is a noteworthy bronze Buddha. The gold shield, crown, and pearls with which he was adorned were stolen in 1949.

Zhaofo Lou Hall

Just a few yards to the west of the Lama Monastery is the former Imperial College (open: Tues.– Fri. 8.30am–7.30pm, Sat. and Sun. 8.30am–5.30pm), where the city library is housed today. It was founded in 1287 by Kublai Khan. The college, also attended by foreign students, maintained its educational pre-eminence until the end of the Qing period (1644–1911). The college masters included various Qing emperors including Shunzhi, Kangxi, Yongzheng and Qianlong. The college was closed in 1900.

★Imperial College (Guozijian)

In the Piyong Hall, the college's main building, the emperor held his lectures. The practically square shaped building (width: about 18m/59ft) dating from 1784, is surrounded by a small round lake which is edged with a finely cut marble balustrade. The roof is covered with yellow-glazed tiles and has a double ledge.

Piyong Hall

The Yilun Tang Hall in the north of the park, also built under the Yang dynasty (1271–1368) is the college library. Before the Piyong Hall was built, the emperor gave his lectures here. The college students were selected from the best candidates chosen by their area in Xiucai and Juren to sit the imperial examinations. After a course of study lasting three years, the students carried out a year's practice in government office, followed by a final examination, which offered them the prospect of employment in the civil service.

Yilun Tang Hall

Marco Polo Bridge (see page 146)

Beijing · Peking

★Confucius Temple (Kong Miao)

The Confucius Temple (open: 9am–4.30pm), built in 1302 and restored in 1411 is situated next to the Guozijian College. The grounds of the two buildings are joined by a wall with several gates.

The great philosopher and teacher Confucius (See Famous People) had a decisive influence on Chinese philosophy; his teachings dominated public and private life throughout centuries. Emperors from many dynasties dedicated magnificent temples to him, this being one of the most famous. The temple honoured him and his ancestors.

Hall of Great Achievements (Dacheng Dian)

This is the main building of the temple complex; commemorations are held here in the second and eighth months of the Chinese calender.

The 198 steles in the side pavilions are engraved with the names and places of birth of the leading 51,624 candidates to sit the imperial examinations between 1416 and 1904. Now the building houses the city museum.

Dongsi Mosque

Further south on the Dongsi Beidajie is the Dongsi mosque which was erected in 1356, modernised in 1447 and renovated at the end of the 1970s. A combination of Chinese and Arab influence can be seen in the architecture.

★Old Observatory (Guguanxiang Tai)

This observatory was built between 1437 and 1446. It lies in the east of the city near the diplomatic quarter, and was continuously in use until 1929. Among the existing instruments is a celestial globe (1669–73) and an armillary globe (1754) both of which are noteworthy.

Shopping Centre (Shangye Qu)

Apart from the friendship shops in the east of the city (Jianguomenwai Dajie 21) and the famous silk shop by the north entrance of the Temple of Heaven, the following centres can to be recommended for purchasing silk, tea, porcelain, handcrafted articles, objets d'art, and antiques:

Wangfujing-Dajie Street

Wangfujing-Dajie Street to the east of the imperial palace, where there is a collection of large department stores and art galleries;

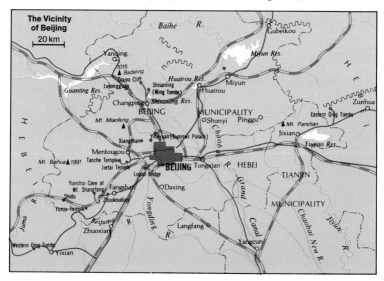

144

Bird's-eye view of the Summer Palace (see page 147)

Marble ship in the Summer Palace (see page 150)

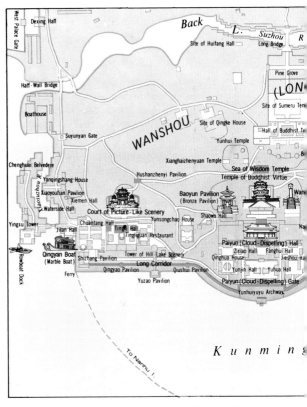

Map labels (top to bottom, left to right):
West Palace Gate; Dexing Hall; Back L.; Suzhou R; Long Bridge; Site of Huifang Hall; Pine Grove; Half-Wall Bridge; (LON; Site of Sumeru Tem; Boathouse; WANSHOU; Site of Qingke House; Hall of Buddhist T; Suyunyan Gate; Yunhui Temple; Chenghuai Belvedere; Xianghaizhenyuan Temple; Sea of Wisdom Temple; Yanqingshang House; Hushanzhenyi Pavilion; Temple of Buddhist Virtue; Xiaoyouhan Pavilion; Baoyun Pavilion (Bronze Pavilion); Wan; Waterside Hall; Xiemen Hall; Court of Picture-Like Scenery; Shaowa Hall; Yingxu Tower; Chuantang Hall; Yunsongchao House; Jilan Hall; Tingli Hall; Tingliguan Restaurant; Na; Qingyan Boat (Marble Boat); Shizhang Pavilion; Tower of Hill-Lake Scenery; Ziziao Hall; Fanghui Hall; Qinghua House; Jieshou Ha; Ferry; Qingyao Pavilion; Long Corridor; Qiushui Pavilion; Yunjin Hall; Yuhua Hall; Yuzao Pavilion; Paiyun (Cloud-Dispelling) Gate; Yunhuiyuyu Archway; Rowboat Dock; Kunming; To Nanhu I.

Xidan-Beidajie Street	Xidan-Beidajie Street which lies to the west of the imperial palace;
Qianmen-Dajie Street	Qianmen-Dajie Street to the south of the Forbidden City, with the famous Tongrentang pharmacy which sells many Chinese remedies.
Liulichang Street	Liulichang Street, which has been reconstructed in Ming style, at right angles to Qianmen Dajie, is famous for many shops in which old books, antiques, original paintings and reproductions can be purchased.

Surroundings of Beijing   M 3

★Marco Polo Bridge (Lugou Qiao)	The Marco Polo Bridge which lies 8km/5 miles to the south-west of Beijing was erected between 1189 and 1192 by the Emperor Shizong.
	Marco Polo crossed this bridge in 1276 and referred to it as Pulisangin in his work "Millions"; Sangin could be a rough transliteration of the name Sanggan, the upper reaches of the river Yongding, over which this bridge runs. Puli is possibly taken from the Persian word "pul" (bridge). In 1444 and 1698 the bridge was repaired after it had been partly destroyed by floods.

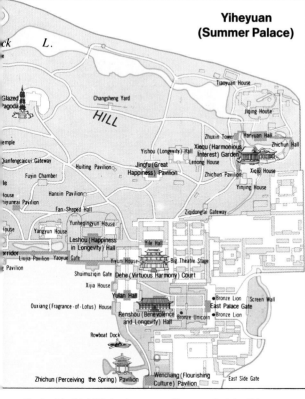

Yiheyuan (Summer Palace)

L.

Tiaoyuan House

Glazed Pagoda

Changsheng Yard

Jinjing House

HILL

emple

Zhuxin Tower   Hanyuan Hall

Yishou (Longevity) Hall   Xiequ (Harmonious   Zhichun Hall
Interest) Garden

Jianfengcaicui Gateway   Huiting Pavilion   Jingfu (Great   Lenong House
Happiness) Pavilion   Zhichun Pavilion   Xiqu House

Fuyin Chamber   Yinjing House

Iouse   Hanxin Pavilion
iyunzai Pavilion

Fan-Shaped Hall   Ziqidongtai Gateway

Iouse   Yunhegingyun House
Yangyun House

Leshou (Happiness   Yile Hall
in Longevity) Hall

rridor   Liujia Pavilion   Yaoyue Gate   Yirun House   Big Theatre Stage
Pavilion   Shuimuziqin Gate   Dehe (Virtuous Harmony) Court

Xijia House

Yulan Hall   ●Bronze Lion   Screen Wall
Ouxiang (Fragrance-of-Lotus) House   East Palace Gate
Renshou (Benevolence   Bronze Unicorn   ●Bronze Lion
and Longevity) Hall

Rowboat Dock

Zhichun (Perceiving the Spring) Pavilion   Wenchang (Flourishing   East Side Gate
Culture) Pavilion

On the July 7th 1937 the Japanese artillery attacked the Chinese troops stationed here and in so doing started the Sino-Japanese War which lasted for eight years.

The 235m/771ft long and 8m/26ft wide bridge is supported by eleven arches, and has 280 side columns decorated with lion sculptures in the balustrades, which have brought fame to the bridge.

At the eastern end of the bridge is a massive stele with an inscription by Emperor Kangxi: "Morning moonlight over the Lugou bridge", (Lugou being the old name for the Yongding river).

The Summer Palace, lies 15km/9 miles to the north of Beijing, its 716 acres making it China's largest park; originally it was a private garden. In 1153 the emperor had the park laid out and named it Jinshui Yuan. During the Yuan period (1271–1368) the lake in the park was enlarged (today called Kunming Hu). From the Ming dynasty (1368–1644) onwards when many pavilions were built here the park was used as imperial gardens. Under Qianlong (reigned: 1735–96) the complex was enlarged to its present size. In 1860 English and French troops burned the park to the ground. Empress Cixi reconstructed the park in 1888, using funds which were in fact intended for the imperial fleet. She named it Yiyeyuan. In 1900 it was once again destroyed by foreign troops and rebuilt yet again by the Empress. It was finally opened to the public in 1924, and since 1949 extensive restoration

★★Summer Palace (Yiyeyuan)

Open
7am–6pm

work has been carried out. Today the park is a favourite destination for excursions.

This 60m/197ft high hill is an outlier of the Yanshan Mountains. Around the middle of the 17th c. the imperial herds were put out to graze here. In 1750, on the occasion of his mother's birthday the Emperor Qianlong gave the hill its present day name; he had numerous buildings erected here, but these were burned down by British and French troops. The present buildings date from the 1880s and 1890s.

Hill of Longeviety (Wanshoushan)

The main entrance of the beautiful park is situated in the east. Just 50m/55yd to the west of this the Hall of Well-being and Longeviety stands on the east bank of the lake. In this hall, where the throne still stands, the Emperor Guangxu and Empress Cixi gave audience to Chinese officials and received foreign ambassadors.

Hall of Well-being and Longeviety (Renshou Dian)

To the north-west of the hall is the Palace of the Jade Waves, where the private chambers of the Emperor Guangxi were situated. He was held here under house arrest by order of Empress Cixi for ten years.

Palace of the Jade Waves Yulan Tang

Leaving the Hall of Well-being and Longeviety and turning left, we soon reach a fenced-in courtyard where stands the Great Theatre. When it was built in 1891 it was the largest theatre of its time. The empress occasionally attended performances of the Beijing Opera which sometimes lasted several days.

Great Theatre

The three-storey stage, into which trap doors were built, is 21m/68ft high and 17m/55ft wide. The empress sat in the Hall of Exhileration (Yile Dian) opposite during the performances.

Slightly to the west of the Great Theatre is the Hall of Happiness and Longevity which stands on the north bank of the lake; it has a connecting courtyard filled with tropical plants and curious rare stones. It served in summer as a private residence for the Empress Cixi; her winters were spent in the Beijing Imperial Palace.

Hall of Happiness and Longevity (Leshou Tang Hall)

To the west of the Hall of Happiness and Longevity is the beginning of the celebrated Long Corridor, which runs along the northern banks of the Kunming Lake. The 728m/796yd long covered walk, made from painted wood, has a roof supported by 273 pairs of columns. It is decorated with 8000 paintings: landscapes, episodes of historical interest and scenes from famous novels of classical Chinese literature.

Long Corridor (Chang Lang)

Half way along the corridor we reach the Pailou (decorated gate), from where the ascent of Wanshoushan Hill begins. The Long Corridor ends at the south-western foot of the this hill.

After passing through the Cloud Dispelling Gate the Yunjin Dian Hall can be seen to the west and the Yuhua Dian Hall to the east. We soon come to the Cloud Dispelling Hall, which is flanked by the halls Fanghui and Zixiao. Empress Cixi's birthdays were celebrated here. In one of the largest halls in this palace are displayed some of the Empress's birthday presents which she received for her 70th birthday. Among these is a painting of Cixi by the Dutch artist Hubert Vos.

Cloud Dispelling Hall (Paiyun Dian Hall)

Two corridors running parallel to another lead to the Hall of Virtuous Light (Dhui Dian), where steep steps go up to the Pavilion of the Fragrant Buddha.

The 41m/134ft high, octagonal pavilion with its 20m/66ft high stone pillar is the most important building on the Hill of Longevity. From the top of this pavilion the whole park can be seen.

Pavilion of the Fragrant Buddha (Foxiang Ge)

To the east of the pavilion is the Zhuanlun Zang, an archive of Buddhist manuscripts. A 10m/33ft high stele in the centre of the building carries the

Zhuanlun Zang

◀ *Pavilion in the Summer Palace*

inscription; "Wanshou Shan, Kumming Hu" (Hill,of Longevity, Kunminghu Lake) by Emperor Qianlong; on the back of the stele is a report on work carried out on the lake.

Pavilion of Precious Clouds (Baoyun Ge)	To the west of the Pavilion of the Fragrant Buddha is the Pavilion of Precious Clouds, finished completely in bronze. On the south side are engraved the names of the craftsman who worked on the building.
Sea of Wisdom (Zhihhuiihai)	On the top of Hill of Longevity stands the Temple of the Sea of Wisdom, which is covered in green and yellow glazed tiles. Inside a gilded Buddha statue is preserved.
Hear the Golden Orioles (Tingli Guan)	Continuing along the Long Corridor towards the west we arrive at the House called Hear the Golden Orioles, where theatrical performances were previously held and which today is a restaurant.
Marble Ship (Shifang)	At the end of the Long Corridor is the Marble Ship also called Qingyan Fang. The base is of marble and the upper part of wood; two stone wheels also protrude from the construction. The ship is ironic evidence of the fact that Empress Cixi used the funds which were intended to modernise the imperial fleet to renovate her private residence.

From this point the South Lake Island can be reached, either by ferryboat or in the south-west on foot over the Seven-arched Bridge (Shiqikong Qiao). This bridge was built over a hundred years ago, and is the longest bridge on the lake, measuring 150m/164yd. Worth noting are the 150 lions on the railings, all of which are carved differently. In front of the bridge stands a bronze ox, which supposedly fends off the water demon.

Kunminghu Lake	The 200ha/543 acre lake is fed by spring water. It was originally only a pool, but Emperor Qianlong had it enlarged in order to carry out naval exercises here in the summer. Bridges and dams subdivide the lake into several sections.

On the South Lake Island stands the Temple of the Dragon King (Longwang Miao).

The Western Dyke (Xidi) connects the north-west part of the park with the south. The dyke and its six bridges including the lovely arched Jade Belt Bridge (Yudai Qiao), are reproductions of the Su-Dongpo Dam in the Hangszhou West Lake.

Garden of Harmony and Pleasure (Xiequ Yuan)	On the eastern foot of Hill of Longevity, hidden in an out-of-the-way corner, is the Garden of Harmony and Pleasure. This "garden in a garden" was laid out in 1751 and modelled on a private park in Wuxi; it was renovated in 1811. There is a lotus pond surrounded by covered paths and buildings.

To the west of the park are the Pavilion of Joy and Farming (Lenong Xuan), the Pavilion of Long Life (Yiahou Tang) and an observatory tower (Jingfu Ge).

Garden of Perfection and Light (Yuanming Yuan)	The Garden of Perfection and Light, the so-called Old Summer Palace, is to be found 500m/550yd from the New Summer Palace. The building of the 350ha/864 acre complex began in 1709. This complex consists of three sections the Garden of Perfection and Light, the Garden of Eternal Spring (Changchun Yuan), and the Garden of the Beautiful Spring (Qichun Yuan). The Emperor Qianlong engaged the Jesuit Giuseppe Castiglione from 1747 until 1760 to build European style palaces. In 1860 the complex was destroyed in a matter of ten days by British and French troops and finally, at the suggestion of the British, it was set on fire. The imperial family began restoring the complex, although they had to stop again because of insufficient funds being available. Furthermore, the stones were used by the Chinese for housebuilding. Today real effort is being put into the restoration work.

The gardens used to be characterised by lakes, intertwined water-courses, and man-made hills and also numerous palaces and pavilions. There are still small traces of the European style palaces (Xiyang Lou) to be seen.

A small exhibition provides information on the history of the complex and a model conveys an impression its former glory.

★★Western Mountains (Xishan)

The Fragrant Mountain (Xiangshan; 557m/1827ft), rises steeply in the Western Mountains, some 25km/15 miles to the north-west of the city in a park which bears the same name. Its peak is reminiscent of incense burners and, as it is often covered by clouds looking from a distance like smoke, it has been named Incense-burner Mountain (Xianglushan, shortened to Xiangshan). In the summer it is a favourite venue for day visitors because of the cool mountain air. In the autumn, the former imperial hunting preserve is particularly attractive owing to the trees with their glowing red leaves.

★★Fragrant Mountain (Xiangshan)

In 1186 a temple and a palace were built here. In 1745 under Emperor Qianlong 28 temples, pavilions, pagodas, and villas were erected and this area was surrounded by a wall. The complex was almost completely destroyed in 1860 and 1900. It is only due to the restoration work carried out in the past few decades that the former glory of the park can be appreciated. The lower station of a lift up to the top of the Fragrant Mountain (Xiangshan) is situated at the northern gate; the main entrance is the eastern gate.

The Spectacle Lake in the northern section of the park actually consists of two lakes connected by a footbridge giving it the appearance of a pair of spectacles.

Spectacle Lake (Yanying Hu)

To the south-west of the Spectacle Lake is the Pavilion of Self Examination, with its sickle-shaped pool.

Pavilion of Self Examination (Jianxin Zhai)

The Temple of Light, situated to the south of the Pavilion of Self Examination, was built in 1780 for the Panchen Lama in the Tibetan style. The archway in front of the temple bears inscriptions in Chinese, Manchurian and Tibetan.

Temple of Light (Zhaomiao)

The small seven storey, octagonal Liuli Ta Pagoda lies to the west of the Temple of Light. It is covered in coloured ceramic tiles and every storey has little bronze bells which tinkle when the wind blows.

Liuli Ta Pagoda

A path leads south past the Lotus Hall (Furong Guan) to the Jade Flower Hill Villa (Yuhua Shanzhuang). To the west is the vantage point of Xishan Qingxue.

The path called "Even the Devil is Afraid" (Gujianchou) leads up to the peak of the Fragrant Mountain.

In the south-east of the park lie the remains of the Xiangshan Temple (with several terraces) dating from 1186.

Xiangshan Temple

The Shuangqing Villa stands to the south-west of the Xiangshan Temple; it has a pool fed by two springs.

Shuangqing Villa

The Temple of the Azure Clouds (1321; temporarily closed for alterations) is situated at the eastern foot of the Fragrant Mountain. In the Ming period (1368–1644) extensions were carried out here by eunuchs who wanted to build themselves a tomb. The Emperor Qianlong had the temple extended in 1748.

Temple of the Azure Clouds (Biyun Si)

Next we pass through the Mountain Gate (Shanmen) and climb the steps to the Hall of the Heavenly King (Tianwang Dian), then to the Maitreya Hall (Milefo Dian) and finally to the Pusa Dian Hall in the third courtyard.

In the Temple of Azure Clouds

500-Luohan Hall
(Luohan Tang)

Next on the left is the 500-Luohan Hall, where can be seen 508 figures 500 of whch are 1.5m/5ft high gilded Luohans, which have all been individually created. Also, in the corridors are seven figures of the gods, and on a roof beam is a figure of the monk Jigon, who was supposed always to arrive late.

Sun-Yat-sen
Memorial Hall

The following main hall belonging to the temple complex is the Sun-Yat-sen Memorial Hall. The body of Sun-Yat-sen (See Famous People) was laid in state here in 1925, the hall is now dedicated to memory of the "Father of the Republic". Kept here are busts of the politician and his silver-plated coffin, a gift from the Soviet Union, although it did not reach here until two weeks after the burial. In the side rooms is an exhibition with photographs about the life and work of Sun-Yat-sen.

In the nearby Spring Courtyard (Shuiquan Yuan), visitors may rest and enjoy the scenery.

Diamond Throne
Pagoda
(Jingangbaozuo
Ta)

Behind the Memorial Hall the 35m/114ft high Diamond Throne Pagoda rises up in the middle of a two part terrace. It is surrounded by four smaller pagodas and two dagobas. Its name is reminiscent of the town Bodh Gaya, where Siddharta Gautama gained inspiration. Here the body of Sun-Yat-sen was laid in state until it was transported to Nanking in 1929. The pagoda still contains his hat and some of his clothing.

**Temple of the
Sleeping Buddha**
(Wofo Si)

The Temple of the Sleeping Buddha (situated to the north-east of the Fragrant Mountain on the Shouanshan Mountain), dates back to the first half of the 7th c., it was enlarged between 1320 and 1331. From 1734 the temple was officially named Temple of Universal Spiritual Awakening (Shifangqujue Si) although it is unofficially named after the great bronze statue of the sleeping Buddha. When visiting this temple the first things to be seen are an 18th c. decorated gate, then a small pool, the bell tower on the left, and the drum tower on the right. To be seen on the second floor of the Hall of the Kings of Heaven (Tianwang Dian) are statues of Maitreya and the four Kings of Heaven. In the third courtyard is the Hall of the Three Saints (Sansheng Dian), where a Shakyamuni statue and eighteen Luohan figures are kept. The Wofo Dian houses the figure of the sleeping Buddha on his way to Nirvana. The statue is surrounded by twelve statues of his pupils. The monumental sculpture, 5.33m/17ft long and weighing 53 tons was created by 7000 craftsmen in 1321.

Hall of the
Kings of Heaven
Hall of the
Three Saints
Wofo Dian

These gardens, situated less than a mile to the north-west of the Temple of the Sleeping Buddha, are popular with day visitors. There is a beautiful view from the hill called the Cloud Peak Half-way to Heaven (Bantian Yunlin).

Gardens of the
Cherry Ravine
(Yingtaogou)

The Badachu comprising eight temples is situated on the Cuiweishan and Lushishan mountains to the south of the Xishan range.

**Eight Great
Sights**
(Badachu)

The Temple of Eternal Peace on the Cuiweishan was erected in 1504. In the first hall is a bronze statue of Guan Yu who was a general at the time of the three empires (220–280); the second hall is dedicated to Shakyamuni.
   A further hall is dedicated to the Goddess Niangniang who is believed to fulfil the wish for children.

Temple of
Eternal Peace
(Chang'an Si)

To the north of the Chang'sn Si is the Temple of Godly Light. Like the nearby octagonal Liaota pagoda (1071), this temple was also destroyed by foreign troops in 1900. According to historical records, one of Buddha's teeth was supposed to have been stored here (one of the four teeth brought to China from India after his cremation). While clearance work was being carried out following the temple's destruction, a wooden box was discovered containing the tooth. This was taken to the Guanji Si temple for some time until a new home was found for it here in the 1950s in the Buddha-tooth Pagoda (Foya Ta).

Temple of
Godly Light
(Ligguang Si)

Further to the north, between the Cuiweishan, Lishishan and the Pingboshan mountains, is the little Monastery of the Three Mountains, the origins of which are unknown. There is a fine view from the pavilion in the temple grounds.

Monastery of the
Three Mountains

Next is the Temple of Great Compassion dating from 1550. Particularly worth seeing are the eighteen Luohan figures, attributed to the famous sculptor Liu Yuan.

Temple of Great
Compassion
(Dabei Si)

Following on to the north-west is the Hall of the Dragon King where, according to legend, the "dragon king" lived. The building, also called The Monastery of the Dragon Spring (Longuan An) dates from the Qing dynasty (1644–1911).

Hall of the
Dragon King
(Longwang Tang)

The next and largest of the eight temples is the Temple of the Fragrant World originating from the Tang period (618–907) when it was called Pingpo Si. It was modernised in 1678 by Emperor Kangxi, and again in 1748 by Emperor Qianlong. At that time an imperial residence and a library for Buddhist manuscripts were founded here. In the main hall, which is flanked by the bell and drum towers, can be seen statues of Buddhas past, present and future.

Temple of the
Fragrant World
(Xiangjie Si)

The monk Haiyou supposedly lived for forty years during the Qing dynasty (1644–1911) in this cave on the peak of Cuiweishan; its name is taken from the pearl-shaped stones at the entrance to the cave.

Cave of the
Wonderous Pearl
(Baozhu Dong)

The Temple of the Cult of Buddha, dating from the Tang period (618–907), is situated on the mountain opposite; Lushishan. It was later renovated several times. In the first courtyard is a 2m/6ft high bronze bell from 1470.
   In the north of the site is the Mimo Yan rock which is shaped like a lion's

Temple of the
Cult of Buddha
(Zhengguo Si)

mouth. Next to this is the Lushi Cave (Lushi Dong), where the monk Lushi is said to have lived during the Tang period (618–907).

Further Sights in the Beijing area

★Temple of the Consecrated Altar (Jietai Si)

This temple, situated 35km/22 miles to the west of Beijing at the foot of the Ma'anshan Mountain, dates from 622. However, nearly all the buildings were reconstructed during the Qing period (1644–1911). The stone altar in the main hall was made during the Ming dynasty (1368–1644). In the 11th c. the monk Fachun lived here; his urn is kept today in one of the two pagodas on the mountain slope. South Chinese influence can be detected in the temple.

The main hall of the complex is the Daxiong Baodian, behind which stands the Pavilon of the Thousand Buddas (Qianfo Ge) with innumerable Buddha statuettes on its walls. Consecration of monks used to take place here on the three-storey white stone terrace.

The steles in front of the Mingwang Hall are among the oldest monuments in the complex; they date from the Liao period (907–1125) and the Yuan period (1271–1368). The complex owes its fame in particular to the five century-pines, which all bear their own name; the pagoda pine, the pine of the reclining dragon, the shaking pine (when a branch is touched the whole tree shakes), the obliging pine and the nine-dragon pine.

★Tanzhe Si Temple

While the Temple of the Consecrated Altar is known for its pine trees, the Tanzhe Si Temple, situated 8km/5 miles further to the west on the Tanzheshan, is known for the temple pond. The foundations of the sacred building were laid in the 3rd c., although the temple we see today did not come into being until the 14th c. The temple's name derives from the words "tan", which is taken from the word "Longtan" (dragon pond), and "zhe" which comes from "Zheshu", the trees which grow on the mountain and were once used for silkworm breeding.

The complex, which lies on a north–south axis, has its entrance in the south. Passing through the Gate of Honour (Pailou), taking the path lined with pines we reach the Mountain Gate (Shanmen). After the Hall of the Kings of Heaven (Tianwang Dian) and the sumptuous Hall of the Great Hero (Daxiong Baodian) the Vairocana Pavilion (Pilu Ge) stands at the far end of the complex's central axis; from here there is a good view of the whole area. Behind one of the halls is a 1000 year old ginkgo tree.

In the eastern part of the site are the imperial family apartments and the quarters of the head of the monastery.

A well-known spring is also situated here, together with the Pavilion of the Floating Beaker (Liubei Ting) where drinking sessions were once held.

At the north-western end of the site is the Avalokiteshvar Hall, where can be seen the stone tablet on which Kublai Khan's daughter apparently knelt every day in penance for her father's sins.

There are numerous pagodas in a courtyard outside the complex which were built after the 12th c. One of these is dedicated to Milao Yan.

★Prehistoric Village near Zhoukoudian

The prehistoric village near Zhoukoudian, situated 43km/27 miles southwest of Beijing, has attracted interest from archaeologists all over the world. Extensive finds prove that hominides settled here about 500,000 years ago. Even before this was discovered, labourers occasionally found fossils in chalk quarries on the Dragon Bone Mountain (Longgushan); they thought the finds were dragon bones, hence the mountain's name.

Peking Man

Since the first complete preserved skull of the Peking man (*Homo erectus pekinensis*) was discovered, finds of equal interest were made in subsequent years: human thigh bones, collar bones, shin bones, skull and teeth, also ashes, stones and bones showing clear signs of burning, suggesting that Peking man knew how to make fire. In all the remains of 40 humans were found. In the 1940s many of the finds disappeared under mysterious circumstances. Later the remains of skeletons and artefacts of early palaeolithic man, who lived 12,000–27,000 years ago, were also discovered in the higher part of the mountain.

Displayed in the exhibition hall are finds from the Dragon Bone Mountain and more fossils from other parts of the country. They are divided into three sections: the evolution of man, the life of the Peking man, and the role of palaeoanthropology and palaeontology in China.

See Great Wall

The Great Wall near Badaling

The tomb site, measuring about 40sq.km/25sq. miles lies in a valley of the Tianshoushan hill, almost 50km/31 miles to the north of Beijing. It is the "monumental graveyard" of the Ming dynasty, where thirteen of the sixteen dynasty's emperors are interred, together with empresses and concubines. In accordance with an old tradition, the rulers had their tombs built during their lifetime. Hence Emperor Yongle (reigned 1402–24) arranged for his tomb site to be decided upon and measured. When choosing the site soothsayers were brought in to arrange, in particular, protection from the wind and against the bad spirits coming from the north. The valley of Tianshoushan was ideal for this purpose, as it is not exposed on the west, north and east sides. Peasants living in the vicinity were forced to leave. This graveyard was used for over two hundred years (1409–1644). During this time the whole area was protected by a surrounding wall and imperial

★★Thirteen Ming Tombs
(Ming Shisanling)

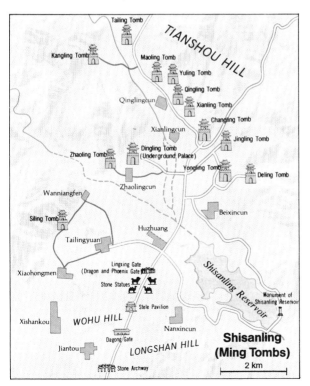

Shisanling (Ming Tombs)

2 km

Ming Mausoleum

guards. All visitors including the emperor were only allowed to enter the area on foot. A large number of labourers maintained the site.

Each funeral site has, in addition to the actual burial hill, its own sacrificial hall and stele pavilion. Until now only the Changling and Dingling tombs have been restored.

Path of Souls (Shen Dao)

The Path of Souls, leading to the imperial necropolis of Changling, can be reached through the marble Gate of Honour (Shi Paifang; erected 1540). Along the path the visitor comes upon the Great Red Gate (Dagong Den), the passage through which had doors to secure it, the middle door being only opened for the ceremonies of imperial burials. Next is the Pavilion of the Great Stele (Dabei Lou), with a 6.5m/21ft high marble stele rising from the back of a statue of a tortoise (1426). Connected to this is the Avenue of Stone Statues (1435), lined with twelve pairs of animals and six pairs of humans.

At the end of the avenue is the Dragon and Phoenix Gate (Longfeng Men) with two arches. We then pass by the Shisanling Reservoir, (constructed in the 1950s).

Changling Tomb

Further north is the Changling (open: 9am–5pm), the tomb of the third Ming Emperor Yongle (reigned: 1402–24) and Empress Xu, who died in 1407. The tomb is surrounded by a magnificent wall.

A red gate with three arches leads to the first courtyard with a stele pavilion of the Qing dynasty (1644–1911) and the Gate of Mercy (Ling'en Men) In the second courtyard is the Hall of Mercy (Ling'en Dian) with 32 sandalwood columns rising from a three-tiered terrace. In the third courtyard is a stele pavilion standing on a square based tower. The stele inside bears the inscription "Tomb of the Emperor Chengzu" (the name given to Yongle after his death). In front of the tower is an altar on which marble ritual vessels have been placed.

The Dingling tomb was erected for Emperor Wanli (reigned: 1572–1620) and his two wives – Xiaoduan (died 1620) and Xiaojing (died 1612), who was only laid to rest here after her son succeeded to the throne and raised her status to that of emperor's widow. The building of the tomb on the orders of Wanli was begun in 1584 and took six years to complete. The excavations, carried out in May 1956 disclosed an "underground palace" consisting entirely of white marble. The tomb, of very similar structure to the Changling tomb, is the only one to be opened so far.

Dingling Tomb

In the first two courtyards there remain only the terraces on which halls once stood. In the diamond wall surrounding the tomb mound is a gate which leads underground to a 1195sq.m/1429sq.yd site complex consisting of five rooms. The middle room houses three marble thrones, several altars and a large blue and white porcelain vessel containing oil, which apparently serves as an "eternal light". The tomb-chamber is the last and largest of these three rooms; this is where the emperor's coffin is kept; the empress lies to the left of the emperor and his concubine to his right.

The Gouya rocks are three steeply rising peaks, the highest of them at 1500m/1641ft. They are situated 10km/6 miles to the north-west of the Ming tombs. The majority of the 72 temples which were established in this area between the 14th and the 19th c. have unfortunately been destroyed. The area still attracts many tourists because of its natural beauty – narrow paths winding through rocks and shrubs, mountain springs, rare birds and many other attractive features.

★Gouya Rocks

The Grotto of Clouds and Waters, richly endowed with stalagmites and stalactites, is hidden on the slopes of the Shangfangshan about 50km/31 miles to the south-west of Beijing. The well-lit grotto has been open to the public since 1980.

Grotto of Clouds and Waters (Yunshui Dong)

The Temple where the Clouds Dwell consists of five courtyards with six main halls and numerous other buildings. It is situated 75km/46 miles to the south-west of Beijing. The buildings were originally constructed over 1300 years ago, but they were destroyed during the war in the 1930s and 40s, since when they have been rebuilt. In the nine grottoes to the north-east of the temple are 4195 stone tablets dating from the 7th c. to the 17th c. They are inscribed with Buddhist inscriptions. A further 10,000 tablets, also with Buddhist inscriptions, were buried in the 12th c. to the south of the temple. The 30m/98ft high pagoda to the north of this site also dates from before the 12th c.; the four smaller dagobas nearby were constructed during the Tang period (618–907).

Temple where the Clouds Dwell (Yunju Si)

15km/9½ miles to the west of the temple is one of the mooring places situated on the upper reaches of the River Juma. This area is known for its picturesque valleys and unusual rock formations; its beauty is often compared to that of Guilin.

★Mooring No. 10 (Shi Du)

In the region of Zunhua, a small city about 100km/62 miles to the east of Beijing, is an area over 125km/78 miles wide and 20km/12 miles long forming the eastern Qing necropolis. In the fourteen tombs lie five Qing emperors (1644–1911), fifteen empresses, 136 concubines and five princesses. The building of this monumental graveyard began in 1663 and took several years to complete. The mausoleums here are built underground like the ones in the Ming Necropolis, and in front of every tomb stand several memorial buildings.

★**Eastern Qing Tombs** (Qing Dongling)

Yuling is the tomb of Emperor Qianlong (reigned: 1735–96). On the walls of the "underground palace" with its four decorative gates, are Buddha reliefs with inscriptions in Sanskrit and Tibetan.

Yuling

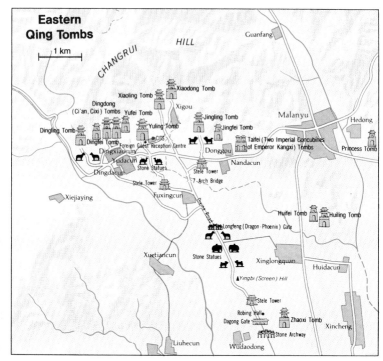

Cixi Tomb	From an architectural point of view the Cixi tomb is the most splendid. It is situated about 1km/¾ mile to the west of the Yuling tomb. The decorative patterning on the ceiling, beams and columns in the hall is completely covered with gold-leaf.

Worth seeing is the high-relief on the enormous stone tablet which takes up the whole middle section of the steps leading up to the main hall of the mausoleum; at the top is a portrayal of a phoenix to symbolise the empress, and at the bottom is a dragon to symbolise the emperor. This representation suggests that the empress is of far greater importance than any emperor.

★Western Qing Tombs (Qing Xi Ling)

The western Qing necropolis, almost 500,000sq.m/598,000sq.yd in size and thus smaller than the eastern necropolis, lies 120km/74 miles to the south-west of Beijing. Buried in the fourteen tombs are four emperors, and 72 members of the family including wives, concubines, sons and daughters. The reason for laying out of two dynastic tomb sites was that the emperor Qianlong made a law which meant that fathers and sons could not be buried in the same graveyard.

Mausoleums

The fourteen mausoleums and the temple buildings belonging to them reflect the strict rules of the feudal hierarchy. The tombs of the emperors and empresses are larger than those of the concubines and princesses; the former have red roofs and the latter have green roofs.

Canton · Guangzhou

广州市

Chinese
equivalent

Capital of Guangdong Province
Altitude 5m/16ft. Area: 1345sq.km/519sq. miles
Population: 3,220,000 (conurbation 5,870,000)

Canton lies in a fertile plain in the centre of the south Chinese province of
Guangdong, in the delta of the Zhujiang, at 113°14'E and 23°12'N.
   Canton can be reached from Hong Kong by air, rail, ferry or bus and from
Beijing by rail or air. There are also regular flights to various other Chinese
cities such as Shanghai (2½hrs), Tianjin (3hrs), Shijiazhuang, Wuhan,
Changzhou, Qinhuangdao and Hohhot.

Situation and
Communications

Canton is not only an economic, but also a cultural centre. The Sun-Yat-sen
University (Zhongshan Daxue) has an importance extending well beyond
the immediate area of Canton, while in the city's opera houses the Chinese
opera tradition continues to be nurtured.
   Cantonese cooking, in which seafood plays a crucial part, is also famous.

Importance

An important Cantonese legend tells the story of how five gods came down
to earth on goats and gave the inhabitants five ears of corn in order to
protect them from famine.
   The city of Canton, which was originally called Fanyu, has a history
dating back over 2000 years. In 214 B.C. Emperor Qin Shi Huangdi nomi-
nated it capital of the administrative area of Nanhai (Southern Sea) in
recognition of its growing importance as a river and sea port. In A.D. 226 it
was renamed Guangzhou. From the time of the Tang dynasty (618–907)
onwards Canton developed into a centre of foreign trade and as a result a
large Islamic community grew up here. Under the Song dynasty (960–
1279) the city enjoyed a golden period. In 1517 the Portuguese landed here,
followed by the Spanish, Dutch, British and French. Over the years the
harbour became larger and larger and in 1684 the East India Company
moved its headquarters here in order to be able to have better control of its
trade in the opium which it was bringing over from India. In 1839 the
Imperial High Commissioner Lin Zexu had 1185 tons of opium destroyed in
Humen, a small village near Canton, and in so doing triggered off the
opium wars between Britain and China. In 1841 the city offered stubborn
resistance to the attacking English troops, with the peasants of Sanyuanli
(today a suburb of Canton) particularly distinguishing themselves. In the
Treaty of Nanking (1842) the city was forced to open its doors to foreign
trade and in 1858 the island of Shamian became a foreign concessionary
area. This contact with foreigners was destined to imbue the Cantonese
from very early on with nationalistic sentiments, a readiness for reform and
revolutionary ideas. At the beginning of the 20th c. Sun Yat-sen started
numerous uprisings against the Qing government.
   In 1918 the city began to be modernised, with wide streets being laid out,
countless shacks torn down, canals filled in and the city walls taken down.
The year 1924 saw the founding of the Whampoa military academy where
Zhou Enlai studied. In the period following, Zhou, Guo Moruo and Mao
Zedong taught at the local institute of the peasants' movement. After the
rupture in relations between the Communists and the Guomindang, more
than 5000 of the former lost their lives at the hands of Guomindang troops
during a workers' revolt in 1927. In 1949 Canton fell to the Communist
regime.
   In the 1950s Canton became an important centre for industry (steel,
chemicals, textiles and foodstuffs) and foreign trade, a development which
was helped by its proximity to Hong Kong. Since 1957 the famous Canton
Fair has taken place twice a year.

History

Buddha statues in the Temple of the Six Banyan Trees

Sights

★Temple of the Six Banyan Trees (Liurong Si)

The temple site, situated in Chaoyang Beilu Street in the old part of the city, was built in A.D. 537 on the orders of the provincial governor of the time, Xiao Yu, in order to house one of Buddha's bones. It is named after the six banyan trees which formerly stood in the courtyard and to which the poet Su Dongpo dedicated a piece of writing.

Hall of the Sixth Patriarch (Liuzu Tang)

In the Hall of the Sixth Patriarch the visitor is able to admire a bronze statue of the monk Huineng, the founder of the Southern School of Chan (Zen) Buddhism. The statue was cast in the Song period (960–1279).

Floral Pagoda

The original floral pagoda, dating from 537, burned down in the 10th c. and was reconstructed in its present form in 1097 from a drawing of the original building. During the restoration work of 1980 some tiles were discovered with inscriptions which probably date from the Song era. The top of the 57m/187ft high pagoda, which can ascended by a flight of steps, is crowned by a richly decorated bronze column weighing 5 tonnes.

Hall of the Goddess of Mercy (Guanxin Dian)

The Hall of the Goddess of Mercy dates from 1663. Inside it a 4m/13ft high 5 tonne bronze sculpture is housed. It represents Guanyin, the Chinese goddess of love.

★Temple of Light and Children's Love (Guangxiao Si)

The Temple of Light and Children's Love, one of the oldest buildings in the city, is only a short distance from the Temple of the Six Banyan Trees. In the 1st c. B.C. Zhao Jiande, the king of the state of Nanyue, lived here. Under the Western Jin dynasty (265–316) the royal residence was turned into a temple. After that the building was chiefly inhabited by Indian monks who came to China in order to disseminate Buddhism. In 1151 the building

River Zhujiang in Canton ▶

received its present name. Of the original 30 temples and palaces only about ten have survived.

Iron Pagodas   The two iron pagodas on either side of the main temple are worth inspecting closely, as they are thought to be the oldest of their kind in China.

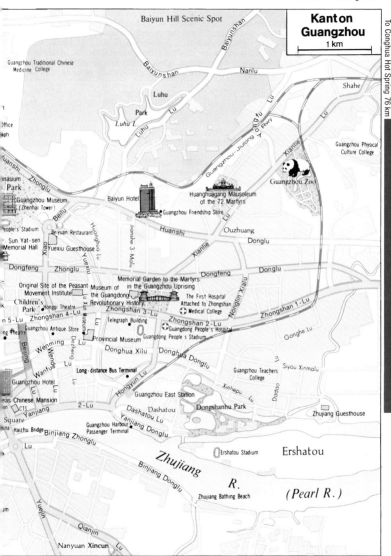

The Eastern Iron Pagoda (Dongtie Ta) dates from 967 and is decorated with over 900 niches with statuettes of Buddha.

The Western Iron Pagoda (Xitie Ta), dating from 963, only retains three "storeys".

Canton · Guangzhou

★Mosque in Memory of the Wise Man (Huaisheng Si)

The Mosque in Memory of the Wise Man, situated in the city centre 300m/330yd south of the Temple of the Six Banyan Trees, is one of the oldest mosques in China. It is supposed to have been built by an Arab in 627 in honour of Mohammed. It is also known as the Lighthouse Mosque (Guangta Si) because its 36m/118ft high minaret is fitted with lighting equipment and in the past was actually used as a lighthouse. Today this house of prayer is the centre of the city's Muslim community.

Ancestral Temple of the Chen Family (Chenjia Ci)

Between 1890 and 1894 the great ancestral temple of the Chen family was built in Zhongshan Lu. It is famous for its wood carvings and sculptures, of which particular mention should be made of the figures on the roof ridges which adopt themes from mythology and classical literature.

Today the temple houses the Folklore Museum, in which arts and crafts from Canton and Guangdong are displayed.

★Yuexiu Gongyuan Park

Yuexiu Gongyuan Park (928,000sq.m/229 acres) is situated at the foot of the hill of the same name in the north of the city. It contains several ponds, a hall of flowers, an orchid garden, a sports complex and an open-air cinema.

The Building Overlooking the Sea (Zhenhai Lou)

On the hill stands a five-storey 28m/92ft high palace, the "Building Overlooking the Sea". It was constructed in 1380 and in 1686 was converted into a watch-tower to guard against pirate attacks.

Today the building is the seat of the Historical Museum of Guangzhou. On the individual storeys there are exhibits on display from the various epochs of Chinese history, while on the top storey there is information available on the Communist movement in Canton.

Sun-Yat-sen Memorial Hall (Zhongshang Jiniantang)

The 49m/161ft high Memorial Hall is located at the south end of Yuexiu Gongyuan Park and is dedicated to the memory of Sun-Yat-sen (see Famous People), who was the first president of the Chinese Republic, which was founded in 1911. This imposing building was erected in 1931 in

Canton: in Yuexiu-Gongyuan Park

the classical Chinese style. The hall, which is used for cultural events, has space for more than 4000 people.

In the gardens in front of the hall can be seen a bronze statue of Sun-Yat-sen while to the west lies a small museum which keeps the politician's memory alive.

The Tomb of the 72 Martyrs on the Hill of the Yellow Flowers commemorates those who lost their lives during the uprising led by Sun-Yat-sen against the Qing government on April 27th 1911. The tomb is situated on the Xianlie Lu, about 3km/2 miles east of Yuexiu Gongyuan Park. It was erected in 1918 and is surrounded by a park. On the arch at the southern entrance are to be found Sun-Yat-sen's words "Eternal Glory". The park also contains an obelisk, pavilion and pyramid-shaped building, the upper section of which consists of 72 stone slabs representing the 72 martyrs.

★Tomb of the 72 Martyrs on the Hill of the Yellow Flowers (Huanghuagang Qishi'er Lieshimu)

A little further to the north-east of the Tomb of the 72 Martyrs on the Hill of the Yellow Flowers lies the Zoo, one of the largest in China. The pandas are especially popular.

Zoo

About 4km/2½ miles east of the city centre, on Zhongshan Lu, a 26ha/ 64 acre cemetery was laid out in 1957 for the victims of the Canton uprising which was led by the Communist party in 1927. The 5700 people shot by the Guomindang government are now buried in a tumulus. In addition the memorial park also contains a pavilion (1957) dedicated to Sino-Soviet friendship and one (1964) to Sino-Korean friendship. These are intended as a reminder that Russians and Koreans also lost their lives in the uprising. In the western section of the park stands the Museum of the Revolutionary History of Guangdong.

Memorial Park to the Martyrs of the Canton Uprising (Lieshi Lingyuan)

Sun-Yat-sen Commemorative Hall

Canton · Guangzhou

The College of the Peasants' Movement (Nongmin Yundong Jiangxisuo)

The College of the Peasants' Movement is to be found to the west of the Memorial for the Martyrs of the Canton Uprising. It was founded jointly by the Communist Party and the Guomindang in July 1924 in a former Confucian temple.

This college, in which the cadre of the Communist Party are educated, was from 1926 under the direction of Mao Zedong and its teachers included Zhou Enlai. Mao's office, a large hall, library, refectory and students' dormitory can all be visited.

★Cathedral of the Sacred Heart (Shengxin Dajiaotang)

The 58m/190ft high Cathedral of the Sacred Heart in Yide Lu Street is the largest Christian church in China. The French architect Guillemin built it between 1863 and 1888 in Neo-Gothic style.

Culture Park (Wenhua Gongyuan)

The 8ha/20 acre Culture Park in the south of the city offers a wide range of entertainments, including exhibition halls, an open-air stage and an opera and concert hall.

★Qingping Market

At the market, consisting of two intersecting covered streets extending along Qingping Lu, there are all kinds of food on sale (fruit, vegetables, fish, snakes, turtles and poultry), animals of every type (dogs, cats, monkeys, etc.), herbs, earthenware and porcelain.

Shamian Island

Shamian Island is 900m/1000yd long and 300m/330yd wide and lies in the south-west of the city, linked with the north bank of the Zhujiang by several bridges. Under Ming rule (1368–1644) the island was used as a harbour.

During the Opium Wars it was vigorously defended by the city leaders because of its strategic position, but in 1861 it was conceded to England and France. The foreign powers erected their consulates here, as well as villas, banks, churches and even a tennis court and sailing club. The Chinese needed special permission to be able to set foot on the island.

It is only since 1949 that Shamian has once again been under Chinese administration. Today some of the larger consulates are still located here.

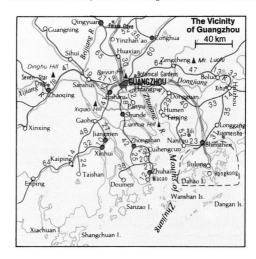

Surroundings

To the north-east of the city rises the mountain range of the White Clouds with more than thirty peaks, the highest of which, The Peak Which Touches the Stars (Moxing Ling), reaches a height of 382m/1253ft. Of the many picturesque places to be found in the mountains, mention should be made of the 2000-year-old Nine Dragons Spring (Jiulong Quan), the tomb of Zhang Erqiao, a famous singer of the Ming period, and the Villa of the Waves in the Sea of Pines (Songtao Bieyuan).

★Mountains of the White Clouds (Baiyunshan)

The Conghua Wenquan thermal springs are to be found in the spa resort of the same name, 80km/50 miles north-east of Canton. The spa comprises a dozen calcium, magnesium and natrium springs, as well as several thermal baths, extending over an area of some 10sq.km/4sq.miles. The water temperatures range from 50° to 70°C (122°–158°F). The resort also has a large number of sanatoria, hotels and boarding houses.

★Conghua Thermal Springs (Conghua Wenquan)

The house in which Sun-Yat-sen (see Famous People) was born in 1866 is situated in the village of Cuiheng (Zhongshan district), about 100km/62 miles south of Canton. It still has the original furniture. In a neighbouring building there is a museum commemorating the founder of the first Chinese republic.

★Birthplace of Sun Yat-sen (Zhongshan Guju)

Changchun

M 3

Chinese equivalent

Capital of Jilin Province
Altitude: 200m/656ft. Area: 1116sq.km/430sq. miles
Population: 1,810,000 (conurbation 5,960,000)

Changchun lies on the banks of the Yitonghe river, at 125°19′E and 43°52′N. There are rail and air links with Beijing.

Situation and Communications

Changchun ("Eternal Spring") is known as "Automobile City" (Volkswagen), because the first Chinese motor car factory was founded here in 1953. Its universities and research institutes also play an important role, as do its film studios.

Importance

Changchun is still a relatively young town, having been founded in the 18th c. Following the construction of the Chinese rail network in the first half of the 20th c. it developed into a focal point for traffic in Inner Mongolia and to North Korea. Between 1933 and 1945 Changchun, as the capital of the Japanese-controlled state, was named Mandchukuo Xinjing ("New Capital"). Puyi, the last of the Qing emperors, was crowned state emperor here in 1934.

History

Sights

The Provincial Museum is housed in the former Imperial Palace (Weiman Huanggong) in the north-east of the town. This magnificent edifice covers an area of 43,000sq.m/47,000sq.yd. The various buildings form two complexes: the inner one served as Puyi's private residence, while the outer was used for official purposes only.

★**Provincial Museum**
(Sheng Bowuguan)

The following sections of the palace are of special historical interest: the Palace of Study and Kindness (Jixu Lou), where the Emperor's bedchamber, study, bathroom and prayer-hall are well preserved; the Palace of Diligence and Love of the People (Qingmin Lou), in which Puyi was crowned ruler of the state of Manchuria; the Palace of Longing for Distant Lands (Huaiyuan Lou), used for banqueting, and finally the Hall of Common Virtue (Tongde Dian), where the Emperor received his relatives.

Palace buildings

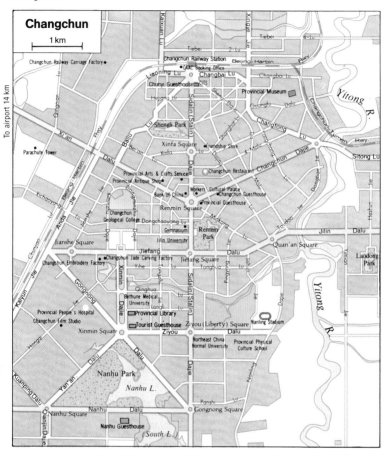

Changchun

1 km

To airport 14 km

Several departments of the present museum house permanent or temporary exhibitions; items on display include provincial archaeological finds, old paintings and calligraphic documents.

Film town

Changchun's well-known film studios lie on Hongqi Jie. Here visitors can see reproductions of streets, shops and other Beijing buildings. Genuine and fake jewellery, furniture and clothing of all kinds are housed in the props store. In the special effects hall visitors are shown some of the tricks employed in filming.

Surroundings

★ **Ruins of Gaojuli**
(Gaojuli Yizhi)

The Ruins of Gaojuli are to be found some 300km/190 miles south of Changchun, near the Korean border. Gaojuli is the name of an ancient kingdom which was founded in 108 B.C. and destroyed in 427 B.C. Today only a few remains bear witness to its existence.

Guoneicheng, the kingdom's capital, was built near the present-day Ji'an, on the west bank of the Yalu river. Its well-preserved defensive walls have a circumference of 2713m/2984yd. Square in plan, the town was also protected by a 10m/11yd wide moat on its east, south and north sides, while the west was bordered by the Donggou river.

Close to the ruins can be seen some ten thousand graves dating from the same period; made of stone or clay, the sepulchres have survived the ravages of time remarkably well. The interior walls are frequently decorated with some wonderful frescos.

Because of its conical shape the tomb of General Zhu Meng is also described as the "Pyramid of the East". The seven-storey edifice is 12m/40ft high and has a circumference of 32m/105ft. As the result of plundering through the centuries nothing now remains of its interior furnishings.

Tomb of
General Zhu Meng
(Jiangjun Mu)

Changjiang · Yangtse River

F 5–L 5

The Changjiang (Yangste) river is over 6000km/3700 miles long, making it the longest and most important river in China and the third longest in the world, after the Amazon and the Nile. It flows from west to east through eight provinces and divides China into northern and southern halves.

For over 2000 years the Changjiang has been China's major transportation route; about 2700km/1680 miles are navigable. At one time it could be crossed only by ferry, but now there are bridges at Chongqing, Wuhan and Nanjing. Its catchment area, with 700 tributaries, covers some 1,800,000sq.km/695,000sq.miles or about one-fifth of the total area of the country, and the average annual volume of water carried is 1,050 billion

Importance

One of the three gorges of the Changjiang (Yangtse)

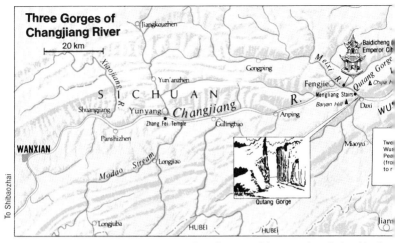

Three Gorges of Changjiang River

cu.m or 230,000 billion gallons. A quarter of the country's agricultural land lies within the vicinity of the river.

Course of the river

The Changjiang rises 5600m/18,380ft up at Geladandong in Tanggulashan in the eastern highlands of Tibet, initially flows east and then turns south to form the border between Tibet and the province of Sichuan. It then zig-zags its way through North Yunnan and continues north-east, forming the border between Sichuan and Yunnan. Where it enters Sichuan near Yibin the river (navigable from here on) flows north-east and then east through Central China to the East China Sea. The delta, 350km/220 miles long and 80km/50 miles wide, begins near Nanjing. Near Shanghai the two arms of the Changjiang enter the sea. The Grand Canal forms a link between the north-east and south of China.

Floods

The low and high water levels of the Changjiang vary according to the season by as much as 80m/260ft; in its lower reaches this variance can be twice as much as that of the Mississipi.

Regular flooding of the river causes much devastation. For example, the flood of 1981 in the province of Sichuan resulted in 920 deaths and 28,000 injuries; 1,500,000 people were rendered homeless.

A major cause of this flooding was the destruction of forests along the upper reaches of the river to provide more land for the growing of cereal crops. Attempts are now being made to solve the problem by means of re-afforestation programmes.

Sanxia Dam

Under construction on the Changjiang near Yichang is the huge and ecologically controversial Sanxia Dam, 2km/1¼ miles long and almost 200m/650ft high, with the generating capacity of 16 nuclear power stations. As well as supplying electricity the dam will provide water for irrigation and enhance flood protection. To build the dam 1.2 million people had to be resettled. The picturesque Three Gorges, which attract hundreds of thousands of visitors each year, will be filled with water.

★Three Gorges of Changjiang River (Changjiang Sanxia)

Scenically the most beautiful section of the Changjiang is the 200km/ 125 mile stretch between Fengjie, a small town 260km/160 miles east of Chongqing, and Yichang in the province of Hubei. This stretch has been made navigable with the aid of blasting operations to remove shallows and by marking out shipping channels.

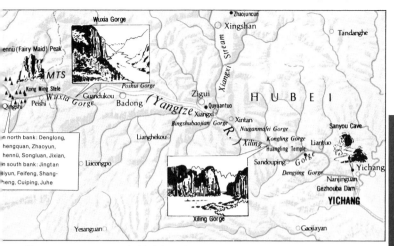

From west to east, one behind the other, lie the three famous and picturesque gorges known as Qutang, Wu and Xiling, forming what has been described as "the most entrancing scenery in the world".

At a number of places the river, a mixture of raging torrents and dangerous shallows, winds its way through the gorges which are lined with rugged cliffs and high mountain peaks. There are many places of interest to tourists.

A sight-seeing tour of the Three Gorges and the historical and cultural monuments can be made only by boat. As a rule the excursion will commence in Chongqing and pass through Changzhou, Fuling, Fengdu, Zhongxian and Wanxian to Yichang.

Between Zhongxian and Wanxian lies the fortified "treasury" built into the rock face and known as the "Pearl of the River". It is 56m/184ft high, making it the highest building of its kind in China. Constructed by Emperor Yongyan c. 1800, it is made up of three parts, the entrance, a twelve-storey edifice and a temple. Inside stand a statue of the Buddha and a stela (upright slab) inscribed with a description of how the temple was built. Legend has it that at one time rice would fall every day from a small hole in the rock and thus provide food for the monks. It was this "treasure" found in the rock that gave the temple its name. When some monks tried to enlarge the hole the rice stopped flowing. *(Treasury in Stone (Shi Bao Zhai))*

On the opposite bank from the town of Yunyang stands the Temple of Zhang Fei Miao, dating from the Northern Song period (960–1127). It was erected in memory of General Zhang Fei, who is said to have been murdered here by mutinous army officers in the year 220. *(Zhang Fei Miao)*

In the Qutang Xia Gorge, where the Changjiang is at its narrowest, the banks reach a height of between 500 and 700m/1650 and 2300ft and the mountains as much as 1000 to 1400m/3300 to 4600ft. The narrowest spot, known as the "place of the monk with his head hanging down", is only 100m/110yd wide. *(Qutang Xia Gorge)*

The gorge is 4km/2½ miles from Fennggjie and is about 8km/5 miles long. At its entrance the ruins of the City of the White Emperor can be seen on the north bank of the Changjiang. It was given this name in A.D. 25 when – according to legend – Gongsun Shu, the founder of the town, saw a white mist rise up out of the Bailon (White Dragon) spring, and thereupon named himself the White Emperor.

Close by stands a temple with the same name (Baidi Si), dating originally from the late 7th c. It is famous mainly for its 70 or more stelae (inscribed pillars) from the Sui period (581–618) and the statues in the main hall (Mingliang Dian) of Liu Bei, Zhuge Liang, Guan Yu and Zhang Fei, who lived in the time of the Three Kingdoms (220–280). Shortly before his death Liu Bei, ruler of the state of Shu, named his chancellor Zhuge Liang as his successor. The temple was built as a memorial to this act of confidence and trust. Guan Yu and Zhang Fei were famous generals who served with glory under Liu Bei.

Near the Fengxiang Xia the visitor should note the wooden coffins protruding from a rock. In ancient times the inhabitants of Sichuan used to safeguard the coffins of their deceased relatives by placing them in natural crevices or hollows in the rock or on massive wooden beams anchored in stone.

Witches' Gorge
(Wu Xia)

The Wu Xia Gorge is 40km/25 miles long in all; the western part belongs to the province of Sichuan, while the eastern section is in Hubei province. Because of the twelve mountain peaks along its bank – the highest being Fairy Mountain (912m/2994ft), dedicated to Yao Ji – and the superb panoramic views, this is regarded as the most beautiful of the three gorges.

Three Little
Gorges

At the western end of Witches' Gorge, near Wushan, the Daninghe river joins the Changjiang. From here visitors can make excursions to the Three Little Gorges (Longmen, Bawu and Dicui), which total 50km/30 miles in length.

Ancient coffins can be seen from the river in Bawu Gorge; these are stored some 500m/1650ft up in caves in the steep cliffs along the east bank.

In Dicui Gorge, with its lush vegetation of bamboos and trees, there is an imposing waterfall. A "boat coffin", an example of an old burial custom, is housed in a hollow in the steep mountain face.

Fairy Peak
(Shennü Feng)

On Fairy Mountain there stands a 7m/23ft high stone pillar in the shape of a woman, which is known as Fairy Peak. According to legend Yi, daughter of the Mother of Heaven Xi Wangmu, helped Da Yu, the ruler of the Chu kingdom, to prevent the river from flooding so frequently. Love blossomed between them, and Yi stayed one night with him in the Gaotang temple, of which now only a few ruins remain. At the northern foot of Fairy Mountain, on a flat rocky ledge known as the Shoushu Tai terrace, she is said to have given Da Yu instructions on how to tame the river.

Zhuge-Liang Stele
(Kong Ming Bei)

Near Fairy Peak lie the Peak of Pines (Songluan Feng) and Peak of the Immortals (Jixian Feng). On a steep mountain face below the latter stands a stele inscribed in a beautiful calligraphic hand with the words "Chong Ya Die Zhang Wu Xia" ("Wu Xia with rocky faces one above the other and mountains one behind the other"). Legend has it that this inscription was the work of Zhuge Liang (also known as Kong Ming), the strategist and chancellor of the state of Chu during the period of the Three Kingdoms (220–280).

Xiling Xia
Gorge

Xiling Xia Gorge, 450km/280 miles east of Chongqing in Hubei province, is nearly 80km/50 miles long, making it the longest of the three gorges. It has some dangerous shallows, heavy rapids and numerous reefs. Its bank are strewn with countless rock formations with the strangest of names – these include the Gorge of Military Writings and The Sword (Bingshu Baiojian Xia), where can be seen a rock protruding from the ground like a sword (General Zhuge Liang is said to have hidden here a textbook he had written when he was unable to find a suitable successor), the Gorge of Ox Livers and Horses' Tongues (Niuganmafei Xia) and the Gorge of the Yellow Cow (Huangniu Xia). At the bottom of the latter stands a temple with the same name, which dated originally from the Han period (206 B.C. to A.D. 220) and was rebuilt in 1618.

On the north bank, about 50km/30 miles east of the exit from the gorge, lies the little town of Xiangxi (Fragrant River), named after the river which flows by it. A legend has grown up around this picturesque name: more than 2000 years ago Wang Zhaojun lived here; she was a beautiful woman who washed her garments in the river and thus in the course of time gave the waters a lovely fragrance.

Xiangxi

Changsha

长沙市

Chinese equivalent

Capital of Hunan Province
Altitude: 44m/145ft. Area: 117sq.km/45sq. miles
Population: 859,000 (conurbation 1,070,000)

Changsha lies on the banks of the Xiangjiang, a large tributary of the Changjiang, in a fertile agricultural region in the north-east of Hunan province, at 112°58′E and 28°12′N. The town is served by the Beijing–Canton railway and by a small airport.

Situation and Communications

Changsha can look back on two thousand years of history. In the Spring and Autumn periods and the period of the Warring Kingdoms (771–221 B.C.) it was known as Qinyang because of the amount and quality of handwork and artistic goods it produced (textiles, metallurgy, lacquer-work). It was given its present name in the Qin period (221–206 B.C.), when it was one of the most important towns in China. Under the Song dynasty (960–1279) Changsha became an educational centre. The town walls, parts of which still stand, were built at the beginning of the Ming period (1368–1644). In 1664 the Qing rulers elevated it to the status of provincial capital of Hunan. In 1904, under pressure from western powers, the town was opened up to foreigners, and Europeans and Americans subsequently settled here. Mao Zedong (Tse-tung) lived in the town from 1911 to 1923; he studied and taught at the College of Education. In the Sino-Japanese war of 1937–45 a large part of Changsha was destroyed and reconstruction did not commence until after the founding of the People's Republic in 1949. Helped by its position on the Xiangjiang, the town developed as a commercial centre; its harbour is now the largest on the river. Today it is also a financial and industrial centre, with light industry predominating.

History

Map see p. 175

The early history of the Communist Party Committee of the province is portrayed in the Qingshuitang, which gets its name from a pond which once lay behind the house. The conference rooms and Mao Zedong's residential quarters can be seen.

Sights
Pond of the Clear Water (Qingshuitang)

Martyr Park (Lieshi Gongyuan) with its memorial pagoda was laid out in 1955 in memory of those who died in the liberation struggle. There is an exhibition hall in the base of the 38m/125ft high pagoda.

Memorial Pagoda to the Martyrs (Leisha Jinianta)

The Provincial Museum lies in the north-east of the town on the bank of Lake Nianjia. Various archaeological finds are displayed in a total of 10,000sq.m/11,000sq.yd of floor space. The exhibits include bronze articles from the Shang era (16th–11th c. B.C.) and painted objects from the period of the Warring Kingdoms (475–221 B.C.). There are also finds from the Mawangdui burial site (see below) dating from the Western Han dynasty (206 B.C. to A.D. 24); these include the mummy of a lady of noble birth (to house which the museum was specially built), which has been painstakingly preserved in its entirety, and the magnificent coffin and gravegoods which accompany it. The corpse is wrapped in about twenty layers of silk and linen sheets. The transmigratory banner placed in an inner coffin

★Provincial Museum (Hunansheng Bowuguan)

is in the form of a T-shaped silken picture displaying outstanding artistic skill and radiant colours and is one of the earliest examples of Chinese silk-painting. It portrays the journey of the deceased into the hereafter and also shows mythological creatures.

★Pavilion of the Heart of Heaven (Tianxin Ge)

The Pavilion of the Heart of Heaven stands above the south-eastern section of the town walls of Changsha. Its date of origin is uncertain; all that is known is that it was restored in 1759. In the 1950s a public park was laid out around the Pavilion.

Hunan College of Education No. 1 (Hunan Diyi Shifan Xuexiao)

The college in the south of the town was burned down in 1938 and faithfully rebuilt after 1949. It was here that Mao Zedong (Tse-tung) studied (1913–18) and taught (1920–21). During that time he organised a student union and evening classes for the workers, as well as founding a Marxist study group. Photos, manuscripts and books in the college document his political career.

★Island of Oranges (Juzi Zhou)

The Island of Oranges – so named after the large numbers of orange trees growing here – is a narrow strip of sand 5km/3 miles long in the middle of the Xiangjiang river. The southern end of the island has been made into a public park. Here the visitor will find a pretty pavilion and a stone tablet on which is engraved a poem about the town written by Mao Zedong. From the southern end of the island there is a particularly good view of the river.

★Yuelushan Hill

Yuelushan Hill, to the west of the Old Town on the west bank of the Xiangjiang, is 297m/975ft high and scenically charming. Historically interesting monuments are scattered over its slopes.

The Yuelu Academy (Yuelu Shuyuan) stands at the eastern foot of the hill; since 1925 it has been the site of the University of Hunan.

Mao's birthplace in Shaoshan (see page 176)

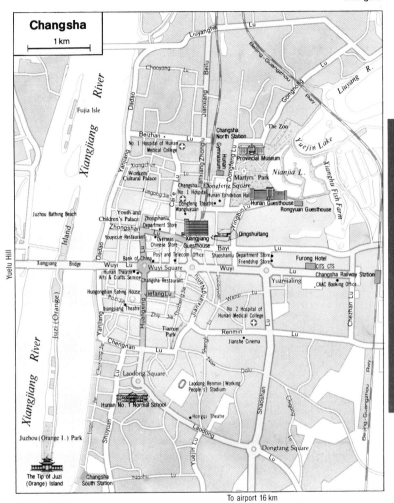

In the evening there is an impressive view to be had from the Pavilion for the Enjoyment of Twilight (Aiwan Ting), which was built in 1792 and restored in 1952. The inscribed pillar (Yuwang Bei) standing on the top of the hill dates from 1212 and describes the struggles of the mythical Emperor Yu against the flooding river.

Lushan-Si Temple, built in 268, is one of the oldest Buddhist sanctuaries in the province. The main doorway and the Cangling Ge pavilion can still be seen.

Close by stands a valuable stone tablet inscribed by the famous calligraphist Li Yong (678–747), which uses more than 1400 characters in describing how the temple was built.

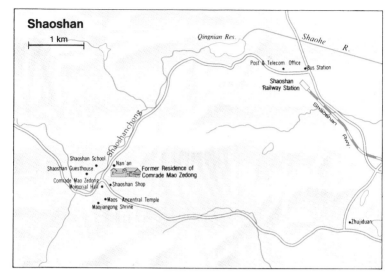

★ Temple of the Beginning of Blissful Happiness (Kaifu Si)

This temple in Kaifu Si Street was erected in 907. After repeated acts of destruction over the centuries the major buildings have now been restored. The complex includes the Halls of Sansheng Dian and Pilu Dian, as well as the Hall of the Great Buddha (Daxiong Badian) which was rebuilt in 1923. The temple houses two inscribed stone tablets dating from the 17th and 19th c.

Surroundings

★★ Han Graves in Mawangdui (Mawangdui Hanmu)

The three Han Graves, 4km/2½ miles north-east of the town, came to light during excavations carried out between 1972 and 1974. They belonged to a noble family who lived at the beginning of the Western Han dynasty (206–24 B.C.).

The first tomb, that of the wife of Prince Li Cang, held a completely preserved mummy together with rich grave-goods which are now housed in the provincial museum in Changsha; these included inscriptions and paintings on silk, books written on bamboo leaves, lacquered objects and silken textiles. The other two graves were for the Prince and his son.

★ The house where Mao Zedong was born (Mao Zedong Guju) in Shaoshan

The house where Mao Zedong (Tse-tung) was born in 1893, the son of a well-to-do farmer, and where he lived until 1910, stands in the village of Shaoshan, 100km/60 miles from Changsha. In 1912 Mao moved to Changsha in order to attend the college there.

Built in typical Hunan style, the house was made into a museum in 1964. On display are personal items owned by the young Mao together with photos from his revolutionary period.

Changzhou

K 5

常州市

Province: Jiangsu
Area: 94sq.km/36sq. miles. Population: 500,000

Changzhou lies on the Nanjing–Shanghai rail route, at 119°57'E and 31°42'N.

It is two hours by air from Beijing or Canton.

The town has been in existence for more than 2500 years. Thanks to its situation on the Grand Canal – the extremely important transportation and trade route which was first constructed in the 5th c. B.C. and has been extended several times since – Changzhou has enjoyed periods of rapid and thriving expansion.

Today it is one of the major industrial towns in Jiangsu province, especially in the spheres of food production, textiles and machinery.

The Temple of Heavenly Peace situated in the Old Town and known as the Monastery of Great Rapture (Guangfu Si) until the year 1111, was built in 901–04. This colossal building complex, which consists of eight temples, 25 palaces and some 500 houses, was once the most important Buddhist monastery in the whole of south-east China. Unfortunately only 500 bas-reliefs and an equal number of arhats have been preserved. The present buildings were rebuilt during the Qing dynasty (1644–1911).

Every sixty years the "Great Buddhist Tonsure" (Chuanjie Dafahui) is celebrated. The last celebrations were held in 1990.

In the centre, in Plum Tree Park, stands the Hongmei Ge Pavilion, built in 1008–16. This two-storey building, 17m/56ft tall, was rebuilt in 1295 after the original had been destroyed by arsonists.

The park is known in particular for the red blossom on the plum trees in March and April.

This garden, landscaped in the Ming style and the only one of its kind in the whole of southern China, was laid out in the Qing period, between 1688 and 1672.

The Imperial Canal in Changzhou

Chengde

Chinese
equivalent

Province: Hebei
Altitude: 46m/151ft. Area: 622sq.km/240sq. miles
Population: 208,000 (conurbation Chengde 302,000)

Chengde lies 250km/155 miles north-east of Beijing in the north-east of Hebei province at 117°54′E and 40°58′N. It is reached from Beijing either by rail or by road.

Situation and
Communications

In the 16th c. Chengde (formerly known as Jehol) was still just a small village. In the early 18th c. the Jiangxi Emperor Xuangye built a summer residence here. Over the years the town gained in importance until finally it became the second seat of the Manchurian government.

History

   Today Chengde is a commercial centre in the north of Hebei province.

Sights

This mountain palace, used by the imperial court as a summer retreat, lies in a valley surrounded by high mountains to the north of the town. Its construction commenced in 1703 under the Jiangxi Emperor Xuangye, but it was not completed until 1790. The Qianlong Emperor Hongli extended it with buildings in various national styles. When the Jiaqing Emperor was struck down by lightning near the palace in 1820 the court regarded this as a bad omen and left the palace never to return. The residence comprises over 110 buildings, covers an area of 560ha/1400 acres and is surrounded by a wall 10km/6¼ miles long. The complex reveals both north and south Chinese building styles and is divided into two sections – the palace area and the landscaped gardens.

**Imperial
Summer Villa**
(Bishu
Shanzhuang)

   Visitors enter the relatively small palace area through the Gateway of Beauty (Lizheng Men), which has three entrance passages, a large central one which was reserved for the Emperor and two smaller ones at the side. The following buildings make up the whole complex: the Main Hall (Zheng Gong), decorated with rich carvings in the finest nanmu wood, where the Emperor received his ministers, generals, representatives of national minorities and diplomatic envoys; the Palace of Foaming Waves (Qing Gong) which contained the Emperor's bed-chamber; The Hall of Pine and Cranes (Songhe Zhai), where the mothers and some of the Emperor's concubines lived; the Hall of The Sighing Pines and Ten Thousand Valleys, which the Emperor used for study and rest.

   The parkland behind the palace covers a large part of the whole complex and is itself divided into three parts – the lake area, which boasts various kinds of summer-houses, pavilions and stone bridges, the hilly part and the flat gardens.

   Its most picturesque and attractive features are the artificially laid-out south Chinese private gardens, in imitation of the grass steppes of Mongolia and the mountains north of the Blue River. At the south end of the lake area a stone bridge with three small Shuixin pavilions spans the Silver Lake and the Lower Lake, and in the northern part stands the House of Mists and Rain (Yanyu Lou), from where the Emperor enjoyed a view of the mountains on rainy days.

   To the north-west will be found Wenjin Ge, built in 1774 and one of the seven libraries of the Qianlong Emperor. Among the well-known works

◄ *Pagoda of the Six Banyan Trees in Changzhou*

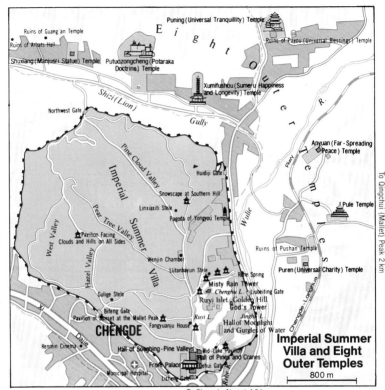

The following labels appear on the map:

Puning (Universal Tranquillity) Temple
Ruins of Guang'an Temple
Ruins of Arhats Hall
Ruins of Puyou (Universal Blessings) Temple
Shuxiang (Manjusri Statue) Temple
Putuozongcheng (Potaraka Doctrine) Temple
Xumifushou (Sumeru Happiness and Longevity) Temple
Shizi (Lion)
Northwest Gate
Gully
Anyuan (Far-Spreading Peace) Temple
Pine Cloud Valley
Huidiji Gate
Snowscape at Southern Hill
Linxiaxiti Stele
Pule Temple
Pagoda of Yongyou Temple
Imperial Summer Villa
Pear Tree Valley
Pavilion Facing Clouds and Hills on All Sides
West Valley
Hazel Valley
Wenjin Chamber
Ruins of Pushan Temple
Lütanbayun Stele
Puren (Universal Charity) Temple
Rime Spring
Misty Rain Tower
Gulige Stele
Chenghu L. Liubeiting Gate
Ruyi Islet Golden Hill
Bifeng Gate
God's Tower
Pavilion of Sunset at the Mallet Peak
Ruyi L. Jinghu L.
Hall of Moonlight and Gurgles of Water
Fangyuanju House
CHENGDE
Renmin Cinema
Hall of Soughing-Pine Valleys
Mid-Lake Pavilion
Hall of Pines and Cranes
Front Palace Dehui Gate
Municipal Hospital
Lizheng Gate

To Qingchui (Mallet) Peak 2 km

Imperial Summer Villa and Eight Outer Temples

800 m

To Chengde Airport 4,5 km

kept here is one of the few copies of the Siku Quanshu collection of literature, comprising 36,304 volumes (the complete works are now stored in the State Museum in Beijing).

Eight Outer Temples (Waiba Miao)

The eight (originally eleven) temples to the north and east of the Imperial Summer Villa were built between 1713 and 1780.

Temple of Universal Charity

The Temple of Universal Charity (Puren Si) was built to the east of the villa in 1713 to mark the 60th birthday of the Jiangxi Emperor.

Temple of Universal Good (Pushan Si)

To the north of the Temple of Universal Charity stands the semi-ruined Temple of Universal Good. This was also built in 1713 but is in the Tibetan style.

Temple of Universal Joy (Pule Si)

The Temple of Universal Joy, about 500m/550yd north-east of the Temple of Universal Charity, dates from 1766 and was constructed to mark the visit of representatives of Mongolian and other minorities from north-western China. Of considerable historical interest is the Pavilion of the Sunrise (Xuguang Ge) or Round Pavilion. It stands on a square terrace with two steps leading up to it, and has a magnificently decorated ceiling.

From here begins the very worthwhile three-hour climb to Toad and Hammer Rock.

Interior of the Imperial Summer Palace

This temple, lying further north, was built in 1764 at the behest of the Jiangxi Emperor to mark the defeat of the Dsungars. Inside, the carved statue of Ksitigarbha, the Ruler of the Underworld, is of interest.

Temple of Far-spreading Peace (Anyuan Miao)

The Temple of Universal Tranquillity, also known as the Temple of the Great Buddha, situated to the north-east of the Summer Villa, was built by the Qianlong Emperor in 1755 in a mixture of Chinese and Tibetan styles after he had subjugated the north-western territories. The temple became known for the wooden statue of Guanyin Bodhisattva, which stands 22m/72ft tall and weighs 110 tonnes. It stands in the Great Hall (Dacheng Ge), which is 37m/121ft high and is flanked by the Hall of the Sun and Moon. Further to the east will be found the Temple of Universal Blessings (Puyou Si). This temple dates from 1760 and also contains statues of the Buddha.

Temple of Universal Tranquillity (Puning Si)

Temple of Universal Blessings

Further to the south-east stands the Temple of Happiness and Longevity of the Sumeru Mountain, one of China's most magnificent historical monuments. It was built by the Qianlong Emperor in 1780 on the lines of the Tashilhunpo monastery in Tibet, to mark the visit of the sixth Panchen Lama. Note particularly the roof of the Great Hall, which is decorated with gilded copper tiles and dragons, each of which is 5m/16½ft long and weighs one tonne; in all, 1500kg/3300lb of gold were used to make them. At the highest point of the complex stands a pagoda with glazed tiles on the outside.

Temple of Happiness and Longevity of the Sumeru Mountain (Xumifushou Miao)

The Temple of the Potaraka Doctrine to the north of the villa is the largest of the Eight Outer Temples and is modelled on the Potala Palace in Lhasa. It was built between 1767 and 1771 to mark the 60th birthday of the Qianlong Emperor Hongli. The main building is the 43m/140ft high Great Red Terrace (Dahongtai). The history of the Turgut tribe from Mongolia is inscribed on large stone tablets; in 1770 this tribe, which had spread as far as the Volga, undertook the 5000km/3000 mile trek back to China.

Temple of the Potaraka Doctrine (Putuozoncheng Miao)

Chengdu

<table>
<tr><td>Temple of the
Manjushri Statue
(Shuxiang Si)</td><td>The Temple of the Manjushri Statue was erected in 1774. It is based on a building of the same name, but of much older date, which stands on the sacred site of Wutaishan in the province of Shaanxi.</td></tr>
</table>

Capital of Sichuan Province
Altitude: 500m/1640ft. Area: 1447sq.km/559sq. miles
Population: 2,540,000 (conurbation 4,420,000)

<table>
<tr><td>Situation and
Communications</td><td>Chengdu lies in an important rice and wheat-growing region in the centre of the province of Sichuan at 104°04′E and 30°35′N.
    Chengdu is linked with Beijing, Shanghai and Canton by air and rail routes. More than twenty express trains and forty direct air flights – including some to Lhasa – connect it with all the major towns in China.</td></tr>
<tr><td>History</td><td>Chengdu was the capital of the Shu (Zhou) kingdom which was conquered by the Qin in 316 B.C. Under the Qin and Han dynasty (221 B.C. to A.D. 220) it advanced to become the political, economic and cultural centre of southwest China. Even at that time the breeding of silkworms and weaving of brocade were already highly developed industries.
    One of China's oldest and most respected state schools was founded here. In the period of the Three Kingdoms (220–280) Chengdu, by now the capital of the state of Shu Han, saw the art of brocade weaving flourish as</td></tr>
</table>

Backyard of a typical quarter of Chengdu

never before. In the 8th c. it became a centre of trade, commerce and industry, which included lacquered and silver filigree work. At the time of the Five Dynasties (907–960) Emperor Meng Chang (919–965) arranged for large numbers of little hibiscus trees to be planted along the town wall and the streets. Chengdu became the capital of Sichuan in 1368.

As a result of its history Chengdu is even today still often known as Brocade City (Jin Cheng) or Hibiscus City (Rong Cheng). It is also a major traffic hub and industrial town with a considerable volume of light and heavy industry. Moreover, its fourteen colleges, including Sichuan University which was founded here in 1927, make it an important cultural centre.

After the Cultural Revolution Chengdu's tradition of tea-houses was revived. Today there are a large number of them, one of the most famous being the Yuelai Tea-house (Yuelai Chaguan).

Tea-houses

In tea-houses guests will receive a cup of tea which will be repeatedly topped up with hot water.

From time to time the Sichuan Opera, a 300 year-old variation on classical opera, is peformed in Chengdu.

This mosque, which towers above the buildings of the Old Town south of the bell-tower, probably dates from the time of the Qianlong Emperor (1736–96), as suggested by the inscription "Seventh year of the empire of Qianlong" found on a beam in the building.

Sights

★Mosque
(Qinzhen Si)

In a Japanese air-raid in 1941 all the mosque buildings apart from the prayer-hall were destroyed.

The rectangular building is 25·7m/84ft long and 11·7m/38ft wide, and completely covered in enamelled tiles.

The first temple was built by a Li Xiong in 302 in honour of Zhuge Liang (181–234), a legendary military strategist and statesman, who was also chancellor of the Shu Han empire (221–263). For his services Zhuge Liang was made a Prince (Marquis) in 223. This temple, which was rebuilt in 1672, is situated in the south-west of Chengdu.

★Temple of Prince Wu
(Wuhou Ci)

In the central hall stands a gilded clay figure of Zhuge Liang, in front of which are three bronze drums dating from before the 6th c. B.C. The two small figures on either side of the Prince are of his son and grandson.

There is also a temple here dedicated to Liu Bei, the ruler of the Shu Han empire. To the west of it lies the 12m/40ft high burial mound which contains his last remains. Twenty-eight terracotta statues of ministers, generals and high officials of the state of Shu Han are displayed in the east and west covered walks. In front of each statue is a small stele inscribed with details of the life of the person concerned.

In the Cultural Park (Wenhua Gongyuan) in the west of the town stands the old Taoist Qinyang Temple, which dates from the Tang period (618–907). The present buildings are of the Qing period (1644–1911). Note the Pavilion of the Eight Trigrams (Bagua Ting) with its eight stone pillars on which are carved dragon patterns, etc.

Qinyang Gong

The house of Du Fu (712–770; see Famous People), the famous poet of the Tang dynasty, will be found in the west of the town on a bend of the Huanhuaxi river. However, this is not the original thatched building in which Du Fu lived for four years from 759 to 763, because that one was destroyed in the middle of the Tang era (618–907). The buildings which the visitor will see today are replicas in stone and wood dating from 1500 and 1811 which were restored in 1949. Nevertheless, the house still retains its original name of Du Fu Caotang (Du Fu's Thatched Cottage).

★Du Fu's Thatched Cottage
(Du Fu Caotang)

The complex comprises several sections which portray the life and work of Du Fu. Adjoining it is a beautiful park with little bridges, pavilions and a garden of bamboo.

Chengdu

Ximen Bus Station

Xicheng (West City) Stadium

Fuhe R. (Jinjie)

Shihui Jie

Xinhua

Xilu

Beijiaochang

Wangjiang Jie

Xi Daile

Babao Jie

Qinglong Jie

Chen

Renmin

Zha

Tomb of Wang Jian

Yihuan

Qingjiang Lu

Huoshu Jie

Changshun Jie

Rongleyuan Restaurant

Chengdu Snack Bar

Yangshi Jie

Xiyulor

Chenmapo Bean curd Restaurant

Hospital Attached to the Chengdu
Institute of Traditional Chinese Medicine

Shi'erqiao Jie

Shi'er Bridge

Er Shiye Jie

Shangye Jie

Dongchengen Jie

Sichuan People's Hospital

Shi'er Bridge

Huimen Jie

Xisheng Jie

Jinhe Jie

Renmin (People's) Stadium

Sichuan Exhibition C

Chengdu-Wenjiang Hwy
Nanhe

Qinganggong Bus Station

Bagua Pavilion

Cultural Park
(Qingyang Palace)

Qingyang Zhengtie

Xijiaochang

Monument to the Martyrs
of the Railway-protecting
Movement in Autumn 1911

Telecommunications Building

Renmin Xilu

Re

Du Fu's Thatched Cottage

Huanhua Creek

Baihua Bridge

Baihuatan Park

Nanjiaochang

Xiduan

Yongpi Bo

Changji Jie

Renmin (People's)
Park

Xiyu Jie

Wang Pang Duck Restaurant

Shaanxi Jie

Xinhua
Bookstore

Renmin
Dongy

Chenge

Produc

Furong Rest.

Sichuan Theatre

Wenmiao Houjie

Wenmiao Qianjie

CITS
CTS

Renmin

Jinjiang

B

Daosongshu Jie

Temple of Marquis Wu

Nanjiao (South
Suburb) Park

Daile

Nanmen Bridge

Jinjiang Bridge

Wuhouci

Ximanqiao

Jianqu

Hospital Attached to the
Sichuan Medical College

Nanlu

Sichua
Co

Southwest Institute
for Nationalities

Yihuan

Lu

Provincial Natatorium

Provincial Stadium

Youraleng

Vicinity of Chengdu

Qingcheng
Mountain

Guanxian

Dujiangyan Irrigation
System

Xindu

CHENGDU

Dayi

Anren

Min jiang R.

To Leshan, Mt. Emei

Heilongtan Res.

Meishan

Renshou

Emei

Leshan

Mt. Emei Baoguo Temple

Wutongqiao

**Vicinity of
Chengdu**

30 km

To Chengdu South Station,

du North Station   To the Zoo 2 km, Xindu 18 km

Chengdu

500 m

Liangjiaxiang
Beiduan
Gymnastics Park
Jiefang
nghua Jie
Shahe
Ershan
Beilu

Wenshu Monastery
Beimen Bridge
Fuqing
Jianshe
Madou
huan
y Factory
Zhizhen
Caoma
Xiang
Yihuan
Jie
Tongzhun
Jinggangshan Cinema
1-Hao Bridge
Dongcheng (East City) Stadium
Xinhua
Feng sheng Jie
Dongfeng
Hongxing
Donghua
Jianshe
Dongjiaochang
Menghui
Renmin Swimming Pool
Dongduan
alace
Anomsheng
Chengdu Telecommunication Bureau
Dongfeng
ce
Xinhong
Lu
ngfeng Hotel
Sichuan Antique Store
2-Hao Bridge
Dongfu Jie
oking Office
Hongqi Theatre
Qingjiang
Huiyuan Jie
aurant
Sichuan Library
Dongfeng
huan
Arts & Crafts Service
urant
Qingjiangpeng Cinema
Dongduan
Friendship
Dajie
Store
Hongxing
Dongbei
Wangjiang Jie
Dongfeng Bridge
Shuangqiao
Chengdu Hotel
Xiaodong
Dajie
Yihuan
Dongfeng
Dongmen Bridge
Niuwangmiao Jie
Shuangqiaozi
Niushikou Longtansi
Hwy
Xinnanmen Bridge
R
erminal
Zhimin
Lu
Yidongqiao Jie
Nanxin
Tongjiang Lu
Lu
Hongyan
Xinsheng Lu
Shengli Cinema
Wangjiang Jie
Juyan Bridge
Niushikou
Wenhua Jie
Nanmen-Shahepu
Daping Jie
Wangjiang Lu
Fuhe R. (Jinjiang)
Nanxin-Shahepu
Laodong Jie
Sichuan University
Shuangnan Lu
Path
incial Museum
Wangjianglou Park
Longzhou Lu

185

Flower Market

Tomb of
Wang Jian
(Wang Jian Mu)

Known as "The Eternal Mausoleum" (Yong Ling), the well-preserved tomb of Wang Jian (847–918), ruler of the Early Shu empire, lies in the north-west of the town. The 15m/50ft high building, divided into three chambers, was opened up in 1942. In the central chamber will be found the king's artistically decorated sarcophagus, and in the chamber behind it is a stone statue of Wang Jian.

★Manjushri
Temple
(Wenshu Yuan)

The Manjushri Temple in the north of the town covers an area of 5ha/12½ acres. The complex comprises five temples in wood and stone, and was built in 1691 above the ruins of an earlier monastery dating from the time of the Southern Dynasties (420–589). The Temple of Shuofa Tang houses ten iron statues of Buddhist guardian gods from the Song period (960–1279) and in the Cangjing Lou are to be found more than 100 bronze sculptures of Buddhas and Buddhist saints from the Qing era (1644–1911).

Daci Si, in Dongfeng Lu Street, dated originally from the Tang period (618–907), but the present buildings are of the Tongzhi period (1862–74). At one time the temple was decorated with some valuable wall-paintings.

★Wangjianglou
Park and Tower of
the View of
the River
(Wangjianglou
Gongyuan)

The park (open; 7.30am–6pm) became well-known through the famous poetess Xue Tao (769–834), who lived here. In the park stands the four-storeyed 30m/100ft high Tower of the View of the River (Wangjianglou). A few yards away the visitor can see a fountain from the Tang period (618–907); the famous poetess is said to have used its water to produce the red paper she used and which still bears her name. In the park stand several buildings, all of which are in her memory; these include the Tower of Poetic Recitation (Yinshi Lou), the Pavilion of the Washing of Paper (Wanjian Ting) and the Tower of the Washing of Brocade (Zhou Lou). She was particularly fond of bamboo plants, and a grove of 140 different species of bamboo was laid out in her memory.

Surroundings

The Monastery of Precious Light is to be found in Xindu, a small town 18km/11 miles north-east of Chengdu. It is thought to date from the Han dynasty (24–220). More than twenty buildings (a pagoda, five temples and sixteen courtyards), almost all of which were constructed in 1670, are scattered over an area of 8ha/20 acres. The 13-storey Sarira Pagoda (Sheli Ta) from the Tang period (618–907) has survived. Archaeologically valuable items on display include a stone tablet with 1000 Buddha reliefs (A.D. 540) and 500 larger-than-life terracotta statues from the Qing period (1644–1911), which depict Luohans in an individual manner.

★Monastery of Precious Light (Baoguang Si)

The irrigation system to be found near the town of Guanxian on the upper reaches of the Minjian river, 55km/34 miles north-west of Chengdu, was constructed in 250 B.C. by Li Bing, prefect of Sichuan at the time of the Warring Kingdoms, in order to prevent catastrophic flooding. He ordered the river to be divided up by means of earth dams, with one section branching out into tributaries and canals which served to irrigate the fields. The whole complex is made up of the "Fish's Jaws" (Yuzhui), which functions as a watershed and dyke, the weir known as "Flying Sands" (Feisha Yan) and the canal, the "Neck of the Precious Bottle" (Baoping Kou). This ingenious system has meant that the Minjian has never again flooded its banks during the last 2200 years, and the Chengdu Plain of central Sichuan has become one of China's most fertile regions.

★★Dujiangyan irrigation system (Dujiangyan)

On Mount Yulaishan, on the east bank of Minjiang, can be seen the imposing Temple of the Two Kings, built in the Qing period (1644–1911) on the ruins of an earlier 6th c. edifice. Statues of the creators of the irrigation system, Li Bing and his son Li Erlang, stand in the halls of the temple.

Temple of the Two Kings (Erwang Miao)

At the northern tip of a small island in the river, on a mound at the mouth of the "Neck of the Precious Bottle" canal, stands another building of historic importance, the Temple of the Slayer of the Dragon. According to legend, the reason the Minjiang river had flooded its banks so often was that a wicked dragon had its lair in the waters. Li Bing and his son succeeded in chaining the dragon so that there was no longer any fear of floods. It is uncertain when the first temple was built here in honour of the slayer of the dragon; it is only known that the present building dates from the Qing period (1644–1911). The impressive stone statue of Li Bing dates from the year 168; it stands 2·0m/9½ft high, weighs 4½ tonnes, and was salvaged from the river in 1974. An inscription on the breast shows the year and month in which it was sculpted.

Temple of the Slayer of the Dragon (Fulong Guan)

16km/10 miles south-west of the Dujiangyan irrigation complex soars Mount Qingchengshan, with its 37 peaks. It is one of China's Taoist pilgrimage shrines. Some impressive palaces, towers and pavilions are scattered over this scenically beautiful mountain.

★Mount Qingchengshan

At the foot of Mount Qingchengshan stands the Taoist Palace of the Creation of Good Fortune (Jianfu Gong), which dates back to the Tang period (618–907). The present buildings were erected in 1888.

Palace of the Creation of Good Fortune

Tradition has it that Zhang Daoling, the legendary founder of the Taoist religion, taught in a cave in this mountain. Since then it has been called the Cave of the Heavenly Master. The temple dates from the Sui period (589–618), but was rebuilt at the end of the Qing dynasty (1644–1911). Visitors can see a terracotta likeness of Zhang Daoling and three 90cm/3ft statues dating from 723 and representing Fuxi, Shengong and Xianyuan, three rulers said to lived in China in prehistoric times.

Cave of the Heavenly Master (Tianshi Dong)

Built between 1860 and 1870, the Temple of the Utmost Purity stands majestically on the Laoxiao Ding mountain peak. It replaced a much older 3rd c. building which burned down in the mid-17th c.

Temple of the Utmost Purity (Shangqing Gong)

Covering an area of 2000sq.km/770sq.miles, this nature reserve lies some 130km/80 miles west of Chengdu. Surrounded by mountains more than 5000m/1930ft high, the reserve is home to 60 different types of mammals, including pandas and snub-nosed apes, 300 kinds of birds and 4000 species of plants, including giant redwood trees. A research station has been set up here to study the habits of pandas.

★★Wolong Nature Reserve (Wolong Gou)

The colossal stone statue of Maitreya is to be seen in Leshan, a small town some 120km/75 miles south of Chengdu, at the western foot of Mount Lingyunshan. 71m/230ft high, it was carved out of the bare rock. A Buddhist monk by the name of Haitong was the first to work on it, from 713 until his death. After that a number of other monks and artists continued the mammoth task until it was eventually completed in 803. The figure is the largest sculpture of the Buddha to be found anywhere in the world.

Leshan

★★Great Buddha of Leshan (Leshan Dafo)

On Mount Lingyunshan stands the Pagoda of the Souls; it is 38m/125ft high and of the Song period (960–1279). Its 13 storeys are bedecked with statues of the Buddha. From here there is a beautiful view of the surrounding countryside.

Pagoda of the Souls (Lingbao Ta)

The Rock Tombs to be found in the suburbs of Leshan are highly impressive. They date from the 1st to the 6th c. and vary in depth between 6 and 90m/20 and 300ft.

Rock Tombs

The Wuyou Temple was built on Mount Wuyoushan during the Tang period (618–907). Its treasures include three Buddha sculptures of gilded camphor wood.

Wuyou Si

35km/22 miles east of Lesha, in Shawan Cheng, the parental home of the famous writer and politician Guo Moruo (1892–1978) is open to visitors.

Parental home of Guo Moruo

Mount Emeishan, the well-known mountain dedicated to the bodhisattva Puxian, stands 160km/100 miles south-west of Chengdu; its highest peak, the Peak of the Ten Thousand Buddhas (Wanfo Ding), reaches a height of 3099m/10,170ft. It is revered by Chinese Buddhists as one of the four Holy Mountains (the others being Mount Wutaishan in Shanxi province, Mount Jiuhuashan in Anhui province and Mount Putuoshan in Zhejiang province), and is shrouded in myths and legends.

★★Mount Emeishan

The first Taoist temples on Mount Emeishan were built during the Eastern Han dynasty (25–220). From the Tang period (618–907) onwards, however, the mountain became one of the major destinations of Buddhist pilgrims because of the 200 or so shrines which had been built on it over the years.

Twenty temples and monasteries still survive, and the provincial government has plans to restore them.

From Chengdu the visitor can take the train to Emei and then proceed by bus to the cable-railway station from where the cars travel up to the top of Mount Emeishan.

Ascent

However, the only real way to enjoy the fascinating flora and fauna is to make the ascent on foot. Take the bus from Emei to Baogua at the foot of the mountain. The climb up the northern face is 44km/27 miles, the southern face 66km/40 miles. Every two to four miles there is a temple, monastery or snack-bar offering food and overnight accommodation if required.

Keep an eye out for monkeys, which are very fond of picking pockets and rifling rucksacks.

◀ *The Great Buddha of Leshan*

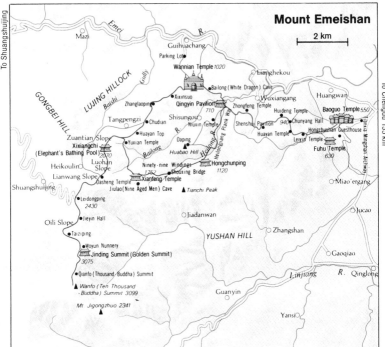

Mount Emeishan

2 km

Temple of Services to the Country (Baoguo Si)

The Temple of Services to the Country stands at the foot of Mount Emeishan at a height of 550m/1805ft. It can be said to form the entrance door to this Buddhist "Mecca". The numerous temple buildings erected during the reign of Emperor Wanli (1573–1620) house many valuable works of art, including a 2·4m/8ft high statue of the Buddha in colourfully ena-melled porcelain which dates from 1415. Visitors can also admire a 7m/23ft high bronze pagoda from the Ming period (1368–1644), decorated with more than 4700 small Buddha figures and the whole Sutra of Avatamsaka.

Temple of the Vanquished Tiger (Fuhu Si)

The Temple of the Vanquished Tiger lies about 1km/1100yd west of the Temple of Services to the Country. The present buildings were erected in 1651 on the foundations of an old shrine built during the Tang period (618–907). As this region was at one time threatened by wild tigers the local inhabitants gave the temple its name in the hope that it would provide them with protection against the beasts.

Pavilion of Clear Sound (Quingyin Ge)

The pavilion of Clear Sound stands 15km/9 miles west of the Temple of Services to the Country, at a height of 770m/2527ft, at the confluence of the White Dragon river (Bailongjiang) and the Black Dragon river (Heilong-jiang); it was named after the soft lapping of the waters of these two rivers. Two stone arched bridges span the rivers.

Temple of Eternity (Wannian Si)

The Temple of Eternity lies about 1km/1100yd north-west of the Pavilion of Clear Sound, at a height of 1020m/3348ft. The original edifice, which was commenced in the Jin era (265–420) and completed during the Ming period (1368–1644), was almost completely destroyed in a conflagration in 1946.

Only the Palace of Tiles (Zhuan Dian), built under Emperor Wanli (1573–1620), remained unharmed and was restored in 1953 when two temples were added. This palace houses a bronze statue of Bodhisattva Puxian of 980, standing 7·3m/24ft tall and weighing 62 tonnes. The Buddhist deity is shown mounted on the back of an elephant with six trunks.

This monastery, situated 1120m/3675ft up the mountain, was built in the Ming period (1402–1644). Note the tall bronze lamp decorated with hundreds of Buddha figures and dragons.

Honchun Ping

Nine old men are said to have lived in this Taoist cave known as Jiulao Dong.

Cave of the Nine Old Men

Situated at a height of 1752m/5750ft, the Temple of the Peak of the Immortals (Xianfeng Si) dates from the year 1612.

Temple of the Peak of the Immortals

The Elephant's Bathing Pool (Xixianchi), at a height of 2070m/6794ft and 14km/9 miles from the Temple of the Peak of the Immortals, is well worth a visit. According to legend Bodhisvatta Puxian used to bathe his favourite elephant in this hexagonal pond. The temple on the edge of the pond dates from 1699.

Elephant's Bathing Pool

Golden Peak, about 5km/3 miles south of Elephant's Bathing Pool, is 3075m/10,092ft high, making it one of the highest peaks on Mount Emeishan.

Golden Peak (Jin Ding)

On Golden Peak stand Huacang Si monastery and also the Monastery of the Reclining Clouds (Woyunan). The latter is famous for its bronze stele dating from the second half of the 15th c.

Monastery of the Reclining Clouds (Woyunan)

A short distance from the monastery lies the well-known Terrace of Beautiful Views (Duguang Tai), from where the visitor can enjoy "the three magnificent views of Mount Emeishan" – the Sunrise, the "Sea of Clouds" and the "Light of Buddha".
　　The "Light of Buddha" is the name given to a halo phenomenon, as a result of which a person looking out from the viewing terrace can see his or her own shadow a short distance away surrounded by a circle of light in the seven colours of the spectrum.

"Light of Buddha"

Chinghai

See Qinghai

Chongqing

重庆市

Chinese equivalent

Province: Sichuan
Altitude: 261m/857ft. Area: 1521sq.km/587sq. miles
Population: 2,650,000 (conurbation 6,510,000)

Chongqing lies in the eastern part of Sichuan province, at the confluence of the Changjiang and Jialingjiang rivers, at longitude 106°29′E and latitude 29°39′N. The Old Town sprawls over a hill which is encircled by the two rivers. Chongqing is accessible by rail from Chengdu, the provincial capital, as well as by air from Beijing and Canton.

Situation and Communications

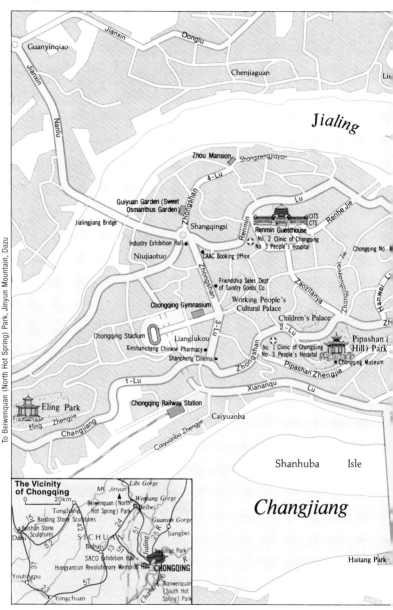

Tschungking
Chongqing

500 m

Xibutang Jie
Guihua Jie
Jiangbei Zhengjie

Liaojiatai Zhengjie

Jinyangmen

Xia Hengjie

Chaotianmen

Chaotianmen No. 4 Wharf

Chaotianmen No. 5 Wharf

Chongqing Harbour
Passenger Terminal

Jialing Cableway

Chaotianmen No. 6 Wharf

Xiaohe Shunchengjie

Cangbai Lu

anlu

Linjiangmen

Bank of China

Xinhua Lu

Snaanxi Lu

Dohe Shunchengjie

al Zhilu

No. 2 Hospital of Chongqing Medical College

Linjiang Lu

Feihongtang

Minzu Lu

Old Sichuan Restaurant

Chongqing Restaurant

Yizhishi Restaurant

Dongshuimen

People's Liberation Monument

ongqing Guesthouse

Minsheng Lu

Chunhuige

Qunlin Market

Friendship Store

Chongqing Arts & Crafts Service

Renmin Theatre

Chongqing Department Store

Zourong Lu

Xinhua Lu

Chongqing Theatre

1-Lu

Guanshengyuan
Restaurant

Xinmin Jie

Minquan Lu

Wuyi Lu

Donglu

Wanglongmen

Renmin Park

Heping
Lu

Laodong Cinema

Jiaochangkou

Kaixuan Lu

Jiefang Lu

Taipingmen

Zhongxing

Shibati

Jiefang   Xilu

Chuqimen Wharf

(Yangtze R.)

Haitangxi-Danzishi

Haitangxi
Lu

Huangjued

anyu

Chongqing: old part of the town

Chongqing, also known as the "Mountain City", is one of the country's most important conurbations, and its mines and shipyards help to make it the political and commercial centre of south-west China. Chongqing University and other colleges mean that it is also of importance in the educational sphere.

History

Chongqing can boast a history going back more than 3000 years. As early as the 13th c. it was the capital of the Ba kingdom. Like many other Chinese towns and cities, it has borne a number of names in the course of its history – under the Sui dynasty (589–618) it was called Yuzhou, and then Gongzhou during the time of the Northern Song (960–1126). Its present name, which roughly translated means "double good fortune", was conferred upon it by the Song Emperor Guangzong in 1189 in order to celebrate two particularly favourable events in his political life, his appointments to Prince and then to Emperor.

At the time of the Japanese occupation the southern office of the central committee of the Chinese Communist party was housed in Chongqing. In 1939 it became the provisional capital of the Chinese Republic, as Nanjing was in the possession of Japanese troops. As a result, millions of people moved here from the eastern provinces and businesses and universities were transferred here too. After 1949 Chongqing's economic development continued apace.

Sights

★Loquat
Hill Park
(Pipashan)

Loquat Hill towers to a height of 280m/920ft in the central/southern part of the Old Town, in the centre of Loquat Hill Park. From here there is a superb view of the whole city. Originally privately owned, the park was opened up to the public in 1955. On the top of the hill stands an octagonal pavilion. Nearby will be found the Municipal Museum in which are exhibited many archaeological specimens discovered in the city and the surrounding countryside.

The Southern Hot Springs, lying 24km/15 miles south of Chongqing among some delightful scenery, are very popular with visitors. Built in the second half of the 19th c., the baths are located in a beautiful park which has a brook running through it. The average temperature of the very sulphurous water is about 40°C/104°F.

Near the hot springs there are some other interesting sights, such as Fairy Mountain (Xiannüyou Yan), the Huaxi river, the Flying Waterfalls and an arched bridge.

The Natural History Museum lies in Bebei, a satellite town 45km/28 miles north-west of Chongqing. There are some 60,000 exhibits, of which the fossilised dinosaur remains are of particular interest; the local region is famous for the fact that these animals roamed here in prehistoric times.

The Northern Hot Springs rise north-west of Bebei (52km/32 miles north-west of Chongqing), in Wenfang Gorge near the Jialingjiang river, at the foot of Mount Jinyunshan. The free-flowing springs have an average temperature of about 35°C/95°F.

As well as the springs, the park-like surroundings also contain four Buddhist temples from the Ming and Qing periods (1368–1911); they are the Hall of the Great Buddha (Dafo Si) from 1432, which houses a giant statue of Shakyamuni, the Temple of Avalokiteshvara, the Temple of Amitabha and the Temple of General Guan Yu.

Red Cloud Mountain, 60km/37 miles north-west of Chongqing, is one of the most impressive mountains in the province. It is named after the Temple of the Red Clouds, built in 423, which was destroyed by fire in the middle of the 17th c. and rebuilt in 1683. The highest of its nine peaks, Jade Peak (Yujian Feng), is 1040m/3413ft high.

There are 50,000 or more stone sculptures at forty different sites all in the vicinity of Dazu, a little town 100km/62 miles west of Chongqing. Most of these historically and artistically valuable works – they include statues, bas-reliefs, high reliefs, etc. – are religious in character and represent Buddhas, Bodhisattvas and Buddhist, Taoist and Confucian saints, although some do portray scenes from everyday life as well as landscapes, animals and plants. The statues are either chiselled out of the hillsides or are housed in caves; the oldest date from the end of the Tang period, i.e. the 9th c., and many others are from the 12th c.

The most valuable of all are to be found on the slopes of Mount North (Beishan) and at the foot of Treasure Chamber Mountain (Baodingshan).

The largest collection of Mount North sculptures, hewn over a period of 250 years starting from 892 A.D., will be found near the town of Fowan (2km/1¼ miles north-west of Dazu), carved out of niches in a rock 7m/23ft tall and 500m/1641ft long. The work in the southern section was carried out between the 9th and 10th c., that in the northern section after the 10th c.

The beneficent Goddess of Mercy (Avalokiteshvara), carved in the middle of the 12th c., is also known as the "Chinese Venus", because of her great beauty.

The Bodhisattvas Manjusri and Samantabhadra, riding on a lion or an elephant, represent the victory of good over evil as told in Buddhist teachings.

Between 1179 and 1249 more than 10,000 sculptures were carved at the foot of Treasure Chamber Mountain (Baodingshan), 15km/9½ miles north-east of Dazu. The most beautiful are to be found in Dafowan, on a rock 15 to 30m/50 to 100ft high and 500m/1650ft wide. They depict Buddhist saints and episodes from their lives and work.

The giant statues of Buddha near Dazu

Goddess of Mercy
In a niche on the southern slope of the rock, quite a way to the east, stands the 3m/10ft tall statue of the Goddess of Mercy (Avalokiteshvara) with her 1002 arms. She is the main attraction in Dazu.

Buddha
Also famous is the 30m/100ft long reclining statue of Buddha entering Nirvana. Many other carvings depict scenes from everyday life, some showing important events in a woman's life, such as pregnancy, the birth and nursing of a child and its later marriage. Another group of figures is intended as a warning against the evils of alcohol – a father rejecting his drunken son, and a man so much under the influence of drink that he fails to recognise his own wife.

★Zigong Dinosaur Museum
The quite exceptional Dinosaur Museum is located at the now famous Dashanpu site some 11km/7 miles north of Zigong and 180km/112 miles west of Chongqing, where a great many, unusually well-preserved, dinosaur fossils were discovered. Skeletons of dinosaurs and other vertebrates are displayed in a 3600sq.m/39,000sq.ft exhibition area.

Dali · H 6

Chinese equivalent

大理市

Province: Yunnan
Altitude: 1980m/6500ft. Population: 2,500,000

Situation and Communications
Dali lies at 100°12′E and 25°37′N, about 400km/250 miles north-west of the provincial capital of Kunming with which it is linked by rail and overland buses.

Dali forms part of the autonomous region inhabited by the Bai minority, who form the bulk of the population. Dali is known both for its places of interest and for its lucrative marble deposits. The marble quarried here is known as "Dali Stone".

Dali's origins lie in the dim and distant past. All that is known is that it was the capital of the Nanzhao kingdom (738–902), when it was called Taihe. For centuries it was an important trading hub. During the Song period (960–1279) an independent kingdom existed here with the name of Dali. At times during the 13th c. it came under the rule of the Mongols.

History

The Sanyue Jie Festival – an open-air market which has been organised by the Bai in the west of Dali for more than 1000 years – is held annually on the 15th day of the third month (hence its name) and usually lasts for between five and seven days. Other national minorities, many of whom travel here from far afield, also take part wearing their festive costumes.

The Great Festival of the Third Month (Sanyue Jie)

This festival was first held in the Tang era (618–907) in honour of Guanyin, the Goddess of Mercy, which is why it is sometimes called the Guanyin Jie. Everything imaginable is offered for sale on the richly stocked stalls, ranging from conventional medicines to everyday objects and even horses, while the people enjoy singing, dancing and various contests such as horse-racing and longship races.

Erhai means "Ear Sea". This name can be explained both by the size of the lake – it measures 7km/4½ miles wide and some 40km/65 miles long and covers an area of 250sq.km/96sq. miles – and by its shape, which resembles a human ear. This beautiful lake, situated 2km/1¼ miles east of the town centre, bears eloquent witness to Dali's glorious past. There are a number of old buildings to visit on an island in the lake and along its banks.

Sights

★**Lake Erhai**

Unfortunately little remains of the former residence of the King of Nanzhao (Nanzhao Bishugong) on the little Isle of the Golden Spindle (Jinsuo).

★Royal Summer Palace

The ruins of the ancient town of Taihe (see History above) can be seen on the west bank of Lake Erhai; these include two walls of rammed-down clay 1·5 and 2km/1600 to 2100yd long respectively, a fort built in 747 and a stone tablet 3·02m/10ft high, 2·27m/7½ft wide and 58cm/2ft thick which dates from 766. The inscription chiselled on the tablet describes a battle and the relationship between the kingdom of Nanzhao and the rulers of the Tang dynasty.

★Ruins of Taihe (Taihecheng Yizhi)

The Temple of the Exalted Holy One, also known as the Temple of the Three Pagodas (Santa Si), stands on the west bank of Lake Erhai. It is known mainly for its three pagodas. The largest of these, the Pagoda of the Thousand Searches (Qianxun Ta), a rectangular building of sixteen stepped storeys, stands 69m/226ft high and is very similar to the Pagoda of the Little Wild Goose in Xian. There are some doubts as to when it was built, although most experts now think it was in the third decade of the 9th c. In the centre of the front of each storey there is a niche containing a marble statue of the Buddha.

Temple of the Exalted Holy One (Chongsheng Si)

The two smaller pagodas are to the north and south of the large one. Both are octagonal and of ten stepped storeys, are 42m/138ft high and date from the time of the Five Dynasties (907–960).

When renovation work was carried out in 1978 large numbers of historically interesting objects were discovered in the foundations and upper structure of the pagodas.

Behind the pagodas lies the Hall of Yutong Guanyin Dian, which houses a particularly interesting bronze statue of the Buddha and a marble stele (1325).

The Cangshan mountain range west of Dali stretches for more than 50km/30 miles from north to south and contains a lot of marble quarries. Its

Surroundings

Lake Erhai in Dali

nineteen peaks are all over 3000m/9,900ft, the highest being Mount Malong, which is 4122m/13,530ft. Between the peaks mountain streams gurgle their way down to Lake Erhai. Those interested in nature will be amply rewarded by the "Four Beauties" of the Cangshan mountains – clouds, snow, peaks and streams.

★Cangshan Mountains

5km/3 miles south of Dali stands Guanyin Tang, dating from the Qing period (1644–1911) and dedicated to Guanyin, Goddess of Mercy. According to legend she, dressed as an old woman and with a giant stone on her back, faced an enemy army and put it to flight.

Guanyin Tang

Also some 5km/3 miles south of the town stands the Gantong Si temple, dating from the Eastern Han period (24–220) but renovated by the Mings (1368–1644).

Gantong Si

It is worth visiting the Pagoda of the Snake Bones, 14km/9 miles south of Dali near the town of Xiaguan. It is over 30m/100ft high and was built in memory of a young man who – according to legend – freed the region from a giant man-eating snake, but lost his life in doing so.

Pagoda of the Snake Bones (Shegu Ta)

Dalian

L 4

旅大市

Chinese equivalent

Province: Liaoning. Area: 1000sq.km/386sq. miles
Population: 1,480,000 (conurbation 4,720,000)

◀ *The South Gate in Dali*

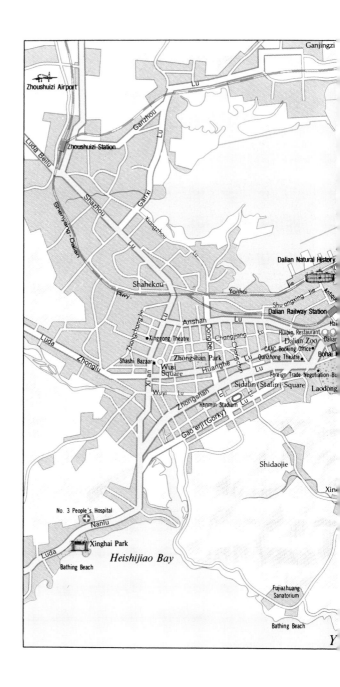

Dalian

Ganjingzi

Zhoushuizi Airport

Zhoushuizi Station

Ganzhou Lu

Luda Beilu

Shazhou

Shenyang–Dalian

Garki Lu

Xiangzhou Lu

Dalian Natural History

Shahekou

Yonhai

Shuangxing Jie

Antique

Rwy.

Luda

Zhonghong Jie

Anshan Lu

Dongbei

Changliong

Dalian Railway Station

Hai

Xinggong Theatre

Chongchun

Lu

Huibin Restaurant

Dalian

Zhonglu

Shashi Bazaar

Zhongshan Park

Dalian Zoo

CAAC Booking Office

Qunzhong Theatre

Bohai

Xi'an

Wusi Square

Huanghe

Foreign Trade Negotiation Bu

Wuyi Lu

Zhongshan

Sidalin (Stalin) Square

Laodong

Renmin Stadium

Lu

Gao'erji (Gorky)

Shidaojie

Xin

No. 3 People's Hospital

Nanlu

Luda

Xinghai Park

Heishijiao Bay

Bathing Beach

Fujiazhuang Sanatorium

Bathing Beach

Y

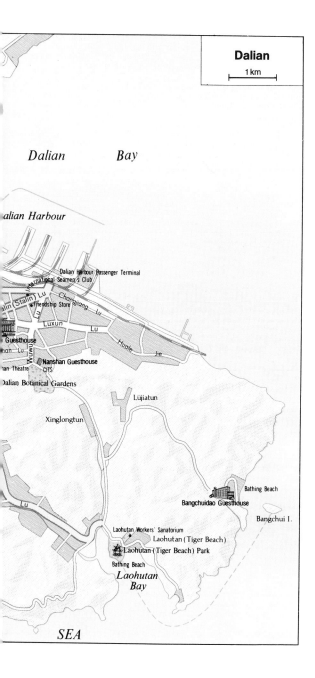

Dalian

1 km

Dalian Bay

alian Harbour

Dalian Harbour Passenger Terminal

International Seamen's Club

Chongqiang Lu

Friendship Store

lin (Stalin) Lu

Luxun Lu

Huale Jie

Guesthouse

han Lu

Nanshan Guesthouse

han Theatre   CITS

Dalian Botanical Gardens

Lüjiatun

Xinglongtun

Lu

Bathing Beach

Bangchuidao Guesthouse

Bangchui I.

Laohutan Workers' Sanatorium

Laohutan (Tiger Beach)

Laohutan (Tiger Beach) Park

Bathing Beach

Laohutan Bay

SEA

Dalian

Situation and Communications	Dalian lies at 121°40′E and 38°52′N, at the southernmost tip of the Liaodong peninsula. It is linked with Shenyang by rail and a motorway, with Shanghai by regular service ships, and with Beijing and Hong Kong by regular flights taking one and three and a half hours respectively.
Importance	Dalian, previously known as Lüda (a contraction formed from Lüshun and Dalian), boasts one of the largest trading ports in China. It forms one of China'a special commercial zones, with shipyards, engineering and rolling-stock works, as well as steel, chemicals, petro-chemicals, cement, textiles and canned foods.
	Dalian is famed for its apples, which the Chinese prefer to any other fruit, and because of its mild climate and many sandy beaches it has become one of the most popular summer holiday resorts in northern China.
History	It is uncertain when the town was founded. All that is known is that after 108 B.C., when Emperor Han Wudi opened a shipping line between the Liaodong and Shandong peninsulas, it expanded considerably. In the late 19th c. the Manchurian government set up a naval base in Dalian which gave it a further economic boost. From 1894 onwards the town was under Russian control, and was expanded and docks built. In 1905 the Japanese took it over, and it was returned to the Soviet Union in 1945. Since 1949 it has grown in importance as an industrial town. In 1976 a large oil-harbour was built.

Sights

Natural History Museum	The Natural History Museum, to the north of the railway station, exhibits mammals and marine creatures, plants and minerals. There is also the opportunity to visit a glassworks.
★Xinghai Gongyuan Park	Covering some 15ha/37½ acres, Xinghai Gongyuan Park lies in the south-west of the town with the sea on three sides. There are facilities for bathing.
Sea View Observation Tower (Wanghai Lou)	On a rocky ledge stands the Sea View Observation Tower, a favourite spot with naturalists.
Cave of Marine Exploration	The sea can also be reached by climbing down into the Cave of Marine Exploration (Tanhai Dong), the entrance to which is concealed on the side of a hill in the south-east of the park. There is a large rocky cliff near the cave.
Tiger Beach Park (Laohutan)	Covered in lush vegetation, this park is situated on a rocky promontory in the south-east of the town. Against the skyline are silhouetted pretty pavilions in the classical Chinese style, their roofs covered in multi-coloured enamelled tiles. The name of the beach is based on the legend that this region was once ravaged by a wild tiger which was then slain by a young man called Shi Cao.
	Two hills nearby serve to remind us of this legend: one is called Hill of the Cleft Tiger's Head (Bania Ling), the other Hill of Shi Cao (Shi Cao Ling).
Tiger Cave (Laohu Dong)	On a hillside in the west of the park can be seen Tiger Cave, with its entrance guarded by a sculpture of a tiger.
Modern Satellite Town (Wucai Cheng)	This curious architectural conglomeration is to be found on the coast, in the north-east of the industrial area of Dalian. Covering 10·5ha/26¼ acres, the suburb is divided into six different quarters designated A, B, C, D, E and F. The buildings in quarters A and B are typically Chinese, while those in B reflect West European styles and those of C that of Asia Minor. Quarter D is dominated by numerous skyscrapers, while E is a mix of western and eastern tastes in dwellings. In quarter F skyscrapers alternate with smaller houses.

Surroundings

This tomb, which dates from the Eastern Han period (25–220). was discovered in 1931 to the south of the village of Shagang in the Ganglinzi region, 25km/15½ miles north of Dalian. It consists of a main chamber, two anterooms, one room at the rear and a side-chamber. Note in particular the frescos on the east, south and north walls of the main chamber. They show the deceased ascending into Heaven.

★ Han Tomb in Yingchengzi (Yingchenzi Hanmu)

The port of Lüshun, known to the western world by its earlier name of Port Arthur, lies some 60km/37 miles south-west of Dalian at the southern tip of the Liaodong peninsula. On its north and east sides it opens out into a bay on the Yellow Sea; the bay is always free of ice and is surrounded by a line of rocky hills at least 5km/3 miles long and more than 200m/660ft high. Well-protected, and accessible from the sea only via a waterway some 350m/385yd wide, the harbour is still an important naval base and therefore public access is restricted.

Lüshun (Port Arthur)

Harbour town

The fortified harbour designed by the Chinese viceroy Li Hung Chang (d. 1901) was captured in 1894 by the Japanese during the Sino-Japanese war, but under the terms of a somewhat dubious 25-year leasing contract it was handed over to Russia in 1898, only to be recaptured by the Japanese in 1904 after a stubborn siege, an act which triggered off the Russo-Japanese war of 1904–05.

Port Arthur fortifications

On February 8th 1904 the Japanese Admiral Togo successfully attacked the Russian fleet which was lying in the roads off Port Arthur. An attack by the Russian ships on April 13th 1904 was repulsed; the flagship "Petropavlovsk", with Admiral Makarov on board, hit a mine and sank.

Siege and bombardment in the Russo-Japanese War 1904–05

After the Russians (under General Stössel) had lost the battle near Chinchou on May 26th 1904 the Japanese (under General Nogi) surrounded the as yet unfinished fort defended by Stössel and began the attack on August 8th 1904. On August 9th 1904 Takunchan Hill (212m/696ft above sea level; to the east) was taken and from there the Russian fleet was subjected to heavy fire until it fled the harbour and was eventually defeated. By November 2nd the beleaguered garrison was forced back to its main line of defence, although the attacking armies had suffered heavy losses – in the attack on Fort Panluchan to the north-east on August 19th 1904 they lost some 15,000 men. The Japanese then changed to mine-warfare, and on November 26th 1904 tried to storm the defences but were repelled and lost some 9000 soldiers in the attempt. On December 5th 1904, after a bombardment lasting several days, the Japanese finally succeeded in taking the key Russian position on High Mountain (203m/666ft; to the north-west); by then their losses had been estimated at 12,000 men. On December 15th the Russian General Kondrakento fell while defending Fort Kikwanschan. After losing Fort Erlungschan and Fort Sungsuchan in the north-east the Russians evacuated the northern front. On January 1st 1905 General Stössel offered to surrender, and this was signed the next day. In the battles for Port Arthur the Russians are thought to have lost about 50,000 men (including 25,000 prisoners), while the total Japanese losses were some 70,000.

In Lüshun, where quite a lot of Colonial-style houses have been preserved, there is a Museum of History and Culture in which are displayed archaeological finds from the surrounding countryside.

Near the harbour quarter, on the way up to Bay Yu Hill (with splendid views), the visitor will find the Wan Zhong Mu Martyry (Tomb of the 10,000 Faithful), which contains the ashes of those Chinese who fell in the Sino-Japanese war of 1894–95, when the Japanese marched into Lüshun on November 21st 1894.

Sights in Lüshun

Datong

Historic plan of Port Arthur (now Chinese Lüshun) from Baedeker's travellers handbook "Russia" (7th edition page 524, Leipzig 1912)

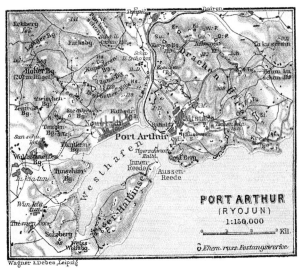

J.-D. = Japanese Monument · K.-M. = War Museum · R.-D. = Russian Memorial

FORMER RUSSIAN FORTIFICA- TIONS	Er.	Erlungshan	O.-P.	East Panlunshan
	HS.	Hsiao an tsu shan	Si.	Silver Hill
	Ich.	Ichinohe	Su.	Sungsushan
	Itz.	Itzuschau	S.-Taj.	South Tajanku
	Ki.	Kikwanshan	T.-R.	Temple Redoubt
	L.	Lao lu tsui	Ta.	Taantzushan
	N.-Taj.	North Tajanku	Tu.	Tungshikvanshan
	N.-Tu.	North Tungshikvanshan	W.-P.	West Panlunshanshan

Datong

J 3

Chinese equivalent

大同市

Province: Shanxi
Altitude: 1216m/3990ft
Population: 605,000 (conurbation 896,000)

Situation

The industrial town of Datong lies at 113°12'E and 40°07'N, in the north of Shanxi province on a plain which is shielded to the north and south by two sections of the Great Wall of China. There is a rail link between Datong and Beijing.

History

It seems probable that Datong was founded in the 5th c. B.C. From A.D. 398 to 495, when it was known as Pincheng, it was the seat of the Northern Wei dynasty. Many works of art which can now be seen in the Yungang Shiku Caves date from this period. Under the Ming dynasty (1368–1644) Datong became strategically important.

The considerable deposits of coal nearby have given Datong the name of the "Coal Capital"; agricultural machinery is another important branch of industry here.

Sights

The Huayan Monastery, to the west of the town centre, is one of the few well-preserved sacred buildings from the Liao period (916–1125). Huayan was a school of Buddhist teaching, of which there were many at that time.

★★Huayan Monastery (Huayan Si)

In 1122 the monastery was destroyed and a new building soon replaced it. In the first half of the 15th c. it was divided into the Lower Monastery (Xia Huayan Si) and Upper Monastery (Shang Huayan Si). It is unusual in that it faces east, an architectural feature unique to the Liao period.

The main hall of the Lower Monastery is the Sutra Temple, dating from 1036, which served as a library of Buddhist writings. At the time there were 38 built-in cupboards (made during the Liao dynasty) which housed some 18,000 volumes from the Ming and Qing periods (1368–1911). The 579 volumes which originally existed have been partially lost. In the centre of the building stand three statues of the Buddha, surrounded by clay figures.

Sutra Temple (Bojijiao Cangdian)

To Wooden Pagoda in Yingxian 70 km

Datong

In each of the four corners a guardian figure in coloured clay sits upon a throne.

Sumptuous Hall of the Great Hero (Daxiong Baodian)

The Upper Monastery is structured around the Hall of the Great Hero, which replaces a former 11th c. building burned down in 1122. It covers an area of 1560sq.m/16,785sq.ft, making it one of the largest Buddhist temples in China. The wood and clay statues are from the Ming period (1368–1644). There are five Buddha statues as well as some sculptures of minor gods. The heads and upper bodies of the 20 heavenly guardian statues on each side of the temple are bent forward about 15 degrees, a feature rarely found anywhere else in China. All the temple walls are painted with frescos; these cover an area of 887sq.m/9540sq.ft and portray the life and works of Shakyamuni, the Dong An at the time of the Emperor Guangxu (1875–1908). The ceiling of 973 panels was decorated in the Qing era (1644–1911) with geometrical patterns and floral decorations.

Another part of the temple houses the Municipal Museum.

★Shanhua Si Monastery

The Shanhua Si or Nan Si (Southern Monastery) lies, as its name suggests, in the south of the town. Construction commenced in the 8th c. but in 1122 a large part fell victim to the fire of that year. It was rebuilt between 1128 and 1143. Today the monastery comprises the Sumptuous Hall of the Great Hero (Liao period, 916–1125), the Hall of the Three Holy Ones (12th c.) and the Puxian Pavilion, or Puxian Ge (1154).

Sumptuous Hall of the Great Hero (Daixong Baodian)

The Sumptuous Hall of the Great Hero contains five statues of Tathagata (one of the ten titles afforded to Shakyamuni) seated on a throne of lotus leaves; each is surrounded by several followers and Bodhisattvas. On each side of the temple stand 24 statues of gods all with different faces. Apart from two guardian statues from the Jing period (1115–1234) all these figures can be attributed to the Liao era (916–1125). Although the wall-paintings are of the Qing period (1644–1911) they are based on the style of the Yuan dynasty (1271–1368).

Hall of the Three Holy Ones

In the Hall of the Three Holy Ones, a typical example of the architecture of the Jin dynasty (1127–1234), visitors can see the statues of the Three Holy Ones, Shakyamuni, Wenshu and Puxian Bodhisattva

★Wall of the Nine Dragons (Jiulong Bi)

The Wall of the Nine Dragons, in Dongjie Street in the town centre, is 45·5m/149ft long, 8m/26ft high and 2·02m/6½ft thick. It was built in 1392 to embellish the residence of Zhu Gui, the thirteenth son of the first Ming Emperor Zhu Yuanzhang. In 1644 the palace burned down, and the only part saved from the flames was the wall, built of coloured ceramic bricks and decorated with bas- and high-relief. The decorations portray nine dragons flying up to the sun, the symbol of immortality.

Surroundings

★★Yungang Shiku Caves

The Yungang Shiku Caves, 16km/10 miles west of Datong on the southern slopes of the Wuzhou Mountains, stretch for over 1km/1100yd in an east-west direction. Like the caves at Dunhuang and Longmen, these too house a number of Buddhist works of art which betray Indian and Ancient Greek influences.

There are 53 caves in all containing more than 51,000 statues, the largest being 17m/56ft high and the smallest a mere 2cm/¾in,

Yungang Shiku Caves

as well as high-reliefs. Most were made between A.D. 460 and 494, on the orders of Emperor Wencheng Di, a practising Buddhist. Ten of thousands of sculptors laboured on this mighty task under the supervision of the monk Tao Yao.

Cave No. 3, the largest of the Yungang Shiku Caves, contains a Buddha and two Bodhisattvas, which are rendered particularly interesting by their impressive stance and elegant clothing. From the way they are presented it is thought that they date from the early Tang period (618–907). Cave No. 3

Cave No. 5 contains the 17m/56ft high statue of Yungang. The seated Buddha was probably carved in the 5th c. but covered in coloured clay during the Tang period. Cave No. 5

In the centre of Cave No. 6 stands a 16m/52½ft high column shaped like a two-storey pagoda. It is decorated with numerous bas-reliefs describing the life of Shakyamuni from his birth until he entered Nirvana. Further episodes from his life are inscribed on the east, south and west walls of the cave. Cave No. 6

Cave No. 7 contains two stone lions in front of a Figure of the Buddha, and six Bodhisattva statues. Cave No. 7

The influence of various styles can be seen in this cave. The way the Indian deities Vishnu and Shiva are portrayed shows an Indian influence, while the guardian with the trident is clearly Hellenistic in style. Cave No. 8

An inscription on the east wall of Cave No. 11 indicates that it was built in the year 483. It boasts 95 large stone carvings and numerous Bodhisattva figures in small niches. Cave No. 11

Cave No. 12 is noted for its carvings of 5th c. musical instruments. Cave No. 12

Datong

Buddhist statues in the Yungang Shiku Caves

Cave No. 13	The 13m/43ft tall statue of Maitreya in Cave No. 13 strikes an unusual stance; its hand is supported by a four-armed figure standing on one leg.
Caves 14 and 15	Although these two caves are severely weathered they are of interest because of the thousands of small Bodhisattva figures in niches in the walls.
Cave No. 16	Cave No. 16 which, together with Nos. 17 to 20, is one of the oldest in Yungang, houses a Buddha and five Bodhisattva sculptures. These are more than 13m/43ft tall and portray five emperors of the Northern Wei dynasty.
Cave No. 17	Cave No. 17 contains a revered statue of Maitreya sitting cross-legged.
Cave No. 18	This cave houses an impressive statue of Shakyamuni on the robe of which are carved countless small Bodhisattva figures.
Cave No. 19	Here can be seen another enthroned figure of Shakyamuni which is 16·7m/55ft high.
Cave No. 20	Cave No. 20 also contains a seated figure of Shakyamuni, this one being 13·7m/45ft tall. This sculpture, which has become the symbol of the Yungang Caves, is a magnificent masterpiece.
Further Sights Wooden Pagoda of Yingxian (Yingxian Muta)	Built in 1056, the Wooden Pagoda of Yingxian stands in Yingxian, about 70km/44 miles south of Datong. It is the oldest wooden pagoda in China and a masterpiece of Chinese timber construction. The octagonal building, put together without the use of a single nail, is of impressive height (67m/220ft). On the ground floor the visitor can see a large statue of Shakyamuni and six frescos portraying Tathagata, one of the ten forms in which Buddha appeared. On the third floor is a statue of Bodhisattva with four faces, each looking towards a different point of the compass. The four

The "Hanging Monastery"

faces symbolise the immeasurable wisdom of Buddha, whose gaze can pass through any object. In the middle of the fifth floor can be seen a sculpture of a seated Shakyamuni surrounded by eight Bodhisattvas. As the likeness of Shakyamuni is an outstanding one the building is also known as the Pagoda of Shakyamuni (Sajia Ta).

72km/45 miles south-east of Datong soars Mount Hengshan, one of the five mythical mountains of China (the others being Mount Taishan in Shandong province, Mount Hashan in Shaanxi province, Mount Hengshan in Hunan province and Mount Songshan in Henan province). At one time it was regarded a a holy mountain, and the Emperors made sacrifices to Heaven here. The highest peak on Mount Hengshan, which is also known as Mountain of the North, reaches a height of 2017m/6620ft.

★ Mount Hengshan

Various monuments are scattered over the slopes of Mount Hengshan. The most famous of these is the Hanging Monastery, 5km/3 miles from Hunyuan, which was built near the Pass of the Golden Dragon (Jinlong Kou) on a rock-face 30m/100ft above the valley floor. Constructed in the 6th c. A.D., the monastery consists of 40 small halls and pavilions. The buildings are supported by beams anchored into crevices in the rock-face. In the buildings the visitor can see 80 bronze, iron, terracotta and stone sculptures dating from different periods.

★★ Hanging Monastery (Xuankong Si)

Dunhuang   F 3

墩煌

Chinese equivalent

Province: Gansu. Altitude: 1100m/3610ft
Population: 10,000 (conurbation 92,000)

Dunhuang

Situation and Communications

Dunhuang lies at 94°38'E and 40°09'N in the west of Gansu province, on the famous Silk Road.

There are air flights from nearby towns and cities; buses run to Dunhuang from Liuyuan, which lies some 150km/93 miles to the north and is the nearest rail station on the Beijing–Ürümqi line.

History

Under the rule of Emperor Han Wudi Dunhuang was elevated to the status of a town in 111 B.C. Its situation on the Silk Road, which divides here into two roads going north and south respectively, helped Dunhuang to enjoy an economic boom. Along this trade route new ideas, religious teachings such as Buddhism and scientific knowledge spread east and west. As a result Dunhuang has developed since the 4th c. to become a centre of Buddhism. In 619, when it was the seat of the administrative district of the same name, its name was changed to Shazhou; the remains of this old town lie to the west of present-day Dunhuang.

Surroundings

★★Mogao Ku Caves

History and origin

The main attraction for visitors to the area around Dunhuang are undoubtedly the unique treasures found in the Mogao Ku caves, also known as the Caves of the Thousand Buddhas (Qianfo Dong). Mogao is a small town 25km/15½ miles south-east of Dunhuang. The caves are a very important centre of Buddhist art and give an insight into the political and economic life of the times during which they were constructed. The first grottoes were hewn out of the rock by monks in the year 366. As Buddhism spread so did the number of such caves, so that over a span of some 1000 years diggings were made into a wall of sandstone measuring 1600m/1 mile in length; by the Tang period (618–907) a thousand metres/eleven hundred yards had been excavated in this way. In the Ming period (1368–1644) the caves gradually became forgotten. It was not until the year 1900 that a monk named Wang Yuanlu found in Cave No. 16 60,000 valuable works of art which had probably been hidden there by monks in the 11th c. in order to safeguard them from their enemies. The find included books, documents, silk-paintings, embroidery and bronze statues dating from the 4th to the 14th c. The books – which embrace Buddhist, Taoist and Confucian writings as well as literary texts and philosophical and natural history treatises – are in various languages (Chinese, Tibetan, Sanskrit, Uigur, etc.) However, the authorities showed little interest in the finds, which were subsequently sold by Wang to British, French and Japanese collectors. It was not until 1949 that the Chinese government made efforts to preserve this unique cultural site and set up a research institute for this purpose. In 1987 UNESCO included the caves in their list of the World's Cultural Heritage Sites.

492 mainly square or rectangular caves, with 2415 statues in coloured clay, 45,000sq.m/484,000sq.ft of wall-paintings and five wooden buildings have survived the ravages of time, but the remaining caves have been destroyed by the effects of weather. The largest grotto is 40m/130ft high and 30m/100ft wide and deep, while the smallest is less than 1m/3ft 4in. high. Each cave has a plaque showing its official number, date of construction and dynasty. The sculptures are all of painted clay, the largest being 33m/108ft and the smallest just 10cm/4in. They are of Buddhas, Bodhisattvas, holy men, youths and Buddhist believers. The wall-paintings cover all kinds of subjects – Buddhist characters, episodes from the Sutras, the teachings of Buddha, legends, fairy-tales, everyday scenes, floral patterns and geometric decoration.

Caves of the Northern Wei dynasty (386–534)

The Wai Caves show unmistakable signs of Indian influence both in the choice of subjects and in the methods employed. The statues are of impressive size; the wall-paintings mainly portray scenes from the life of the historical Shakyamuni Buddha.

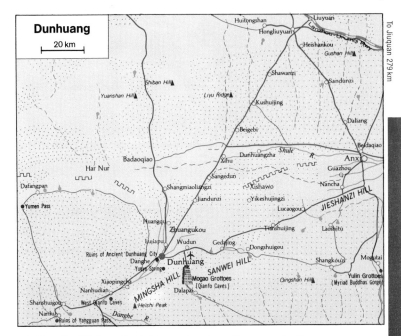

In Cave No. 254 the wall-paintings are based on a theme dear to the hearts of Buddhists – sacrificing self for the good of others. One picture shows Prince Sudana cutting flesh from his own body with a piece of dried bamboo cane in order to feed it to a hungry tiger lying next to him. The next scene shows his parents and siblings in mourning for the dead prince.

Cave No. 259 contains the statue of a Buddhist saint. Her white face and mysterious smile have earned her the nickname of "Mona Lisa".

Cave No. 275, dating from the second half of the 4th c., is famous for its painting showing the self-sacrifices of Shakyamuni in an earlier life. Shakyamuni, then King Sivi, is sitting cross-legged and watching with satisfaction a dove which he has saved, while an executioner is cutting flesh from his body to feed an eagle. His serene countenance is in stark contrast to the grim face of the executioner. Other beautiful examples of the art of this period are Caves Nos. 248, 257, 260, 263, 272, 428, 431, 435 and 439.

On the walls of Cave No. 249, one of the caves of the Western Wei dynasty, can be seen scenes of a tiger and antelope hunt; they show one hunter on horseback following three gazelles and a second who has just killed a tiger.

Caves Nos. 285 and 432 are also worth a visit.

Caves of the Western Wei dynasty (535–557)

Cave No. 428 of the Northern Zhou dynasty (557–581) portrays the self-sacrifice of Prince Sudana. Cave No. 296 is also of interest.

Caves of the Northern Zhou dynasty

95 caves remain from the time of the Sui dynasty, when Buddhist art showed marked Chinese characteristics.

Cave No. 419 houses a group of coloured clay statues, including a Buddha, two Bodhisattvas and Ananda (Buddha's favourite disciple). Note

Caves of the Sui dynasty (581–618)

211

in particular the sculpture of the ascetic Mahakasyapa, who reflects the joy felt by one who has passed all the tests that life can impose. His decayed teeth, deeply-lined face and the protruding veins in his neck all show how this ascetic suffered.

The wall-painting in Cave No. 423 shows the God of the East, an immortal being from Chinese mythology.

Note also Caves Nos. 244, 294, 295, 305, 404, 420 and 427.

The 213 preserved caves from the Tang period, where again a degree of Indian influence can be seen, make up the largest group. The largest Dunhuang statue, a 33m/108ft high Buddha Amitabha, will be found in Cave No. 96.

Cave No. 136 contains a 26m/85ft high figure, and No. 158 a reclining figure of Buddha as he enters Nirvana.

The wall-painting in Cave No. 220 shows a concert with musical instruments of the period – a valuable contribution to our knowledge of Chinese musical history.

In Cave No. 329 can be seen the famous wall-painting of "The Land of Buddha", the Land of Purity. In the centre of the picture sits Amitabha on a throne of lotus blossom, with a Bodhisattva on each side. In front of him several young ladies are dancing and an orchestra is playing. Asparas, Buddhist angels, float between the clouds in the sky.

Also of interest are Caves Nos. 45, 112, 156, 217, 320–322, 328 and 445.

Caves of the Tang dynasty (618–907)

The persecution of Buddhists in 845 brought a stagnation of Buddhist art in its wake. As there was no space for any further caves to be built the existing ones were later restored. From that period 33 caves remain, and of these No. 16 is of particular interest. It contains a painting measuring 13·5m by 5m/44ft by 16ft of the Wutaishan Mountains and everyday scenes from this mountain region. It is a sort of map of the country, one of the oldest of its kind in China. Note also Cave No. 98.

Period of the Five Dynasties (907–960) and of the Early Song (960–1279)

During the Western Xia period little other than restoration work was carried out on the caves, while in the Yuan period nine new caves were constructed. Cave No. 465 is from this era and boasts 60 well-preserved frescos showing shepherds and craftsmen at work.

Western Xia (1032–1227) and Yuan period (1271–1368)

Other Sights

Mingshashan, 5km/3 miles south of Dunhuang, is 40km/25 miles long and 20km/12½ miles wide. It was formed from quicksand. If someone slides down the hill it makes a whistling or ringing sound, from where it gets its name of the Ringing Mountain of Sand.

The Ringing Mountain of Sand (Mingshashan)

7km/4½ miles south of Dunhuang lies this lake, which gets its name from its crescent-like shape. The formation of the lake resulted from a geological peculiarity – the north and south slopes are higher than the east and west – and from the wind which blows from west to east. The wind initially blows in a south-easterly direction, is then forced upwards where it rotates spirally before finally retreating in an easterly direction. As a result, the lake has never once become silted up with sand in 1000 years.

Lake of the Crescent Moon (Yueyaquan)

30km/19 miles south-west of Dunhuang will be found the Western Caves of the 1000 Buddhas. These are of rather less importance. They contain paintings from the Northern Wei period (386–534), the Tang period (618–907) and the period of the Five Dynasties (907–960).

Western caves of the 1000 Buddhas (Xi Qianfo Dong)

◄ *Statue of the Tang period in the Mogao Ku Caves*

Foshan

J 7

Chinese
equivalent

佛山市

Province: Guangdong
Altitude: 5m/16ft. Area: 77sq.km/30sq. miles
Population: 333,000 (conurbation 2,630,000)

Situation

Foshan lies in the centre of the south of Guangdong province, about
20km/12½ miles south-west of Canton, at 113°10′E and 23°04′N.

History

Archaeological finds in Foshan prove that the region was inhabited 2000
years ago. In 628 three bronze Buddha statues were discovered, and these
gave the town its name – Foshan literally means "Buddha Mountain". It
became an important Buddhist site. Under the Song dynasty (960–1279)

To Guangzhou 26 km

Foshan was known as a centre of the porcelain industry (Shiwan porcelain), metalworking and silk-weaving. Porcelain manufacture is still a major industry, together with skilled crafts such as that of folding and cutting paper patterns.

The Temple of the Ancestors dates originally from the second half of the 11th c., and was restored in 1372 following a fire. It is dedicated to the God of the North, Ruler of the Waters, and not – as is often wrongly assumed – to ancestors as such. The Chinese name "Foshan Zumiao", or "Temple of the Ancestors", simply implies that it is the oldest temple in the town. The rich ceiling decoration with many figures is its most interesting feature.

The complex covers an area of 3000sq.m/32,300sq.ft and includes the following buildings: the portico (Qian Dian), the main hall (Zheng Dian), the Festival Hall of Truth (Qingzhen Lou), the Pond of Scented Brocade (Jin-xiang Chi) and the Theatre of a Thousand Good Fortunes (Wanfu Tai).

In the walled pond in front of the portico there is a stone turtle, a symbol of long life. At one time performances were held in the theatre, which is decorated with gilded carvings.

The Institute of Folk Art is now housed in the former Temple of Brotherly Love and Long Life (Ren Shou Si) with its red pagoda. Porcelain, paper designs and Chinese lanterns made of various materials are produced here.

Fujian

Province
Area: 121,380sq.km/46,865sq. miles
Population: 30,790,000. Capital: Fuzhou

Fujian province lies on the south-east coast of China, between 115°50′ and 120°47′E and 23°30′ and 28°19′N. It is separated from Taiwan by the Formosa Strait.

Some 90% of the province is mountainous country, running from south-west to north-east parallel to the coast. The few areas of plains lie in the east towards the sea. There are 6,500,000ha/16,250,000 acres of forest.

The subtropical climate of this zone is very strongly influenced by monsoons. The period in which frosts occur is limited to 100 days of the year.

Between the 8th and 1st c. B.C. Fujian alternated between being independent or forming part of the Chinese Empire, where it remained apart from a period during the first half of the 10th c. As early as the 11th c. foreign trade developed, and this was always an important factor for Fujian. Increasing overseas trade saw the beginning of a wave of emigrants to south-east Asia, among other places, After 1949 the Taiwan question brought a reduction in external trade.

Fujian is classed as a Special Economic Zone, which resulted in somewhat frenzied economic development during the 1980s. Important factors in its economy are the cultivation of rice (two harvests each year), tea and sugar-cane, as well as the timber industry and fishing. Other agricultural products include sweet potatoes, citrus fruits, bananas, wheat, ground-nuts, rape and tobacco.

China

Fujian Province

HEILONGJIANG

JILIN

INNER MONGOLIA
(NEIMENGGU)

LIAONING

XINJIANG

©Baedeker

GANSU

INNER MONGOLIA **BEIJING**
(NEIMENGGU) **(PEKING)**

TIANJIN

HEBEI

NINGXIA

SHANXI

SHANDONG

QINGHAI

GANSU

SHAANXI

HENAN

JIANGSU

XIZANG (TIBET)

HUBEI

ANHUI

SHANGHAI

SICHUAN

ZHEJIANG

JIANGXI

GUIZHOU

HUNAN

FUJIAN

YUNNAN

GUANGXI

GUANGDONG

TAIWAN

XIANG GANG
(HONGKONG)

AO MEN
(MACAO)

HAINAN

The People's Republic of China

Zhonghua Renmin Gongheguo

In the industrial sector food, steel and chemicals are of importance. Major minerals include coal, iron-ore, copper and wolfram.

Places to visit

In addition to the capital Fuzhou, Xiamen and Quanzhou (see entries) possess places of interest to tourists.

Fushun

L 3

Chinese equivalent

抚顺市

Province: Liaoning. Area: 200sq.km/77sq. miles
Population: 1,190,000 (conurbation 2,060,000)

Situation and Communications

Fushun lies on the Hunhe river in the east of Liaoning province, about 50km/30 miles from Shenyang. at 123°51′E and 41°50′N. There are bus and train services to Fushun from Shenyang.

History

Fushun is about 4000 years old; however, it was not given its present name until 1384. Before the Manchurians conquered the whole of China they chose the town as their seat of government and changed its name to Xinjing ("New Capital").

In the early 20th c. a start was made in mining the region's rich coal deposits, and this soon grew apace.

From the 1950s onwards other important branches of industry developed, such as oil-refining and iron-smelting, electronics and engineering.

Sights

Gao'ershan Pagoda
(Gao'ershan Ta)

The Gao'ershan Pagoda, built under the Liao dynasty (916–1125), stands in the north of the town behind the Pavilion of the Goddess of Mercy (Guanyin Ge). Its details, such as the octagonal substructure, reflect the style typical of its period.

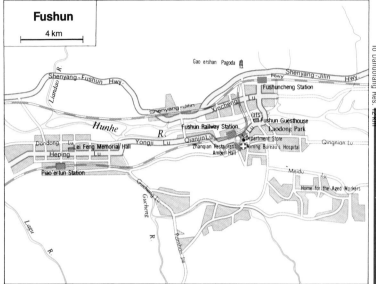

Surroundings

Dahoufang Reservoir, situated in some beautiful countryside 15km/9 miles from Fushun, was built between 1954 and 1958 and measures 110sq.km/42½sq. miles in area.

Dahoufang Reservoir

Adjoining the reservoir is the Yuanshualin Tomb, originally built in 1929 as the last resting-place of the commander-in-chief Zhang Zuolin.

Yuanshualin Tomb

When the Japanese invaded in 1931 work on the building had to be interrupted. The many stone carvings and sculptures from the Ming and Qing periods (14th–20th c.) are of interest; many of them come from the Temple of Long'en Si in Beijing.

This 70m/230ft high mountain to the south-east of the reservoir was the scene of a battle in which the Qing were victorious over the Ming. To commemorate the event Emperor Hongli erected an inscribed stone stele here in 1776.

Mount Sa'erhushan

Built in 1598, this mausoleum 100km/62 miles east of Fushun is one of the three Qing Imperial Tombs (1644–1911) in the north-east of China; the other two are to be found near Shenyang, the capital of Liaoning province.
    Covering an area of 11,880sq.m/3 acres, this burial site is the last resting place of the father, grandfather and great-grandfather of the first Qing emperor.
    The complex is divided into three parts – the entrance courtyard (qianyuan) with four memorial stelae, the rectangular fortress with the Temple of Good Fortune (qiyundian) and the citadel (baocheng) containing the four graves.

★Yongling Mausoleum

Fuzhou

Chinese
equivalent

福州市

Capital of Fujian Province
Altitude: 10m/33ft. Area: 1043sq.km/403sq. miles
Population: 1,170,000 (conurbation 1,830,000)

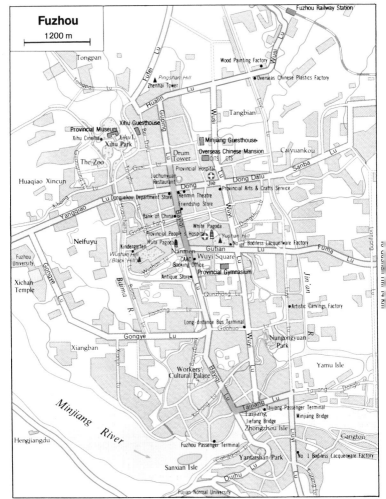

To airport 6 km

Fuzhou lies on the Minjian river in the east of Fujian province and some 50km/30 miles from the sea, at 119°18'E and 26°06'N.

The town can be reached by rail or air from Beijing, Shanghai, Canton, Tianjin and Hangzhou.

Fuzhou has a past stretching back more than 2000 years. In 202 B.C. it was the capital of the Yue kingdom and in the 10th c. of the Min kingdom. It was given its present name in 725. Fuzhou is known as "Banyan Town" because of the subtropical banyan trees planted during the Song period (960–1279). Since that time overseas trade has developed more and more, as a result of which many foreigners have settled in the region, especially on the island of Nantai. In 1842, following the Opium Wars, Fuzhou became one of the five ports which were declared open to foreign trade.

In 1949 industrialisation commenced when Fuzhou was linked to the major rail routes and the Minjiang river was extended to accommodate shipping; the main branches are engineering and light industry.

Sights

Yushan Hill with its fine views dominates the town centre; it is known particularly for the hundred or more inscriptions, dating from the 10th to 19th c., which decorate its rock faces.

The town's symbol, the 41m/135ft high, seven-storey White Pagoda at the western foot of the hill, was built in 904 as a wooden-clad brick building; however, it burned down in 1534 after being struck by lightning. It was rebuilt in brick in 1548.

Behind it stands a temple (Baita Si) built in the Qing dynasty (1644–1911) on the foundations of a Buddhist temple dating from 905. Today it houses a library.

The temple to the east was built in 1918 in honour of General Qi Jiguang (1528–87), who had fought against Japanese pirates in 1562.

On the top of the hill can be seen the Hall of the Great Master, or Guanyin Hall (Guanyin Ge), built in 1713. In 1911 it was used as the headquarters of the revolutionary army. An inscription by the Emperor Qianlong (1736–96) on a stone tablet relates how Bodhisattva Avalokiteshvara changed into a woman, the Goddess of Mercy (Guanyin), who is so revered by Chinese Buddhists.

Also in the town centre, 1·5km/1 mile west of Yushan Hill, stands Black Hill, which has been a popular spot for outings for hundreds of years. More than 200 inscriptions are engraved on its rock faces, the best-known being that made in 772 by Li Yangbing, a notable Tang calligrapher. Of historical importance are inscriptions made by some eunuchs from the Ming period (1368–1644) giving detailed descriptions of their many duties, especially of their work in the shipyards.

On the eastern foothills stands the 35m/115ft high granite-built Black Pagoda, dating from the year 941 and so named as a counterpart to the White Pagoda. It stands on the site of a stupa from the Tang period (618–907). In the course of extensive restoration work in 1957 measures were taken to halt the subsidence which had occurred on one side. Near the Black Pagoda can be seen a stele from the Tang era.

West Lake, situated in Xihu Park in the north-west of the town, was named after the better-known lake of the same name in Hangzhou (see entry), and is a favourite leisure spot. Banyan trees and meadows are a feature of the land along the banks. The lake was dug out in A.D. 282 as part of of an irrigation project. The Provincial Museum is in Xihu Park.

Temple of
Hualin Si

On the southern slopes of Mount Pingshan in the north of Fuzhou stands the Hualin Si temple, from the Tang period (618–907). The main building, the Sumptuous Hall of the Great Hero (Daixong Baodian) built in the Tong era (960–1279), is all that remains of the early edifice, the other buildings having been added during the Qing dynasty (1644–1911).

Tomb of Lin Zexu

This tomb lies in a northern suburb of Fuzhou. In 1839 the supreme commander Lin Zexu (1785–1850) confiscated and burned 20,000 cases of opium which the British had smuggled into China from India, and this led to the outbreak of the Opium Wars.

Surroundings

Temple of Sublime
Good Fortune
(Chongfu Si)

The Temple of Sublime Good Fortune, at the foot of Mount North (Beiling), 8km/5 miles north of Fuzhou, was founded back in 977. However, the buildings which have survived date from the Guangxu period (1875–1908).

Drum Mountain
(Gushan)

Drum Mountain, 969m/3180ft high and lying 14km/9 miles east of the town, was named after a rock on one of its peaks which is said to emit drum-like sounds during storms and rain. It offers much in the way of interesting sights.

Temple of the
Bubbling Spring
(Yongquan Si)

This monastery, built on a hillside 455m/1490ft up in the year 908 on the orders of the Duke of Fujian in order to provide accommodation for the monk Shen Yan, was destroyed by fire in 1542 and rebuilt in 1627. Its cultural treasures include an extensive Buddhist library with over 10,000 sutra volumes and a statue in white jade of a reclining Buddha. Some of these books were written with the blood of ascetics who pricked their index finger with a needle and then used the finger as a brush.

Ceramic Pagodas
of a Thousand
Buddhas
(Qianfo Taota)

These two nine-storey pagodas in front of the temple are scarcely 7m/23ft high and date from 1082. They originally formed part of the Temple of the Dragon of Good Fortune (Longrui Si) on Nantai Island, and were moved here in 1972. A total of 1078 Buddha miniatures are attached to the external walls.

The rock-inscriptions (moya shike) which can be found everywhere in the vicinity of Fuzhou and number more than 400 in all range in date from the Song period (960–1297) to the 20th c.; some of them are by famous calligraphers, academics and statesmen.

Temple of
Linyang Si

On Mount Beifengshan, 19km/12 miles from Fuzhou, lies Linyang Si temple, from the year 931. However, the buildings which remain date from the end of the last century.

Luoxing Ta

The Luoxing Ta pagoda, from the Song period (960–1279), stands on the mountain of the same name near the port of Mawei Gang, 21km/13 miles south-east of the town.

According to legend, it was built by a woman in memory of her husband who was hanged for a crime he did not commit. The edifice, which is visible from afar because of its elevated position, was restored between 1621 and 1627.

★**Mount Wuyishan**

Mount Wuyishan lies in the north of Fujian province on the border with Jiangxi province. From Fuzhou take the train to Nanping and then continue by bus.

This mountain has been famous for centuries as a place of great scenic beauty, and also because of Lake Wulong and the various healing herbs which grow there. The terrain has been declared a nature reserve in view of the many different species of plants and animals.

When walking on the mountain be very careful of poisonous snakes.

Note

The main area of interest is that along the River of the Nine Meanders (Jiuqu Xi), which flows through this region for a distance of 7km/4½ miles. A boat trip down-river takes about 1½ hours.

Places to visit

On the first bend in the river stands the Great Royal Peak (Dawang Feng); it can be climbed by way of a narrow rocky path leading up its south side.

On the third bend, in crevices high up in the rocks, the visitor can see wooden boats in which the Guyue used to bury their dead more than 2000 years ago.

Near the fifth bend in the river there was a private school, where the philosopher Zhu Xi (1130–1200) was a teacher.

Gansu

F–I 3–5

甘肃省

Chinese equivalent

Province
Area: 451,000sq.km/174,130sq. miles
Population: 22,850,000. Capital: Lanzhou

Gansu province lies in the north-west of China, between 93°28′ and 108°44′E and 32°36′ and 42°48′N.

Situation

The height of the province above sea-level varies between 1000m and 3000m/3300ft and 9900ft, the highest peak being 5808m/19,060ft and the lowest point 600m/1970ft. Plateaux predominate in the north and east, with steppes covering almost 30% of the land in the south and west. The eastern part of Gansu is a loess (fine, windblown soil) region through which flows the Huanghe river.

Topography

China

Gansu Province

The People's Republic of China
Zhonghua Renmin Gongheguo

Houses of compressed mud in Gansu

To the north-west, between the north-eastern edge of the Qinghai-Tibet Plateau and the Gobi Desert, the province is in the form of a long "corridor", with oases fed by water from the Qilianshan Mountains marking the course of the Silk Road.

Climate

The climate has a Continental character, with cold, dry winters and warm, humid summers.

History

Gansu became part of the Chinese empire back in the time of Emperor Shihuang of the Qin dynasty (221–206 B.C.). Being surrounded by oases the region was well suited to serve as a part of a route linking east to west. Buddhism found its way here along this route as early as the 1st c. B.C. As a result a number of trading centres along the Silk Road, such as Dunhuang and Jiuquan, became centres of the new religion, accompanied by the construction of numerous cave temples, the most famous of which being those in Dunhuang.

Economy

Traditionally a poor region, the province has enjoyed rapid industrial development in recent years, with Lanzhou becoming the centre of industry and transport. Crude oil exploration has become of great importance, and other natural resources include coal, copper, lead and zinc.

There is a water shortage in most parts of the province, so irrigation projects are essential to agricultural development. However, such projects often result in serious problems brought about by large-scale resettlement programmes, since most peasants have no desire to leave their land. The major agricultural products are wheat, maize, millet, cotton, linseed and melons. Pigs, sheep, cattle and horses are also reared.

Sights

The towns of Dunhuang and Jiuquan (see entries) offer much of interest to the visitor.

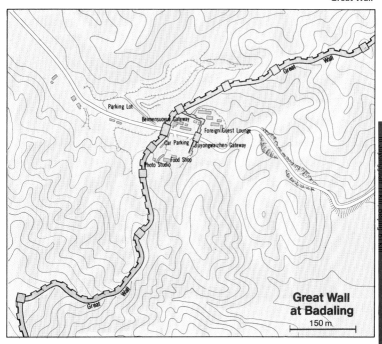

Parking Lot

Beimensuoyue Gateway

Foreign Guest Lounge

Car Parking   Jiyongwaizhen Gateway

Photo Studio   Food Shop

Great Wall at Badaling

150 m

Great Wall

万里长城

Chinese equivalent

"Nobody can be a true hero unless he has travelled along the Great Wall" goes the popular saying, and this clearly demonstrates the great importance which the Chinese attach to this unique monument. The Great Wall (in Chinese Wanli Chang Cheng, or The Wall That Is Ten Thousand Li In Length) today stretches about 6000km/3700 miles in all, from Shanghaiguan Pass in the east to Jiayuguan Pass in the west. It passes through Hebei, Tientsin, Beijing, Shanxi, Inner Mongolia, Ningxia, Shaanxi and Gansu. It averages 6 to 8m/20 to 26ft in height, rising to 16m/52ft in places, and is 6 to 7m/20 to 23ft wide at the top with battlements and watch-towers. Because of the poor condition of much of it only some sections are open to visitors. Along the wall will be found many cultural monuments and historical towns. There are a large number of walls in China with a total length of 50,000km/30,000 miles.

Building of the wall began in the Spring and Autumn periods, between the 8th and 5th c. B.C., and work continued during the subsequent period of the Warring Kingdoms (475–221 B.C.). Fearing attacks by neighbouring states and by the Huns and other tribes who had settled in north and west China, the individual emperors built massive defensive complexes along their boundaries. Following the unification of the country in 221 B.C. Emperor Qin Shi Huangdi (221–210 B.C.) ordered the various defensive walls to be joined up to form one great wall. 300,000 soldiers and 500,000 peasants,

History

223

The Great Wall near Beijing

many of whom died, were forced to work for several years on his mammoth construction of rammed earth. After completion it measured some 5000km/3000 miles in length and reached from Lintao in the west to Liadong peninsula in the east. Under the Han dynasty (206 B.C. to A.D. 220) it grew to 10,000km/6000 miles. In the Ming period (1368–1644), when the country was attacked by Mongols from the north and tribes of hunters from the north-east, the wall was strengthened and lengthened; many sections were completely rebuilt in brick and stone, and watch-towers erected at intervals of between 200 and 300m/220 and 330yd. The first Ming Emperor Zhu Yuanzhang ordered his General Xu Da to improve and renew the wall and defend the passes. Nine commanders, under the direct command of the Emperor himself, were put in charge of the defences. Most of the Great Wall as we see it today was built under this dynasty, although parts were destroyed by local inhabitants who stole stones from it to build houses and roads.

★Jugongguan Pass

Jugongguan Pass begins 50km/30 miles north-west of Beijing, extends for over 20km/12½ miles through a valley and ends 5km/3 miles from Badaling. After the Great Wall had been completed Emperor Qin Shi Huangdi settled the workers in a number of villages scattered along this valley; none of which survive today. At one time the pass was strategically very important as it safeguarded the northern approach to Beijing. The fortress here dates from the 14th c. The Terrace of the Clouds (Yuntai), built of marble *c.* 1345, measures 10m/33ft high, 27m/89ft long and 18m/59ft wide, and once had three towers and later a temple. Today it boasts an arched gateway decorated with reliefs of deities, guardians of the heavens and mythological animals as well as Buddhist inscriptions in Sanskrit, Tibetan, Mongolian. the Xixia language, Uigur and Chinese.

★★Badaling

One of the best-maintained sections of the Great Wall (restored in 1957) is unquestionably that near Badaling Pass, at a height of 1000m/3300ft above

China

The People's Republic of China
Zhonghua Renmin Gongheguo

sea-level and 85km/53 miles north-west of Beijing, from where it can be reached by train or bus. This section of the wall is between 7 and 8m/23 and 26ft high and 5 to 6m/16 to 20ft wide. Ten men or five horses can stand side by side across the top. It is faced with three layers of bricks. Along the inside runs a parapet 1m/3ft high and along the outside are battlements twice that height. The wall was also important as a traffic route.

In this mountain pass there is a fort built in 1502 which covers an area of 5000sq.m/53,000sq.ft. In the exhibition hall in front of it visitors can see terracotta figures of warriors from the Qin period (221–206 B.C.).

The section of the Great Wall near Gubeikou, 130km/80 miles from Beijing, is also very impressive. It was built on Mounts Panlong and Wohu and there is a wonderful view from here. The defensive tower built during the Ming period (1368–1644) is now just a ruin.

Gubeikou

Guangdong

I–K 6–7

Chinese equivalent

Province
Area: 198,500sq.km/76,640sq. miles
Population: 64,390,000. Capital: Canton

Traversed by the Tropic of Cancer, Guangdong lies in south China, between 108°13′ and 119°59′E and 3°28′ and 25°31′N. Its jurisdiction covers a mainland region together with a number of islands scattered over the South China Sea. The main dialect is Cantonese, which is spoken mainly in the west and north of the province, while the Hakka dialect will be heard in the north and Fujian in the eastern coastal region.

Situation and Dialects

Guangxi

Topography	Guangdong is distinguished by mountainous country, which in the north is separated from the Changjiang river valley by the 2000m/6600ft high Nanling Mountains, and by flatlands at the mouth of the Xijiang and on the Leizhou peninsula.
Climate	The monsoon climate is typical of tropical and subtropical areas of China. Temperatures often climb as high as 40°C/104°F, and most of the rain falls during the summer months, when Guangdong is often struck by typhoons.
History	Under the Qin Emperor Shi Huangdi (reigned 221–210 B.C.), at a time when Guangdong was inhabited by minority peoples and not by the Han, some areas of the province became part of the Chinese Empire, which subsequently swallowed up the whole region during the Han period (206 B.C. to A.D. 220). As a result of its coastal situation foreign influences have been evident here ever since the Tang period (618–907), when a mosque was built in Canton. Trade with other countries developed considerably until the 12th c. At that time, and in the centuries which followed, many Han came to Guangdong. From the 16th c. onwards European influence began to be felt in Guangdong; in 1553 Macau became Portuguese, in 1841–42 Hong Kong was taken over by the British and in 1898 Canton came under French administration. Large numbers of people emigrated to south-east Asia and North America, and half of the Chinese overseas population hailed originally from Guangdong.
Economy	Guangdong is China's richest province, and produces an eighth of the country's total income. In 1992 it showed a growth rate of about 19%; local investment grew by 35% and almost one-half of overseas investments in China were made in the province. Its proximity to Hong Kong and Macau aided its economic growth. Light industry (food and textiles) plays an important part, and mention should also be made of such heavy industry as metal-working, engineering and shipbuilding. Only about 15% of the total area of the province is suitable for agricultural purposes. Two-thirds of the agricultural land is devoted to rice growing, and the climate means that two annual rice harvests are possible. Fruit-growing – mainly bananas, mandarins, pineapples and lychees – is also of importance. Other agricultural products include sugar-cane, tea, tobacco and ground-nuts. Fishing in the South China Sea makes an important contribution to the economy.
Places to visit	In addition to the provincial capital Canton (see entry), Foshan, Zhaoqing, Shenzhen, Shantou, Zhanjiang and Zhuhai (see entries) are all of interest.

Guangxi   H–J 6–7

Chinese equivalent	广西壮族自治区

Autonomous Region
Area: 236,000sq.km/91,000sq. miles
Population: 43,240,000. Capital: Nanning

Situation and People	The autonomous region of Guangxi lies in south China, between 104°29′ and 112°03′E and 20°54′ and 26°23′N. In addition to the Han population, a large proportion of the people living in Guangxi belong to the ethnic minority known as the Zhuang, whose language is similar to that of the Thais. In addition, the Yao, Miao, Dong, Maonan, Hui, Jing, Yi, Shui and Gelao ethnic groups all live here. It was for that reason that in 1958 the central government established the Autonomous Region of Guangxi, one of the five such autonomous regions for

China

Autonomous Region Guangxi

HEILONGJIANG

JILIN

INNER MONGOLIA (NEIMENGGU)

LIAONING

XINJIANG

© Baedeker

GANSU

INNER MONGOLIA (NEIMENGGU)

BEIJING (PEKING)

TIANJIN

HEBEI

NINGXIA

SHANXI

SHANDONG

QINGHAI

GANSU

SHAANXI

HENAN

JIANGSU

XIZANG (TIBET)

SICHUAN

HUBEI

ANHUI

SHANGHAI

ZHEJIANG

JIANGXI

GUIZHOU

HUNAN

FUJIAN

YUNNAN

GUANGXI

GUANGDONG

TAIWAN

XIANG GANG (HONGKONG)

AO MEN (MACAO)

HAINAN

The People's Republic of China
Zhonghua Renmin Gongheguo

national minorities with a status similar to that of a province (the other four being Xinjiang, Inner Mongolia, Tibet and Ningxia). The birth-control regulations which apply to all Han people do not apply to the minorities, with the result that in some cases their rate of population growth clearly exceeds that of the Han population.

Some 85% of this region on the upper reaches of the Xijiang river is boldly structured mountainous country of karst stone rising from the coastal plain on the Gulf of Tonkin (Beibu Wan) in the south (which extends as far as the central part of the region) up to the plateaux of Guizhou and Yunnan. The highest peak is Mount Miao'ershan (2142m/7030ft), in the northern Yuecheng Ling chain.

Topography

The subtropical monsoon climate is characterised by long, hot summers and generally mild winters. In July the average temperature reaches 27°C/81°F in the north and 32°C/90°F in the south, while in the month of January it is 4°C/39°F in the north and 16°C/61°F in the south. Rain falls in the months of April to September, with annual amounts of between 1000 and 2000mm/40 and 80in.

Climate

Conflicts have been the dominating factor in Guangxi's history. Up until the 19th c. the Han and the ethnic minorities fought for possession of the region, and then the French and the British tried to gain control. At the end of the 19th c. Longzhou, Wuzhou and Nanning were obliged to open themselves up to foreign trade. In 1939 and 1944 Guangxi was occupied by the Japanese.

History

After 1949 Guangxi's industry grew at a fast rate; major branches are food (sugar factories), metallurgy and chemicals, engineering, cement and electronics. Mineral resources include crude oil, natural gas, coal, iron, zinc, nickle and bauxite. Agriculture is Guangxi's major industry, however, even though only 12% of the total land area is suitable for cultivation. Tropical fruits such as bananas and pineapples are important crops. The climate in

Economy

the south in particular means that rice (two crops every year) and sugar-cane can be grown. In the wooded north sandalwood and cork are produced. Fishing also has an important role to play.

Places to visit

The province is one of the most beautiful regions of China. In addition to the capital Nanning (see entry), Guilin, Luizhou and Wuzhou (see entries) have much to offer.

Guangzhou

See Canton

Guilin   J 6

Chinese equivalent

Autonomous Region of Guangxi
Altitude: 150m/492ft
Area: 54sq.km/21sq. miles
Population: 290,000 (conurbation 685,000)

Situation and Communications

Guilin lies at 110°17′E and 25°16′N, in the middle of some fabulously beautiful countryside in the north-east of the autonomous region of Guangxi.

As Guilin is one of China's main tourist attractions there are frequent air flights from Beijing, Canton and Hong Kong. From Nanning, the capital of Guangxi, it is an eleven hour train ride to Guilin.

★★Town features

Several crystal-clear rivers meander through the town, which is encircled by a ring of mountains with bizarre rock-formations and caves. The landscape was formed over a period of some 200 million years, when the sea still reached this far inland. Layers of *muschelkalk* (chalk formed from fossilised shells) were deposited; then the earth's crust was formed, the chalk stratified and was shaped by wind and water to produce vast numbers of caves.

All that makes Guilin a unique natural experience. For hundreds of years poets and artists have been fascinated by the the sheer splendour of the unique scenery, around which many fairy-tales and legends have been woven. In autumn the scent of cinnamon trees fills the air.

History

The Qin Emperor Shi Huangdi (reigned 221–210 B.C.) laid the Lingqu Canal which links the Lijiang and Xiangjiang rivers. Although today it is used mainly for irrigation purposes, for many centuries the canal was the main traffic route between south and central China. Guilin has now become the capital of the administrative region of the same name. It obtains its name ("Forest of Cinnamon Trees") from the subtropical cinnamons which have been a feature of the town since ancient times. In the mid-17th c. the Ming government took up residence here when fleeing from the Manchurians. When the Qing dynasty (1644–1911) succeeded the Mings Guilin was made the capital of Guangxi and attained this status again between 1936 and 1949, after which it was finally replaced by Nanning. During the Sino-Japanese War many people from the north fled to Guilin. Its economic situation has improved considerably during recent years.

Beautiful scenery around Guilin ▶

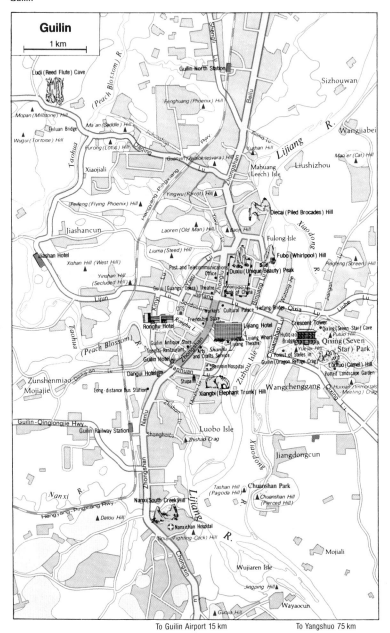

Guilin

1 km

Ludi (Reed Flute) Cave
Guilin North Station
Sizhouwan
Mopan (Millstone) Hill
Peach Blossom R.
Fenghuang (Phoenix) Hill
Ma'an (Saddle) Hill
Beilu
Lijiang R.
Wangjiabei
Feiluan Bridge
Taohua
Daqing Lu
Juhuatang
Wugui (Tortoise) Hill
Furong (Lotus) Hill
Xinma Lu
Yushan Hill
Mao'er (Cat) Hill
Hengyang–Pingxiang
Guanyin (Avalokitesvara) Hill
Zhongshan
Liushizhou
Xiaojiali
Mahuang (Leech) Isle
Feifeng (Flying Phoenix) Hill
Yingwu (Parrot) Hill
Lu
Diecai (Piled Brocades) Hill
Jiashancun
Laoren (Old Man) Hill
Baoji Hill
Fulong Isle
Xiaodong R.
Jiashan Hotel
Liuma (Steed) Hill
Fubo (Whirlpool) Hill
Pingfeng (Screen) Hill
Xishan Hill (West Hill)
Yinshan Hill (Secluded Hill)
Post and Telecommunications Office
Duxiu (Unique Beauty) Peak
Lijun
Taoyuan
Guilin (Guangxi) Opera Theatre
Wenhua Lu
Bank of China
Peach Blossom R.
Xinyi Lu
Ronghu L.
Sanduoli
Jiefang Lu
Jiefang Bridge
Qixia Lu
Liuhe Lu
CITS
Workers' Cultural Palace
Zhongshan
Crescent Tower
Qixing (Seven Star) Cave
Putuo Hill
Ronghu Hotel
Friendship Store
Lijiang Hotel
Forest of Steles in Huaqiao Bridge
Qixing (Seven Star) Park
Guilin Antique Store
Arts and Crafts Service
Shanhu
Lijiang Wharf
Lijiang Theatre
Yueya Hill
Tonglai Restaurant
Renmin Hospital
Guilin (Dragon Refuge Crag)
Luotuo (Camel) Hill
Guilin Hotel
Wanhuan
Potted Landscape Garden
Dangui Hotel
Stupa
Zizhou Isle
Wangchenggang
Huixian (Immortals Meeting) Crag
Zunshenmiao
Mojiajie
Long-distance Bus Station
Xiangbi (Elephant Trunk) Hill
Guilin–Qinglongjie Hwy.
Guilin Railway Station
Nanlu
Luobo Isle
Jiangdongcun
Shanghaitu
Zhishan Crag
Xiaodong R.
Zhishan
Nanxi R.
Zhongshan
Lijiang R.
Tashan Hill (Pagoda Hill)
Chuanshan Park
Chuanshan Hill (Pierced Hill)
Nanxi (South Creek) Hill
Hengyang–Pingxiang Hwy.
Datou Hill
Nanxishan Hospital
Mojiali
Douji (Fighting Cock) Hill
Chonglian
Wujiaren Isle
Jingping Hill
Guota Hill
Wayaocun

To Guilin Airport 15 km   To Yangshuo 75 km

Sights

A steep path of 306 steps leads up to the top of the Mount of Unique Beauty in the town centre. It is 152m/500ft high, and from the top there is a magnificent view over the town and the surrounding area. The peak is dominated by an arched edifice known as The Southern Gateway to Heaven (Nantian Men). There are a number of caves on the mountain slopes, the inner and outer walls of which are covered in inscriptions from the Tang (618–907) and Qing (1644–1911) eras. To the south of the mountain, on the land belonging to the teacher training college, stands the Wangcheng, once the residence of the King of Jingjiang. All that remains are parts of the walls together with some balustrades and staircases.

★Peak of Unique Beauty (Duxiu Feng)

Whirlpool Hill lies 300m/330yd to the east of the Peak of Unique Beauty. The iron bell weighing 2½ tonnes and the giant Pot of a Thousand Men are from the Dingyue Si temple of Diecaishan and date from the Qing period (1644–1911).

Whirlpool Hill (Fuboshan)

The Cave of the Returned Pearls lies at the foot of the Mountain of the Gentle Waves. According to legend, this was the lair of a dragon which owned a glowing string of pearls. A fisherman found them and took them, but he was plagued by pangs of conscience and finally returned the jewels to their owner. In the cave will be found the touchstone on which swordsmen tested their weapons. On Qianfo Yan Rock can be seen over 200 Buddhist sculptures and inscriptions from Tang and Song era (7th–13th c.).

Cave of the Returned Pearls (Huanzhu Dong)

The Mountain of Piled Brocades (or Mountain of Cinnamon Trees, because these evergreen trees once grew on its slopes) has a number of peaks and stands in the north of the town on the banks of the beautiful Lijiang river. It was a popular place with visitors more than 1000 years ago, largely because of the many pavilions and monuments which public and literary figures had erected here; unfortunately, none of these have survived the

Mountain of Piled Brocades (Diecaishan)

"Elephant Trunk" Hill

River Lijiang

ravages of time. In the caves can be found Buddhist sculptures and in-scriptions from the Tang and Song period (7th–13th c.). From the highest peak, Mingyue Fen (223m/732ft) there is a picturesque view of the town and its surroundings.

★Seven Star Park
(Qixing
Gongyuan)

Seven Star Park lies in the east of the town. It covers an area of 40ha/100 acres, making it Guilin's largest public park, and derives its name from its seven hills, the layout of which is similar to that of the stars in the Great Bear constellation. At the entrance will be found the Bridge of Flowers (Huaqiao) from the Song period (960–1279). The four northernmost hills, the Putuoshan, contain a number of caves, including Seven Star Cave. The three southern peaks form the Yueshan Hills. The woods containing stone inscriptions, mostly from the Song period, will be found interesting.

Camel Hill
(Luotuoshan)

Camel Hill, 22m/72ft high, is in the south-east of the park; as its name suggests, it looks rather like a sitting dromedary. Peach trees are scattered over it, and these give it a pink tinge in spring. The Municipal Zoo at its western foot is open to visitors.

Seven Star Cave
(Qixing Yan)

Seven Star Cave, formed from a subterranean river-bed, measures 800m/880yd in length overall and is made up of several grottos, both small and large, linked by zig-zag passageways. It has attracted visitors for centuries. The largest cave is 43m/140ft wide and 27m/89ft high, with a constant internal tem-perature of about 20°C/68°F. Its walls are covered with writings and poems by famous calligraphers, statesmen and men of letters, the oldest inscription dating from the year 590.

Dragon Refuge
Cave
(Longyin Yan)

Dragon Refuge Cave in the west of the park contains over one hundred inscriptions, ranging in date from the Northern Song period (960–1126) to the early 20th c.

★Elephant Trunk Hill
(Xiangbi Shan)

Elephant Trunk Hill can be found on the west bank of the Lijiang river, in the south of the town. Its shape is reminiscent of an elephant dipping its trunk in the river. Legend says that an elephant which belonged to the Emperor of Heaven came down to earth to help the people in their work. This angered the Emperor of Heaven, who stabbed the elephant as it was drinking at the river's edge and turned it to stone. The cave between the "body" and the "trunk" is of a particularly interesting shape and has inspired poets and writers old and new to engrave verses on its walls. The poems of Lo You, Fan Chengda and other poets of the Song dynasty (960–1279) are of inestimable literary and archaeo-logical value. On the top of the hill stands the Puxian Ta Pagoda in the shape of the handle of the dagger with which the elephant was killed.

On the southern edge of the town towers South Creek Hiil, with its two symmetrical peaks. It is rich in caves and artistically inscribed rock-faces. The writings number 200 and date back to the Tang (618–907) and Song (960–1279) eras. On the north edge of the hill lies a park of the same name.

South Creek Hill (Nanxishan)

Reed Flute Cave, situated in a completely concealed spot on Guangming Hill, 6km/3¾ miles north-west of the town, is Guilin's largest and most impressive cave. Its name is explained by the fact that reeds for making flutes and pipes have been grown in this region since ancient times. This dripstone cave is 240m/790ft deep, and visitors will walk for some 500m/550yd through a sea of stalactites and stalagmites, with the artifical lighting provided by floodlights and neon lamps emphasising the ever-changing shapes. One grotto, called The Crystal Palace of the Dragon King, will hold 1000 people; a pillar of stone represents the Dragon King's magic wand. Over 70 wall-inscriptions from the Tang period (618–907) bear eloquent witness to the cave's long history.

Surroundings

★★Reed Flute Cave (Ludi Yan)

10km/6 miles south of the town, at the foot of Mount Dushan, will be found the cave known as Zengpi Yan, where traces of a Stone Age settlement were found in 1965. The finds – stone and bone tools, pottery, traces of fires and graves – can be seen in an exhibition hall.

Zengpi Yan

A trip along the Lijiang river is one of the high spots of a holiday in China. From Guilin to Yangshuo the river meanders its way through 83km/52 miles of beautiful countryside, with bamboo forests, dense reed-beds and incredibly bizarre rock formations.
   Now and again the visitor will see a fishing boat glide by with two or more cormorants on board. Many fishermen use these birds to help them find fish. The journey will continue past Pierced Hill (Chuanshan), Clean Vase Hill (Jingpingchan), Embroidery Hill (Xiushan) and, at about the half-way point, Picture Hill (Huashan).
   The local tourist office arranges trips on the river, with a guide, which last about five hours.

★★**Lijiang River**

Trip on the river

Where the boats moor in Yangshuo there is a pretty market offering arts and crafts for sale. Green Lotus Peak (Bilian Feng) outside Yangshuo is worth seeing. A few miles south of Yangshuo stands a mighty banyan tree which is hundreds of years old. 3km/2 miles from the tree is Moon Hill (Yueliangshan), the peak of which resembles a crescent-shaped crater.

Yangshuo

Guiyang

I 6

Chinese equivalent

Capital of Guizhou Province
Altitude: 1070m/3512ft. Area: 54sq.km/21sq. miles
Population: 800,000 (conurbation 1,310,000)

Guiyang, also known as Zhu, lies at 106° 37′E and 26°34′N, in the centre of Guizhou province and in the middle of a plateau flanked by high mountains. It stretches along the banks of the Nanminghe river, a tributary of the Wujiang. There are rail links with Chongqing and Kunming and air links with Beijing, Shanghai, Canton and other large Chinese cities.

Situation and Communications

Guiyang's origins lie in the dim and distant past. There is evidence that there was a town here at the time of the Han dynasty (206 B.C. to A.D. 220). It

History

served as a military base in the Yuan era (1271–1368). Under the Mings (1368–1644) Xingui, as it was then called, enjoyed a considerable boom; the town walls which still stand date from that period. It has been called Guiyang since 1913. In recent years heavy industry has become established here, as well as chemicals, textiles and consumer-goods.

Sights

This triple-roofed building in the town centre stands 20m/66ft high and was built in 1689. The forecourt is adorned with two iron columns, one dating from 1732 and the other from 1797. There are pillars on the inside walls and tablets hanging from the ceiling contain many old inscriptions.

★ Pavilion of the Man of Letters (Jiaxiu Lou)

Qianlingshan Gongyuan Park lies 1·5km/1 mile north-west of the town and covers an area of some 300ha/750 acres. It is in fact a miniature nature park, with trees, medicinal herbs, 2500 different species of plants, dozens of rhesus monkeys and 50 species of birds. The park also boasts a picturesque lake encircled by hills.

★ Qianlingshan Gongyuan Park

In the centre of the park towers Mount Qianlingshan (1300m/4267ft). From its western peak there is a superb view of the town.

Mount Qianlingshan

The Temple of Great Fortune was built on Mount Qianlingshan in 1672. It contains several halls.

Temple of Great Fortune (Hongfu Si)

Behind the mountain an obelisk pierces the skyline above a pine forest. It is dedicated to the victims of the Civil War of 1949.

Obelisk

Nearby will be found Guiyang Zoo, with over 80 rare species of animal such as snub-nosed monkeys, tigers and pandas.

Zoo

In another corner of the park lies the Cave of the Unicorn, which was discovered in 1531. For many years Generals Chang Hsueliang and Yang Hucheng were imprisoned here by the Guomindang (Kuomintang) nationalist government after having been found guilty in 1937 of collaborating with the Communist Party when Chiang Kai-shek was captured in Xi'an.

Cave of the Unicorn (Qilling Dong)

Surroundings

Huaxi Gongyuan Park, 17km/10½ miles south of the town, lines the banks of the River of Flowers (Huaxi), which forms the Huaxi Waterfall near Bashang Bridge.
   This area is called "Flower of the Guizhou Plain" by the local people because of the beautiful scenery. Features of the park include islands, bridges, pavilions and tea-houses.

Huaxi Gongyuan Park

The Underground Gardens in an extensive cave some 23km/14 miles south of Guiyang were first discovered in 1965. The path through the 587m/1930ft deep cave leads past a number of stalactites and stalagmites, the surreal effect of which is intensified by an effective system of lights.

★ Underground Gardens (Dixia Gongyuan)

The Huangguoshu Waterfall is over 60m/200ft high and 80m/260ft wide, making it the largest waterfall in China. It lies 150km/93 miles south-west of Guiyang, where for more than 2km/1¼ miles the Baishui river winds its way over nine steep tiers of rocks and the same number of waterfalls.

★ Huangguoshu Waterfall (Huanggshu Pubu)

◄ *Huangguoshu Waterfall*

Guizhou

Chinese equivalent	贵州省

Province
Area: 170,000sq.km/65,600sq. miles
Population: 33,150,000. Capital: Guiyang

Situation and People

Guizhou province lies in south-west China, between 103°37′ and 109°32′E and 24°37′ and 29°13′N.

Many national minorities (Dong, Hui, Yao, Zhuang) live in Guizhou, with the Miao in the majority.

Topography

85% of Guizhou is a high plateau crossed by mountain ranges, the highest peak being 2900m/9520ft. The level of the land drops in three stages from east to west, and the dense network of rivers and valleys produces a very complex natural structure.

Climate

The climate is the typical monsoon type. with mild winters and warm summers. In the capital Guiyang the average temperature in July is 24°C/75°F and in January 4°C/39°F.

Rainfall amounts are very large (1000–1500mm/40–60in. per annum), and very few days have completely cloud-free skies. When talking about Guizhou province the Chinese are fond of the saying "There are never three days of clear skies nor three dry feet of earth to be seen in Guizhou".

History

This region was originally inhabited by minorities, mainly the Miao. Its history has been marked by constant uprisings against the ever-increasing influence exerted by the Chinese central government.

Economy

Guizhou's industries – iron and steel, engineering, electronics, tyres, cement and fertilisers – are centred mainly in Guiyang and Zunyi. The major mining products are mercury, coal, bauxite and manganese ore.

China

Guizhou Province

The People's Republic of China
Zhonghua Renmin Gongheguo

In the field of agriculture the main crops are of rice, wheat, maize, rape, potatoes and tobacco. Silkworm breeding and the production of tung oil are also of importance.

The spirit known as maotai jiu, made from wheat and sorghum, is known worldwide.

In addition to the capital Guiyang (see entry), Maotai (see entry) and Huangguosha (see Guiyang) have much to offer the visitor.

Places to visit

Haikou

J 7

Chinese equivalent

Capital of Hainan Province
Area: 218sq.km/84sq. miles. Population: 290,000

Haikou lies at the northern end of Hainan Island, at 100°18′E and 20°01′N.

There are air flights to Haikou from Canton, Beijing, Shanghai and other Chinese cities.

Situation and Communications

Haikou was known as a port back in the Song period (960–1279). Between 1911 and 1926 it rapidly grew into a modern town.

Today Haikou is the political, economic and cultural centre of Hainan province as well as being a major port and traffic hub.

History

This temple on the southern edge of the town was built in 1889 in memory of five statesmen from the Tang and Song period (618–1279) who had been banished to Hainan Island. On a stone tablet in front of the temple visitors can see the relevant legend written by the Song Emperor Huizong (1082–1135), who was famous as a calligrapher.

Sights

★Temple of the Five Dignataries (Wugong Ci)

Near the Temple of the Five Dignataries stands the Temple of Su Shi, which was built in 1617, on the foundations of the Monastery of the Golden Millet (Jinsu An), in memory of the famous poet Su Shi, who spent some time here in 1097.

★Temple of Su Shi (Sugong Ci)

The two fountains which the poet Su Shi caused to be built here are still standing. They are called the Fountain of the Cleansing of the Heart (Xixin Quan) and the Fountain of the Floating Millet (Fusu Quan).

Fountains

The Temple of the Two Dignataries stands on the same site as the Temple of the Five Dignataries. The dignataries referred to are Hai Rui, a minister during the Ming dynasty (1368–1644), and his contemporary, the philosopher Qui Xun. Both were born near Haikou.

Temple of the Two Dignataries (Ergong Ci)

The Tomb of Hai Rui lies close to the village of Binya near Haikou. In 1566 Hai Rui (1514–87), a minister at the Ming court, was bold enough to accuse the Emperor of neglecting affairs of state and devoting too much of his time to Taoism. This foolhardy act resulted in several years imprisonment. Shortly after his release he was again stripped of all office because he criticised a number of ministers and generals.

The harsh criticism directed by Mao Zedong against Wu Hans' play "The Removal from Office of Hai Rui" marked the beginning of the Cultural Revolution (1966–76).

Surroundings

★Tomb of Hai Rui (Hai Rui Mu)

Built in 1710, Qiongtai Shuyuan Academy, in the small town of Qiongshan just south of Haikou, originally comprised several buildings. Today, however, only the Red Building (Hong Lou) remains; it houses a teacher training establishment.

Qiongtai Shuyuan Academy

Hainan   17–J 8

Chinese
equivalent

海南岛

Province
Area: 34,380sq.km/13,274sq. miles
Population: 6,740,000. Capital: Haikou

Situation

Surrounded by the South China Sea, the province of Hainan, the southern-most island of China, lies between 108°34' and 111°02'E and 18°16' and 20°13'N, 48km/30 miles off the coast of Guangdong.

Known as "China's Hawaii", the island measures 260km/160 miles from east to west and 210km/130 miles from north to south, and has enjoyed an enormous increase in tourism in recent years. After the Han, the major population group is the Li. In addition, there are some 60,000 Miao and 5000 Moslem Hui.

Topography

Two-thirds of the island is flat. Contrary to most Chinese mountain ranges, the mountains stretch from north-east to south-west and none is more than 2000m/6600ft high. The highest peak is Five Finger Mountain (Wuzhishan), which is 1879m/6166ft.

Until the 1950s almost a third of Hainan was covered in tropical rain forest, but apart from some 2400sq.km/930sq. miles it was then all cut down to provide agricultural land. Since then attempts have been made to make good the damage through a re-afforestation programme. Three nature reserves have been set up to protect wild life.

Climate

The subtropical and tropical climate produces high average temperatures and high rainfall; in the south of the island the annual rainfall can be as high as 2000mm/80in.

History

During the Tang and Song period (7th–13th c.) undesirable officials and intellectuals were sent into exile on the island. In the 15th c. the Li, the

China

Hainan Province

HEILONGJIANG

JILIN

INNER MONGOLIA
(NEIMENGGU)

LIAONING

XINJIANG

© Baedeker

GANSU

INNER MONGOLIA
(NEIMENGGU)

BEIJING
(PEKING)

TIANJIN

HEBEI

NINGXIA

SHANXI

SHANDONG

QINGHAI

GANSU

SHAANXI

HENAN

JIANGSU

XIZANG (TIBET)

HUBEI

ANHUI

SHANGHAI

SICHUAN

ZHEJIANG

JIANGXI

HUNAN

GUIZHOU

FUJIAN

YUNNAN

GUANGXI

GUANGDONG

TAIWAN

**The People's
Republic of China**
Zhonghua Renmin Gongheguo

XIANG GANG
(HONGKONG)

AO MEN
(MACAO)

HAINAN

original inhabitants, were driven into the hills and forests in the south by Han Chinese immigrants from the mainland. In 1939 the Japanese occupied the island. Hainan became a province in its own right in 1988; prior to that it had formed part of Guangdong.

In 1988 the province was declared a Special Economic Zone. Its economy is based on rubber production, iron-ore mining and – with 50% of the area being used for agriculture – on the cultivation of tropical fruits such as bananas and pineapples. In addition, coal and non-ferrous metals are mined and oil is extracted off the coast. Fishing is also of importance.

Economy

In addition to the provincial capital Haikou the town of Sanya (see entries) is of interest to tourists.

Places to visit

Handan

J 4

Chinese equivalent

Province: Hebei
Altitude: 60m/197ft. Area: 420sq.km/162sq. miles
Population: 800,000 (conurbation 1,800,000)

Handan lies on the eastern foothills of the Taihang massif, in the south of Hebei province, at 114°23′E and 36°32′N. It stretches along the west bank of a tributary of the Huanghe river. Handan is linked by rail with Beijing.

Situation and Communications

Handan's beginnings lie shrouded in the mists of time. There are records of it having been a rich settlement in the Spring and Autumn periods (770–476 B.C.). In the time of the Warring Kingdoms (476–221 B.C. it was the capital of

History

People's festival in Handan

the Zhao kingdom from 386 to 228 B.C. and was then destroyed by the armies of the Qin kingdom (221–206 B.C.). During the Eastern Han era (206 B.C. to A.D. 24) Handan was rebuilt and became one of the five largest Chinese states. However, in succeeding centuries it suffered so severely from the effects of lengthy wars that by the end of the 1940s its population numbered a mere 30,000. From the 1950s onwards its fortunes revived and today it is one of the major industrial centres of Hebei province.

Sights

★**Ruins from the time of the Zhao kingdom** (Zhaowangcheng Yizhi)

The ruins of the old Zhao capital lie 4km/2½ miles south-west of the present town centre. The town was divided into three districts, eastern, western and northern. In the western section visitors can see the remains of the 284m/312yd long and 265m/290yd wide Dragon Terrace (Longtai), where the main palace is thought to have stood.

Congtai Platform

The Congtai Platform, 26m/85ft high, will be found in the north-eastern section of the site. Experts differ regarding the date of this terrace. Legend has it that it was built for King Vuling (reigned 325–299 B.C.), the ruler of the Zhao kingdom, and served him as a viewing platform during military exercises and also for watching singing and dancing performances.

Temple of the Seven Wise Ones (Qixian Ci)

Near the platform stands the Temple of the Seven Wise Ones. dedicated to Lin Xiangru, Lian Po and five more personalities from the time of the Warring Kingdoms (474–221 B.C.).

Surroundings

Temple of the Ancestors (Lüzu Ci)

This temple 10km/6 miles north of Handan was founded in the Tang period (618–907), but the present building dates from the Ming dynasty (1368–1644). It is dedicated to Lü Weng the Immortal One (b. 798). A stone statue of him stands in the Hall of Our Ancestor Lü (Lüzu Dian).

★**Caves of the Echoing Mountain** (Xiangtangshan Shiku)

There are sixteen of these caves, which are to be found on Mount Shigushan some 25km/15½ miles south-west of Handan. Seven lie in the southern foothills and nine on the west side 15km/9 miles away. The largest cave is 13·3m/44ft wide and 12·5m/41ft deep. The first caves were dug in the 6th c. and the latest during the Ming period (1368–1644). In all they contain about 3,400 statues; the Cave of a Thousand Buddhas (Qianfo Dong) alone is home to 1028 figures and many high-relief carvings.

Hangzhou   L 5

Chinese equivalent

杭州市

Capital of Zhejiang Province
Altitude: 5m/16ft. Area: 429sq.km/166sq. miles
Population: 1,220,000 (conurbation 5,440,000)

Situation and Communications

Hangzhou (Hangchow) lies in the north of Zhejiang province, in the Qiantangjiang delta, about 40km/25 miles west of Hangzhou Bay, at 120°12′E and 30°15′N.

There are rail links with Shanghai, Nanjing, Beijing and Canton. It can also be reached by air from the major Chinese cities and from Hong Kong.

Hangzhou, popularly known as "Silk City", is one of China's most beautiful towns; in the words of the well-known Chinese proverb "In Heaven is Paradise, here on earth are Suzhou and Hangzhou". The famous "Dragon Well" tea (Longjing cha) is grown in this region.

Hangzhou, one of China's six historical capital cities, can boast of 2100 years of history. It was first mentioned as an important urban settlement known as Qiantang in 221 B.C. It was given its present name in the year 589 during the Sui dynasty (581–618); when the Grand Canal was then built between Beijing and Hangzhou the town grew rapidly in importance. From the 9th c. onwards, over a period of 237 years and under fourteen emperors, Hangzhou was repeatedly chosen to be a capital city. Its truly halcyon days began when the rulers of the Southern Song dynasty (1127–1279) fled here after they had lost control of north China and their capital city of Kaifeng and sought to make Handan their new capital. With them came artists and academics.

History

Marco Polo visited Hangzhou in the 13th c., was immediately captivated by this "Heavenly City", as it was then known, and described it as the most beautiful in the world. Although he was impressed by the "beautiful palaces", the "wonderfully built houses" and the twelve thousand stone bridges, the streets surfaced in stone and brick and the Turkish baths, he waxed even more enthusiastic about the town's navigational system which made it a port on both the river and the sea, and the many and varied craft workshops and their size ("every workshop employed at least ten, often fifteen, twenty, thirty or even forty men, apprentices as well as master craftsmen").

West Lake, 5·66sq.km/2·2sq. miles in area and with an average depth of 1·5m/5ft, lies west of the Old Town of Hangzhou and is surrounded by hills on three sides. It is divided into five sections by the Sudi and Baidi Causeways; these sections are known as Outer Lake (Wai Hu), the largest of all,

★★West Lake (Xihu)

Hangzhou

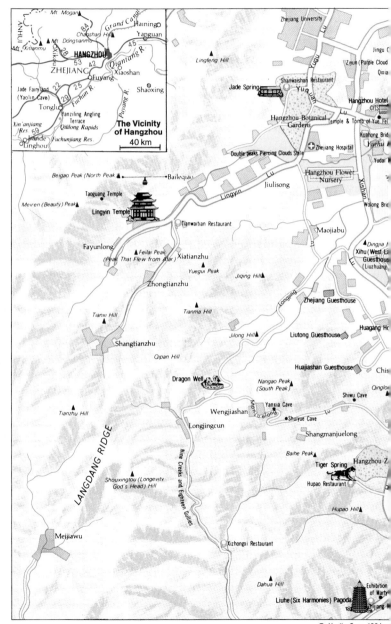

The Vicinity of Hangzhou

40 km

To Yaolin Cave 120 km

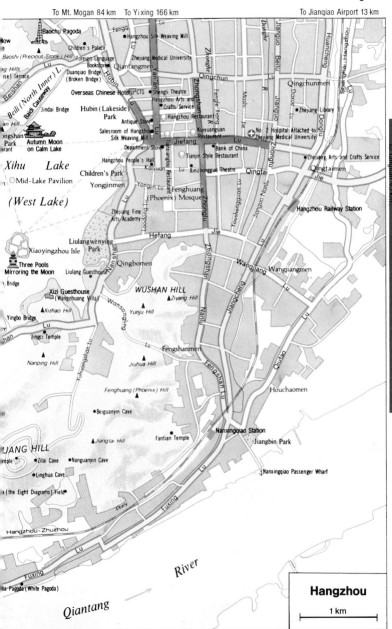

To Mt. Mogan 84 km   To Yixing 166 km   To Jianqiao Airport 13 km

Baochu Pagoda

Fenghu

now

Children's Palace

Hangzhou Silk Weaving Mill

Baoshi (Precious Stone) Hill

Zhejiang Medical University

ng Hills

Dunhe

Jianguo

Huancheng

Beilu

Dongpo(Zhongguanxiang

ise) Terrace

Foreign Language

Bookstore   Qiantangmen

Zhongshan

Zhongshan

Qingchun

Qingchun

Qingchunmen

Beili (North Inner) L.

Baidi Causeway

Hubin

Duanqiao Bridge
(Broken Bridge)

Yan an Lu

Fenghe Kong

Mashi

Jie

Jianguo

Dongru

Overseas Chinese Hotel   CTS

Shengli Theatre

Zhejiang Library

Jindai Bridge

Hubin (Lakeside)
Park

Hangzhou Arts and
Crafts Service

an Hill

Antique Store

Hangzhou Restaurant

Zhongshan

Zhejiang Medical University

ngshan

Park

Autumn Moon
on Calm Lake

aurant

Salesroom of Hangzhou
Silk Weaving Mill

Jiefang

Kuiyuanguan
Restaurant

Lu

No 2 Hospital Attached to

Jie

Xihu   Lake

Department Store

Bank of China

Tianchang Lu

Zhejiang Arts and Crafts Service

Tianjin Style Restaurant

Qingtaimen

Hangzhou People's Hall

Kaiyuan

Lu

Xinzhongguo Theatre

Qingtai
Jie

Mid-Lake Pavilion

Children's Park

Yongjinmen

Yongjin lu

Yonglin lu

Fenghuang
(Phoenix) Mosque

Qingbo Lu

Zhonglu

Fengshan Lu

(West Lake)

Hengluxiaozhong

Zhejiang Fine
Arts Academy

Jie

Hangzhou Railway Station

Nanlu

Liulangwenying
Park

Hefang

Jie

Xiaoyingzhou Isle

Wansong

Qingbomen

Zhongcheng

Wangjiang

Wangjiangmen

Three Pools
Mirroring the Moon

Liulang Guesthouse

Lu

Bridge

Xizi Guesthouse
(Wangzhuang Villa)

WUSHAN HILL

Jiangcheng

Wansong

▲Ziyang Hill

Lu

▲Xizhao Hill

Yuhuangshan Lu

▲Yunju Hill

Qiutao

Yingbo Bridge

Lu

shan

Jingci Temple

Lu   Fengshanmen

Nanping Hill

▲Jiuhua Hill

Fengshan Lu

Houchaomen

Fenghuang (Phoenix) Hill

●Beiguanyin Cave

JIANG HILL

▲Jiangtai Hill

Fantian Temple

Nanxingqiao Station

mple●   ●Zilai Cave   ●Nanguanyin Cave

Jiangbin Park

●Linghua Cave

Lu

a (the Eight Diagrams) Field●

Nanxingqiao Passenger Wharf

Hangzhou-Zhuzhou

Fxwy

Fuxing

Lu

Lu

Fuxing

River

ta Pagoda (White Pagoda)

Qiantang

Qiantang

To Yanguan 45 km

Hangzhou

1 km

243

West Lake surrounded by mountains

North Inner Lake (Beili Hu), West Inner Lake (Xili Hu), South Lake (Xiaonan Hu) and Lake Yue (Yue Hu). There are also four islands in West Lake – Gushan, Xiaoyingzhou, Ruangongdun and Huxinting (Mid-Lake Pavilion).

★Sudi Causeway

Known also as "Mr Su's Dyke" (Sugongdi), this 2·8km/1¾ mile long cause-way was built in 1089 by order of the famous poet Su Shi, who was then prefect of Hangzhou. It lies in the west part of the lake and links the north bank with the south. To build the causeway mud was dredged from the lake, dried in the sun and then reinforced by adding algae.

There are few experiences more pleasurable than an early morning stroll across the causeway in spring, past beautiful flower-beds, peach trees in blossom and weeping willows casting their shadows on the six arched stone bridges. Watching the sunrise in spring from the Sudi Causeway is one of Hangzhou's most wonderful experiences.

Baidi Causeway

In the north of the lake lies this 1km/1100yd long causeway; it is also known as "Mr Bai's Dyke" (Baigong Di), after Bai Juyi, a famous poet from the Tang period (618–907). It begins near Broken Bridge (Duanqiao) and ends on the Isle of the Hill of Solitude (Gushan).

Broken Bridge (Duanqiao)

Broken Bridge links the Baidi Causeway with the shore. It is particularly beautiful in winter when covered with snow. A well-known Chinese love story relates how on this bridge many hundreds of years ago the White Snake, in the shape of a beautiful woman, met the academic Xu Xian for the first time. They fell passionately in love, but a malicious monk forced them to part.

★Isle of the Hill of Solitude (Gushan)

This island gets its name from the 38m/125ft high hill which stands in the middle of it; from the top of the hill there is a fine view of the surrounding scenery. The following buildings are scattered over an area of 20ha/50 acres – Sun-Yat-sen Park (Zhongshan Gongyuan), the provincial museum,

Typical Chinese pavilion on Lake West

the provincial library, and the headquarters of the Xiling Masonry Company (Xiling Yinshe), founded in 1903.

Built in 1699, the Pavilion of the Autumn Moon on the Calm Lake stands at the end of the Baidi Causeway, at the eastern end of Gushan Isle. Anyone staying in this region in autumn would do well to spend an evening here watching the moonlight spread its mystery and magic over the whole lake.

    The Pavilion was built for the Qianlong Emperor Pinghu (reigned 1735–96), who also used to enjoy the moonlit view over the lake from here in autumn; an inscibed column bears his description of these magical moments, and this is why this spot bears his name.

★Pavilion of the Autumn Moon on the Calm Lake (Pinghu Qiuyue)

In the north of the island is the Pavilion of the Cranes, built in the Yuan period (1279–1368) in honour of the poet Lin Hejing (967–1028). Disenchanted with corrupt officialdom he retired here to lead a quiet life. His grave is situated near the pavilion.

Pavilion of the Cranes (Fanghe Ting)

A small alabaster building owned by the Xiling Masonry Company houses the oldest stone tablet in Zhejiang province, the Sanlao Stele (Sanlao Bei) dating from the Eastern Han period (25–220) and discovered in 1852.

Sanlao Stele

7ha/17½ acres in area, this island was made in 1607 from mud dredged from the lake. It contains four "mini-lakes", linked by a zig-zag bridge, the Bridge of the Nine Arches (1727), and with lotus blossom and waterlilies floating on their surface. The pavilions, terraces and plants combine to produce the magic atmosphere of West Lake.

Little Paradise Island (Xiaoyingzhou)

These three round stone pagodas, each little more than 2m/6½ft high and known as The Three Pools Mirroring the Moon, rise up out of the lake near the south bank of The Island in the Little Ocean.

    They were erected in 1621 on the spot where the prefect Su Shi had built three older pagodas which were soon destroyed. The original intention

★Three Pools Mirroring the Moon (Santan Yinyue)

Zigzag bridge on Little Paradise Island (Lake West)

was that the buildings would serve to prevent the local people from growing aquatic plants there and thus avoid mud collecting around them.

Today the pagodas serve quite a different purpose – they entertain tourists with subtle illuminated displays. In the twilight of the evening a burning candle is placed behind one of the five round windows which is covered with tissue paper. When the moonlight falls on the pagodas charming lighting effects are then mirrored on the surface of the water.

★ Bay of Flowers (Huagang)

The Bay of Flowers, or Huagang Park, on the south bank of West Lake, covers 20ha/50 acres and is filled with flower beds, containing mainly paeonies, and lawns. This was a popular excursion spot back in the times of the Song dynasty (1127–1279), and thousands of multi-coloured fish can be seen at play in a small lake which was laid out at that time.

Park of the Song of the Nightingale of the Willow Branch

The Park of the Song of the Nightingale of the Willow Branch (Liulang Wenying Gonyuan) is 17ha/42½ acres in size and covered with willow and cherry trees. Under the Southern Song dynasty (1127–1279) it was the Imperial Garden. In the middle stands a monument commemorating the peace treaty signed between Japan and China.

Other Sights

★ Shopping Centre (Shangye Qu)

Hangzhou is one of the best towns for shopping anywhere in China. Silk is the chief local product. Other good buys include brocade, tea ("Dragon Well" brand) and scissors made by Zhang Xiaoquan. These can be bought especially in shops along Zhongshan Zhonglu, Jiefang Lu, Hubin Lu and Yan'an Lu, the streets which form the town's main shopping quarter.

Market

The market, held each evening, is an experience in itself. Everything imaginable is on sale and a vast range of culinary delights can be savoured. Craftsmen of all kinds also ply their trades.

This pagoda was built in 1933 on the north bank of West Lake, on the foundations of an older pagoda built in the second half of the 10th c. for a high-ranking state official who sought the protection of Buddha for Qiang Hong Chu, ruler of the Wu kingdom. This led to the pagoda being given the name "Baochu", which means "Protector of Chu". It stands 45m/148ft high and is one of the town's landmarks.

Baochu Ta Pagoda

Yellow Dragon cave lies some 500m/550yd west of Baochu Ta Pagoda, at the foot of Qixia Ling hill. In the first half of the 13th c. a monk lived here; he built a hut in front of the cave, and towards the end of the Qing dynasty (1644–1911) this was extended into a Taoist monastery.
Note the spring gushing forth from the jaws of a dragon. There is a bamboo grove near the cave.

Yellow Dragon Cave (Huanglong Dong)

This temple (open: 9am–6pm) at the northern end of the Sudi Causeway on West Lake was built in 1221 in honour of General Yue Fei (1103–42). Although the General had successfully repelled several Tartar raids the emperor and chancellor accused him of high treason and sentenced him to death. He was hanged together with his son Yue Yun. After his rehabilitation in 1163 two tombs were built to the west of where the temple now stands, and the bodies were reinterred there. A statue of the General stands in the temple hall, the ceiling of which is decorated with cranes, a symbol of immortality. The temple also contains 86 stone plaques on which the Song Emperor Gaozong (1107–87) and his wife engraved classical texts by Confucius. The most valuable treasure, however, is a stone celestial globe showing many of the constellations, which dates from the time of the Five Dynasties (907–960) but was not rediscovered until 1956. It is thought to be the oldest stellar map in the world. The road leading to the tombs to the west of the temple is lined with stone figures of important officials, tigers, sheep and horses. In front of the tombs are wrought-iron statues of the persons who were responsible for passing judgement on the General, the chancellor, his wife and two high officials; these are all kow-towing. In the two corridors visitors can admire 125 stelae engraved with poems by the General and inscriptions by many famous personages praising his achievements.

★Temple of General Yue Fei (Yue Miao)

To the west of the Temple of General Yue Fei lie the Botanical Gardens, covering an area of more than 200ha/500 acres and boasting some 4000 different species of plants. The herb gardens and the large number of different kinds of bamboo are particularly worthy of attention. Water from the Jade Spring flows into a fish-pond.

Botanical Gardens

The Jade Spring gushes forth 2km/1¼ miles west of the Temple of General Yue Fei, in a garden which was laid out in 1964 on the site of an old 5th c. monastery. The inscription on the wooden plaque which hangs above the ledge of the building surrounding the spring is by the well-known artist Dong Qichang (1555–1636). The Chinese characters "Yu Le Guo" mean "Kingdom of the Happy Fishes". Various kinds of fish still swim in the waters of the spring.

★Jade Spring (Yu Quan)

The Temple of the Hidden Immortals, 3km/2 miles south-west of Jade Spring, dates from 326 B.C. and is one of the most famous temples in China. It is thought that in the 10th c. there were some 300 buildings here housing 3000 monks. After having been destroyed during the Taiping Uprising (1851–64) the building was rebuilt.

★★Temple of the Hidden Immortals (Linying Si)

In the Hall of the Celestial Kings sits a sculpture of Maitreya and a wooden statue of Weituo from the Southern Song period (1127–1279). To the side can be seen the statues of the Four Celestial Kings.

Hall of the Celestial Kings (Tianwang Dian)

Hangzhou

Sumptuous Hall of the Great Hero (Daxiong Baodian)

The Sumptuous Hall of the Great Hero stands 33·6m/110ft high. Pilgrims come to pay homage to a gilded statue of Shakyamuni, 19·6m/64ft tall and made of 24 pieces of camphor-wood. Behind the statue can be seen a figure of Guanyin.

The Peak That Flew From Afar (Feilai Feng)

A little to the south towers The Peak That Flew from Afar, separated from The Temple of the Hidden Immortals by a mountain stream. According to legend an Indian monk who came here in the year 326 asked "In which year did this Indian mountain fly here? When Buddha was alive it was the favourite resting place of immortal souls." It was thus that the mountain and the monastery built in that same year both got their names.

The mountain is 168m/223ft high and riddled with numerous caves and niches, the latter containing about 380 Buddha statues which date back to the 10th c., the time of the Five Dynasties. The three oldest examples, dating from 951, can be seen on the east wall of the Qinglin Cave; one is of Shakyamuni, one of Avalokiteshvara and the third is a Bhaisajya (or "Medicine Buddha") statue.

The largest sculpture on this peak is to be found on its northern slope; it is a Maitreya from the Song period (960–1279), wearing a satisfied smile and holding a rosary in one hand.

North Peak (Beigao Feng)

To the north of the Temple of the Hidden Immortals is North Peak (Beigao Feng), with steps leading up to it. From the top there is a superb view of West Lake and the surrounding scenery.

Surroundings

★ **Dragon Well (Longjing)**

3km/2 miles south-west of West Lake, to the east of the village of the same name, lies Dragon Well in the midst of some beautiful countryside, a feature of which are the tea plantations which produce the fine Dragon Well tea (Longjiang Cha). According to the villagers the spring which provides water for the well was discovered some time before 1800.

A visit is recommended to one of the tea factories in which the fresh tea-leaves are refined, processed and packed.

Pagoda of the Six Harmonies

The Spring of the Running Tiger, 5km/3 miles south of West Lake, is one of three best known springs in China. A legend describes how it was discovered in 819 with the help of two tigers. The spring produces 0·37cu.m/80 gallons of water per second; the quality is regarded as being extremely good and it is ideal for making tea. The high surface tension of the water is an interesting factor; visitors can test this by placing a coin on the surface and watching it float. There is a tea-house in the former temple nearby.

★Tiger Spring
(Hupao Quan)

About 8km/5 miles south of the town, on the north bank of the Qiantang-jiang river, the visitor will find the 60m/200ft high Pagoda of the Six Harmonies. When it was rebuilt in 1899 the original brick core was retained and wood-cladding added to the exterior.
　　On this site there once stood a former pagoda towering to a height of 150m/500ft or so, built in 970 but burned down by a foreign army in 1121. The pagoda is thought to offer protection from floods and also serves as a lighthouse.
　　Although from the outside the octagonal building appears to have thirteen storeys, in fact there are only seven. A staircase incorporated in the wood-cladding enables visitors to climb almost to the top. From there the view includes the 1322m/1450yd long road and rail bridge over the Qiantangjian river which was built between 1934 and 1937 to designs by the architect Mao Yisheng.

★★Pagoda of the Six Harmonies
(Liuhe Ta)

Collected together in a park at the Pagoda of the Six Harmonies are 80 or so reconstructions of pagodas from all over China.

Pagoda Park

Mount Moganshan, 719m/2360ft high, lies 50km/31 miles north-west of Hangzhou and 200km/124 miles south-west of Shanghai. There are bus services from both those cities.
　　The word "Mogan" is formed from two separate names, Mo Xie and Gan Jiang, being those of a married couple who lived in the 5th c. B.C. Both were very skilled swordsmiths who devoted their lives to making two incomparably beautiful swords for the emperor.

★Mount Moganshan

Of the many picturesque spots which the countryside around Hangzhou has to offer, special mention should be made of Sword Lake, on the banks of which – so legend has it – Mo Xie and Gan Jiang would sit and polish the swords they had just forged. An impressive three-stage water-fall, 100m/330ft high, feeds water into the lake.

Sword Lake
(Jian Chi)

Harbin

M 2

哈尔滨市

Chinese
equivalent

Capital of Heilongjiang Province
Altitude: 143m/469ft. Area: 156sq.km/60sq. miles
Population: 2,590,000 (conurbation 4,520,000)

Harbin lies on a fertile plain on the banks of the Songhuajiang river, in the south of China's northernmost province, at 127°08′E and 45°41′N.
　　It is linked by rail and air with the capital Beijing. There are also flights to Harbin from other Chinese cities such as Shanghai, Canton, Xiamen and others.

Situation and
Communications

Manchurians first settled here 900 years ago and founded a small village called Arjin. Several centuries later the name was changed to Harbin. From the late 19th c. onwards the village gradually grew into a town, aided by the building by the Russians of the first rail link, part of the Trans-Siberian Railway. As well as other foreigners, many Russians settled here in the early years of this century, especially in the wake of the October Revolution

History

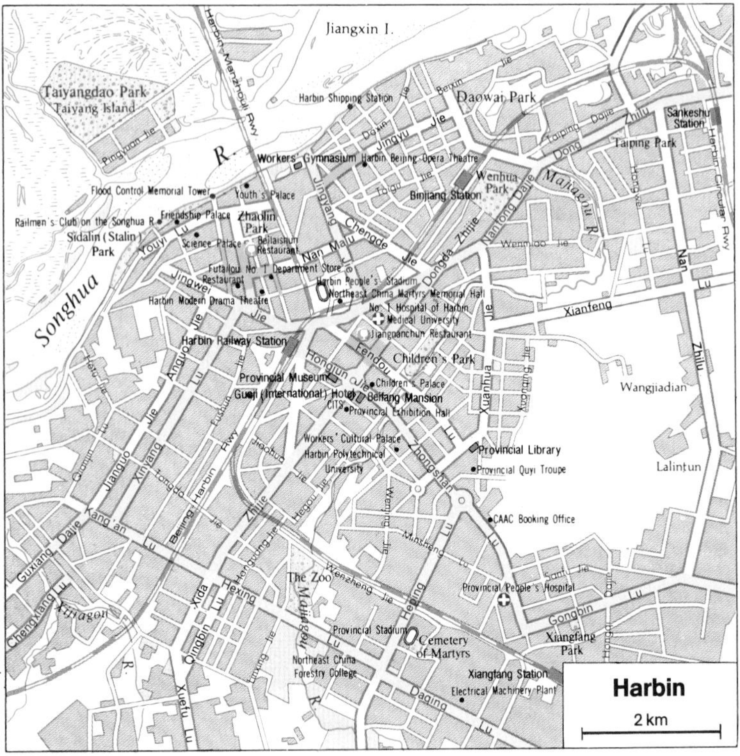
Jiangxin I.
Taiyangdao Park
Taiyang Island
Pingyuan Jie
Harbin Manzhouli Rwy
Harbin Shipping Station
Daowai Park
Beixin
Jie
Jingyu Jie
Sankeshu Station
Taiping Dajie
Taiping Park
Zhilu
Harbin Circular Rwy
R.
Workers' Gymnasium
Harbin Beijing Opera Theatre
Wenhua Park
Binjiang Station
Majiagou R.
Flood Control Memorial Tower
Youth's Palace
Railmen's Club on the Songhua R.
Friendship Palace
Zhaolin Park
Sidalin (Stalin) Park
Science Palace
Beilaishun Restaurant
Jingyang Jie
Chengde Jie
Nan Malu
Dongda Zhijie
Nantong Dajie
Wenmiao Jie
Youyi Lu
Futailou No. 1 Department Store
Restaurant
Harbin People's Stadium
Jingwei Jie
Harbin Modern Drama Theatre
Northeast China Martyrs Memorial Hall
No. 1 Hospital of Harbin Medical University
Xianfeng
Songhua
Harbin Railway Station
Jiangpanchun Restaurant
Children's Park
Provincial Museum
Hongjun Jie
Fendou
Children's Palace
Guoji (International) Hotel
Beifang Mansion
CITS
Provincial Exhibition Hall
Xuanhua
Wangjiadian
Anguo Jie
Xinyang
Jianguo
Qiqihar
Workers' Cultural Palace
Harbin Polytechnical University
Zhongshan
Provincial Library
Provincial Quyi Troupe
Lalintun
Harbin Rwy
Zhijie
Hegou Jie
Wenjing Jie
Minsheng
CAAC Booking Office
Kang'an Lu
Beijing Lu
Guxiang Dajie
Chengxiang Lu
Xiangong
The Zoo
Wenzheng Jie
Hexing
Xida
Majiagou
Heping Lu
Provincial People's Hospital
Gongbin
Qingbin
Provincial Stadium
Cemetery of Martyrs
Xiangfang Park
Northeast China Forestry College
R.
Xiangfang Station
Electrical Machinery Plant
Xuefu Lu
Daqing Lu
Harbin
2 km

To airport 25 km

of 1917, and this is witnessed by the large number of Russian churches and houses to be seen in the town.

After 1946, following the amnesty granted by Stalin, many of these refugees returned to their homeland. Today Harbin is one of the major industrial centres of northern China.

Sights

★Temple of Paradise
(Jile Si)

The Temple of Paradise, at Dongda Zhijie No. 5 in the city centre, covers an area of 2·6ha/6½ acres; it dates from 1924 and ranks as the largest Buddhist temple in Heilongjiang province.

It consists of four large halls – the Hall of the Four Heavenly Kings (Tianwang Dian), with statues of Maitreya and the Four Heavenly Kings, the Sumptuous Hall of the Great Hero (Daixong Baodian), the Hall of the Three Holy Ones (Sansheng Dian), containing statues of Amitabha, Guanyin and Dasizhi, and the Pavilion of the Holy Scriptures (Cangling Lou).

As well as the halls, the seven-stepped Pagoda of Qiji Futu Ta deserves special attention. The niches on the exterior walls contain over 30 small statues of the Buddhist saint, Arhat. Inside, a wooden staircase leads to the upper floors.

From the ground floor there is access to a neighbouring temple containing seven statues of Shakyamuni, Guanyin, Bhaisajya (the "Medicine Buddha"), and four Bodhisattvas.

Ice-lantern Festival: frozen sculpture ▶

Harbin

Church of St Nicholas

The orthodox church of St Nicholas near the Temple of Paradise was built in 1899 in the Neo-Gothic style. The framework is entirely of wood and richly decorated with sculptures. This church is one of the largest of Harbin's seventeen Christian churches.

Temple of Confucius (Wenmiao)

Also situated in Dongda Zhijie is the Temple of Confucius, built in traditional style in 1926. It comprises a main hall and two side-halls. The main hall contains statues of Confucius and other men of learning.

Children's Park (Ertong Gongyuan)

The Children's Park is a special attraction. Children can ride on a 2km/1¼ mile long miniature railway.

Heilongjiang Provincial Museum

The most interesting section of the museum is its Natural History department with exhibits describing the history of mankind.

Zoo

The Zoo in the south of the town boasts 140 species of animals; the tiger from northern China is particularly rare.

Zhaolin Gongyuan Park

In the north-west of the town, not far from the Songhua river, lies Zhaolin Gongyuan Park, named after General Li Zhaolin (1908–46). His grave can be found in the northern section of the park.

Festival of the Ice Lanterns

This festival is held every year between January 5th and February 5th, when all the roads and houses in the town are decorated with lanterns and carvings sculpted from ice. The park itself is covered in a sea of lanterns, statues, miniature houses, temples, animals, plants, boats and other vehicles, all made in ice by local artists. At this time of year the temperatures range between −20 and −30°C/−4 and −22°F.

Stalin Park (Sidalin Gongyuan)

Stalin Park, close by on the south bank of the Songhuajiang, offers many kinds of water-sports and other leisure activities. The monument in the park commemorates the flood of 1957 and the many volunteers who helped at the time.

Sunny Island Park (Taiyang Dao Gongyuan)

Sunny Island is a sandbank of 38sq.km/14½sq. miles on the opposite bank of the Songhuajian river. It is a popular excursion spot and health resort with sanatoriums. In summer whole families often come here to picnic.

Surroundings

★Historic town of Huining (Shangjing Huiningfu)

Between 1115 and 1153, before the Jin conquered almost the whole of northern China, their capital city was Huining, sited about 30km/19 miles south-east of Harbin, where the town of Ancheng is today.

Two sections of the old city wall and the foundations of the Wuchong Palace have survived. 300m/330yd west of the palace ruins can be seen the 10m/33ft high burial mound of Taizu, the first emperor of the Jin dynasty. In 1908 a memorial slab dated 1188 was discovered, with inscriptions describing the life and work of the Buddhist monk Bao Yan. This memorial slab is today housed in the Provincial Museum in Harbin.

Daqing Oil-fields (Daqing Youtian)

The Daqing oil-fields, among the largest in the whole of China, were opened up in March 1960. They lie 159km/99 miles west of Harbin to which they are linked by rail. Annual oil production amounts to some 50 million tonnes. Thanks to these immense oil-fields China has been self-sufficient in the sphere of crude oil production since 1964.

The ruins of Longquan lie in the commune of Bohai (Ning'an district), about 300km/190 miles south-east of Harbin. At one time Longquan was the capital of the kingdom of Bohai, which was founded by the Manchurians in 698 but laid waste by another tribe in 926, when Longquan was also almost completely razed to the ground. All that now remains are some sections of the walls, a few stone buildings and sculptures.

★Historic town of Longquan (Longquan Gucheng)

The Enamel Well, used only by the king and noble personages, is also of interest.

Enamel Well (Liuli Jing)

The Temple of Prosperity, built in the Qing peiod (1644–1911), comprises the Hall of the God of War (Guandi Dian) and the Hall of the Three White Men (Sansheng Dian) which contains a large stone Buddha.

Temple of Prosperity (Xinglong Si)

The 6m/20ft high Pagoda of the Stone Lamp (Shi Dengta) is from the Tang period (618–907) and consists of twelve basalt sections.

Pagoda of the Stone Lamp

Covering an area of 95sq.km/37sq. miles and situated 10km/6 miles south of Bohai at a height of 350m/1150ft, the Lake of Mirrors is of volcanic origin. Deposits from an erupting volcano blocked the upper reaches of the Mudan river and resulted in the formation of the lake. At its northern end a 40m/130ft wide waterfall plunges down 20m/65ft into the lake, which is surrounded by a string of ten craters. At the bottom of four of them (diameter 50–500m/160–1600ft, depth 40–45m/130–150ft) grow all sorts of different trees, forming what is known as the Underground Forest (Dixia Senlin).

★Lake of Mirrors (Jingpo Hu)

The Five Linked Lakes, situated in the middle of volcanic mountains 300km/186 miles north of Harbin, are also of volcanic origin. The whole surrounding terrain is covered in volcanic rock and hot springs.

The Five Linked Lakes (Wuda Lianchi)

Hebei

J–K 3–4

河北省

Chinese equivalent

Province
Area: 190,000sq.km/73,360sq. miles
Population: 62,200,000. Capital: Shijiazhuang

Hebei province lies on the Gulf of Bo Hai in northern China, between 113°27' and 119°53'E and 36°04' and 42°37'N. Beijing and Tientsin lie within this province. It obtains its name from its geographical position – Hebei actually means "north of the river", namely the Huanghe.

Situation

Some 60% of the total area is accounted for by the mountain ranges scattered over the north and west of the province, the remaining 40% being taken up by the fertile, alluvial Hebei Plain. Most of Hebei lies within the catchment area of the Haihe river.

Topography

The climate is continental in character, with cold, dry winters and warm, humid summers.

Climate

From an historical aspect, until the 11th c. Hebei was of importance only because it was a border region. It was only when the Yuan (1271–1368) made Beijing their capital that it found itself in the centre of the new kingdom and so was able to develop its trade and crafts.
    From 1421 to 1928 the region was called Chihli. Industrialisation began in the mid-1800s. Since ancient times flooding had been an ever-present problem in Hebei, but after 1949 this danger was removed as a result of a

History

China

HEILONGJIANG

JILIN

Hebei Province

INNER MONGOLIA
(NEIMENGGU)

XINJIANG

LIAONING

© Baedeker

GANSU

INNER MONGOLIA
(NEIMENGGU)

BEIJING
(PEKING) •

TIANJIN

NINGXIA SHANXI HEBEI

QINGHAI SHANDONG

GANSU HENAN

SHAANXI JIANGSU

XIZANG (TIBET)

SHANGHAI

HUBEI ANHUI

SICHUAN ZHEJIANG

JIANGXI

HUNAN

GUIZHOU FUJIAN

YUNNAN

GUANGXI GUANGDONG

TAIWAN

XIANG GANG
(HONGKONG)

AO MEN (MACAO)

HAINAN

The People's Republic of China
Zhonghua Renmin Gongheguo

programme involving afforestation of the mountain region together with the building of water reservoirs and irrigation and drainage systems.

Economy

Available minerals include coal, iron and copper ore. Sea-salt is obtained from the salt-marshes along the Gulf of Bo Hai.

Hebei is also one of China's main cotton-growing regions. Wheat, maize, millet, soya beans, sweet potatoes and olives are also grown, together with fruit in the mountain regions.

Places to visit

In addition to the provincial capital Shijiazhuang (see entry), Chengde, Handan, Qinghuangdao and Tangshan (see entries) are all of interest to the visitor.

Hefei   K 5

Chinese equivalent

合肥市

Capital of Anhui Province
Altitude: 26m/85ft. Area: 458sq.km/177sq. miles
Population: 930,000 (conurbation 3,530,000)

Situation and Communications

Hefei lies at 117°16′E and 31°51′N, in the centre of Anhui province, at the confluence of the Dogfei and Nanfel rivers.

It is six hours by train from Nanjing and eleven from Shanghai. By air it is a two-hour flight from Beijing or Canton and one hour from Shanghai; there are also air links with other major Chinese cities.

History

The town's history goes back over 2000 years, to the Western Han period (206 B.C. to A.D. 8). Even then it was an important trading centre for agricultural products, cattle and handicrafts. Hefei was a military base during the time of the Three Kingdoms (220–265) and again under the Southern Song

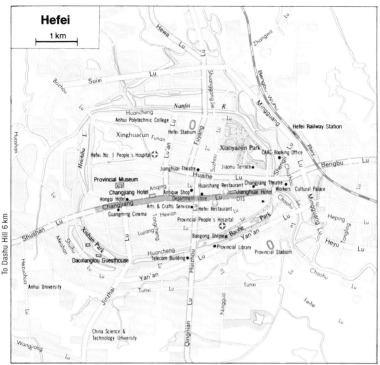

Hefei

1 km

To Dashu Hill 6 km

To Luogang Airport 2 km

dynasty (1127–1279). In 1949 it was made the capital of Anhui province. Since then politics, industry, culture and science have set the tone of the town. The well-known University of Science and Technology is here.

The platform erected in the east of the town, 5m/16½ft tall and 3700sq.m/44440sq.yd in area, was erected in the 2nd c., on instructions from Cao Cao, the chancellor of the state of Wei, for the purpose of providing instruction in the use of the crossbow. 500 bowmen were trained here to defend the town. On the platform stands a fountain, dating from 269, the balustrade of which is marked by deep furrows where it was used to sharpen arrows.

The Temple of Clear Instruction, built in the mid-1800s, replaces an 8th c. Buddhist temple.

Adjoining the Platform for Instruction in Crossbow Shooting on its north-east side lies the Park of the Easy Ford, which covers 2ha/5 acres. A lake is surrounded by flower beds and lawns. The park also contains a monumental tomb which once housed the helmet and armour worn by General Zhang Liao of the Wei Empire. It was here that the General put the Wu army to flight in 215.

The Temple of Bao – in the south-east of the town, at the western end of tranquil Baohe Gongyuan Park – was built in 1882 on the foundations of a

Sights

★ **Platform for Instruction in Crossbow Shooting** (Jiaonu Tai)

Temple of Clear Instruction (Mingjiao Si)

★ **Park of the Easy Ford** (Xiaoyaojin)

★ **Temple of Bao** (Baogong Ci)

255

14th c. temple and restored in 1946. It stands on the spot where Bao Zheng (999–1062), a native of Hefei and holder of various high offices including those of prefect of Kaifeng and vice-minister, pursued his studies. He was very popular with the people because of his moral integrity and incorruptibility. He even condemned to death one of the Emperor's sons-in-law.

Near the temple is a well roofed over by a pavilion. Popular tradition has it that its water suits honest officials but gives corrupt ones a headache.

Provincial Museum

On display in the museum are a large number of exhibits relating to the history of Anhui province.

The most valuable exhibit is a magnificent burial robe, made of little pieces of jade, in which a noblemen from the Han period (206 B.C. to A.D. 220) was buried.

Heilongjiang   L–O 1–3

黑龙江省

Province
Area: 469,000sq.km/181,000sq. miles
Population: 35,750,000. Capital: Harbin

Situation

Heilongjiang, the northernmost province of China, lies between 121°13′ and 135°06′E and 43°26′ and 53°34′N. It is separated from Russia by two rivers, the Heilongjiang (Amur in Russian), which gave the province its name, and the Wusulijiang (Ussuri in Russian).

Topography

Heilongjiang comprises the Little Chingan Range, the northern section of the Central Manchurian Mountains, and the marshlands along the lower reaches of the Songhuajiang and Wusulijiang rivers.

Climate

The climate is continental, with long and very hard winters (on February 13th 1969 the thermometer fell to −52.3°C/−62°F) and extremely short,

China

Heilongjiang Province

HEILONGJIANG

JILIN

INNER MONGOLIA (NEIMENGGU)

LIAONING

X I N J I A N G

© Baedeker

GANSU

INNER MONGOLIA (NEIMENGGU)

BEIJING (PEKING)

TIANJIN

HEBEI

NINGXIA

SHANXI

SHANDONG

Q I N G H A I

GANSU

SHAANXI

HENAN

JIANGSU

X I Z A N G (TIBET)

SICHUAN

HUBEI

ANHUI

SHANGHAI

ZHEJIANG

JIANGXI

GUIZHOU

HUNAN

FUJIAN

YUNNAN

GUANGXI

GUANGDONG

TAIWAN

The People's Republic of China
Zhonghua Renmin Gongheguo

HAINAN

AO MEN (MACAO)

XIANG GANG (HONGKONG)

warm summers. On the plains the average January temperatures are −20°C/−4°F, −30°C/−22°F in the mountains, and 23°C/73°F in July. In some regions in the extreme north-west there is hardly any summer at all.

Until well into the 19th c. Heilongjiang was a region which knew only cattle-raising and fishing. Industrialisation began with the building of the railway between 1896 and 1903. In the years 1900–05 it was occupied by the Russians and from 1931 by the Japanese. After 1949 it became an important part of the new China. The plains were cultivated and forests utilised. | History

In the industrial sector the wood-processing industry (including paper factories) and sugar-mills play an important part. Rich coal deposits are mined near Shuanggyashan and other places, and near Anda lies the giant Daqing oil-field. Important agricultural products include wheat, sugar-beet, sunflower seed and flax. The province is also a major supplier of timber. | Economy

The capital Harbin (see entry) and its surroundings are of particular interest. | Places to visit

Henan   J–K 4–5

河南省 | Chinese equivalent

Province
Area: 167,000sq.km/64,500sq. miles
Population: 87,630,000. Capital: Zhengzhou

Henan, one of China'a most densely populated provinces, lies in central China, on the lower reaches of the Huanghe river, between 110°22′ and 116°38′E and 31°23′ and 36° 22′N. Henan means "south of the river", because most of the province does lie south of the Huanghe. | Situation

China

Henan Province

© Baedeker

The People's Republic of China
Zhonghua Renmin Gongheguo

Topography	Henan can be divided into two topographical areas, the hilly region in the west and parts of the North China Plain in the east. Three river systems flow through the province – the Huanghe in the north, the Huaihe in the south and the Tanghe and Taohe in the south-west.
Climate	The climate is largely continental, being cold and dry in winter and humid in summer. Average January temperatures are −2°C/28°F in the north and plus 2°C/36°F in the south, while in July temperatures on the plains average 28°C/82°F. In spring Henan suffers from long periods of drought and violent sandstorms which cause considerable damage.
History	Signs of settlements dating back to Neolithic times (the Yang-shao culture) have been discovered in Henan. It is believed that the Shang dynasty (16th–11th c. B.C.) had its capital city near Anyang after 1384 B.C. From the 8th to the 3rd c. B.C. Luoyang was the capital of the Zhou rulers, and, alternating with Chang'an, it remained so until the 10th c. A.D. Subsequently Kaifeng was the capital for a short time.
Economy	The only mineral of any importance to Henan is coal. Much of the soil is very fertile (the result of extensive and rich loess deposits), 60–70% of the land under cultivation being found in the east of the province. The main crops are wheat, oleaceous plants, maize, sorghum, soya beans and fruit as well as cotton and tobacco. In addition Henan is a major producer of sesame seeds, walnuts and tea, and has a long tradition of silk manufacture.
Places to visit	Henan is one of the birthplaces of Chinese civilisation, and there are many historical buildings of interest to the visitor, especially in and around Luoyang, Kaifeng and Zhengzhou (see entries).

Hengyang J 6

Chinese equivalent	恒源县

Province: Hunan
Area: 34sq.km/13sq. miles. Population: 383,000

Situation and Communications	Hengyang lies on the Xiangjiang river, in the interior of Hunan province, at 112°38′E and 26°52′N. It is linked to Changsha, the provincial capital, by the Beijing–Canton railway. It is also possible to fly to Hengyang from Canton; the flight lasts one and a half hours.
History	Hengyang can boast a long history, as witnessed by the works of poets from the Tang era (618–907) and by writers and politicians of later periods. Today it is the second largest economic and cultural centre in Hunan province.
Sights ★ Stone Drum Mountain	Stone Drum Mountain (Shigushan), near the north gate to the city, is at the confluence of the Zhengshui and Xiangjiang rivers. A rock on the mountain, 2m/6½ft high, is shaped like a drum. Li Daoyuan (472?–527) described it in his "River Sketches".
Stone Drum Academy	In the year 997 an institute of higher education was built at the foot of the mountain and in 1035 it was given the name of Stone Drum Academy. At that time it was one of China's four leading educational establishments (the other three being the Yingtian and Yuelu Academies and the School of the White Stag Caves). In the 1940s the original academy buildings were burned down by Japanese troops; only a few stelae and some inscriptions from the Ming and Qing periods (1368–1911) survived.

A few hundred yards south of the town towers the Mountain of the Return of the Wild Geese. According to tradition, wild geese flying north were unable to fly over this mountain and had to return south. The monastery, built in 742, was destroyed during the Second World War apart from a temple which survived.

Mount Hengshan, 1290m/4234ft in height, is one of China's Five Holy Mountains. Even emperors came here on pilgrimages to bring offerings to the gods.

Situated 50km/30 miles north of Hengyang, this mountain – also known as South Mountain (Nanyue) – is renowned for its beautiful scenery, its 72 peaks and its historical importance. Numerous inscriptions carved by academics and poets can still be seen.

The temple and monastery, situated at the foot of South Mountain near the little hamlet of Nanyue Zheng, is an enormous complex on a site of 9·8ha/24½ acres. It was built in 725 but has been much restored and extended since. The main hall (Zhengdian), reconstructed in 1882, is 22m/72ft from floor to ceiling; the 72 richly-sculptured pillars on the façade symbolise the 72 peaks of Mount Hengshan.

Other buildings of note are the Imperial Library (Yushu Lou), the Pavilion of the Imperial Memorial (Yubei Ting), the Imperial Residence (Qing Gong) and the Temple of Consecration, 300m/330yd east of the above-mentioned monastery. The Temple of Consecration, rebuilt in 1714, comprises the Hall of the Buddha (Dafo Dian), the Temple of San Guan (Guansheng Dian), the Temple of the Medicine Buddha (Yaoshi Dian) and the Palace of Arhat (Luohan Tang). The east and west walls of this palace are adorned with 500 alabaster statues of Buddhist saints.

The Temple for the Safekeeping of the Tripitaka, built in 1931 on the foundations of a previous building dating from 568, once housed a volume of the Tripitaka (holy writings of Hinayana Buddhism) donated by the first Ming Emperor Zhu Yuanzhang. Unfortunately the book went missing some time ago.

Dating from the 16th c. the Temple of the God of Fire is built on the slopes of Zhurong Feng, at 1290m/4234ft the highest peak of Mount Hengshan. The temple is unusual in being roofed with slates made of iron.

The Temple of the South Terrace is situated 4km/2½ miles north-west of the Temple and Monastery of South Mountain. In its present form it dates from 1902 to 1906; the original 6th c. building no longer exists.

As well as several Buddhist temples it also comprises the tomb of the monk Xi Qian, who came here in 743 in order to spread the word of Buddha. He is regarded as the founder of a Japanese school of Buddhism. The temple of Fangguang Si, to the north-west, was founded in 503.

Surroundings

Mountain of the Return of the Wild Geese (Huiyanfeng)

★★Mount Hengshan

Temple and Monastery of South Mountain (Nanyue Damiao)

Temple of Consecration (Zhusheng Si)

The Temple for the Safekeeping of the Tripitaka (Cangjiang Dian)

Temple of the God of Fire (Huoshang Miao)

Temple of the South Terrace (Nantai Si)

Hohhot   J 3

呼和浩特市

Chinese equivalent

Capital of the Autonomous Region of Inner Mongolia
Altitude: 1080m/3545ft. Area: 65sq.km/25sq. miles
Population: 778,000 (conurbation 1,420,000)

Hohhot (Huhehaote) lies in the centre of Inner Mongolia, south of the Daqingshan river, at 111°32'E and 40°28'N. There are rail and air links with Beijing, as well as flights from Shanghai (4 hours), Canton (4½ hours), Nanjing (4 hours), Shenyang (3½ hours), Xi'an (3½ hours), etc.

Situation and Communications

Hohhot

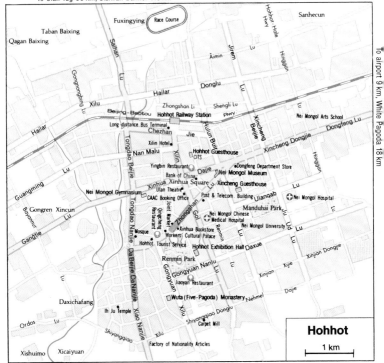

To Ulan Tug 90 km, Siziwan Banner 110 km

Fuxingying Race Course

Taban Baixing
Qagan Baixing

Sanhecun

To airport 9 km, White Pagoda 18 km

Áimin Jirem Lu

Donglu Lu

Hailar Zhongshan Li Shengli Lu

Beijing–Baotou Hohhot Railway Station Pwy

Long-distance Bus Terminal Chezhan Jie Nei Mongol Arts School

Dongfeng Lu

Xincheng Beijie

Xilin Hotel CITS Xincheng Dongjie

Nan Malu Xilin Hohhot Guesthouse

Yingbin Restaurant Dajie Dongfeng Department Store

Bank of China Nei Mongol Museum

Xinhua Xinhua Square Xincheng Guesthouse

Nei Mongol Gymnasium Ulan Theatre

CAAC Booking Office Post & Telecom Building Ulanqab

Qingzheng Restaurant Joint Market Nei Mongol Hospital

Mosque Medical Hospital Manduhai Park

Xinhua Bookstore Nei Mongol Chinese

Workers' Cultural Palace Nei Mongol University

Hohhot Tourist Service Hohhot Exhibition Hall Daxue Lu

Renmin Park

Gongyuan Nanlu Xinjian Dongjie

Gongyuan Lu Xinjian Xijie

Jiaoyan Restaurant Daoje

Wuta (Five-Pagoda) Monastery Nehmei

Daxichafang

Ih Ju Temple Xiao Nanlie

Shiyangqiao Dongli

Shiyangqiao Carpet Mill

Ordos Lu

Xishuimo Xicaiyuan Factory of Nationality Articles

Hohhot

1 km

To Zhaojun Tomb 9 km

History

In contrast to many other Chinese towns Hohhot is still comparatively young, having been founded in 1581 by the Mongol prince Altan Khan, under the name of Kuku-khoto (Blue Town). The Kangxi Emperor Xuanye (reigned 1661–1722) ensured Chinese supremacy over the Mongols and stationed troops in the town. In 1947, when Inner Mongolia was made an Autonomous Region, it was decided that Hohhot would be its capital.

Today Hohhot is the political, cultural and industrial centre of the region. Manufacture of wool and leather products, metal, building materials, engineering and chemical industries all play an important role.

Sights

Lama Temple of Xilitu Zhao

The Lama Temple of Xilitu Zhao in the Old Town was founded in the Ming period (1368–1644); it was home to the famous Huofo Xitiuke, who was tutor to the fourth Dalai Lama. To the south-east of the Main Hall, which is laid out in Tibetan style like all the other halls, stands a 15m/50ft high stupa (Buddhist shrine), one of the most beautiful to be found anywhere in Inner Mongolia.

Dazhao Monastery

Dazhao Monastery, to the east of Xilitu Zhao, was built in Sino-Tibetan style in 1567 by Altan Khan, who converted the Mongols to the teachings of the Tibetan Gelupga sect. It boasts a silver statue of the Buddha, which is why the site is also known as the Silver Buddha Temple.

Museum of Inner Mongolia

This museum at Xinhua Dajie No. 1 provides information about Mongolia and its people, including displays of traditional crafts.

Inside a Buddhist temple

The Temple of the Five Pagodas (Wuta Si), in the south of the town about 200m/220yd from the People's Park (Renmin Gongyuan), was built during the reign of Yongzheng (1723–35); unfortunately, only the Diamond Pagoda has survived. Its base, decorated with floral and animal motifs, geometric patterns and quotations in Chinese, Mongolian, Tibetan and Sanskrit, is surmounted by five pagodas placed close together, the central one being the highest. They are adorned with figures of the Buddha and Bodhisattva. Set into a decorative wall behind the pagoda is a stone tablet, 144cm/58in. in diameter, engraved with an astronomical map showing the twelve signs of the zodiac, the twelve signs of the Chinese horoscope and some two thousand stars. The inscriptions are in the Mongolian language. This map bears witness to the high standard of knowledge acquired by 18th c. Chinese astronomers.

★ Temple of the Five Pagodas

This mosque in the Chinese style is to be found to the north-west of the Temple of Five Pagodas, at the old north gate of the town. It was founded in the 18th c. and restored in 1933. The Islamic community numbers about 20,000. In addition to the Main Hall the mosque has a Moslem bath. The temple houses 30 volumes of the Koran in Arabic which are two hundred years old. The minaret has a small pavilion on the top of it.

★ Hohhot Mosque (Qingzhen Si)

The race course in the north of the town is the scene of traditional Mongolian equestrian games as well as horse and camel races.

Race course (Sai Ma Chang)

The 33m/108ft high sepulchral mound to be found 9km/5½ miles south of the town, is the last resting-place of Wang Zhaojun (Zhaojun Mu), the concubine of one of the emperors of the Western Han dynasty. In 33 B.C. she was married to a Xiongnu prince in order to cement relations between the Xiongnus and the Hans. The life of Wang Zhaojun is the subject of many

Surroundings

★ Tomb of Wang Zhaojun

A mosque

legends and poems, and she is regarded as a symbol of peace. Her tomb is mentioned in a book written as long ago as the Tang era (618–907).

The tablet in front of the tomb bears an inscription by Dong Biwu (1885–1975), the former President of the People's Republic of China. A nearby exhibition hall provides information on the life of Wang Zhaojun.

★White Pagoda (Bai Ta)

Standing 43m/141ft high and made of wood and brick, the White Pagoda, 18km/11 miles east of the town centre, was built at the end of the 10th c. The exterior walls contain inscriptions – the oldest dating from 1162 – written in Chinese, Ancient Persian, Ancient Syrian and other languages which are no longer spoken.

Grasslands

From Hohhot visitors can make excursions lasting one or several days into areas of grassland, such as that of Xilamuren (87km/54 miles to the north) or Gegentala ("Radiant Grass", 145km/90 miles to the north). Visitors will spend the night(s) in *yurts* (Mongolian nomads' circular skin- or felt-covered tents), and will be offered a varied programme including horse- and camel-rides, visiting a shepherd's family, watching wrestling bouts and enjoying evenings round the camp-fire. There will also be an opportunity to sample typical Mongolian cooking.

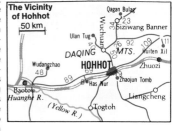

Hong Kong

Chinese
equivalent

British Crown Colony
City state
Area: 1071sq.km/413sq. miles. Altitude: 0–958m/0–3144ft
Population: at least 6,000,000. Capital: Victoria (Central District)

The following short description is included in view of the fact that in 1997   **Note**
Hong Kong is to be returned to Chinese rule. Detailed coverage can be
found in the separate Baedeker guide for "Hong Kong · Macau".

The city state of Hong Kong (Chinese: Xiang Gang) is situated about   Situation and
145km/90 miles south-east of Canton on the South China coast within the   Territory
bounds of the delta formed by the Canton River and its various tributaries,
which reaches a width of as much as 30km/19 miles. Hong Kong's exact
location not far south of the Tropic of Cancer is between 22°9' and 22°37'N
and 113°62' and 114°30'E. To the north it is bordered by the People's
Republic of China (Guangdong/Kwantung Province), while to the south lies
the South China Sea. The name Hong Kong ("fragrant estuary") refers not
only to the offshore island bearing that name but also to the whole of the
independent territory, which has the status of a Crown Colony under British
administration. The colony consists of Hong Kong Island itself with its
administrative centre Victoria (originally an independent town; more
recently referred to as Central District), the peninsula of Kowloon, which
includes the urban area of the same name, and the still relatively rural New
Territories, which include almost all the nearby islands and islets.

The complete surface area of the colony, including expanses of water, is   Area and
2911sq.km/1124sq. miles. The land surface amounts to 1071sq.km/   Topography

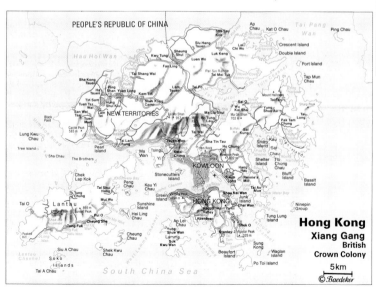

Hong Kong
Xiang Gang
British
Crown Colony
5km
© Baedeker

414sq. miles, with 78sq.km/30sq. miles making up Hong Kong Island, 10sq.km/4sq. miles Kowloon and 977sq.km/377sq. miles the New Territories.

Hong Kong's highly fragmented topography can be likened to a labyrinth, consisting of rocky islands (over 230) and promontories with narrow coastal plains and countless hidden bays. Between the main island of Hong Kong and the Kowloon peninsula lies the harbour of Victoria.

The highest point of elevation is Taimo Shan (958m/3144ft) situated in the New Territories.

Climate

The climate is basically sub-tropical. The summers are hot and humid, the winters cool, but always dry and sunny. Spring and autumn are very short. Rainfall occurs primarily in spring and summer, often in the form of heavy showers. The difference between day and night temperatures is small, averaging only 5.5°C/10°F. Daytime temperatures in summer usually lie between 25 and 31°C/77 and 88°F. The high humidity, often as much as 90%, makes the climate at this time of year very oppressive. Between May and September Hong Kong is frequently hit by typhoons. In winter the temperatures seldom fall below 10°C/50°F and on fine days can climb to as much as 20°C/68°F. Late autumn and early winter (October–December) can be the most agreeable months for a visit with deep blue skies and pleasantly warm sunshine. In spring (February/March) it is wet and misty, while by May the summer sun's effects are felt.

Population

At Hong Kong's first census in 1851 the colony had a population of 32,983, of whom 31,463 were Chinese. In 1931 there were 878,947 inhabitants, including 859,425 Chinese. The flood of legal and illegal immigrants and refugees from the People's Republic of China and other crisis-torn areas of the south-east Asian sub-continent have caused the population to increase to at least 6,000,000 since 1949/1950. About 98% of the population of Hong Kong are Chinese, predominantly Cantonese and Hakka. The British community totals some 20,000 (excluding military personnel). There are over 15,000 US citizens and more than 100,000 nationals of other states (particularly the British Commonwealth). About 60% of the inhabitants were born in the colony.

The population density is extremely high with an average of about 5500 people per sq.km/14,250 per sq. mile, while the built-up area of Kowloon has the highest density to be found anywhere in the world with a staggering 200,000 per sq.km/520,000 per sq. mile. The annual rate of population growth is at present around 1.5%, average life expectancy 78 years, illiteracy about 11%. Those in employment work predominantly in industry and the service sector, and the proportion of Hong Kong citizens with jobs is well over 90%.

Bearing in mind Hong Kong's considerable material prosperity it is surprising how under-developed the social infrastructure is. Government spending on education, health, and care of the sick and elderly is extremely low, with the result that abject poverty and excessive wealth are to be found glaringly juxtaposed. The refugee problem represents an extraordinary burden for the city.

Living
conditions

Despite all the efforts of the British administration the problem of housing in the colony has proved intractable; over a million people live in households numbering more than seven to a room.

One of the worst manifestations of Hong Kong's housing shortage are the so-called container homes. These 1.5×2.2m/5×7ft "cages", stacked side by side and one on top of another, are in reality little more than places to sleep.

Squatter people

Poverty is most in evidence among the half-million or so "squatter people", settlers without any legal rights, too poor to afford proper accommodation, living in slums or makeshift shacks on the hillsides or at the water's edge among the 15,000 "tanka", the "boat people" whose own numbers have noticeably declined thanks to an intensive programme of house building.

Buddhism, Taoism and Confucianism are the most widespread religions (about 600 temples), but there is a substantial Christian minority (some 500,000) as well as Muslims, Hindus, Israelites and other minority faiths. Indeed places of worship of the various religions and philosophies – temples, churches, mosques and synagogues – all co-exist peacefully alongside one another.

Religion and Culture

The culture of China, which can trace its history back to the middle of the 3rd millennium B.C., entered Hong Kong with the flood of Chinese immigrants to the colony. Even today it is this tradition which defines the spiritual life of the city, notwithstanding colonisation and immigration from other Asiatic countries, Europe and America.

The official languages are Chinese (Cantonese; since 1974) and English.

Language

Hong Kong is a British Crown Colony (since 1842), to which were annexed the Kowloon peninsula in 1860 and the New Territories in 1898 (a 99-year lease). Each of these three territories is divided into districts.

State and Administration

The government of the colony consists of a legislative council, an executive council, and a governor as representative of the British crown.

The city's future status has been decided by a treaty signed in 1984 which lays down that the sovereignty of the whole of Hong Kong will revert to the People's Republic of China on July 1st 1997.

As long ago as the Longshan period (around 3000 B.C.) Hong Kong had settlements, and right up to modern times it can be said to share essentially the same history as the rest of the Chinese area of civilisation.

History

In the 18th c. the British merchant fleet set out from England and eventually reached China. Using the Portuguese trading post of Macau the British conducted their trade all the way up the Zhujiang as far as Canton. The Chinese, who believed themselves to be culturally superior to the newcomers, chose to limit their contact merely to trade; they were content to accept silver in exchange for their tea and silk, the latter being a much prized commodity among the British. In time, however, the balance of payments between the two countries became an increasing burden to the British, and they turned to opium as a countermeasure. The drug had originally reached China in the 17th and 18th c. through the Portuguese. With only a small part of the quantities imported actually being used for medicinal purposes, the lion's share of the drug ended up being consumed illicitly, with the result that in 1729 the Emperor of China declared the opium trade illegal. Nevertheless, opium imports continued to increase, especially after 1773 when the British East India Company was granted a monopoly of the Bengali opium harvest, and imports rapidly rose to the massive figure of over 1000 chests a year. In 1796 the Emperor of China renewed the original ban on importation of the drug, but by 1836 the British were selling 26,000 chests of opium in China. The situation had reached crisis proportions. The Chinese demanded an end to the opium trade, but the British declared their wish to continue it, making great play of the sanctity of free trade. This eventually led to the First Opium War (1840–42), as a result of which part of present-day Hong Kong became a British Colony.

The island of Hong Kong had already been occupied previously, but by the terms of the Treaty of Nanking (Nanjing) in 1842 it was ceded unconditionally to Great Britain by the Chinese. Furthermore, as a result of the Second Opium War 1856–58) China was forced to give Britain the Kowloon peninsula and Stonecutters Island by the terms of the First Peking Convention (1860).

It was not until 1898 that Britain, seeking to defend its colony and safeguard its territorial claims in the face of the challenge from rival trading nations along the Chinese coast, secured the 99-year lease on the

959sq.km/370sq. miles of the New Territories and the numerous outlying islands. Thus the island of Hong Kong and the Kowloon peninsula legally became British territory, to which in theory China could lay no claim at all, whereas in contrast the New Territories, which is where the new burgeoning industrial base was to a large extent centred, would have to be returned to China in 1997, come what may.

From the time of the First Opium War to the 1950s – with the exception of the Japanese occupation during the Second World War (1941–45) – Hong Kong served as the international port and trans-shipment centre linking China and the West. However the Korean War (1950–53) and the US embargo on the supply of strategically important goods to China has diminished the significance of this role. In order to be able to survive, Hong Kong has had to slim down its industrial base and develop its potential as a financial centre. The colony was also caught up in the events of the Chinese cultural revolution of 1966–68 and was severely shaken by anti-British riots.

Political Perspectives

In September 1984 Great Britain and the People's Republic of China signed an agreement which laid down the following terms: the whole of Hong Kong would be placed under Chinese sovereignty on July 1st 1997, but at the same time the city would retain its special status as an autonomous region for a further fifty years and this status would guarantee the retention of existing commercial, economic, legal and cultural structures.

Economy

Trading and financial operations are the most important elements of the economy. Industries include the following: agricultural products (fruit and vegetables), fishing, minerals (quartz, felspar and kaolin), textiles and clothing, metal-working, artificial fibres, electrical and electronic products. Imports include machines, precision tools, yarns and dyes for textile production. Exports include textiles, furniture, chemical products, electrical goods and toys.

Leading international commercial and financial centre

Hong Kong is today a leading world finance and trade centre. Well over a hundred international banks have opened up branches here and the gold market is one of the largest in the world. The existence of a market economy and free trade are guaranteed by the authorities and taxes are relatively low. Except for tobacco, alcohol, perfume, cosmetics and certain petro-chemical products there are import duties or limits but the movement of capital is not subject to any restrictions. These favourable conditions have attracted many foreign businessmen and industrialists, in particular expatriate Chinese. Hong Kong is in addition a leading centre for trade in diamonds, jewellery and clocks.

As a city state with the role of a world trading centre, Hong Kong also has a modest local economy, of which agriculture, fishing and the construction industry are the most important elements. But within the overall economic picture it is imports, exports and re-exports which dominate. Over half the working population is in industry, with a good fifth involved in commerce.

International meeting-point

Hong Kong is an important international meeting-point in the fields of trade, finance, communications and industry. Originally it gave the British access to the continent of Asia, as well as providing the Chinese with an additional trade outlet. Fortunes have been made and lost here, usually at the arbitrary dictates of fate, with the result that people have adapted how they think and act to prevailing circumstances and have learnt to alter their plans and tactics at just the right moment and to live through tough times. This individual flexibility, coupled with the reluctance of the colony's government to interfere in matters of economic regulation, has enabled Hong Kong to attain its privileged international position.

Important industries

The most important areas of industrial production are textiles and clothing. Next in importance are electronics and the processing of artificial fibres. To these can be added toy production, an area where Hong Kong has for many years led the world, and clock-making and jewellery, both of which are of great importance. There is no doubt that these areas of industrial production have contributed to Hong Kong's present position as one of the world's leading centres of trade, relying on an international communications network, a liberal legislative system and a plentiful supply of cheap labour.

For the People's Republic of China, Hong Kong has become an important source of foreign exchange, as the colony has imported Chinese consumer goods, foodstuffs, building materials and other goods on a large scale. Furthermore Chinese people from Hong Kong and south-east Asia also transfer considerable sums of money to their relatives in China, while on visits there and also through banks. The government in Hong Kong, in consultation with the authorities of the neighbouring Chinese province of Guangdong, maintains friendly relations with the People's Republic of China.

Source of foreign exchange for the People's Republic of China

The nerve centre of Hong Kong is Victoria Harbour. Situated between Hong Kong Island and the Kowloon peninsula, it has an area of some 6000ha/23sq. miles and a width of between 1.6 and 9.6km/1 and 6 miles. It counts as one of the finest natural harbours in the world and in terms of tonnage ranks at the top of the world list. The container terminal (in the north-west of Kowloon) is one of the four largest in the world. An important part of passenger transport within the colony is conducted on water.

Important seaport

The official currency is the Hong Kong dollar (HK $), which is equal to 100 cents (c).

Currency

Within Asia Hong Kong plays a very special role on many different levels. With its lively ethnic mix it is possibly the most cosmopolitan of all cities. The green hills of Hong Kong Island and the mountains of the New Territories soar up into the deep blue skies above the mists of the large city or in the dry season are shrouded in thick clouds. But the attractiveness of the scenery contrasts starkly with the wretchedness of the colony's hopelessly overcrowded built-up areas. As well as the delightful islands of the South China Sea, with their unspoilt sandy bays, there are plenty of other attractions created by the hand of man: reservoirs stretch out through green valleys and skyscrapers tower up to a height of almost 375m/1230ft. But there is much that is less edifying: slums, unsightly factories, eroded mountains, quarries, large areas of development, crowds of people and an enormous amount of noise.

Cosmopolitanism and contrasts

Although superficially Hong Kong may appear westernised, it is nevertheless Chinese through and through. Even in the prosperous centres of Victoria and Kowloon there are many streets with shop-fronts and houses which differ very little from those of other East China ports of the last century, save for the incomparably wider range of goods on display.

If Singapore makes an ideal introduction for visitors to Asia, Hong Kong is better suited to the requirements of the more experienced traveller. Those who immerse themselves too hastily into the city's hectic and feverish whirl can easily be overwhelmed by the scale of their impressions and are quite likely to develop an aversion to the place. Those who take their time to acclimatise themselves to this very different world, will realise the extraordinary riches which Hong Kong has to offer. The city's charm lies in its contradictions. If you leave behind you the ultra-modern skyscraper surroundings of Hong Kong Island and Kowloon and venture into the New Territories you will find a quite different world: in the fields ploughs will be pulled by water-buffaloes and peasants will still be tilling their land in the time-honoured way. In those areas of the colony which hitherto have not fallen under the grip of modern industrialisation, including the remote offshore islands, the centuries-old way of life of peasants and fishermen continues to survived untouched by the hand of progress. Most Chinese eating-houses have preserved their old customs and usages; only the beer which is on sale everywhere is a concession to modernity. The authentic old Chinese atmosphere can still be experienced every evening in the numerous cinemas where the programmes can include both films in Mandarin produced in Hong Kong as well as Cantonese films. Chinese operas are broadcast regularly on the radio and television and the traditional festivals are celebrated every year with a wealth of colour and extravagance.

In the everyday hurly-burly of this vast city, visitors are scarcely noticed – something which is surprising, given the huge number of foreign tourists who pass through. The wheeler-dealing of Hong Kong's traders is conducted with much hustle and bustle at all levels, the shops being crammed full of every conceivable commodity. Particularly noticeable is the range of hand-crafted goods on offer, while there are outstanding restaurants where probably the very best Chinese cuisine in the world is available. The harbour is packed with ships, yachts, boats, junks and sampans. What probably most impresses the visitor is the sheer bubbling vitality and dynamism of the colony's people. Relaxation and recreations play a relatively minor role in the lives of most of Hong Kong's inhabitants, and it is to be regretted that courtesy and consideration for others are not infrequently neglected in people's struggle for prosperity and advancement.

In Hong Kong drive on the left

In spite of the dominant role which money and business play in Hong Kong, the city still possesses attractive, quiet and untouched corners with interesting things to see. The New Territories and the many islands were once oases of rest for the local people. But although they have been increasingly taken over by modern industrial development, they are still very much an alternative for the visitor who is not solely interested in the downtown shops. For the short-stay visitor to Hong Kong there are plenty of fascinating things to see and do and the serious problems which the colony's infrastructure are posing are scarcely likely to impinge on his enjoyment. One thing, however, will very quickly become clear: Hong Kong is no longer cheap. Over the last few years practically all goods and services have become enormously more expensive, but even so, it is true to say that on the whole the visitor still gets good value for money.

Hong Kong Island

★Victoria Peak

To get the best view of Hong Kong it is best to make the ascent of Victoria Peak, at 554m/1818ft the highest point on Hong Kong Island (in the north-west). The summit station of the Victoria Peak Tramway is situated at 379m/1243ft and it takes about eight minutes to make the precipitous, breathtaking ascent from the base station at Murray Building behind the Hilton Hotel on Garden Road in Central District (Victoria). This cable-railway has operated since 1888 without any accidents and is therefore one of the oldest and safest methods of transport in the colony. Both trains maintain a balance of weight as the one climbs the mountain and the other descends. For the ascent the Peak Tramway is often overcrowded, while by contrast on the downward journey it tends to be less full. It is therefore a good idea to take a taxi or minibus to go up the mountain and then travel down using the tramway.

★★View

The summit station of the cable-railway, known as Peak Tower, redesigned to plans by the British architect Terry Farrell, incorporates a shopping precinct with restaurants and a viewing terrace which offers a fascinating panorama over Victoria, the harbour, Kowloon and the mountains of the New Territories.

In clear weather a walk around the summit, which takes about an hour, should on no account be missed. To the south and south-west there is a view across the whole of Hong Kong Island and the offshore islands. The sunsets are particularly impressive and this is an ideal time for taking photos, especially just as night is falling, when Hong Kong turns into a gigantic sea of lights. It is also well worthwhile to continue up to the Victoria Peak Garden, a park situated on the upper south slope of Victoria Peak.

The area around Victoria Peak used to be inhabited exclusively by foreigners and it was not until after the Second World War that the Chinese were also allowed to settle here. In springtime the mountain is frequently shrouded in mist and it can be extremely cool. In summer, on the other hand, it can be a place to take refuge from the oppressive heat which pervades the lower-lying built-up areas of the city.

Victoria, generally known nowadays as Central District of Hong Kong Island and occupying the northern part of the central area, is both the capital and the vibrant commercial centre of the colony. This is where the skyscrapers of the banks and trading houses are to be found, built on land whose value in the past few years has rocketed to astronomic heights. These new buildings have almost completely replaced the older ones of the earlier colonial era. If one looks around in the streets and on the spacious squares between the Mandarin and Hilton Hotels, it is difficult to imagine that up until thirty years ago four or five-storeyed whitewashed houses with verandas stood there. The lawns and fountains of Statue Square were not completed until 1966. Modern high-rise buildings now dominate the skyline of this business district and are also gradually starting to be built further down in place of the old commercial houses and offices along the harbourside.

Victoria (Central District)

The last remaining relics of the colonial period consist of the following: the Supreme Court opposite the War Memorial, the old Officers' Mess, a long grey two-storeyed building with verandas to the east of the Hilton Hotel, St John's Cathedral, built in 1847–49 and situated opposite the base station of the Victoria Peak Tramway, and Government House in Upper Albert Road, the residence of the British governor.

Government House

South-west of Government House lie the Zoological Garden and the Botanical Garden, separated from one another by Albany Road. The Chinese regularly meet here in the early morning for traditional shadow-boxing.

Zoological Garden, Botanical Garden

One of Hong Kong's oldest buildings is the luxurious Hotel Mandarin, located next to the Prince's Building, which is famous for its ceramic relief decorations and excellent range of shops.

Hotel Mandarin

The most impressive building in the area is, however, "The Landmark", a five-storey complex which is laid out around a large inner courtyard (1860sq.m/20,000sq.ft; fountain) and accommodates around 100 shops. At weekends there is regularly a wide range of free entertainment on offer here.

The Landmark

As we go westwards along Queen's Road, the open shop-fronts lend the townscape an increasingly Chinese appearance. Steep narrow stepped alleyways branch off from the main street in a south-westerly direction, scaling the hillside. In the tiny stalls and small shops to be found here there is an immense array of goods for sale. Ladder Street, famous for its junk shops, is particularly picturesque, while curiosities of all kinds are bought and sold on Cat Street (Upper and Lower Lascar Row). It is also worth visiting the two Taoist temples on nearby Hollywood Road (both at No. 124): Man Mo Temple (1848) and Lit Shing Kung Temple.

Ladder Street

Cat Street

★Man Mo Temple
Lit Shing Kung Temple

Further to the north-east below Queen's Road is Connaught Road, which runs alongside the ferry piers. The road begins in the east by the Connaught Centre skyscraper, where the Hong Kong Tourist Association (HKTA) has its headquarters (information office).

Opposite, to the north-east, are the General Post Office and the Government Publication Centre. Here in the Government Information Service Bookshop there is a wide range of literature relating to Hong Kong.

Further east, at Edinburgh Place (Queen's Pier by the harbour) is City Hall, seat of the city administration and a gathering place for all those interested in culture and art (concert hall, theatre, exhibition rooms).

City Hall

Traditional Chinese junks, framed by modern skyscrapers of Hong Kong

**Flagstaff House
(★Museum of Tea
Ware)**

Just to the south of City Hall on Cotton Tree Drive is Flagstaff House, built in 1844, which was formerly the residence of the British military commander. It has been completely restored in the 19th c. style and now houses the interesting Museum of Tea Ware with Chinese tea services dating from the sixth dynasty to the present.

Westwards from City Hall along the harbourside are the quays serving the Star Ferry, which crosses to Kowloon, and the other ferries which serve the outlying islands. At the end is the Macau Terminal (ferries and hydrofoils to and from Portuguese Macau in 1–3½ hours). In the immediate vicinity there is a colourful bazaar or street-market held every evening, known as "Poor Man's Nightclub", where traders set out their wares, flying cooks prepare tasty fish specialities, while travelling entertainers and musicians perform. In the daytime it is well worth taking a walk along the harbour quaysides and watching the lighters, boats and junks from the People's Republic of China (mainly from Canton on the Zhujiang) unload their wares (foodstuffs, building materials, etc.).

**University of
Hong Kong
(★Fung Ping
Shan Museum)**

Further up, going in a south-westerly direction from Connaught Road and Queen's Road, there is a series of roads, one of which, Bonham Road, is the location of the University of Hong Kong. In 1953 the noteworthy Fung-Ping-Shan Museum (94 Bonham Road) was opened inside the university. Its collections are devoted mainly to Chinese ceramics and bronzes.

Wan Chai

Immediately to the east of Central District (Victoria) is the district of Wan Chai, the home of Susie Wong, the character in the novel (who came from the "Luk Kwok" Hotel). Wan Chai is an entertainment area for sailors and the glitter of the bars and the brightly-lit signs in the shops reflect the night-time scene here. Apart from a few small temples, mention need only be made of the 66-storey Hopewell Centre and the Arts Centre (theatre, stage shows).

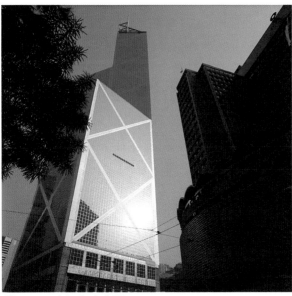

Skyscraper of the Bank of China

Going east from Wan Chai we cross into the district of Causeway Bay, which has developed into a popular shopping and restaurant area since the opening of the road tunnel running under Victoria Harbour to Kowloon (Cross-Harbour Tunnel). In Typhoon Shelter, which is a specially constructed harbour with protection against typhoons, the luxury boats and pleasure yachts of the Royal Hong Kong Yacht Club are moored, along with some 7500 boats and junks belonging to the "Boat People".

A little way to the south of the yacht club building stands the World Trade Centre.

★ Causeway Bay

Further east we reach the districts of North Point, Quarry Bay and Shau Kei Wan, where the ramshackle shacks of the squatters can be seen stretching out above the modern residential areas.

North Point, Quarry Bay, Shau Kei Wan

Inland to the south of Wan Chai is the district of Happy Valley with its large-scale sports facilities (including a racecourse). An interesting document of local history is provided by the four cemeteries – one Persian, one Catholic, one Muslim and one from the Colonial period – which lie along the road behind the Royal Hong Kong Jockey Club.

Happy Valley

Further over to the south-east lies Tiger Balm Garden (Tai Hang Road), a well-known but also controversial leisure park, which was laid out in 1935 and named after the "Tiger Balm" menthol ointment invented by the Chinese Aw Boon Haw. Often on the border between art and kitsch, the park contains plaster figures of fabulous animals from Chinese mythology, artificial mountains with caves and grottoes and representations of life in old China. The park's symbol is its 50m/165ft high white pagoda.

Tiger Balm Garden

On the south-west coast of Hong Kong Island lies the old fishing port of Aberdeen. About 20,000 people live in boats and junks in its harbour, most of them working as fishermen or as stevedores on the surrounding

Aberdeen (Chek Pai Wan)

wharves. A trip round the harbour on a sampan and a visit to the big fish market can be recommended. Aberdeen is also well-known for its floating restaurants. Lying beyond the harbour and linked to the town by a bridge is the island of Ap Lei Chau ("duck's tongue") with its large electricity station.

★★Ocean Park

South-east of Aberdeen the Shum Shui promontory extends southwards. At its tip lies Ocean Park with one of the largest "oceanariums" in the world. The park is divided into two sections on different levels, linked by a 1.4km/1 mile long cable-car. The journey from the lower level to the higher takes seven minutes and at the top the visitor will find the "Ocean Theatre" (performances with dolphins and sea-lions, etc.) and the "Wave Cove", a pool with simulated waves. The biggest attraction is, however, the deep-sea aquarium, Atoll Reef, in which over 30,000 different marine animals can be viewed.

Bathing beaches

Along the south coast of Hong Kong Island, with its many small bays, there are a number of beaches of variable quality. The best, which tend to be very crowded during the summer season, are to be found along Deepwater Bay, Repulse Bay and South Bay (less spectacular).

Stanley

The Stanley promontory is the southernmost extension of Hong Kong Island. The colony's main prison is located here (formerly an internment camp at the time of the Japanese occupation during the Second World War). At Stanley itself the market is enjoyable to visit (particularly good for textiles), while the narrow beach at Stanley Bay is suitable for bathing. Mention should also be made of the Tin-Hau temple of 1767.

From Stanley it is well worth taking a walk northwards to the Tai Tam reservoir.

Big Wave Bay
Shek O

On the east coast of Hong Kong Island there are beaches at Big Wave Bay (surfing also possible) and further south at Shek O.

Kowloon

Situation and Importance

The wide reaches of Victoria Harbour to the north of Hong Kong Island are crossed by a railway tunnel (MTR) and a road tunnel (Cross Harbour Tunnel; there is a second one further east). On the far side lies the Kowloon peninsula, the second urban area of the Crown Colony of Hong Kong.

Tsim Sha Tsui
Ocean Terminal

The southern end of the peninsula is occupied by the district of Tsim Sha Tsui. At the south-western end is the large overseas passenger ship terminal, known as the Ocean Terminal, which has a shopping centre, and the Star Ferry Pier, which is the dock for harbour ferries to and from Hong Kong Island. The Clock Tower is a relic of a railway station which was formerly situated here.

★ Cultural centre

★ Museum of Art
★ Space Museum

The quayside area to the east has been widened with embankments and turned into a "cultural centre". This complex includes a concert hall, theatre and two extremely interesting museums, the Museum of Art and the Space Museum, the latter boasting a Zeiss planetarium (housed in a hemispheric building) and a section devoted to solar science.

Hung Hom
Railway Terminus

Further west in the area around Salisbury Road leading up to the Hung Hom Railway Terminus, Hong Kong's main railway station, various new hotels and shopping complexes have sprung up ("East Tsim Sha Tsui").

★ Nathan Road

From the northern dock area of Victoria Harbour, Nathan Road runs for about 4km/2½ miles in a dead straight line northwards as far as Boundary Road, the northernmost limit of the city area of Kowloon. This busy major traffic artery, which has the MTR underground line running beneath it, is often referred to as the "Golden Mile". Both sides of it are lined with hotels, restaurants, department stores, cinemas, shops and night clubs. Indeed it can almost be said that there is a surfeit of goods and entertainments on offer.

Along the west side of Nathan Road, about 500m/¼ mile north of the harbour, is the extensive Kowloon Park, in which are to be found an Islamic centre (with mosque) and the Museum of History (entrance on Haiphong Road) with exhibits concerned with the local history.

Kowloon Park

★Museum of History

The north side of Kowloon Park borders on the district of Yau Ma Tei. This area, which is bounded by Nathan Road to the east, Public Square Street to the north, Temple Street to the west (Chinese night-time market) and Market Street to the south, has four Chinese temples: Tin-Hau Temple, Fook Tak Tse Temple, Shing Wong Temple and Shea Tam Temple. This temple area was established on a different site in 1870, but moved to its present position in 1876 and most recently renovated in 1972. A little way to the west, at the junction of Kansu Street and Reclamation Street, the well-known "Jade Market" is held every day. By day a trip can be taken by sampan through the typhoon-protected harbour known as Yaumati Typhoon Shelter and the life of the boat-dwellers, known as the "Water People", can be seen at close quarters.

Yau Ma Tei
Chinese night market
Four Chinese temples

Jade market

Nathan Road leads from Yau Ma Tei to the shopping area of Mong Kok, where in tiny Hong Lok Street (south of Argyle Street) the Bird Market is held. Anyone who is anxious to buy one of the splendid exotic birds (kakadus, parrots, etc.) on display here, ought to seek advice at the nearby "Kowloon Veterinary Hospital" (9 Tung Fong Street).

Mong Kok
★ Bird market

Further north-west is the Lei Cheng Uk tomb, which was discovered in 1955 in the district of Sham Shui Po (41 Tonkin Street) and has been assigned to the latter part of the Han dynasty (A.D. 25–220). The earthenware and bronze objects which have been uncovered are set out in a small museum. The burial site is situated in the middle of a large social housing area.

Sham Shui Po
★★ Lei Cheng Uk Tomb

Right in the very north-west of Kowloon lies the Lai Chi Kok amusement park with the Sung Dynasty Village, completed in 1979, which is a miniature reproduction of a village from the time of the Song dynasty (960–1279). Wooden pavilions, in which "villagers" in period costume demonstrate various types of work, are arranged along the banks of an artificially created river. Besides a herb shop, tavern and shop selling fans there are various traditional craft workshops. Other features include a villa in a rock and flower garden, a wax figure museum, a temple and a restaurant, the food of which is prepared using traditional old Song recipes. Occasionally special events are held, such as wedding ceremonies, folk-dancing demonstrations, kung-fu exhibitions, performances by trained monkeys and court displays.

Lai Chi Kok
Amusement Park
★ Sung Dynasty Village

New Territories

In terms of area, the mainly mountainous New Territories form by far the largest part of the colony of Hong Kong. In the north they stretch from Kowloon as far as the Chinese border, while also extending far to the east and west (here fringed by numerous bays and coves). In addition – apart from the main island of Hong Kong and Stonecutters Island – the numerous outlying islands, including the largest, Lantau Island, also come under the administrative jurisdiction of the New Territories.

Situation and Territory

About 10km/6 miles north of Victoria Harbour, which separates Kowloon from Hong Kong Island, lies the new satellite town of Sha Tin, in which it is anticipated that some 500,000 people will eventually live. The quickest way to reach Sha Tin is to take the train from Hung Hom Railway Terminal in Kowloon.

Satellite town
Sha Tin

Hong Kong

★★Temple of 10,000 Buddhas

The most important place of interest at Sha Tin is the Temple of 10,000 Buddhas, which stands at an altitude of 320m/1050ft and can only be reached by climbing a steep flight of steps. The temple complex is on two levels – the principal temple on the lower level and the second temple, consisting of four separate structures, on the upper. The principal temple of 10,000 Buddhas (there are now in fact over 12,800 figures) was begun in 1950 and is dedicated to its founder, Kuan Yin, who died in 1965 (his embalmed body is preserved in the Buddha posture and visible behind glass). In the forecourt there is a nine-storey pagoda.

★Art Gallery of the Institute of Chinese Studies

Another attraction in Sha Tin is the Art Gallery of the Institute of Chinese Studies, the art gallery of the Chinese university, which has valuable collections (paintings, calligraphy, seals, etc.) from different periods of Chinese history. In 1978 the Royal Hong Kong Jockey Club opened a second racecourse in Sha Tin (the first is at Happy Valley on Hong Kong Island) and races are regularly held here at weekends. Towering up to the south of Sha Tin is the highly distinctive Amah Rock, whose shape suggests a woman carrying a child on her back.

Country parks

The New Territories also possess various areas under environmental protection which are known as "country parks". Here the visitor can find plenty of greenery, extensive stretches of water, attractive duck-ponds, beaches (Clearwater Bay in the extreme south-east has a good beach for bathing) and high points which offer excellent views. These all make a welcome change from the hectic bustle of the built-up areas of Kowloon and Victoria. However, even away from the centres of population, new industrial zones and residential districts are continually springing up and these threaten the continued existence of these protected natural areas. A popular area for

Tai Lam Chung Reservoir

walking is provided by the surroundings of the large Tai Lam Chung Reservoir in the south-west of the mainland.

Castle Peak

The most westerly part of the New Territories and a popular place with beachgoers is the area known as Castle Peak, which takes its name from the hill of that name (583m/1913ft), which is said to have been the scene of a number of battles. The district has villa developments in green surroundings, as well as large social housing complexes. Among the industrial installations here the seawater desalination plant at Lok On Pai should be mentioned.

Po Toi Monastery

On the slopes of Castle Peak Hill stands the Buddhist monastery of Po Toi, with a small temple and the "Dragon Gardens" (with reproductions of old Chinese buildings).

Ching Chun Temple

Near Castle Peak Hospital stands the Taoist Ching Chun Temple (1959) with remarkable roof decorations.

Yuen Long

In the north-west of the New Territories we come to the little country town of Yuen Long, which, with its picturesque little streets and Chinese craft workshops, is well worth a visit. It is also worth making a detour further

★Lau Fau Shan

north-westwards to the little town of Lau Fau Shan, situated on a tongue of land extending into Deep Bay (Hau Hoi Wan). Here oysters, fish and ducks are farmed and the fish restaurants enjoy an excellent reputation.

★★Kam Tin

Some 4km/2½ miles east of Yuen Long lies the 16th/17th c. village of Kam Tin (real name Kat Hing Wai), which is surrounded by a wall and moat and can only be reached along a single narrow entranceway (admission fee). Descendants of the founding Tang family still live there. In the nearby area there are another five such walled villages.

In the far north of the New Territories is the border with the People's Republic of China. The border is surrounded by a no-go zone which can only be visited with a special permit. It is possible, though, to look over into China from certain raised viewing points – such as Lok Ma Chau in the west.

Border with the People's Republic of China

Just the other side of the border the People's Republic of China has set up the "special industrial zone" of Shenzhen (including a large amusement park) which can be visited with a special visa valid for three days. This is usually done by taking the train from the Lo Wu border station; for information and bookings contact travel agencies in Hong Kong.

Special industrial zone of Shenzhen

The islands of Lantau, Chek Lap Kok, Cheung Chau and Peng Chau

The islands to the west of Kowloon and Hong Kong can be reached by regular ferry connections. The boats berth on Hong Kong Island at the "Outlying Islands" quay on Connaught Road. There are also circular boat trips available to the islands.

Boat connections

Lantau is by far the largest island in the colony (about double the size of Hong Kong Island), but only about 30,000 people live there. The largest settlement, Tai O (pop. 12,000, mainly fishermen; crab paste), with houses built on stilts above the river, lies at the western end.

★Lantau Island

In the centre west of the island, at an altitude of 800m/2600ft, is the monastery of the "precious lotus" or Po Lin, the building of which was begun in 1921. The massive Buddha figure has a height of 35m/115ft and it measures 52m/171ft in diameter. It is possible to spend the night in the monastery (Spartan sleeping-places and vegetarian food). In the early morning hours one can be taken up to Lantau Peak (933m/3061ft) by a monk. It is the highest point on the island and the sunrise is superb. To the south of the monastery lie the tea plantations of the Ngong Ping Plateau, the only ones in the colony (overnight accommodation available in small bungalows).

★Po Lin Monastery

It is well worth a walk around the Shek Pik reservoir which lies amid picturesque scenery to the south-west of Lantau Peak. Underwater pipelines take water stored here to islands of Cheung Chau and Hong Kong.

Shek Pik Reservoir

In the centre north of the island of Lantau stands Fort Tung Chung, which was built by the Chinese in 1817 as a defence against the invading Europeans.

Fort Tung Chung

Another attraction on Lantau Island is the Trappist monastery of the Catholic Cistercian order, known as Tai Shui Hong ("Trappist Haven"), situated in the north-east of the island. It was founded in 1956 by monks who had fled from the Chinese dictators in Beijing and who now run a highly lucrative dairy farm. It is also possible to spend the night here.

★Trappist Haven of Tai Shui Hong

Chek Lap Kok, an island lying off the north shore of Lantau Island, is the location of Hong Kong's new airport, due to be completed in 1997, which should relieve the pressure on the severely overstretched Kai Tak Airport (south-east of Kowloon). The rocky surface of the island has been both flattened (90 million cu.m/3180 million cu.ft of rock will have been blasted away) and raised (75 million cu.m/2650 million cu.ft of sand and gravel), so that the overall area of the island has been increased by about 13sq.km/5sq. miles. The massive site, complete with motorway and rail connections and a satellite settlement, must rank as one of the largest construction projects in history.

Chek Lap Kok Island (new airport under construction)

The two small islands of Cheung Chau and Peng Chau, which lie off the east coast of Lantau Island to the south and north respectively, are densely populated (mainly fisher people) but have no motorised transport. These typically Chinese islands throng with visitors at weekends.

Cheung Chau and **Peng Chau** Islands

Huai'an

Chinese equivalent	淮安县

Province: Jiangsu
Area: 1644sq.km/635sq. miles. Population: 1,100,000

Situation and Communications

Huai'an lies at 119°09'E and 33°29'N, about 200km/125 miles north of the provincial capital of Nanjing. The west side of the city is surrounded by the Great Imperial Canal. There is a bus service between Nanjing and Huai'an.

History

Huai'an can look back on five thousand years of history. First it was an important military stronghold. Then with the opening of the Imperial Canal the town experienced a boom in trade and business during the 6th and 7th c. In the 16th c. the townspeople had to defend themselves repeatedly against attacks from Japanese pirates. During the Japanese-Chinese War (1939–45) Huai'an served as a garrison for guerrilla units.

The city is the birthplace of Wu Cheng'en (1500–82), the author of the famous novel "Travels in the West", and the politician Zhou Enlai (see Famous People).

Sights

Huai River Guardian Tower (Zhenhuai Lou)

This two-storeyed 8m/26ft high wooden tower on a brick pedestal in the centre of the city dates back in its present form to 1881. As the Huai River frequently broke its banks, causing high loss of life and extensive damage, the inhabitants gave the tower its name in the hope that by constantly keeping guard they could curb the river. It is also known as the Drum Tower (Gu Lou), after the building which previously stood here during the Song dynasty (960–1279) and which had to make way for the new building. There is a small museum inside the tower.

★Birthplace of Zhou Enlai (Zhou Enlai Guju)

The house in which the famous statesman was born on August 5th 1898 lies 300m north-west of the Zhenhuai Lou (Drum Tower) in a small street. Zhou Enlai (see Famous People) lived here until 1910, when he was taken to Shenyang by his uncle. After his death in 1976 the house was restored and opened to the public.

★Wentong Pagoda (Wentong Ta)

The 44m/144ft high Wentong Pagoda, a brick building with wooden ledges, in the north-west of the city, on the east bank of the Great Imperial Canal, was erected in 984 and restored on several occasions over the centuries. Its parabolic shape is highly unusual in architectural terms.

Surroundings

★Ming Dynasty Tombs (Mingzu Ling)

The tombs on the west bank of Lake Hongzehu, about 150km/90 miles south-west of Huai'an, were built at the orders of the first emperor of the Ming dynasty (1368–1644) in 1387, so that his ancestors – his grandfather, great-grandfather and great-great-grandfather – might all have a place of interment befitting their rank. The approach to the tombs is lined with various holy temples and numerous stone statues of riders, officials, soldiers, lions and unicorns, etc.

Hubei   I–K 5–6

Chinese equivalent	湖北省

Province
Area: 180,000sq.km/69,500sq. miles
Population: 55,120,000. Capital: Wuhan

China

Hubei Province

HEILONGJIANG

JILIN

INNER MONGOLIA
(NEIMENGGU)

XINJIANG

© Baedeker

GANSU

INNER MONGOLIA
(NEIMENGGU)

LIAONING

BEIJING
(PEKING)●

TIANJIN

(HEBEI)

NINGXIA SHANXI

SHANDONG

QINGHAI

GANSU

SHAANXI HENAN

JIANGSU

XIZANG (TIBET)

SICHUAN

HUBEI

ANHUI SHANGHAI

ZHEJIANG

JIANGXI

HUNAN

GUIZHOU

FUJIAN

YUNNAN

GUANGXI GUANGDONG

TAIWAN

XIANG GANG
(HONGKONG)

HAINAN

AO MEN
(MACAO)

The People's
Republic of China
Zhonghua Renmin Gongheguo

The province of Hubei lies north of Lake Dongting Hu (hence its name: Hubei means "north of the lake"), along the middle course of the Changjiang, between 108°21'–116°07'E and 29°01'–33°16'N.

Situation

A large part of Hubei, often known as the "land of the thousand lakes", consists of a river depression opening southwards caused by the wide meanderings of the Changjiang and by the Hanshui, the area being bounded to the west, north and east by mountain ranges. In the west lies the 3105m/10,187ft high mountain of Shengnongjia, which is surrounded by an enormous rain forest. This area has been declared a nature reserve.

Topography

The province has features of both continental and monsoon climates, with all four seasons being very well defined. Winters are short and cold, summers hot and moist. The average temperature is 4°C/39°F in January and 30°C/86°F in July. The provincial capital of Wuhan ranks with Tschungking and Nanjing as one of the hottest cities in China, with temperatures in summer often rising above 40°C/104°F. Rainfall (600–700mm/23–28in.) occurs mainly in spring and at the beginning of summer.

Climate

During the Zhou dynasty (11th c.–221 B.C.) Hubei belonged to the kingdom of Chu. Then it was incorporated into the empire of China by the Qin-Emperor Shi Huangdi (reigned 221–210 B.C.). Because of its position on the Changjiang the area attained considerable importance. In 1644 the province of Hubei was formed. Since 1860 certain towns in the province have been open for trade to the western powers. Wuhan was the starting-point of the revolution of 1911, which led to the downfall of the Qing dynasty.

History

The iron and steel combines of Wuhan and Huangshi were established as a result of the discovery of extensive iron deposits. In addition gypsum quarrying and copper and phosphate mining are all important. Industries of note include machine construction, shipbuilding and chemicals.

Economy

Hubei is one of the most important rice-producing (wet rice cultivation) areas in China. Other key crops are cotton, tea (in the mountain areas),

277

wheat, maize, soya beans, sesame and fruit. The many lakes support both fishing and fish-farming.

Places to visit   Wuhan, the capital, Shashi, Xiangfan and Yichang are all worth visiting (see entries for all four towns).

Hunan   I–J 5–7

Chinese
equivalent

湖南省

Province
Area: 210,000sq.km/81,000sq. miles
Population: 62,090,000. Capital: Changsha

Situation   The province of Hunan lies in Central China, mainly to the south of Lake Dongting Hu (its name means "south of the lake"), between 108°47'–114°13'E and 24°38'–30°08'N.

Topography   Hunan basically falls within the catchment area of Lake Dongting Hu, which lies along the northern edge of the province, and its affluent rivers Xiang-jiang, Zishui, Yuanjiang and Lishui. The north is flat, while the west, east and south parts of the province are hemmed in and indented by hilly uplands and mountain ranges.

Climate   The climate is continental, but heavily influenced by monsoons. Winters are short and bring plentiful precipitation in the form of both rain and snow. Summers are hot and moist. The average temperatures in Changsha are 30°C/86°F in July and 6°C/43°F in January.

History   At the time of the Warring Kingdoms (475–221 B.C.) Hunan belonged to the Kingdom of Chu. From the 3rd c. onwards Han Chinese migrated over and over again into the region, which was inhabited by Miao and Yao. From the time of the Yuan and Ming dynasties (13th–17th c.), when Hunan and Hubei

China

Hunan Province

The People's
Republic of China
Zhonghua Renmin Gongheguo

were amalgamated to form the province of Huguang, Hunan played an important role in providing rice for the country, resulting in the proverb "When the harvest has been good in Huguang, the whole country prospers!" Hunan became an independent province in 1664 and as the home region of Mao Zedong was a focal point for the revolutionary movement in the 20th c.

Hunan is rich in minerals, particularly in tungsten and antimony ore, as well as manganese, lead, zinc, tin, copper, coal and phosphates. The most important industrial towns lie along the Xiangjiang. | Economy

Hunan is, however, still largely an agricultural province and counts as one of China's main rice-producing areas, the crop occupying approximately a half of all the land available for cultivation (one fifth of the province). Tea, cotton, maize, cereals, soya beans, sorghum and sweet potatoes are the other main crops. Timber production (pine, maple, bamboo, cedar and spruce) is also important.

As well as the capital Changsha (see entry), it is worth going to Hengyang (see entry) with nearby Hengshan, one of the five holy mountains of China, as well as Xiangtan and Yuegang (see entries). | Places to visit

Huzhou   L 5

湖洲 | Chinese equivalent

Province: Zhejiang. Area: 10sq.km/4sq. miles
Population: 111,000 (conurbation: 936,000)

Huzhou lies 50km/31 miles north of Hangzhou and 200km/124 miles southwest of Shanghai, at 121°07′E and 30°52′N. There are bus services from both Hangzhou and Shanghai. | Situation and Communications

Nothing definite is known of the origins of Huzhou. All that is certain is that there must have been an important settlement there as early as 602, as in that year it was raised to the status of capital of an administrative district directly under the rule of the province. From the 7th c. onwards the town developed into one of the most important silk centres in south-east China. Under the last two imperial dynasties (from the 14th c. to the early 20th) it became the leading producer of artists' brushes, a position which Huzhou can still lay claim to today. Feather fans are another well-known product. | History

This building, which stands in the city centre, is often referred to as the "pagoda within a pagoda" (Tali Ta), as it consists of two concentric octagonal structures. The inner pagoda is made of heavy stone, the outer one of bricks and wood. The original 8th c. building was destroyed by lightning in 1150. The inner part was rebuilt in the same year, the outer in 1234. | **Sights** / ★Feiying Ta Pagoda

The Temple of the Iron Buddha in the west of the city dates from 1369. It is also known as the Temple of the Goddess of Mercy, because in the main hall a 2m/6½ft iron statue of the Avalokiteshvara dating from 1022 is kept. | ★Temple of the Iron Buddha (Tiefo Si)

Inner Mongolia   I–L 1–4

内蒙古自治区 | Chinese equivalent

Autonomous region
Area: 12,000,000sq.km/4,630,000sq. miles
Population: 21,840,000. Capital: Hohhot

China

Autonomous Region Inner Mongolia

The People's Republic of China
Zhonghua Renmin Gongheguo

Situation	The autonomous region of Inner Mongolia lies between 97°12'–126°04'E and 37°24'–53°23'N in the north of China along the borders with Russia and Mongolia. The vast majority of the population is Han-Chinese, only about 13% being Mongols.
Topography	This region consists largely of steppeland and desert and takes in part of the Mongolian plateau, which has an average height of 1000m/3280ft, the desert area of the Ordos Plateau, around which the Huanghe flows, and in the north-east the Great Chingan.
Climate	The extreme continental climate brings long, bitterly cold winters (the average temperature in January is −10°C/14°F) and only three to five months in summer are free of frost. Rainfall is scarce, with only 150–500mm/6–20in. falling each year. The warmest and at the same time wettest months are July, with an average temperature of 21°C/70°F, and August. 60% of the annual rainfall occurs in these two months.
History	As early as the 10th c. B.C. the area of Xiongnu was settled. From the 5th c. the Chinese started to build the Great Wall as a defence against the tribes from the steppes. Emperor Wudi of the Han dynasty (206 B.C.–A.D. 220) occupied parts of Inner Mongolia as a way of protecting trade routes with the west. In the 5th c. Turkish peoples brought the land under their rule. Under Genghis Khan the Mongols defeated the Jin kingdom in the 13th c. and founded the Yuan dynasty. But as early as 1368 the last emperor of this dynasty had to flee back to Mongolia from Beijing. At the beginning of the Manchurian Qing dynasty (1644–1911) the region was annexed to the empire. During this period there was an increase in Han Chinese coming here to settle and this led to uprisings and a struggle for independence. In 1911 the Mongol freedom fighters succeeded, with Russian support, to achieve independence for Outer Mongolia.

Grazing camels

The invasion of Manchuria by the Japanese in 1931 brought Inner Mongolia into that country's sphere of influence. Underground groups fought for the region's independence with help from the Chinese communists.

The autonomous region of Inner Mongolia was established on May 1st 1947, thus before all the other regions which eventually gained autonomy status (Xinjiang, Ningxia, Guangxi and Tibet). In 1949, when Mongolia again came under Chinese rule, as well as on several other occasions during the last 50 years, the region was enlarged. In 1979, after the Cultural Revolution (1966–76), which had led to the territory being reduced in size by almost a third as a result of the Chinese dictators' fears of separatist aspirations, the boundaries were restored to what they had been in 1956.

Economy

Coal, chromium, copper, precious metals and iron ore are all mined (iron and steel works in Baotou). In the salt lakes of the desert areas both salt and soda are also extracted.

About half the province's area can be used as grazing land (mainly sheep and goats, but also cattle, horses and camels). The government is trying to use financial inducements to persuade the nomads to take up a settled existence.

The only fertile and successfully cultivated area of Inner Mongolia is the valley of the Huanghe, which in its upper course flows for hundreds of kilometres through the province. In these areas given over to agriculture, which is only possible on the 110 to 160 frost-free days in the year, cereals, sugar-beet, oil-seed, potatoes, maize and kauliang are produced.

Places to visit

The towns of Hohhot and Baotou (see entries) can be visited by tourists. Anyone seeking a more unusual experience can try sleeping in a yurt (nomad's skin-covered tent).

281

A Mongolian family outside their jurt

Jiangsu

K–L 4–5

Chinese equivalent	江苏省

Province
Area: 102,600sq.km/39,600sq. miles
Population: 68,440,000. Capital: Nanjing

Situation
Jiangsu extends along the east coast of China, around the lower course of the Changjiang. It lies between 116°21'–121°54'E and 30°46'–35°08'N.

Topography
17% of the surface area of the province is taken up with waterways and lakes, while the rest consists of plains broken up by isolated hills. The region includes the low-lying alluvial plain of the Changjiang and the old estuarial area of the Huanghe (diverted in 1863), a flat coastal region criss-crossed by canals. The mud brought down by the two rivers has in the course of thousands of years pushed the coast several kilometres out to sea, at the same time causing the formation of large lakes (Taihu, Gaoyou Hu, Hongze Hu).

Climate
The climate shows considerable variations: while the south has a moist temperate climate, the north is cooler. The annual rainfall, which decreases as one goes northwards, is about 1000mm/39in. In summer and autumn the area is subject to typhoons.

History
Up until the 6th c. B.C. the region belonged mainly to the Wu Kingdom. When the Mongols conquered northern China in the 12th c., the Song dynasty fled to the south, causing south Jiangsu to develop into an economic, cultural and political centre. The province, whose name is derived from its two prefectures, Jiangning and Suzhou, was set up in 1667 by the

China

Jiangsu Province

HEILONGJIANG

JILIN

INNER MONGOLIA
(NEIMENGGU)

LIAONING

XINJIANG

©Baedeker

GANSU

INNER MONGOLIA **BEIJING
(NEIMENGGU) (PEKING)**

TIANJIN

HEBEI

NINGXIA

SHANXI

QINGHAI

SHANDONG

GANSU

SHAANXI

HENAN

JIANGSU

XIZANG (TIBET)

SICHUAN

HUBEI

ANHUI

SHANGHAI

ZHEJIANG

JIANGXI

GUIZHOU

HUNAN

FUJIAN

YUNNAN

TAIWAN

GUANGXI

GUANGDONG

XIANG GANG
(HONGKONG)

AO MEN
(MACAO)

HAINAN

The People's
Republic of China
Zhonghua Renmin Gongheguo

Kangxi Emperor of the Qing dynasty. Between 1839 and 1842 the English advanced into the Changjiang delta area and during the Japanese War (1931–45) Japan occupied Jiangsu, which suffered considerable damage as a result.

Since 1949, besides the traditional textile and food industries, machine engineering, motor vehicle and chemical industries have also gained prominence. In the agricultural sector vegetables, cereals, cotton and rape should be mentioned. In addition salt is extracted in the coastal region. Wuxi and Suzhou are centres of silk production, which has made Jiangsu famous both in China and abroad.

Economy

Visitors will find the following of particular interest: Nanjing, Changzhou, Huai'an, Lianyungang, Suzhou, Wuxi, Xuzhou, Yixing and Zhenjiang (see individual entries).

Places to visit

Jiangxi

J–L 5–7

江西省

Chinese
equivalent

Province
Area: 166,000sq.km/64,000sq. miles
Population: 38,650,000. Capital: Nanchang

The province of Jiangxi in south-east China, to the south of the Changjiang, lies between 113°34′–118°28′E and 24°29′–30°15′N.

Situation

Running through the middle of Jiangxi Province from south to north is the Ganjiang (hence the abbreviation "Gan" for the province) with the largest freshwater lake in China, Poyang Hu (3583sq.km/1383sq. miles). It is surrounded by a plain extending over more than 20,000sq.km/77,000sq. miles, which to the south, east and west is bounded by mountains as high as 2000m/6500ft.

Topography

China

Jiangxi Province

The People's Republic of China
Zhonghua Renmin Gongheguo

Climate

The climate is very mild, the average temperature in January being 6°C/43°F. The province also has plentiful and regular rainfall.

History

The area was originally inhabited to a large extent by non-Chinese, but in the 3rd–6th c. was settled by Han-Chinese, who fled there to escape the steppe peoples in the north. During the Ming period (1368–1644) the province emerged with its present boundaries. In the 20th c. Jiangxi was the first power base of the communist revolutionaries.

Economy

The large coal reserves and deposits of tungsten ore in the Dayu Ling Mountains are important industrially. Kaolin is also mined, with porcelain production in Jingdezhen. The main agricultural product is rice, which is cultivated for 10 to 11 months in the year (wet rice-growing area around Poyang Hu) and occupies 70% of the available arable land. Other crops include tea, barley, wheat, sesame, rape, maize and sweet potatoes. Jiangxi is also an important fruit-growing area, producing water melons, pears, date-plums, apples, oranges and the famous pipless mandarin and has a significant forestry industry (cedar, camphor, maple and pine).

Places to visit

The capital Nanchang and the towns of Jingdezhen, Jinggangshan and Juijiang all merit a visit (see individual entries).

Jiaxing   L 5

Chinese
equivalent

嘉兴市

Province: Zhejiang
Area: 13sq.km/5sq. miles. Population: 117,000 (conurbation 666,000)

Situation and
Communications

Jiaxing is situated at 120°45′E and 30°43′N, in the extreme north of the province of Zhejiang, north-east of the provincial capital Hangzhou, in the middle of a fertile rice-growing area. Jiaxing can be reached by rail from Hangzhou in two hours, from Shanghai in three.

The great age of the town can be demonstrated by a document from the Qin era (221–206 B.C.). At that time it was known as Youquan, its present name going back to the period of the Three Kingdoms (A.D. 220–280). In 1921 the founding of the Communist Party of China was proclaimed from a ship on Lake Nanhu. Jiaxing has been an important rice and silk trading-centre for centuries.

History

South Lake in the south of the town consists of two connected halves and occupies an area of some 35ha/86 acres. Lying at anchor on the south-eastern shore of the island known as "Heart of the Lake" (Huxin Dao) is the famous ship which witnessed the launching of China's Communist Party.

Sights

★**South Lake**
(Nanhu)

The small island has yet another monument, the Palace of the Smoking Rain, which was built in 1549 over the ruins of a building dating from the year 940. Fifty old cut gems are kept in the palace.

Palace of the Smoking Rain
(Yanyu Lou)

Yi Yuan Garden – also known as the garden of the Feng family, who had it laid out in 1871 – is situated in Haining, a small town about 25km/16 miles south-east of Jiaxing. It is the largest and best preserved private garden in the province. It has been open to the public since 1964.

Surroundings

★Yi Yuan Garden

Jilin

L–N 2–3

吉林省

Chinese equivalent

Province
Area: 187,400sq.km/72,355sq. miles
Population: 25,090,000. Capital: Changchun

China

The People's
Republic of China
Zhonghua Renmin Gongheguo

Jilin

Situation	Jilin lies in north-east China, on the border with Russia and North Korea, between 121°38′–131°17′E and 40°52′–46°18′N. The province is called "Jilinwula" in Manchurian, which means "along the Song-hua River". Around 30 ethnic minorities, including Koreans, Hui, Manchurians and Mongols, live here.
Topography	Jilin takes in parts of the fertile Manchurian plains belonging to the catchment area of the Soghuajiang, the most important river in the province, and also part of the East Manchurian wooded mountain areas.
Climate	The continental climate brings long cold winters and short summers. The temperature regularly falls below zero on as many as 240 days each year. Most of the rainfall, which decreases as one goes west, occurs between May and September.
History	The province, which was founded in 1907, formed part of the puppet state of Manchuguo after the Japanese occupation. In 1945 Russian troops marched into Jilin, followed by Chinese nationalists, who were subsequently driven out by the Communists in 1948.
Economy	There is a wide-ranging industrial base supported by rich mineral reserves (coal, slate, iron, copper, lead, zinc, silver and gold). Agricultural products include soya beans, maize, sugar-beet, kauliang, rice, sorghum and millet. Timber (27% of the province is forested) and furs are also important.
Places to visit	The province of Jilin is one of the birthplaces of the Manchurian civilisation and therefore can offer many places of interest, of which the most important are Changchun (see entry) and Jilin, which has given the province its name.

Jilin M 3

Province: Jilin. Altitude: 150m/492ft. Area: 271sq.km/105sq. miles
Population: 837,000 (conurbation 1,070,000)

Situation and Communications	The city of Jilin lies on the Di'er Songhuajiang in the centre of the province of Jilin at 126°30′E and 43°48′N. It is situated about 100km/62 miles from the provincial capital Changchun and can be reached from there in about 2 hours by train or bus.
History	Jilin is over 300 years old, the city's beginnings dating back to 1673 when a wooden defensive ring was built. This was replaced by clay ramparts in 1727: Today Jilin is an important provincial centre for trade and industry (foodstuffs, chemical and electrical goods).
Sights Beishan Park	Beishan Park, situated in the south-west of the city, consists mainly of hills rising to a height of some 200m/650ft. In the eastern part are the Temple of the War God (Guandi Miao; 1692) and the Pavilion of the Jade Emperor (Yuhuang Ge; 1725). These temples and a viewing pavilion provide a fine panorama of the city.
Surroundings Lake Songhua Hu	24km/15 miles south-east of Jilin lies the reservoir, Lake Songhua Hu. It is situated next to the hydro-electric power station of Fengman, which receives its water from the Songhuajiang. The picturesque and peaceful lake with its clear water extending over an area of 550sq.km/210sq. miles is a popular place with visitors. Five Tiger Island (Wuhu Dao) is a favourite spot for bathing, boating and fishing.
Ruins of the Bohai Kingdom	The ruins of the Bohai Kingdom, which was founded in 698, are to be found in the south-east of Dunhua, about 150km/93 miles south-east of Jilin. They comprise the remains of the walls surrounding the capital Aodong and about eighty tombs in which members of the royal family are buried.

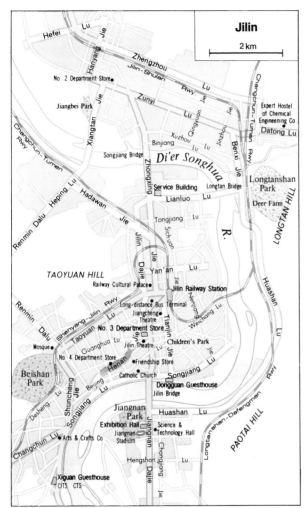

To Fengman 18 km

The nature reserve of Changbaishan is the largest such area in China, covering 220,000ha/850sq. miles. It begins 250km/155 miles south-east of Jilin and extends to the Korean border.

★ Changbaishan Nature Reserve (Changbaishan Ziran Baohuqu)

It formed part of UNESCO's international nature protection scheme. The rocks of Changbaishan have a white shimmer, hence the area's name (changbai ''always white'').

In the park there are over 1500 plants and about 300 types of animal, including martens, tigers, leopards and deer. To reach the nature reserve travel from Jilin to Erdobaihe and thence by bus.

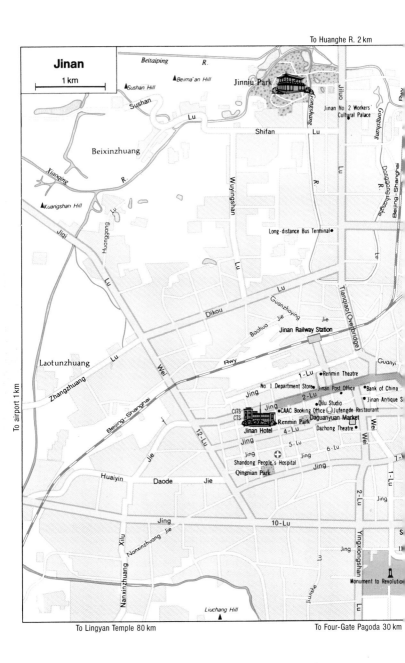

Jinan

1 km

To Huanghe R. 2 km

Beitaiping R.

Sushan Hill

Beima'an Hill

Jinniu Park

Jiluo

Gongshang

Sushan Lu

Jinan No 2 Workers
Cultural Palace

Beixinzhuang

Shifan Lu

Xiaoqing R.

Kuangshan Hill

Huanggang Lu

Wuyingshan Lu

Gongshang R.

Donggang zhonglu

Beijing-Shanghai

Jiqi

Lu

Long-distance Bus Terminal

Laotunzhuang

Zhangzhuang Lu

Dikou

Wei

Guanzhaying Jie

Baohua Jie

Jing

Lu

Tianqiao (Overbridge)

To airport 1 km

Jinan Railway Station

Guanyi

Rwy

1-Lu • Renmin Theatre

No 1 Department Store • Jinan Post Office • Bank of China

2-Lu • Jinan Antique S

CITS
CTS • CAAC Booking Office

Qilu Studio

Jufengde Restaurant

Daguanyuan Market

Jinan Hotel Renmin Park 4-Lu Dazhong Theatre •

Wei

12-Lu

Jing

5-Lu 6-Lu

1-L

Huaiyin Daode Jie

Jing

Shandong People's Hospital
Qingnian Park

Jing

Jing

Wei

2-Lu

Nanxinzhuang Jie

Xilu

Jing

10-Lu

Jing

Jing

Yingxiongshan

Nanxinzhuang

Jianshe

Liuchang Hill

Monument to Revolutio

Lu

To Lingyan Temple 80 km

To Four-Gate Pagoda 30 km

288

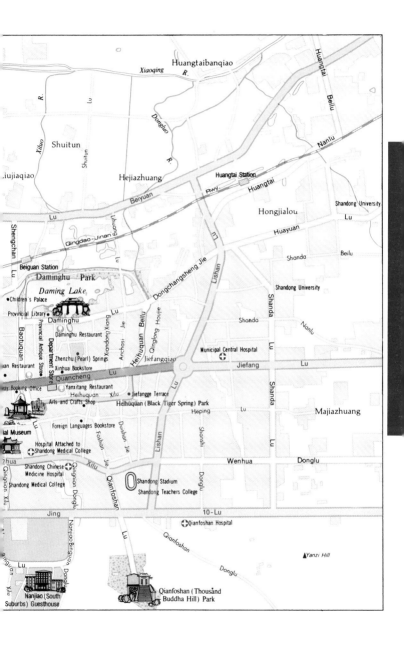

Xiaoqing R.

Huangtaibanqiao

Xiluo R.

Lu

Dongjiao R.

Shuitun

Shuitun

Liujiaqiao

Hejiazhuang

Huangtai Station

Beiyuan

Huangtai

Rwy.

Huangtai Beilu

Nanlu

Shandong University

Lu

Hongjialou

Lu

Shengchan Lu

Qingdao—Jinan

Lu

Uhuang Lu

Huayuan

Shanda

Beilu

Beiguan Station

Daminghu Park

Dongchangsheng Jie

Shandong University

Daming Lake

Lishan

Shanda

Children's Palace

Provincial Library

Daminghu

Xiandong Xiong Lu

Qinglong Houjie

Shanda

Lu

Nanlu

Baotuquan

Provincial Antique Store

Daminghu Restaurant

Anchasi Jie

Heihuquan Beilu

Municipal Central Hospital

Department Store

Zhenzhu (Pearl) Springs

Jiefangqiao

Jiefang

Lu

uan Restaurant

Quancheng

Xinhua Bookstore

Shanda Lu

way Booking Office

Yanxitang Restaurant

Lu

Arts and Crafts Shop

Heihuquan

Xilu

Jiefangge Terrace

Heihuquan (Black Tiger Spring) Park

Heping

Majiazhuang

Foreign Languages Bookstore

Dushan Jie

Heping

Lu

ial Museum

Foshan Jie

Shanshi

Hospital Attached to

Shandong Medical College

zhua

Shandong Chinese

Medicine Hospital

Qingnian Donglu

Xilu

Lishan

Wenhua

Donglu

Qingnian Xilu

Shandong Medical College

Qianfoshan

Donglu

Jing

Nanjiao Binguan Donglu

Shandong Stadium

Shandong Teachers College

10-Lu

Qianfoshan Hospital

Lu

Qianfoshan

Qianfoshan

▲Yanzi Hill

nguan Lu

Xilu

Donglu

Nanjiao (South

Suburbs) Guesthouse

Qianfoshan (Thousand

Buddha Hill) Park

Ji'nan

| White Head Mountain (Baitoushan) | One of the most beautiful peaks in Changbaishan is White Head Mountain (2155m/7070ft), an extinct volcano. |

Heaven Lake (Tian Chi)

On the summit of White Head Mountain lies the famous 9.2sq.km/3.6sq. mile Heaven Lake, a crater over 300m/1000ft deep, which formed during a volcanic eruption in 1702 and then filled with water. The lake, which has an average depth of 204m/669ft and is surrounded by steep rocks, is frozen over for half the year. A monster is supposed to live here.

An opening on the north bank of the lake releases large amounts of water which, at an altitude of 1250m/4100ft, plunge 68m/223ft into an abyss, thereby forming the famous waterfall known as the Changbai Pubu. This water supplies the Erdao Baihe, one of the two source rivers of the Songhuajiang.

On the north side of Baitoushan there is an extensive area of thermal springs, about 900m/half a mile away from the waterfall, which reach temperatures as high as 82°C/180°F.

Ji'nan   J 4

Chinese equivalent

济南市

Capital of Shandong province
Area: 483sq.km/186sq. miles
Population: 1,400,000 (conurbation 3,550,000)

Situation and Communications

Ji'nan is situated in the west of the province of Shandong, between the Huanghe in the north and the Taishan in the south, at 117°E and 36°41'N. The city can be reached by train or air from Beijing, Canton, Nanjing, Shanghai and other large cities in China. There is also an extensive bus network linking it with other provincial centres.

Ji'nan is famous for its feather paintings and its woven articles.

The traditional local opera (lüju) is particularly popular. It is not governed by such strict rules as the Peking Opera, so the characters tend to have more opportunities to develop.

History

It is not known when Ji'nan was founded, only that it already existed 2700 years ago. Under the Western Han dynasty, in other words about 2100 years ago, it received its present name Ji'nan ("south of the River Ji", which is the name the Huanghe had in antiquity). From very early on the town was well-known as a trading centre and under Ming rule (1368–1644) it became the political centre of the province.

Ji'nan also used to be known as "city of springs" and a stone plaque from the Jin period (1115–1234) named 72 springs. Today there are over a hundred, with a constant temperature of 18°C/64°F.

Sights

★Spring with the Vertical Jet

The "Spring with the Vertical Jet" (Baotu Quan) is to be found in the Baotuquan-Gongyuan Park in the city centre, in among buildings which date in part back to the Song era (760–1279). From earliest times the spring has had the reputation of being one of the most beautiful in China, as is borne out by a tablet with the inscription "The first spring in the world". It owes its name to the tremendous force with which the water shoots out of the ground into three fountains (at about 1600 litres/350 gallons per second).

Memorial Hall to Li Qingzhao

Baotuquan-Gongyuan Park also contains a memorial hall to the famous and much venerated poetess Li Qingzhao, who was born in Ji'nan (1084– c. 1151).

Pavilion of the Roaring Waves

In the Pavilion of the Roaring Waves (Gualan Tang) there are some stone tablets which were completed in the 14th c. and later.

The Provincial Museum to the south of the Spring with the Vertical Jet possesses a natural history and historical section.

Provincial Museum

On display are bronzes and cut stones from the Shang (16th–11th c. B.C.), Zhou (11th c.–221 B.C.) and Han (206 B.C.–A.D. 220) periods. The calendar which can be seen here dates back to c. 130 B.C. and lays claim to being the oldest in China.

The Pool of the Five Dragons, which measures several hundred square metres, is to be found 200m/220yd north of the Spring with the Vertical Jet and is fed by five springs. It was already famous at the time of the Tang dynasty (618–907).

★Pool of the Five Dragons (Wulong Tan)

In the north of the city lies the Lake of the Great Light, which extends over 46ha/114 acres and receives water from several springs. Pavilions and covered walks have been erected around the lake.

★Lake of the Great Light (Daming Hu)

Many old buildings line the banks of the lake. The North Pavilion on the north shore was built in the Yang period (1271–1368).

North Pavilion (Beji Ge)

On the opposite shore stretches the Fantasy Garden (Xia Yuan), which was laid out in 1909.

Fantasy Garden

The Pearl Spring is to be found in a public park to the south of the Lake of the Great Light. The visual effect of the water bubbling out of the ground resembles a chain of pearls.

★Pearl Spring (Zhenzhu Quan)

The regional government had its seat in the vicinity from the 15th to the 19th c.

The Spring of the Black Tiger, which was discovered in the 12th c., lies 1km/½ mile to the east of the Spring of the Vertical Jet. The water gushes out of fissures in three black rocks which form the shape of a tiger's head.

Spring of the Black Tiger (Heihu Quan)

The 285m/935ft high Thousand Buddha Mountain rises up about 2.5km/1½ miles south of the city centre. According to tradition, the garden of the Emperor Shun lay at the foot of this mountain. He was one of the mythical rulers of the Chinese in prehistoric times.

★Thousand Buddha Mountain (Qianfoshan)

The slopes of the mountain, the grottoes at its foot and the 7th c. Monastery of the Prosperity of Life (Xingguo Si) conceal a wealth of Buddhist statues – hence its name – which are 1400 years old.

Near the summit of the mountain stands the Pavilion of the Fine View. From here there is a marvellous panorama across Ji'nan.

Pavilion of the Fine View (Yilan Ting)

Surroundings

Only a few buildings remain of the old Shentong Monastery, 30km/19 miles south of Ji'nan on the Mountain of the Green Dragon (Qinglong Shan).

Shentong Monastery

These include the square Four Gates Pagoda, the restoration of which in 1972 led to the discovery in the upper part of a small stone tablet in which was engraved the year in which the pagoda was built – A.D. 611. The 15m/49ft high alabaster building is one of the oldest stone pagodas in China.

★Four Gates Pagoda (Simen Ta)

The Dragon and Tiger Pagoda is the burial monument to a monk, who is thought to have lived between the 10th and 14th c. The monument is constructed out of four richly sculpted stone slabs and stands on a three-tiered base, which is also decorated with many bas-reliefs. The upper brick building has a double ledge.

Dragon and Tiger Pagoda (Longhu Ta)

★Rock of the Thousand Buddhas (Qianfo Ya)	The 65m/213ft high rock has over 100 niches, in which 200 Buddhist sculptures, principally from the early Tang period (618–907) are stored.
★★Temple of the Divine Rock (Lingyan Si)	The construction of the Temple of the Divine Rock, 80km/50 miles south of Ji'nan in the Changqing district, was begun under the Northern Wei (386–534) and finished under the Song (960–1279). The holy site, which used to be one of the most famous Buddhist monasteries in China, comprises 40 buildings and 500 rooms.
Hall of the Thousand Buddhas (Qianfo Dian)	The main hall is the Hall of the Thousand Buddhas, dating from the Ming period (1368–1644). Among the many statues on display here the 40 Luohan clay sculptures are particularly impressive and, because of their vividness, are considered to be the finest of their type in the whole of China. There has been some controversy over when they were actually created, although most art historians believe them to date from the Song period (960–1279).
Pizhi Ta Pagoda Grove of the Burial Pagodas (Muta Lin)	While visiting the temple area, one should on no account miss the 11th c. octagonal Pizhi Ta Pagoda and, further to the west, the monumental Grove of the Burial Pagodas with its 167 pagodas. The oldest burial pagoda (Huizong Ta) was erected in the 8th c. in honour of the monk Huizong, who lived here from 742 to 756.

Jingdezhen   K 6

Chinese equivalent	景德镇
	Province: Jiangxi. Area: 140sq.km/54sq. miles Population: 268,000 (conurbation: 497,000)
Situation and Communications	Jingdezhen is situated at 117°11′E and 29°19′N, in the north-east of the province of Jiangxi, about 150km/93 miles north-east of the provincial capital, Nanchang. Jingdezhen can be reached from there by rail and air, and regular flights also connect the town with many other Chinese cities.
History	Before the 11th c. the small village of Xinping on the site of the present town was already known for the high quality of its porcelain production. Emperor Jingde (1004–07) declared the village to be the centre of production for imperial porcelain and ordered all pieces produced thereafter to bear the words "Manufactured in the Jingde period". In the course of time the town's original name was replaced by that of the emperor. Under the Ming dynasty (1368–1644) Jingdezhen was one of the four centres of porcelain manufacture and had a total of 100 small factories and workshops. This porcelain is famed for being white as jade, clear as a mirror, thin as paper and having an unsullied reputation. Today the city can claim pride of place in the Chinese art of porcelain-making. Half the population is in one way or another involved in this highly profitable industry. Kaolin, the raw material from which porcelain is made, comes from the mountain of Gaolin, hence its name.

Sights

Sights	The museum in Fengling Lu contains exquisite items on display which illustrate the history and development of porcelain manufacture.

Porcelain production in Jingdezhen

On the edge of the city it is possible to visit the remains of old kilns, the most famous being those at Baihuwan (9km/5½ miles east of the city centre), Liujiawan (22km/14 miles from the centre), Huangnitou (7.5km/4½ miles east of the centre) and Hutian.

On display are large numbers of porcelain objects, both fired and unfired, dating from the 10th–17th c.

Surroundings

★ Kilns
(Guyao Zhi)

Jinggangshan

J 6

Chinese equivalent

Province: Jiangxi. Area: 714sq.km/276sq. miles
Population: 47,000

Jinggangshan is situated at 114°09′E and 26°33′N, in the south of Jiangxi Province, on the border with Hunan.

Buses run from the provincial capital, Nanchang; alternatively one can fly to Ganzhou and continue by bus.

Situation and Communications

In the 1920s this region, together with the Jinggangshan Mountains, was the scene of Mao's first revolutionary struggles, thereafter becoming the base of the Red Army, which Mao formed. It was from here that the Communists began their famous Long March in 1934.

Today the region is a popular place to visit on account of its interesting architectural monuments and its many picturesque villages.

History

Jinghong

Sights	Ciping Zhen is the most important district in Jinggingshan and was where Mao's peasant army had its headquarters.
★ Ciping Zhen	
Mao's House	The headquarters of the New 4th Army Corps, Mao's house and the Town Museum can all be visited.
Dajing Zhen	The district of the town known as Dajing Zhen occupies a valley surrounded by high mountains. There are several buildings here which bear testimony to the Maoist revolution: the Red Army dormitory, Mao's dwelling and the field hospital.
Surroundings	The 1000m/½ mile long Grotto of the Stone Swallow lies 9km/5½ miles north-east of Ciping Zhen. In the lower section there are seven small dripstone caves with stalactites and stalagmites. These caves have become joined together by tiny narrow passages. The cave was formed by centuries of erosion taking place in the limestone.
★ Grotto of the Stone Swallow (Shiyan Dong)	

Jinghong   H 7

Chinese equivalent	景洪

Province: Yunnan
Area: 1920sq.km/741sq. miles. Population: 700,000

Situation and Communications	Jinghong lies on the Lancangjiang (Mekong) at 100°51′E and 22°01′N, in the south of Yunnan Province, on the border with Myanmar (Burma). There are bus services and flights to Kunming.

Dai houses

Jinghong has a rich folk tradition and is the capital of the autonomous district of Xishuangbanna, whose inhabitants consist predominantly of Dai (45% of the population), as well as other ethnic groups (Hani, Bulang, Jinuo,Yi, etc). The Dai's traditional dwellings are built on stilts.

Although Buddhism was very widespread here and there were many temples and pagodas, very little has been preserved.

Many tourists come to Jinghong in order to experience the water festival which takes place every year in April, the New Year festival in the Dai calendar. In joyous mood the local people make their way to the banks of the Lancangjiang and shower one another with water; the wetter people become, the more good luck will come their way. These celebrations are linked to an old legend in which the people are said to have cleansed a maiden with bucketfuls of water because she had cut off the head of a monster and in so doing had soiled herself with his blood. During the festival longship races are also held.

Water Festival (Poshui Jie)

The nature reserve of Xishuangbanna Ziran Baohuqu surrounds Jinghong and stretches over an area of more than 200,000ha/770sq. miles as far as the borders with Laos and Myanmar (Burma). It is the largest in China and enjoys a completely balanced ecosystem. A notable feature of this nature reserve is the tropical rain forest in which rare plants, such as the podocarpus and the cyatheaceae, flourish. The reserve also offers the perfect habitat for many species of animals, e.g. elephants, tigers, gibbons.

Surroundings

★Xishuangbanna Ziran Baohuqu Nature Reserve

The 16m/52ft high White Pagoda of Damenglong (50km/31 miles south of Jinghong) was built in 1204 in honour of Shakyamuni Buddha and is surrounded by eight 9m/30ft high stupas. It is considered to be one of the most beautiful Buddhist buildings in the region. The base for the building is furnished by a large rock with an indentation which resembles a giant's footprint. According to tradition it was left behind by Shakyamuni.

★White Pagoda of Damenglong (Feilong Baita)

The Octagonal Pavilion of Jingzhen is at least 15m/49ft high and stands some 50km/31 miles west of the city, 14km/9 miles west of the village of Menghai on Jingzhenshan Mountain. The building, which was constructed in 1701, consists of three parts: the brick base, the middle section, also made of bricks, the walls of which are decorated with colourful glass patterns, and the conical wooden roof, which is supposed to have been adapated from a head-covering of Buddha. The architectural style evinces well-defined Buddhist influences.

Octagonal Pavilion of Jingzhen (Jingzhen Bajiaoting)

Jinhua

K 6

金华市

Chinese equivalent

Province: Zhejiang. Area: 301sq.km/116sq. miles
Population: 125,000 (conurbation 833,000)

Jinhua is situated at 119°35'E and 29°09'N, in the centre of Zhejiang Province.
    The city is 185km/115 miles from the provincial capital Hangzhou and can be reached from there by rail (4 hours) or bus. There are also rail and bus links with other Chinese towns.

Situation and Communications

The town, which was mentioned as early as the Eastern Han era (25–220), received its present name in the Sui era (581–618). At the time of the Southern Song (1127–1279) an important philosophical movement sprang up here, the Jinhua school, an eclectic derivative of Confucianism.

History

From the earliest times Jinhua has been an important trading centre, dealing in both timber and agricultural produce.

In previous centuries the city acquired a certain distinction by virtue of a culinary speciality, Jinhua ham.

Sights

★Tower of the Eight Poems (Bayong Lou)

The original Tower of the Eight Poems in the north of the city was erected in 494 at the instigation of the prefect Shen Yue, who on completion of the building climbed to the top of the tower and recited eight poems. Since then it has been a meeting-place for literati.

The present-day building was rebuilt during the Qing period (1644–1911) as a faithful replica of the original.

From the tower there is a fine view across the city and the surrounding area.

Surroundings

★Grotto of the Two Dragons (Shuanglong Dong)

The Grotto of the Two Dragons lies on the slopes of the North Mountain (Beishan), 15km/9 miles north of the city. At the entrance there are two massive stalagmites which have the shape of a dragon's head.

The grotto is divided into two parts, an outer and an inner, 1200m/$^3\!/_4$ mile and 2100m/1$^1\!/_4$ mile long respectively, which are connected by a narrow 12m/40ft long channel. As the grotto is under water, visitors travel in a small boat.

Grotto of the Ice Vase (Binghu Dong)

The 50m/164ft long Grotto of the Ice Vase lies 200m/220yd further up from the Grotto of the Two Dragons. It owes its name to its shape, which calls to mind a vase, and the low temperatures which are to be found here even on warm days.

In the middle of the grotto the visitor will be astonished to see a small 20m/66ft high waterfall which disappears between clefts in the rocks.

Grotto of Homage to the True Immortals (Chaozhen Dong)

The Grotto of Homage to the True Immortals lies 1km/$^1\!/_2$ mile further up from the Grotto of the Ice Vase, concealed between the rocks.

According to a legend a Taoist hermit, who is purported to have lived here, by practising alchemy over a number of years, successfully attained immortality.

Jiujiang   K 6

Chinese equivalent

九江市

Province: Jiangxi. Area: 555sq.km/214sq. miles
Population: 364,000

Situation and Communications

Jiujiang lies at 115°58′E and 29°47′N, in the north of Jiangxi Province.

The city is 135km/84 miles from the provincial capital, Nanchang, which can be reached by rail (3 hours) or bus. There are two airports. Ships also travel to Jiujiang from Wuhan, Chongqing, Nanjing and Shanghai.

History

The city, which in antiquity went under the names Xunyang, Chaisang and Jiangzhou, can definitely claim to be over 2000 years old, as a prefecture was established here during the period of Qin rule (221–206 b.c.). Over the centuries the town became a major trading centre in tea and porcelain. Many artists came to Jiujiang and left behind an enormous number of paintings, sculptures, inscriptions and drawings on stone. In 1862 the city was forced to open its doors to foreign trade. Since 1949 light industry has played an important role in the economic life of the city.

Lushan Mountain ▶

To Lianhua (Lotus) Cave

Mount Lushan

| 1 km |

Hillside Pavilion

Xiaotian (Smaller Heaven) Pool

River-Viewing Pavilion

Rizhao Peak
▲ 1313

Friendship Store
● Bus Station
Arts & Crafts Service

The Second Branch of Lushan Sanatorium
Jinxiu Valley

Moonlit Pine Wood

Mt Dayue
1453

● CTS
● Lushan Guesthouse

Floral Path

Fairy Cave

The Zoo

Yunzhong Guesthouse

● Lushan Sanatorium

Wenshu
Terrace
Tianchi Pagoda
Round Buddha Hall

G U L I N G

Tianchi
Temple
● Longyu (Dragon Fish) Pool

Lushan Mansion

● Lushan People's Theatre
Lushan Museum

● The First Branch of Lushan Sanatorium

Longshou (Dragon
Head) Cliff
Wulongtan (Black Dragon Pool) Falls

Hydropower Station Dam

Lulin Bridge

● Friendship Club

Huanglongtan (Yellow Dragon Pool) Falls
Three - Treasure Trees

Yuping (Jade Screen) Peak

■ Lulin Hotel

Botanical Gardens

Hanpokou Archway

Hangpo Pavilion

Litou (Plough) Peak
▲ 1293

Jiuqi (Nine Grotesque) Peak

To Hanyang Peak

To Guanyin Bridge

Sights	Lake Gantang Hu in the city centre covers an area of 18ha/44 acres and receives its water from springs on Mount Lushan. The lake is divided by a 50m/164ft dam, on which is situated the Bridge of the Wise Men's Longing (Sixian Qiao), dating from the Song period (960–1279).
★Lake Gantang Hu	
★Wave Spring (Lang Jing)	The wave spring, which was formed in 201 B.C., is in the north of the city on the bank of the Changjiang. For many hundreds of years a very strange phenomenon could be observed: if a strong swell or wave built up in the river, the water in the spring would also ripple at the same time. When the course of the Changjiang was diverted northwards, this phenomenon ceased to occur, although to this day the name of the spring serves as a reminder of it.

Surroundings

★★Mount Lushan	Mount Lushan, which occupies an area of 250sq.km/97sq. miles, is one of the most popular recreational and holiday areas in China. It lies to the south of Jiujiang (bus connections), between Changjiang and Lake Poyang Hu. The massif comprises over 90 separate peaks, the highest, Hanyang Feng, having an altitude of 1474m/4836ft. Under the Han dynasty (206 B.C.–A.D.

220), Lushan developed into a Buddhist centre. Poets and writers in later centuries waxed lyrical about the irresistible charms of this mountain landscape. According to one such poet, Lushan has at least 2000 scenes of natural beauty with which to captivate the observer. The mountain also boasts intriguing rock formations, waterfalls, springs, pools, pavilions, temples and stone inscriptions.

The Temple of the East Wood on the north-west slopes of Mount Lushan is of extraordinary significance for Buddhists, as it was here that the monk Huiyuan (334–416) founded the School of the Pure Country (Jingtu Zong), a Buddhist sect. In 381 the monk had the temple built and lived in it for many years, interpreting and commenting on the teachings of Buddha.

Temple of the East Wood (Donglin Sin)

The Pagoda of the West Wood, which rises up to the west of the temple, dates from the 8th c.

Guling is a spa situated in the middle of the Lushan massif at an altitude of 1167m/3829ft. Often referred to as the "Garden among the Clouds", the resort has several modern hotels providing accommodation for visitors.

Guling

2km/1 mile to the south-west of Guling stands the Dragon Head Rock, from which there is a magnificent view across pine-woods, waterfalls, criss-crossing paths and highly unusual rock formations.

Dragon Head Rock (Longshou Ya)

The Cave of the Immortal is practically 10m/33ft deep and lies to the north-west of Guling. According to legend, it was once the dwelling of the immortal Taoist monk Lü Dongbing (b. 798). The inscription at the entrance to the cave dates from 1255.

Cave of the Immortal (Xianren Dong)

The Floral Path, which lies to the east of the Cave of the Immortal, was celebrated by the poet Bai Juyi back in the Tang period (618–907). A stone tablet with the inscription "Floral Path", which is said to have been engraved by Bai Juyi himself, is kept in the main pavilion.

Floral Path (Hua Jing)

The Pavilion of the Imperial Stele, not far in a north-westerly direction from the Cave of the Immortal, was built by the Ming Emperor Taizu in the 14th c. to commemorate a meeting with the immortal Taoist Zhou Dian. The inscription on the stele dates from the time of this emperor.

Pavilion of the Imperial Stele (Yubei Ting)

The Three Precious Trees, about 1km/½ mile south of Guling, are said to have been planted by the Buddhist monk Tan Xi 1500 years ago. They are described in the "Travel Sketches of Xu Xiake", which date from the Ming period (1368–1644).

Three Precious Trees (San Baoshu)

Hanpokou Hill, about 2km/1 mile south-east of Guling, is dominated by two pavilions, Hanpo Ting and Wangpo Ting. From the hill the visitor has a picturesque view of Lake Poyang Hu and the Changjiang.

Hanpokou Hill

The Summit of the Five Old Men in the south-east of the massif resembles, as its name suggests, the shape of five old men or five lotus blossoms.

Summit of the Five Old Men (Wulao Feng)

The waterfall of Sandie Quan, which lies in the eastern part of the Lushan massif, forms a series of three cascades as it tumbles down into the valley below.

Sandie Quan Waterfall

The School of the White Stag Cave, situated in the valley of the Wualo Feng, is one of the four most famous places of learning of the Song era (960–1279), in which the famous Confucian philosopher Zhu Xi (1130–1200) taught. Behind the school there is a cave with the stone sculpture of a white stag dating from the 16th c. It was fashioned to commemorate the brothers Li Bo and Li Shu, who sought refuge in the cave in 785 and spent their days there in the company of a white stag.

School of the White Stag Cave (Bailudong Shuyuan)

Jiuquan

G 4

Chinese equivalent	酒泉市

Province: Gansu
Altitude: 1400–1800m/4593–5905ft
Area: 3300sq.km/1275sq. miles. Population: 250,000

Situation and Communications

Jiuquan is situated at 98°29'E and 39°47'N, on the Silk Route, in the western part of the province of Gansu. It has rail, air and road connections with the remainder of the country.

History

According to a legend General Huo Qubing (140–117 B.C.) stopped off here after defeating a northern steppe people. In order to show him his gratitude, Emperor Wudi sent him wine. Wishing to share the present with his soldiers, the general poured all the wine into a spring. This is the origin of the name Jiuquan ("wine spring"). Jiuquan was founded in 343, although initially it was known as Suzhou. It was a stopping-place on the Silk Route. The town also became important economically because of its rich mineral deposits.

Sights

★Park of the Wine Spring

The Park of the Wine Spring (Jiuquan Gongyuan) lies in the east of Jiuquan and surrounds the legendary old spring which gave the town its present name. The source water of this spring is provided by a small lake. The park is a charming place with its pretty pavilions, bridges and lavishly decorated covered galleries.

★Museum of the Great Wall (Changcheng Bowuguan)

The Museum of the Great Wall (see entry) was opened in 1989 and is the only one devoted exclusively to the Great Wall and its history. In the seven rooms, which together occupy an area of 3120sq.m/33,580sq.ft, the visitor can learn about the history of the wall's construction and see the results of recent scientific investigations.

The wealth of exhibits include archaeological finds, photographs, miniature models of various sections of the wall and a piece of electronic apparatus which can project onto a screen the various changes of direction of the wall from the beginning of its construction up to the Ming dynasty (1368–1644).

Surroundings

Tomb of Dingjiazha Gumu

This tomb, with wall paintings of great importance from a historical point of view, lies in the desert 3km/2 miles west of Jiuquan. It is thought that the deceased was a nobleman who lived some 1600 years ago. One wall of the vault, which is completely decorated with frescos, is still well preserved. In the upper section there is a representation of the sky with sun, moon and two deities, who are surrounded by birds, flying horses, stags and toads, etc. At the bottom, on the other hand, the earthly world is depicted with hunting and pasture scenes, banqueters and concerts, etc.

Wenshushan Mountain

15km/9 miles south-west of Jiuquan rises the mountain of Wenshushan, which was the location of an important Buddhist centre from the 4th c. Several temples and caves have still been preserved, of particular interest being the Thousand Buddha Grotto (Qianfo Dong), the Ten Thousand Buddha Grotto (Wanfo Dong), the Old Buddha Grotto (Gufo Dong) and the Guanyin Grotto (Guanyin Dong).

★Jiayuguan Pass

A railway line and bus route both go to the Jiayuguan Pass, situated 25km/15½ miles west of Jiuquan. It has air connections with Dunhuang and Ürümqi. The pass is dominated by a fortress dating from 1372 which occupies an area of 33,500sq.m/8¼ acres and marks the western end of the Great Wall. It is surrounded by two walls, a low exterior one and an inner

The fort on the Jiayuguan Pass

one, 12m/39ft high. The latter is enclosed by a ring of battlements and has two 17m/56ft high three-storeyed towers, dating from 1506, in the east and west.

The plans of the fortress are supposed to have been so exact that at the end of its construction only one building stone was left over. The stone in question has been preserved right up to the present day.

The Monastery of the Great Buddha was built in 1098 and is situated in the town centre of Zhangye, 150km/93 miles to the south-east of Jiuquan. It contains a 34m/112ft high Buddha made of variegated clay and with a wooden centre. The monastery's wall frescos are of particular interest and are inspired by Taoist writings and old fairy tales.

★Monastery of the Great Buddha (Dafo Si)

Kaifeng

J 5

Chinese equivalent

Province: Henan
Altitude: 77m/253ft. Area: 359sq.km/139sq. miles
Population: 300,000 (conurbation 580,000)

Kaifeng ("break the seal") is situated at 114°21′E and 34°41′N on the railway line from Lianyungang to Ürümqi.

Rail and bus services link Kaifeng with the provincial capital Zhengzhou, with Beijing, Shanghai, Nanjing, Canton, Xi'an and other towns.

Situation and Communications

Excavations have proved that Kaifeng already existed at the time of the Shang dynasty (16th–11th c. B.C.). In addition remains of a Neolithic settlement have been found in the surrounding area. In the Spring and Autumn Periods (770–476 B.C.) the settlement was a border post of the Zheng kingdom and the ruler Zheng Zhuanggong established a grain store here. From then on Kaigfeng's importance grew significantly. Under the Wei rulers (220–280) it became capital for the first time and gained this status agian in the period of the Five Dynasties (907–960). Kaifeng's golden period, however, was under the Northern Song dynasty (960–1127), when it was capital for a period of 167 years and developed into a large city with a population of about one million. The extension of the canal system brought a further economic upswing. It has also been reliably attested that Kaifeng possessed a substantial Jewish community. The famous picture scroll of this period, "The Qingming Banquet by the River" (Qingming Shanghe Tu; today in the Imperial Palace in Beijing) illustrates the wealth and opulence of this epoch. With the collapse of the Song dynasty the town suffered severe damage and declined in importance. Around the middle of the 17th c. it suffered a number of appalling floods from the Huanghe. In 1644

History

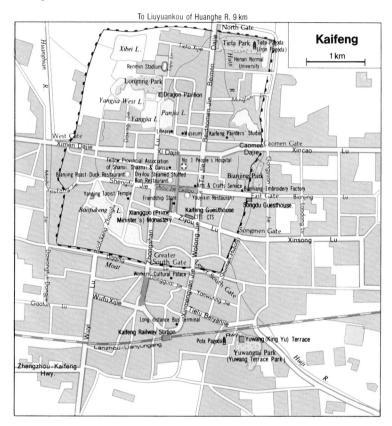

To Liuyuankou of Huanghe R. 9 km

Kaifeng

1 km

Huanghun R.

Xibei L.

North Gate

Tieta Park   Tieta Pagoda (Iron Pagoda)

Henan Normal University

Tieta Xijie

Renmin Stadium

Longting Park

Dragon Pavilion

Yangjia West L.

Yangjia L.

Panjia L.

Beimen

Baogonghu Jie

Minglun

Caomen

West Gate

Ximen Dajie

Daxing

Library

Museum   Kaifeng Painters' Studio

Caomen Gate

Xincao   Lu

Xi Dajie

No 1 People's Hospital

Fellow Provincial Association of Shanxi, Shaanxi & Gansu

Bianjing Roast-Duck Restaurant

Shengfu   Diyilou Steamed Stuffed Bun Restaurant

Jie   Zhou Jie   Gulou

Arts & Crafts Service

Bianjing Park

Gongyuan

Bianjing Embroidery Factory

Bianjing   Lu

Youfang Jie

Yanqing Taoist Temple

Baofukeng L.

Xiangguo (Prime Minister's) Monastery

Friendship Store

Youyixin Restaurant

East Gate

Songdu Guesthouse

Kaifeng Guesthouse

CITS   CTS

Ziyou   Lu

Zhongshan

Baofukeng Zhonglu

Songmen Gate

Xinsong   Lu

Liaodong   Lu

Greater South Gate

Moat

Biaojing

Workers' Cultural Palace

Dongguai-jie

Zhongshan

Wangfu

Shanmen Beijie

South Gate

Wufu Xijie

Gaofun   Lu

Dowanglu Dongjie

Yanwuting Jie

Tietu Beiyanjie

Long-distance Bus Terminal

Kaifeng Railway Station

Wlu

Lanzhou-Lianyungang

Hwy.

Pota Pagoda

Yuwang (King Yu) Terrace

Yuwangtai Park (Yuwang Terrace Park)

Huili   R.

Zhengzhou-Kaifeng Hwy.

the town's dykes were opened as a defensive measure against invading Manchurians and as a result 300,000 people lost their lives. For this reason there are only very few architectural monuments surviving from the Song period. Today silk and embroidery provide an important source of income for Kaifeng.

Sights

In the old centre of Kaifeng a 400m/440yd long street with 36 buildings in the Song style has been reconstructed, with products and services characteristic of the period on sale.

Street in the Song style

The most interesting feature is the reproduction of the old Fan restaurant, mentioned in many old classical works. In one of these works the story is told of how the Song Emperor Huizong used to leave his palace in unobtrusive apparel and come to the restaurant, where he would spend many a merry evening in the company of the famous actress Li Shishi, later to become his favourite concubine.

Between the streets of Beitu Jie and Nanjiaojing there are still traces of the old Jewish quarter, where from the 12th c. onwards the largest Jewish community in China lived.

In the Chancellor's Temple ▶

★Temple of the Chancellor (Xiangguo Si)	The Temple of the Chancellor in the city centre was built in 555 and for centuries was a renowned Buddhist centre. It was destroyed on several occasions – including the floods of 1644 – and then rebuilt, the last time in 1766. It was given its present name by a chancellor of the Tang era (618–907) who had made an outstanding contribution to restoration work on the building.
Octagonal Ceramic Palace (Baijiao Liulidian)	The most important building on the site is the Octagonal Ceramic Palace, the contents of which include a 7m/23ft high Guanyin statue. The gilded likeness of the goddess, with her four faces, 1000 arms and 1000 eyes, was created out of a single piece of Ginkgo wood. In the neighbouring bell-tower hangs an enormous 4m/13ft high bronze bell, weighing over 5 tons and dating from the Qing period (1644–1911).
Dragon Pavilion (Longting)	The Dragon Pavilion, situated 1.5km/1 mile to the north of the Temple of the Chancellor in the Dragon Park, was built in 1692 on the site of a Ming palace which had been destroyed in the floods of 1644. The staircase leading to the pavilion is decorated with a dragon motif, while inside there is a stone bench, likewise ornamented with dragons.
★Iron Pagoda (Tieta)	The Iron Pagoda, which dates from 1049, is located in the north-east of the city, in the centre of the park of the same name. Owing to the rust-brown ceramic tiles with which it is covered, one could be forgiven for thinking it is made of iron – hence its name. The ascent to the top of the 55m/180ft high 13-storey pagoda is well worthwhile, rewarding the visitor with a beautiful view over Kaifeng and the surrounding area.
Terrace of King Yu (Yuwangtai)	The terrace lies in a park of the same name in the south-east of the city, south of the railway line and 3km/2 miles from the Temple of the Chancellor. According to tradition the legendary Da Yu stayed here while he was subduing the Huanghe. On the terrace stands the Temple of King Yu (Yuwang Miao). To the south there is a wooden arch on which hangs a small plaque with the words "Ancient Terrace of the Musician". Another legend has it that the famous musician Shi Kuang gave concerts here in the Spring and Autumn Periods (770–476 B.C.). For this reason the terrace is also known as the Music Terrace (Guchui Tai). One of the halls is dedicated to famous poets of the Tang era (618–907) who composed verses here, such as Du Fu and Li Bai.
Pagoda Pota	The hexagonal Pagoda Pota, formerly part of a temple from the Northern Song period (960–1127), is situated to the west of the Terrace of King Yu. It originally consisted of six storeys, of which only three survived the partial destruction of the building in the 14th c.

Kashgar   C 4

Chinese equivalent	日喀则市
	Autonomous region of Xinjiang Altitude: 1289m/4229ft. Population: 100,000 (conurbation 300,000)
Situation and Communications	The oasis town of Kashgar (also Kaxgar, Chin. Kashi) lies on the old Silk Road in the west of the autonomous region of Xinjiang, at 75°58′E and 39°35′N. It is about 1000km/620 miles from Ürümqi, the capital of the region, and is connected with it by regular flights (about 4hrs) and buses (3–5 days). Kashgar, the most westerly town in China, is predominantly inhabited by Uigurs and is heavily influenced by Islam. The traditional craftwork includes carpets, embroidery and musical instruments.

Kashgar: Id Kah Square

Mausoleum of Abakh Hoja

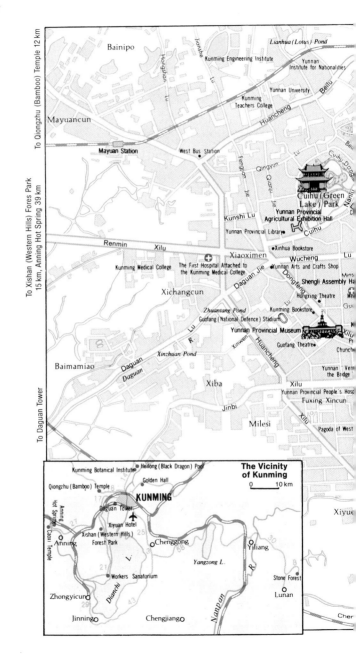

To Qiongzhu (Bamboo) Temple 12 km

To Xishan (Western Hills) Fores Park
15 km, Anning Hot Spring 39 km

To Daguan Tower

Bainipo

Kunming Engineering Institute

Lianhua (Lotus) Pond

Yunnan Institute for Nationalities

Jianshe

Hongshan Lu

Mayuancun

Yunnan University

Kunming Teachers College

Huancheng

Mayuan Station

West Bus Station

Qingyun

Fengrun Jie

Cuihu Dong

Nan

Beili

Cuihu (Green Lake) Park

Yunnan Provincial Agricultural Exhibition Hall

Yunnan Provincial Library

Cuihu

Renmin   Xilu

Qianju Jie

Kunshi Lu

Xinhua Bookstore

Xiaoximen

Wucheng

Lu

Kunming Medical College

The First Hospital Attached to the Kunming Medical College

Yunnan Arts and Crafts Shop

Dongfeng

Mins

Shengli Assembly Ha

Xichangcun

Daguan Jie

Hongxing Theatre

Kunming Bookstore

Gui

Me

Zhuantang Pond

Guofang (National Defence) Stadium

Yunnan Provincial Museum

Lu

Xinwen

Huancheng

Guofang Theatre

Xilu

Pr

Chunch

Baimamiao

Daguan

Daguan

Xinzhuan Pond

Xiba

Jinbi

Milesi

Yunnan Vern
the Bridge

Xilu

Yunnan Provincial People's Hosp

Fuxing Xincun

Xilu

Pagoda of West

Kunming Botanical Institute

Heilong (Black Dragon) Pool

Qiongzhu (Bamboo) Temple

Golden Hall

The Vicinity of Kunming

0   10 km

KUNMING

Daguan Tower

Anning Hot Springs

Xiyuan Hotel

Xishan (Western Hills) Forest Park

Caoxi Temple

Anning

Chenggong

Yiliang

Xiyue

Yangzong L.

Workers Sanatorium

Dianchi

L.

Stone Forest

Zhongyicun

Lunan

Jinning

Chengjiang

Nanpan R.

Cher

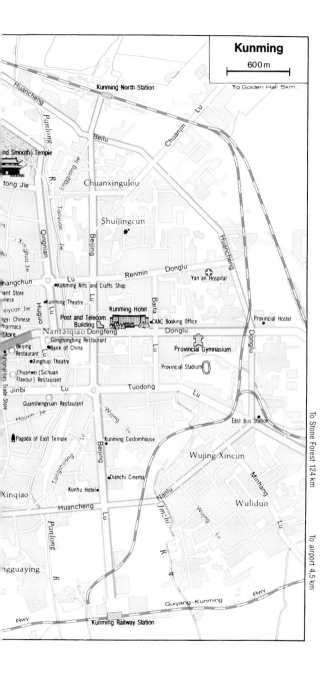

Kunming

600 m

To Golden Hall 5km.

Kunming North Station

Huancheng

Panlong R.

Beilu

Chuanjin Lu

(nd Smooth) Temple

Imgguang Jie

Chuanxingulou

tong Jie

Taoyuan Jie

Shuijingcun

Xinghua Jie

Qingnian Jie

Beijing

Huancheng

hangchun

Renmin

Donglu

Yan'an Hospital

nent Store
inese

Lu

•Kunming Arts and Crafts Shop

eiyuan Jie

•Kunming Theatre

Huguo

Baita

ngyi Chinese
harmacy

Lu

Post and Telecom
Building

Kunming Hotel

•CAAC Booking Office

Provincial Hostel

Store

Nantaiqiao Dongfeng

Donglu

Donglu

Beijing
Restaurant

•Gongnongbing Restaurant

Lu

Nationalities Trade Store

•Bank of China

Provincial Gymnasium

•Xinghuo Theatre

Chuanwei (Sichuan
Flavour) Restaurant

Provincial Stadium

Jinbi

Lu

Tuodong

Lu

Guanshengyuan Restaurant

Houxin Jie

Wujing Lu

East Bus Station

Tangshuang Lu

Pagoda of East Temple

Beijing

Kunming Customhouse

Wujing Xincun

Minhang Lu

Xinqiao

Dianchi Cinema

Wuliduo

Kunhu Hotel•

Huancheng

Nanlu

Jinzhi

Wujing Lu

Lu

Panlong R.

gguaying

R.

To Stone Forest 124 km

To airport 4.5 km

Rwy

Guiyang-Kunming

Rwy

Kunming Railway Station

Kunming

History

Kashgar was founded over 2100 years ago by Huns, Indoscyths, Uigurs and other ethnic groups. With the establishment of the Silk Road and the formation of a municipal administration under the Western Han dynasty (206 B.C.–A.D. 8), the settlement underwent considerable development. At the time of the Tang dynasty (618–907) it was also used as a military base.

Sights

★Id Kah Mosque
(Aitiga Qingzhensi)

The Id Kah Mosque, the largest in Xinjiang, situated on the square of the same name in the centre of the town, can accommodate up to 8000 worshippers and has an area of 1ha/12,000sq.yd. It was built in 1798, since when it has been restored and extended several times. The roof, which is lavishly decorated with floral motifs, is supported by 140 green pillars with sculptured ornamentation. Nearby there is a traditional and very characteristic bazaar ("bazha").

★Market

Every Sunday a market is held on the north-east edge of the town. Local products of every conceivable kind are on sale here: carpets, hats, jewellery, Uigur knives and even donkeys and horses. With an average of 150,000 visitors it is thought to be the largest open-air market in the world.

★Tomb of
Abakh Hoja
(Aba Heijia Mu)

The tomb of Abakh Hoja, a typical 17th c. Islamic monumental tomb which was completely restored in 1807, lies on the eastern edge of the town. It is almost completely composed of green ceramic tiles. The entrance is decorated with geometric patterns, the walls with stuccoed bas-reliefs. Up to 50 years ago the domed roof was crowned by a massive gold figure weighing 1.5kg/3lb. In the interior 72 members of the Abakh Hoja family are interred, their ancestor being an Islamic saint of the 17th c.

Surroundings

★Grottoes of the
Three Immortals
(Sanxian Dong)

The Grottoes of the Three Immortals date from the Eastern Han period (25–220) and lie 10km/6 miles to the north of the town, on the slopes of a steep hill. Each one of the three long interlinking caves is divided into a front and rear section. A badly damaged Buddha statue is kept in the rear section of the middle cave. On the walls of the left-hand cave there are some 70 likenesses of Buddha, dating back 1700 years. One of the Buddhas on the rear wall is depicted with a bare back – an unusual phenomenon in the wall paintings of that period.

Hanoi

The sparse remains of the town of Hanoi, dating from the Tang era (618–907), are to be found 30km/19 miles north-east of Kashgar.

Kunming

Chinese
equivalent

Capital of Yunnan Province
Altitude: 1893m/6211ft. Area: 6235sq.km/2407sq. miles
Population: 1,430,000 (conurbation 1,990,000)

Situation and
Communications

Kunming lies at 102°43′E and 25°05′N, in the centre of the province of Yunnan on the northern shore of Lake Dianchi. There are flights to Kunming from Beijing, Shanghai, Chengdu, Canton, Xi'an and other Chinese cities, as well as from Hong Kong. Kunming can also be reached from Chengdu and Guiyang by rail.

Kunming is famed as the "City of Eternal Spring" because of its mild climate and lush vegetation although within the space of a single day it is possible for the city to experience considerable variations in temperature. The city is also the cultural capital of the province, possessing universities, colleges and an institute for minorities.

People of many different nationalities live together in the city, a fact immediately apparent just from external appearances. There is a wide range of handmade goods available, e.g. embroidered blouses and caps. A

Shopping centre in Kunming

special attraction are the colourful markets, the parks and the beautiful wooden house-fronts, which give the city a rather provincial air.

In the 3rd c. B.C. General Zhuang Qiao retreated to the shores of Lake Dianchi and founded the city of Kunming. Under the Tang dynasty (618–907) it had the role of a military base. A little later on it became the capital of the Nanshao Kingdom. Kunming developed into an important trading centre, supplying India, Indochina, Burma and Sichuan. Marco Polo described it in 1287 as a "fine city" with inhabitants of many different races. In addition he mentioned the wealth of its trading houses and its salt production. Around 1650 the last hereditary prince of the Ming dynasty sought refuge in Kunming and founded the Southern Ming kingdom, which was destroyed eleven years later by Qing troops. In 1855 the city started a rebellion against its foreign Manchurian rulers but it was brutally put down. After 1910, when the railway line to Haiphong (now Hanoi) was opened, Kunming developed into a modern city. At the time of the Japanese invasion a large number of factories and research establishments were transferred here, in order to save them from destruction. In the last forty years Kunming has experienced another enormous spurt of growth and become a major economic centre.

This museum, which was opened in Dongfeng Xilu in 1964, contains over 50,000 exhibits, including valuable bronze implements belonging to the national minorities.

Jade Lake, into which nine springs feed, lies in the north-west of the city in the park of the same name. The late 17th c. Pavilion of the Green Waves (Biyi Ting) stands on an island in the middle of the lake. Two dams dominate the lake: the one running in a north–south direction and crossed by three bridges is known as the Dyke of Governor Ruan (Ruan Di) and was

History

Sights
Provincial Museum

Jade Lake
(Cuihu)

309

erected towards the end of the 18th c. The other one, called Tang Dyke (Tang Di), was built in 1919 and runs east–west.

★★Temple of Perfection and Success (Yuantong Si)

The Temple of Perfection and Success, situated in the north of the city and just to the south of the zoo of the same name, was built during the Tang period (618–907), rebuilt between 1301 and 1320, and subsequently restored on several occasions during the next few centuries. An octagonal pavilion situated in a square lake is of particular interest. In the main temple, the Hall of Perfection and Success (Yuantong Baodian), the visitor should look out for some 14th c. Buddhist statues and two Ming period (1368–1644) dragons made from coloured clay which are coiled around two pillars.

Pagoda of the West Temple, Pagoda of the East Temple

In the south of the city two pagodas rise up in close proximity to one another, the Pagoda of the West Temple (Xisi Ta) and the Pagoda of the East Temple (Dongsi Ta), both dating from the Tang period (618–907) and both having been faithfully rebuilt after the Muslim uprising of 1868.

Surroundings

★★Lake Dianchi

Lake Dianchi has a surface area of 297sq.km/115sq. miles and an average depth of 5.5m/18ft. Now known as Lake Kunming, it lies about 4km/2½ miles south-west of the city and is fed by 20 rivers and streams. There are thought to have been settlements here more than two thousand years ago.

Daguan Lou Gongyuan Park

On the shores of the lake there are many places to visit, for example Daguan Lou Gongyuan Park with its tower of the same name on the west shore. The tower, which was completed in 1691, originally had two storeys but in 1828 a third storey was added. For a number of years the tower served as a meeting-place for local men of letters. In 1857 it was destroyed

Statue of Buddha in the Temple of Perfection and Success

A park near Kunming

during the war but rebuilt in 1869. The building has a double roof which is covered with yellow-glazed tiles. In 1888 the famous calligrapher Sun Ranweng engraved the longest "parallel poem" (duilian) in China (180 characters) on the two front pillars.

The Western Mountains, which rise to over 2300m/7500ft, lie along the west shore of Lake Dianchi, about 15km/9 miles from Kunming, from where they can be reached by bus. Between the highest summit, Taihuashan, and the lake there is a difference in altitude of 470m/1542ft. Hidden away in the mountain valleys there are several Buddhist and Taoist temples, while at the foot of Gaoraoshan the visitor will come across the tomb of the Kunming-born composer Nie Er (1912–35), who composed the Chinese national anthem. His tomb is approached by 24 steps, symbolising the age of the deceased.

Western Mountains (Xishan)

The construction of the Taoist Pavilion of the Three Pure Ones took place over six centuries, during the Yuan, Ming and Qing periods (1279–1911).

Pavilion of the Three Pure Ones

From here one can reach the cave of Ciyun Dong, and from there proceed to the Dragon's Gate (Longmen). The Stone Pavilion (Datian Ge) is reached by a tunnel with stone steps and offers a wonderful view across Lake Dianchi.

At the foot of Taihuashan lies the temple of the same name, dating from the Yuan period (1279–1368). Nearby stands the "Lakeview Tower" (Wang-hai Lou).

To the north of the temple we come to Huating Si, dating from the Song period (960–1279), the main hall of which contains three gilded Buddha sculptures and 500 Luohan figures.

The Golden Hall, built in 1671 and situated to the north-east of the city on Minfeng Shan Mountain, is modelled on an earlier building dating from 1602, which was moved to Binchuan near Dali in 1637.

Golden Hall (Jin Dian)

311

The building has a square ground-plan with 6.2m/20ft sides and is 6.7m/22ft high. It is made completely of bronze, as are its fittings and statues. It gets its name from the way its roofs shine like gold in the sun.

★Bamboo Temple
(Qiongzhu Si)

On a foothill of Yu'anshan Mountain, 10km/6 miles north-west of Kunming stands the Bamboo Temple. As yet the exact date of its construction has not been determined, but it can be said with certainty to have been before the end of the 13th c.

The temple contains several valuable works of art: the Yuan period (1271–1368) statue of the Buddhas of the Three Worlds made of variegated clay (in the Buddha Hall); a small stone tablet on which is engraved in Chinese and Mongolian an imperial edict of 1316 calling on the army and the civilian population to protect the temple; the 500 Luohan statues of clay (1883–90) by the sculptor Li Guangxiu (in the Buddha Hall and two neighbouring buildings), which represent the various social strata in a very vivid and individual way.

★Pool of the
Black Dragon
(Heilong Tan)

The Pool of the Black Dragon, situated 14km/8½ miles north of the city in the park of the same name, is famous mainly for the Taoist Temple of the Dragon Spring (Longquan Guan), which is believed to have been founded under the Han dynasty, i.e. some 2000 years ago.

Palace of the
Black Dragon
(Heilong Gong)

Further down, on the west bank of the pool, stands the second part of the temple complex, the Palace of the Black Dragon, dating from 1454. Growing on the temple site today are a plum tree from the Tang period (618–907), a cypress from the Song era (960–1279) and a camellia from the Ming period (1368–1644).

Thermal Springs
of Anning
(Anning Wenquan)

The Thermal Springs of Anning lie 40km/25 miles to the south-west of Kunming near the village of Anning. They were discovered as early as the Eastern Han period (25–220), but were not made use of until the early 15th c.

The Stone Forest (see page 314)

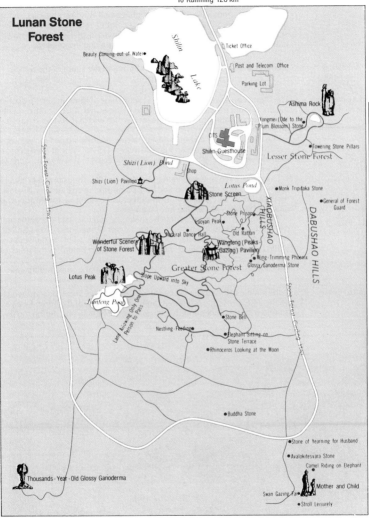

Lunan Stone Forest

To Kunming 126 km

Shilin Lake

Ticket Office

Post and Telecom Office

Parking Lot

Beauty Coming out of Water

Ashma Rock

Yongmei (Ode to the Plum Blossom) Stone

CITS

Shilin Guesthouse

Towering Stone Pillars

Lesser Stone Forest

Shizi (Lion) Pond

Shop

Shizi (Lion) Pavilion

Lotus Pond

Monk Tripitaka Stone

Stone Screen

General of Forest Guard

Stone Prison

Guoyan Peak

Natural Dance Hall

MAOBUSHAO HILLS

DABUSHAO HILLS

Old Rattan

Wonderful Scenery of Stone Forest

Wangfeng (Peaks Gazing) Pavilion

Wing-Trimming Phoenix

Glossy Ganoderma Stone

Greater Stone Forest

Lotus Peak

Slope Upward into Sky

Lianfeng Pond

Land Allowing Only One Person to Pass

Stone Bell

Nestling Feeding

Elephant Sitting on Stone Terrace

Rhinoceros Looking at the Moon

Stone Forest Circling Hill

Buddha Stone

Stone of Yearning for Husband

Avalokitesvara Stone

Camel Riding on Elephant

Thousands-Year-Old Glossy Ganoderma

Swan Gazing Far

Mother and Child

Stroll Leisurely

The 45°C/113°F hot springs contain calcium, magnesium, natrium and other minerals; they are particularly recommended for skin diseases and rheumatism.

To the west of the thermal springs (1km/½ mile) stands the Caoxi Si Temple, erected under the Tang dynasty (618–907) and later rebuilt on several occasions. In honoured place in the main hall dating from the Song period (960–1279) is a Buddha statue which by some strange phenomenon is

★ Caoxi Si Temple

313

invested with almost mythical powers of attraction. Every 60 years on the evening of the 15th of the Chinese month (according to the Chinese calendar) a ray of moonlight passes through a small window and falls on the middle of the Buddha's brow, forming a point of light there; as the moon slowly rises up in the sky, the point of light moves further and further down, until finally it reaches the navel of the sculpture and disappears.

Pearl Spring
(Zhenzhu Quan)

Mention should be made of the Pearl Spring to the south of the temple.

★★Lunan Stone
Forest (Shilin)

The Stone Forest lies 120km/75 miles south-east of Kunming in the district of Lunan. After the sea receded millions of years ago, tectonic movements caused deep fissures to occur in the rock, which was then further shaped by erosion processes.

The forest consists of thousands of narrow, weirdly-shaped rocks towering up to a height of between 5 and 30 metres (15–100ft), scattered over an area of over 26,000ha/100sq. miles. 80ha/200 acres of this area are open to visitors.

The rocks have memorable names such as Ten Thousand Year Mushroom (10m/33ft high), Mother and Son, Camel Riding on Elephant, Avalokitesvara Rock, Buddha Stone, Rhinoceros Looking at the Moon and Beautiful Maiden Ascending from the Water.

The Stone Forest is accessible by means of carefully laid-out paths and can be divided into three sections: the Lesser Stone Forest (Xiao Shilin), which is to be found just beyond the north entrance, a little to the south of Shilin Lake (Shilin Hu); the Greater Stone Forest (Da Shilin), to the south of the Lesser Stone Forest, with Jianfeng Pool and numerous grottoes; and the Outer Stone Forest (Wai Shilin) which takes in the surrounding area.

Torch Festival

In the middle of the Lesser Stone Forest there is a 2ha/5 acre meadow which on the 24th day of the 6th moon month is the scene of the Torch Festival, mounted by the Sani minority group. It lasts 24 hours and during the day

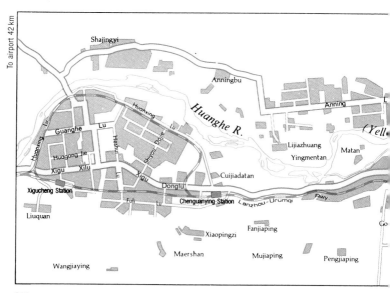

sports contests are held in national costume (a kind of wrestling match, martial arts, target shooting and horse racing). Finally throughout the night there is an imposing torchlit procession with interludes of song and dance.

Lanzhou

H 4

兰州市

Chinese equivalent

Capital of Gansu Province
Altitude: 1508m/4947ft. Area: 2122sq.km/819sq. miles
Population: 1,430,000 (conurbation 2,400,000)

Lanzhou lies at 103°42′E and 36°02′N, in the east of the province of Gansu. The city is not only a road and rail junction but also has a modern airport linking it to all the other large cities in China.

Situation and Communications

Lanzhou was founded over 2000 years ago. In 81 B.C. it had already acquired the dimensions of a town and later developed into an important stopping-place on the Silk Road. In 581 it was given the name "Lanzhou". Through the construction of the Longhai Railway in the 20th c., which extends from Jiangsu to Xinjiang, the city acquired considerable importance as a meeting-point between east and west.

History

After 1949 Lanzhou underwent enormous economic development, becoming an important industrial centre (petro-chemicals, weaving, metal processing) and achieving prominence in the field of atomic energy research. Today the city is the political, economic, scientific and cultural centre of Gansu Province and the second largest city in north-west China. It is also famous for its fruit, notably its melons.

Lanzhou

3 km

Sights

Provincial Museum (Sheng Bowuguan)	The museum's exhibits include ceramics, some of which date from Neolithic times. The most famous item is the bronze sculpture "Flying Horse from Gansu", with its hoof resting on a bird. It comes from a tomb from the Eastern Han period (24–220) which was discovered in 1969.
Mountain of the White Pagoda	In the north of the city stands Baitashan, named after the seven-storey 17m/56ft high White Pagoda, which was erected on the summit under the Yuan dynasty (1271–1368) and subsequently rebuilt in the middle of the 15th c. From here there is a superb view. Together with the sacred buildings surrounding it, the pagoda forms the focal point of a public park, laid out in 1958, which covers an area of 8000sq.m/1½ acres.
★Park of the Five Springs (Wuquanshan Gongyuan)	In the south of the city lies Wuquanshan, about 1600m/5250ft high and named after the Five Springs at the foot of the mountain. Scattered over its slopes are several monuments of considerable cultural and archaeological significance. The Park of the Five Springs has been laid out here.
Temple of Reverence and Solemnity (Chongqing Si)	The most important of these monuments is the Temple of Reverence and Solemnity, built in 1372. Here it is possible to see a 3m/10ft high iron bell, dating from 1202 and with a weight of some 5 tons, and a bronze Buddha sculpture, dating from 1370 and with a height of over 5m/16ft. From the top of the mountain there is a wonderful view of the city.

Surroundings

★★Grottoes of the Thousand Buddha Temple (Bingling Si Shiku)	These grottoes in the mountain of Xiaohishishan, about 90km/56 miles west of Lanzhou and 35km/22 miles south-west of Yongling, can be reached by bus. The cave complex was constructed in 420 but achieved eminence during the Tang dynasty (618–907). At the time of the Yuan dynasty (1271–1368) it was turned into a Tibetan monastery. The Chinese name "Bingling" is the transliteration of a Tibetan term, which means "Thousand Buddhas" or even "Hundred Thousand Buddhas". The temple site includes 34 grottoes and 149 niches with 679 stone sculptures, 82 clay statues – the largest statue is 27m/89ft, the smallest 20cm/8in. high – and 900sq.m/9700sq.ft of wall paintings. In the 40m/130ft high grotto No. 169 there is an inscription on the north wall which confirms the year of the temple's construction: "in the first year of Jian Hong", i.e. A.D. 420.

Between 1964 and 1974 the hydro-electric power station Liujia Xia was built, which provides Gansu and areas of the neighbouring provinces with energy. During the construction a 200m long dam was constructed in order to protect the grottoes from any flooding. As a result it is possible to visit them by boat. |
Temple of the Thunder God (Leizu Miao)	The Terrace of the Thunder God, 8.5m/28ft high, 106m/348ft long and 60m/197ft wide, is located 250km/155 miles north-west of Lanzhou, near the town of Wuwei. On it stands the Temple of the Thunder God, which was reconstructed under the Qing dynasty (1644–1911). In October 1960 a Han grave, dating from the early 2nd c., was discovered under the terrace. Among the valuable burial gifts is the famous statue of a galloping horse (known as the Flyiing Horse) which was chosen as its symbol by the Municipal Tourist Office.
Labrang Monastery	About 250km/155 miles south-west of Lanzhou (and accessible from there by bus), near the town of Xiahe, stands the Labrang Monastery, an important religious building of the Gelupka sect. The monastery was founded in about 1710 and was once inhabited by between 3000 and 4000 monks.
★Grottoes of Maijishan (Maijishan Shiku)	The Grottoes of Maijishan, situated 300km/185 miles south-east of Lanzhou on the outskirts of the little town of Tianshui, can be reached from Lanzhou by train. The 194 grottoes, which date from the 4th c. onwards, were hewn

out of two walls of rock and contain over 7000 sculptures and 1300sq.m/14,000sq.ft of frescos. Among the motives represented here there are Buddhistic themes and scenes from the political and everyday life of the era.

Lhasa

F 6

拉萨市

Chinese
equivalent

Capital of the Autonomous Region of Xizang (Tibet)
Altitude: 3685m/12,090ft. Area: 38sq.km/15sq. miles
Population: 107,000

Lhasa (Tibetan = "Place of the Gods") is also known by the name "City of Sun", because it is situated high on the Tibetan plateau, the "Roof of the World", which is very well favoured by the sun. Lhasa lies on the banks of the river of the same name (Lasahe; Kyichu), at 91°04′E and 29°33′N, in the south of Tibet.

Lhasa's airport lies 120km/75 miles outside the city. From here there are flights to Beijing (4½hrs) and Chengdu (2hrs). Chengdu also has bus connections (2 weeks), while Katmandu in Nepal can be reached by road.

Situation and
Communications

Lhasa was once called Rasa ("goats' earth") and 1300 years ago was the capital of the renowned Tufan kingdom. Both in the 7th and 8th c. marriages took place between a Chinese princess and the ruler of Lhasa, the Han Chinese and Tibetans being well disposed to one another at this time. In the succeeding centuries these harmonious relations worsened to a considerable degree, however, leading to endless conflicts and military

History

Lhasa: detail on the Tsuglagkhang Temple

317

confrontations. In 1951 Lhasa was conquered by Communist troops of the People's Republic of China and in 1959 the Dalai Lama was forced to leave Lhasa and seek refuge in India after one of the many revolts which took place in protest against the centralised power of the Chinese.

Today Lhasa is by far the most important economic, cultural and religious centre in Tibet.

Sights

Octagon Street (Bajiao Jie)

The city's market takes place daily on this street in the centre of Lhasa. Every morning at about 10 o'clock crowds of people begin to throng round the countless white-canopied stalls and Tibetan shop-windows. All manner of things are to be found here, including clothes, felt hats, cushions in every conceivable colour, lacquered boxes both large and small, rings, bangles, chains and silver earrings. There is also no shortage of craftware from the neighbouring lands of Nepal, Bhutan and Sikkim.

★ City Temple of Tsuglagkhang/ Jokhang Temple (Dazao Si)

The Temple of Tsuglagkhang in the centre of the city is thought to have been built in the 7th c. to a design by the Chinese princess Wen Chang. In fact the building reveals many features which belong to the Chinese style of the Tang period. Of interest in the main hall is the golden statue depicting the 12-year-old Shakyamuni, which the princess brought from the imperial capital of Chang'an. The present-day statue, however, is thought to date from the 12th c. The corridors and rooms of the temple are full of wall paintings representing events from Tibetan history and mythology.

In the two side pavilions there are sculptures of Songtsen Gampo, his wife Wen Cheng and a Nepalese princess.

The Barkhot, or holy path of transformation, runs right round the temple complex.

★★ Potala Palace (Budala Gong)

Potala Palace (open: daily except Sun.), designed as the winter residence of the Dalai Lamas, is 110m/360ft high and 360m/1200ft wide and occupies an area of some 130,000sq.m/155,500sq.yd in the north-west of the city, on the

Potala Palace

south-facing hillside. Songtsen Gambo, the ruler of the Tufan kingdom, had the palace built in the 7th c. after his marriage to Princess Wen Cheng of the imperial Tang family.

In subsequent years the palace was badly damaged through weathering and pillaging by enemy soldiers. When the 5th Dalai Lama (1617–82) of the Qing dynasty (1644–1911) was proclaimed spiritual and temporal overlord of the Tibetans, he ordered the royal residence to be rebuilt. His successors continued the work which he had begun, until the palace attained its present dimensions. The whole building, which was left undamaged by the Cultural Revolution (1966–67), underwent restoration between 1989 and 1994.

The complex, towering to a height of over 100m/330ft, can be divided into three sections: the palaces (Gongbao), the defensive fortifications (Chengbao Xue) and the gardens (Linka). This jewel of Tibetan architecture, which also reveals Chinese influences, has some thousand rooms, and its buildings are as many as 13 storeys high.

The Red Palace contains eight gilded burial stupas of the Dalai Lamas, inlaid with precious stones. The largest of these, 15m/49ft high and containing 3.7 tonnes of gold, is the tomb of the 5th Dalai Lama.

Red Palace (Hong Gong)

The stupa of the 13th Dalai Lama is also magnificently fitted out and contains wall paintings of great interest, including one depicting the ruler's visit to the Dowager Empress Cixi in Peking.

The White Palace includes the residence of the Dalai Lamas, the reigning kings and the tutors to the Dalai Lamas, as well as dwellings and offices. The private apartments of the 14th Dalai Lama have remained unaltered since his flight in 1959.

White Palace (Bai Gong)

Many of the palace walls are covered with frescos depicting episodes from Buddhist scriptures, landscapes from the surrounding area and historical events such as the arrival of the two Tang princesses or the journey of the 5th Dalai Lama to Beijing.

The oldest part of the whole complex is the Avalokiteshvara Chapel in the north-east part of the Red Palace, also known as the bridal chamber (of Songtsen Gampo and Wen Cheng). It contains, among other things, a figure of Avalokiteshvara.

Dragon King Lake, situated behind Potala Palace, was formed as a result of excavation work carried out for the construction of the palace. Today the area around the lake is a public park. A pair of steles recall the two great victories on Tibetan soil which were gained by the Manchurian government in 1720 and 1792 against the Mongol invaders.

Dragon King Lake (Longwang Tan)

On the small island in the lake stands a temple consecrated to the Dragon King.

Another important religious building is the Ramoche Temple, built in the 7th c. After being devastated on several occasions, it was finally renovated in the 1980s.

Ramoche (Xiaozhao)

These gardens, situated 4km/2½ miles away on the western edge of the city, are the most frequented park in Lhasa. The summer residence of the Dalai Lama, construction of which began in the 1840s, was once situated in the park, although the buildings to be found there today date for the most part from 1954–56.

★★Jewel Gardens (Norbulingka/ Luobulinka)

The 360,000sq.m/90 acres of parkland encompass everything from grand palaces and every possible kind of pavilion to pergola and small lakes.

Sera Monastery, 5km/3 miles to the north of Lhasa, was founded in 1419 by Lamaists as a monks' dwelling-place. The monastery contains a Tibetan copy of the Tripitaka from the 15th c. and a portrait embroidered on silk from the Ming period (1368–1644).

Surroundings

Sera Monastery (Sela Si)

Drepung Monastery

★Drepung
Monastery
(Zhebang Si)

Drepung Monastery is located on a hillside 10km/6 miles north-west of Lhasa. It was built in 1416 in the typical Tibetan style by adherents of the Yellow Cap Order (Gelupka) and became the political centre of the sect, with four Buddhist seminaries being housed here. The sacred buildings, which can accommodate up to 8000 monks, form the largest Lamaist monastery in Tibet. The burial stupas of the 2nd, 3rd and 4th Dalai Lamas are to be found here.

To the south-west of the monastery lies the palace, dating from 1530, in which the Dalai Lama resided.

The nearby monastery of Nechong was the seat of the Tibetan state oracle.

Lianyungang   K 5

Chinese
equivalent

连云港

Province: Jiangsu. Area: 740sq.km/286sq. miles
Population: 380,000 (conurbation 2,930,000)

Situation and
Communications

Lianyungang lies at 119°28'E and 34°38'N, in the north-east of Gansu Province on the Yellow Sea.

The city marks the beginning of the intercontinental railway line, crossing the whole of China and then Russia and ending finally at Rotterdam (total length: 10,700km/6,500 miles). This "Eurasian bridge" was opened to traffic at the end of 1990.

In a document dating from A.D. 65 mention is made of a Buddhist community in the area of Lianyungang which is also thought to have been responsible for the bas-reliefs on Kongwangshan Mountain. Wu Cheng'en, author of the famous novel "Travels in the West" (Xiyou Ji), was born in Lianyungang in the 16th c. On the eastern edge of the town a harbour was constructed by the Dutch in 1933. Salt extraction plays an important part in the economy of the town.

Kongwangshan Mountain, 2km/1 mile south of the city, is famous for its 108 sculptures in high relief, which are chiselled into a rock 16m/52ft long and 10m/33ft high. They date from the Eastern Han period (25–220), in other words two centuries earlier than the Dunhuang Grottoes. In front of these relief figures stand two groups of sculptures: an elephant with its keeper and a gigantic toad in a crouching position.

Surroundings

★★**Kongwangshan Mountain**

At the foot of Kongwongshan lies the Dragon's Cave, its walls covered with 24 inscriptions. The oldest date from 1072.

Dragon's Cave (Long Dong)

In the Peach Blossom Gorge (Taohua Gou) of Jinpingshan, situated 10km/6 miles outside the city, the visitor will find a rock in which the Yi tribe carved large numbers of anthropomorphs and geometric motives 4000 years ago. At that time the rock was used as a sacrificial altar.

★**Jinpingshan Mountain**

15km/9 miles south-east of the city rises the 625m/2050ft high Huaguoshan Mountain. At about 400m/1300ft up the mountain stands the temple of Sanyuan Gong dating from the 7th c.
The cave of Shuilian Dong ("Water Curtain Cave") is where the king of the apes Sun Wukong from the novel "Travels in the West" (Xiyou Ji) by Wu Cheng'en is supposed to have lived.

Huaguoshan Mountain

The 625m/2050ft high mountain of Yuntaishan, famed for the weird shapes formed by its rocks, rises 20km/12½ miles to the east of the city.
Some scholars are of the opinion that Yuntaishan Mountain inspired Wu Cheng'en to create the "Mountain of Flowers and Fruit" in his novel "Travels in the West".

★**Yuntaishan Mountain**

At a height of 400m/1310ft stands Sanyuan Gong Monastery, a Taoist building complex dating back 1300 years. At the foot of the mountain stands a tiled pagoda (1026).

Sanyuan Gong Monastery

Liaoning

K–M 2–4

Chinese equivalent

Province
Area: 145,700sq.km/56,255sq. miles
Population: 39,900,000. Capital: Shenyang

The province of Liaoning lies between 118°53'–125°46'E and 38°43'–43°26'N in the southern part of north-east China.

Situation

The overwhelming majority of the population are Han Chinese. More than two thirds of the minorities consist of Manchurians, but there are also Koreans, Hui and Mongols.

The eastern part of the province, including the Liaodong peninsula, is almost completely taken up with the wooded Changbai massif. The west consists of hilly countryside, rising in the north-west to the Great Chingan

Topography

China

Liaoning Province

The People's Republic of China

Zhonghua Renmin Gongheguo

at over 2000m/6500ft. Between these two areas of elevation lies the plain of the Liaohe, occupying over 30% of the land area of the province.

Climate

The climate has a continental character but this effect is tempered by monsoons. The overall average temperature for the year is 8°C/46°F, while in Shenyang average temperatures for January and July are −13°C/9°F and 25°C/77°F respectively. There are often as many as 200 days a year when frost is experienced, while three-quarters of the annual rainfall occurs between June and September.

History

The plain of the River Liaohe was settled from a very early date, while in the peripheral areas Manchurians and Mongols practised livestock farming and forestry. In the course of time more and more Han Chinese migrated into Liaoning. During the 19th c. foreign powers were particularly interested in the rich mineral potential of the province. Between 1932 and 1945 it formed part of the Japanese-controlled state of Manzhouguo. Since 1949, with the expansion of the industrial base, there has been particular emphasis on heavy industry.

Economy

Rich mineral deposits enabled the present-day dominance of heavy industry to develop during the period of Japanese occupation. In addition there are the traditional textile and food industries. Liaoning also has reserves of coal and iron ore, as well as magnesite deposits and supplies of copper, lead, zinc and molybdenum ore.

Energy supplies are ensured through thermal power stations and a hydro-electric power station at Yalujiang which is shared with North Korea.

In the agricultural sector the staple foods grown are kauliang, millet and maize, while the province is also an important producer of cotton and tobacco. On the Liaodong peninsula silkworm breeding and fruit-growing (especially apples) are important activities.

Places to visit

For the visitor Dalian, Anshan and Fushun (see entries) are of interest.

柳州市

Chinese
equivalent

Autonomous Region of Guangxi
Altitude: 90–120m/295–395ft. Area: 541sq.km/209sq. miles
Population: 470,000 (conurbation 590,700)

Liuzhou lies on the Liujiang, at 109°24'E and 24°19'N, 130km/80 miles from
Guilin and 255km/158 miles from Nanning, the capital of the region. It is an
important railway junction on the Hunan–Guangxi, Guizhou–Guangxi and
Zhicheng–Liuzhou lines. Guilin, Nanning and other towns can be reached
by bus, while there are flights taking 1½hr to Canton.

Situation and
Communications

The area around Liuzhou was settled as long as 15,000 years ago. By 219
the place had achieved a certain eminence and since 634 it has had its
present name. Liu Zongyuan (773–819), a famous man of letters and minister of rites under the Tang dynasty, was exiled to Liuzhou in 815 after failed
attempts at gaining reforms but by his merits rose to be a town elder and
enjoyed great prestige among the population. He has left a splendid
description of the town.
    Today Liuzhou is predominantly an industrial centre.

History

This park in the city centre is named after Liu Zongyuan. He was granted the
title of prince posthumously by the Song Emperor Huizong at the beginning of the 12th c.

Sights

★**Prince Liu Park**
(Liuhou Gongyuan)

In the park there are two monuments which commemorate the poet: a
tomb, which in fact only contains his head covering and a few articles of
clothing, and the ancestral temple of Prince Liu, built in 821 and rebuilt in
1729. A large number of old stone slabs with inscriptions by scholars from
the Tang, Song and Yuan periods (9th–13th c.) are stored here, as well as a
portrait of Liu Zongyuan engraved on a stele.

Ancestral Temple
of Prince Liu
(Liuhou Ci)

The 150m/500ft high Horsesaddle Mountain, which gets its name from its
shape, is situated in the south of the city. As long ago as the Tang era
(618–907) it aroused the interest of many travellers. One of its main attractions is a deep dripstone cave full of stalagmites and stalactites. Visitors
have left over 100 inscriptions on the mountain rock faces, including one
dating back to 1112.

Horsesaddle
Mountain
(Ma'anshan)

The summit of the 80m/260ft high Yufengshan (Fishpeak Mountain), situated in the park of the same name, is reflected in the Little Dragon Pool
(Xiaolong Tang) and suggests a fish leaping out of the water – hence the
mountain's name. The mountain and pool are linked to an old legend:
many hundreds of years ago a maiden named Liu Sanjie lived in the area
and she used to climb up the mountain and sing songs of lament protesting
at the local rulers. The latter thereupon started to pursue her by all possible
means. Eventually the maiden could bear it no longer and threw herself
into the pool. Immediately a heavy thunderstorm broke out and two fishes
sprang out of the pool. One bore the maiden up to heaven, the other fell
onto the earth, changed into a mountain and overwhelmed the tyrants. On
Yufengshan stands a stone statue of the maiden. In memory of Liu Sanjie a
song festival is held every year on the 15th day of the 8th moon month.

★Fishpeak
Mountain
(Yufengshan)
Little Dragon
Pool
(Xiaolong Tang)

Luoyang

South of the city (4km/2½ miles) lies the Great Dragon Pool. Its name also refers to a legend, this time that of a heavenly dragon who could conjure up thunder and lightning and rain and lived at the bottom of the pool. The 100ha/240 acre pool is in the middle of evergreen woods and rugged rocks covered with inscriptions.

Luoyang   J 5

Chinese
equivalent

洛阳市

Province: Henan. Area: 544sq.km/210sq. miles
Population: 582,000 (conurbation 978,000)

Situation and
Communications

Luoyang is situated at 112°27′E and 34°41′N, in the west of the province of Hena, on the River Luohe. Its name means "north of the Luo".

The city is connected by rail with Beijing, Shanghai, Canton, Xi'an and Zhengzhou, while a small airport makes flights possible to Canton, Shanghai, Xi'an and Ürümqi.

History

Finds from the area show that settlements existed here even in Neolithic times (Yangshao and Longshan civilisation). Luoyang was from 770 B.C. the capital of nine dynasties – firstly the Eastern Zhou dynasty (770–221 B.C.) under the name Wangcheng – and was therefore the military, economic and cultural centre of the country.

During the period of the Eastern Han dynasty (25–220), who likewise resided here, a large imperial academy was founded with some 30,000 students and a huge library was built. This period coincided with the invention of paper by Cai Lun and the advent of Buddhism. In A.D. 68 the White Horse Temple, the oldest Buddhist monastery in China, was built.

During the era of the Three Empires Luoyang was the capital of the Wei empire and subsequently of the Western Jin dynasty (265–316). The rulers of the Northern Wei dynasty (386–534), who also had their residence here, were great patrons of Buddhism and during this time more than 1000

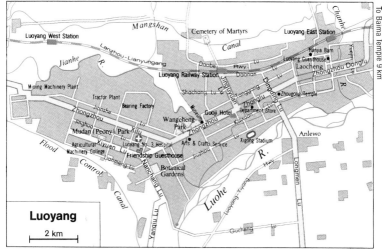

To Longmen Grottoes 7 km

temples were established. At the end of this period Luoyang was destroyed and rebuilt under the Sui (581–616).

In the Tang period (618–907) the city was the eastern capital alongside Chang'an. Since this time Luoyang has been known as the City of Peonies, reputedly a symbol of wealth.

The famous poets Du Fu and Li Bai lived and worked here. Empress Wu Zetian (reigned 690–705) had a special affection for Luoyang.

After the Jin moved their capital to Kaifeng in 937, the city had only a subordinate role and was overshadowed by Xi'an.

It was not until the second half of this century that Luoyang experienced a revival – thanks to two important industrial concerns, a tractor works and a ball-bearing factory.

The manufacture of lamps and lanterns also has a long history here.

Sights

Wangcheng Gongyuan Park lies in the heart of Luoyang on the site of the former royal city (Wangcheng), built by the Zhou in the 11th c. B.C. The park is renowned for its wealth of peonies. Most of the 180 types of peony are represented here and tradition has it that the flower has been grown here for more than a thousand years.

★Wangcheng Gongyuan Park

Of historical interest are two tombs from the Han period (206 B.C.–A.D. 220) which were discovered in the 1950s near the old city centre and then transferred here. The older of the two dates from the 1st c. B.C. and contains wall paintings which are among the earliest in China. The second tomb dates from the Eastern Han period (24–220) and contains two stone doors decorated with carvings.

The museum was opened in 1958 and is housed in the Guandi Miao temple dating from the Ming period (1402–1644). On display are finds made by archaeologists during the 1950s in the area surrounding the city. Exhibits include Neolithic ceramics and bronze vessels dating from the Zhou era (11th c.–221 B.C.).

Municipal Museum

Surroundings

The Dragon's Gate Grottoes are, with the caves of Datong and Dunhuang, among the most important cave temples in China. They extend for over 1km/½ mile along the slopes of Longmenshan Mountain 12km/7½ miles south of the city. This Buddhist religious site includes not only the 1352 grottos but also 750 niches and 40 pagodas, containing many wall paintings, 3680 rock inscriptions and almost 100,000 statues. The first caves were created in A.D. 494 when the Northern Wei dynasty (386–534), which actively supported Buddhism, moved its capital to Luoyang. Over the last few centuries a large part has been destroyed, partly by erosion, partly by people, including even collectors.

★★Dragon's Gate Grottoes (Longmen Shiku)

The 7th c. temple of Qianxi Si contains a sculpture of the Buddha Amitabha with two pupils. In addition two Bodhisattvas and two guardians of heaven can be seen.

Qianxi Si Temple

Binyang Dong Grotto on the north-west slope of the mountain consists of three interconnecting chambers which were created between the 6th and 7th c. on the orders of the Xuanwu Emperor as an act of veneration to his parents. The middle one dating from 500–523 is of particular interest. It contains statues of Shakyamuni and ten Bodhisattvas. These sculptures are distinguished by their narrow faces, outstretched bodies and richly draped clothes – all features which are characteristic of the art of sculpture in the Northern Wei epoch.

Binyang Dong Grotto

Only three of the original four bas-reliefs on the two side walls have survived. They depict episodes from the life of Shakyamuni.

Dragon's Gate Grottoes . . .

. . . near Luoyang

The Ten Thousand Buddha Grotto was constructed on the south-west slope in 680. It contains not 10,000 but 15,000 Buddhistic sculptures, which are to be found in high relief on the south and north walls. On the ceiling an enormous lotus blossom can be seen.

Ten Thousand Buddha Grotto (Wanfo Dong)

Lotus Blossom Cave, which was created in the late Wei period, is named after the lotus blossom on its roof. In the middle of the cave there is a large sculpture of Shakyamuni.

Lotus Blossom Cave (Lianhua Dong)

The 36m/118ft wide and 41m/135ft deep grotto known as Fengxian Si Temple, also situated on the south-west slope, was created between 672 and 675 and is the biggest in the whole complex. It was once protected by a wooden porch. There are 11 Buddhist statues – scholars, heavenly kings and guardians – and the largest, a Buddha Losana, is 17m/56ft high. With its round-cheeked face this sculpture is typical of the early – prosperous and peaceful – Tang era.

Fengxian Si Temple

In the Remedy Cave established by the Empress Wu Zetian (624–705) the visitor will come across over 140 inscriptions from the early 7th c. which give medical advice for the treatment of digestive complaints, angina, malaria and other illnesses. It is therefore of particular interest to those carrying out investigations into traditional Chinese medicine.

Yaofang Dong (The Remedy Cave)

Guyang Dong Grotto on the south-west slope of the mountain was created in 493 before any of the others. On the niches in the cave walls numerous sculptures with white contours protrude. This grotto also contains a large number of stone inscriptions which are masterpieces of calligraphy. Both the statues and the inscriptions date from the time of the cave's inception.

Guyang Dong Grotto

On Xiangshan the grotto of Kanjing Si is of special interest. The walls of the 7th c. grotto are decorated with 29 Luohan figures.

Kanjing Si Grotto

Other places of interest in the surrounding area

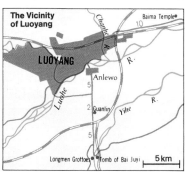

The Vicinity of Luoyang

Chanhe R.
Baima Temple
10
LUOYANG
R.
Anlewo
5
Luohe R.
2 Guanlin Yihe
R.
5
Longmen Grottoes • Tomb of Bai Juyi   5 km

The head of Guan Yu (?–219), a general of the Shu kingdom who was beheaded on the battlefield, is reputed to lie under the great burial mound, 7km/4½ miles south of the city. For the Chinese people he is still a symbol of loyalty, trust and moral integrity, even today, because of his self-sacrificing deeds.

Tomb of General Guan Yu (Guan Lin)

The tomb of Bai Juyi is to be found on the Summit of Poetic Perfection (Pipa Feng) on Xinagshan Mountain on the east bank of the Yihe. The famous poet (772–846) was for many years court tutor to some of the hereditary princes of the Tang dynasty and spent the last years of his life at the foot of Xiangshan.

Tomb of the poet Bai Juyi (Bai Juyi Mu)

9km/5½ miles from Luoyang, on the eastern edge of the city, stands the White Horse Temple, built in A.D. 68, which is one of the oldest in China. Its name is linked to a legend: the Han Emperor Mingdi sent two monks to India in 64, in order that they should study the holy scriptures of Buddha there. The two monks made friends with two Indian priests called Kasyapa-matang and Dharmaranya and asked them to bring the sutras to China and

★★White Horse Temple (Baima Si)

promulgate their teachings. The two Indian priests came to Luoyang with the Buddhist writings on two white horses (hence the temple's name). In order to provide safe storage for the sutras the emperor had this temple built. More than 1000 monks came here in order to hear the teachings of the two priests. When the latter died they were buried in the temple. Their tombs can be seen in the gateway of the temple. The present buildings occupying the site date from the Ming period (1368–1644). In front of the temple stand two equestrian sculptures made of stone, dating from the Song period (960–1279).

★Skyscraper Pagoda (Qiyun Ta)

South-east of the White Horse Temple towers the 24m/79ft high thirteen-storey Skyscraper Pagoda, which was built under the Later Tang dynasty (618–907) and rebuilt under the Jin dynasty. It is a typical example of the Tang dynasty style.

★★Songshan Mountain

Songshan, 50km/31 miles south-east of Luoyang and 15km/9 miles north-west of the district capital Dengfeng, is one of the five sacred Buddhist mountains in China to which the emperors made pilgrimages in order to offer up gifts to heaven. The others are Taishan (Prov. Shandong), Heeng-shan (Prov. Hunan) and Huashan (Prov. Shaanxi). Many old architectural monuments stand on the slopes and in the vicinity of the 1440m/4725ft high Songshan, which is also often familiarly called Centre Mountain.

Shaolin Monastery

The monastery of Shaolin, which was built in 495 on the western slopes of Songshan, is the birthplace of Chan Buddhism, which was founded by the Indian monk Bodhidharma (Damo) at the beginning of the 6th c. Being bodily very weakened as a result of long phases of meditation, he thought up with his disciples a series of exercises which were designed to restore strength and mobility to the body. It was this which led to the famous boxing school of Shaolin (Shaolin Quan), which is still practised today by countless Buddhists and non-Buddhists in its later form, Kungfu. Under both the Ming and Qing dynasties, from the 14th to the early 20th c., the monastery was almost completely rebuilt. The inscription "Shaolin Si" over the door of the main entrance dates from the time of Emperor Kang XI of the Qing dynasty (1662–1723).

Thousand Buddha Hall (Qiabfo Dian)

Thousand Buddha Hall, one of the main buildings of the monastery, is decorated by a 300sq.m/3225sq.ft Ming period (1368–1644) wall painting, on which 500 Luohans are depicted rendering homage to Vairocana. The hollows in the ground are thought to stem from centuries of practice of Shaolin martial arts.

Pagoda Wood (Talin)

A few hundred metres to the west of the monastery begins the Pagoda Wood, in which more than 220 burial pagodas stand in close proximity one to another. Between 791 and 1803 the most famous abbots and monks of the monastery were buried here.

Palace of the Martial Arts

The Palace of the Martial Arts was opened in the monastery of Shaolin in 1988. It is a training centre where followers of Shaolin boxing or Kungfu can attend courses (Length: 7 days to 1 year). In addition instruction in Budd-hism, traditional Chinese arts of healing and the Chinese language are also given. The courses are also open to foreigners.

Temple of the Earliest Forefather

To the north of the monastery stands the Temple of the Earliest Forefather (Chiuzu An), which was built in the 6th c. and restored in 1125.

Songyue Ta Pagoda

The tiled Pagoda of Songyue Ta belonging to the Temple of Songyue Si, 5km/3 miles north-west of Dengfeng is the oldest of its kind in China. This dodecagonal building dates from 520 and is 40m/130ft high.

Songyang Academy

Songyang Academy, situated at the foot of the Junyi Peak, the highest point on Songshan, was formed in the 11th c. out of the Songyang Temple of 484 and counts as one of the four most important places of education in

Pagoda Wood (burial place of monks)

old China. The two cypresses in the courtyard are supposed to be the oldest in the whole of China.

Zhongyue Maio Temple lies 4km/2½ miles east of Dengfeng. It was built in the 3rd c. B.C. and enlarged in 110 B.C. The present buildings date from the Qing period (1644–1911). With its surface area of some 100,000sq.m/ 120,000sq.yd it is the most monumental Buddhist building in the province. The complex of over 400 buildings is symmetrically arranged.

Zhongyue Miao Temple

In front of the Great Hall (Zhongyue Dadian) four 3m/10ft high cast iron figures dating from 1064 keep guard.

Dengfeng Observatory, which is situated 14km/8½ miles from Dengfeng at the south-eastern foot of Songshan, was built in 1276 and is the oldest observatory in China. The stone and tile building is 13m/43ft high and is equipped with a 31m/102ft long stone sundial.

Dengfeng Observatory (Dengfeng Guanxingtai)

This is where the famous astronomer and mathematician Guo Shoujing worked. In 1199, after many long observations and exact calculations, he was able to prove how long the earth takes to orbit the sun and was in fact only out by a mere 26 seconds.

Ma'anshan   K 5

马鞍山

Chinese equivalent

Province: Anhui
Area: 278sq.km/107sq. miles. Population: 350,000

Macau

Situation and Communications

Ma'anshan lies at 118°29'E and 31°42'N, on the Changjiang in the east of the province of Anhui.

It is situated about 80km/50 miles from Nanjing with which it has rail, bus and ship connections. It can be reached from the provincial capital Hefei by rail and bus.

History

Ma'anshan means "Horsesaddle Mountain", a name which is derived from an old legend. In 202 B.C. Xiang Yu, King of the Chu kingdom, committed suicide in this region after being defeated by his arch-rival, the Han King Liu Bang. His horse was disturbed by his master's non-appearance and ran up a hill in the hope of being able to espy him on the horizon. After the faithful steed had vainly kept a look-out for many days, he let out a long despairing sigh and died, the saddle falling to the ground. In memory of this the hill was named "Horsesaddle Mountain".

Until the 1930s Ma'anshan was only a small village with barely 300 inhabitants. When rich reserves of iron were discovered in the vicinity 60 years or more ago, Ma'anshan very quickly developed into an industrial town which today possesses one of the most important iron foundries in China.

Surroundings

★The Coloured Pebblestone Rocks (Caishi Ji)

The Coloured Pebblestone Rocks are located 7km/4 miles south of the town on the banks of the Changjiang. Owing to their strategic position the rocks were fought over for hundreds of years.

Today there is an extensive park here with many monuments, some of which commemorate famous people.

Li Bai Pavilion (Taibai Lou)

The Pavilion of Li Bai (see Famous People) was originally built in the 9th c. but in the succeeding periods has been destroyed and rebuilt on several occasions. It is consecrated to the outstanding poet Li Bai who spent the last years of his life in a nearby village. The present three-storey building dates from the second half of the 19th c. On the first floor stand two statues of the poet in boxwood, while on the second floor there is a view across the beautiful surrounding area.

Terrace for Capturing the Moon (Zuoyue Tai)

The Terrace for Capturing the Moon is a sheer rock overhanging the Changjiang. Tradition has it that the drunken Li Bai leapt from the terrace into the waters of the river in an attempt to capture the moon's reflection and in so doing drowned.

★Mountain of the Green Snail (Cuiluo Shan)

The 131m/430ft high Mountain of the Green Snail lies 7km/4½ miles south of the town on the banks of the Changjiang. It owes its name to its luxuriant vegetation and its shape, which resembles that of a snail.

Li Bai's Tomb (Li Bai Yiguan Jiong)

In the midst of this vegetation are hidden several places of interest including the tomb of Li Bai, where the clothing of the drowned poet is kept. His corpse could not be saved.

Macau
J 7

Chinese equivalent

澳門

Chinese territory under Portuguese administration
Area: about 18sq.km/7sq. miles (increasing as a result of land reclamation)
Altitude: 0–174m/0–571ft
Population: approx. 500,000. Capital: Macau

The short description which follows must be read in the light of the fact that Macau is to be returned to Chinese sovereignty in 1999. More detailed coverage is provided by the separate Baedeker guide "Hong Kong · Macau".

The Chinese territory under Portuguese administration, known as Macau, in Chinese Ao Men or An Men (from "A Ma Gao" = Bay of A Ma, the Chinese goddess of seafarers and fishermen), lies about 90km/56 miles south of Canton (Guangzhou) on the South China coast, about 60km/37 miles west-south-west of the British colony of Hong Kong on the west side of the Canton delta, the broad estuarian expanse of the Canton or Pearl River (Zhujiang/Chukiang).

Situation and Territory

The territory of Macau extends between 22°06' and 22°12'N (only a short distance south of the Tropic of Cancer) and 113°34' and 113°35'E, and is bounded to the north by the People's Republic of China (province of Guangdong/Kwantung). Its area of 18sq.km/7sq. miles is steadily increasing as a result of land reclamation and includes the 7sq.km/2½sq.mile hilly peninsula of Macau with its capital of the same name (originally in Portuguese "Cidade do São Nome de Deus de Macau, Não Há Outra Mais Leal"), as well as the offshore islands of Taipa (about 4sq.km/1½sq. miles) and Coloane (about 7sq.km/2½sq. miles) which are linked to Macau and one another by a bridge (a second is under construction) and causeway.

The climate of Macau is subtropical, the weather warm to hot with an annual average temperature of around 20°C/68°F (average maximum of 28°C/82°F), a relative humidity level of 73–90% and most rainfall occurring between April and October. However, a cool sea-breeze makes the hot period of the year more bearable than in Hong Kong. The winter half of the year is low in rainfall and less hot (under 20°C/68°F). The most pleasant weather conditions are in November and December, while from May to September there are occasional typhoons.

Climate

PEOPLE'S REPUBLIC OF CHINA
GUANGDONG PROVINCE

Macau
Ao Men

3 km
© Baedeker

Macau A

B

Pearl River Delta

Chinese territory under Portuguese administration

Taipa

Hongkong

Macau International Airport

C

D D E

Coloane

NEW PROJECTS
A Second Ferry Terminal
B Second Taipa High-level Bridge
C Rail and Bus Connection
D Land Reclamation
E Ka Ho Container Port

South China Sea

95% of the population of about half a million are Chinese, with the remainder comprising small minorities of Portuguese and other Europeans. A large proportion of the Chinese inhabitants are refugees who migrated there during the occupation of China and Hong Kong by Japanese troops during the Second World War or during Mao Zedong's "cultural revolution".

Population

The population of Macau is predominantly Buddhist (about 77%). Although there are only 25,000 Catholics, Macau is the see of a bishop.

Religion

The official languages are Portuguese and Chinese (Cantonese), but English is the language mainly used for trade and communications.

Language

On February 17th 1976 Macau was granted a statute of autonomy which guaranteed the territory's full internal self-government under Portuguese sovereignty.
The government consists of a

Administration

legislative assembly, at the head of which stands the Governor, appointed by the Portuguese President, who is aided by a Consultative Council. The Governor and his secretaries look after all executive decisions.

There are several parties, including the Beijing-oriented Electors' Union and the Pro-Macau Group.

History

Macau is the oldest European colony in China. After military skirmishes the mandarins governing the Chinese province of Canton granted a lease of the Macau area to the Portuguese, subject to payment of an annual rent. From very early on Macau was a missionary centre and then in 1575 the diocese was founded with responsibility for Christianity in China and Japan.

In the first century of its existence Macau became prosperous as a result of its trade with China and Japan, but it was not long before this turned into a steady decline, caused primarily by Japan's decision to sever contacts with the rest of the world. In addition the Portuguese had to contend with both a large amount of competition and also the activities of pirates, whose ranks included a considerable number of adventurers from the Netherlands and other European countries.

In 1845 Macau was declared a free port (a status it still holds today) and henceforth no longer had to pay import, turnover and leasing duties to China. The Governor João Ferreira do Amaral, who took office in 1846, pursued this policy even further and drove out the Chinese tax-collectors. His harsh rule later led to his being attacked and killed by outraged peasants. The Treaty of Tientsin in 1862 confirmed Portuguese sovereignty over Macau and the islands of Taipa and Coloane but was not ratified by China until December 1st 1887. In return Portugal undertook never to sell Macau and the islands without the consent of China. As a result of favourable commercial conditions more and more Chinese merchants were attracted to Macau and the territory was quickly to become the preferred summer residence of British traders, who would await the start of the next season here.

In the Second World War Macau remained neutral and was therefore not occupied by the Japanese. In 1951 the territory was declared a Portuguese overseas province. In 1966 in the course of demonstrations in favour of Macau's becoming part of the People's Republic of China there were deaths and injuries but peace soon returned with China apparently still having good reasons for maintaining the status quo. However, the change of power in Portugal, which followed the bloodless military coup carried out in 1974 against the dictator Salazar, brought with it a movement for decolonisation. Initially, however, China rejected Portugal's offer to return Macau. Nevertheless in 1976 the territory received a new statute of autonomy which guaranteed its internal independence. Since then Macau has been a "Chinese territory under Portuguese administration".

Political
perspectives

In 1986 Portugal and the People's Republic of China agreed that, in accordance with the lease agreement in operation since 1557, Macau should be handed back to China on December 20th 1999 (after 442 years!). Macau will then be conceded a special status similar to that which Hong Kong will receive in 1997. All Macauans born in the territory up to December 31st 1979 will automatically become Portuguese citizens and be entitled to travel to Portugal and the other countries of the EU whenever they wish.

Economy

Agricultural products: sweet potatoes, ground-nuts, tobacco; fishing; industries: textiles, clothing, matches, fireworks, porcelain, ceramics, optical and electrotechnical goods, plastics; exports: textiles, leather goods, foodstuffs, fireworks, optical instruments; gold (government monopoly); tourism (including casinos).

The economy of the territory is based above all on textiles and clothing, electrical and optical equipment, and fireworks. Small and medium-sized businesses predominate. A very important role is also played by tourism, in particular the Hong Kong Chinese who come to Macau in order to gamble (forbidden in the British colony).

1 pataca (Pat.,M-$) = 100 avos (Avs). Banknotes are in the following denominations: 5, 10, 50, 100 and 500 patacas, and there are also coins with the values 10, 20 and 50 avos and 1 and 5 patacas.

Currency

In recent years Macau has been almost totally dependent on Hong Kong for its transport services, with ferries, hydrofoils, hovercrafts, motorboats and helicopters connecting the two territories. On the east side of the peninsula of Macau lies the Outer Harbour (Porto Exterior) with its ferry terminals, while on the west side is the Inner Harbour (Porto Interior), which is protected from typhoons.
  Vehicles travel on the left in Macau.

Transport

In recent times a major effort has been made to effect every possible improvement in the transport infrastructure. Thus on the Macau peninsula, a short distance to the north-east of the Shun Tak Centre, a second ferry terminal, the New Macau Ferry Terminal, has been built. A second road bridge between Macau and Taipa (the New Macau-Taipa Bridge) is under construction. Macau's first fully international airport, built on newly reclaimed land off the east coast of Taipa, came into operation in 1996. On the north-east coast of the island of Coloane a new deep-water harbour is being built for container ships (Ka Ho Container Port). A land reclamation project aims to fill in all the waters between the islands of Taipa and Coloane, something which would lead to a radical environmental change for the whole area. Furthermore, the introduction of rail and motorway links with China are envisaged.

New Installations and Projects

Recent milestones in the promotion of tourism include the greatly increased hotel capacity offered by the territory (between 1991 and 1993 almost doubled) and the establishment of an extensive leisure area in the south-east of Coloane.

Promotion of Tourism

Macau Peninsula

Both from the Shun Tak Centre, the first terminal for ferry traffic to and from Hong Kong, situated in the Outer Harbour, and also from the new ferry terminal just to the north, it is possible to travel into the town centre by bus or taxi, and this is where most of the hotels are to be found. Just past the grandstand belonging to the motor-racing track one comes to the unusual Hotel Lisboa, where there is a monument to Governor Ferreira do Amaral, the founder of independent Macau.

Macau
Ferry Terminals in the Outer Harbour
Motor-racing Track
Hotel Lisboa

Situated near the Outer Harbour is the Macau Forum, opened in 1985, a centre for culture, sports and leisure activities.

★Macau Forum

The broad tree-lined Rua da Praia Grande leads from near the Outer Harbour to the beach. Between the Hotel Lisboa and the Inner Harbour (home to the floating casino Macau Palace) extending diagonally across the whole of the peninsula, is the Avenida Infante Dom Henrique, later the Avenida Almeida Ribeiro, the most important shopping street in Macau.

Rua da Praia Grande

Avenidas Infante Dom Henrique and Almeida Ribeiro

In the centre the Avenida Almeida Ribeiro widens to become the Largo do Leal Senado, which is where the imposing senate building, the Leal Senado, is located. The epithet "leal" (legal, loyal) was given to the senate of Macau because in 1809 it sent a battleship in support of the Portuguese royal court, which had had to flee to Brazil in the face of Napoleon's advancing troops. The present senate building is supposed to have been built in 1784 on the site of an older building. The façade was not added until

★Leal Senado

1870 and the complete building was completely restored in 1939–40. It encloses a charming inner courtyard; on the first floor is the council chamber and the library (a number of books dating back to the 16th c.)

Santa Casa
da Misericórdia

At the north-eastern end of the square stands Santa Casa da Misericórdia, the premises of a charitable institution set up in 1498. The Casa da Misericórdia owes its inception to the Jesuit Dom Melchior Nunes Cameiro Leitão, the first Bishop of China and Japan. His head is preserved in a glass reliquary. A few steps to the east stands the Sé Catedral (cathedral), built between 1844 and 1850 on the site of a 17th c. church and rebuilt in 1938. It is built in the style of a basilica with two sturdy towers. In a shrine above the chapel lie the relics of Japanese martyrs who died during the persecution of Christians in the early 17th c.

★Sé Catedral

Santo Agostinho

From the Leal Senado the Rua Central leads south-westwards to the Church of Santo Agostinho (St Augustine), the largest church in the area, which was built in 1586, renewed in 1814 and extensively rebuilt in 1875.

★Teatro de
Dom Pedro V

Opposite stands the Teatro de Dom Pedro V, which todays belongs to the Club de Macau. A short distance further on stands the Church of São Lourenço (St Laurence; originally 16th c., but substantially renovated during the 19th c.) with its Baroque-style interior. Extending up the hill behind lies the traditional old residential district of the town.

Directly behind the Church of São Lourenço stands the St Joseph Seminary with its church built between 1746 and 1758, the façade of which is approached by a flight of steps. A museum of sacred art is housed here.

Museum of
Sacred Art

Palácio
do Governo

From São Lourenço a narrow street leads down to the Baia da Praia Grande, where the Palácio do Governo, the seat of government in Macau, a three-winged Classical building, is situated.

Running southwards from the Praia Grande towards the tip of the peninsula is a road which leads up to the hill or Penha with its chapel and Residência Episcopal (bishop's residence; at present unoccupied). Here there is a good view of the town and harbour; a little further down stands the pink-stuccoed Governor's House.

Residência
Episcopal
★View

★Pousada de
São Tiago
Ma Kok Temple

A pathway around the tip of the peninsula (on the far side of the walls of the former Fort Barra, in which the Pousada de São Taigo is now housed, and on the other side of the naval arsenal) leads to Ma Kok Temple, which is dedicated to the sea goddess A Ma. The temple, which is reputedly six hundred years old, is built on rock which was cut nearby. The colourfully painted relief of the ship by which the goddess is supposed to have landed can be seen here. Opposite the temple stands the Museu Marítimo de Macau (the Macau Nautical Museum).

Museu Marítimo

★Camões
Gardens

On the west side of the peninsula (in the area to the north of the Porto Interior and the Avenida Almeida Ribeiro) lie the Camões Gardens, from where there is a view across the Inner Harbour to the hills of the nearby Chinese mainland. The gardens boast a grotto dedicated to the great Portuguese poet Luís Vaz de Camões (1524–80), who in all probability was living in Macau at the time of the city's foundation.

On the same site as the gardens stands a building built about 1770 which once served as the administrative headquarters of the East India Company and from 1940 to 1992 contained a fine museum devoted to Camões. As a result of a change of ownership of the building, the valuable artistic collections (including Kwantung ceramics and early 19th c. paintings) are being stored elsewhere and for the time being are not available for viewing.

Protestant
Cemetery

Near the Camões Gardens lies the old Protestant Cemetery with a total of 162 gravestones.

Probably the most famous site in Macau is the massive façade of the Church of São Paulo, the only remaining part of the church which was built between 1601 and 1637 by Japanese Catholics under the direction of Italian Jesuits and destroyed by fire in 1835. The impressive façade displays a remarkable marriage of European and Far Eastern architectural styles and to examine all its details it is well worth having a pair of binoculars.

★★ Remains of the Façade of São Paulo

A good view of the whole building can be obtained from the former hill fort of São Paulo do Monte, which was established in 1620. In among the ruins of the fort stand several old guns.

Guia Hill (174m/571ft) is also dominated by an old fort (1637). There is also a chapel and a lighthouse which began operations in 1865 and is the oldest of its type along the Chinese coast. This is the highest point in Macau and offers a splendid view across the whole of the territory and the wide estuary of the Pearl River.

Guia Hill
★ Lighthouse

★★ View

To the north of the city centre, on the Avenida do Coronel Mesquita, stands the fascinating labyrinth-like Kuan Yin Temple, also known as Kun Iam Tong. The interior contains some fine Buddha figures and a carved picture of the Goddess of Mercy in the main hall. In the temple garden lies the stone slab on which the first treaty between China and the USA is purported to have been signed in 1844. There is also a legend which claims the temple is consecrated to Marco Polo.

★★ Kung Iam Tong
(Kuan Yin Temple)

Further on northwards is the Lin Fong Temple, also known as the Lotus Temple. It was built by Taoists in 1592 and for a long time was used as a resting-place for travellers to China. At the entrance to the temple garden stone creatures from Chinese mythology stand guard.

The "Portas do Cerco" are the gates on the northern edge of Macau which form the only border crossing with the People's Republic of China.

★ Portas do Cerco

Macao: ruined façade of the former Church of São Paulo

Maotai

★Sun-Yat-sen
Memorial House

On the way back to the senate building a visit can be made to the memorial house of Dr Sun-Yat-sen (Mansão Evocativa de Sun-Yat-sen) on the Avenida Sidónio Pais. This Moorish-style building was built in memory of the founder of the first Chinese republic, Sun-Yat-sen (1866–1925), who for some time practised as a doctor in Macau. The actual house he lived in was subsequently used as a store for explosives and was actually destroyed by an explosion.

Monuments

Further south the visitor will pass a monument commemorating the Portuguese victory over the Dutch fleet, which attacked Macau in 1622, and one to Vasco da Gama, who discovered the sea route to India.

Macau Archives

The restored colonial buildings along the Avenida Conselheiro Ferreira de Almeida house archives comprising books, documents and extensive records on microfilm relating to the Portuguese colonial empire and the links between Macau and both the Portuguese motherland and its Asiatic neighbours.

Taipa and Coloane

Taipa

These two islands lying just offshore from the Macau peninsula are a little world on their own. The southern end of the high curved bridge, known as the Ponte Macau-Taipa, leads on to the island of Taipa (a second bridge running parallel to the east of the first is under construction).

The island is soon likely to gain in importance as a result of the Macau International Airport (Macau's first), which has been under construction since 1988 on reclaimed land off the eastern shore of the island. The airport is expected to begin operations in 1995.

A trotting course is located in the south-western corner of the island while the University of Macau is to be found in the north. Also of interest are the old Church of Senhora do Carmo, which is approached by a flight of steps and offers a good panoramic view, and the museum of furniture which is located in a restored colonial-style house on the beach in Taipa Village.

There are five Chinese temples on the island, of which Tin Hau Temple is probably the best known. It was built just under 200 years ago and contains a decorated shrine with the picture of a goddess.

The fireworks factories which are so important for Macau's economy are located on Taipa.

Coloane

A causeway links Taipa to the island of Coloane. Coloane has a number of quays for junks, two bays with shaded bathing beaches, and an interesting church dating from the early 20th c., which was built in memory of Portuguese soldiers who had set children free from the clutches of pirates. There is an old temple nearby with a ship carved out of an enormous whalebone. The Pousada de Coloane (hotel) is situated near Cheoc Van Bay (in the south; leisure facilities).

Hac Sa Bay in the south-east can offer similar facilities with the opening of a new leisure complex, the Macau Golf & Country Club.

Maotai

Chinese
equivalent

茅台

Province: Guizhou
Area: 4sq.km/1½sq. miles. Population: 10,000

Situation and
Communications

Maotai is situated at 106°22′E and 27°49′N, about 150km/90 miles north of the provincial capital of Guiyang.

From the latter it is possible to proceed by train to Zunyi and from there by bus to Maotai.

A few hundred years ago Maotai was just a small village. In 1741 a harbour was built which became the main shipping centre for salt imported from the province of Sichuan. In the ensuing period the port underwent rapid development as a result of the growing number of distilleries established there.
    Although today Maotai has become an important trading centre for the provinces of Guizhou and Sichuan, it has retained its almost medieval townscape with stone steps, narrow alleyways and houses built in the traditional Chinese style.

History

Maotai is famous all over the world for its spirit, which has the same sort of reputation as Scotch whisky and French brandy.
    The high percentage (53°) spirit is distilled from sorghum and wheat, using a complicated distillation procedure. In China the drink symbolises hospitality and is served at almost all official banquets and celebrations. Its unmistakable aroma is a result of the lengthy and costly production process, which involves eight fermentation and seven distillation stages, as well as several years' storage in a special cellar.
    The factory lies in the centre of the town and produces an average of 1500 tons of Maotai spirits a year.

Sights

★Maotai
Distillery
(Maotai
Jiuchang)

Nanchang

K 6

Chinese
equivalent

Capital of Jiangxi Province
Altitude: 20m/65ft. Area: 65sq.km/25sq. miles
Population: 850,000 (conurbation 2,450,000)

Nanchang lies at 115°53′E and 28°41′N, in the north of the province of Jiangxi, on the River Ganjiang.
    The city can be reached from Beijing, Shanghai and Canton by rail and there are air connections with almost all the large cities in China.

Situation and
Communications

The first settlement in this area has been proved to have existed 5000 years ago. In the 2nd c. B.C. this settlement had acquired the dimensions of a town, was given the name Nanchang ("flourishing town of the south") and started to become a trading centre for agricultural produce. On August 1st 1927 the Chinese Communists under the leadership of Zhou Enlai organised an armed insurrection here and drove the troops of Chiang Kaishek out of the town for a short time. This date is considered the historical starting-point of the Red Army.
    Today Nanchang is the political, economic, cultural and scientific centre of the province of Jiangxi.

History

Sights

The Park of the 1st of August, which was laid out in 1932, contains East Lake (Dong Hu) and Hundred Flowers Island (Baihua Zhou). During the Southern Song period (1127–1279) the lake was used as a training-ground for imperial troops. Subsequently, right up to the beginning of this century, the park was the scene of imperial state examinations at district and provincial level.

★**Park of the
1st of August**
(Bayi Gongyuan)

On Hundred Flowers Island lies Master Su's Garden, named after the scholar Su Yunquin, who laid it out some 1000 years ago.

Master Su's
Garden
(Suweng Pu)

The Museum of the Revolution (Baiyi Qiyi Jinianguan) is situated in the west of the city, on Zhongshan Lu. Originally a five-storey hotel, it was

Museum of the
Revolution

337

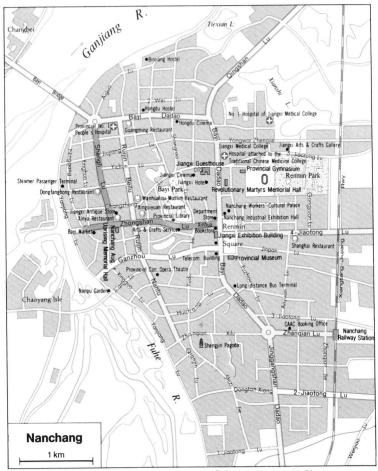

Nanchang

1 km

To Qingyunpu Taoist Temple 5 km

turned into the Communist headquarters following the uprising on August 1st 1927.

Temple of Great Peace (Da'an Si)

The Temple of Great Peace, which dates back to the 4th c., stands on Yuzhanghou Jie. Inside, a large iron vessel dating from the period of the Three Kingdoms (220–263) is kept.

Memorial Hall to the Martyrs of the Revolution

The Memorial Hall to the Martyrs of the Revolution (Geming Lieshi Jiniantang) is on Bayi Dadao and commemorates ten civil war battles and the revolutionaries who fell in them.

Provincial Museum

The Provincial Museum, which was opened in 1958, displays archaeological finds, calligraphy and ceramics from the Ming and Qing periods (1368–1911), as well as technical exhibits.

Street scene in Nanchang

The 45m/148ft high Memorial Pagoda to the Nanchang Uprising on Bayi Guangchang Square was erected in 1977 on the occasion of the 50th anniversary of the 1927 uprising.

Memorial Pagoda to the Nanchang Uprising (Bayi Nanchang Qiyi Jinianta)

The marble and granite clad building bears inscriptions recalling the events of that time.

The Gold Wire Pagoda in the south of the city dates from the early 10th c. During excavation work in the immediate surrounding area four bundles of gold wire and three swords were brought to light.

★Gold Wire Pagoda (Shenjin Ta)

The pagoda collapsed in 1708 but was rebuilt five years later. In 1788 it was surmounted with a gold tripod which was supposed to ward off fires. The octagonal 59m/194ft high pagoda has seven storeys, each with a canopy.

The actual date of the Taoist Temple of the Blue Clouds, situated in a southern suburb of the city, is a matter of controversy, with opinions ranging from 321 to 641.

Temple of the Blue Clouds (Qingyunpu)

The temple houses a museum in which are displayed works by the painter Badashanren and his pupils. Zhu Da (*c.* 1626–*c.* 1705), better known by the pseudonym Badashanren (Man of the Eight Great Mountains), was one of the greatest painters of his age.

His work, which departs radically from the style of the time, exerted a lasting influence on the modern impressionists. Badashanren disapproved of the Qing dynasty, which ruled from 1644, and in 1661 retreated to this temple for a period of 26 years.

The three main halls are dedicated to the god of war Guandi, the Taoist saint Lü Dongbin and the legendary dragon-slayer Xu Dun.

Nanjing · Nanking   K 5

Chinese
equivalent

南京市

Capital of Jiangsu Province
Altitude: 15m/49ft. Area: 867sq.km/335sq. miles
Population: 2,130,000 (conurbation 3,740,000)

Situation and
Communications

Nanjing lies on the Changjiang, in the west of the province of Jiangsu, at
118°42'E and 32°07'N. In the east of the city rises the Purple Mountain
(Zijinshan) and in the west the Stone City (Shitou Cheng), which together
are likened to a rolled-up dragon or tiger.

The city is connected to Beijing, Shanghai, Tianjin and other major
Chinese cities by rail, road, air and river-boat. There are regular charter
flights to Hong Kong.

Nanjing is the political, economic – with heavy industry of prime importance – and cultural centre of the province of Jiangsu. For centuries the city
has been famous for its velvets, silks and brocades. Important agricultural
products from the surrounding area include rice, cereals, fruit, vegetables
and tea. Nanjing University is famous both in China and abroad.

Cityscape

Nanjing owes its present appearance to the first emperor of the Ming
dynasty (1368–1644), who had a high "perimeter wall" and many buildings
erected. The building work, which began in 1369 and lasted 18 years,
turned Nanjing into an enormous city stretching over more than 33km/
21 miles. The city wall, which is built out of large bricks, rested on granite
foundations and contained numerous watch-towers which were connected by a wide stone-paved passageway.

History

The area around Nanjing was already settled over 5000 years ago. In
495 B.C., at the time of the Warring Kingdoms, an armaments foundry was
established here, around which a town gradually developed, going on to
become the capital of the Wu Empire (220–280). In later centuries there was
a succession of dynasties: the Eastern Jin, Song, Qi, Liang, Chen and first
Ming (1368: the city was called Yingtian at this time). The leaders of the
Taiping rebellion of 1853 came from here, then in 1911 the Chinese republic
followed and in 1928 the Guomindang, following the example of the Wu,
chose Nanjing as their seat of government.

Over the centuries many families from the north, fleeing from unknown
invaders, took refuge in Nanjing. The town started to acquire real economic
and cultural importance and even when the capital was moved to Beijing in
1421, the town, under its present name of Nanjing (southern capital), held
on to its economic (shipbuilding) and cultural hegemony, to which the
presence of the imperial academy made a not inconsiderable contribution.
In 1842 Nanjing saw the signing of the first treaty which laid down far-
reaching concessions to the colonial powers. After the crushing of the
Taiping uprising in 1864 Nanjing was almost completely destroyed and its
reconstruction took many years. In 1937 the city fell into the hands of the
victorious Japanese who carried out a massacre against its civilians. In
1949 the People's Liberation Army conquered Nanjing, which was declared
capital of the province of Jiangsu three years later.

Sights

★Drum Tower
(Gu Lou)

Built in 1382, the Drum Tower stands in the city centre on the west side of
the People's Square and is today used for exhibitions of paintings and
calligraphy, etc. In the Ming period (1368–1644) it constituted the centre of
the city, an honour which is now held by Xinjiekou, about 2km/1 mile to the
south.

Bell Pavilion
(Dazhong Ting)

Close to the Drum Tower stands the Bell Pavilion, which was built in the
19th c. to take the place of a tower which had collapsed in the 17th c. It
contains a 14th c. bell weighing 23 tonnes.

The Palace of the Heavenly King in the city centre dates from the time when Nanjing was the capital of the ''heavenly kingdom'' of the leaders of the Taiping Uprising. Only a small part of the original extensive building has been preserved.

Palace of the Heavenly King (Tianwang Fu)

The 395ha/1½sq. mile Black Dragon Lake in the north of the city occupies a large area of the park of the same name. It contains five small islands interconnected by bridges and causeways: Cherry Tree Island (Yingzhou), Beam Island (Liangzhou), Round Island (Huanzhou), Water Chestnut Island (Lingzhou) and Emerald Island (Cuizhou). The lake gained its name back at the beginning of the 5th c. after a black animal was seen there – supposedly a dragon, but in reality probably a crocodile.

★Black Dragon Lake (Xuanwuhu)

Under the Ming dynasty (1368–1644) Beam Island was used to house the largest state archive in China. It consisted of two parts, the register of inhabitants (Huang Ce) and the register of land tenure (Yuling Ce). The archive was manned by over 80 clerks but after a census, which was carried out every ten years, an additional thousand workers would be employed on a temporary basis.

Beam Island (Liangzhou)

Today Beam Island is the lake's main tourist attraction because it boasts many architectural monuments set in picturesque surroundings. These include the Temple of the Spirits of the Lake (Husheng Miao), the Lotus Blossom Pavilion (Shanghe Ting) and the Tower with the Beautiful View (Lansheng Lou).

Today it is still possible to see certain sections of the city wall which was built at the beginning of the Ming dynasty (1368–1644) and which at one time encircled the whole of the old centre of Nanjing. This defensive wall was originally 33km/21 miles long, 12m/39ft high and 8m/26ft thick.

★City Wall from the Ming period (Mingdai Chengqiang)

Sun-Yat-sen Mausoleum

341

To Yangzhou 82 km

Changjiang R.

Zhongshan Wharf
Monument of Crossing Changjiang
Xiuqiu Park
Yijiang Gate
Nanjing Bus Terminal
Zhongyangmen
Rehelu Square
Yancangqiao Square
Zhongshan
CITS
CTS
Shuangmenlou Guesthouse
Xinmofan   Malu
Liangzh
Dingshan Guesthouse
Nanjing Hotel
Children's Palace
Dinghuai Gate
Shanxilu Square
Xuanwu Gate
Hunan Lu
Friendship Store
Overseas Chinese Store
Jiangxin Isle
Sanchahe
Caochangmen
Beijing Xilu
Drum Tower
Jiming (Cockcrow)
Nanjing Muslim Restaurant
Beijing
Telecom   Arts & C
Bldg
Huadong (East China)
Hydraulic Engineering College
Nanjing University
Gulou Hospital
United Ticket Office of Railway
Highway and Waterway
Na
Co
Shitoucheng
(Stone Citadel)
g
el)
Qingliangshan Park
Gongren Hospital
Guangzhou
Wutaishan Gymnasium
Zhujiang
S & N China Native
Produce Grocery
Dasanyuan Restaura
Shengli Hotel
Old Guangdong Restaurant
Jinling Hotel
Bank of China
Hanzhong
Hanzhongmen
Jiangsu Chinese Medicine Hospital
Antique Store
Tongqinglou Restaurant
Xinjiekou
CAAC Booking
Jiangdongmen
Chating Dongjie
Mochou Lake
Mochouhu Park
Shuiximenwai Dajie
Renmin Market
Renmin Theatre
Chaotian (Heaven
Worshiping) Palace
Nanhu L.
Shuiximen
Shengzhou
Tongrentang
Chinese Pharmacy
Jiankang
Zhanyuan Garden
Fuzi Confu
Museum of the His
Bailuzhou P
Changle
Zhonghua Gate
Wengcheng (Jar Fortress)
Yuhua Gate
Zhonghuamen Station
Yuhua
Yuhuatai Mausoleum of M
Yuhuatai Terrace of Raining Flowe

To Zutang Hill 14 km

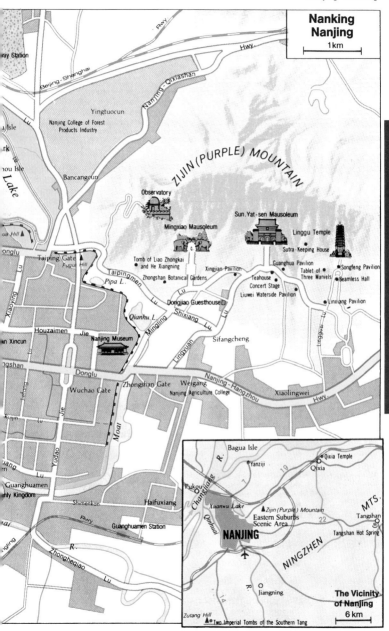

Nanking
Nanjing
1km

way Station

Beijing-Shanghai Hwy.

Nanjing-Qixiashan

Yingtuocun

Nanjing College of Forest
Products Industry

n Isle

rk

hou Isle

Lake

ZIJIN (PURPLE) MOUNTAIN

Bancangcun

ua Hill

onglu

Observatory

Mingxiao Mausoleum

Sun.Yat-sen Mausoleum

Linggu Temple

Taiping Gate

Fugui Hill

Tomb of Liao Zhongkai
and He Xiangning

Taipingmen

Pipa L.

Zhongshan Botanical Gardens

Xingjian Pavilion

Sutra-Keeping House

Guanghua Pavilion

Tablet of
Three Marvels

Songfeng Pavilion

Beamless Hall

Xiaoying

Lu

Mingling

Dongjiao Guesthouse

Teahouse
Concert Stage
Liuwei Waterside Pavilion

Linxiang Pavilion

Lu

Qianhu L.

Shixiang Lu

Houzaimen Jie

Lingyuan

Sifangcheng

Linggu

an Xincun

Nanjing Museum

gshan

Donglu

Wuchao Gate

Zhongshan Gate

Weigang

Nanjing-Hangzhou

Xiaolingwei Hwy.

Nanjing Agriculture College

Rujin

Lu

Jie

Yudao

Moat

iang
m Lu

Guanghuamen

hly Kingdom

Shimenkon

Haifuxiang

Hwy.

Guanghuamen Station

gling

Zhongheqiao Lu

R.

The Vicinity
of Nanjing
6 km

Bagua Isle

Changjiang R.

Pukou

Yanziji

Qixia Temple

Qixia

19

Xuanwu Lake

▲ Zijin (Purple) Mountain

Eastern Suburbs
Scenic Area

Qinhuai R.

NANJING

22

Tangshan

Tangshan Hot Spring

NINGZHEN MTS.

7

Jiangning

R.

14

Zutang Hill

▲ Two Imperial Tombs of the Southern Tang

343

Nanjing · Nanking

Sun-Yat-sen Gate (Zongshan Men)	The best preserved sections of the wall are to be found on either side of Sun-Yat-sen Gate in the east of the city, built in 1927.
Nanjing Museum (Nanjing Bowuguan)	Nanjing Museum is housed near Zongshan Gate in a wooden building based on the architectural style of the Liao period (907–1125). The history of the province of Jiangsu is dealt with and exhibits include ceramics and bronzes.
Remains of the former Imperial Palace	Not far from the museum, in Noongate Park (Wumen Gongyuan), lie the ruins of the former Imperial Palace, which was built between 1368 and 1379 for the first Ming Emperor Zhu Yuanzhang and later served as the model for the imperial palace in Peking. After the capital was transferred to that city in 1421 the palace in Nanjing fell into disuse and was partially destroyed. Only the Noon Gate (Wumen) and the Five Dragon Bridge are left to testify to the building's former greatness.
Tomb of the first Ming ruler (Mingxiao Ling)	On the eastern edge of the city, at the foot of the Purple Mountain (Zijin-shan), lies the Tomb of the first Ming Emperor Zhu Yuanzhang (1328–1398). It was built between 1381 and 1383 and is the largest of the 14 Ming tombs (the other thirteen are to be found on the northern edge of Peking). Over the years the mausoleum has suffered considerable damage.
	The burial site is on a massive scale, comprising not only the actual tomb chamber, but also, besides several memorial buildings, a broad "path of the soul", lined with stone sculptures arranged in pairs, representing animals, mythological creatures, dignitaries, etc.
★Mausoleum of Sun-Yat-sen (Zhongshan Ling)	To the east of the Ming tomb the visitor will come to the memorial to Sun-Yat-sen (see Famous People), occupying 8ha/20 acres on the top of a hill. The body of the famous statesman, who died on March 12th 1925, was transferred to Nanjing from the Peking Temple of the Azure Blue Clouds in 1929 and interred here. The politician's famous aphorism "The world belongs to everyone" (Tianxia Wei Gong) is inscribed over the main door-way. The main building contains the memorial hall built of white granite and the burial chamber. In the middle of the memorial hall there is a statue of Sun-Yat-sen in a seated position. His "general programme for the reconstruction of the nation" is engraved on black marble on the walls.
★Temple of the Valley of Spirits (Linggu Si)	The Temple of the Valley of Spirits is situated to the east of the Mausoleum of Sun-Yat-sen. Founded in the 6th c., it originally stood on the site now occupied by the Tomb of the first Ming Emperor. When the latter sought a site for his mausoleum, the temple was moved to its present position in 1381. It owes its fame primarily to the main hall (Wuliang Dian), still well preserved, which is remarkable for having no beams. Only bricks were used in the temple's construction and these, skilfully interlocked, support the ceramic tiled roof with its double ledge. The central and largest of the five arches which divide up the pavilion is 14m/46ft high and 11m/36ft wide.
★Purple Mountain Observatory (Zijinshan Tianwentai)	The observatory, which is situated on a western summit of the Purple Mountain, was founded in 1934 and is the largest astronomical research institute in China. It possesses many modern astronomical instruments, but also some from previous centuries, including a bronze armillary sphere from the Ming era (1368–1644).
Confucius Temple (Fuzi Miao)	The Confucius Temple consists of several buildings and is situated in a quarter of the city which frequently plays host to cultural events and other leisure activities. It was built in 1869 on top of the remains of an earlier existing building which was burned down in the early 12th c.
★Garden with the Fine View (Zhanyuan)	The Garden with the Fine View, which lies to the west of the Confucius Temple, was the private garden of General Xu Da at the beginning of the Ming dynasty (1368–1644). It was given its present name by Emperor Qianlong (reigned 1736–96), who was responsible for the two ideograms on the plaque over the entrance.

Lake Mochouhu

Bridge over the Changjiang (Yangtze-Kiang)

Museum of the Taiping Uprising	This building originally formed part of a palace belonging to the first ruler of the Ming dynasty, Zhu Yuanzhang (1328–98). In 1853, when the Heavenly Taiping Kingdom chose Nanjing to be its capital, one of its most important military leaders, Yang Xiuqing, resided here. In 1958 the Museum of the Taiping Uprising (Taiping Tianguo Lishi Bowuguan) was housed in the building.
Flower Rain Terrace (Yuhuatai)	The Flower Rain Terrace lies on a hill in the south of the city. According to legend it was here that a Buddhist monk preached so movingly that a rain of flowers from heaven fell down – hence the name. A memorial recalls the victims who were executed on the orders of Chiang Kaishek in 1927.
Mochouhu Lake	Mochouhu Lake extends over 47ha/116 acres in the west of the city. It derives its name from a beautiful woman who lived in this area in the 5th c. and whose statue can be seen to the west of the Tulip Pavilion (Yujin Tang). The present buildings date from the 1950s.
Tower of the Victorious Game of Chess (Shengqi Lou)	Close by stands the Tower of the Victorious Game of Chess, dating from 1871. Its name commemorates a game of chess which the Ming Emperor Taizu played against General Xu Da. On losing the match the emperor presented his victor with the lake and its monuments.
Stone Wall (Shitoucheng)	In the west of the city, along the bank of the Qinhuai River, stands a 3000m/ 2 mile long stone wall (averaging between 0.3 and 0.7m/1 and 2¼ft in height; 17m/56ft at its highest point), the only remaining evidence of the original fortifications built by Sun Quan, King of Wu, in the 3rd c., which also included a fortress and a defensive ring.
Bridge over the Changjiang (Changjiang Daqiao)	The bridge over the Changjiang in the north-west of Nanjing was built between 1960 and 1968 and consists of two levels: a 6772m/4¼ mile long railway bridge and a 4589m/1½ mile long road bridge. The Chinese are particularly proud of this piece of construction because it was designed and built without any foreign aid.
Surroundings Swallow Stone (Yanzi Ji)	About 12km/7½ miles north of the city rises the Swallow Stone of Yanshan Mountain on the Changjiang. On top of the rock, which resembles a swallow in flight, there is a pavilion with a stone stele with calligraphy by the Qianlong Emperor (reigned 1735–96).
★Temple of the Dwelling of the Evening Clouds (Quixia Si)	The Temple of the Dwelling of the Evening Clouds, situated 22km/13½ miles north-east of the city on the 440m/1444ft summit of Quixiashan, was originally built in 483 by the hermit monk Ming Sengshao, but was destroyed by a fire in 1855. Most of the present buildings date from 1908; they contain many sculptures from the Tang and Song periods (618–1279). The 15m/50ft high Sarira Pagoda (Sheli Ta) is thought to date back to 601.
Amatayus Hall (Wuliang Dian)	Only a short distance away stands the Amatayus Hall, built by the son of Ming Sengshao in 484 in order to pay homage to the 10m/32ft high statue of the Buddha of Eternal Life (Wuliangshou Fo). The Buddha is framed by two Bodhisattva figures.

Nanning

17

Chinese equivalent	南宁市

Capital of the autonomous region of Guangxi
Altitude: 80–100m/260–330ft. Area: 68sq.km/26sq. miles
Population: 525,000 (conurbation 866,000)

Nanning lies at 108°16'E and 22°49'N in the south of the autonomous region of Guangxi, on the banks of the Yongjiang. It is connected with other major cities by air and rail.

Nanning is a lively industrial city which enjoys a climate where everything is green and in blossom all the year round. The most important agricultural products are rice and sugar-cane, while thanks to the favourable climatic conditions it is possible to harvest subtropical fruits such as mangoes and lychees.

The Longship Festival, which takes place at the beginning of June (on the 5th day of the 5th month according to the lunar calendar) attracts countless visitors every year who come to see the longship races which are conducted with dedicated zeal on the Yongjiang.

Longship Festival

The city, which was already the political centre and military stronghold of south-west China over 1600 years ago, received its present name during the Yuan period (1271–1368). In 1912 Nanning became the capital of the province of Guangxi and in the 1950s was declared the seat of government of the Zhuang national autonomous region of Guangxi. In 1952 a minorities institute was founded here.

History

The Museum of the Autonomous Region of Guangxi is near the city centre and has a floor area of 12,900sq.m/139,000sq.ft. It was built in 1954 and extended in 1978.

Sights

It provides an introduction to the history of the various different nationalities in Guangxi. The exhibits include 320 old bronze drums, made by ethnic minority groups in the region.

★Museum of the Autonomous Region of Guangxi (Guangxi Bowuguan)

The People's Park in the north-east of the city is one of the most picturesque places in Nanning. 200 rare types of tree and flower are to be found in this very popular park.

★People's Park (Renmin Gongyuan)

South Lake extends over an area of 93ha/230 acres in the south-east of the city. Of special interest are an orchid garden and a bonsai exhibition.

South Lake (Nanhu)

On the east shore of the lake there is an excellent restaurant offering delicious fish dishes.

In the nearby Botanical Garden over 1900 different medicinal herbs are cultivated.

Yiling Yan Grotto is located on top of a hill 29km/18 miles to the north of the city (accessible by bus). Popular tradition has it that about 1500 years ago a Taoist hermit lived here. The people used to take refuge in the cave when faced with adversity. In the 1100m/1200yd long dripstone cave the visitor will see stalagmites and stalactites of every conceivable shape, while neon illuminations provide fantastic lighting effects.

Surroundings

Yiling Yan Grotto

The 1km/½ mile long lake, Waters of the Soul, lies 43km/27 miles north of Nanning in the district of Wuming. It is fed by springs which are always clear. The water temperature is 18–22°C/64–72°F all the year round. The shores of the lake are lined with bathing pools, pavilions, kiosks and other facilities.

★Waters of the Soul (Ling Shui)

Nantong

L 5

南通

Chinese equivalent

Province: Jiangsu
Area: 18sq.km/7sq. miles. Population: 293,000

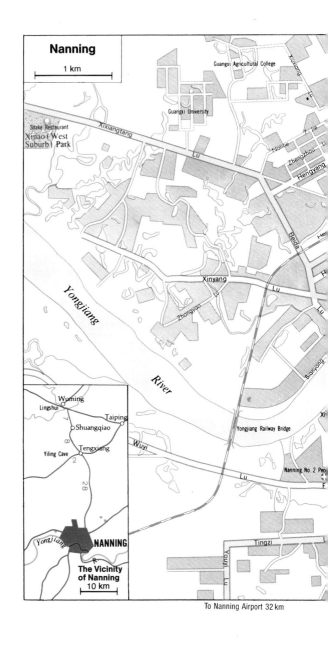

Nanning

1 km

Guangxi Agricultural College

Guangxi University

Snake Restaurant
Xijiao (West
Suburb) Park

Xixiangtang Lu

Nonie

Zhengzhou

Hengyang

Xiujiang

7 Jie

Beida

He

Xinyang

Lu

Lu

Zhongyao

Lu

Yongjiang

River

Bianyang

Wuming
Lingshui
Taiping
Shuangqiao
Tengxiang
Yiling Cave

Wuyi

Yongjiang Railway Bridge

Xi

Nanning No 2 Peo

Lu

NANNING
Yongjiang

Tingzi

You

The Vicinity
of Nanning
10 km

To Nanning Airport 32 km

348

To Yiling Cave 29 km

Renmin (People's) Park
Guangxi Stadium
Monument to Revolutionary Martyrs
Nanning Binyang Hwy
Yongwu
You'ai
Hwy
Lu
Station
Bailong Restaurant
CAAC Booking Office
Bus Terminal
CTS Guangxi Exhibition Hall
CTS
Chaoyang
Mingyuan Hotel
Gonoyuan Lu
Jiadong
Yongzhou
Hotel
Minzhu
Yuelin
Jianzheng
No 1 Hospital of Guangxi
Traditional Chinese Medicine College
Jinor
Workers' Cultural Palace
Xinmin
Cinema Bamboo and Wood
Handicrafts Store
Chaoyang Theatre
Nanning Hotel
Department Store
rts and Crafts Service
ing Restaurant
Minsheng
Dongfeng Lu
Friendship Store
Lu
Hongxing Theatre
Post & Telecom
Building
Qiyi Square
Minzu Cinema
arbour
Wharf Winter Swim-
ming Pavilion Yongjiang Hotel
Guangxi Museum
iang Bridge
Qixing
Lu
Xinghu Lu
iatre
Zhongshan Lu
Guangxi Gymnasium
Bank of China
Guangxi Arts College
(South L.)
Taoyuan
Fish Restaurant
Nanhu
Guangxi People's Hospital
Tianhu
(South L.) Park
rafts Factory
Cinema
Hed
Nanning Stadium
Lu
Nanhu Lake
Guangxi
Medical College
Lu
Jintou
Hospital of Guangxi Medical College
Tingzi
Yongjiang
River
ngzi Lu
Baishacun
Jiangbin Hospital

Nantong lies at 120°51'E and 32°02'N, in the south-east of the province of Jiangsu, on the northern bank of the estuary of the Changjiang. It can be reached by river-boat from Shanghai in six hours, while there are connections by both bus and water with the provincial capital Nanjing.

Situation and Communications

Although Nantong can boast a history stretching back a thousand years, it remained until the 1950s a quiet backwater with only a few thousand inhabitants. Today, however, it has become an important industrial centre in the province of Jiangsu.

History

The Temple of Heavenly Rest in the town centre dates from the second half of the 9th c. Most of the buildings were, however, rebuilt in 1430.
  Documents are stored here which are of particular interest for specialists in Chinese architecture of the Ming period (1368–1644).

Sights

★Temple of Heavenly Rest (Tianning Si)

The importance of this museum, which was founded in 1905 in the east of the town, lies in the fact that it is the earliest modern museum in China. Its exhibits include numerous archaeological finds from Nantong and the surrounding area.

★Museum of Nantong (Nantong Bowuyuan)

Towering up about 10km/6 miles south of the town on the north bank of the Changjiang is the 107m/351ft high Wolf Mountain.

Surroundings

★**Wolf Mountain** (Lang Shan)

The summit of Wolf Mountain is dominated by the 15th c. Pagoda Holding up the Clouds, a square five-storeyed building made of wood and tiles.
  On the north-east slope of the mountain there is an old inscription, left on a rock in 937 by the then prefect of the district, Yao Cun.

Pagoda Holding up the Clouds (Zhiyun Ta)

Ningbo   L 6

宁波市

Chinese equivalent

Province: Zhejiang. Area: 1033sq.km/399sq. miles
Population: 1,040,000 (conurbation 4,980,000)

Ningbo is situated at 121°32'E and 29°51'N, in the north-east of the province of Zhejiang, 25km from the East China Sea, at the confluence of the Yaojiang and Yongjiang Rivers.
  This important port with its network of navigable canals is also a busy industrial and trading centre and has been dubbed "Little Shanghai".
  The city has connections by bus, train, plane and ship with both the provincial capital, Hangzhou, and Shanghai.

Situation and Communications

As long ago as the Qin period, about 2300 years ago, the city was of considerable importance. Under the Tang dynasty (618–907) it grew to be one of the most important ports in China. When the Song dynasty moved its seat of government to Hangzhou in 1127, Ningbo's prosperity grew in leaps and bounds. By the 16th c. foreign ships were also calling at the port and the local merchants were gradually able to extend their commercial connections to Japan, Korea, south-east Asia, Europe and even America. The first modern factories were established around the middle of the 19th c. and about this time the port was forced to open itself up to foreign powers. As a consequence of being awarded the status of "coastal port open for foreign trade", Ningbo has been able, in the last few years, to make considerable progress in the industrial and service sectors.

History

◄ *Curious dripstone formations in the Yiling-Yan Grotto (see p. 347)*

Ningbo

Sights

★Unique Pavilion under the sky (Tianyi Ge)

The Unique Pavilion under the Sky, in the west of the city, was built by the high-ranking official Fan Qing between 1561 and 1566 in order to house his private library, which is one of the oldest of its kind in China. In front of the two-storey wooden building an artificial pond was laid, which was intended to provide water in the event of a fire. Originally the library collection consisted of 70,000 volumes, but over the centuries the stock has been decimated by theft. Today, however, the library has recovered its former glory and at present can boast a collection of over 80,000 books, incunabula, old manuscripts and a large number of inscriptions in stone dating from the 14th–19th c.

Tianfeng Ta Pagoda

The seven-storey Tianfeng Ta Pagoda (approx. 55m/180ft high) is situated in the south of Ningbo and dates back to 695, in other words the Tang era – hence its popular nomenclature of Tang Ta (Tang pagoda). Fire and lightning have damaged and even destroyed the hexagonal building on several occasions. The building's present appearance goes back to the year 1330, while its last restoration occurred in 1957.

It is well worth climbing up to the top storey of the pagoda in order to enjoy the superb panorama of the city.

Surroundings

★**Baoguo Si Temple**

Baoguo Si Temple, 15km/9 miles north of Ningbo, comprises a number of buildings.

Treasure Hall of the Great Hero (Daxiong Baodian)

The main hall of the temple, the Treasure Hall of the Great Hero, is consecrated to Buddha and is the oldest wooden building in the province, dating back to 1013. The temple's much venerated sculpture of Buddha dates back to 1102, as the inscription on the base of the statue testifies.

★Tiantong Si Monastery

35km/22 miles east of Ningbo, at the foot of Taibaishan, stands Tiantong Si Monastery, which was built in 300 and has been rebuilt and extended many times. The present buildings date from the Qing era (1644–1911). The monastery exerted a great influence on the course of Japanese Buddhism. In the 13th c. the monk Dogen came to study here. He founded the Sotoshu sect, a branch of the Buddhist religion which is still important today in Japan. Its adherents still continue to visit the monastery.

In the main hall three sculptures can be seen which depict Buddha in the past, present and future. The two small statues in front are of Ananda and Mahakasyaoa, two of the ten favourite disciples of Buddha. Nearby there are another 18 portraits of Arhat.

★Ashoka Monastery (Ayuwang Si)

The Ashoka Monastery was founded in 425, not far from Tiantong Si, and achieved fame through a stupa which is said to contain a bone belonging to Shakyamuni. According to tradition it was found by Liu Sake in 282. The bone is today kept in a wooden dagoba inside the stone stupa, for the protection of which a temple was specially erected. Behind the stupa can be seen a statue which represents Shakyamuni entering Nirvana, while on the back wall of the temple four guardians of heaven are depicted in high relief. On the terrace in front of the building a number of stelae are displayed, the oldest of which dates from 833. The 36m/118ft high tiled pagoda to the west of the temple was built in 1365.

★Ruins of the Hemedu Civilisation (Hemedu Wenhua Yizhi)

In the village of Hemedu, about 50km/30 miles north-west of Ningbo, the remains of an ancient civilisation were discovered in 1973. The first and second of the four excavation layers have been assigned to the Neolithic period. Among the finds should be mentioned terracotta objects, tools made of wood and bone, grains of rice, bones of breeding pigs and buffaloes. These all confirm the advanced state of development attained by these people, who must have settled in this area six to seven thousand years ago.

Putuoshan rises up some 100km/60 miles east of Ningbo (accessible from there by ship) on an island just 12sq.km/4½sq. miles in area, which belongs to the Zhoushanquando group of islands. Together with Wuteishan, Emeishan and Jiuhuashan it belongs to the Holy Mountains of Buddhism. Many legends have grown up around the mountain and island: in 916 a Japanese monk tried to bring a statue of the Goddess of Mercy (Guanyin) to his country, but when he came to this region, an iron lotus flower rose up from the water and barred his way to his ship. Thereupon the monk took a vow to build a temple, at which the lotus flower vanished. A short time later the "Temple of Guanyin, who does not wish to depart" (Bukengqu Guanyi-nyuan) was built on the slope of the mountain. According to another legend, after a long period of meditation, the Goddess of Mercy is supposed to have received enlightenment on nearby Luojiashan. She then crossed the sea with a single leap and came to rest on Putuoshan where she left behind a footprint. Between the 10th and early 12th c. 218 monasteries, accommodating some 3000 monks, were built on the mountain.

★★Putuoshan Mountain

Among all these religious buildings the Monastery of Universal Salvation stands out. Built in 1080 it covers an area of 14,000sq.m/3½ acres and comprises seven temples, 12 pavilions and 16 other buildings. The Yuan-tong Baodian Hall, the largest of all the temple buildings, will accommodate 1000 people. The second largest monastery is Fayu Si. In the Yangzhi convent the stone likeness of Guanyin is of particular interest. The prince's stupa (Duota) dates from the 14th c.

Monastery of Universal Salvation (Puji Si)

Tiantaishan, about 100km/60 miles south of Ningbo, lays claim to being the birthplace of the Buddhistic Tiantai School.

★★Tiantaishan Mountain

On the slopes of Tiantaishan there are a number of Buddhist monuments to be found. The most famous is Guoqing Si Monastery, dating from the year 598. In 805 the Tiantai School even began to be promulgated in Japan by a Japanese monk who had undertaken a pilgrimage to Tiantaishan the year before. The monastery possesses 14 halls and many works of art of incalculable value, including stone tablets, stone inscriptions and votive plaques. In the main hall a bronze statue of Shakyamuni (6.8m/22ft high; weighing 13 tonnes) from the Ming era (1368–1644) is held in great veneration. The 18 carved wooden sculptures from the 13th and 14th c. represent Luohan.
   On the hill to the east of the monastery rises a 60m/20ft high tiled pagoda which is estimated to be some 1300 years old. It has a hexagonal ground-plan and is made up of nine floors.

Guoqing Si Monastery

Ningxia

H–I 3–4

宁夏回族自治区

Chinese equivalent

Autonomous region
Area: 66,400sq.km/25,600sq. miles
Population: 4,800,000. Capital: Yinchuan

Ningxia is the smallest of the five autonomous regions of China. It lies between 104°17'–107°40'E and 35°14'–39°22'N, in the north-west of the country.

Situation

The Huanghe flows through the central and northern parts of the province, which also has a dense network of canals which has been created over many hundreds of years. Three quarters of the territory is composed of high-lying plateaux – with Liupanshan in the south – and the other quarter consists of lowland plains (around Yinchuan). The highest mountain is Helanshan (3556m/11,667ft).

Topography

China

Autonomous Region Ningxia

HEILONGJIANG

JILIN

INNER MONGOLIA
(NEIMENGGU)

LIAONING

XINJIANG

© *Baedeker*

GANSU

INNER MONGOLIA
(NEIMENGGU)

**BEIJING
(PEKING)**●

TIANJIN

(HEBEI)

NINGXIA

SHANXI

SHANDONG

QINGHAI

GANSU

SHAANXI

HENAN

JIANGSU

XIZANG (TIBET)

HUBEI

ANHUI

SHANGHAI

ZHEJIANG

SICHUAN

JIANGXI

HUNAN

GUIZHOU

FUJIAN

YUNNAN

GUANGXI

GUANGDONG

TAIWAN

XIANG GANG
(HONGKONG)

AO MEN
(MACAO)

HAINAN

The People's Republic of China

Zhonghua Renmin Gongheguo

Climate	Ningxia is dominated by a typical continental climate with an annual mean temperature of 7°C/45°F. Winters are very harsh indeed (the average January temperature being as low as −10°C/14°F), while the summers are not particularly hot (the average July temperature is 20°C/68°F). The annual rainfall is less than 200mm/8in.
Population	The Muslim Hui constitute an ethnic minority which, with 1.2 million people, forms a significant proportion of the population. In addition there are Mongols and Manchurians. Ningxia was declared an autonomous region in 1958.
History	Since the time of the Qin dynasty (221–206 B.C.) Ningxia was assigned to various different administrative areas, until it became a province in its own right in 1928. In 1958 the Autonomous Region of Ningxia Huizu Zizhiqu was formed.
Economy	Ningxia's most significant mineral is coal, while the northern plain, which is well irrigated by a canal system, is regarded as the "granary" of northwest China. Rice, wheat, millet, cotton, sugar-beet and melons are all produced, while the main livestock farmed is sheep.
Places to visit	The many places of interest are concentrated in the capital Yinchuan (see entry) and the surrounding district.

Qingdao   L 4

Chinese equivalent	青岛市
Town map pp. 356–57	Province: Shandong Altitude: 77m/252ft. Area: 244sq.km/94sq. miles Population: 1,180,000 (conurbation 6,410,000)

Qingdao is situated on the Yellow Sea, in the east of Shandong province, at 120°14'E and 36°06'N.

There are rail and air links with Beijing, Shanghai, Canton, Nanjing, Xi'an, Jinan and other Chinese cities. Qingdao can also be reached by sea from Shanghai and Dalian.

The town boasts one of China's major sea ports, which is free of ice all the year round, and it is also the chief industrial centre of Shandong province.

Qingdao is known for its beer (Qingdao Pijiu, produced by a German brewery which was established here in the 1930s) and the mineral water from Mount Laoshan (Laoshan Kuanghuanshui).

Qingdao's mild climate and beautiful, clean beaches attract both Chinese and foreign tourists.

Qingdao ("Green Island") was a small trading port as long ago as the Song era (960–1279). From 1874 onwards it grew in strategic importance as first fortifications and then military harbour installations were built. After 1898, when Germany enforced a 99-year lease for the Jiazhou region, Qingdao developed into a "European" town, and signs of this are still to be seen today. The town was occupied by the Japanese during the First World War and was promised to them when the war ended; this led to the formation of the May 4th Protest Movement in 1919. It was 1922 before Qingdao was returned to China.

Since the 1950s Qingdao has shown rapid industrial development.

This market in the town centre is renowned for the rich array of goods on sale. It is estimated that some 200,000 people visit it every day. As well as Qingdao beer and Laoshan mineral water, old furniture, second-hand bicycles, straw baskets and much, much more is here to tempt the buyer.

The pier built in 1891 in Qingdao Bay in the south of the town is 440m/480yd long and 10m/11yd wide.

At the southern end of the pier stands the octagonal Pavilion of the Rebounding Waves, built in classical Chinese style. Inside, a spiral staircase leads up to the upper storey.

The pier and this pavilion are regarded as Qingdao's emblems.

This park, named after the writer Lu Xun (see Famous People) lies in the south of the town on a rocky promontory close by the sea, and gives a wonderful view over the water.

The Marine Museum in Lu Xun Gongyuan Park is divided into two sections. In one section the exhibits cover the development of marine creatures and plant life, while the other houses an aquarium.

South of the museum a pier leads to the Little Green Isle, on which stands a lighthouse 15m/50ft high.

In all there are seven bathing beaches, the most popular being those numbered 1, 2 and 3.

The largest is Beach No. 1, in the south of the town, which is 580m/640yd long. No. 2 is a little way further east, where more than 80 hotels and health clinics lie in a row. About 1km/1100yd further east still is Beach No. 3, which is not as large as the other two.

Sun-Yat-sen Park, Qingdao's largest, lies in the east of the town.

The beautiful plants which grow there make it a favourite place for outings.

Zhanshan Temple, also situated in the east of the town and encircled by hills, was built in 1934 and is the only Buddhist edifice in Qingdao. In the

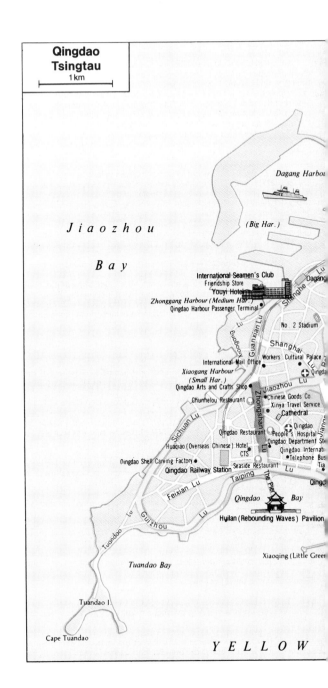

Qingdao
Tsingtau
1 km

Jiaozhou

Bay

Dagang Harbou

(Big Har.)

International Seamen's Club
Friendship Store
Youyi Hotel
Zhonggang Harbour (Medium Har.)
Qingdao Harbour Passenger Terminal

Dagang

No. 2 Stadium

Shanghai
Workers' Cultural Palace
International Mail Office

Qingda

Xiaogang Harbour
(Small Har.)
Qingdao Arts and Crafts Shop
Jiaozhou Lu
Chinese Goods Co.

Chunhelou Restaurant
Xinya Travel Service
Cathedral

Qingdao
People's Hospital
Qingdao Restaurant
Qingdao Department St
Huaqiao (Overseas Chinese) Hotel
Qingdao Internati
CTS
Telephone Bus
Qingdao Shell Carving Factory
Seaside Restaurant
Tia
Qingdao Railway Station

Qingd

Taiping

Qingdao Bay

Hyilan (Rebounding Waves) Pavilion

Xiaoqing (Little Green

Tuandao Bay

Tuandao I

Cape Tuandao

Y E L L O W

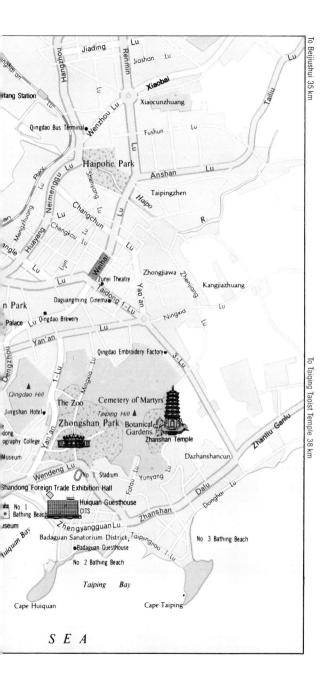

To Taiqing Taoist Temple 38 km

eastern section of the complex towers an octagonal stone pagoda of seven storeys.

Surroundings

★★Mount Laoshan

Mount Laoshan, around which countless legends have been woven, lies 30km/19 miles north-east of Qingdao and falls steeply away towards the coast. Its tallest peak, Laoding, reaches a height of 1133m/3720ft. The mountain, rich in mineral water springs, displays bizarre rock formations, waterfalls and caves.

Many years ago it was revered as the "Home of Eternal Life", where grew magic herbs which could cure all known diseases and make man immortal. It was in order to search for these wondrous plants that the Qin Emperor Shi Huangdi (259–210 B.C.) and the Han Emperor Wudi (156–87 B.C.) climbed this mountain. In the 8th c. the Tang Emperor Xuanzong sent two high officials to find and collect the magical herbs and to prepare for him the Elixir of Life. After the 10th c. more and more Taoist monasteries sprung up here, but most of them were destroyed in later years.

Temple of Supreme Purity (Taiqing Gong)

The Taoist Temple of Supreme Purity, or Lower Temple (Xia Gong), stands near the coast at the south-eastern foot of Mount Laoshan. It dates originally from the Song period (960–1279), but the present buildings were built during the reign of the Emperor Wanli (1573–1620).

The two stone tablets on the walls of the Hall of the Three Emperors (Sanhuang Dian) contain two inscriptions, one by Kublai Khan and the other by Genghis Khan. There is a superb view of the sea from here.

Temple of Great Purity (Shangqing Gong)

The Temple of Great Purity, or Upper Temple (Shang Gong) – built between 1297 and 1307 but later extended several times – lies up above the Temple of Supreme Purity, on the south-eastern slope of Mount Laoshan. In front of the temple stand some ginkgo trees which are several hundred years old.

Longtan Pu Waterfall

South of the Temple of Great Purity the Longtan Pu Waterfall plunges down from a height of 20m/66ft.

Temple of Supreme Peace (Taiping Gong)

The Temple of Supreme Peace on the northern slopes of Mount Laoshan was built in the Song period (960–1279) and has been restored several times. It is known for the strange stone formations which encircle it.

Temple of Huayan Si

The Temple of Huayan Si, on the eastern slopes, is the region's only Buddhist temple. The original mid-17th c. building was soon destroyed during subsequent wars and was rebuilt a number of years later.

The Jiushui river, some 12km/7½ miles long, snakes its way through the northern part of Mount Laoshan. Waterfalls, rock formations and monuments combine to make this region quite idyllic.

Qinghai

青海省

Chinese
equivalent

Province
Area: 720,000sq.km/277,920sq. miles
Population: 4,540,000. Capital: Xining

Qinghai lies in the north-west of China between 89°35' and 103°03'E and
31°40' and 39°19'N.
   The province was named after the Qinghaihu Lake, (Koko Nor in Mongolian). After Tibet it is the least populated province in China.
   The population, concentrated mainly in the eastern region, consists
chiefly of ethnic minorities; Tibetans, Mongolians, Kasachen and Hui. Each
minority lives in its own autonomous district.

Situation

The Qinghai-Tibet Plateau; over 400m/1312ft high, covers the territory.
The 220,000sq.km/84,920sq. mile basin Qaidam Pendi lies on this plateau
reaching heights of 2600–3000m/8530–9843ft. It is part of the Kulunshan
mountain range, which has average heights of 5000–6000m/16,405–
19,686ft, and of the Bayan Har Shan.
   In the province is the source of the rivers Huanghe, Lancangjiang
(Mekong) and Changjiang. High mountain steppes and deserts dominate
the area, only 2% of which consists of forests.

Topography

The climate is typically continental; low average yearly temperatures,
great changes in temperature, seldom, but concentrated, downpours and
long periods of sunshine.

Climate

Originally the region was chiefly inhabited by Tibetans and Mongolian
nomads. From the 3rd c. B.C. Chinese influence was felt here, becoming

History

China

Qinghai Province

**The People's
Republic of China**
Zhonghua Renmin Gongheguo

more pronounced from the 6th c. onwards. Later Qinghai was included in the places which came under Tibetan and Tangut control, until it finally became completely Chinese.

Trade and Industry

Industry mainly consists of the manufacture of agricultural products textiles and food. From the rich natural resources oil, uranium and coal are mined; salt is extracted from the salt water lakes.

Of great importance is livestock farming (yak, sheep, camels, and horses). In the river valleys near Xining and on the southern edge of the Qaidam Pend basin arable farming includes barley, oats, maize, millet, and sweet potatoes.

Places to visit

Tourism in this province is still very underdeveloped except in the capital Xining (see entry); its mosques and the nearby salt-water lake, Quinghai Hu, attract a number of visitors.

Qinhuangdao   K 3–4

Chinese equivalent

Province: Hebei. Area: 363sq.km/140sq. miles
Population: 460,000 (conurbation 2,390,000)

Situation and Communications

Qinhuangdao lies at 119°37′E and 39°52′N, in the north-east of the Hebei province, on the Bohai Sea, 260km/161 miles from Tianjin and 400km/ 248 miles from Beijing.

There are rail connections with Beijing (4–5 hours), Tientsin (3 hours) and Shenyang (about 6 hours).

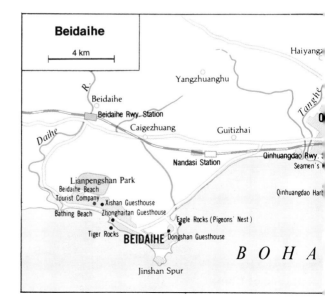

The city's port plays an important role in Chinese trade. The city itself is separated into three districts about 15km/9 miles apart: Beidaihe in the west, Qinhuangdao in the centre and Shanhaiguan in the east.

The Shanhaiguan is the most important pass in the east of the Great Wall. The fortress, originally constructed in 1381 – the present structure dating from 1639 – is situated in the centre of Shanhaiguan. It has four gates protected by towers. There are 68 embrasures in the wall for archery purposes.

Sights

★★ Shanhaiguan Fortress

Hanging on the east gate roof ledge is a large wooden tablet bearing the inscription: "First gate on earth" (Tianxia diyiguan). It was engraved by one of the graduates of the imperial examinations.

The extension of the citadel leading to the sea is known as the Head of the Old Dragon and forms the eastern end of the Great Wall.

Head of the Old Dragon (Laolongtou)

The Meng Jiangnu Miao Temple lies about 5km/3 miles to the west of the Shanhaiguan Fortress. By order of the Qin Emperor Shi Huangdi hundreds of thousands of labourers had to rebuild the Great Wall in the 2nd c. B.C. According to an old legend, Meng Jiangnu came to Shanhaiguan from far away to search for her husband who was doing socage work here. When she discovered that he had long since died from the hard labour, she cried so much that a completed section of the wall collapsed, thus releasing her husband's corpse. Meng carried the section to the coast and threw it and him into the sea.

★ Meng Jiangnu Miao Temple

The temple, consisting of two halls, was erected several hundred years ago by the residents in this area. The front hall houses a terracotta statue of Meng Jiangnu. Some of the dedications engraved on the many stone tablets here originate from the Qing emperors Qianlong, Jiaqing and Daoguang.

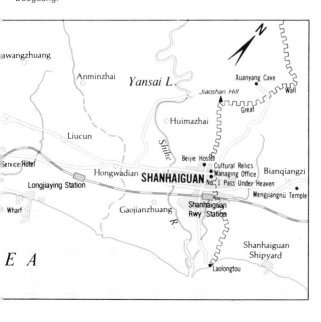

Quanzhou

★★ Beidaihe	Beidaihe is one of the most popular holiday and health resorts in China with numerous guesthouses and sanatoriums. The beach, the mild climate and the many parks attract large numbers of visitors. In 1898 the status of Beidaihe was raised when, by imperial decree, it was chosen as a health resort. At that time Europeans and wealthy Chinese built their villas here, but after 1949 Beidaihe became the health resort for the workers and sanatoriums were then erected.
Climate	The climate on this coastal stretch is very mild; in the summer the average temperature is around 23°C/72°F. The bathing season normally lasts from May to October.
Beidaihe Beach (Beidaihe Haibin)	The 10km/6 mile long, 2km/1 mile wide beach, with its many rocks and cliffs, is situated in the west of Beidaihe. In addition to a number of bathing establishments, some of which date back to the late 19th c, there are also five public gardens. The beach is divided into east, west and central sections, the west section being reserved for foreigners. Walking along the beach towards the east we reach the Tiger Rocks.
The Lotus Blossom-stones Park (Lianshuashi Gongyuan)	The Lotus Blossom-stones Park, also known as the Lianpengshan Gongyuan, extends from the west of Beidaihe on the pine covered hill of Donglian Feng. Here visitors can find the Guanyin Si temple.

Quanzhou   K 7

Chinese equivalent	泉州市
	Province: Fujian Altitude: 200m/656ft. Area: 530sq.km/204sq. miles Population: 120,000 (conurbation 400,000)
Situation and Communications	Quanzhou lies at 118°35′E and 24°52′N in the south-east of the Fuijian province on the Jinjiang estuary. From Xiamen and Fuzhou it is accessible by air or by sea.
History	Already in the 6th c. Malayan ships docked in Quanzhou, and it was founded in about 700. Quanzhou grew until in the 10th c., under the Tang, it had become with Canton and Yangzhou one of the three largest Chinese international trading ports. From the 11th c. to the 14th c. the city had its greatest flowering. At this time the woven satin which was manufactured here was even sold in the European market. Some expert linguists think that the word satin is taken from "Zaiton", which is the name Marco Polo gave to Quanzhou in his work "Millions". The Venetian travelled back to Italy from Quanzhou in 1292, and noted in his travel journal: "Zaiton is the biggest port in the world". During the following centuries, the city attracted many foreign dealers, missionaries, and travellers, many of whom finally settled here. In the 15th c. the city lost its status as a trading centre.
Sights ★Mosque of Peace and Clarity (Qingjing Si)	The Mosque of Peace and Clarity, situated in the Tumen Jie in the south-east of the city, was erected in 1009 in the style of a prayer house of Damascus. The construction was financed by donations from foreign Muslims. It was restored in 1310. Islamic merchants were already coming here in the 7th c. to seek trade. As the mosque is one of the oldest in the whole of China, the government placed it under its protection. For this reason an order by the Ming Emperor Chengzu is engraved on a stone tablet inside the mosque which dates from 1407. The order begs respect for this important building and reverence for

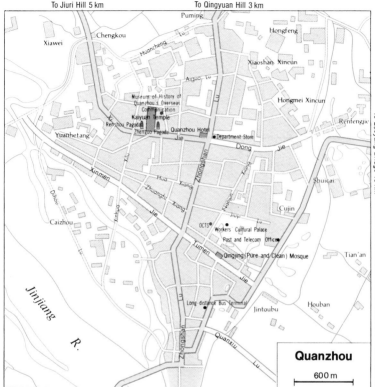

To Jiuri Hill 5 km   To Qingyuan Hill 3 km

Puming

To Luoyang Bridge 10 km

Quanzhou

600 m

To Cao'an 15 km   Shijing 42 km   To Houzhu Harbour 10 km

the Islamic faith. The impressive main gate is still preserved. On the mosque walls passages from the Koran are engraved in old Arabic.

The Temple of the Beginning of the New Age, situated to the north-west of Quanzhou, in Xi Jie street, dates from 686. It is one of the largest temples in China with an area of 70,000sq.m/22,967ft. At one time more than one thousand monks were reported to have lived here.

★★Temple of the
Beginning of the
New Age
(Kaiyuan Si)

The 20m/66ft high main building, the Buddha Hall, was erected between 1368–1644 under Ming rule on the remains of the previous building. The 24 extremely finely chiselled statuettes on the columns represent Apsaras. The base of one of the columns is decorated with sphinxes; a sign that the early Chinese were aware of Mediterranean culture. On an altar in the rear section of the hall there is an interesting statue only 50cm/19in. high, the "thousand armed goddess of mercy". Note that no two arms are exactly alike.

The Buddha Hall
(Daxiong Baodian)

More than ten thousand books of sacred writings are kept in the Pavilion of the Sacred Books (Cangjinag Ge).

Pavilion of the
Sacred Books
(Cangjiang Ge)

Towering in front of the temple are two stone pagodas, the emblems of Quanzhou. The eastern pagoda Zhenguo Ta (48m/157ft high) dates from

Stone Pagodas
(Shuangta)

363

Temple of the Beginning of the New Age

the end of the Tang period (618–907). The pagoda has five floors and an octagonal ground plan. Its substructure is decorated with 39 bas-reliefs crafted from alabaster, portraying events in the life of Shakyamunis. The 44m/144ft high western Pagoda of Longevity (Renshou Ta; from the first half of the 10th c.), is similar to the Zhenguo Pagoda, except that its base is decorated with stylised patterns of birds and flowers.

★Museum of the History of Foreign Trade (Haiwai Jiaotongshi Bowuguan)

To the east of the Kaiyuan Si temple is the Museum of the History of Foreign Trade (founded 1959). It is divided into three sections: in the first section is a 24m/26yd long, 9m/10yd wide sailing ship from the Song period (960–1279). It was discovered in 1974, near the port of Houzhu in Quanzhou Bay about 10km/6 miles south east of the city. The second section displays hundreds of sculptures and stone tablets with inscriptions in old Chinese, Latin, Syrian and old Arabic; they date back to the Song and Yuan era (10th–14th c.). In the last section over 300 ceramic pieces are displayed; these were crafted in Quanzhou from the 10th c. onwards and were intended for export.

Surroundings

Mountain of Clear Springs (Qingyuan Shan)

The 490m/1608ft high Mountain of Clear Springs is also known as the Beishan (north mountain), its name being taken from Quanzhou "city of springs". It is said that there were once many Daoist temples here.
 The 5m/16ft high Rock of Laotse (Laojun Yan), a figure of the philosopher, dates from the Song period (960–1279).
 In a building on the Amitabha rock (Mituo Yan), can be seen a tall statue of the Amitabha Buddha.

★Ninth Day Mountain (Jiurishan)

The Ninth Day Mountain is situated 5km/3 miles to the west of the city on the bank of the Jinjiang River. Even in the Song period it was a popular goal of pilgrims. According to tradition many people moved to Fujian from the north in the 3rd and 4th c. Every year on the ninth day of the ninth month of the moon, the people came to Jiurishan to look in the direction of their home and this has given the mountain its name.

The slopes of the twin-peaked mountain are decorated with more than 70 inscriptions, some of which are the work of poets who came to this place. Thirteen of these inscriptions are in memory of the sacrificial ceremonies which the Governor of Quanzhou held here between 1104 and 1266 to beg the gods to protect the Chinese traders at sea.

The western peak is crowned with a 4.5m/15ft high Buddha sculpture on a lotus-flower throne, dating from the 10th c.

On the Mountain of Souls (Lingshan) on the eastern edge of Quanzhou, are buried two students of the prophet Mohammed. They came here in the early 7th c. to spread the word of Islam. Behind the graves is a marble plate dating from 1323 inscribed in Arabic.

★Holy Islamic Grave Yard (Yisilanjiao Shengmu)

The bridge, erected in the years 1053 to 1059, which spans the Luoyang river 10km/6 miles to the north-east of the city is 843m/2765ft long and 7m/23ft wide. The pavilion on the middle of the bridge is covered with many stone tablets, with inscriptions up to 1000 years old. The 46 pylons were part of the original structure which was seriously damaged by an earthquake in 1607.

Luoyang Qiao Bridge

In the little village of Shijing stands the House of General Zheng Chenggong (42km/26 miles to the south of Quanzhou). He was born here in 1624. Zheng freed Taiwan from the Dutch rulers on February 4th 1662 and died only three months later. His body was buried in the family graveyard of Shuitou, some 10km/6 miles to the north of this house. In 1962 the house was converted into a museum in order to keep the memory of the national hero alive.

House of General Zheng Chenggong (Jinianguan)

Qufu

K 4

Chinese equivalent

Province: Shandong
Altitude: 63m/206ft. Area: 895sq.km/345sq. miles
Population: 510,000

Qufu lies at 116°58′E and 35°36′N, in the south of the Shandong Province, some 170km/105 miles to the south of the provincial capital of Jinian, with which there are connections by rail and bus.

Situation and Communications

In the "spring and autumn periods" (770–476 B.C.) Qufu was the capital of the dukedom of Lu. As this is the birth place of Confucius (see Famous People), the city has remained a "mecca" for his followers.

History

Sights

The temple complex (22ha/54 acres) was built in 478 B.C., only one year after the death of the philosopher at the instigation of Duke Lu Aigong. The temple stands on the site of the house where Confucius was born. In the course of centuries the building has been repeatedly damaged, restored over 60 times and extended. The alterations finally ceased in the 18th c., and since then the building has remained unchanged.

The 1km/½ mile long and over 200m/218yd wide temple grounds, surrounded by cyprus trees, incorporate nine courtyards lined by groups of 466 buildings of various designs. Together with the Imperial Palace in Beijing and the Imperial Summer Palace in Chengde, the temple is one of the three outstanding creations of ancient Chinese architecture.

★★Confucius Temple

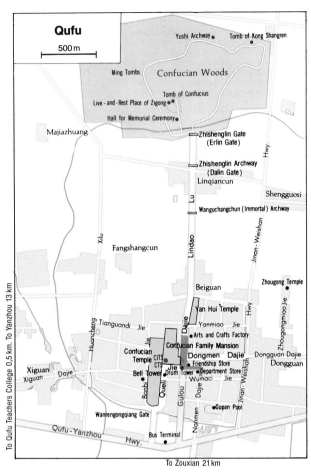

There is a defence tower on each of the four sides of the red curtain wall. The main buildings are arranged along a north–south axis, with the side buildings lying symmetrically next to them.

The Star Gate forms the main entrance and leads to the first courtyard with its decorative gates of the Ming period (1368–1644).

The second courtyard is entered by the Gate of the Omniscient (Sengsi Men) which also dates from the Ming period; this courtyard is guarded by two stone warriors of the Han period (206–220 B.C.), former grave goods. They stand 2.54m/8ft to 2.30m/7ft high; one is armed with a sword, the other with a lance.

The core of the temple complex is entered through the Dazhong Men Gate.

Tongwen Men Gate

The Tongwen Men Gate leads into a courtyard with four imperial steles dating from the Ming period.

Confucian Temple

To the north-east and north-west of this are two guest houses which once offered hospitality to the people who carried out the ceremonies held in honour of Confucius.

The Pavilion of the Literary Star, erected in 1018, was rebuilt in 1191 and extended in 1500. Collections of handwriting by several emperors were once housed here. The structure is an outstanding example of traditional Chinese architecture.

Pavilion of the Literary Star (Kuiwen Ge)

The Thirteen Pavilions of the Imperial Steles (Shisan Yubei Ting) date from various eras.
They contain 53 steles which were engraved by emperors.

Thirteen Pavilions of the Imperial Steles

The next courtyard is entered by the Dacheng Men Gate where another pavilion, the so-called Apricot Altar, is situated. This was where Confucius taught his students, and a stone tablet dating from the 12th c. can be seen on the altar. In 1569 a pavilion was erected around this historically important altar. The rectangular structure housing two steles has a two-tiered roof, covered in yellow ceramic tiles.
In front of the pavilion can be seen a stone censer dating from the Song period (960–1279).

Apricot altar (Xintan)

This hall is 32m/105ft high, 34m/111ft long and 54m/177ft wide. It dates from the 11th c. and is the main building of the complex. Here were held the ceremonies in honour of Confucius. Throughout the centuries it has been damaged several times, and in 1724 it was completely rebuilt. The hall, which stands on a 2m/6ft high terrace, has stone columns, dragon reliefs, and a yellow ceramic tiled roof. Apart from the statue of Confucius, statues of his sixteen pupils are also housed here. All the statues are made of painted earthenware.

Hall of Great Achievements (Dacheng Dian)

The Hall of Sleep, dating from 1019, is dedicated to the wife of Confucius. It was restored and extended in 1500 and completely rebuilt in 1730.

Hall of Sleep (Qingdian)

Qufu

Hall of the Signs of the Wise Man (Shengji Dian)

In the Hall of the Signs of the Wise Man (1592) are 120 engravings in stone, portraying scenes from the life of Confucius; they were engraved by famous painters and calligraphers between the 8th c. and the 13th c.

Apart from the main buildings the following monuments are of interest: Old Fountain of Confucius (Kongzhai Gujin) to the east of the Xintan, and the Red Lu Wall (Lu-Bi), where the works of Confucius were hidden when the Qin Emperor Shi Huangdi buried his followers alive and burnt all the master's writings. The Hall of Songs and Rites (Shili Tang) is supposed to commemorate the important teachings of Confucius. In the western part of the park is the Jinsi Tang Hall where are kept old musical instruments which were played at the ceremonies.

★Kong Family Residence (Kong Fu)

This is the residence of Confucius, which is the Latinised name for Kong Fuzi, the equivalent of Master Kong. Lying to the east of the Temple of Confucius, it has a total area of 16ha/39 acres. In the Han period (206–220 B.C.) the family, already titled and possessing considerable wealth, had to administer the master's temple and supervise the rites and ceremonies. During the Ming period (1368–1644) residences were built for them next to the temple. The residential quarters, consisting of nine courtyards, numerous buildings and a garden, is divided into three sections. In the middle section are various offices, the former seat of the local government of Qufu and the bedchambers of the family members. The eastern section is reserved for religious ceremonies and rituals. The western section, which originally housed a library and several studies, has now been converted into a hotel.

Yanmiao Temple

The Yanmiao to the north of Qufu was erected in 200 B.C. for Yan Hui, the favourite pupil of Confucius. The untimely death at 32 of the extremely gifted Yan Hui affected Confucius deeply. The main hall is supported by four stone columns which are decorated with dragon motives, the roof is covered with green glazed ceramic tiles.

Surroundings

★Kong Family Woods (Konglin Woods)

In these 200ha/494 acre woods (situated 1.5km/1 mile from the city), Confucius, his son, his uncle, and many more of his direct and indirect ancestors were laid to rest. Growing here are more than 20,000 old trees some of which are said to have been planted by Confucius himself.

From the centre of Qufu a wide straight road leads to the cemetery. On the way we pass the three great gate arches: the Arch of Eternal Spring (Wanguchangchun Fang), the Arch of the Sacred King (Zhishenglin Fang) and the Gate of the Sacred King (Zhishenglin Men) – the entrance to the cemetery.

Grave of Confucius

The master's grave mound – although it is not certain whether he is actually buried here – rises up in the centre of the cemetery. The gravestone (1443) carries the inscription "Grave of the Sacred King of Culture, who achieved Absolute Perfection". To the east of the grave are buried his son and grandson.

Grave of Shangren Kong

In the north-eastern corner of the the cemetery Shangren Kong is buried; he also was a descendent of Confucius and a well known dramatist who lived between the 17th c. and 18th c.

★Nishan Mountain

30km/18 miles to the south-west of Qufu rises the Nishan Mountain. On its eastern slope stands a 10th c. Confucius temple. Behind the temple lies the well-known Grotto of Confucius (Kongzi Don).

Qufu: a ceremony in the Confucian Temple ▶

Sanya

Grotto of Confucius (Kongzi Dong)	According to tradition Confucius was born in a nearby village and brought here soon after his birth by his father, who abandoned him at the foot of the Nishan because he was so ugly. A tigress brought him to this grotto and nursed him day and night until the repentant parents returned to collect their child.
Pavilion of the River View (Guanchuan Ting)	A few yards above the grotto stands the Pavilion of the River View, where Confucius according to local legend, uttered the famous phrase "as the river flows, so everything flows".
★★Han Tombs on the Yinqueshan and the Jinqueshan	In Linxin, some 200km/124 miles to the south-east of Qufu at the foot of the Yinqueshan and the Jinqueshan are situated old graves, most of them dating from the early Western Han period (Yinqueshan, Jinqueshan, Hanmu; 206 B.C.–A.D. 23).
Tomb No. 1	Discovered in tomb No. 1 on the Yinqueshan in 1972 were 4942 bamboo strips covered in closely written Chinese characters. These are fragments of two thousand year old works from an era before paper was invented. Before this significant find only the titles of a few works were known, eg.: "The art of war of Sun Bin".
Tomb No. 2	Grave No. 2, also opened in 1972, contains 32 strips of bamboo which clearly represent sections of a calender of the year 134 B.C.
Tomb No. 9	In tomb No. 9 on the Jinqueshan archaeologists came across a coffin lid in 1976 which was decorated with a 200cm/78in. long, 42cm/16in. wide magnificently coloured silk painting. It shows heaven, the mortal life of the buried person and hell.

Sanya

18

Chinese equivalent	三亚
	Province: Hainan Area: 1878sq.km/725sq. miles Population: 70,000 (conurbation 420,000)
Situation and Communications	Sanya, China's southern-most city, lies at 109°29'E and 18°10'N on the southern tip of the Hainan Island. It has connections by air with the provincial capital Haikou and Canton. On the clean white beaches of Sanya bathing is possible throughout the year. Extensive construction work on new hotels and holiday villages is in progress.
Surroundings Stag Cape (Lu Huitou)	Stag Cape is the southern tip of Hainan island 6km/4 miles south of Sanya. Its shape is reminiscent of a deer with its head facing backwards. The rocky beach is rich in coral-reefs.
★Cave of the Fallen Paintbrush (Luobi Dong)	The over 3m/10ft deep Cave of the Fallen Paintbrush lies 10km/6 miles to the west of the city on the south-western slope of a mountain. Here can be seen a stalactite which looks like a giant paint brush. Underneath a bulging stone catches the lime drops which fall from its roof. Before the local residents send their children to school for the first time they put them to a little test in this grotto: If the child succeeds in catching a falling drop in the palm of his hand then he will achieve good marks and a successful journey through life; otherwise other possibilities must be explored.

Sanya: "End of the World" Cape

The Cape at the End of the World, some 24km/15 miles to the west of Sanya, was once renowned as "the most remote spot in the world".
   On the rocks which lie around the cape numerous ideograms can be identified; they were carved in 1733 by the provincial governor and other civil servants of the time. The inscriptions repeatedly concern the remote geography of this stretch of land: "Absolute End of the World", "Beginning of the Sea", "Pillars of the Southern Firmament", etc.

Cape at the
End of the World
(Tianyahaijiao)

Shaanxi

I–J 4–5

陕西省

Chinese
equivalent

Province
Area: 195,000sq.km/75,270sq. miles
Population: 33,630,000. Capital: Xi'an

Shaanxi lies between 105°29'–111°15'E and 31° 42'–39°35'N in the north of China with the River Huang flowing through the province from west to east. In the east the River Huanghe separates Shaanxi from the province of Shanxi. The southern border runs over the Micangshan and Dabashan mountains (up to 2709m/8888ft).
   The plain of the Huang, where about half the population lives, is the main residential and industrial area of the province.

Situation

Shaanxi incorporates a loess plateau (1000–2000m/3281–6562ft), dominated by the mountainous area of Baiyushan with its deep valleys. To the south is the adjoining Huang plain which lies at 300–600m/984–1968ft, and which is bordered by the Qinlingshan (the highest mountain is the Tai-

Topography

China

Shaanxi Province

The People's Republic of China
Zhonghua Renmin Gongheguo

baishan 3767m/12,359ft), which in turn falls steeply to the south into the valley of the Hanshui river.

Climate

The Qinlingshan forms the border separating the steppe climate in the north from the humid subtropical climate in the south. Precipitation, which declines towards the north, falls between May and October.

History

Finds from the mesolithic and neolithic period verify that the valley of the Huang was among the earliest areas in China to be inhabited by humans. The Zhou dynasty resided here (11th c.–221 B.C.), as did the Qin dynasty (221–206 B.C.).

Until the 9th c. Shaanxi remained the political, industrial and cultural centre of China, when the seat of government was transferred to the east and the north. The area suffered a decline between 1876 and 1879, and in 1928 several million people starved to death here.

Economy

In the development of trade and industry Shaanxi stands far behind that of the coastal provinces. Its most important branches of industry are cotton manufacture and engineering, followed by coal and oil production, iron metallurgy, chemicals, building materials and electronics. Coal and iron-ore are mined, and oil, gold and salt extracted. Energy is produced by thermal and hydro-power stations on the Hanshui.

Varying climatic zones determine the type of agriculture here. The growing period in the south is 260–280 days a year, in the Huang valley it is 240 days and in the north only 190 days a year. In the Huang plain, wheat and cotton are cultivated, in the south rice, maize, and pulses are grown, also oranges and tea. The most important agricultural produce in the north is millet and wheat. Roughly a third of the arable land is irrigated.

Places to visit

The capital Xi'an (see entry) and its surroundings offer countless sights. A visit is recommended to Yan'an (see entry), the birthplace of the Maoist revolution.

Shandong

山东省

Chinese
equivalent

Province
Area: 153,300sq.km/59,173sq. miles
Population: 85,700,000. Capital: Jinan

The densely populated province of Shandong lies between 114°36'–
122°43'E and 34°25'–38°23'N on the Bohai and the Huanghai seas.

Situation

The territory consists of 55% flat land, 35% hills and mountains, 9%
swamp, and 1% lakes and rivers. In the east lies the peninsula of Shandong
Bandao with its many bays, separating Huanghai Bay from the Yellow Sea.
The province is predominantly hilly, with some higher areas (Laoshan up to
1087m/3566ft). The western area joins the alluvial plains of the lower
Huangha. In the central part of the province rise the Shandong mountains
which consist of several ranges, with the Taishan at 1525m/5003ft.

Topography

The climate is of the continental type, with hot dry summers and cold
winters. The peninsula of Shandong, however, enjoys a mild climate.

Climate

The Longshan culture came into being in this area in the 3rd c. B.C. Since
the 4th c. Shandong has been an important centre of maritime trade. The
19th c. brought catastrophic flooding. The Huanghe shifted its bed in the
middle of this century but was brought under control by extensive dyke
construction. At the end of the 19th c. the area came under German influence and in the 20th c. was at times occupied by the Japanese. Since
1940 Shandong has developed, particularly in the industrial sphere.

History

Favourable natural resources and rich minerals have led to the development of extensive agriculture and industry here – particularly since

Trade and
Industry

China

**The People's
Republic of China**
Zhonghua Renmin Gongheguo

the constant high water-level of the Huanghe was brought under control by dams and regulation. Wheat and maize, millet, groundnuts, sweet potatoes, tobacco, cotton and fruit are grown. Also playing an important role are silkworm cultivation, livestock rearing and freshwater and sea fishing.

Mining of coal, oil, iron-ore, bauxite and graphite is of great importance. Apart from the dominant food and textile industry (cotton production), there has developed since the early 1960s an iron and steel industry supplying tool-making machines, vehicle, locomotive and waggon construction, as well as oil production and chemical plants. Tsingtau and Yantai are important sea ports.

Places to visit

Shandong can boast many old towns and places of tourist interest including: the seat of the government, Jinan (see entry) called the city of springs; Tsingtau, which is well-known not only for its beer and mineral water (see entry); Yantai (see Qufu) the birthplace of Confucius; Tai'an (see entry) with the nearby Taishan Mountain, and finally Weifang (see entry) where paper dragons are made.

Shanghai
L 5

Chinese equivalent

上海市

Autonomous City
Altitude: 4m/13ft. Area: 6200sq.km/2393sq. miles
Population: 8,300,000 (conurbation 14,000,000)

Situation and Communications

Shanghai lies at 121°29'E and 31°18'N in eastern China, on the Huangpujiang estuary in the East China Sea.

Shanghai is 1460km/906 miles away from Beijing from where it can be reached in a two hour flight or a seventeen hour train journey. There are also connections by rail and air with Nanking, Hangzhou, Canton and other main cities. There are three shipping lines operating services to Dalian, Tsingtau and Ningbo.

The name Shanghai means "over the sea". It is the largest city in China and the centre of the nation's trade and industry, with the biggest and most important port in the land. The city is experiencing a meteoric economic expansion, one result of which has been a massive building boom. Much of this activity is focused on the new industrial zone of Pudong, a district in the east of the city reached via the longest suspension bridge in the world.

Almost 200 universities, technical colleges and research institutions also make the city a centre for the sciences.

Owing to the high population density Shanghai has great housing and traffic problems; these should be alleviated somewhat by the opening in 1995 of the city's underground railway and by the construction in the suburbs of modern dwellings replacing the traditional houses known as lilongs.

History

The first settlement here was in the Song period (960–1279); it then became a fishing village, and in the middle of the 13th c. a small city grew up on the west bank of the Huangpujiang called Shanghai. Its size and importance increased considerably because of a flourishing foreign trade and it almost reached its present size. In the 16th c. silk and cotton weaving developed. During this period a city wall was erected.

From 1843 onwards, after China's defeat in the opium wars, Shanghai became the free port of various western powers, which forced the Chinese government to concede several districts. It became a European style metropolis, separated into Chinese, French and international sectors. The Chinese viewed the foreigners as a restrictive force, and resistance to them increased.This finally found expression in protest demonstrations by students and workers.

In July 1921 the Communist Party of China was proclaimed here. Chiang Kai-shek brutally brought down the people's uprising of 1927. After the outbreak of war between the USA and Japan in 1941 the latter occupied the foreign concession. In 1949 following the occupation by the Red Army, foreign concessions and private ownership were abolished. However, Shanghai was still able to continue to assert its industrial pre-eminence. During the Cultural Revolution (1966–76) the city was the base for the "gang of four" led by Jiang Qing. Subsequently, despite the beginnings of liberal economic reforms, Shanghai lost its leading role.

The Zongshan Lu, a river promenade running along the west bank of the Huangpujiang, is also known under the Anglo-Indian name of "Bund" (Waitan). The left side of the road is lined with numerous buildings put up by the English and French at the time of the occupation; today many of these have been taken over by banks.
    Moving from south to north we see the city hall, the bell tower (the former port customs office), the Peace Hotel, the Bank of China, and the Friendship Stores. The right side is taken up by the promenade, lawns and flower beds.
    The Oriental Pearl TV Tower (open: 8am–8.30pm), on the opposite side of the river in Pudong Park, offers a quite outstanding view.
    From Shiliupu Quay, just off Zongshan Lu, it is possible to take a sightseeing tour by passenger steamer around the port and the confluence of the Huangpujiang and Changjiang rivers.
	Sights
	
	★Waitan

The Nanjing Lu, the principal shopping street of Shanghai was constructed in the second half of the 19th c.; it runs from the Zongshan Lu for several miles towards the west. Here can be found shops of every description, restaurants and cinemas, also the department stores Yibai and Jiubai.	Nanjing Lu
This open green area came into being in the colonial period on the grounds of the racecourse. The former "start" and "finish" buildings today house the city library. The northern part of the site forms the People's Park, the southern part the People's Square, which is used for parades.	People's Park (Renmin Gongyuan)
Displayed in a small museum here are, among other exhibits, bronzes and ceramics.	People's Square (Renmin Guangchang)

This museum occupies a new building in the People's Park (open: Mon.–Sat. 8.30am–5pm). Because of its large collection of art, displayed on three floors, it is one of China's most important museums.
    The bronzes date from the Shang and Western Zhou period (16th c.–770 B.C.) and the porcelain from the Song, Yuan and Ming eras (960–1644). The oldest ceramics date back to neolithic times (about 7000–2000 B.C.). Also to be seen is a picture and calligraphy collection.
    Particularly worth mentioning are the terracotta figures from the tomb sites of Qin Shi Huangdi from Xi'an.
	★Shanghai Museum (Bowuguan Shanghai)

To the south-east of the city centre, bordered by the Renmin Lu and Zongshan Lu streets, extends an area riddled with a maze of little lanes, which was formerly surrounded by a city wall. The hustle and bustle of life and dealing dominates the area. Wandering through the Old Town offers opportunities for shopping or eating and drinking.	Old Town (Yuyuan)
The Yuyuan Garden (open: 8.30am–4.30pm) situated to the north east of the Yuyuan, covers an area of over 20,000sq.m/21,880sq.yd and consists of an outer and an inner garden. The garden was laid out in 1559 by a high state official in the style of Suzhou. Outside the garden can be found the very popular Tea-House in the Heart of the Lake, reached from the bank by a zig-zag bridge.	★Yuyuan Garden
The Outer Garden, dating from 1559, which was extended in 1577 and renovated in 1760 has a few buildings. The best known of these is the Hall of	Outer Garden

Shanghai

To Minhang 22 km   To Shanghai Botanical Gardens 1 km

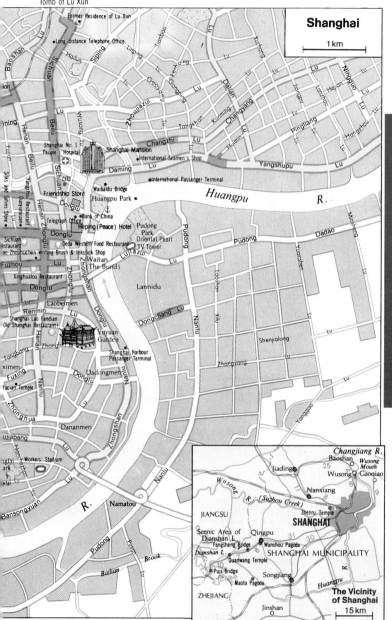

Hongkou Park
Tomb of Lu Xun

Shanghai

1 km

Former Residence of Lu Xun

• Long distance Telephone Office

Shanghai No. 1
People's Hospital
Shanghai Mansion
• International Seamen's Shop
Daming
• International Passenger Terminal

Waibaidu Bridge
Friendship Store
Huangpu Park

Huangpu R.

Bank of China
Telegraph Office
Heping (Peace) Hotel
Pudong
Park
Oriental Pearl
TV Tower
Deda Western Food Restaurant
Zhouhuchen Writing Brush & Inkstick Shop
Waitan
(The Bund)
Xinghualou Restaurant

Lujiazui

Pudong

Dadao

Lannidu

Laobeimen

Dongchang Lu

Renmin
Shanghai Lao Fandian
Old Shanghai Restaurant
Yuyuan
Garden

Shenjialong

Shanghai Harbour
Passanger Terminal

Dadongmen

Zhangyang

Dananmen

Workers' Stadium

Namatou

Pudong

Brook

Baflian

Changjiang R.

Baoshan
*Wusong
Mouth*
Jiading
Wusong Gaoqiao

Nanxiang

Wusong R. (Suzhou Creek)

JIANGSU

Zhenru Temple
SHANGHAI

Scenic Area of
Dianshan L.
Qingpu
Fangsheng Bridge
Wanshou Pagoda
Dianshan L.
SHANGHAI MUNICIPALITY
Guanwang Temple
Puji Bridge
Songjiang
Maota Pagoda
Huangpu

ZHEJIANG
**The Vicinity
of Shanghai**
Jinshan
15 km

Teahouse in the Yuyuan Garden

Spring (Dianchun Tang), where the Company of the Little Swords (Xiaodao Hui) had its headquarters between 1853 and 1855, when it ruled Shanghai. Today weapons and coins from the society are on display.

Inner Garden (Neiyuan)

The inner garden, or Park of the Purple Clouds (Qiuxia Pu) dating from 1709, once belonged to the nearby Temple of the City God (Chenghuang Miao). The patron was often a person to whom the inhabitants were under a moral obligation. Today a shop can be found in the temple.

Although the garden is only slightly more than 1ha/0.2 acres it includes all the typical features of a medieval Chinese garden: attractive little palaces, tree-lined paths, flower beds, loggia, and magnificent decorated dividing walls. Of particular interest here are the huge limestone rocks (Yulinlong Shi) and a long wall, its upper section in the shape of a dragon.

Meeting Place of the first Congress of the Communist Party of China

In July 1921 the foundation meeting of the Communist Party of China took place in the south of the city, in the French concession district. Thirteen of the 53 party members took part including chairman Mao. As there was a danger of being searched by the concessionary police, the delegates finished the meeting early. They then completed their deliberations on a ship in Jiaxing in the province of Zheijiang.

The Meeting Place (open: 8.30–11am and 1–4pm except Mon. and Thur. when 1–4pm only) is situated at the corner of Xingye Lu and Huangpulu. Displayed in a small museum are various exhibits documenting the history of the revolution.

Fuxing Gongyuan Park

The Fuxing Gongyuan Park in the south of the city was created in 1909 in the former French concessionary district. It is a favourite resting place, with trees providing shade.

Shanghai: the harbour and the Bund waterside promenade

Shanghai: in the Old Town

Exhibition Centre

Former residence of Sun-Yat-sen (Sun Zongshan Guju)	Near the Fuxing Gonyuan Park is the former residence of Sun-Yat-sen (see Famous People), situated at No. 7 Xianshan Lu, where the statesman lived from 1920. The house, which has been converted into a small museum, still has the original furniture.
★Longhua Park (Longhua Gongyuan)	The Longhua Park lies in the south-west of the city. It contains a temple and a pagoda which reportedly date from the year 247, but have been des-troyed and rebuilt many times. The present 40m/131ft high, seven-storey pagoda of brick and wood dates back to 977. Around every storey runs a balcony with a canopy-roof over it. The last time the various temple build-ings were restored was at the end of the 19th c. Buddhist ceremonies are regularly held here.
Botanical Garden	The botanical garden, founded in 1954, is situated in the south of the city in Longwu Lu. Here can be seen reproductions of landscape scenes.
Church of Xujianhui (Xujianhui Tianzhutang)	The church, built between 1906 to 1911 in Neo-Romanesque style, is situated to the south of Shanghai in the city district of Xujiahui near the municiple sports palace. It is the largest Catholic place of worship in Shanghai and the nave can accommodate 2500 people. Both of the bell-towers are over 50m/164ft high.
★**Jade Buddha Temple** (Yufo Si)	The temple (open: 8am–5pm), situated in the north-west of the city in Anyuan Lu, houses two Shakyamuni statues which the monk Huigen brought with him from Burma. In order to find a fitting place to accommo-date the statues, he collected funds for building a temple at Jiangwan in the north-east of Shanghai. The work was completed in 1882 but the building was destroyed in 1911 during the revolution. Seven years later an under-taking was made to rebuild the temple on a site nearer the old city, and this is how the present Jade Buddha Temple came into being. The building work took ten years to complete, from 1918–28. The temple is divided into three halls and two courtyards.
Hall of the Kings of Heaven (Tianwang Dian)	In the Hall of the Kings of Heaven stand statues of the four heavenly kings, a gilded Maitreya and a gilded Weituo. The charming Hall of the Great Hero (Daxiong Baodian) has Buddhas of the past, present and future, and also eighteen Luohan figures.
Shakyamuni Statues	The two Shakyamuni sculptures were carved from a single piece of white jade. The 1.9m/6ft high statue of the seated Shakyamuni can be found on the upper floor of the Wentang main hall, where a collection of Buddhist manuscripts is also kept. The small reclining Shakyamuni (barely 1m/3ft long), portrayed entering Nirvana, is situated in a building in the west courtyard of the temple.
Zhenru Si Temple	The Zhenru Si Temple (1320) is situated in the north-western edge of Shanghai, near the Zhenru railway station. Of the original complex only the main hall of brick and wood is still preserved.
Former Residence of Lu Xun (Lu Xun Guju)	In the north of the city in Shanyin Lu is the Lu Xun (see Famous People) terrace, where the writer lived from April 11th 1933 until his death on October 19th 1936. In his study on the upper floor he translated, among other works, Gogol's novel "The Dead Souls".
Tomb of Lu Xun (Lu Xun Mu)	In the Hongkou Gongyuan Park, to the north of the house where Lu Xun resided, is the poet's tomb which was put up on the occasion of the twentieth anniversary of his death.

Surroundings

★Garden of Natural Beauty (Guyi Yuan)	The 6.6ha/16 acre Garden of Natural Beauty in Nanxiang, a little village 8km/5 miles to the north-west of Shanghai, was laid out in the 16th c. It was extended in 1746, seriously damaged in 1937 and completely relaid in 1959.

Statues in the Jade Buddha Temple

Today it is embellished with numerous pavilions, small villas, pagodas, lakes and flowerbeds. There is also a dagoba dating from the Song period (960–1279) and several stone pillars from the Tang era (618–907) with inscriptions from the Buddhist Sutra.

The north-eastern section of the roof is missing from the rectangular Buque Ting Pavilion (bu que meaning to correct a mistake). The building was erected in 1931 during the Japanese occupation of Manchuria; the missing roof section was meant to remind the Chinese of this occupation.

The Confucius Temple, situated to the south of Jiading 19km/12 miles north-west of Shanghai, was built in 1219 and restored during the Yuan, Ming and Qing dynasties. In 1958 the municipal museum of Jiading was erected here where, among other exhibits are kept 90 stone tablets with old inscriptions.

Confucius Temple of Jiading (Jiading Kongmiao)

The 48.5m/158ft high nine-storey pagoda, also known as the Four-cornered Pagoda (Fang Ta), was built during the rule of the Northern Song between 1068 and 1094 and was renovated between 1975 and 1977. It is situated 30km/18 miles to the south-west of Shanghai in the city of Song-jiang. Its rectangular ground plan makes it exceptional as pagodas from the Song period were usually octagonal; the rectangular shape is typical of the Tang period (618–907).

★Xingsheng-jianosi Ta Pagoda

It can be seen that the pagoda's substructure leans slightly to the south-east and that the canopies on the south-east façade are longer – these are precautions taken by the builders of the Song period against typhoons from the south-east.

Near Songjiang on the Tianmashan mountain stands the Pagoda for Guarding Pearls, also known as the Leaning Pagoda (Xie Ta). It dates from 1079 and was almost burned down in 1788. Afterwards bricks were torn from the building which is why it leans towards the west.

Pagoda for Guarding Pearls (Huzhu Ta)

Garden of Natural Beauty

Pagoda of Longevity (Wanshou Ta)	The Pagoda of Longevity was erected in 1743 by the occupants of the town of Qingpu, 31km/19 miles to the west of Shanghai, to wish the emperor Qianlong a long life. He did in fact answer their prayers and considerably lowered the taxes to be paid. The pagoda was originally made from bricks and wood, although the wooden section was destroyed by fire in 1883.
Freedom Bridge (Fanshang Qiao)	The Freedom Bridge, some 10km/6 miles to the south-west of the Pagoda of Longevity, is 71m/230ft long and 6m/19ft wide, the longest stone bridge in Shanghai. It was built in 1571 with funds collected by the monk Xing Chao. He was also responsible for stopping the local people fishing under the bridge, and even suggested to them that they should throw back the fish which they had already caught. The original bridge collapsed in 1814; the present bridge was built a little later at the instigation of another monk.
★Dianshan Hu Lake	The 60sq.km/23sq. mile Dianshan Hu Lake extends out some 50km/31miles to the west of Shanghai.
Garden of Grand Scenery (Daguan Yuan)	The Garden of Grand Scenery is situated on the east bank of the lake. Some of the buildings, including the Guawang Temple and the Aofeng Pagoda have survived through the years. On the east bank of the lake is a large public bathing area.
Bridge of General Wellbeing (Puji Qiao)	The single-arched Bridge of General Wellbeing, 10m/32ft 27m/29yd long and 2.75m/3yd wide, is situated 54km/33 miles from Shanghai. It was built in 1265 during the Song period (960–1279) and all its features are typical of its time of origin – purple bricks, restricted width and a single arch with a long span. The structure is without doubt a magnificent example of bridge architecture of the Song period.
Mao Ta Pagoda	The Mao Ta Pagoda, built in the second half of the 9th c., stands 20km/12 miles to the east of the Bridge of Wellbeing, towering up on a small island in the River Mao. For a long time it served as a lighthouse.

Shantou K 7

汕头

Chinese
equivalent

Province: Guangdong. Area: 246sq.km/95sq. miles
Population: 787,000 (conurbation 9,400,000)

Shantou lies on the South China Sea, in the east of the Guangdon province, at 116°38′E and 23°24′N, some 450km/279 miles to the east of the provincial capital of Canton.

Situation and
Communications

    From Canton the city is accessible by plane (1 hour), by bus or by ship.

As with other cities in the Guangdong province the origins of Shantou are uncertain. The only fact which is definitely known is that the city was already an important centre with a lucrative ceramic industry during the Song period (960–1279).

History

    Throughout the centuries the local ceramic craftsmen developed a unique style. The decoration was carried out with particular care, even before the application of separately fired layers of glaze.
    In the previous centuries the importance of the city grew with the construction of a port.
    At present Shantou is one of China's special economic areas which in return for the promotion of foreign trade and economic co-operation with other countries has been granted a whole range of privileges.

The Queshi Gongyuan Gardens, situated 1.5km/1 mile to the south of Shantou, are separated from the city by a strait. Many tropical plants surround the two pools.

Surroundings

Queshi Gongyuan
Gardens

    In the surrounding area are 43 hills with many caves, grottoes, pavilions, arbours and flowerbeds.

Shanxi J 3–5

Chinese
equivalent

Province
Area: 156,000sq.km/60,216sq. miles
Population: 28,420,000. Capital: Taiyuan

The province of Shanxi is situated in the north of China between 110°15′–114°32′E and 34°35′–40°45′N. It is bordered in the west by the province of Shaanxi and in the centre by the Huanghe; in the north the Great Wall separates it from Inner Mongolia, and in the south lies the province of Henan. In the east the western mountain ranges of the Taihangshan wi·ich reach heights of from 1500m/4921ft to 1850m/60,698ft form the border.

Situation

The greater part of the Shanxi plateau lies at over 1000m/3281ft and is covered by a massive loess layer some 100m/328ft thick. It is only plateau-like in character in the western part, otherwise it is heavily structured by several mountain ranges – the Wutaishan 3058m/10,033ft, the Luliangshan 2831m/9288ft, the Zhongtiashan 2359m/7739ft, the Taiyueshan 2347m/7700ft, the Hengshan 2017m/6617ft – and basins (some at only 300m/984ft). The River Fenhe flows through a valley from north to south; in parts it broadens into a basin.

Topography

Shanxi has a predominantly continental climate, influenced by monsoons; the winters are cold, the summers not very hot. The average temperature is

Climate

China

Shanxi Province

The People's Republic of China

Zhonghua Renmin Gongheguo

between 6 and 14°C. Rain falls mainly between July and September; annual amounts are between 4–6cm/1–2in.

History

Shanxi can look back over a long and turbulent history. Because of its strategically important position the district was always a guarantor of power for the kingdoms of central Asia – the Jin (265–420), the Northern Wei (386–534) and the Northern Qi. Liu Yuan, the founder of the Tang dynasty, overran the Sui dynasty from Taiyuan. The foundation of the province dates from the 14th c.

Trade and Industry

Shanxi is the leading Chinese province for coalmining; also mined here are iron, titanium, vanadium, silver, zinc and copper ores. Apart from iron-ore smelting important branches of industry include engineering, cotton manufacture, and chemical and food production. Arable farming is mainly based in the Fenhe valley, in the centre of the Shanxi basin, and in the Xin Xian basin, its success depending on artificial irrigation. Crops include grain (wheat, millet, maize), soya beans, cotton, hemp, sugar-beet, tobacco and groundnuts. Cattle, donkeys, and mules are kept as draught animals.

Places to visit

The province owes its considerable number of architectural monuments, in particular those around Datong and Taiyun (see entries) to its long history.

Shaoxing   L 5

Chinese equivalent

绍兴市

Province: Zhejiang
Altitude: 5m/16ft. Area: 100sq.km/38½sq. miles
Population: 265,000 (conurbation 4,000,000)

Situation and Communications

Shaoxing is situated at 120°34′E and 30°00′N in the north of the Zhejiang province.

There are connections by rail and bus with the provincial capital of Hang-zhou 60km/37 miles away.

Shaoxing lies in a picturesque landscape between the Mirror Lake and the Kuaijishan Mountain. A network of small canals, bridges and white-washed buildings make their impression on the lovely townscape.

For over 2000 years the famous rice wine Shaoxing Jiu has been pro-duced here. Silk and tea production also have a long-standing tradition.

The history of Shaoxing began over 400 years ago. Its origins go back to a legend about Yu the Great, a heroic figure who harnessed several rivers and founded the Xia dynasty (2116 c. B.C.). According to this legend Yu was laid to rest at the foot of the Kuaijishan Mountain.

History

In the Spring and Autumn Period (770–467 B.C.) the city was called Yue and was the capital of the empire of the same name. During the following centuries many artists and scholars were either born or chose to live in the city. The famous calligrapher Wang Xizhi (321–379) lived here for a long while; the celebrated writers Lu You (1125–1210), Qiu Jin (1875–1907) and Lu Xun (1881–1938 see Famous People) were all born in Shaoxing.

The 40m/131ft high pagoda in the city centre, dating from the year 504, has been restored several times.

Sights

Dashansi Ta Pagoda

Nearby stands a memorial to Qiu Jin, who was executed here.

Qiu-Jin Memorial

This two-storey wooden house, with a garden in Lu Xun Lu street in the city centre, is where Lu Xun lived from his birth in 1881 until 1899 and then again from 1910 until 1912 when he taught at the teacher training institute here.

★Birthplace of Lu Xun Guju (Lu Xun Guju)

To the east of the house is the Sanwei Shuwu studio, a kind of private school which the author attended from 1892–97. The original furnishings still remain, including the desk used by Lu Xun.

Studio of the Three Perfumes (Sanwei Shuwu)

In the Lu Xun Exhibition Hall (Lu Xun Jinianhuan), near the birthplace of Lu Xun, photographs, letters and works by the author are displayed.

The Lu Xun Exhibition Hall

In the south of the city is the former residence of Qiu Jin. The house has been furnished as a memorial, where the life of the poet has been recorded in photographs and documents.

Former Residence of Qiu Jin (Qiu Jin Guju)

In 140 the prefect of Shaoxing at that time had the Mirror Lake excavated 1.5km/1 mile to the south of the city and let 36 rivers from the surrounding area flow into it. Since then the lake has been made famous by many literary figures. Today the lovely scenery can still be enjoyed. Valuable minerals are extracted from the water which are necessary in the fer-mentation process of the famous rice-wine Shaoxing Jiu.

Surroundings

Mirror Lake (Jian Hu)

3km/2 miles to the east of the city lies the East Lake on the spot where, around two thousand years ago, a rocky hill is believed to have existed. According to legend the Qin emperor Shi Huangdi was out riding, over-seeing the area, when he stopped at the foot of the hill to water his horse. In the Han period (206 B.C.–A.D. 220) the local residents began to remove stone from the hill to surface roads and build houses and bridges. Finally the hill disappeared completely, and in its place the East Lake expanded. Nowa-days this area is a popular place where Chinese people can spend a day's holiday.

★East Lake (Dong Hu)

Nine stone bridges divide the lake into three sections. On the banks of the lake lie two secluded caves which can only be reached by boat.

Shashi

Tomb of the Ruler Yu (Yu Ling)	In front of the tomb of the mythical ruler Yu (which lies 4km/2 miles to the south-east of Shaoxing), stands a pavilion which was restored in 1979. It houses a stele dating from the Ming period (1368–1644) with the inscription "Tomb of the great Yu". Yu was a legendary king of the Xia dynasty (21–16 c. B.C.).
Temple of the Ruler Yu (Yu Miao)	To the right of the tomb stands a temple dedicated to Yu. It dates from the 6th c. although it was destroyed and has been rebuilt. The greater part of the buildings belonging to the complex date from the Qing era (1644–1911), except for the main hall which was erected in 1934.
★Orchid Pavilion (Lanting Pavilion)	The Orchid Pavilion, set in impressive natural scenery with bamboo woods and winding streams, is situated 14km/9 miles to the south-west of the city. A stele with an inscription by the Emperor Kangxi (reigned: 1662–1723) is housed in the pavilion. Outside the pavilion a picturesque little lake extends for some 30m/32yd. In the centre of this lake is a stone tablet with two ideograms which, roughly translated, mean "goose pond". They are attributed to Wang Zizhi (see Famous People), who in the year 335 wrote the famous "Preface to the Orchid Pavilion Poetry Ccollection". The pavilion was therefore already in existence in the 4th c.
Wang Zizhi Memorial Hall	In the Wang Zizhi Memorial Hall, a statue of Wang Zizhi is worshiped. On both the side walls can be seen a few stone tablets into which several 7th c. inscriptions are carved concerning the above mentioned preface. Very near to this stands a further pavilion which houses steles with inscriptions by the emperors Kangxi and Qianlong (reigned: 1736–96).

Shashi J 5

Chinese equivalent	沙市
	Province: Hubei. Area: 12sq.km/5sq. miles Population: 198,000 (conurbation 240,000)
Situation Communications	Shashi lies on the north bank of the Changjiang, in the centre of the province of Hubei at 112°13'E and 30°22'N. It is 240km/149 miles from the provincial capital Wuhan (1 hour by air), and can also be reached by bus or by ship. There are air services to Shanghai (4 hours), Canton (2½ hours), and Changsha (1½ hours).
History	The city has a long history dating from the Xia dynasty (21–16 c. B.C.). Under Zhou rule (1066–221 B.C.), the city was called Jiangjin, which means "port on the river". In 689 B.C. Shashi became a kind of outpost to the Chu dynasty capital of the time. The great poet Qu Yuan was born here in the 4th c. In the Tang era (618–907) trade considerably improved and under Ming rule (1368–1644) the city expanded even further. At that time Shashi had 99 main roads, each of which was intended for a specific business or craft. In recent times some branches of industry have developed rapidly in Shashi, especially light industry, textiles, electronics, chemicals and engineering.

Sights

★Sun-Yat-sen Park (Zongshan Gongyuan Park)	This park, situated in the city centre, is best known for its two monuments: the tomb of the Chancellor Lun Shu'ao Mu and the Spring and Autumn Pavilion. The tomb lies in the north-eastern corner of the park. Sun Shu'ao, chancellor of the Chu empire, gained an important military victory near the city and was therefore buried here. The present tomb however was only built in 1757, long after his death.

The Spring and Autumn Pavilion was erected at the beginning of the 19th c. on the western outskirts of Shashi and was moved here in 1931. It houses a statue portraying General Guan Yu (?219) reading the classical work "Spring and Autumn".

Spring and Autumn Pavilion (Chunqiu Ge)

In the south of the city on the bank of the Jingjiang (a tributary of the Changjiang river) is the Pagoda of Longevity, completed in 1552 after four years building work.
   The octagonal seven-storey building of wood and stone, over 40m/131ft high, has 94 niches in the façade which are decorated with white marble statues. In the gold plated bronze chapel the complete text of a Buddhist manuscript has been engraved. From the top floor there is a beautiful view over the city.

Pagoda of Longevity (Wanshou Ta)

Surroundings

The ruins of Jinan are situated about 20km/12 miles to the north-west of Shashi on the southern slopes of the Jishan. Jinan, capital of the Chu empire from 689–278 B.C., was the largest city in China at that time.
   Archaeological excavations have shown that the city had a rectangular ground plan and massive defence walls, which were up to 7m/22ft high and 4.5km/3 miles long (east–west) and 3.5km/2 miles long (north–south), covering a total area of 16sq.km/6sq. miles. In the south-eastern section of the city the foundations of a building were discovered (60m/65yd long and 14m/15yd wide) which once formed part of the imperial palace.
   The city district of Fenghuangshan was transformed into a large grave-yard during Qin and Han rule (221 B.C.–A.D. 206). In addition to a 2000 year old mummy, numerous objects of immeasurable worth were discovered here, including bamboo strips with inscriptions and decorated ceramic crockery.

★Ruins of Jinan (Jinan Gucheng)

Following the other discoveries three necropolises from the Chu dynasty were found outside the defence walls with over 700 large tombs of noble families. Around the city walls thousands of Chu graves were also discovered.

Chu Tombs

Shenyang

L 3

Chinese equivalent

Capital of the Liaoning Province
Altitude: 40m/131ft. Area: 173 sq.km/67sq. miles
Population: 4,140,000 (conurbation 5,320,000)

Shenyang is situated in the centre of the Liaoning province at 123°24′E and 41°43′N. From Beijing it can be reached in 11 hours by train and from Tianjin in 9 hours; from the other main Chinese cities it can be reached by air. The city is connected with the port of Dalian by rail and a 375km/232 mile long motorway.
   Shenyang is the most important centre for trade, industry and culture in the north-east of China. It is an important engineering centre and has chemical and textile works.

Situation and Communications

Over 2000 years ago, at the time of the western Han (206 B.C.–A.D. 24) Shenyang (under the name of Honcheng) was already one of the greatest cities in north-eastern China. It has been known under its present name since the Yuan era (1271–1368), perhaps because of the military impor-tance it gained three hundred years before that as the stronghold of the Liao dynasty. Mukden is the Manchurian name for the city.

History

Shenyang

Youyi (Friendship

Liao

Xinkai

Liaoning Univers

Chongshan

Xilu

Bainiao Park

Dacheng Station

Ningsha

Minglian   Lu

Huibinlou Restau

Beijing-Harbin

Qishan

Tawan Jie

Kunshan

Huashan

Hwy

Bei

1-Lu

Huashan

Transhon   Lu

Huanggutun Station

Jie

Bei

Jie

Bei

Jie

Jie

Bei

Xinggong

Jie

Korean Departme

Jianshe Park

3-Lu

2-Lu

Bei

Zhaogong

Jianshe

Jie

Jie

4-Lu

Shenyang Institute c
Traditional Chinese Medici

Qigong

Weigong

Baogong

Cuigong

Datie

Friendship Store

Nan

Zhongshan

Nan

Nan

Dalu

5-Lu

Shenyang Railway Station

CITS

Nan

Nan

Xinhua

6-Lu

Xinggong

Yinghong

Nanjing

Overseas Chinese Hotel

Provincial Art

Nan

7-Lu

Cuihua

Joint Department Store

Zhonghua

Laodong
Park

11-Lu

10-Lu

Zhonghua Theatre

Zhonghua Lu

12-Lu

Heping Cinema

Shenyang Cultural Palace

CAAO Booking C

Shengli

Xinhua

Mizhun

Zhongshan
Park

Yingbin Restaurant

Nan

Nanjing

Shenyang Stadi

Shenyang-Xinmin   Hwy

Nan

Taiyuan

Torince

Heping

Xinhua Square

Nan

Xinhua

Heping Square

5-Ma

Nan

Matu

10-Matu

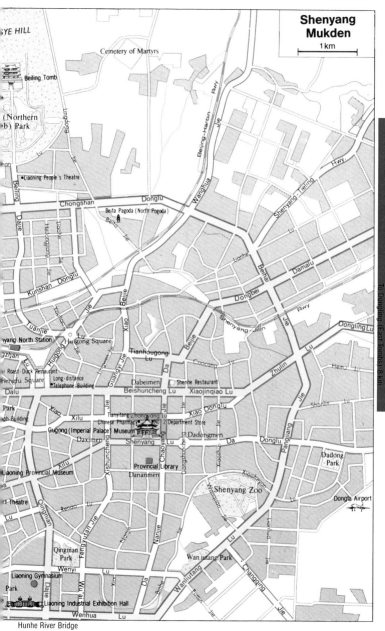

Shenyang
Mukden

1 km

YE HILL

Cemetery of Martyrs

Beiling Tomb

(Northern
b) Park

Lingdong Jie

Beijing-Harbin Rwy

•Liaoning People's Theatre

Beiling

Dalie

Chongshan

Donglu

Wanghua

Shenyang - Tieling

Hwy.

Beita Pagoda (North Pogoda)

Beita Jie

Heilongjiang Jie

Beijia Jie

Kunshan Donglu

Tuanjie

Lianhe

Dongbei

Shenyang-Jilin

Beihai Jie

Damalu

Dongbei

Beilie Jie

Xiao Da Jie

Beilie Jie

Shenyang-Jilin Jie

Dongling Lu

To Dongling (East Tombs) 8 km

yang North Station

Huigong Square

Tianhougong Lu

Caocong Lu

Zhulin Lu

Shenlin Lu

gzhan

Huigong Jie

Guangyi Jie

i Roast-Duck Restaurant
hengfu Square Long-distance
•Telephone Building

Dabeimen

Shenhe Restaurant

Beishuncheng Lu

Xiaojinqiao Lu

Hami Lu

Dalu

Park

ch Building

Xiao Dalu

Xilu

Tianyitang Zhongyang Lu
Chinese Pharmacy NO.2 Department Store

Xiao Donglu

Pangjiang Lu

Gugong (Imperial Palace) Museum
Daximen

Shenyang

Chaoyang Lu

Dadongmen

Da Jie

Dongshuncheng Jie

Donglu

Dadong
Park

Liaoning Provincial Museum

Provincial Library

Dananmen

Xiaoshan

Xiaoheyan Lu

t Theatre

Qingnian

Renao Lu

Nanjie

Wanliutang Lu

Shenyang Zoo

Dongta Airport

Fengutan Jie

Qingnian
Park

Wenyi Lu

Liaoning Gymnasium

Wan jutang Park

Changqing Jie

Park

Dalie

Xiao Lu

Da Jie

Wanliutang Lu

Jie

Liaoning Industrial Exhibition Hall

Wenhua Lu

Hunhe River Bridge

Between 1625 and 1644 Mukden was the Manchurian seat of government of the Qing dynasty which ruled the whole of China from here. Towards the end of the 19th c. it came into the sphere of influence of Russia, although the city and southern Manchuria had to be handed over to the Japanese following the defeat near Mukden in 1905.

The murder of a Japanese General in 1931 was the cause of the so-called "Mukden incident", which ended with the Japanese occupation of the whole of Manchuria. Japanese foreign rule lasted until 1945, when the Russians declared war on Japan and took Shenyang. After they had exploited the south Manchurian minerals, the new occupiers dismantled the industrial sites. In 1948 the city was captured by the communists.

Sights

★★Imperial Palace (Gugong)

The magnificent and imposing 60,000sq.m/71,760sq.yd Imperial Palace, dating from the the the early Qing era, is situated in the east of Shenyang. It is, after the Imperial Palace in Beijing, the second largest completely preserved palace complex in China. The building work took over ten years to complete (1625–36). The complex served as an imperial palace to both of the first Qing emperors, Nurhachi (1559–1626) and Huang Taiji (1592–1643). The palace complex includes several courtyards, around which are grouped numerous buildings, and is separated into eastern, central, and western sections.

Hall of Exaulted Government (Chongzheng Dian)

The Hall of Exaulted Government, built before 1632, is the centre of the middle section and houses the imperial throne and a screen with a gilded dragon as a bas-relief. It served as the audience building to the second Qing emperor Huang Taiji, and was also used for carrying out daily business.

Phoenix Tower (Fenghuang Lou)

The three-storey Phoenix Tower (1627) behind the Hall of Exaulted Governments was used for banquets.

Shenyang: detail in the Imperial Palace

The adjacent Palace of Clarity and Rest, built in 1625, housed the imperial couple's sleeping chambers and sacrificial rooms.

Palace of Clarity and Rest (Qingning Gong)

The Pavilion of the Source of Culture in the rear section of the western wing functioned as the emperor's private study. The only complete edition of the Siku Quanshu, a Chinese encyclopedia which appeared in 1772 in only seven editions, was previously kept here.

Pavilion of the Source of Culture (Wenshuo Ge)

Situated at the far end of the eastern wing, this is the oldest palace building and dates back to the early 17th c. Although the octagonal building is reminiscent of a nomadic tent, the building otherwise reveals many features of Chinese architecture. Held here were the most important ceremonies concerning the emperor.

Hall of the Great Government (Dazheng Dian)

In the Ten Princely Pavilions, which are set in two rows in front of the Hall of the Great Government, were the offices and reception halls of the ten leading princes of the Qing era, those of the princes of the right wing, the princes of the left wing, and the eight banner commanders who led the Qing army. Some of the buildings in the complex house the palace museum.

Ten Princely Pavilions (Shiwang Ting)

Also known as the "Mausoleum of Light" (Zhaoling), the northern tomb is a popular place with day visitors. It is situated in the north of the city in the middle of a park. The architectural style represents a successful combination of the traditionally arranged Chinese burial sites and the castle-like buildings of the early Qing period – a masterpiece of an amalgamation of Han and Manchurian art. Buried here is Huang Taiji (reigned 1626–35) and his wife. The building work on the 180,000sq.m/215,280sq.yd tomb site was begun in 1643 and completed eight years later. It is the best preserved and largest of the three imperial mausoleums in and around Shenyang.

The "Path of Souls" is lined with stone columns and two stone sculptures of horses, depicting the emperor's two favourite animals.

★★Northern Imperial Tomb (Bei Ling)

In the largest steam engine museum in China various types of steam engines are displayed in an area of barely 10,000sq.m/11,960sq.yd. The engines date from the beginning of the century to the 1950s, and come from several countries. Visitors can ride on one of the engines and view a locomotive and waggon factory, and a rail service headquarters.

Steam Engine Museum

Surroundings

The Eastern Imperial Tomb, also known as the "Mausoleum of Good Fortune" (Fu Ling), lies on a hill 11km/7 miles to the north-east of the city. It is the resting place of the first Qing emperor Nurhachi and his wife. The necropolis, built between 1629 and 1651, covers an area of 194,800sq.m/232,980sq.yd, the style of the structure corresponding to the Northern Imperial Tomb. The beautiful scenic surroundings add to the particular charm of the monument.

★Eastern Imperial Tomb (Dongling)

Some 20km/13 miles south of the the city is the battle field of Mukden, where the decisive fighting took place in the war between Japan and Russia (February 25th–March 10th 1905).

The Battle of Mukden (1905)

The Russian army, under the command of General Kuropatkin, consisted of the First Army under General Linewitsch on the left flank, the Second Army under General Baron Kaulbars on the right flank to the west, and the Third Army under General Baron Bilderling in the centre. In all there were 310,000 men with 1100 guns. Their strongly established position was about 150km/93 miles long and about 20–25km/12–15 miles wide.

The Japanese forces, under the command of Marshall Oyama, had dug themselves in deeply opposite the Russian position. They consisted of five armies: the First Army under General Kurok, the Second Army under

Position of Troops

General Oku with reserves, and the Fourth Army under General Nodzu in the centre, the Third Army under General Nogi on the right flank to the west, and the Fifth Army under General Kawamura on the right wing to the east. In total there were 300,000 men at the most, with 892 guns. The front was about 80km/50 miles to 100km/62 miles wide and about 30km/19 miles to 50km/31 miles deep.

Course of the Battle

Towards the end of February 1905 the Japanese attacked the Russian left flank, simultaneously their Third Army began to surround the Russian right wing. Until March 1st 1905 they achieved no particular advantage, then the Russians were forced back even further. On March 7th 1905 Kuropatkin admitted defeat, and ordered a retreat, which partly degenerated into a rout.

Losses

The losses to the Russian amounted to over 87,000 men, of whom 29,000 were taken prisoner; the Japanese lost an estimated 67,000

Shenzhen   J 7

Chinese equivalent

深圳

Province: Guangdong
Area: 327.5sq.km/126sq. miles. Population: 1,000,000

Situation and Communications

Bordering on Hong Kong, Shenzhen lies at 114°04'E and 22°31'N, 140km/ 87 miles to the south of the provincial capital of Canton, in the midst of beautiful scenery.

From Canton and Hong Kong the city can be reached by bus and train, in addition to which there is a hydrofoil service between Hong Kong and Wenjindu (Shenzhen's port).

History

Until 1979 Shenzhen was only a small village with a few streets, four factories and about a dozen shops. Then the central government transformed it into a special centre for trade and industry, which led to an economic boom. The signs of rapid growth are everywhere. Old districts are being demolished and new buildings appear almost out of thin air – shopping and office complexes, as well as numerous hotels and holiday villages catering for the increasing flow of tourists – with inevitable consequences for the cityscape.

Surroundings

★Splendid China
(Jinxiu Zonghua)

In this beach park, which extends over 20km/12 miles to the east of the city on the banks of Dapeng Bay, the best known of the Chinese natural and architectural monuments have been reproduced. In addition, in the adjacent Cultural Folk Village, miniature villages of nearly all the 56 Chinese nationalities have been set up.

The park has also been equipped for bathing, and holiday houses can be rented in the immediate vicinity.

Holiday Village
(Xili Dujiacun)

32km/21 miles to the north-west of Shenzhen, on the banks of the Xili lake, is the Xili holiday village which is surrounded by a covered walk. It includes a place for barbecues, a rifle range, a revolving restaurant situated on a beautiful slope and several secluded villas.

Included in the attractions of the holiday village are Unicorn Hill (Qiling-shan) and the Water Paradise (Shuishang Leyun).

Shenzhen: holiday village

Shigatse

See Xigaze

Shijiazhuang

J 4

Chinese
equivalent

Capital of the Province of Hebei
Area: 284sq.km/110sq. miles
Population: 1,300,000 (conurbation 1,710,000)

Shijiazhuang lies at 114°29′E and 38°N in the south-west of the Hebei province, 280km/174 miles to the south-west of Beijing, from where the city can be reached in 3 hours by train or by bus. The city also has an airport.

Situation and
Communications

Until the beginning of the 20th c. Shijiazhuang was just an unimportant village. From 1902, when the railway from Beijing to Wuhan came into being, it gradually grew in size to become a small city. Five years later the building of a second railway between Zhengding and Taiyuan accelerated the expansion of Shijiazhuang. In 1926 it finally reached the size of a major city and in 1947 its name was changed to Shimen.
    Since the end of the 1940s Shijiazhuang developed so quickly that it not only became the present political, economic and cultural centre of the Hebei province, but is now also one of the most important industrial metropolises in the north of China.

History

Shijiazhuang

To Pilu Temple 10 km Xibaipo 89 km To Longxing Temple 14 km

Shijiazhuang

1 km

To Cangyan Hill 78 km

To Anji Bridge 40 km

| Sights | The hospital in the west of the city bears the name of the Canadian doctor Norman Bethune who was responsible for medical care in the Red Army during the revolution. The first senior consultant was Kortis, an Indian. In the hospital grounds are the Bethune and Kortis halls. |

Sights

Bethune Hospital of Peace

The hospital in the west of the city bears the name of the Canadian doctor Norman Bethune who was responsible for medical care in the Red Army during the revolution. The first senior consultant was Kortis, an Indian. In the hospital grounds are the Bethune and Kortis halls.

Surroundings

Vairo Cana Temple (Pilu Si)

The Vairo Cana Temple, situated 10km/6 miles to the north-west of the city, dates from the Tang period (618–907). Of the many buildings in the former temple complex only two have been preserved, the Shakyamuni and the Vairocana Halls. The former has walls decorated with Buddhist frescos and houses a Shakyamuni statue. The Vairocan temple, rebuilt in 1342, contains an earthenware statue of the Buddha Vairocana, hundreds of wall-paintings representing scenes from paradise, hell and the mortal world and religious (Buddhist, Daoist, Confucian) and human figures (emperors, empresses, queens, ladies-in-waiting, etc.). All the statues and wall paintings date from the 14th c.

★★Temple of Lavish Prosperity (Longxing Si Temple)

The Temple of Lavish Prosperity, erected in 586, is situated 14km/9 miles to the north-east of Shijiazhang in Zhengding. It is also known as the Great Buddha Temple (Dafo Si), because housed in the main building, the Dabei Ge, is a 22m/72ft high bronze statue of the Guanyin with 42 arms dating from 971.

In the temple complex, which measures about 50,000sq.m/59,800sq.yd, there are further historically important buildings of artistic interest. These include two pavilions each with an imperial stele, and the Moni Temple where five Buddhist earthenware statues dating from the Song era (960–1279) and a painted sculpture also modelled from earthenware of the goddess of mercy from the Ming period (1368–1644) are revered.

The monastery also contains a large collection of stone tablets with engraved prose texts, poems or portraits. The oldest engraving dates back to the 6th c.

The 51m/56yd long Anji Qiao Bridge was built between 605–616 by Lu Chun from 28 blocks of stone. The colloquial name of the bridge, which lies 40km/25 miles to the south-east of Shijiazhuang in the district town of Zhaoxia, is Zhaozhou Qiao. It is the oldest arched stone bridge in the world. The structure spans the river with a single arch 37m/40yd long and 9.6m/10yd wide. To relieve the strain on the main arch and to relieve the pressure of the water, the builder added two small arches to the end of each bridge with a width of about 3.80m/4yd–2.80m/3yd. The structure represents without doubt an innovation in bridge construction.

★★Anji
Qiao Bridge

78km/48 miles to the west of the city rises the Green Rocks Mountain. Its slopes and the surrounding landscape are scattered with monasteries and temples dating from the 6th c. onwards. Of particular interest are the Temple of Good Fortune and Festivities (Fuqing Si) and the Palace of the Rainbow Bridge (Qiaolou Dian).

**★Green Rocks
Mountain**
(Cangyan Shan)

The Temple of Good Fortune and Festivities, probably of the Sui period (589–618), is dedicated to the daughter of the Sui emperor Yangdi. One of the main buildings, dating from the early Tang period (618–907), is the Hall of Princess Nanyang who converted to Buddhism following the death of her father. At the far end of the hall is a grotto which apparently served as the princess's bedroom. Also kept in the temple, in addition to the painted earthenware statue of the princess, are ten statues of ladies-in-waiting playing old musical instruments. There is also a wall fresco portraying the conversion and life's work of the princess, who became a nun.

The brick pagoda behind the temple dates from the late Ming period (1368–1644).

Temple of Good
Fortune and
Festivities
(Fuqing Si)

As its name implies, the Palace of the Rainbow Bridge, which belongs to the Temple of Good Fortune and Festivities, stands on a arched stone bridge 15m/16yd long and 9m/10yd wide; it is reminiscent of a rainbow with two steeply rising rock walls joining to meet each other. The bridge is 1400 years old, although the palace was not built until the middle of the 17th c.

Palace of the
Rainbow Bridge
(Qiaolou Dian)

The two tombs in Mancheng dating from the time of the western Han (206 B.C.–A.D. 23) are situated about 150km/93 miles to the north-east of Shijiazhuang and are the last resting place of the prince Liu Sheng and his wife. The two underground mausoleums (a true reproduction of the residence of the ruling pair with bedrooms, living rooms, bathrooms, etc.), are 50m/164ft long, 38m/125ft wide and 7m/22ft tall. The two tomb chambers are covered by a hermetically insulating sheet of cast iron. The clothes on both the bodies are made from small pieces of jade, held together with gold thread (the prince's have 2498 jade pieces and 1100g of gold thread, the princess's have 2160 jade pieces and 600g of gold thread). Also discovered in the tomb is an extremely charming gilded bronze statue, 48cm/18in. high, of a kneeling lady-in-waiting holding a lamp. By this specimen the direction and the strength of the light could be regulated.

★★Han Tombs
in Mancheng
(Mancheng
Hanmu)

A further priceless addition to the grave goods is a bronze incense-burner which has picture subjects with gold thread running through them; they portray towering mountain ranges on the far side of a sea.

Sichuan

G–J 5–6

Chinese
equivalent

Province
Area: 567,000sq.km/219,000sq. miles
Population: 108,970,000. Capital: Chengdu

The province of Sichuan lies in the south-west of China, on the upper
reaches of the Changjiang river, between 97°22′ and 110°10′E and 26°03′
and 34°20′N.

Situation

About 109 million people live in Sichuan, making it the most heavily
populated province in China. In the western regions are found national
minorities such as Yi, Tibetans, Miao, Qiang and Hui. Chongqing is the
largest town in the province, followed by the capital Chengdu.

The Sichuan Basin covers an area of 220,000sq.km/85,000sq. miles and
takes up most of the eastern region; because of the large amounts of red
sandstone found here it is also known as the Red Basin. It is surrounded on
all sides by high mountains – by the Yunnan Guizhou plateau in the south,
the Dabashan range in the north-east, the Wushan in the east and the edge
of the Qinghai Highlands in the west. The countryside is hilly – between 400
and 800m/1300 and 2600ft above sea-level – with some sunken plains,
particularly the Chengdu Plain in the west.

Topography

The continental and monsoon climate means that the plains enjoy mild
winters, early springs and long warm summers, with only moderately
harsh winters and temperate summers in the higher lands to the south-
west, while the inhabitants of the mountains in the north-west must endure
winter temperatures for most of the year. In Chengdu the average January
temperature is about 7°C/45°F and that in July 26°C/79°F.

Climate

◀ *Shijiazhuang: gilded bronze statue from the Han tombs in Mancheng*

Sichuan

History

The region was first inhabited by Han Chinese in the 4th c. B.C. Until the 10th c. it was an independent kingdom for part of the time and under the control of the central government at other times. After the demise of the Qing dynasty, under which it had attained provincial status, Sichuan was broken down into individual regions. In 1938, after the Japanese invasion, the National Government returned here. It was at this time that industrialisation began with the transfer of many businesses from eastern China, and this trend intensified after 1950.

Economy

The fertile soil, mild subtropical climate and rich mineral deposits combine to make the Sichuan Basin the main economic and industrial area of the province. Natural gas, coal, oil, salt, manganese, sulphur and iron-ore are all extracted, while engineering, automobile manufacture, iron-smelting, chemicals, cotton and foodstuffs are the major industries. International tourism is on the increase. In the agricultural sphere rice, maize, wheat, millet, sweet potatoes, sugar-cane, tea, soya beans and groundnuts are all grown. The breeding of silkworms and the raising of pigs and poultry are also of importance. In the west sheep- and yak-breeding play a major role.

Places to visit

The numerous tourist attractions include Chongqing and the provincial capital Chengdu (see entries).

Suzhou   L 5

Chinese equivalent

苏州市

Province: Jiangsu. Area: 119sq.km/46sq. miles
Population: 700,000 (conurbation 5,310,000)

Situation and Communications

Suzhou (120°36'E, 31°19'N) lies south of the river delta of the Chiangjian on the eastern bank of the Taihu Lake in the south-east of Jiangsu province. It is a good hour by train from Shanghai, four hours from Nanjing and sixteen hours from Beijing. A dense network of roads connects it with other cities in the province and also with Shanghai and Hangzhou. As the city is on the Imperial Canal Suzhou can offer tourists the possibility of a short cross-country cruise as far as Hangzhou.

The Imperial Canal is one of the many canals which flow through the city and which have given it the title of "Venice of the East". Suzhou is also famed for its gardens which gave it another name, "Heaven on Earth". As far as trade is concerned, Suzhou lies at present in fourth place after Shanghai, Tientsin and Beijing. The manufacture of cotton and silk play a central role in the economy, followed by chemical production and light industry. Traditionally the art of embroidery is important.

History

Suzhou is over 2500 years old. He Lu, the ruler of the Wu state, proclaimed Suzhou as capital of the empire in 484 B.C., and in 514 B.C. he built a defence wall surrounding the city; this is no longer in existence. According to some old documents the wall was 23.5m/26yd long and had sixteen gates. Despite numerous urban attacks which took place throughout the centuries, the historic city centre is barely unchanged in its plan. Of the eight gates, which are not situated by the water, only two have been preserved.

From the 5th c. onwards many civil servants, traders, and scholars settled here and laid out magnificent gardens to enhance the appearance of their houses. Suzhou developed into an economic and cultural centre, mainly as a result of the building of the Imperial Canal in the 6th c.

Under the Ming dynasty (1368–1644) this was the wealthiest city in the south-east of China. In 1860 during the Taiping uprising Suzhou was the victim of destruction.

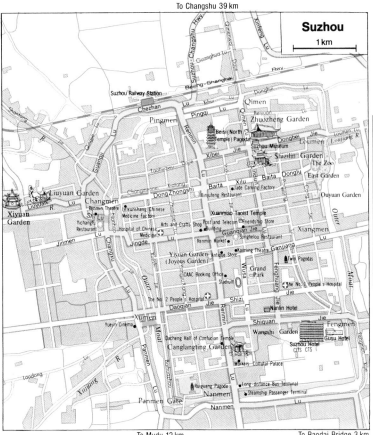

To Mudu 12 km   To Baodai Bridge 3 km

Under the Ming dynasty (1368–1644), at a time when the city was experiencing an unprecedented flourishing, there were no less than 271 gardens here. In the 20th c. many parks were left neglected and today there remain only about a dozen gardens. They were replicas of landscapes with mountains, trees and flowers, to which were added towers and pavilions.

Recently an effort has been made to restore them.

The Gardens

The one-acre Garden of Harmony, situated in the city centre in Renmin Lu, offers the visitor enchanting scenery which seems to change with every step. These grounds were the private property of the Chancellor Wu Kuan during the Ming period (1368–1644), and were referred to as the "Daguan Yuan" in the famous novel "The Dream of the Red Room". Towards the end of the 19th c. the gardens were relaid by a government official in accordance with the plans of a well-known artist, incorporating features from other gardens. A pathway divides the garden.

Garden of Harmony (Yiyuan)

399

Suzhou: Garden of the Master of the Nets

★Garden of the
Master of the Nets
(Wangshiyuan)

The Garden of the Master of the Nets is situated in the south of the city near the modern Suzhou hotel. In 1140 the chief of the imperial chronicler's office, whose nickname was "Master of the Nets", had a residence built here. This garden, known particularly for its scenic beauty and variety, also incorporates several buildings.

★★Garden of the
Pavilion of
Azure Waves
(Canglangting)

The Garden of the Pavilion of Azure Waves, also situated in the south of the city, is one of the oldest in China. Even in the middle of the 10th c. it surrounded a general's villa. A century later a famous poet bought the villa and had a pavilion built in the garden. He gave it the poetic name Pavilion of the Azure Waves. Between the 13th and 14th centuries the estate served as a Buddhist monastery; during the Ming dynasty (1368–1644) it reverted to private ownership. Owing to Buddhist influence the two-acre garden offers some features of special interest which distinguish it from other gardens in the city. These include a low surrounding wall with large openings, and a double arcade connecting the inner and outer sections. In the middle of the grounds is an artificial hill on which stands the Pavilion of the Azure Waves.

★★Garden of
Lingering
(Liuyuan)

This seven-acre garden in the west of the city was laid out by a Mr Liu in 1800 on the site of a park of the Ming period (1368–1644); it is joined to the neighbouring West Gardens. With the Garden of the Humble Administrator, the Summer Palace in Beijing and the Imperial residence in Changde it enjoys special protection as one of the most famous garden complexes of China.

The garden is certainly the most beautiful in Suzhou. It boasts a pool, several buildings, a man-made hill and a grove of peach trees. Particularly impressive is the pool with its surrounding pavilions and hills. Across the water leads a covered pathway on the walls of which hang over three hundred stone tablets engraved with old characters.

Also noteworthy are the delightful carvings in the Yuanyang and Wufengxian Halls.

Pavilion in the Garden of the Master of the Nets

A peculiarity is the Cloud-high Summit (Guanyun Fen), a 7m/22ft high Taihu stone.

The West Garden lies to the west of the Garden of Mr Liu, with which it was originally connected. In the 16th c. the park was the private property of a high official of the imperial court. Following his death his son converted the site into a Buddhist monastery. In 1860 the garden was destroyed in the war, although it was relaid only a few years later.

West Garden (Xiyuan)

Among the numerous buildings, the Luohan Hall (Luohan Tang) is particularly impressive, it houses over 500 gilded statues of Buddhist saints, and a statue of the thousand-armed goddess of mercy carved from the stump of a camphor tree.

The Lion Grove to the north of Suzhou is famed for its man-made hills formed from the unusual Taihu stone (limestone from the Taihu Lake). It was laid out in 1350 in a temple area, and is one of the most famous old gardens in the city.

★Lion Grove (Shizilin)

The garden's name derives from the largest rock, which has the shape of a lion.

The picturesque Garden of the Humble Administrator, one of the best known in Suzho, came into being in the 16th c., on the site of a former Buddhist monastery, to the north of the Lion Grove. The first owner, the retired minister Wang Xiancheng who named this garden, was inspired by the old saying "water the garden and plant vegetables, this is the occupation of the knowledgeable civil servant". His son apparently lost the garden in a game of chance. The site is divided into western, middle and eastern sections, the middle section is of particular interest to the visitor. Numerous towers and pavilions rise up on the banks of the pools, which occupy three fifths of the area, creating the impression that the whole garden is floating on water.

★★Garden of the Humble Administrator (Zhuozheng Yuan)

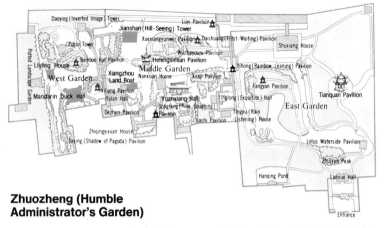

Zhuozheng (Humble Administrator's Garden)

Directly beyond the entrance is the beginning of the eastern section. Following the visitor's route the sights are: the Orchid and the Snow Palaces, the Hill of Cloud Hunting (Zhuiyun Feng), the Pavilion of the Spring of Heaven (Tianquan Ting), the Villa of the Fragrant Journey (Shuxiang Guan) and the Pavilion of the Beautiful Landscape (Fangyan Ting). In the middle garden are several pavilions, small villas and bridges arranged around a pool, in the middle of which rises a hill. Among the best-known buildings here are the Palace of the Distant Fragrance (Yuanxiang Tang), The Pavilion of the Four Winds (Hefengsimian Ting), the Pavilion of the Wind in the Pinewood (Songfeng Ting), the Pavilion of Waiting for Frost (Daishuang Ting) and the Bridge of the Fleeing Rainbow (Xiaofeihong).

Palace of the Mandarin Duck (Yuanyang Ting)

The most beautiful building in the western section of the garden is, without doubt, the Palace of the Mandarin Duck with the Hall of Thirty-six Mandarin Ducks (Sanshiliu Yuanyang Guan), and the Hall of the Eighteen Camellias (Shiba Mantuohua Guan).

Further Sights

★Temple of Secrets Xuanmiao Guan

The Daoist Temple of Secrets in the city centre dates back to the second half of the 3rd c. The original buildings are no longer preserved; the complex was newly erected in the 12th c.

Hall of the Three Pure Ones (Sanqing Dian)

The main building is the Hall of the Three Pure Ones which was built in 1179 according to the plans of Zhao Boxiao. It is 45m/49yd long and 25m/27yd wide. The 1.75m/6ft high main altar is crowned with gilded earthenware statues of the three most important Daoist godheads, the jade emperor, the god of supreme cleanliness, and the god of superior cleanliness. The sculptures, which were finished in the 12th c. are of particular artistic value.

The North Temple Pagoda (Beisi Ta)

The North Temple Pagoda, situated some 500m/547yd to the west of the Garden of the Humble Administrator, was erected in the 12th c. over the foundations of a 6th c. pagoda The octagonal brick and wooden building has galleries around it. There are good views from the upper floor.

★Tiger Hill (Huqiu Hill)

The Tiger Hill on the north-western edge of Suzhou, only 36m/118ft high covers an area of about 13ha/32 acres. 2500 years ago King He Lu (the ruler of the Wu state) was reportedly buried here with 3000 swords. A tiger is said to have guarded the grave, which accounts for the name of the hill.

In the garden of the Humble Administrator

At the foot of the hill stands the Er Shanmen gate from the Tang period (618–907), its supporting beams are not made from one single piece, which is why the hall is also known as the Hall of Broken Beams (Duanlinag Dian).

Second Hill Gate (Er Shanmen)

It is said that in the 3rd c. attempts were made to unearth the swords of King He Lu without success. Digging caused a waterhole to be formed which was given the name Sword Lake (Jianchi).

Sword Lake (Jianchi)

On the top of the hill towers the famous "leaning tower" of China, the Pagoda of the Cloud-rock Temple, dating from 961. Four hundred years ago the 47.5m/155ft high building began to lean. For a long time the pagoda has been the emblem of Suzhou.

Pagoda of the Cloud-rock Temple (Yunansi Ta)

The Monastery of the Cold Mountain is situated on the city's western edge on the banks of the Imperial Canal. In the Tang period (618–907) a poet sang the praises of the monastery: "At the Monastery of the Cold Mountain, behind the city of Suzhou, my boat is moored, the bells strike midnight".
   The site dates from the year 502, although the present buildings only came into existence in 1905. It is named after the prominent monk Hanshan (7th c.).
   Items kept in the monastery include a few dozen stone tablets with inscriptions by well known personalities from earlier centuries.
   The bronze bell which hangs on the right hand side of the main hall is a reproduction of a lost bell from the Tang era.

★Cold Mountain Temple Monastery (Hanshan Si)

Surroundings

The Bridge of the Precious Belt, first built in 806, spans the Imperial Canal 3km/2 miles to the south-east of Suzhou. It is 317m/346yd long and has 53 arches.

Bridge of the Precious Belt (Baodai Qiao)

Tai'an

Mountain of the Wonderful Rocks (Lingyanshan)	In Mudu, 12km/7 miles from Suzhou, rises the 82m/269ft high Mountain of the Wonderful Rocks. It is known for its unusual and bizarre rock scenery.
	According to legend Fu Chai the king of the Wu empire lived here over two thousand years ago with his favourite concubine Xi Shi, who was said to be the most beautiful Chinese woman of all time. Even poets such as Li Bai and Bai Juyi who lived under Tang rule (618–907) believed in the legend and wrote exquisite verse about this mountain.
Lingyan Si Temple	The Buddhist Lingyan Si Temple on the Mountain of the Wonderful Rocks was rebuilt in the years between 1919 and 1932.
Duobao Ta Pagoda	The Duobao Ta Pagoda belonging to the Lingyan Si Temple dates from the 12th c. and was restored in 1977.

Tai'an   K 4

Chinese equivalent	泰安
	Province: Shandong. Altitude: 25m/82ft Area: 2500sq.km/965sq. miles. Population: 1,200,000
Situation and Communications	Tai'an lies at 117°08′E and 36°12′N, in Shandong province, 70km/43½ miles south of Shandong, the provincial capital. There are rail and bus links with Shandong.
History	One of the oldest towns in the province, Tai'an enjoyed considerable prosperity as long ago as the 2nd c. B.C. In the early 12th c. it was a military base and became the capital of an important administrative district in 1182. In the centuries that followed, thanks to its proximity to Mount Taishan, it continued to gain in importance, both politically and economically.
	In recent years tourism has been a growth industry. Many hotels and guest-houses have been built or extended to cater for the increasing numbers of both Chinese and foreign visitors to Mount Taishan.

Sights

★**Temple of the Mountain God** (Dai Miao)	The Temple of the Mountain God, in the town centre, covers an area of 9·6ha/23·7 acres and comprises 813 palaces, temples, pavilions and covered walkways. Originally built in the Qin period (221–207 B.C.) it has been frequently extended and restored right up to the present day, and is dedicated to the God of Mount Taishan.
Hall of Heavenly Gifts (Tiankuang Dian)	The main building, the Hall of Heavenly Gifts, dates from 1009, and was restored in 1956.
	It is said that, in a vision, the emperor saw a cloth of gold silk both at his court and on Mount Taishan. He regarded it as a gift from the God of Heaven and built this temple to express his gratitude.
	The building can be compared with the Hall of Supreme Harmony in the Imperial Palace in Beijing and with the Hall of Great Achievements in the Temple of Confucius at Qufu. Measuring 49m/160ft long, 20m/66ft wide and 22m/72ft high, the temple stands on a terrace and is surrounded by a white balustrade and roofed with yellow tiles. Inside can be seen a wall-painting, 62m/203ft long and 3·3m/11ft high, from the Song period (960–1279), entitled "Departure and Return". It portrays the Mountain God going in procession up the mountain, and shows 657 figures, numerous birds and mythical creatures, as well as some magnificent scenery.

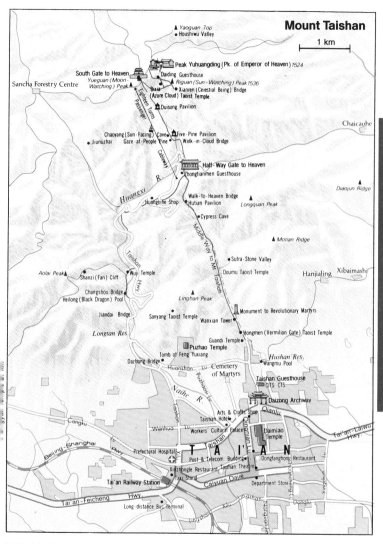

Mount Taishan

1 km

- Yaoguan Top
- Houshiwu Valley
- Peak Yuhuangding (Pk. of Emperor of Heaven) *1524*
- South Gate to Heaven
- Daiding Guesthouse
- Yueguan (Moon-Watching) Peak
- Riguan (Sun-Watching) Peak *1536*
- Sancha Forestry Centre
- Xianren (Celestial Being) Bridge
- Bixia (Azure Cloud) Taoist Temple
- Duisong Pavilion
- Chaicaohe
- Chaoyang (Sun-Facing) Cave
- Five-Pine Pavilion
- Jiunuzhai
- Gaze-at-People Pine
- Walk-in-Cloud Bridge
- Half-Way Gate to Heaven
- Zhongtianmen Guesthouse
- Diaojun Ridge
- Walk-to-Heaven Bridge
- Huangxihe Shop
- Hutian Pavilion
- Longquan Peak
- Cypress Cave
- Motian Ridge
- Sutra-Stone Valley
- Wuji Temple
- Doumu Taoist Temple
- Hanjialing
- Xibaimashi
- Aolai Peak
- Shanzi (Fan) Cliff
- Changshou Bridge
- Heilong (Black Dragon) Pool
- Linghan Peak
- Jiandai Bridge
- Sanyang Taoist Temple
- Wanxian Tower
- Monument to Revolutionary Martyrs
- Longtan Res.
- Puzhao Temple
- Guandi Temple
- Hongmen (Vermilion Gate) Taoist Temple
- Tomb of Feng Yuxiang
- Dazhong Bridge
- Cemetery of Martyrs
- Wangmu Pool
- Hushan Res.
- Taishan Guesthouse
- CITS CTS
- Daizong Archway
- Arts & Crafts Shop
- Taishan Hotel
- Workers' Cultural Palace
- Daimiao Temple
- Prefectural Hospital
- Post & Telecom Buildings
- Dongfanghong Restaurant
- Xinzhongle Restaurant
- Taishan Theatre
- Tai'an Railway Station
- Taxi Stand
- Department Store
- Caiyuan Dajie
- Tai'an-Feicheng Hwy
- Long-distance Bus Terminal
- Tai'an-Laiwu Hwy

T A I ' A N

Behind the Hall of Heavenly Gifts lie a number of courtyards, including the well-known Han Courtyard of Pine Trees, where five pine-trees which are said to have been planted by the Han Emperor Wudi in 110 B.C. are still standing.

Han Courtyard of Pine Trees (Hanbai Yuan)

The Bronze Pavilion dates back to 1615 and originally stood on Mount Taishan.

Bronze Pavilion

405

Nearby is the Iron Pagoda (1533); three of the original thirteen floors have survived.

Iron Pagoda

In another courtyard can be seen the Eastern Seat of the Emperor, where at one time various rulers stayed when they came on a pilgrimage to Mount Taishan. It houses various offerings made by these emperors, such as the three "Treasures", a lion, a jade sceptre and a porcelain calabash.

Eastern Seat of the Emperor (Dongyu Zuo)

In the temple precincts can be found large numbers of commemorative stones from various periods, including an inscribed stone tablet from 209 B.C., one of the oldest in China. The text of the inscription was composed by the Qin Emperor Ershi and calligraphed by his chancellor Li Si; of the original 222 ideograms only the last ten can still be deciphered.

Also known as Mount of the East (Dong Yue), Mount Taishan to the north of Tai'an is the most famous of China's Five Holy Mountains. The other four are Hengshan in Hunan province, Huashan in Shaanxi province, Hengshan in Shanxi province and Songshan in Henen province. Because it is in the east of the country, where the sun rises, Mount Taishan is treated with special reverence. For over 2000 years rulers came here to pay homage to the Gods of Heaven and Earth. The mountain stands 1545m/5070ft high and its picturesque scenery is always in the clouds. Large numbers of waterfalls, temples and pagodas all add to its natural splendour. Mount Taishan is visited by numerous Chinese and foreign walkers who also come to experience the magnificent sunrise over the mountain top.

★★Mount Taishan

The mountain can be climbed by either the eastern (central) or western route. It is best to choose the main route, the eastern one, because this contains most of the sights and places of interest. The climb to the top is about 9km/5½ miles, with a difference in altitude of 1350m/4430ft. Climbers can follow a flight of 6293 steps, parts of which between the Middle Gateway to Heaven and the Southern Gateway to Heaven are almost vertical.

Climb

However, there is also a mini-bus which goes to the Zongtian Men Gate, from where there is a cable-railway up to Moon View Peak (Yueguan Feng).

The climb up Mount Taishan begins at the Archway of the Mountain God, constructed of granite and supported by four pillars and dating from the mid-16th c. Further north, along a path going off to the right, the climber will pass the Pool of the Heavenly Queen (Wangmu Chi) and then come to the Hall of the Heavenly Queen (Wangmu Dian).

Archway of the Mountain God (Daizong Fang)

The actual climb begins at the Palace of the Vermilion Gate, where at one time the Emperor would don his ceremonial robes before setting out on his pilgrimage climb up Mount Taishan. The date the palace was originally built is not known. It was last completely renovated in 1626, but since then a number of restoration attempts have proved necessary.

Palace of the Vermilion Gate (Hongmen Gong)

In front of the palace stand three gateways of white marble, one of which is named after Confucius (Kongzideng Lin Chu), who rested here for a short while before setting off up the mountain.

The next stop is the Archway of the Ten Thousand Immortals, built in 1620 and restored in 1954. Here the climber can see some commemorative stones with inscriptions dating from the Ming period (1368–1644).

Archway of the Ten Thousand Immortals (Wanxian Lou)

Next will be seen the Taoist Palace of the Goddess of the Great Bear (Doumu Gong).

Palace of the Goddess of the Great Bear

From the main route a path leads off to Sutra Stone Valley, where the text of the Diamond Sutra was engraved on a giant stone more than 1400 years ago.

Sutra Stone Valley (Jingshi Yu)

◀ *Taishan Mountain*

Taiwan

<table>
<tr><td>Hutian Ge Pavilion</td><td>Continuing north the visitor will come to he Hutian Ge Pavilion, or Pavilion of the Heavenly Cauldron.</td></tr>
<tr><td>Halfway Gate to Heaven (Zhongtian Men)</td><td>Having completed two-thirds of the climb and arrived at the junction of the east and west routes, the climber will now reach the Halfway Gate to Heaven, a stone edifice from the Qing period (1644–1911).

Those who will find the next stretch too difficult can travel from here to the top by cable-railway.

To the north of the Halfway Gate to Heaven is Walk-in-Cloud Bridge (Yunbu Qiao), which leads over a fast-flowing stream, followed by the Pines of the Fifth Class (Wudaifu Song), which were planted in 1730. Further north stands the Pavilion of the Facing Pines (Duisong Ting).

The Staircase of Eighteen Bends (Shiba Pan) has more than 1000 steps and leads up to the Southern Gateway to Heaven.</td></tr>
<tr><td>Southern Gateway to Heaven (Nantian Men)</td><td>The Southern Gateway to Heaven, another stone edifice, was built in 1264. Under the ledge can be seen the three Chinese characters "mo kong ge", meaning "pavilion which reaches up to heaven".

It is now only 1km/1100yd to the top. On the way the climber will pass a Taoist temple just below the peak.</td></tr>
<tr><td>Temple of the Princess of the Azure Cloud (Bixia Ci)</td><td>The Temple of the Princess of the Azure Cloud, built between 1008 and 1016, is now reinforced with heavy metal struts. In the main hall stands a bronze statue of the princess, who is revered as the tutelary goddess of Mount Taishan. In the courtyard can be seen two stelae, also in bronze, with inscriptions dating from 1615 and 1625.</td></tr>
<tr><td>Daiding</td><td>The most important of the many inscriptions carved on the group of rocks known as Great View (Daguan) on the nearby Daiding peak is the essay about Taishan (Ji Taishan Mingbai). Standing 13·3m/44ft high and 5·3m/17ft wide, the stone contains 996 ideograms, each of which is 1m/40in. in diameter. The calligraphy was the work of the Tang Emperor Xuanzong in 726.</td></tr>
<tr><td>Sun-Watching Peak (Riguan Feng)</td><td>To the south-east of Daiding lies Sun-Watching Peak, from where visitors can enjoy the beautiful sunrise.</td></tr>
<tr><td>Peak of the Emperor of Jade (Yuhuang Ding)</td><td>The climb ends on the Peak of the Emperor of Jade (or Emperor of Heaven), dominated by the Temple of the Emperor of Jade (Yuhuang Dian).</td></tr>
</table>

<table>
<tr><td>Chinese equivalent</td><td>

Ta Chung-Hwa Min-kuo · Republic of China (ROC)
Area: 36,179sq.km/13,965sq. miles. Altitude: 0–3952m/0–13,003ft
Capital: Taipei</td></tr>
<tr><td>**Note**</td><td>In the following brief description the spelling of Chinese proper names follows the Wade Giles System in preference to Pinyin transliteration.</td></tr>
<tr><td>Situation and Region</td><td>The East Asian island of Taiwan (meaning "terraced strand"; formerly known as Formosa) lies between 21°45'E and 25°38'N and 120°1' and 122°6'E, on either side of the Tropic of Cancer. It is separated from the Chinese mainland by the 160km/100 mile wide Taiwan (Formosa) Strait, with the East China Sea to the north, the Pacific Ocean to the east and the South China Sea (Bashi Channel/Luzon Strait) to the south. It is the heartland of the Republic of China (also known as Nationalist China), or Ta</td></tr>
</table>

PEOPLE'S REPUBLIC OF CHINA
FUJIAN PROVINCE

East China Sea

Keelung

Taipei

Hsinchu

Quemoy

Formosa Strait

Taichung

TAIWAN

Changhua
Yuanlin
Puli
Sun Moon Lake

Hualien

Pacific

Penghu (Pescadores)

Chiayi

Tropic of Cancer

Tainan

Taitung

Lu Tao

Kaohsiung Pingtung

Taiwan Republic of China

Lan Yu

100km

South China Sea

Oluanpi

Ocean

© Baedeker

Chung-Hwa Min-kuo in Chinese, which also comprises the 64 Penghu Islands (Penghu Lieh Tao) or Pescadores (area 127sq.km/49sq. miles and of volcanic origin) in the Taiwan Strait, the two small Pacific islands of Lan Yu (Island of Orchids) and Lu Tao (Green Island) lying to the south-east of Taiwan, and also – in addition to numerous other islets – the groups close to the Chinese mainland known as Quemoy (Chinmen; 175sq.km/67sq. miles) and Matsu (Lienkiang; 29sq.km/11sq. miles) further north.

The island of Taiwan is over 36,000sq.km/13,900sq. miles in area, and measures at the most 400km/250 miles from north to south and 140km/87 miles from east to west.

Area and extent

The topography of Taiwan is characterised by three roughly parallel mountain chains running from north to south which are well over 2500m/8200ft high at some points. Situated almost exactly on the Tropic of Cancer, Yu-shan (Jade Mountain, or Mount Morrison) is 3952m/12,970ft high, making it the island's highest peak. These ranges of fold mountains were formed comparatively recently in geological terms. Taiwan lies exactly on the spot where the Philippine Islands and the Japanese Ryukyu Islands converge. The frequency of earthquakes (more than 150 each year!) shows that the faults which once caused the mountains to form are still present. The central mountain range is the watershed of the short rivers flowing west and eastwards to the sea. The east coast is steep and not really suitable for cars, but the west coast slopes more gradually down to the sea with coastal plains which are more than 40km/25 miles wide in places, making them ideal for habitation.

Topography

Life on Taiwan is largely ruled by the alternately humid and subtropical climate. The warmest time is in July, when temperatures average above 28°C/82°F. The coldest month is February, when levels often drop to below 15°C/59°F. Nevertheless, the annual averages are 25°C/77°F at sea-level in the south and 21°C/70°F in the north.

Climate

The fierce south-west monsoons are the main reason for the heavy rainfall figures. Most of the rain (up to well over 300mm/12in. per month!) falls in the months of June and July. In summer atmospheric humidity reaches 80%. On the other hand, it becomes very dry in late autumn and winter, especially in the south-west of the island. Taiwan is often the victim of raging typhoons during the typhoon season from July to October.

Flora

As a result of the prevailing climatic conditions plant life on Taiwan varies considerably, but can roughly be allocated to four different altitude levels. The lowest level is where forests of evergreen laurel trees flourish. This is followed by mixed forests of many different species found on land as high as 2600m/8500ft above sea-level. The mountain slopes are covered by coniferous forests, while on the highest peaks (over 3600m/12,000ft) only grass and pulvinate succulents can survive. At present some 60% of Taiwan is wooded, some of which is mangrove forest. About a third is utilisable arable land (especially in the west, where some land is irrigated), the main crops being rice, sugar-cane and tea.

Fauna

Ever since settlers first set foot on Taiwan its native animal population has been gradually decimated and seriously so in recent years. In the more remote forests, however, one can still find such animals as wild boar, deer, wild cats and monkeys (macaques). Mention should also be made of the many species of butterflies.

Population

With a population of some 21 million – mainly Han Chinese, together with 338,000 Gaochans (an ancient Malay-Polynesian people) and small foreign minorities – and an average density of 580 inhabitants per square kilometre/1500 per square mile (somewhat more on the coastal plains in the west). Taiwan is 2½ times more densely populated than the United Kingdom, for example. After the Communists gained power in China in 1949 the size of Taiwan's population increased considerably when hundreds of thousands of mainland Chinese sought refuge here; the number of births also now far exceeds the number of deaths. A glance at the statistics produced by the capital Taipei will give an indication of the way the population has increased. Shortly after the Second World War about 400,000 people lived in the city; by 1993 this figure had increased more than sixfold! At present the annual growth rate is 1·1%, average life expectancy is 74 years and the urban population accounts for more than 50% of the total.

Language

The official language of Taiwan is Mandarin Chinese, but colloquially a number of Chinese dialects are spoken, especially Amoy or South Fukien and Hakka. English is the main commercial language. Many older Taiwanese also speak Japanese.

Religion

The two main religions are Buddhism and Taoism. There is also a sizeable Christian minority as well as small numbers of Moslems and Animists.

Education

Educational standards are comparatively high. Since 1968 all children between the ages of six and fifteen must attend school. It is therefore not surprising that the number of illiterates almost halved between 1970 and 1981; today only 7% of the population cannot read and write.

The needs of those seeking higher education are served by technical colleges, grammar schools and universities.

State and government

On March 1st 1950 Chiang Kai-shek proclaimed the Republic of China on Taiwan, based on the Constitution of 1947 (revised many times, the last revision being in 1992). The Republic sees itself as the legitimate successor to the first National Chinese Republic set up by Sun-Yat-sen in 1912, and regards Taipei as the provisional capital of the whole of China.

The highest governing body is the National Assembly, with the President as head of state. The Executive Yüan is responsible for internal and foreign policy, with its president acting as prime minister; it is supervised by the

Legislative Yüan, or Central Parliament. The Judicial Yüan is responsible for all matters of law, while the State Regulatory Yüan controls the civil service. The Control or Supervisory Yüan constitutes the supreme court of appeal.

There is universal suffrage. The government party is the Chinese People's Party (Kuomintang/KMT; first party split was in 1993); other major parties include the Democratic Progress Party (DPP), the Chinese Social Democratic Party (CSDP) and the Workers' Party (Kungtang/KT); there are also more than 60 other minor parties and political groups.

As well as the Central Parliament (Legislative Yüan) Taiwan Province and the capital Taipei have their own parliaments.

The Chinese Province of Taiwan is divided into 16 administrative districts (Hsi), the five independent towns of Keelung, Taichung, Tainan, Hsinchu and Chiayi, as well as two Special Regions, namely, the capital Taipei and the port of Kaohsiung.

The island of Taiwan was originally settled by Austronesian tribes who, in pre-historical times, brought the old Malayan aboriginals under their yoke. It was not until the seventh century A.D. that Chinese immigrants arrived from the mainland.

In 1206 Taiwan became part of the kingdom of China. In the 16th and 17th c. Portuguese (they named it Formosa, meaning "beautifully-formed island"), Spanish, French and Dutch colonists arrived on the island. In 1624 the Dutch built a fort on the site of the present town of Tainan. Shortly after this the Spanish founded a settlement in the north of the island. In the second half of the 17th c. Chinese forces led by Cheng Cheng-kung who were retreating from the advancing Manchu arrived here and defeated the European colonists. In 1684 Taiwan became part of the south Chinese coastal province of Fukien (Fujian). For a short time in 1884 the French occupied the island and the Pescadores. By 1887 Taiwan had become a province of China.

Following the Sino-Japanese War of 1894–95 and the Treaty of Shimonoseki Taiwan came under Japanese control. The inhabitants of the island resisted and declared the "Republic of China" (the first Asian republic). However, the Japanese resorted to harsh measures and it was 1945 before Taiwan again became part of China. In 1949, after suffering defeat at the hands of the Communists, the Kuomintang government of Chiang Kai-shek took refuge on Taiwan. A year later they proclaimed the "National Republic of China". With the support of the USA the Chinese Nationalists were able to retain their state and territory here, including the small surrounding islands.

The Communists refused to acknowledge Taiwan as an independent state, claiming it was in fact an integral part – the 23rd province – of the People's Republic of China. After Nationalist China had been expelled from the United Nations in 1971 and replaced by the People's Republic it ceased to carry any weight as a political power, and only some twenty countries maintained diplomatic relations with Taiwan. Nevertheless, the Taiwan government still claimed sovereignty over China.

After a short interregnum period Chiang Ching-kuo, the son of Chiang Kai-shek who had died in 1975, became head of state. He suffered a severe blow in 1979 when the USA severed diplomatic relations with Nationalist China and annulled the 1954 security pact. After the death of Chiang Ching-kuo in 1988 his successor, the Taiwanese-born Lee Teng-hui, pursued liberal domestic policies and one of rapprochement with the People's Republic of China. In 1991, after 44 years, free elections were held to elect members to the National Assembly.

Today Taiwan can be regarded as one of the world's newly-industrialised countries. As regards its agricultural economy, the island ranks among the most progressive regions of East Asia; a decisive step in this connection were the agricultural reforms carried out in 1949. Land which had previously been owned by or leased to a few large landowners passed into the

History

Economy

hands of those who worked it, and the previous owners received compensation in the form of shares in the new state industries which were set up. The USA exercised considerable influence on Taiwan's industrial development; in co-operation with the Taiwan government it set up the Joint Commission on Rural Reconstruction (JCRR) and invested considerable sums of money in improving the infrastructure, intensifying fishing and cattle-breeding, manufacturing fertilisers and improving standards of education and health care. Now many farms are able to harvest three rice crops every year. Taiwan has become a major exporter of agricultural products.

Industry is mainly export-orientated and relies heavily on labour-intensive production. Many individual stages of production are carried out which would result in high labour and ancillary costs in the Western world. Examples of these include the textile, precision engineering and electronic industries, especially those concerned with the manufacture and assembly of photographic equipment and computers. Taiwan's major trading partner is the USA, followed by Japan. Indirect trade with the People's Republic of China via Hong Kong, Japan and Singapore is gaining in importance.

Obtaining raw materials is a problem for Taiwanese industry. As the island has relatively few natural resources of its own (these are mainly hard coal, natural gas, marble and asbestos) it is obliged to pay for the import of raw materials much of what it earns from its exports.

The major exports – mainly to the USA, Hong Kong and Japan – are electronic equipment, machinery, electrical goods, textiles, metal, plastics and rubber goods, as well as agricultural produce such as rice, tea, sugar, fruit and vegetables.

Imports – mainly from Japan, the USA and Germany – are electronics, machinery, chemicals, crude oil and motor vehicles.

Service industries contribute 54% of the gross domestic product, industry 42·3% and agriculture 3·7%.

The National Economic Development Plan for the years 1991–96 aims to increase the income per capita from US $8000 (1990) to US $14,000 (1996).

Currency

The legal currency of Taiwan is the New Taiwan Dollar (NT$; Kuai) and, since 1992, the Renminbi Yüan (RMB ¥), the "people's currency" of the Chinese People's Republic.

Transport and Communications

The state pays great attention to the matter of public transport, in attempts to ensure that there are good links between the mountainous east of the island and the industrial and economic centres in the west.

In all, the Taiwan Railway Administration is responsible for some 2500km/1550 miles of railway track, of which 1200km/750 miles is used for scheduled services, with two main lines in the east and west of the island – with an extension for high-speed trains planned for the stretch between Taipei and Kaohsiung – and 1300km/800 miles for transport of special freight such as timber and sugar.

The road network (note: driving is on the right) has a total length of 20,000km/12,500 miles, of which 17,000km/10,500 miles are asphalted. Since 1978 a motorway – the Sun-Yat-sen Freeway, over 370km/230 miles long – has linked the capital Taipei in the north with the port of Kaohsiung in the south. In recent years several east–west link roads have been constructed. All parts of the island are linked by good bus services.

There are two international airports at Taipei and Kaohsiung, as well as a further eleven smaller airports catering for domestic flights on Taiwan and to the outlying islands. In all there are seven Taiwan airlines, but only China Airlines (CAL) operates scheduled international flights.

The Taiwan trading fleet owns over 13,200 ships, but 12,000 or so of these are just small fishing vessels. Overseas traffic uses the four international sea ports of Kaohsiung, Chilung, Taichung and Hualin.

Tourism

In the last twenty years or so tourism has developed considerably and now makes an important economic contribution to the economy of Taiwan. Whereas in 1970 less than 410,000 foreign tourists visited the island, in

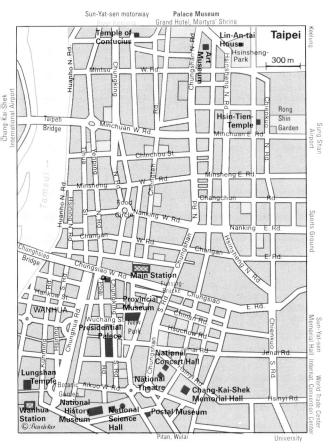

Taipei

Temple of Confucius

Lin-An-tai House

Art Museum

Hsinsheng-Park

300 m

Keeling

Hsin-Tien-Temple

Rong Shin Garden

Chang Kai-Shek International Airport

Taipeh Bridge

Tamsui →

Minchuan W. Rd

Minchuan E. Rd

Sung Shan Airport

Chinchou St

Minsheng E. Rd

Minsheng

Changchun Rd

Sports Ground

Food Circle

Nanking W. Rd

Nanking E. Rd

Changan W. Rd

Changan E. Rd

Chunghsiao Bridge

Chungsiao W. Rd

Main Station

Fuhsing-Brücke

Chungsiao E. Rd

WANHUA

Hankow St

Provincial Museum

Wuchang St

New Park

Chimai Rd

Hsuchow Rd

Presidential Palace

Jenai Rd

National Concert Hall

Jenai Rd

Sun-Yat-sen Memorial Hall Internat. Convention Center

World Trade Center Memorial Hall Internat. Convention Center

Lungshan Temple

Botanic Aikou W. Rd Garden

National Theatre

Chang-Kai-Shek Memorial Hall

Hsinyi Rd

Wanhua Station

National History Museum

National Science Hall

Postal Museum

©:Baedeker

Pitan, Wulai

University

1991 this figure had risen to more than 1,800,000. More than a half of the tourists come from Japan. Apart from Chinese living abroad who come to visit their families, the second largest contingent, some 13% of the total, is from the USA, followed by Koreans (9%). For their part, the Taiwanese travel mainly to Hong Kong, Japan and Thailand.

Taipei (pop. 2,700,000), the capital of the Republic of China (a "city state" since 1967) and – through the eyes of the Taiwanese – also the provisional capital of the whole of China (see History), lies in the north of the island of Taiwan. In recent years the city, one of the fastest-growing in the whole of Asia, has became a major industrial and commercial centre. Taipei will provide the tourist with a plethora of interesting places to visit, some containing cultural treasures brought over from the Chinese mainland.

The Capital Taipei

Situation and Importance

The city's oldest quarter is Wanhua, lying between Chunghua Street and the Tamsui (Tanshui) river. Wanhua, with its colourful and noisy markets, still boasts a large number of old houses built in the traditional style.

Wanhua Quarter

Taiwan

Visitors to the markets will be urged to purchase items ranging from religious objects and herbal remedies to live snakes and exotic delicacies.

★Lungshan Temple

In the south of Wanhua Quarter stands Lungshan Temple (Dragon Mountain Temple), the oldest and most famous Buddhist shrine in Taipei; it is dedicated to the God of Grace and Mercy.

The original temple, built in 1740, was the victim of an earthquake in 1817. The new building completed a few years later was badly damaged in a typhoon in 1867, and the remains – with the sole exception of a camphorwood statue of the Goddess of Mercy Kuan Yin – were completely destroyed in bombing raids in 1945. The present building dates from 1957.

Presidential Palace

The Presidential Palace lies in the city centre. On the forecourt the flag is raised and lowered at sunrise and sunset, accompanied by the national anthem. Huge events and celebrations are held here annually on October 10th, a national holiday.

New Park

Behind the Presidential Palace lies New Park, a veritable green oasis in the centre of the city with a three-storey pagoda, pavilions and a small pool. In the evenings fortune-tellers erect their tents on the lawns.

Provincial Museum

The Provincial Museum in New Park has collections of natural history and anthropological items. The exhibition pertaining to Taiwan's original native inhabitants is particularly interesting.

The National University Anthropological and Archaeological Department boasts an excellent collection giving an insight into the history of pottery, carving, textiles and jewellery, weapons and other everyday items. Admission is by special arrangement only.

Botanical Gardens

Along the southern edge of the city lie the charming Botanical Gardens, where visitors can see more than 700 species of plants and a pretty lotus-pool.

National History Museum

The nearby National History Museum houses a good collection of Chinese art and objets d'art (including imperial robes, embroidery, religious utensils, bronze work, etc.). Prime examples of the engraver's art include ivory carvings inscribed with Chinese characters which are so minute they can be read only with the aid of a strong magnifying glass. From time to time there are temporary exhibitions of contemporary Chinese painting.

Culture Complex

The Culture Complex on Nanhai Street includes the National History Museum described above and also the National Science Hall.

At 243 Kuei-Yang Street will be found the Museum of the History of the Taiwanese Forces.

There is an interesting Postal Museum on Chungking Street (southern section 3, No. 45).

★Insect Museum

Visitors to the Insect Museum at 71 Chinan Street can admire the colourful display of all the 400 or so species of butterfly found on Taiwan.

Chiang Kai-shek Memorial Hall

In the middle of a magnificent park on the south-western edge of the town centre stands the massive Chiang Kai-shek (Chung Cheng) Memorial Hall, which was opened on April 4th 1980. The building stands 70m/230ft tall and is a classic example of Chinese architecture. The 80m/260ft wide and 30m/100ft tall entrance gate to the 25ha/62 acre park is also most imposing.

National Concert Hall National Theatre

Between the entrance gate and the Memorial Hall stand the National Concert Hall and the National Theatre.

Sun-Yat-sen Memorial Hall

A second large memorial hall in the west of the city is dedicated to Sun-Yat-sen; there are seats for over 2600 in the auditorium.

Chiang Kai-shek Memorial Hall in Taipei

Entrance to the National Palace Museum in the north of Taipei

Taiwan

Hsing Tien Temple	Hsing Tien temple, on Sungchiang Street on the north-eastern edge of the city centre, is dedicated to the God of War Kuan Kung (Kuan Yu), an important figure featured in the Chinese classic "The Adventure Story of the Three Kingdoms".
★Municipal Art Museum Yesterday's World	To the north-west of Hsing Tien Temple, between Mintsu Street and the Keelung river, stands the modern Municipal Art Museum. To the west, opposite the Art Museum, an old Chinese village has been re-constructed and given the name "Yesterday's World".
Temple of Confucius	The Temple of Confucius further to the north-west is not actually a place of worship but rather a memorial to the academic and philosopher who is still revered by many Chinese. Commemorative celebrations are held on September 28th, his birthday, together with Ming style court dancing. The peaceful temple surroundings are very conducive to quiet contemplation.
Pao An Temple	The Taoist Pao An Temple will be found in Hami Street. It dates from the 17th c., making it one of the oldest temples on Taiwan.
Linchi Temple	Linchi Temple in Chiuchuan Street exudes an atmosphere of mystical peace and quietness.
Academy of Opera	The nearby Tapeng Academy of Chinese Opera is one of the best educational establishments of its kind on Taiwan and has already produced a number of star performers. Here even young children take very demanding singing courses or undergo strenuous gymnastic training.
Grand Hotel Shrine of the Martyrs	To the north, on the far side of the Keelung river and beyond the imposing Grand Hotel, the visitor will find the impressive Shrine of the Martyrs of the National Revolution.
Chinese Culture and Film Centre	On the way to the National Palace Museum (see below) the visitor will pass the Chinese Culture and Film Centre. The buildings of this small complex are in the styles of various dynasties; Chinese feature films are shown here.
★National Palace Museum	In the midst of the thickly-wooded hills of the suburb of Waishuanghsi lies the world-famous National Palace Museum. The building itself is most impressive, with its crescent-shaped archways and colourfully glazed bricks and tiles. Inside are housed treasures beyond compare. The most valuable items come from an imperial collection started in the 12th c. These precious objects were brought here from Nanking (Nanjing) in 1948. Because of lack of space only about 11,000 of the many hundreds of thousands of objets d'art can be displayed at any one time; the exhibits are changed every three months. The remainder are stored behind thick steel doors deep down in catacombs below the museum. However, those which are on display are impressive enough – Tang and Sung paintings, jade carvings, exquisite Ming porcelain, calligraphy, bronze-work up to 3000 years old, objects decorated in enamel and delicate filigree, lacquer-work, rare books and documents, tapestries and toys once played with by the Manchu emperors when they were children.
Close surroundings Yangmingshan National Park	The many charms of Yangmingshan National Park, 15km/9 miles north of the capital, attract large numbers of visitors, especially in spring when the cherry-trees and azaleas are in bloom. Rock-gardens and pavilions by the side of pools give it a unique character. There are several hotels with thermal baths. Many of Taipei's more well-to-do inhabitants live hereabouts.
Peitou	The road from Taipei to the town of Peitou to the north-west is home to a number of potteries and stoneware factories. At the "China Arts Pottery Co." pottery can be purchased and the individual stages of ceramic manufacture observed.

On the far side of Peitou lies the fishing port of Tamsui, on the northern side of the river of the same name. At one time Tamsui was a flourishing harbour town, as evidenced by the lavish façades of the beautiful brick buildings of which many have survived. There are a number of good fish restaurants. Just outside the town lies a splendid golf-course.

Tamsui

High above the mouth of the river towers the old fort of Santo Domingo (Red Fort); built by the Spaniards in 1628 and later taken over by the Dutch, it is encircled by red walls which have resulted in its popular name of "Hung Mao Cheng", or "Fort of the Red Barbarians". Now empty, the fort was occupied by the British consulate until 1972.

On the far side of the river mouth towers the strangely-shaped Mount Kuamyin-shan (612m/2008ft). It is named after the Goddess of Compassion, whose face is said to be discernible in the rock.

The holiday resort of Pitan, 14km/9 miles south of Taipei, is very popular with the people of Taiwan. The Green Lake has facilities for bathing and boat-trips.

Pitan

Near Mucha, a suburb of Taipei, one of Asia's largest zoos has come into being. Animals from all over the world enjoy greatest possible degree of freedom here.

★Zoo

After passing through Mucha, the Chihnan Temple will be found 16km/ 10 miles south-east of Taipei. It is also known as the "Temple of the Eight Immortals" or "Temple of the Thousand (actually 1275!) Steps". The Chinese believe that worshippers who spend the night here receive divine revelations from Lu Tung-pin in the form of dreams.

Chihnan Temple

In Sanshia, 22km/13½ miles south-west of Taipei, the Tsu Shih Temple which was destroyed during the Second World War is being rebuilt. Visitors can watch the artists and sculptors at work.

Sanshia

About 30km/19 miles north-east of Taipei lies Taiwan's second largest sea-port, Keelung (Chilung; pop. 354,000). It is situated on the East China Sea and a number of arterial roads terminate here.

More distant surroundings

Keelung

The town can look back on a very eventful history. The Spaniards occupied it in 1626 and named it "Santisima Trinidad" (Blessed Trinity). Later the Dutch settled here until they in turn were driven out by Cheng Cheng-kung (Koxinga) in 1661. A disastrous earthquake destroyed the town in 1867. In 1884 French marines were stationed here for a time. Eleven years later a Japanese expeditionary force gained control of this strategically important town.

Known as "Rain Harbour" because of its extremely wet climate (up to 3000mm/120in. of rain falls in the course of 200 days), the main item of interest to visitors is the 22·55m/73ft high statue of Kuan Yi (Goddess of Mercy), which stands on a base of black marble and towers over the harbour.

10km/6 miles north-east of Keelung lies Yehliu National Park, with its bizarre rock formations jutting out sheer into the sea. Adjoining it is an Oceanarium with dolphins.

Yehliu National Park

There are a number of good fish-restaurants in the fishing village of Yeliu.

Yeliu

The beautiful bathing beaches of Chinsan lie 6km/4 miles north of Yehliu.

Chinsan

The seaside resort of Fulung, 52km/32 miles east of Taipei near a most delightful peninsula protruding far into the Pacific Ocean, also offers excellent bathing beaches.

Fulung

The resort of Wulai, 35km/22 miles south of Taipei, offers plenty in the way of leisure facilities. An excursion train runs from here to an Ataya village (the original native inhabitants of the island), who still perform their traditional songs and dances and wear the old forms of dress.

Wulai

417

Taiwan

City in Miniature
"Window on
China"
near Lungtau

50km/31 miles south-west of Taipei, near Lungtau, visitors can view the "Window on China", a "city in miniature" with several dozen models of famous Chinese buildings constructed to a scale of 1:25; these include the Imperial Palace in Beijing and the Great Wall of China.

Shihmen
Reservoir

A holiday resort has been built around the Shihmen (Gate of Stone) reservoir with its impressive dam, which is situated 55km/34 miles south-west of Taipei.

Tzuhu

On the way there the visitor will pass by the peaceful Tzuhu Lake, which has a special significance for the Chinese apart from being just a leisure spot. In a mausoleum (wear respectable clothes) can be seen the glossy black tomb of President Chiang Kai-shek (see Famous People), who died in 1975. Tzuhu, where he used to come to meditate, is regarded by many Taiwanese as being merely his temporary resting-place; their intention is that when the Chinese Nationals finally take over the mainland once more he will be able to lie at peace for ever in Nanjing (Nanking), the Kuomintang capital.

Hsinchu

110km/68 miles south-west of Taipei and to the south of the town of Hsinchu towers the "Lion's Head", a mountain on which can be found the Buddhist centre of Taiwan. This is a group of four temples with various ancillary buildings. For a small payment the monks will provide visitors with refreshment and accommodation for the night if required.

Other places to visit

Hualien

Hualien (pop. 150,000) is the capital of the Hualien district in the east of central Taiwan. Some 80,000 descendants of the island's original native inhabitants live in this region, a predominant feature of which is the central mountain chain which runs through the island from north to south. The town itself is a centre of the Taiwan marble industry and for some years now has been an important traffic hub with a modern harbour.

In one of Hualien's marble works visitors can watch the local metamorphic crystalline limestone being processed.

Toulan

A few miles south of Hualien lies the folklore village of Toulan, where descendants of the Ami tribe will give visitors an insight into their culture through their traditional dances, songs and dress. A visit to the South Sea Garden is also to be recommended.

Suao

The drive from Hualien along the east coast to the fishing port of Suao on the north-east coast will be found particularly charming. En route the visitor will pass some spectacular and jagged cliffs jutting out into the sea.

Central Cross
Island Highway

One of the tourist highlights of a stay in Taiwan is the drive from Hualien to Tungshih along the 193km/120 mile long Central Cross Island Highway, constructed in 1960. The route this major arterial road takes across the island has led to its being known locally as the "Treasure Island Rainbow". It provides access to a large number of scenic and charming places.

★ Taroko Gorge

The first 19km/12 mile section of the road has been bulldozed through the imposing Taroko Gorge, a wildly romantic pass through rocky terrain composed mainly of marble and other forms of limestone. The construction of this length of road involved the blasting of 38 tunnels and numerous "windows" in the rock. Look out particularly for the "Marble Bridge", the Shrine of Eternal Spring" and the place where blocks of smooth marble are heaped one on top of the other like ice-floes.

Tienshiang

At the upper end of the gorge lies the pleasant resort of Tienshiang (450m/1477ft); an exposed suspension bridge leads to a temple and a pagoda. Further west, in Tayuling, a side road leads off to the Hohuanshan massif (highest peak 3422m/11,230ft), so popular with winter sports enthusiasts and climbers, and then down to Wushe and on to the Lake of the Sun and the Moon (see subsequent entry).

6km/3¾ miles beyond Wushe lies the spa town of Lushan.

Lushan

To the north-east of Lushan will be found the resort of Lishan, which attracts visitors all the year round. It boasts a large hotel built in the classical palace style.

Lishan

The road now continues westward downhill, past the Techi and Kukuan reservoirs and through large banana plantations, to Tungshih.

Tungshih

Taichung (pop. 763,000), with its artificially-constructed harbour, is the most important town in central Taiwan. Now the island's third largest town, it was founded by Chinese settlers from the mainland in 1721 and was initially named Tatun (Great Hill). When the Japanese came to Taiwan in 1895 they renamed it Taichung and made it into one of the island's major towns. Its status was further enhanced when the sea-port 26km/22 miles further to the west came into operation. A ten-lane motorway links the port with the town itself.

Taichung

Taichung's town emblem is the 26·8m/88ft high statue of the Buddha, which is one of the largest of its kind to be found anywhere in Taiwan; it contains a number of rooms, including even a small library.

Places of interest near to Taichung include the Pan Chue Temple, with a bell-tower and a Buddha figure, as well as the Christian University of Tunghai with its many Oriental style buildings and the fine Luce Chapel, designed by the internationally famous architect Ieoh Ming Pei.

In Wufeng, 10km/6 miles south of Taichung, the Hall of the Provincial Collection and, a little way away, a huge statue of the Buddha 21·8m/71½ft tall, are well worth seeing; large stone dragons guard the road to the statue.

Wufeng

The town of Chunghsinghsintsun, 25km/15½ miles south of Taichung, is the seat of Taiwan's provincial government (as opposed to the central government).

Chunghsingh-sintsun

10km/6 miles further south, near Yuanlin, lies what is probably the largest rose garden on Taiwan.

★ Rose Garden near Yuanlin

Chitou Woodland Leisure Park, some 80km/50 miles south of Taichung, extends over 2488ha/6145 acres and is sponsored by the Taiwanese National University. Most of the woodland is covered in bamboo, but its pride and joy is a cypress tree, about 2800 years old and 46m/150ft tall, regarded by many of the local people as a holy tree.

Chitou Woodland Park

Large numbers of pilgrims come to pay homage to a 21·8m/72ft tall figure of the Buddha seated on his throne, on a mountain peak 19km/12 miles south-west of Taichung. The base of the statue is 4·2m/13¾ft high and covered with lotus blossom.

Buddha statue near Changhua

The well-known Sun Moon Lake (Jihyuetan) lies 70km/43½ miles south-east of Taichung in the midst of some charming countryside offering much in the way of holiday and leisure facilities, a native village and a number of temples. Near the south bank of the lake stands Hsuan Chang Temple, the shrine of which contains the remains of the famous monk of that name. Under the Tang dynasty Hsuan Chang brought some Buddhist writings back to China and these enabled him to spread the gospel. A little further south towers the nine-storey T'zu En Pagoda.

★★ Sun Moon Lake

A magnificent Butterfly Garden has been laid out close to the nearby town of Puli. The whole garden is covered with a large net so that visitors can observe the insects at close quarters.

★ Butterfly Garden near Puli

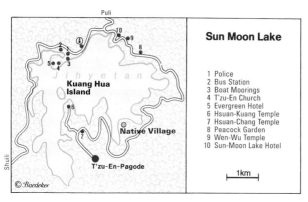

Puli

Sun Moon Lake

Kuang Hua Island

Jihyetan

Native Village

T'zu-En-Pagode

Shuili

© Baedeker

1 Police
2 Bus Station
3 Boat Moorings
4 T'zu-En Church
5 Evergreen Hotel
6 Hsuan-Kuang Temple
7 Hsuan-Chang Temple
8 Peacock Garden
9 Wen-Wu Temple
10 Sun-Moon Lake Hotel

1km

15km/9½ miles north-east of Sun Moon Lake lies an extensive woodland holiday centre together with the Geographical Centre of Taiwan.

Geographical Centre of Taiwan

The holiday region of Alishan, situated in the mountain range of the same name in the interior of Taiwan, is one of the most beautiful on the island. It can be reached along Highway 18 which crosses Taiwan from east to west, or by train from Chiai. The journey by mountain railway is particularly charming; it leads through tropical countryside along a 72km/45 mile stretch of track laid by the Japanese in 1912 which includes 80 bridges and 50 tunnels, up to the pleasantly cool or temperate mountain village of Alishan (2190m/7187ft). The train from Chiai usually stops en route at the Holy Tree, a 3000 year-old cypress which was struck by lightning in 1947. It is over 18m/60ft tall and 14·6m/48ft in circumference. Steam-train enthusiasts will be pleased to know that some old locomotives still operate in Alishan.

★Alishan

In Alishan itself, where there is good accommodation to be had, the small museum, a botanical garden, the romantic Two Sisters Pool and the Tree of the Three Generations are all worth a visit. Many visitors take the opportunity to climb up to the viewing platform on Mount Chu from where they can admire the sea of clouds below and the Yushan massif (Jade Mountains; highest peak 3997m/13,118ft). Watching the sunrise from Mount Chu is also an unforgettable experience.

Tainan (pop. 660,000), the "City of A Hundred Temples" (at present more than 200!) is the oldest town in Taiwan. Its history – from 1684 to 1887 it was the island's capital – is closely linked with the name of Cheng Cheng-kung (Koxinga), the great Chinese hero who expelled the Dutch colonists from the island.

Tainan

The chief place of interest is the Cheng Cheng-kung (Koxinga) Shrine, a complex of buildings in the Chinese temple style with a statue of the hero in the main hall. Nearby is a Folk Art Museum, while to the north stands the oldest Temple of Confucius on Taiwan; it was built by General Chen Yung-hua, a follower of Koxinga, in the 17th c. and carefully restored some time ago.

Chihkan Tower, a little further north, was built in 1875 in place of the Dutch fort known as "Providentia", which was destroyed in an earthquake in 1862. On a rampart opposite the entrance can be seen stone turtles and stelae engraved with Chinese characters and picture-symbols. Originally Fort "Providentia" was connected to Fort "Zeelandia" by an underground

◀ *T'zu-En Pagoda near the Sun Moon Lake*

421

tunnel. It was in the latter fort, the walls of which were built with Dutch bricks, that Koxinga died in 1662.

In Kai Yuan Temple, one of the oldest Buddhist shrines on the island, visitors will be interested in the statue of the thousand-armed Goddess of Mercy and the "Shrine of the Five Concubines" (five women who committed suicide in 1683 when the last Ming fortress surrendered to the Qing dynasty).

Kuantzeling Yi Tsai Lu Erh Men

Situated fairly close to Tainan, the thermal spa town of Kuantzeling, Yi Tsai, a fort built by the French in 1874, and Lu Erh Men (where Koxinga landed in 1661), are all worth a visit.

Coral Lake

30km/19 miles north-east of Tainan stretches Coral Lake (Wushantou reservoir), a reservoir bespattered with over 100 islets and cliffs and in rural surroundings. The region around the lake – on which boat trips can be made – is rapidly becoming a holiday area.

Kaohsiung

Kaohsiung (pop. 1,400,000), on Taiwan's south-west coast, is the capital of Kaohsiung province and the country's largest port. It is the site of the largest breaker's yard for ships, the second largest dry dock and the fifth largest container terminal to be found anywhere in the world. In addition to being home to numerous export-orientated industrial firms Kaohsiung also boasts the country's second international airport.

Places of tourist interest in Kaohsiung include the Buddhist temple known as "Kings of the Three Mountains", the Taoist Wen Wu Shrine and the "Three Phoenix Palace", where buskers play.

★View from Shou-shan

From Shou-shan ("Mountain of Long Life"), on which stands an interesting shrine to the martyrs, there is a magnificent view. The modern Temple of Confucius (built in 1976), the Pavilion of Spring and Autumn near the Tsoying naval base, the Pagodas of the Tiger and the Dragon and the charming Lotus Lake are all most impressive.

Cheng Ching Lakeland District

★Chung Hsing Pagoda

10km/6 miles outside Kaohsiung lies the Cheng Ching Lake District, which has much to offer in the way of attractions, such as a zig-zag bridge, a lovers' bridge, three pavilions, and some of Taiwan's best-known landmarks, the Chung Hsing Pagoda, the Moon Pavilion and a Road of Orchids. The Kaohsiung Golf and Country Club course lies near the Chung Hsing Pagoda.

★Kenting National Park

Much of the southern tip of the island of Taiwan is studded with coral reefs, and a large part of the total of 32,631ha/113,230 acres of land here forms part of the Kenting National Park, which also takes in the coastal waters.

Oluanpi

The southernmost point is the holiday town of Oluanpi, where traces of prehistoric settlements have recently been discovered. One prominent feature is the local lighthouse, built in 1882, from which on a clear day it is possible to see as far as the Philippines, on the far side of Bashi Strait. The beaches of Oluanpi and other places nearby, especially Kenting north-west of Oluanpi, are excellent for bathing, snorkelling, diving and collecting shells. However, beware of sea snakes which hide in the rocks and coral reefs both on and off the coast.

★Chuan Fan Hsih Coral Rock

Halfway between Oluanpi and Kenting towers the very impressive coral rock known as Chuan Fan Hsih; it is 18m/60ft high and 115ft wide.

Kenting Wild Life Park

A short distance inland lies Kenting Wild Life Park, on the site of a tropical botanical garden which was laid out in 1906. Here visitors can admire more than 1200 different species of plants and lumps of coral retrieved from the sea.

A few miles south-west of the little town of Hengchun lies Lake Lungluan, 175ha/437 acres in area and up to 3·5m/11½ft deep. It contains large numbers of fish and every autumn thousands upon thousands of migratory birds settle on its banks.

Lake Lungluan near Henchun

Everywhere on Taiwan's south coasts will be found tropical vegetation, which has germinated from seeds brought here by wind and sea from the islands of south-east Asia.

Chihpen, on Taiwan's south-east coast, is a popular spa town; it lies 15km/9 miles from the port of Taitung which was at one time extended by the Japanese.

Chihpen
Taitung

Taiwanese Islands of Penghu, Lan Yu and Lu Tao

The 64 Penghu or Pescadores Islands (Penghu Lieh Tao) in the Formosa (Taiwan) Strait have a combined area of 127sq.km/49sq. miles and a population of 100,000.

Penghu Lieh Tao
(Pescadores)

Their beautiful beaches make the islands popular with holidaymakers. However, they should be avoided between October and March, because it can be very stormy during those months. The name "Pescadores" (meaning fishermen) stems from the Portuguese who fished these seas in the 16th c.

★Bathing beaches

Makung, the chief town on Penghu Island, is a busy fishing port. Interesting sights include the bridge (5541m/6060yd long including ramps at either end) over Penghu Bay, Matsu Temple or Temple of the Goddess of the Sea, dating from 1539 and the oldest of all Taiwanese temples, and the Holy Banyan Tree, the roots of which cover half a hectare/1¼ acres of the temple courtyard.

Makung

The island of Lan Yu ("Isle of Orchids") is 45sq.km/17½sq. miles in area and lies in the Pacific Ocean 75km/47 miles off the south coast of Taiwan. On it live 2600 descendants of the Yami, immigrants who settled here before the Chinese came. Living mainly from fishing, the Yami still sail their traditional black and white, canoe-like boats and live in flat-roofed, low-built houses which afford protection from the frequent typhoons.

Lan Yu

Naturalists and all those interested in botany will find on the island an incredible variety of orchids. All who like a beach holiday will also get their money's worth here.

★Orchids

The Pacific island of Lu Tao (Green Island, area 16·3sq.km/6·3sq. miles, pop. 3800), about 30km/19 miles east of the Taiwanese port of Taitung, is catering more and more for tourists. It offers excellent facilities for bathing, diving, shell-collecting, fishing and walking.

Lu Tao

Taiyuan

J 4

Chinese
equivalent

Capital of Shanxi Province
Altitude: 800m/2626ft. Area: 3044sq.km/1175sq. miles
Population: 1,840,000 (conurbation 2,230,000)

Taiyuan lies in the centre of Shanxi province in northern China, on the northern edge of the fertile Taixuan Basin, at 112°32′E and 37°42′N.

Situation and
Communications

The town is 11 hours by rail or 1½ hours by air from Beijing. In addition there are regular flights from a dozen other Chinese cities, including

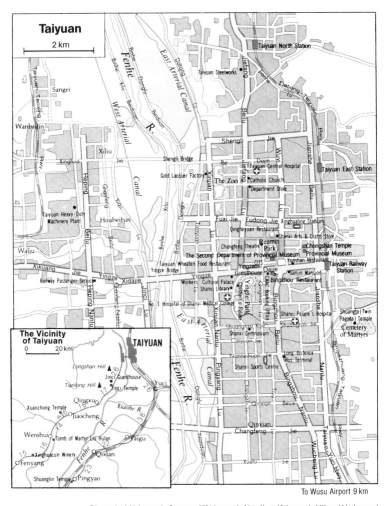

Taiyuan

2 km

Fenhe River
East Arterial Canal
Datong–Taiyuan Jiefang
Taiyuan North Station
Taiyuan Steelworks
Beilu
Wuyi Jie
Jianshe Beilu
Datong–Taiyuan Rwy
Sangei
Xinhua
West Backstrom
Bandon
Taiyuan Tieoning
Wanbailin
Xiliu
Heping
Xinghuo
Qingheng
Xiqu
West Arterial Canal
Shengli Bridge
Shengli
Bei
Jie
Doije
Taiyuan Central Hospital
Catholic Church
Department Store
Taiyuan East Station
Gold Lacquer Factory
The Zoo
Xinjuan
Taiyuan Heavy-Duty Machinery Plant
Houbeitun
Beilu
Dongli
Binhe
Fuxi Jie
Fudong Jie
Xinghualing Stadium
Qingheyuan Restaurant
Shanxi Arts & Crafts Store
Changfeng Theatre
Beimin Park
Chongshan Temple
Waliu
Xikuang
Jie
Yingze
Xidajie
Railway Passenger Service
Heping
Shenheng
Nanlu
The Second Department of Provincial Museum
Taiyuan Wheaten Food Restaurant
Yingze Bridge
Yingze Jie
Yingze Dajie
Provincial Museum
Yunshan Restaurant
Taiyuan Railway Station
Binzhou Restaurant
Sanjin Mansion
Workers' Cultural Palace
Shanxi Library
Yingze Guesthouse
Children's Palace
Qingnian
Binzhou Beilu
Jianshe
No 1 Hospital of Shanxi Medical College
East Arterial Canal
Binhe
Yingze Park
Shuangtas Xiije
Shanxi People's Hospital
Shuangta (Twin Pagoda) Temple
Shuangtasi Jie
Cemetery of Martyrs
Shanxi Gymnasium
Caiyuan Jie
Nannehuan
Shanxi Sports Centre
Long-distance Bus Terminal
Nannehuan
Pingyang
Chang-an
Fenhe River
Canal
Binhe
Dongli
Beijie
Xuefu
Qixian Nanlu
Qixian
Changfeng Jie
Taiyuan–Yuci Highway
Wucheng Lu

To Wusu Airport 9 km

The Vicinity of Taiyuan

0   20 km

TAIYUAN
Longshan Hill
Jinci Guesthouse
Tianlong Hill
Jinci Temple
Yuci
Xuanzhong Temple
Qingxu
Jiaocheng
Xiaohe R.
Wenshui
Tomb of Martyr Liu Hulan
Taigu
Xinghuacun Winery
Qixian
Fenghe R.
Fenyang
Shuanglin Temple
Pingyao

Shanghai (2 hours), Canton (2½ hours), Nanjing (3 hours), Xi'an (1½ hours)
and Tianjin (1½ hours).

History   There were settlements in this region back in Neolithic times. The town was
founded about 2400 years ago, under the name of Jinyang. It found itself
under constant attack from tribes from the north who used it as a base for
further conquering sorties. In the early 7th c. Li Yuan led a peasants'
uprising, overturned the Sui dynasty and in 618 established the Tang
dynasty. Wars brought about the destruction of Jinyang in 979. It was
rebuilt three years later and renamed Songcheng. In 1375 the town
expanded enormously, became the seat of government for the Taiyuan
region from which it took its name. The viceroys of Shanxi province resided

here during the Ming period (1368–1644). The "White Lotus" secret society, which had been in existence since the 11th c., supported the xenophobic movement which led to the outbreak of the Boxer Rebellion.

Today Taiyuan is not only the political and cultural focus of Shanxi province but also one of northern China's major industrial centres.

Located in the east of the city, the Provincial Museum is housed in a former Jin (1115–1234) temple; on display are finds from the Neolithic Age, as well as bronzes, lacquer-work and paintings from various dynasties.

    Another department of the museum can be found in the Chungjang Gong Palace to the west.

Sights

Provincial Museum (Shanxi Sheng Bowuguan)

The Temple of Respect for Kindness opposite the Provincial Museum dates from the Tang era (618–907). In 1381 Zhu Gang, the third son of the emperor of the day, ordered that it be completely rebuilt in honour of his mother, the empress. From the same period are the three Buddha statues, each 8·5m/28ft high, of Guanyin, Goddess of Mercy (with a thousand arms, a thousand eyes and eleven faces) and of the bodhisattvas Wenshu and Puxian, which are to be found in the Hall of Great Compassion (Dabei Dian). The temple also contains large numbers of Buddhist scriptures from the Song, Yuan and Ming period (10th–17th c.).

Temple of Respect for Kindness (Chongshan Si)

The Temple of the Double Pagodas in the south-east of Taiyuan was so named because of its two pagodas, each 54m/177ft high, which serve as the city's emblem.

    A winding internal staircase enables visitors to climb up to the 13th floor of either pagoda, from where they can enjoy a superb view over the city.

★Temple of the Double Pagodas (Shuangta Si)

Surroundings

The Taoist caves on Mount Longshan, 20km/12½ miles south-west of Taiyuan, date from the Yuan period (1271–1368). They contain more than 40 sculptures and inscriptions.

Caves on Mount Longshan (Longshan Shiku)

25km/15½ miles south-west of Taiyuan, at the foot of Mount Xuanweng-shan near the source of the Jin river, lies the Temple of Jinci. This mighty shrine, thought to be dedicated to Prince Shuyu, was founded about 1400 years ago, but has been frequently extended over the centuries right up to the present day. It now comprises about 100 halls, palaces, towers and pavilions. When the town was destroyed during the conflicts of 979 the temple remained unscathed.

    Entrance to the complex is to the south, near the old Gateway of the Clear View (Jingqing Men). Visitors then go direct to the Terrace of the Water Surface (Shuijing Tai), which is used as a theatre, and will see the Shengy-ing Lou Pavilion on the left. They then pass over the Bridge of the Meeting with the Immortals (Huixian Qiao) and come to the Terrace of the Iron Men (Jinren Tai), in the corners of which stand four iron statues dating back to the 11th c. A doorway then leads to the Opera Hall (Xiandian; 12th c.) and across the Flying Bridge, supposed to symbolise a bird in flight, to the Hall of the Holy Mother.

★★Temple of Jinci (under restoration)

This hall was built between 1023 and 1031 in memory of Yijiang, the mother of Prince Shuyu. It contains 43 painted terracotta statues; the largest in the wooden niche represents the Holy Mother, the other 42 are ladies of her court in varying poses and with different facial expressions.

    Near the temple stands an extremely ancient cypress tree, which dates back to the Zhou era (1066–221 b.c.). Another very ancient tree, an acacia which is some 1400 years old, stands a few yards away in the Temple of Guan Gong.

Hall of the Holy Mother (Shengmu Dian)

Taiyuan

Temple of the Goddess of Water	Further to the west is the 16th c. Temple of the Goddess of Water (Shuimu Lou).
Spring of the Fountain of Youth	In front of the temple bubbles the Spring of the Fountain of Youth (Nanlao Quan), the main source of the Jinshui river; by it towers an eight-storeyed 6th c. pavilion.
Shanli Quan Spring	South-east of the Temple of the Holy Mother this spring also bubbles forth under a pavilion.
Cave systems	To the north lies a system of caves, in one of which the academic and calligrapher Fu Shan (1608–84) is thought to have lived. To the south-east of Shanli Quan Spring stands the Temple of Prince Shuyu of the Tang (Tang Shuyu Ci), and in front of it is the Pavilion of the Tang Stela (Tangbei Ting), which houses an inscribed pillar with 1023 characters engraved by the Emperor Taizong in 646.
Caves on Mount Tianlongshan	The twenty or more caves on the slopes of Mount Tianlongshan 40km/ 25 miles to the south-west date mainly from the Tang period (618–907); some are even older. Unfortunately, most of the sculptures are very poorly preserved, but the Buddha statue in Cave 9 is in good condition.
The Hanging Temple (Xuanzhong Si)	Some 60km/37 miles south-west of Taiyuan, in the Jiaocheng district, a Buddhist temple dating from 472 has been built on a steep rock-face – hence its name. It is the Shrine of the Denomination of the Land of the Pure (Jingtuzong). In the second half of the 19th c. it was almost completely burned down; only the Pavilion of a Thousand Buddhas (Qianfo Ge) remained intact. The edifice was restored to its former glory when it was rebuilt in 1955, and it is now home to more than 70 sculptures in wood, clay and wrought-iron.
Hall of the Heavenly Kings	The Hall of the Heavenly Kings (Tianwang Dian) dates from 1605 and is the oldest building in the complex.
Village of the Apricot Blossom (Xinghuacun)	The village of Xinghuacun, 105km/65 miles south-west of Taiyuan, is known worldwide for its Fen Jiu and Bamboo liqueurs (Zhuyeqing). They are both distilled from corn, using pure water from the Heavenly Spring (Shenjing). Such spirits have been produced in Xinghuacun for 1500 years and still make an important contribution to its economy.
★Medieval town of Pingyao (Pingyao Gucheng)	The little town of Pingyao, 107km/66 miles south of Taiyuan, is only 2·1sq.km/⅞sq. mile in area, and has succeeded in retaining its medieval appearance and atmosphere for more than 600 years. Its defensive walls, streets, houses and temple buildings are for the most part well-preserved. The town walls are 6157m/6754yd in length, 6 to 10m/20 to 33ft high, defended by six gate-towers, 72 small watch-towers and 3000 merlons which represent the most famous disciples of Confucius and his 3000 pupils.
★Temple of the Two Forests (Shuanglin Si)	This temple 7km/4½ miles south-west of Pingyao covers an area of some 1·5ha/4¼ acres; founded in 571, it was rebuilt during the Ming dynasty (1368–1644). There are three courtyards around which are grouped ten temple halls. Its 2052 clay sculptures make it a truly representative museum of the Buddhist sculptor's art.
★Temple of the Great Victory (Guangsheng Si)	The Temple of the Great Victory, 200km/124 miles south-west of Taiyuan near the town of Hongtong, includes the well-known Pagoda of the Flying Rainbow (Feihong Ta). This originally dated from the year 147, but was destroyed together with all the other temple buildings in a heavy earthquake in 1303. Between 1515 and 1527 a new pagoda – 47m/154ft high, octagonal in shape, with three storeys, and clad with glazed bricks coloured red, orange, yellow, green, blue and violet – was erected on the old foundations. Visitors who climb the internal staircase can admire the richly-decorated walls.

Mount Wutaishan is one of the four mountains which are holy to Buddhists, the other three being Putuoshan in Zhejiang province, Jiuhuashan in Anhui province and Emeishan in Sichuan province. The word "wutai" means "five terraces"; the mountain was so called because of its five terrace-shaped peaks. The north peak (Dou Feng), at 3058m/10,036ft, is the highest in the chain. Mount Wutaishan lies some 200km/77 miles from Taiyuan, from where there is an overland bus service which passes through some impressive mountain scenery en route to Wutaishan.

★★Mount
Wutaishan

As long ago as the Eastern Han period (24–220) there was a monastery on the mountain dedicated to Wenshu Pusa, God of Wisdom; over the centuries the number of monasteries has increased to several hundred. From the beginning of the Tang era (618–907) the monks living on Mount Wutaishan maintained close contact with their fellow believers in Japan, Indonesia and Nepal. Mount Wutaishan enjoyed a further halcyon period during the Ming period (1368–1644).

Today there are 58 monasteries in all on the mountain, most of them containing Buddhist sculptures. Attempts are at present being made to restore those buildings which remain.

The Temple of the Manifestation, north of Taihuai, a village in the central part of Mount Wutaishan, is one of the oldest Buddhist temple complexes anywhere in the world. It was founded in the 1st c. A.D. and later frequently altered and extended until its total area reached its present 8ha/20 acres. Numerous ancillary buildings are grouped around the seven main temples. Note particularly the Bronze Hall and Bronze Pagodas.

Temple of the
Manifestation
(Xiantong Si)

The Temple of the Pagodas lies to the south of the Temple of the Manifestation, of which it originally formed a part. It was in the Ming period (1368–1644) that it became a temple in its own right. It was then that the 50m/164ft high pagoda – the emblem of Mount Wutaishan and which houses a Shakyamuni relic – and the wooden arched gateway at the entrance were built.

Temple of
the Pagodas
(Tayuan Si)

According to a legend dating back to the Northern Wei period (386–534), the Monastery of the Bodhisattva north of the Temple of the Manifestation on Lingiju Feng Peak was the residence of Wensha Pusa. The Kangxi and Qianlong emperors stayed here quite often and left behind inscriptions carved on two stelae which can still be seen today. Particularly impressive is the rectangular stone tablet, measuring 6m/20ft tall and 1 by 1m/39 by 39in. across, with Qianlong's calligraphy in four languages (Chinese, Manchurian, Mongolian and Tibetan).

Monastery of the
Bodhisattva
(Pusa Ding)

The Temple of the Manjushri Image, about 1km/1100yd south of the Monastery of the Bodhisattva, was founded during the Tang era (618–907), but rebuilt in 1487 following a fire.

Temple of the
Manjushri Image
(Shuxiang Si)

The Wenshu Ge Pavilion contains a 9m/30ft high figure (1496) of Wenshu Pusa (Bodhisattva Manjushri) seated on a lion's back. The other 503 statues (three Buddhas and 500 Luohans) also date from the same period.

Wenshu Ge
Pavilion

The Temple of Rahula, 1km/1100yd east of the Temple of the Manifestation, was originally built during the Tang period (618–907), but re-built in 1492. All the buildings and statues are from the latter period. According to tradition, every year on the 14th day of the sixth lunar month Rahula, son of Shakyamuni, would organise a masked ball to mark the anniversary of Manrushri's birth. This tradition was carried on for many centuries after Rahula's death.

Temple of
Rahula
(Luohou Si)

The Temple of the Radiance of Buddha, built in the 5th c., lies in the south-western part of Mount Wutaishan.

Temple of the
Radiance of
Buddha
(Foguang Si)

Paintings and sculptures from the Tang period (618–907) can be seen here.

★**Monastery of Eternal Joy** (Yongle Gong)

The Taoist Monastery of Eternal Joy near Ruicheng, a small town 400km/250 miles south-west of Taiyuan, was originally built between 1247 and 1262 by the Huanghe near Yongle, the birthplace of the immortal Taoist Lü Donghin (8th c.). The whole complex of buildings we see today took about 120 years to complete; the famous wall-paintings are also from that same period. In 1959, when the Sanmenxia hydraulic engineering project was carried out in the region around Yongle, the monastery was moved to the slopes of a picturesque hill near Ruicheng.

Today the complex comprises four temple buildings erected in a line going from north to south, which have wall-paintings covering an area of some 960sq.m/10,300sq.ft.

The first temple, the Hall of Dragons and Tigers (Longhu Dian), contains murals depicting deities, court officials and warriors.

Hall of the Three Pure Ones (Sanqinq Dian)

The 1325 wall-painting in the adjoining Hall of the Three Pure Ones, which is dedicated to the three major Taoist deities, is 95m/312ft long and 4m/13ft high. It bears the title "Homage to the Founder of Taoism", and shows 286 immortal souls prostrated before the Great Wise One.

Hall of the Pure Yang (Chunyang Dian)

The walls of the Hall of the Pure Yang, which is also known as the Hall of Lü Dongbin, are decorated with 52 frescos dating from 1358 which portray the life of this Taoist saint.

Hall of Chongyang Dian

In the Hall of Chongyang Dian visitors can admire 49 wall-paintings which are dedicated to Wang Chongyang (1112–70), a spiritual Taoist leader.

Tianjin   K 3–4

Chinese equivalent

天津市

Special Self-governing Municipality
Altitude: 4m/13ft. Area: 4276sq.km/1651sq. miles
Population: 9,280,000

Situation and Communications

Tianjin lies in the north of China, 137km/85 miles south-east of Beijing. at 117°13′E and 39°09′N. It can be reached from Beijing by rail, bus or air. As Tianjin is an important rail, road, air and shipping hub – it lies at the confluence of five tributaries of the Haihe river – it is also easy to get to from other large Chinese cities. There are also daily scheduled flights to Hong Kong.

History

The first settlements in the region date back to the times of the Warring Kingdoms (475–221 B.C.). Tianjin was well known as a trading settlement in the 12th c., when it was a centre for the sale and distribution of corn and other foodstuffs from the south.

In 1404 the town – then known as Tianjinwei – was given a town-wall and made into a military garrison. It became increasingly important as a commercial centre during the Qing dynasty (1644–1911). In 1858 the Chinese government was obliged to sign the "Treaty of Tianjin" which provided trading concessions to foreigners, something which the population found abhorrent and which led to serious conflicts. Two years later foreign powers occupied Tianjin and declared its port open to all trading ships. In the years that followed Great Britain, France, Japan, Germany, Russia, Italy, the Austro-Hungarian Empire and Belgium were all granted trading franchises here, and they gave the town a certain European character which it still retains to some degree.

By 1860 Tianjin had grown into an important sea-port, and ten years later the first Chinese textile factory opened up here. In the 130 years since then about 4400 firms of various kinds have become established.

During the Boxer Rebellion in 1900 the town-walls were destroyed. In 1937 the Japanese occupied Tianjin. After 1949 industry, especially heavy

Tianjin: a bridge over the Haihe

industry, developed apace. Floods, which had previously been a frequent menace, were kept at bay by means of various engineering projects. In 1976 a devastating earthquake destroyed large parts of the city.

Tianjin, the third largest city in China, is one of northern China's leading industrial cities. Although heavy industry predominates, light industry, chemicals, textiles and the famous carpet factories all make an important contribution to the economy. The city co-operates to a major degree with countries overseas.

Economy

Xingang, one of China's largest ports, is only 48km/30 miles from the centre of Tianjin.

This hall was built in 1976 in memory of Zhou Enlai (see Famous People), who attended Nankai School here between 1913 and 1917 and promoted a patriotic movement.

Sights

Zhou Enlai
Memorial Hall

The Grand Mosque built of wood and located in the north-west of Tianjin dates from 1644. Although the architecture is Chinese the decorative patterns such as flowers and geometric designs clearly show an Islamic influence.

Grand Mosque
(Qingzhen Dasi)

Erected in 1326 and several times restored, this temple at the confluence of the Haihe river and Grand Canal is dedicated to the Heavenly Goddess, patroness of seafarers. The main hall, subsidiary halls and bell and drum tower can still be seen.

Palace of the
Heavenly Goddess
(Tianhou Gong)

The Temple of Great Mercy in the north of the town is one of the best-preserved temples to be found in Tianjin or in the surrounding countryside. It was restored following the 1976 earthquake.

★Temple of
Great Mercy
(Dabei Si)

429

To Jixian 130 km

**Tientsin
Tianjin**

1 km

Dingzigu Gongrenxincun

Xigu Park

Tianjin-Baxian Hwy.

Beijing-Tianjin Hwy.

Qinjian Dao

Ziyahe

Beilu

Daxin Jie

Xiheqiao Beidajie

Yonghe Dajie

Beiyunhe C.

Zhicheng

Xinko

Huangwei

Yuanwei

Meijian Dong-dabao

Xiheyan

Ziya

R.

Tianwei

Beijing-Shanghai Rwy.

Tianjin West Station

Beiyingmen Ximalu

Xiqing Dao

Xizhan Qianjie

(Grand

Santiaoshi History Museum ●

Dabei (Grand Me

Nanyunhe

Canal

Malu

Hebei Dajie

Canal)

Xinheyan

Dateng Lu

The Grand Mosque

Yanhe Malu

Erduoyan Fried-Cake Snack Bar

Xianyang

Taiping Jie

Hongqiao Restaurant

Bei Malu

Xiaoxiguan Dajie

Qiangzi

Xi Malu

Xibeijiao

Dongbeijiao

Beimennei Dajie

Nanmennei Dajie

Dong Malu

Fenshui Dao

Xiyingmen

Dalie

Xiguan Dajie

Ximennei Dajie

Dongmennei Dajie

Hongqi Lu

Limang Lu

Nan Dadao

Qiangzi R.

Huanghe Lu

Dao

Guangkai 2-Wei Lu

Xinanjiao

Nan Malu

Dongnanjiao

Yanchunlou Restaurant

Quanjude Restaurant

Xishi Dajie

5 Zhou Enlai Memorial Hall

Nanshi

Nankai 2-Wei Lu

Nankai Dajie

Tianjin Department Store

Changjiang Dao

Nankai Dao

Nankai 3-Malu

Nankai 2-Malu

Fu'an Dajie

Bayi Auditorium ●

Qiangzi R.

Changjiang Dao

Shengli

Duolun Dao

Gou Stuffed Bun

Gansu Lu

Sh

Nanfeng

Nanyingmen Lu

Laoxikai Chur

Hongqi R.

Xihu Dao

Xihucun

Anshan

Xinxing

Kunming

Yingkou

Yunna

Weijin Lu

Shad

Renm

Qixiangtai Lu

Xikang Lu

Ch

Hongqi Lu

Tianjin University

Weijin R.

Nankai University

Shuihang (Aquatic) Park

To Yangliuqing 11 km

Ningyuan Park

Hongxing Lu

Jinzhong R.

Yueya R.

Jianchi Lu

Tianjin North Station
Zhongshan Lu

Beijing-Harbin Pwy.

Zhongfang Qianjie

Xinda

Kunwei

Wanliucun Dajie

Jinzhonghe

Zengchang

5-Hao Dao

7-Hao Dao

an Park

Jinzhong Lu

Jinzhong Lu

Wangchuanchang
Gongrenxincun

uitizi Dajie

Xinglu

1-Hao Dao

Zhengyi Dao

Dao

Jintang Zhilu

Xinkai

Zhenli

Lu

Lu

Weiguo Dao

Xinguanxun Dajie

Lu

Beijie

Weiguo Dao

Dongchengfang

Tianjin Railway Station

Fuxingzhuang

Shiqiongzi

Cultural Palace
Jiefang Bridge

Hedong Lu

Dajie

Tangkou
Dajie

Beichong

Xiao

Malu
Tangjiakou
Gongrenxincun

Chenglinzhuang Dao

engyinglou Restaurant
Arts Museum

Dao

6-Jing 6-Wei

8-Wei

Zhangguizhuang

chang
orium

ngguo Theatre

Bank of China

Da'erzhong Lu

10-Jing Lu

Dazhigu

Tianjin-Tanggu

15-Jing Lu

Beijing-Harbin

Yueya R.

gxin Park
iakou

Jianshe

Jiefang

Dagu

14-Jing

Lu

Zhigu

ship Guesthouse

Tianjin Hotel

Friendship Store

Tianjin No. 1 Hotel

Tai'an Dao

CTS

Zhongxin

Overseas Chinese Store

15-Jing Lu

Hwy.

Qishilin Restaurant

Lu

Beilu

6-Wei Lu

15-Jing Lu

Foreign Trade Building
Xiaoyingmen

CITS

Lu

Doo

ourist Co

Hebei Lu

Pukou Dao

Fujian

Daqiao

11-Hao Lu

Dao

Guangdong

Dao

Shaoxing

Dagu

8-Hao Dao

No. 2 Workers'
Cultural Palace

Yong'an Dao

Shaoxing

Renmin Park

Qiongzhou

Xiawafang

Haihe

Tianjin History Museum

To airport 7 km

The older part, rebuilt in 1669, houses hundreds of old bronze, iron, wooden and stone statues, a few of which date back as far as the 3rd c. The new section, built in 1949, is the headquarters of the local Buddhists.

Art Museum
(Bowuguan)

The Art Museum in Jiefang Beilu, south of the main railway station, exhibits paintings from the Yuan to the Qing periods (1271–1911).

French Church
(Laoxikai Jiaotang)

This church, built in the early 20th c, in Neo-Romanesque style and located about 1km/1100yd west of the Friendship Guesthouse, is the largest in Tianjin. Its three aisles are decorated with frescos and its ground plan is in the form of the Cross of Lorraine.

★Park on the Water
(Shuishang Gongyuan)

This park in the south-west of the city covers 200ha/500 acres and is a popular place for a day's outing.

Three lakes with thirteen islands in all take up about a half of the park; they are linked with one another by a network of causeways and bridges. Green lawns surround the lakes. There is a zoo in the south of the park.

Surroundings

★Temple of Unique Joy
(Dule Si)

In Jixian, about 120km/75 miles north of Tianjin, the visitor will find the Temple of Unique Joy, which was built in 984 and probably superseded an earlier building from the Tang period (618–907). It is one of China's oldest wooden buildings.

Hall of Guanyin Ge

The Hall of Guanyin Ge is 23m/75ft high and contains a 15m/50ft tall clay statue of Guanyin. The wall-paintings date from the Ming period (1368–1644).

★Mount Panshan

Mount Panshan near Jixian has been described as "the most beautiful mountain east of Beijing". Its highest peak is about 1000m/3300ft. Numerous famous people have visited it ever since the 3rd c.

Temple of Tiancheng Si

Of the many picturesque and historical sites hereabouts, special mention must be made of the Temple of Tiancheng Si on the northern slope of the mountain; it dates from the Tang period (618–907). The original buildings were destroyed during the conflicts of the 1940s and rebuilt in 1980.

Tibet · Xijang   B–G 4–6

Chinese equivalent

西芷自治区

Autonomous Region
Area: 1,221,000sq.km/471,538sq. miles
Population: 2,260,000. Capital: Lhasa

Situation

Tibet lies in south-west China, between longitudes 78° 25′ and 99° 06′E and latitudes 26° 44′ and 36° 32′N.

Tibet, or Bodjul in Tibetan, is China's most thinly populated region, with the majority of the population – more and more of whom are now Chinese – living in the south of the country.

The very religious Tibetans profess Buddhism or Lamaism, a unique mixture of Indian Buddhism and animistic or magical beliefs. The spiritual and temporal head of state is the Dalai Lama ("Broad Sea of Knowledge"), whose succession is assured because Tibetan Buddhists believe that each Dalai Lama is a reincarnation of his predecessor.

The present head of state is the 14th Dalai Lama (Tenzin Gyatso, b. 1935), who received the Nobel Peace Prize in 1989.

China

**Autonomous Region
Tibet (Xizang)**

HEILONGJIANG

JILIN

INNER MONGOLIA
(NEIMENGGU)

LIAONING

XINJIANG

© Baedeker

GANSU

INNER MONGOLIA
(NEIMENGGU)

BEIJING
(PEKING) •

TIANJIN

HEBEI

QINGHAI

NINGXIA

SHANXI

SHANDONG

GANSU

SHAANXI

HENAN

JIANGSU

XIZANG (TIBET)

SICHUAN

HUBEI

ANHUI

SHANGHAI

ZHEJIANG

JIANGXI

HUNAN

GUIZHOU

FUJIAN

YUNNAN

GUANGXI

GUANGDONG

TAIWAN

XIANG GANG
(HONGKONG)

AO MEN
(MACAO)

HAINAN

**The People's
Republic of China**
Zhonghua Renmin Gongheguo

The whole territory occupies the barren Tibetan Plateau, known as the "Roof of the World" because of its average altitude of more than 4000m/13,000ft. The highest section is on the border with Nepal, and Mount Everest is, of course, the highest peak (8848m/29,039ft). This plateau, the highest and most extensive in the world, consists of almost uninhabited steppes and deserts in the west and north and the populated region in the south, in the relatively fertile mountain valleys (average 3900m/12,800ft), especially that of the Yarlung Zangbo Jiang (Brahmaputra) river, between the Trans-Himalayas and the Himalayas. The plateau is bordered in the north by the Kunlun Mountains, the highest peak of which is the Muztag (7723m/25,347ft).

Topography

In southern Tibet rise the rivers Indus and its tributary the Sutlej, the Yarlung Zangbo Jiang, Irawadi, Nujiang and Lancangjiang (Mekong); they all flow from west to east. The upper reaches of the Changjiang form the eastern border with Sichuan.

In 1993 the Chang Tang region in northern Tibet, an area of some 300,000sq.km/116,000sq. miles, was declared a national park – the second largest in the world.

Tibet has to endure an extremely harsh climate, although the sun shines quite often. Average temperatures vary between 23°C/73°F in summer and −15°C/5°F in winter. On the inhospitable Northern Plateau, however, where snow and sandstorms can often rage for weeks on end, the thermometer can fall to below −50°C/−58°F.

Climate

In the 7th c. a Buddhist kingdom was founded in Tibet, and this soon developed into a sizeable military power. In the 9th and 10th c. Buddhism was ousted and replaced by Lamaism, the spiritual leader of which also exercised temporal power over the people. Under the Mongolian Yuan dynasty (1271–1368) Tibet became a kind of vassal state. Chinese influence became evident from the 14th c. onwards. In 1642 the fifth Dalai Lama established a theocratic state. In the 18th and 19th c. the influence of the Chinese emperors increased. In 1903–04 a military expedition into Tibet led by the British officer and explorer Francis Edward Younghusband

History

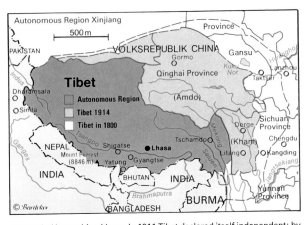

succeeded in reaching Lhasa. In 1911 Tibet declared itself independent; by 1949 it was in reality an autonomous state based on Theocratism (a belief in union of the soul with God through contemplation) and Lamaism. In 1950 troops of the Chinese People's Liberation Army (PLA) occupied the country and a year later it was incorporated into the union of Chinese states. In 1959 an uprising was suppressed by the PLA, prompting tens of thousands of Tibetans, including the Dalai Lama, to flee to India and neighbouring countries; a number even sought refuge in Europe, especially in Switzerland. On September 9th 1965 Tibet was declared an Autonomous

Potala Palace in Lhasa (see p. 318)

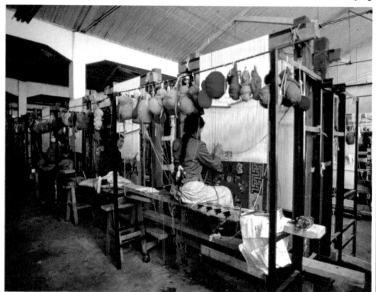

A carpet factory in Tibet

Region within the Chinese People's Republic. In 1966 and 1967 the Cultural Revolution made itself felt in Tibet also. The Red Guards prohibited any religious activity of any kind and destroyed almost all Tibet's historical monuments, especially Lama monasteries; by the time these excesses, which cost the lives of countless Tibetans, finally came to an end a mere thirteen of the original 3800 or so temples and monasteries remained.

After 1976 the leadership in Beijing adopted a more liberal and pragmatic attitude towards Tibet and the region's infrastructure benefited from the construction of a network of roads and the promotion of trade, commerce and industry (especially hydro-electric power, oil, precious metals and coal). In 1980 the Chinese introduced a programme of reform for Tibet, the main points of which were the reintroduction of religious freedom and the partial re-privatisation of agriculture.

Since 1987 there have been more and more demonstrations, particularly of monks and nuns, demanding Tibet's independence; many have been forcibly suppressed by Chinese troops. In 1992, when the central government opened Tibet up to international trade and tourism, and again in 1993 the protests by the Tibetan people against Chinese dominance increased in number. However, China continues to refuse to grant sovereignty to Tibet.

Animal farming with yaks, goats, sheep, horses and donkeys is Tibet's main form of production. About a quarter of the people are nomads. The main agricultural products include barley (in the north this is grown on land as high up as 4600m/15,000ft above sea-level), wheat, pulses, fruit and vegetables.

The industrial sector includes electric power stations, coal mines, engineering, building materials, chemicals, foodstuffs and timber.

Economy

Xigaze and the capital Lhasa (see entries) are the major tourist centres.

It is important that visitors are in good health (normal blood pressure, no respiratory or heart problems). The high altitude soon affects those who

Places to visit

are not used to it and who have come from countries which are not very high above sea-level.

Turpan

Chinese equivalent

Autonomous Region of Xinjiang
Altitude: 154m/505ft below sea level
Area: 10,300sq.km/3977sq. miles. Population: 180,000

Turpan lies in north-west China, at 89°09'E and 42°55'N, in the centre of the Autonomous Region of Xinjiang, in the valley of the same name; the latter covers an area of 50,000sq.km/19,300sq. miles and, being 154m/505ft below sea-level, is the second lowest region on earth after the Dead Sea. Turpan is three hours by train or five hours by bus from the regional capital Ürümqi.

Situation and Communications

The average summer temperature is 32°C/90°F, but in July this sometimes reaches as high as 50°C/122°F. The winters are cold and dry. The number of frost-free days is between 220 and 270. Average annual rainfall is a mere 10mm/0·4in.

Over the years, in attempts to counteract the drought conditions, more than 1000 wells and an underground canal network more than 3000km/1900 miles long have been dug, to conduct water from Tianshin into the Turpan Valley.

The main crops grown are grapes, melons and cotton, the "three treasures of the Turpan Valley". The very sweet and seedless Turpan grapes are dried to make Xinjiang raisins which are sold throughout China and abroad. The sweet Hami melons, which have been grown here for over 1000 years and can weigh as much as 15kg/33lb, are famous throughout the country.

The Turpan district on the Silk Road was known as a busy trading region as long as 2200 years ago.

History

Between the 2nd c. B.C. and the 5th c. A.D. the rulers of the Cheshi kingdom resided in Jiaohe, 10km/6 miles west of present-day Turpan. Around the middle of the 7th c. the Tang dynasty established a government in Turpan to ensure better control of the surrounding regions.

The Emin Mosque was built in the Afghanistan style in the second half of the 18th c. Its tapering minaret (sugong ta in Chinese) is 44m/145ft high.

Sights

Emin Mosque

The Museum contains some valuable pre-15th c. finds from the Astana Tombs.

Museum

2200 years ago Jiaohe, 10km/6 miles west of Turpan, was the capital of the Cheshi kingdom. After the 10th c. it declined rapidly, and in the 14th c. was razed to the ground by Genghis Khan's armies.

Surroundings

★Ruins of the town of Jiaohe (Jiaohe Yizhi)

The Jiaohe site measures 1km/1100yd from north to south and 300m/330yd from east to west. Remains from the Tang period (618–907) include a number of roofless houses, a large but collapsed temple and several roads leading to a main street.

Remains of Buddhist statues can still be seen in the temple niches.

On the road from Turpan to Gaochang stands the Mount of Flames, so called because the sun shining on its reddish rocks makes them glow as if on fire. The rocks are scarred by deep furrows formed by the action of

Mount of Flames (Huoyanshan)

◀ *Minaret of the Emin Mosque*

Turpan: the town centre

flowing water during a wet period in a prehistoric age. In summer temperatures of more than 50°C/122°F are reached here.

The mountain is well-known to the Chinese through the 16th c. novel "Journey to the West" ("Xiyou Ji") by Wu Cheng'en.

★Ruins of the town of Gaochang (Gaochang Yizhi)

Gaochang, 40km/25 miles south-east of Turpan, was built about 2100 years ago. In A.D. 630 the monk Xuanzang stayed here during his pilgrimage to India.

In the mid-9th c. a tribe of Uigurs emigrated from what is now Mongolia, established a kingdom here and chose Gaochang as their capital. However, the settlement became deserted in the 14th c.

Today little remains of Gaochang's former glory – just the towns walls, made of compressed clay, 5m/16ft tall and some 5km/3 miles long; in the south-west, the ruins of a temple complex which once covered an area of 1ha/2½ acres; the network of streets which divided Gaochang into three sections, the outer town, the inner town and the palace district, a lay-out which is reminiscent of that of Chang'an, the seat of the Tang government (618–907).

Astana Tombs

To the north-west of Gaochang lie the Astana Tombs, where the dead were buried from the 3rd to 9th c.

Hundreds of tombs have been uncovered, and three are open to visitors.

★Thousand Buddha Caves of Bezeklik (Baizikelike Qianfodong)

Near Turpan lie the Thousand Buddha Caves.

The best known are undoubtedly those at Bezeklik (some 50km/30 miles north-east of Turpan), a collection of retreats once inhabited by Buddhist monks. Many of the important wall-paintings, a testimony to the heyday of Chinese Buddhism, were discovered by European archaeologists, many of them German, prior to the First World War.

In all visitors can see 57 caves, all numbered, which contain fragments of frescos dating from the 6th to the 14th c. and portraying Buddhist themes.

Wall painting from the Thousand Buddha Caves of Bezeklik

In Cave No. 39 can be seen a group of mourners accompanied by thirteen disciples of Buddha.

Cave No. 39

The north wall of Cave No. 37 shows a painting of a bodhisattva, dressed in red and with blue eyes and a long, straight nose. The explanatory inscriptions are almost all in Chinese and Uigur; this suggests that at this time the cultures of China and Asia Minor complemented and influenced one another.

Cave No. 37

At the approach to the Bezeklik Caves is a mini leisure park where the history of the Silk Road is vividly presented.

Leisure park

Ürümqi

E 3

Chinese equivalent

Capital of the Autonomous Region of Xinjiang
Altitude: 913m/2996ft
Area: 70sq.km/27sq. miles. Population: 870,000

439

Ürümqi

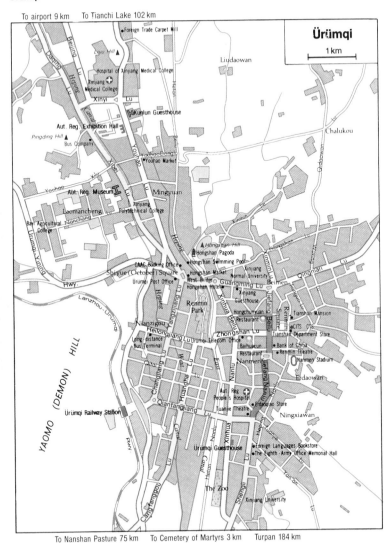

Ürümqi

1 km

To airport 9 km   To Tianchi Lake 102 km

Foreign Trade Carpet Mill
Liudaowan
Leyu Hill
Hospital of Xinjiang Medical College
Xinjiang Medical College
Xinyi Lu
Kunlun Guesthouse
Chalukou
Aut. Reg. Exhibition Hall
Pingding Hill
Bus Company
Youhao Penglu
Youhao Market
Aut. Reg. Museum
Mingyuan
Laomancheng
Xinjiang Polytechnical College
Bayi Agricultural Nongchang College
Hongshan Hill
Hongshan Pagoda
Hongshan Swimming Pool
CAAC Booking Office
Hongshan Market
Shiyue (October) Square
Xinjiang Normal University
Beimen
Qingnian
Urumqi Post Office
West Bridge
Hongshan Hotel
Guangming Lu
Xinjiang Guesthouse
Renmin Park
Hongchunyuan Restaurant
Nianzigou
Heilongjiang Lu
Zhongshan Lu
Tianshan Mansion
CITS CTS
Tianshan Department Store
Long-distance Bus Terminal
Urumqi Telecom Office
Baihuacun
Bank of China
Renmin Theatre
Nanmen
Restaurant
Nanmen Stadium
Erdaowan
Aut. Reg. People's Hospital
Qiantangjiang
Urumqi Railway Station
Tuanjie Theatre
Endaoqiao Store
Ningxiawan
YAOMO (DEMON) HILL
Foreign Languages Bookstore
Urumqi Guesthouse
The Eighth Army Office Memorial Hall
The Zoo
Xinjiang University

Situation and Communications

Ürümqi lies in a oasis in a large desert near the northern foothills of Mount Tianshan, in the north of the Autonomous Region of Xinjiang, at 87°41'E and 43°40'N. The town is on the rail route from Lianyungang (80 hours away by train) to Kazakhstan. There are direct air flights to Beijing, Shanghai, Canton, Xi'an and other large towns and cities. From Ürümqi good roads lead to the furthest corners of the region, as well as to Tibet and Qinghai.

Ürümqi: view of the town

Lake of Heaven to the east of Ürümqi

History	The name Ürümqi comes from the Mongolian and means "Beautiful Pastures". Various tribes grazed their cattle here more than two thousand years ago. In the 1st c. A.D. the Han government sent troops to reclaim the land, but it was not until the Tang era (618–907) that the first urban settlement was formed. In 1758 the town was fortified and shortly after that it was given the name of Dihua. In 1884 Xinjiang was elevated to the status of province and Dihua made the seat of government. It was renamed Ürümqi in 1954, and during the last forty years or so has developed into an industrial town, with coal and iron-ore mining.
Sights Red Mountain (Hongshan)	The Red Mountain towers up amid green countryside to the north of Ürümqi. The mountain itself is bleak and barren with its steep slopes covered in red rock. The peak is surmounted by a nine-storey pagoda, from where there is a beautiful view over the town. After 640, when Buddhism spread through Xinjiang, Red Mountain was for a long time a goal for pilgrims coming from far and wide. At that time there were a large number of monasteries on the mountain.

Surroundings

Southern Mountain Pastures (Nanshan Muchang)	These lush green meadows, surrounded by dense pine forests, lie 75km/47 miles south of Ürümqi in a valley of the Southern Mountain (Nanshan). Shepherds' tents are dotted about everywhere, and several waterfalls can be seen in the distance.
★Heavenly Lake (Tian Chi)	The Heavenly Lake, some 5sq.km/2sq. miles in area, lies 102km/63 miles east of Ürümqi, 1980m/6500ft up on Mount Bogdashan (5445m/17,870ft). The lake, its banks lined with pine-trees and surrounded by snow-capped peaks, is a most impressive sight. It is fed with meltwater from the encircling mountains. A ruler from the Zhou dynasty is said to have held a banquet here 3000 years ago in honour of the Mother of Heaven.

Weifang

Chinese equivalent	潍坊

Province: Shandong
Area: 18,000sq.km/6950sq. miles
Population: 356,000 (conurbation 780,000)

Situation and Communications	Weifang lies in the east of Shandong province, on the railway line from Jinan to Qingdao, at 119°07′E and 36°42′N. There are also buses from Jinan and Qingdao. Weifang has a small airport, but the only flights are to Beijing.
History	During the time of the Three Kingdoms (220–280) Weifang was a major military base. Over the centuries it became less important from a military point of view and more of a cultural centre. For example, Zheng Banqiao, one of the most famous 18th c. Chinese painters, was born here. In more recent years, however, the town has become known all over the world for the manufacture of kites; this has led to Weifang being given the nickname "World Kite Capital". The International Kite Society has its headquarters here and has organised a large kite festival every year since 1984.
Sights ★Shihu Yuan Garden	A large number of buildings in miniature (something frequently found in China, where building land is often at a premium) occupy a small green space measuring only 200sq.m/235sq.yd in the town centre. Laid out in the 18th c., the gardens were originally privately owned by a mandarin, and were opened up to the public only quite recently.

Here visitors can find a small museum with works by the painter and calligrapher Zheng Banqiao, who also held the office of prefect of Weifang for a number of years.

The Kite Museum, 13,000sq.m/140,000sq.ft in total area, lies a few yards from the town centre on the banks of the Bailang river. One large main hall and ten smaller rooms house an exhibition of kites of every conceivable size and shape from many countries, including traditional folk-lore designs as well as some shaped like animals. Visitors can also watch kites being made.

Kite Museum (Fengzheng Bowuguan)

Weihai   L 4

威海市

Chinese equivalent

Population: Shandong. Area: 37sq.km/14sq. miles
Population: 170,000 (conurbation 2,340,000)

Weihai lies at 122°08′E and 37°31′N, in the north-eastern corner of Shandong province, 88km/55 miles east of Yantai, with which it is linked by a good road.

Situation and Communications

In the 14th c. Weihai was a fortified coastal town. In the 1870s the Manchurian government set up a base here for its newly-formed navy, which was completely wiped out by the Japanese in the naval battle off Weihai in 1895. From 1898 to 1930 the town was under British rule, after which it was returned to the Chinese.

History

Mr Liu's Island, just off the coast, is a 20-minute trip by ferry from Weihai. It was here that the base of the ill-fated Chinese navy was situated. Today visitors can still see the headquarters building, the parade ground and some of the battle equipment.

Surroundings

★Mr Liu's Island (Liugong Dao)

The Cape of Chengshan is a rocky promontory on the eastern tip of the Shandong peninsula, about 60km/37 miles east of Weihai.
    According to legend, the Qin Emperor Shi Huangdi came here twice seeking a herb which would provide him with everlasting life.
    On the south side of the cape stand two temples; one is dedicated to the Qin Emperor Shi Huangdi, to commemorate his two visits, while the Temple of the Sun God (Rizhu Ci) was built by the Han Emperor Wudi after he had paid homage to the Sun God on this cliff.

★**Cape of Chengshan** (Chengshan Jiao)

Wenzhou   L 6

温州市

Chinese equivalent

Province: Zhejiang. Area: 25sq.km/10sq. miles
Population: 970,000 (conurbation 6,100,000)

Wenzhou is situated in the south-east of Zhejiang province, on the Quijiang river, at 120°38′E and 28°01′N.
    An important sea and inland port, the city is linked by passenger ship with Shanghai and Ningbo and by bus with Hangzhou, the provincial capital. Wenzhou airport was opened in 1990 and there are now flights to many Chinese towns and cities, including Beijing, Shanghai, Xiamen, Hangzhou, Ningbo, Canton, Chengdu, Wuhan and Nanjing.

Situation and Communications

Wuhan

History

The date when Wenzhou was founded is not known. According to tradition, a town by the name of Yongjia existed here 1600 years ago. When the inhabitants one day saw a white deer on the street they considered this a good omen and changed the name of the town to "Realm of the Deer" (Lu Cheng). It was under the Tangs (618–907) that it was given the name Wenzhou, or "Temperate Town", because of its mild climate. However, the deer remains its symbol, and statues of the animal can still be seen in many places in the town.

In the Song period (960–1279) Wenzhou was one of China's major ports.

Under the Qing dynasty (1644–1911) arts and crafts enjoyed a halcyon period.

Over the years large numbers of people have emigrated from Wenzhou, and many thousands of its former citizens now live in Europe, America and South-East Asia.

Sights

Island in the Heart of the River (Jiangxin Dao)

Measuring 450 by 200m/500 by 550yd, the Island in the Heart of the River lies on the northern edge of town, in the Quijiang river. Its historical buildings and picturesque sites make it a major tourist attraction.

Of particular interest are the 9th c. Temple in the Heart of the River (Jiangxin Si), and the Temple of Wen Tianxiang (Wen Tianxiang Si), built in the 15th c. The latter is dedicated to Wen Tianxiang, a patriotic general who was executed by the Mongols in 1279.

Of the two pagodas on the two hills on the island, the eastern one dates from 869 and the western from 969.

The Museum here documents the history of Zhejiang province.

Surroundings

★Northern Mountain of the Wild Geese (Bei Yandangshan)

This mountain rises near the town of Leqing, about 100km/60 miles northeast of Wenzhou. Its highest point, the Peak of the Gods (Ling Feng), lies 1057m/3470ft above sea-level. Every autumn whole flocks of wild geese fly here in order to spend the winter by one of the lakes, and this is how the mountain got its name.

Bei Yandangshan is known above all for the three waterfalls (Sandie Pu) to the south-west of the Peak of the Gods.

Waterfall of the Great Dragon (Dalong Pu)

The most impressive and most famous is the Waterfall of the Great Dragon, with a fall of 109m/360ft. The strange shapes of the surrounding peaks are such as to transport the observer into the realms of fantasy.

Wuhan   J 5

Chinese equivalent

武汉市

Capital of Hebei Province
Altitude: 24m/79ft. Area: 1557sq.km/600sq. miles
Population: 3,340,000 (conurbation 6,240,000)

Situation and Communications

Wuhan lies at the confluence of the Changjiang and Hanshui rivers, in the east of Hebei province, on the Beijing–Canton rail route, at 114°17′E and 30°32′N.

Wuhan can be reached by rail or air from all the major Chinese cities. There are also ships going to Chongqing, Nanjing and Shanghai.

Importance

Wuhan is a traffic hub and vital industrial and commercial centre as well as being a city of culture and politics. There are rich deposits of iron-ore in the surrounding countryside, and a giant iron and steel combine has grown up here.

River harbour on the Changjiang

The city can be divided into three districts – Wuchang in the east, Hankou in the north and Hanyang in the south; at one time these were all independent towns and separated from one another by the Changjiang and Hanshui rivers. Wuhan's name is in fact formed from the first syllables of the names of these three towns.

Wuchang, the oldest of the three towns, was provided with fortifications as long ago as the Han period (206 B.C. to A.D. 220) and was the capital of Huguang province. The peasants' revolutionary army led by Chen Youliang made it its headquarters in the second half of the 14th c. Wuchang has functioned as the provincial capital since the early 20th c. In 1911 an uprising against Qing rule broke out here.

History

Hanyang was founded in the Sui period (581–618). China's very first iron and steel works came into operation here at the end of the 19th c. Today light industry predominates.

Hankou was just a village until 1858, when the Western powers made it a trading port. Britons, French, Germans and Russians settled here and soon made it into a commercial centre. This development was assisted by the building of the Beijing–Hankou railway. This in turn produced a proletariat which formed the basis of the revolutionary movement.

Much of Hankou's architecture still betrays a strong European influence.

Yellow Crane Tower, extolled as the "eternal sight of the city", stands proudly on the top of Snake Mountain (Sheshan) in the west of Wuchang district. The original building was erected in 1223 in memory of an immortal being who was said to have flown down to the mountain on the back of a yellow crane.

Sights

★Yellow Crane Tower
(Huanghe Lou)

The five-storey, 51m/167ft high tower has been destroyed several times and subsequently rebuilt. It last burned down in 1984 and was rebuilt in 1985. The first tower is said to have been built here 1600 years ago.

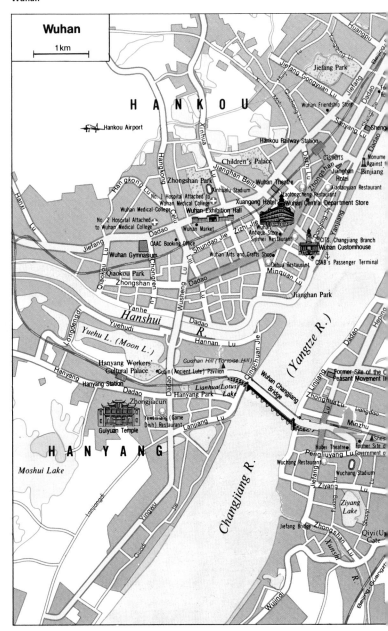

Wuhan

1km

HANKOU

Hankou Airport

Jiefang Gongyuan Lu   Jiefang Park

Wuhan Friendship Store

Hankou Railway Station

Children's Palace

CITS CITS

Jianghan   Binjiang
Hotel

Monume
Against

Jianghan Beilu   Wuhan Theatre
Zhongshan Park

Xiaotaoyuan Restaurant

Xinhualu Stadium   Laotongcheng Restaurant

No. 1 Hospital Attached To   Xuangong Hotel   Wuhan Central Department Store
Wuhan Medical College
Wuhan Medical College   Wuhan Exhibition Hall

No. 2 Hospital Attached   Wuhan Market
to Wuhan Medical College   Zizhi Jie   Wuhan
Antique Store
CAAC Booking Office   Shundao Jie   Sijimei Restaurant   CITS, Changjiang Branch
Wuhan Customhouse

Wuhan Gymnasium   Wuhan Arts and Crafts Shops   CSAB's Passenger Terminal

Qiaokou Park   Dehua Restaurant

Zhongshan Dadao   Minquan Lu

Jianghan Park

Hanshui   Yanhe

Yuehudi

Yuehu L. (Moon L.)   Hannan Lu

(Yangtze R.)

Gushan Hill (Tortoise Hill)   Former Site of the C
Hanyang Workers'   Guqin (Ancient Lute) Pavilion   Wuhan Changjiang   Peasant Movement In
Cultural Palace   Qingchuan Jie   Bridge

Hanyang   Hanyang Station   Lianhua (Lotus)   Zhonghua Lu
Dadao   Lake
Zhongjiacun   Hanyang Park   Minzhu

Yeweixiang (Game   Laniiang Lu
Dish) Restaurant
Guiyuan Temple   Hubei Theatre   Former Site o
Penghuyang Lu   Government o
HANYANG   Wuchang Restaurant

Moshui Lake   Wuchang Stadium

Ziyang Lu

Ziyang
Lake

Changjiang R.   Jiefang Bridge   Zhongshan Lu   Qiyi (U
Gate

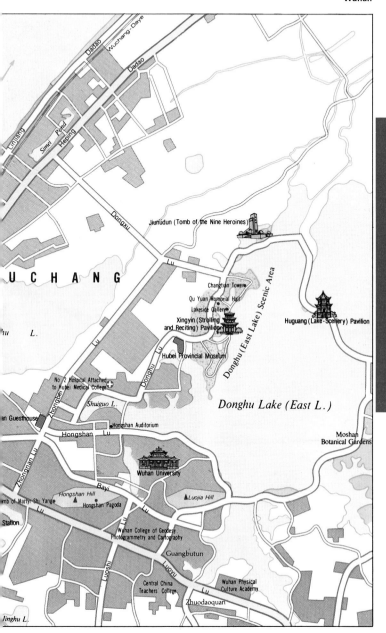

U C H A N G

Jiunüdun (Tomb of the Nine Heroines)

Changtian Tower
Qu Yuan Memorial Hall
Lakeside Gallery
Xingyin (Strolling and Reciting) Pavilion

Huguang (Lake-Scenery) Pavilion

Donghu (East Lake) Scenic Area

Hubei Provincial Museum

hu L.

No. 2 Hospital Attached to Hubei Medical College

Shuiguo L.

Donghu Lake (East L.)

n Guesthouse

Hongshan Auditorium

Hongshan Lu

Moshan Botanical Gardens

Wuhan University

Hongshan Hill

Bayi

mb of Martyr Shi Yang

Hongshan Pagoda

▲Luojia Hill

Station

Wuhan College of Geodesy Photogrammetry and Cartography

Guangbutun

Luoyu

Zhongnan Lu

Zhongbei

Luoshi

Central China Teachers' College

Wuhan Physical Culture Academy

Zhuodaoquan

Jinghu L.

Dadao

Wuchang-Daye

Dadao

Simei Pond

Heping

Linjiang

Dongxu

Lu

Lu

447

Bridge over the Changjiang

From the tower there is a good view of the Changjiang river and the countryside around Wuhan.

Shenxiang Baota Dagoba

The Shenxiang Baota Dagoba near Yellow Crane Tower is at least 9m/30ft tall and dates from the year 1343. It had to be removed to enable the Changjiang Bridge to be constructed, and in 1957 it was rebuilt close by.

Nearby can be seen the former headquarters of the military government during the 1911 uprising.

Mount Hongshan

Mount Hongshan lies east of Yellow Crane Tower. Its temples, pagodas, caves and rocks combine to make it an interesting place to visit.

Special mention must be made of Baoting Si Temple on the southern slope of the mountain, the seven-storey, 43m/140ft high Lingji Ta Pagoda which dates back to the Tang period (618–907), and the 11m/36ft high Xingfusi Ta Pagoda (1270) on the western slope. Also of interest is the Tomb of Shi Yang, one of the leaders of the Great Strike of February 7th 1923, who was arrested that same day and executed a few days later. When the tomb was moved here in 1953 a monument was erected over it.

★East Lake
(Donghu)

East Lake is 33sq.km/12¾sq. miles in area and – as its name suggests – lies in the east of Wuhan. Indented with numerous small bays, the lake is also embellished with bridges, pavilions and villas.

Hubei
Provincial
Museum

This museum on the west bank of East lake documents the history and revolutionary background of Hubei province. Of particular interest are the burial objects which were found in 1978 in the grave of a nobleman who died in 433 B.C. Mention should also be made of a *bianzhong*, a "glockenspiel" with 65 bells of various sizes on a wooden frame; visitors can hear a tape-recording of it being played.

In this hall, built of wood and stone, there is a tea-room and a restaurant.	Hall in which waves can be heard (Tingtao Xuan)
In front of the Strolling and Reciting Pavilion, which can be reached by means of a bridge leading from the bank of the lake, stands a statue of the poet Qu Yuan (c. 332 B.C. to A.D. 295). The pavilion is of three storeys and nearly 23m/75ft high.	Strolling and Reciting Pavilion (Xingyin Ge)
Paintings and seals are displayed in the Lakeside Gallery. Nearby stands the Qu Yuan Memorial Hall. There is a tea-house in Changtian Luo, to the north.	Lakeside Gallery (Binhu Hualang)
On the Hill of the Nine Heroines on the north-west bank of East Lake will be found the Tomb of the Nine Heroines of the Taiping kingdom, who in 1855 valiantly defended Wuhan against the Manchurian army and lost their lives in doing so. They were interred by the populace, and their tomb was rebuilt after 1949.	Hill of the Nine Heroines
Lake Scenery Pavilion is 19m/62ft high and stands on a small island in the lake. It provides a beautiful view.	Lake Scenery Pavilion (Huguang Ge)
Changjiang Bridge leads to Tortoise Hill, in the north-east of the Hanyang district of the town. Here visitors can see the Memorial Temple of the Mythical Ruler Yu (Yugongji Ci), the Tomb of General Lu Su (172–217) and that of the revolutionary Xiang Jingyu (1895–1929).	Tortoise Hill (Guishan)
The Guqin Tai Terrace was laid out probably in the 11th c., in memory of the famous qin player (a qin is a seven-stringed zither-like instrument) Yu Boya, who lived over 2000 years ago and is thought to have come here often to sit and seek solace in his music. It seems that his close friend, Zhong Ziqi, was the only one who appreciated the quality of his composition "Mountain Brook"; when Zhong Ziqi died Yu Boya decided never to play his zither again. On the terrace stands a small pavilion on the ledge of which hangs a small wooden plaque with four Chinese characters which mean "mountain brook"; a commemorative column marks the spot where Yu Boya used to sit and play.	★Guqin Tai Terrace
The Temple of Regained Perfection, about 1km/1100yd south-west of Guqin Tai Terrace, was built in the Qing period (1644–1911), through the efforts of the monk Bai Guang, on the site of a mandarin's private garden, and the architecture is to some degree secular. The main buildings – evenly distributed over the courtyard which is adorned with pools, trees, flower-beds and artificial hillocks – are similar to all other Buddhist temples in China; they include the Buddha Hall, the Luohan Hall (Luohan Tang) containing 500 Luohan statues, and the Changjian Ge Pavilion with sutras (Buddhist teachings).	Temple of Regained Perfection (Guiyuan Si)
This bridge, erected in 1955–57 and the first to be built across the Changjiang river, links the Wuchang and Hanyang districts. 1670m/1832yd long and on two levels; the lower is used by trains and the upper by road traffic.	Changjiang Bridge (Changjiang Daqiao)
Mount Tonglushan lies some 75km/47 miles south-east of Wuhan. Excavations in this region have revealed several hundred underground tunnels, together with tools for mining copper-ore and nine smelting furnaces, some of which date from the Spring and Autumn period (770–221 B.C.). The mining area covers about 8sq.km/3sq.miles, most of which is covered by a layer of slag weighing 40 tonnes, the waste product of copper-smelting.	**Surroundings** ★Old Mines on Mount Tonglushan (Tonglushan Gukuang)
Cockerel Mountain, 200km/125 miles north of Wuhan on the border with Henan province, is famous for its springs, forests and mild climate (the average summer temperature is 24°C/75°F). The mountain is named after a	Cockerel Mountain (Jigongshan)

449

peak, 784m/2573ft high, the shape of which reminds one of a sleeping rooster.

Wuhu

Chinese
equivalent

芜湖市

Province: Anhui. Area: 1124sq.km/444sq. miles
Population: 456,000 (conurbation 946,000)

Situation and
Communications

Wuhu lies in some beautiful countryside in the centre of Anhui province, at the confluence of the Qingyijiang and Changjian rivers, 118°22′E and 31°20′N.

It is 130km/80 miles from Nanjing and 140km/87 miles from Hefei, the provincial capital, and is linked by rail, road and water to these and many other Chinese towns and cities.

History

Wuhu has a history going back more than 2000 years. There was a major settlement here back in the Spring and Autumn period (770–476 B.C.), and it was given its present name during the Han dynasty (206 B.C. to A.D. 220). From the Ming era (1368–1644) onwards it was one of China's richest trading towns and during the Qing period (1644–1911) it became one of the country's four largest centres for the transhipment of rice (the other three being Changsha, Jiujiang and Wuxi). The port was opened to external trade in 1876.

Today Wuhu, with its shipyards, iron foundries and many textile and engineering factories, is an important industrial centre.

Sights

★Lake of Mirrors
(Jinghu)

The crystal-clear waters of the Lake of Mirrors cover an area of 18ha/45 acres. In the second half of the 19th c. the lake was for a number of years the very hub of Wuhu's social life, and its banks were studded with dozens of tea-houses, inns, restaurants and theatres. Today it is still a popular spot for excursions and a leisure centre for the local people, with a library, exhibition building and restaurants.

**Park of the
Reddish-brown
Mountain**
(Zheshan
Gongyuan)

The Park of the Reddish-brown Mountain stretches over an area of some 4sq.km/1½sq. miles in the north-west of Wuhu. Two hills of shimmering red give the park its name. The higher of these (86m/282ft) is dominated by a 16th c. pavilion from which there is a wonderful view over the town. The park also has a small zoo.

Temple of
Universal
Well-being
(Guanghi Si)

The Temple of Universal Well-being was built in the 9th c. on the south-west slope of Reddish-brown Mountain. It comprises three halls in an echelon formation on the hillside. The present buildings date from the Qing period (1644–1911).

Prior to climbing the Mountain of the Nine Blossoms, pilgrims would rest in this temple and light joss sticks.

Surroundings

★★Mountain of
the Nine Blossoms
(Mount
Jiuhuashan)

The Mountain of the Nine Blossoms, 150km/93 miles south-west of Wuhu, is one of the Four Holy Mountains revered by Chinese Buddhists (the other three being Mounts Putuoshan in Zheijang province, Emeishan in Sichuan province and Wutaishan in Shanxi province. Its highest point is the Peak of The Ten Kings (Shiwang Feng), which is 1431m/4696ft.

The mountain's name comes from a poem writen by the Tang poet Li Bai (see Famous People), who compared the nine most beautiful peaks to lotus blossoms. However, its fame goes back much further than that. Large numbers of monasteries were built here in the Eastern Jin period (317–420); there were some 300 in existence in the 17th c., providing accommodation for more than 5000 monks. 56 such sacred buildings still remain and house over 1300 old documents, including seals, letters, calligraphy samples, paintings and Buddhist scripts. Particularly valuable are some palm-leaves from India on which texts from the Sutra were carved 1000 years ago.

The first Temple of Huacheng Si was built in the 8th c.; however, the present buildings – with the exception of Cangjing Lou, which was built between 1426 and 1434 – are from the Qing period (1644–1911).

Temple of
Huacheng Si

South of the Temple of Huacheng Si stands Zhantanlin Temple (late 18th c.). It contains statues of Sakyamuni, Guanyin and Dizang.

Zhantanlin
Temple

The best-known temple on Mount Jiuhuashan is that of Roushen Baodian, first built in 794 and rebuilt in the second half of the 19th c. Today it houses some valuable writings from the Song and Yuan period (10th–14th c.).

Temple of
Roushen Baodian

The Temple of Zhiyuan Si (to the east of Huacheng Si) was built during the rule of Jiajing (reigned 1521–67). Special mention should be made of the three gilded statues of the Buddha in the main hall.

Temple of
Zhiyuan Si

The Palace of the Centenarian on Mount Mokangling contains the mummy, encased in gold, of the monk Haiyu or Wuxia, who lived during the Wanli period (1573–1620) and died at the age of 126.

Palace of the
Centenarian
(Baisui Gong)

On the way to the Peak of the Heavenly Terrace (Tantai Feng) the visitor will pass Bamboo Lake (Zhuhai). From the peak, which is 1325m/4349ft high, Mount Huangshan can be seen to the south and the Changjiang river in the north.

Yellow Mountain, some 150km/93 miles south of Wuhu, has 72 peaks; the highest is Lianhua (1860m/6104ft). The name of the mounain is linked to a legend according to which it was here that the Yellow Emperor carried out his alchemical experiments in an attempt to discover the elixir of life.
    Mount Huangshan is famous for its "four natural wonders" – the steep rock-faces, the pine-trees growing in the strangest shapes imaginable, the grotesquely-formed masses of stone and the sea of cloud through which the peaks protrude. The saying is that Yellow Mountain combines everything that other mountains possess individually – the importance of Mount Taishan, the bleakness of Mount Taishan, the mists and low clouds of Mount Hengshan, the waterfalls of Mount Lushan and the freshness of Mount Emeishan. The flora and fauna, largely unspoiled, are also unique. Many Chinese artists have included it in their paintings (Wushan Painting) and it is the subject of many a book.
When he saw it the famous traveller Xu Xiake is said to have cried "When one has seen the Five Holy Mountains all the others count for nothing; when one has seen Mount Huangshan the Five Holy Mountains suddenly count for nothing".
    A visit to this picturesque region, where the climate is always cool because of the elevated location, usualy begins in Tangkou on the southern edge of the mountain. There are paths linking all the main buildings and places of interests (peaks, waterfalls, trees, temples, pavilions, etc.).

★★Yellow
Mountain
(Mount Huangshan)

In the Wenquan Binguan guesthouse visitors can bathe in the hot springs which maintain a temperature of 42°C/108°F all the year round. They are considered particularly good for the treatment of rheumatism and skin problems.
    Peach Blossom Peak (Taohua Feng) towers over the route north from Tangkou.

Hot Springs

From the "Observe the Waterfall" viewing pavilion there is a fine view of the waterfall.

Guanpu Lou
Pavilion

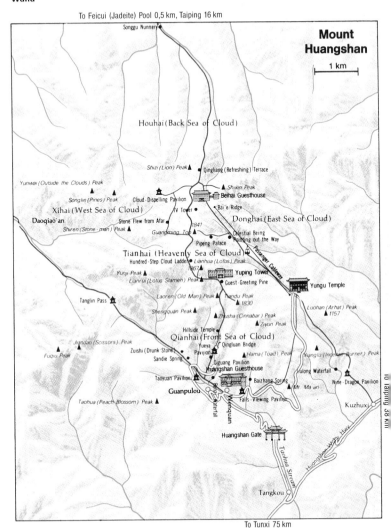

To Feicui (Jadeite) Pool 0,5 km, Taiping 16 km

Songgu Nunnery

Mount Huangshan

1 km

Houhai (Back Sea of Cloud)

Shizi (Lion) Peak ▲   Qingliang (Refreshing) Terrace

Yunwai (Outside the Clouds) Peak ▲   ▲ Shixin Peak

Songlin (Pines) Peak ▲   Cloud-Dispelling Pavilion   ■ Beihai Guesthouse

Xihai (West Sea of Cloud)   TV Tower   ● Bai'e Ridge

Daoqiao'an   Stone Flew from Afar   **Donghai (East Sea of Cloud)**

Shiren (Stone-man) Peak ▲   Guangming Toh ▲ 1841   ● Celestial Being Pointing out the Way

Pipeng Palace

Tianhai (Heavenly Sea of Cloud)   Passenger Cableway

Hundred-Step Cloud Ladder ● Lianhua (Lotus) Peak ▲

Yunji Peak ▲   ▲ 1867 ▦▦▦ Yuping Tower

Lianrui (Lotus Stamen) Peak ▲   ● Guest-Greeting Pine   ■ Yungu Temple

Laoren (Old Man) Peak ▲ ▲ Handu Peak

Tanglin Pass ☖   ▲ 1830   Luohan (Arhat) Peak ▲
                                         ▲ 1157
Shenquan Peak ▲   ▲ Zhusha (Cinnabar) Peak

▲ Ziyun Peak

Hillside Temple ●

Qianhai (Front Sea of Cloud)

Jiandao (Scissors) Peak ▲   Zuishi (Drunk Stone) ● Yueya ● Qingluan Bridge   Xianglu (Incense-Burner) Peak ▲

Fuqu Peak ▲   Sandie Spring ●   Pavilion ● Hama (Toad) Peak

Ciguang Pavilion ☖   Jiulong Waterfall ●

Taoyuan Pavilion ☖   **Huangshan Guesthouse**   ▲ Mi Ma'an   ■ Nine-Dragon Pavilion

Guanpulou   ● Baizhang Spring

Renzi Waterfall   Kuzhuxi

Taohua (Peach-Blossom) Peak ▲   Wenquan   ● Falls Viewing Pavilion

Huangshan–Wuhu Hwy

Huangshan Gate 卄

Taohua Stream

To Taiping 38 km

Tangkou

To Tunxi 75 km

Renzi Pu Waterfall	Next will be seen a further waterfall, Renzi Pu, the branching cascades of which actually form the Chinese character *ren*, meaning "mankind", from which the waterfall gets its name.
Ciguang Ge Pavilion	Further north stands the Ciguang Ge Pavilion, which once formed part of a monastery; only a part of the latter has survived and now houses a restaurant.

The Yellow Mountain ▶

Wuxi

Peak of the Heavenly Capital	When climbing the 1810m/5940ft high Peak of the Heavenly Capital (Tiandu Feng) the visitor will pass Fishback Rock (Jiyu Bei).
The Pine of Welcome	South of the Tower of the Jade Curtain (Yuping Lou) stands the mighty Pine of Welcome (Yingke Song), said to be a thousand years old and which appears in a painting hanging in the Great Hall of the People in Beijing.
Tower of the Jade Curtain	The Tower of the Jade Curtain, standing at a height of 1680m/5513ft above sea-level, houses a guesthouse. In front of it lies the Wenshu Terrace. A temple once stood here, but was destroyed by fire in 1952.
Lotus Blossom Peak	Further north towers Lotus Blossom Peak (Linhua Feng, 1880m/6170ft); it is surrounded by a number of smaller peaks, giving the whole the appearance of a lotus flower.
Peak of Light, The Peak Which Just Flew Here	Further north lie the Peak of Light (Guangming Ding, 1840m/6040ft) and the Peak Which Just Flew Here (Feilai Feng); the latter is named after a 10m/33ft high rock (Feilai Shi) which looks as if it does not belong here.
The Cloud Dispelling Pavilion	A little further north there is a turn off to the west which leads to the Cloud Dispelling Pavilion (Paiyun Ting).
Brush Peak, Cool and Refreshing Terrace, Peak of Conviction	North of the Beihai Guesthouse, with Brush Peak close by, lies Cool and Refreshing Terrace (Qingliang Tai).

To the east of the guesthouse looms Peak of Conviction (Shixin Feng, 1668m/5474ft), the beauty of which is said to affect all who see it. |

Wuxi   L 5

Chinese equivalent	无锡市
	Province: Jiangsu. Area: 403sq.km/156sq. miles Population: 637,000 (conurbation 799,000)
Situation and Communications	Wuxi lies north of Lake Taihu, in the south-east of Jiangsu province, at longitude 120°16′E and latitude 31°37′N. There are rail links with Shanghai (136km/85 miles), Suzhou (42km/26 miles), Nanjing (178km/111 miles), Beijing 1334km/830 miles) and other Chinese cities, as well as regular air flights to Beijing and Canton. An excellent road network connects Wuxi with all the nearby towns. Moreover, as Wuxi lies near the Grand Canal it is also possible to reach Suzhou, Hangzhou, Yangzhou, Zhenjiang, etc, by boat. Because of its fertile soil and mild climate this region, one of China's major rice trading centres, is known as the "Land of Fish and Rice". Wuxi is a well-known health resort with several sanatoriums dotted around Lake Taihu. The town is also a leading manufacturer of textiles, electronic goods, precision instruments and so on. Silk and cotton manufacture has a long tradition, and painted terracotta figures have been made here for over 400 years, the raw material coming from Mercy Mountain (Huishan) in the west of the town.
History	Wuxi is one of the oldest Chinese towns west of the Changjiang river. During the Zhou dynasty (11th–3rd c. B.C.) it was called Youxi ("has tin"), because of its tin deposits. Back in the early Han dynasty, in the 2nd c. B.C., it was already a major urban settlement. From then onwards it became known as Wuxi ("without tin"), which suggests that by then the tin deposits had already been worked out. Many of the writers of the Tang period (618–907) waxed poetic about the town's streams. Shortly after the

The Imperial Canal near Wuxi

opening of the Grand Canal in the 7th c. Wuxi became a major centre for trade in rice and corn. In the early 20th c. the first textile factories soon opened up, and since the 1930s it has developed into a commercial and transport centre.

Sights

The Park of Tin and Mercy lies in the west of Wuxi at the foot of two charming hills, Tin Mountain (Xishan, 75m/246ft) and Mercy Mountain (Huishan); hence its name. The park covers an area of 46ha/115 acres and is home to numerous interesting historical monuments.

★ **Park of Tin and Mercy** (Xihui Gongyuan)

This spring, on the mountain of the same name, is also known as "The Second Most Beautiful Spring under the Heavens" (Tianxia Dierquan).

Mercy Mountain Spring (Huishan Quan)

The Qianlong Emperor found the Garden of Delight (dating from the Ming period 1368–1644) so entrancing that he used it as a model for the "Garden of Harmony and Pleasure" which he had built at his summer palace in Beijing.

Garden of Delight (Jichuang Yuan)

Surroundings

Lake Taihu lies a few miles south of Wuxi. It is 2200sq.km/850sq. miles in area, making it the fifth largest lake in China. It snuggles between wooded hills on the slopes of which crystal-clear springs bubble forth and beautiful gardens have been laid out.

★★ **Lake Taihu**

The Garden of Plums on the northern bank of Lake Taihu is particularly attractive in spring, when thousands of plum trees are in blossom.

Garden of Plums (Meiyuan)

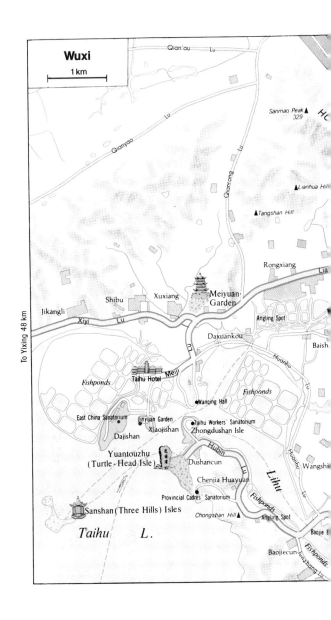

Wuxi

1 km

Qian'ou Lu

Qianyao Lu

Sanmao Peak 329

HU

Lianhua Hill

Qianrong Lu

Tangshan Hill

Rongxiang

Lia

Meiyuan Garden

Xuxiang

Shibu

Angling Spot

Jikangli

Xiyi Lu

Daxuankou

Baish

Huanhu

Fishponds

Meili

Taihu Hotel

Wanqing Hall

Fishponds

To Yixing 48 km

East China Sanatorium

Jinyuan Garden

Taihu Workers' Sanatorium

Dajishan

Xiaojishan

Zhongdushan Isle

Yuantouzhu
(Turtle-Head Isle)

Hubin

Dushancun

Wangshi

Huanhu Lu

Lihu

Chenjia Huayuan

Provincial Cadres' Sanatorium

Fishponds

Sanshan (Three Hills) Isles

Chongshan Hill

Angling Spot

Baojie E

Taihu L.

Baojiecun

Fishponds

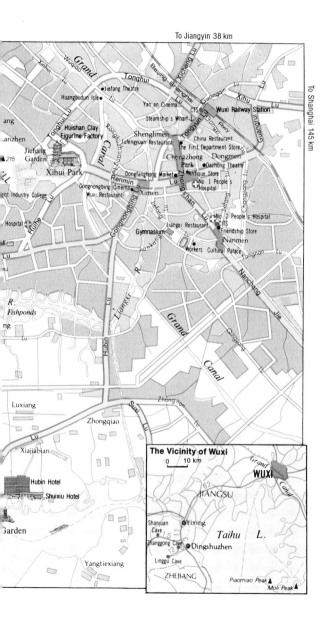

To Jiangyin 38 km

To Shanghai 145 km

Xinhu

Grand

Wuqiao

Tonghui

Beijing Shenghai

Yichang Lu

Jiefang Theatre

Huangbudun Isle

Gwongun

Xihu

Lu

Lu InDuping

Huishan Clay Figurine Factory

Tonghui Lu

anzhen

Yan'an Cinema

Steamship's Wharf

CTS

China Restaurant

Wuxi Railway Station

Shenglimen

Jufengyuan Restaurant

The First Department Store

ang

Rongxiang

Canal

Chengzhong
Park

Dongmen

Dazhong Theatre

Tonghui

Gongji

Fwy

Jichang
Garden

▲ 215

Xihui Park

Dongfanghong Market

Zhongshan Lu

Antique Store

No.1 People's
Hospital

Gongnongbing Cinema
Wuxi Restaurant

Renmin

Ximen

ght Industry College

Hume

Lu

Gongnongbing Lu

Jiefang

No.2 People's Hospital

CITS

Friendship Store

Hospital

Jiangxi Restaurant

Gymnasium

Nanmen

Lu

Jiankang

Workers' Cultural Palace

Tonghan

Lu

Nanchang

ll

R

Lu

Jie

Liangxi

Lu

Hubin

R

Grand

Fishponds

ng

Lu

Qingyang

Canal

Luxiang

Zhongnon

Lu

Zhongqiao

Suxi Lu

Xiajiabian

Lu

Hubin Hotel

Shuixiu Hotel

Garden

Yangtiexiang

The Vicinity of Wuxi

0   10 km

Grand

WUXI

Canal

JIANGSU

Shanjuan
Cave

Yixing

Zhanggong Cave

Dingshuzhen

Taihu L.

Linggu Cave

ZHEJIANG

Piaomiao Peak ▲

Moli Peak ▲

Lake Taihu

Pagoda of Plums (Mei Ta)	In the middle of the garden stands the Pagoda of Plums, built in the traditional style.
Turtle Head Peninsula (Yuantouzhu)	Turtle Head Peninsula – its shape is rather like a turtle's head – forms the tip of a peninsula in the north of the lake. The landscape here is quite fascinating, with steep cliffs and winding paths.
Three Hill Isle (Sanshan Dao)	Three Hill Isle, 3km/2 miles west of Turtle Head, is a small garden floating on the water.
Sea-shell Garden (Li Yuan)	Sea-shell Garden, 5km/3 miles east of Turtle Head, is known for the artificial hills built on it. They are made of rough blocks of stone dug out from the bottom of Lake Taihu; such stones are also used in many other gardens in China.

Xiamen   K 7

Chinese equivalent	厦门市

Province: Fujian. Area: 10·5sq.km/4sq. miles
Population: 480,000 (conurbation 960,000)

Situation and Communications	Xiamen lies in the south-east of Fujian province. at 118°07′E and 24°25′N. It can be reached by rail from Shanghai, or by air or ferry from Hong Kong. There are also flights to Beijing. Xiamen's ancient town centre – Amoy in the Fujian dialect – on the island of the same name is joined to the mainland by a long causeway built in 1956. Xiamen has a favourably-located natural harbour.

Being situated in the subtropical zone, this coastal town enjoys a very mild maritime climate.

Xiamen was founded in 1394 to provide a defence against pirate attacks; later it became a sea-port. It was named Xiamen after the original fortress of Da Xia Zhi Men, known as the "Gateway to the Great Edifice"; the term "Great Edifice" refers to China itself. General Zheng Chenggong (1624–62) set up a naval base here. In 1842, after China had been defeated in the Opium Wars, Xiamen became one of the five free ports which the government was forced to open up to international trade.

By the mid-1950s it had developed into an important industrial centre. Since 1980 Xiamen has been one of the four Special Economic Zones, where a kind of free market economy operates.

History

The botanical gardens known as the Park of Ten Thousand Rocks lie on Lion Mountains (Shishan) in the east of the town. The dominant features of the park are bizarre-shaped rocks, lush vegetation, caves, temples and pavilions. There is also an artificial lake of the same name.

Particularly interesting are the Temple of the Kingdom of Heaven (Tianjie Si) and the nearby Chang Xiao Dong caves which contain inscriptions dating from the Ming period (1368–1644).

Sights

Park of Ten Thousand Rocks (Wanshi Yan)

South Putuo Temple, at the foot of the Mountain of the Five Old Men (Wulaoshan) in the south of the town, was built during the Tang dynasty (618–907).

★South Putuo Temple (Nanputuo Si)

South Putuo Temple

In the front hall stand statues of Maitreya Buddha and the Four Heavenly Kings.

Sumptuous Hall of the Great Hero (Daxiong Baodian)

Three further Buddha figures and one of Guanyin are to be found in the Sumptuous Hall of the Great Hero. Statues of Guanyin can also be seen in the Temple of Dabei Tang.

Cangjing Ge Pavilion

In Cangjing Ge Pavilion there are some interesting writings and a bell from the Song period (960–1279). In the University of Xiamen is a memorial to the writer Lu Xun (see Famous People), who lectured here in 1926–27.

★ Island of the Blown Waves (Gulang Yu)

The Island of the Blown Waves, 2sq.km/¾sq. mile in area and lying 1km/1100yd south-west of Xiamen, boasts some pretty little houses in the midst of rich flora, which has led to their being popularly known as "Gardens of the Sea".

Sunlight Rock (Riguang Yan)

Dominating the island is Sunlight Rock. also known as the Peak of Flying Sparks (Huang Yan) or Dragon's Head Hill (Longtoushan). A Buddhist temple stands at the foot of it.

Zheng Chenggong Memorial Hall

In 1962 this memorial hall (Zheng Chenggong Jinianguan) was built on the north side of the island in honour of the national hero of that name who had liberated Taiwan from the Dutch three hundred years earlier.

Shuzhuang Huayan Gardens

South of Sunlight Rock lie Shuzhuang Gardens, which once belonged to a Taiwanese businessman who moved to Gulang Yu Island in 1895 after his home had been taken over by Japanese. Gangzihou beach is to the west.

Cave of the White Stag (Bailu Dong)

The Cave of the White Stag lies hidden on the southern slopes of Mount Yuping to the north-east of the town. Two wall inscriptions bear witness to the resistance put up by the local populace against its Dutch masters in the first half of the 17th c. In the middle of the cave stands a white clay sculpture of a stag, the symbol of the School of the White Stag on Mount Lushan, which was founded in the Song era (960–1279) and devoted itself to the study of the classical writings of Confucius.

Xi'an

15

西安市

Chinese
equivalent

Capital of Shaanxi Province
Altitude: 412m/1352ft. Area: 861sq.km/332sq. miles
Population: 2,280,000 (conurbation 3,010,000)

Xi'an is situated in central China, between the Weihe river in the north and the Qinling Mountains in the south, at 108°55'E and 34°16'N.

Situation and
Communications

The city lies on a major rail route which runs from Lianyungang on the Yellow Sea via Ürümqi in the Autonomous Region of Xinjiang and on to Kazakhstan. There are direct rail links with Beijing and Shanghai, and flights to most large Chinese cities as well as to Hong Kong.

Xi'an is one of north-west China's chief textile centres, where cotton grown in the artificially irrigated paddy-fields in the neighbouring countryside is treated and processed. Other major branches of industry are chemicals and engineering.

It probably possesses more items of archaeological interest than any other town or city in China, the most important, of course, being the world-famous Terracotta Warriors, which attracted 1,700,000 domestic and foreign visitors in 1992.

Xi'an is one of China's six historic capital cities. From 1027 B.C. onwards eleven dynasties chose it as their seat of government. In fact, however, its history probably goes back 6000 years. In Banpo, a village 6km/4 miles to the east, archaeologists have excavated a settlement once inhabited by over 500 people which dates back to the 4th c. B.C.

History

The Emperor of the Western Zhou dynasty (1066–771 B.C.) elected to reside in Feng, near present-day Xi'an. The capital city during the Qin era in the 3rd c. B.C. was Xianyang (also near where Xi'an lies today), with 500,000 to 600,000 inhabitants, or a third of the total population of China at that time. Under the Western Han (206–8 B.C.) the capital, sited north-west of where Xi'an now lies, was called Chang'an (Long-lasting Peace) and covered an area of 35sq.km/13½sq. miles. Here was the beginning of the famous Silk Road, which wound its way through Central Asia and the Middle East as far as the Mediterranean and thus linked Xi'an with such cities as Istanbul, Rome and Venice. From then until the 14th c. A.D. the Silk Road was an extremely important route along which spread the world's oldest cultures, those of China, Persia, Egypt, Turkey, Greece and Italy.

Under the Sui dynasty (581–618) the town developed even further and its name was changed to Daxing (Great Prosperity). In the Tang era (618–907), named Chang'an once more, it enjoyed a further halcyon period; its area increased to 84sq.km/32sq. miles, making it the largest city in the world at that time. Chang'an was a busy trading centre and the setting-out point for journeys to Central Asia, Russia, India, the Mediterranean and Africa as well as a place where all kinds of ethnic groups came together. Almost all the buildings of that period were destroyed in the countless wars which devastated the country during the Late Tang period, but two which survived were the Pagoda of the Great Wild Goose (Dayan Ta) and that of the Small Wild Goose (Xiaoyan Ta). When the Tang dynasty fell Chang'an became less important. At the beginning of the Ming dynasty (1368–1644) a number of changes were made to the town and it was finally given the name it still holds today, Xi'an (Westerly Peace). However, it was only one-sixth of the size that Chang'an had been during the Tang period. The

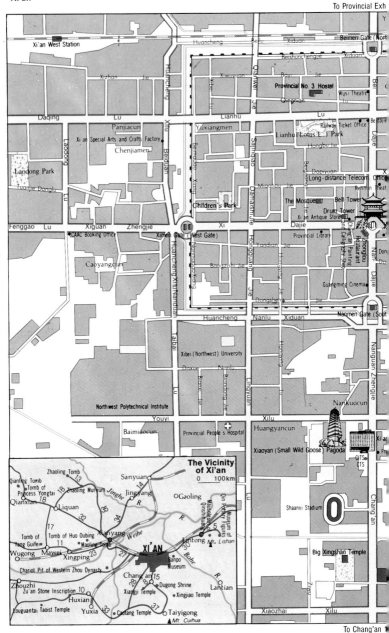

Xi'an

1 km

To Banpo Museum 4 km

Xi'an Railway Station   Hwy.

Beilu   Dongduan   Changying

Jiefang Restaurant

Dong 7 Lu

Jiefanglu Department Store

Bank of China

Jieming (Revolutionary) Park

5-Lu   Dong 5-Lu   Changle   Xilu   Changle Zhonglu

Xi'an Stadium

Jiefang   Huancheng   Donglu   Beilu

Sichuan Cuisine Restaurant   Yongxin Jie   Fang

Dong 3-Lu   Changle   Benlu

Minsheng Restaurant

People's Hotel   Xi'an Jade Carving Factory

ngxin Jie   Renmin Lu   Suoluo   Xiang   Hazhu Lu

Dong 1-Lu   The Zoo

Honsen Lu

Friendship Store   Dorgmen Gate (East Gate)   Dongguan   Zhengjie

Dong   Dajie

an Restaurant   Heping Restaurant

Museum   Heping   Chang'an Cinema   Xingqinggong Park   Jinhho Lu

of Steles)   Lu

Hepingmen   Xianning

Nanlu   Dongduan   Xi'an Jiaotong University   Lu

Huangfuzhuang

Anren   Nanlu

tionxi   he   liandong   he   Yanta

Youyi   Donglu

Liujiazhuang

Changsheng   Jitaicun

lianshe   Lu

Canal   Tielumiao

Flood Control   Tielu Xincun

Wenbaozhai   Guanyingmiao

Xi'an Geological Institute

Xi'an Mining Institute   Lu

Donglu   Xiying

town has changed little in appearance in the last six hundred years. Although its boundaries have expanded considerably since the 1950s the historic town centre remains unaltered.

Urban development

The Tang dynasty built its capital Chang'an 7km/4½ miles north-west of where Xi'an lies today.

Its defensive walls, 22km/14 miles in length, formed an irregular quadrilateral with twelve gates, each with three entrances. The main gate was reserved for the use of the emperor. The north side of the wall is shaped rather like the Ursa Major constellation, and the south side like Ursa Minor.

The town was served by eight main streets and 160 side streets together with large numbers of palaces (none of which survive) and an excellent drainage and sewerage system using pentagonal clay pipes.

On the excavation site, in addition to the remains of the town walls to the south-west, the visitor can still see a large mound of earth which is all that is left of the Han imperial residence, the Palace of Weiyang, around which countless legends have been woven. At one time the palace comprised more than 40 separate buildings, the main one being 183m/600ft long, 164ft wide and 12m/39ft high.

During the Tang era (618–907) what is now Xi'an formed a part of Chang'an, which at that time was 37km/23 miles in circumference and had a population of a million or so. The town was divided into two parts. The inner embraced the northern district with the imperial palace and the southern with the seats of government and administration, while the outer part, lying to the east, west and south of the inner districts, was where the ordinary people lived. Its 25 main streets were lined with numerous markets, shops and workshops. Archaeological research indicates that the western section of the town wall was 2656m/2920yd long, the northern 1135m/1248yd and the eastern (divided into three sections) 2610m/2870yd.

Sights

Bell Tower (Zhonglou)

The Bell Tower in the town centre stands 36m/118ft high. It was originally built in 1384 on a site a little further west, and rebuilt here in 1582.

Visitors can climb up inside as far as the penultimate floor from where they can enjoy a beautiful view of the city.

Drum Tower (Gulou)

Further west from the Bell Tower stands the Drum Tower. It dates from 1370, is 33m/108ft high and stands on a base which is 8m/26ft tall. Apart from this rectangular base it is similar in construction to the Bell Tower.

Temple of the Town God

On Xi Dajie Street stands the Temple of the Town God (Chenghuang Miao), built in 1433. The main hall dates from 1723.

★The Mosque (Qingzhen Si)

The Mosque covers an area of 12,000sq.m/130,000sq.ft and lies about 300m/330yd to the north-west of Drum Tower, in a district inhabited mainly by the Moslem Hui minority. There is said to have been a mosque here back in the Tang period (618–907).

The buildings comprises five courtyards with various buildings in traditional Chinese style but with Islamic decorative patterns. Built during the Ming period (1368–1644) the mosque still has a number of its original stelae. The prayer-hall in the main building will hold up to 1000 worshippers.

★★Provincial Museum

The Provincial Museum, housed in a former Temple of Confucius in the Old Town, contains 2300 old stelae, and is known locally as the "Forest of Stelae" (Beilin).

These stone tablets, which were first collected and brought together in the one place in 1090, are now distributed over six rooms, six corridors and a pavilion. The oldest date from the Han period (206 B.C. to A.D. 220). Particularly well-known is the "Nestorian Stela", dating from 781, the inscription on which calls to mind the introduction of the doctrine of Nestorianism into China in the Tang period (618–907).

Xi'an: town walls

Drum Tower

The town walls were built between 1368 and 1398 on the foundations of the old Tang (618–907) defensive walls. After extensive restorations they have now been incorporated into a "round park", 14km/9 miles in circumference, which encircles the inner town. Averaging 12m/40ft in height and 18m/60ft wide at the base, the wall is furnished with four gates and a large number of watch-towers and bastions.

★★ Town Walls from the Ming period (Xi'an Chengqiang)

The Pagoda of the Small Wild Goose, in the south of the city near the local CITS travel bureau, is square in plan, stands 43m/140ft high and was built in 684 in honour of the Tang Emperor Gaozong. Two of the fifteen original storeys have collapsed as a result of frequent earthquakes.

★★ Pagoda of the Small Wild Goose (Xiaoyan Ta)

The Temple of Daxingshan Si, to the south of the Pagoda of the Small Wild Goose, dates back to the 3rd c., but the present buildings are from the Ming and Qing period (1368–1911) and were restored in 1956. It was once an important Buddhist centre, and Indians also lived here.

Temple of Daxingshan Si

This modern museum to the south-east of the Temple of Daxingshan Si is 44,000sq.m/474,000sq.ft in area and consists of several buildings containing a large number of rooms in which more than 3000 exhibits, displayed in seven chronologically arranged sections, illustrate the story of the city of Xi'an and Shaanxi province from prehistoric times up to the Opium Wars of the mid-19th c. On display are bronze vessels from the Shang and Zhou period (16th–3rd c. B.C.), porcelain from the Tang and Song era (7th–13th c.), gold and silver jewellery from the Tang period (618–907), terracotta warriors from the tomb of Shi Huangdi, a rich collection of frescos from the tombs of Tang rulers which depict scenes from court life, and musical instruments. Evidence of trade with the west is provided in the shape of gold dishes, brooches and silver-plate from the Sassanid (Persian, A.D. 211–651) empire.

★★ Historical Museum of Shaanxi Province (Shaanxi Lishi Bowuguan)

In company with that of the Small Wild Goose, the Pagoda of the Great Wild Goose is the second religious building to survive from the Tang period (618–907). It formed part of the Temple of Great Mercy and Goodness (Ci'en Si), built by Prince Li Zhi in the first half of the 7th c. in honour of his mother. Originally the complex would have had numerous courtyards and almost 2000 rooms in which 300 monks lived, but today it is much smaller. Three Buddha figures can be seen in the main hall.

The Gaozong Emperor Li Zhi built the Pagoda in 652 in order to house more than 650 Buddhist writings which the monk Xuanzang had brought from India and later partially translated. Originally there were only five storeys, but five more were added between 701 and 704. Later three storeys were destroyed during hostile attacks, so today the pagoda has only seven floors and is 64m/210ft tall. It is constructed in rectangular sections which taper towards the top. Two stone plaques are let into the wall on either side of the entrance; these bear inscriptions by the Tang Emperors Taizong and Gaozong.

★★ Pagoda of the Great Wild Goose

Celebration Park covers 50ha/125 acres around a small lake in the east of the city. The modern buildings are modelled on the Tang period style (618–907), in memory of the magnificent residence which stood here 1300 years ago. In 714, when Li Longji, was crowned emperor, he had the residence converted into an imperial palace. Its name is thought to commemorate his accession to the throne.

Celebration Park (Xingqing Gongyuan)

This museum lies 4km/2½ miles east of Xi'an on a site where, in the 1950s, archaeologists unearthed a 6000 year-old village which had operated on a matriarchal structure. About 500 people would have lived in the village, which was surrounded by a ditch 6m/20ft wide and equally deep. The houses, all facing south, were square or round in plan and arranged around a large house 160sq.m/1720sq.ft in area. Corn and other supplies were kept

Surroundings

★ Banpo Museum (Banpo Bowuguan)

◀ *Little Goose Pagoda*

in the store rooms. Adults would have been buried in graves outside the living area, while children were interred near the houses.

Visitors can see the remains of 45 houses, 2 stables, more than 200 cellars, 6 kilns and about 250 graves. Tools and equipment made of stone, terracotta and bone have also been found. The pottery items, which are attributed to the Yangshao culture, are frequently decorated with fishes and have marks scratched on them which are probably the forerunners of a form of writing.

Mausoleum of Jing Di

In 1990, when constructing the road from Xi'an to the new airport, the builders stumbled upon the tomb of Jing Di (reigned 157–141 B.C.), the fifth ruler of the Han dynasty. It lies on a burial site of 9·6ha/24 acres where more than 800 more graves were traced. Some 70,000 workers were forced to labour for 37 years to build the mausoleum.

Investigations indicate that the mausoleum complex contains 24 graves in all. Eight of these have been unearthed and they contain 700 naked terracotta figures. These warrior figures, each about 60cm/2ft tall, have different facial expressions but no arms – something which is a mystery to scientists – and were dressed in silk uniforms. They are equipped with various items in miniature, the *mingqi*, such as coins, corn-measures and arrowheads. In a cemetery nearby were found the mortal remains of an estimated 10,000 people, many of them workers who died while building the mausoleum.

Ruins of Efang Palace (Efang Gong)

The ruins of the Palace of Efang lie 15km/9½ miles west of the city. They are the remains of part of a complex of buildings constructed on the orders of the first emperor of the Qin dynasty (221–206 B.C.). Whenever the emperor defeated an enemy army he would have a building erected him in the architectural style of the enemy country concerned. There are said to have been more than 270 such buildings; in 206 B.C., however, an insurgent general reduced them all to ashes.

Today a few ruins are all that remain of the once magnificent imperial palace – a terrace of compressed clay 20m/66ft high and 31m/100ft round, and a platform, also of compressed clay, 6m/20ft tall and 5m/16ft deep. These were probably the foundations of two of the 270 palace buildings.

Palace No. 3

An archaeological find made in the 1970s proved very interesting to the experts. In the ruins of Palace No. 3 a row of wall-paintings were uncovered which depict a carriage and pair and soldiers on horseback. The tints of these 2000 year-old paintings are incredibly fresh and full of life.

★Mount Lishan

The twin peaks of Mount Lishan, 1200m/3940ft high, lie 26km/16 miles east of Xi'an.

Laojun Temple sits on top of the western peak. According to legend, it was here that the Tang Emperor Xuanzong swore everlasting devotion to his concubine.

A pavilion rises up out of thick grass on the slope approaching the Huaqing Hot Springs (see below). It was at this spot that on December 12th 1936 Chiang Kai-shek (see Famous People) was taken prisoner by two of his officers and forced to join with the Communists in the struggle against the Japanese invaders.

★★Huaqing Hot Springs (Huaqing Chi)

The Huaqing Hot Springs are to be found 26km/16 miles east of Xi'an at the foot of Mount Lishan in a large park containing a number of public baths and some modern palaces built in the Tang style. The hot springs, rich in minerals and with a temperature of 43°C/109°F, were highly regarded more than 3000 years ago. The Tang Emperor Xuanzong often spent the winter here in the company of his favourite concubine Yang Guifei. Shortly afterwards, however, all the buildings were destroyed by war. The new baths constructed in 1956 include one called the Bath of Yang Guifei (Guifei Chi).

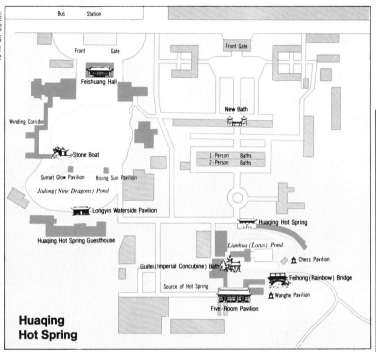

Bus   Station

Front   Gate

Front Gate

Feishuang Hall

New Bath

Winding Corridor

Stone Boat

1 - Person   Baths
2 - Person   Baths

Sunset Glow Pavilion   Rising Sun Pavilion

Jiulong (Nine Dragons) Pond

Longyin Waterside Pavilion

Huaqing Hot Spring

Huaqing Hot Spring Guesthouse

Lianhua (Lotus) Pond

Chess Pavilion

Guifei (Imperial Concubine) Bath

Feihong (Rainbow) Bridge

Source of Hot Spring

Wanghe Pavilion

Five-Room Pavilion

**Huaqing
Hot Spring**

To Mt. Lishan

The Mausoleum of Qin Shi Huangdi (reigned 221–210 B.C.) lies 30km/
18½ miles north-east of Xi'an, near the town of Lintong, under a 46m/150ft
high hill. The emperor was only 13 years old in the year 246 when he gave
instructions for this edifice to be constructed. The work involved a labour
force of 700,000 men.

★★ Mausoleum of
Qin Shi Huangdi
(Qin Shihuang
Ling)

To date it is not known exactly how deep the tomb was and what it
contained. Some archaeologists are of the opinion that it was at least
50m/165ft below ground level, while others think it could have been as
much as 500m/1650ft. Old documents show that the actual tomb was
hermetically sealed with a sheet of bronze to prevent the entry of water.
One letter, written soon after the mausoleum was completed, says "It is full
of rare and valuable items. A refined system of loaded crossbows will kill
anybody who approaches the grave in an attempt to rob it. The floor is
shaped like a broad piece of land with rivers and lakes running through it,
but instead of water they contain quicksilver . . . Candles of whale-oil burn
perpetually". The emperor's sarcophagus is thought to be made of stone or
bronze. In spite of the combined efforts of some famous foreign and
Chinese scientists no satisfactory solution has yet been found to the problem of how to open the tomb without causing damage to the contents.

The site is enclosed by an inner and an outer wall.

In March 1974, when digging wells some 1·5km/1 mile west of the Qin Shi
Huangdi mausoleum, some peasants made a sensational discovery – the
now famous Terracotta Army, distributed over three large underground
platforms and forming part of the emperor's burial objects. Numbering
more than 7000, the figures are cultural assets of considerable quality.

★★ Terracotta
Army (Bingma
Yong)

The famous terracotta army . . .

. . . near Xi'an

Since they have been uncovered the figures, standing 5m/16ft down, have been at risk from the weather; a giant hall has been constructed over the first excavation site to provide protection.

Although the faces of the individual warriors all have different expressions it is known that some were mass-produced in large workshops.

Tomb No. 1, 1·26ha/over 3 acres in area, contains the right wing of the underground army which is guarding the Emperor in his eternal rest. There are 6000 life-sized clay soldiers and horses, numerous chariots and weapons. During the Qin period an army was made up of three sections – the right wing, the left wing and the central unit; even this underground army had to follow the same battle order.

Tomb No. 1

A second section, quite near Tomb No. 1 and measuring 600sq.m/6450sq.ft in area, was also uncovered. It contained the 1500 terracotta figures which comprised the left wing of the army – foot-soldiers, cavalrymen, horses, chariots, etc. The dig also brought to light 2000 weapons and other interesting items.

Tomb No. 2

The third section, some 520sq.m/5600sq.ft in area, houses what is presumably the "headquarters" of the underground army. The finds here include 73 chariots, soldiers and horses, all made of terracotta.

Tomb No. 3

A fourth tomb was opened up between Tombs 1 and 2; this was the store of the central unit of troops and measured 4600sq.m/49,500sq.ft. Unfortunately, however, it was empty, and the opinion of the archaeologists is that work on this grave had to be interrupted because rebellious peasants were marching on the town.

Other Places of Interest in the Surroundings

80km/50 miles north-west of Xi'an, near the town of Qianxian, will be found the tombs of nineteen Tang emperors.

Tang Tombs

The Qianling Tomb dates from the heyday of the Tang dynasty and contains the mortal remains of the third Tang Emperor Gaozong (reigned 649–683) and of his Empress Wu Zetian. The seventeen further tombs are those of relatives and high dignitaries, including Prince Zhanghuai and Princess Yongtai. The road to the tombs is lined with statues of men and animals.

Qianling Tomb

The tomb of Prince Zhanghuai, the second son of Emperor Gaozong, lies 3km/2 miles south-east of the Qianling Tomb.; it contains wall-paintings which give an insight into court life, such as that showing a game of polo. This tomb had been robbed and the archaeologists found only a few burial objects.

Tomb of Prince Zhanghuai (Tang Zhanghuai Taizi Mu)

Close to the Zhanghuai Tomb lies that of Princess Yongtai, the granddaughter of Emperor Gaozong. It is 87m/285ft long and is also decorated with wall-paintings. Burial objects found here included gold and silver jewellery and china; these are now on display in the Qianlin Museum.

Tomb of Princess Yongtai (Yongtai Gongzhu Mu)

To the north-east of the town of Liquan lies the Zhaoling Mausoleum, built in the years 636 to 649 for Emperor Taizong and covering an area of 10,000ha/25,000 acres. The burial site includes 167 tombs of relatives, high officials and generals.

Zhaoling

The finds made here – coloured clay figures, paintings and stone engravings – are in the Zhaoling Museum.

This temple complex – 10km/6 miles north of the village of Fufeng, which itself is some 100km/60 miles west of Xi'an – is famous for its pagoda, in which is kept one of Shakyamuni's finger bones. The bone was brought here on the instructions of the Tang Emperor Xianzong (806–821).

★Temple of the Gateway to Dharma (Famen Si)

The thirteen-storey brick pagoda, 28m/92ft high, was rebuilt in 1988. It towers up in front of the main hall of the monastery which houses a statue

Exhibition hall of the terracotta Imperial Army

of the Buddha. To the sides stand a bell-tower and a drum tower. On the façade of the main hall can be seen an inscription dated 978.

Shakyamuni's finger bone, known to Buddhists as the "Holy Bone", and three copies of it (known as the "Shadow Bones"), were discovered in April

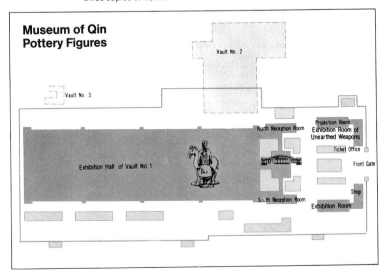

1987 in an underground palace below the foundations of the previous pagoda. This palace, which had remained hidden for 1000 years, contained much valuable treasure from the Tang period, including numerous objects in gold, silver, semi-precious stones, jade or lacquer, many porcelain vessels and woven silks. In 1988 a museum was built here specially to house these finds.

Mount Huashan, also known as Xi Yue (West Mountain), lies some 100km/60 miles from Xi'an and dominates the east of Shaanxi province. It is one of the Five Holy Taoist Mountains. Steep and rocky paths wind their way up between its five peaks to the east, west, north and centre. The highest point is Lotus Peak (Lianhua Feng) to the south, which is 2100m/6892ft. Mount Huashan has been famous since time immemorial. Along the paths which lead past precipitous rock faces and yawning chasms the scenery changes at every step and seems to cast a magic spell over all who pass.

★★ **Mount Huashan**

To get to Mount Huashan take the train to Huayin. The ascent of the mountain begins 8km/5 miles from there, in the Garden of the Jade Spring (Yuquan Yuan). The path winds through what are known as the Eighteen Bends, past some interesting rock formations and a stone gateway, and thence to the Gateway of Clouds (Yunmen), from where there is a magnificent view of the mountainous scenery. From here onwards the path gets steeper. Stone steps lead up to North Peak (Beifeng). The path which follows is dangerous and is only for those with a good head for heights. The climber will pass The Place Where the Ear Scrapes the Rock (Ca'er Ya) and the Ridge of the Blue Dragon, where the rock faces fall away precipitously.

The ascent

Those who decide to climb the South Peak must scramble up using the footholds cut in the face of an extremely steep slope, holding tightly on to an iron chain for safety. One of the most difficult sections is the 100ft long gorge, which is so narrow that only one person at a time can squeeze through.

Xiangfan

J 5

市

Province: Hebei. Area: 18sq.km/7sq. miles
Population: 250,000 (conurbation 310,000)

Xiangfan lies along middle reaches of the Hanjiang river, a major tributary of the Changjiang, in the north of the central Chinese province of Hebei, at 112°07′E and 32°02′N.

Situation and Communications

It is linked by rail and a good road with the provincial capital Wuhan, about 300km/190 miles away.

Xiangfan was already 3000 years old when it was made the capital of a principality during the Western Zhou era (11th c.–770 B.C.). It was given its present name during the Qin period (221–206 B.C.). For the 2100 years or so since then it has been the political and economic centre of the north-western part of Hubei province. In 1950 the new Xiangfan emerged as a result of the merging of the towns of Xiangyang and Fancheng. In the last 40 years the various branches of the textile and light industries have developed rapidly.

History

The Wall of the Green Shadow, in the south-east of Xiangfan, is 7m/23ft high, 25m/82ft wide and 1·6m/5ft 3in. thick; a decorative wall of green stone with white marble edges, it was constructed in the 15th c. in front of the residence of a Ming prince, but burned down in 1641. The bas-reliefs depict over 100 dragons in various poses.

Sights

★Wall of the Green Shadow
(Lüying Bi)

The Temple of Migong Si, in the south-west of the town, was built in memory of the calligrapher Mi Shi (1051–1107), whose work is displayed here.

Temple of Migong Ci

Xiangfan

Surroundings

★Temple of Great Virtue (Guangde Si)

The Temple of Great Virtue, 13km/8 miles west of the town, dates from the Han period and is therefore more than 2000 years old. However, the original buildings were destroyed and rebuilt in the 15th c.

The complex comprises five late 15th c. pagodas standing on a base structure. In the centre, 17m/56ft high, is the round Sumptuous Pagoda of the Buddha (Duobao Fuota, 2nd half of the 15th c,), Lamaist in character and ringed by four smaller, hexagonal buildings.

★Residence of Zhuge Liang

On Mount Longzhongshan, among scenic surroundings 15km/9½ miles west of Xiangfan, will be found the buildings in which Zhuge Lian, a great academic and military strategist, lived from 198 to 207. In 207 his fame reached the ears of Liu Bei, the ruler of the Shu kingdom, who thereupon journeyed here three times in order to bestow on Zhuge Liang the office of Grand Chancellor. The latter gave Liu Bei some good military advice and was consequently held to be the very embodiment of wisdom. After his death the academic was posthumously awarded the title of count.

There are many buildings on Mount Longzhongshan in memory of Zhuge Liang; most of them date originally from the Tang period (618–907) but were rebuilt during the Qing dynasty (1644–1911).

Temple of the Count

The Temple of the Count (Wohou Ci) contains some of Zhuge Liang's literary works.

Palace of the Three Visits (Sangu Tang)

The Palace of the Three Visits, so called to commemorate the meetings between Liu Bei and Zhuge Liang, contains a stela which is engraved with the advice on military policies which the sage gave to the emperor.

Pavilion of the Thatched Hut (Calou Ting)

The Pavilion of the Thatched Hut, built on the very spot where the meetings between Zhuge Liang and Liu Bei took place, houses a stone tablet baring an inscription dated 1540.

★Tomb of Count Yi (Zenghou Yi Mu)

Discovered in 1978, this tomb lies on the southern edge of Suxian, about 100km/60 miles south-east of Xiangfan. It is the last resting place of Count Yi from the state of Zeng, who lived in the early part of the Warring Kingdoms era (475–221 B.C.).

Archaeologists have uncovered an estimated 7000 burial objects, including 124 musical instruments of eight different kinds (64 bronze bells, several zithers with five or six strings, drums, etc.), 140 finely-worked ritual vessels in bronze and numerous painted objects.

★Mount Wudangshan

Stretching over a distance of more than 400km/250 miles, the Mount Wudangshan range (150km/93 miles west of Xiangfan) is one of the Taoist Holy Mountains. Its highest point, Peak of Heavenly Pillars (Tianzhu Feng), is 1612m/5290ft; there are 71 other mountains in the range which, although not so high, are no less impressive. All have fairy-tale names such as the Peak of The Taoist Child, The Young Maiden, The Heavenly Steed and The Five Old Men.

The Temple of the Five Dragons was first built on one of the mountain slopes during the Tang period (618–907). Other religious buildings were added between the 10th and 13th c., but nearly all of them were victims of wars during the late Yuan era (1271–1368). In 1412 the Ming Emperor Chengzu ordered large numbers of Taoist temples to be built on Mount Wudangshan. This mammoth task took more than 300,000 workers nearly ten years to complete; they erected 8 palaces, 38 monasteries, 72 temple halls, 39 bridges and 12 pavilions, most of which have survived to this day. The various complexes were extended in 1552–53.

Gateway to the Mysterious Mountain (Xuanyue Men)

Entrance to the religious precincts is through Gateway to the Mysterious Mountain, 20m/66ft high and 13m/43ft wide and built in the year 1552. The finely-carved bas- and high-reliefs on the four gate pillars portray the legends of the Eight Immortal Taoists.

1km/1100yd from the Gateway to the Mysterious Mountain the visitor will see the Palace of the Meeting with the True Immortal, which was built in 1417 in memory of Zhang Sanfeng who was known as the "True Immortal", because he turned down an invitation from two Ming emperors.

Palace of the Meeting with the True Immortal (Yuzhen Gong)

The palace contains several large rooms, a gateway and covered walks. In the main hall there is a bronze statue of Zhang Sanfeng.

The Temple of Yuxu Gong was built in 1413, and at that time it had 2000 rooms, making it the largest such temple on Mount Wudangshan. Only the Red Gate, the Red Wall and a pavilion with steles have survived.

Temple of Yuxu Gong

The Temple of Fuzhen Gong, also built during the reign of the Yongle emperor (1402–14), blends harmoniously with the surrounding landscape.

Temple of Fuzhen Gong

7km/4½ miles further on stands the Palace of Purple Clouds, built in 1413 and still in a good state of preservation. In the main hall pilgrims pay homage to several Taoist deities, including the Jade Emperor and the God of Reason.

Palace of Purple Clouds (Zixiao Gong)

On the way to the Peak of Heavenly Pillars (Tianzhu Feng) the climber will pass the Palace of the Greatest Harmony, built in 1416. The main hall is flanked by a Drum Tower (Gu Lou) and a Bell Tower (Zhong Lou), in which hangs a bronze bell which also dates from 1416.

Palace of the Greatest Harmony (Taihe Gong)

The main purpose of climbimg the Peak of Heavenly Pillars is to visit the Hall of Gold; standing on a stone platform, this building appears to be made of wood but in fact is all in gilded bronze. The individual bronze sections were cast in 1416 and then fixed together. This masterpiece of the art of casting is 5·54m/18ft 2in. high, 14ft 6in. tall and 10ft 4in. deep. The statues, furniture and ritual plate are also all made of bronze. The most important object is the sculpture of the Taoist god Zhenwu Dijun, which weighs ten tonnes. The statues surrounding him are of his successors – the Golden Child, the Jade Maiden, the Fire General and the Water General.

Hall of Gold (Jindian)

Xigaze · Shigatse

E 6

Chinese equivalent

Autonomous Region of Xizang (Tibet)
Altitude: 3836m/12,590ft. Population: 50,000

Xigaze lies in southern Tibet, 345km/214 miles west of Lhasa, the region's capital, and some 500km/310 miles north-east of Katmandu, at 88°27′E and 29°14′N. It is linked to Lhasa and Katmandu by overland bus.

Situation and Communications

More than 500 years old, Xigaze is the second largest town in the Autonomous Region and has always been the political, religious and economic centre of southern Tibet.

History

On Mount Zongshan in the town there once stood a palace which served as a model for the Potala Palace in Lhasa. It was destroyed during the Cultural Revolution.

On the southern edge of town lies the Monastery of Tashihunpo (Mount of Eternal Blessing), built in 1447 and for a long time the place where the Panchen Lamas performed their political and religious tasks.

Sights

★Tashihunpo Monastery (Zhashilunbu Si)

The complex of buildings, extended several times in the 17th and 18th c. and measuring 15ha/37½ acres in area, houses a giant statue of the Buddha which stands 26m/85ft tall and is cast entirely in bronze. The monastery also includes several silvered *dagobs* (conical shrines) each containing the

The Tibetan Monastery of Tashihunpo

mortal remains of a Panchen Lama. Note particularly the magnificent wall-paintings in the chapel of the first Dalai Lama.

Surroundings

Monastery of Palkhor (Baiju Si)

The monastery town of Palkhor, situated 120km/75 miles south-east of Xigaze near the town of Gyangze (Jiangzi) dates from the 14th c. and is known particularly for its octagonal stupa, the Chorten d'Or (Baijiao Ta). This contains a number of sculptures and frescos in Indian, Nepalese and Chinese styles.

A masterpiece of Tibetan architecture is the early 15th c. Kumbum Chorten, with a mandala-like circular ground plan. All kinds of sculptures and frescos are to be found in dozens of wall-niches.

★Sakya Monastery (Sajia Si)

Sakya Monastery stands 150km/93 miles south-west of Xigaze. The Tibetan word "sakya" means "greyish earth", referring to the colour of the soil in this region. The monastery was the centre of the Sakyapa sect. Its abbots were both the religious and secular heads of Sakya and owners of large estates. The last incumbent was obliged to seek asylum in India in 1959.

The whole monastery complex consists of two sections 500m/550yd apart – the North Monastery dating from 1073 and the South Monastery built in 1268. The huge Assembly Hall or Tsuglagkhang in the South Monastery – it is 10m/33ft high and covers an area of 5500sq.m/59,000sq.ft – can accommodate 10,000 people. The roof is supported on 40 pillars, the stoutest of which was a gift from Kublai Khan. The interior fittings of the hall are magnificent. The right side wing contains stupas in memory of deceased Sakya abbots as well as frescos dating from the 13th c. Bronze figures can be seen in the galleries of the left side wing.

The monastery houses more than 1000 volumes of Buddhist, historical and philosophical writings as well as a large number of porcelain vessels, statues and embroiderings from the Yuan period (1271–1368).

Mount Everest, the highest mountain in the world ▶

Xining

★★Mount Everest
(Qomolangma,
Zhumulangma
Feng)

Mount Everest, at 8848m/29,039ft the highest mountain in the world, has attracted many international climbers over the years. This imposing and majestic summit lies 220km/137 miles south-east of Xigaze on the Sino-Nepalese border. Its Tibetan name of Qomolangma means "Third Goddess". The Indians gave it the name of Everest in 1858 in memory of Sir S. G. Everest, head of the Indian State Institute of Geodetics. Mount Everest was discovered by the British mountaineer George Mallory in 1921.

The first attempts to scale the mountain were in 1921, from the Rongbuk glacier on the north (Tibetan) face, followed by more after 1950 which elected to tackle the south-west face from the Khumbu glacier in Nepal. By 1952 a total of fifteen expeditions had been attempted. The first successful climb was by a British expedition in 1953, which chose to go via the West Basin, the South Saddle (7986m/26,200ft) and the South-east Ridge. The New Zealander Edmund Hillary and Sherpa Tenzing Norgay reached the summit on May 19th 1953. Since then it has been conquered several times, including the first attempt without oxygen apparatus by Reinhold Messner and Peter Habeler in 1978.

Xining   H 4

Chinese
equivalent

西宁市

Capital of Qinghai Province
Altitude: 2275m/7467ft. Area: 350sq.km/135sq. miles
Population: 577,000 (conurbation 910,000)

Situation and
Communications

Xining lies in the north-east of Qinghai province, on the Huangshui river, at 101°42′E and 36°35′N. There are train, bus and air links with Lanzhou, the provincial capital, which is 200km/124 miles away. There are also flights to Beijing (5½ hours) and Taiyuan (3½ hours).

History

Xining came into being more than 2200 years ago. Thanks to its strategically favourable situation – one of the few roads to Tibet passed close by – it was for centuries a fortress town of considerable importance.

In the transitional period between the Qin and Han dynasties, in the 3rd c. B.C., the town was called Huangzhongdi. It was not given its present name until 1104. In the 1950s the town enjoyed a period of rapid economic development. Today it is the political centre of Qinghai province and an important industrial hub of north-western China.

Sights

★Great Mosque of Dongguan
(Dongguan
Qingzhen Si)

This mosque in the town centre is built in the Chinese style and consists of a prayer hall 1100sq.m/11,800sq.ft in area, a courtyard of 8400sq.m/90,400sq.ft and several ancillary buildings.

Surroundings

★★Kumbum Monastery

In the Lusha'er district, 25km/15½ miles south-west of Xining, lies Kumbum Monastery, built in 1560–77 and covering a total area of 40ha/100acres. It is also known as the Temple of the Infinite Number of Pictures of the Buddha (Ta'er Si). It is one of the six largest Lamaist temple complexes in China. In the course of various restorations over the centuries Chinese features have been incorporated in the original Tibetan architecture. The latest restoration work was done in 1979. The whole is a giant complex of religious buildings including pagodas, palaces, temples, loggias and monastic cells. A 14m/46ft high stupa stands at the monastery entrance.

Xining: the mosque

On the monastery forecourt can be seen eight round *chortens* (the Tibetan form of a stupa, or Buddhist shrine), decorated with high-reliefs; they represent the eight basic phases in the life of Shakyamuni – such as Birth, Victory over the Demons, Nirvana, etc.

Eight Chortens (Ruyi Dagoba)

The Great Hall of the Gold Roof, the monastery's principal building, is of three storeys and in the Chinese style. The undulating roof is covered in tiles of gilded bronze. A 11m/36ft tall silver stupa stands in the inner courtyard; it is dedicated to Tsongkhapa (1357–1419), the reformer and founder of the Yellow Cap School (Gelupka). According to legend, he was born here and on the spot where his mother's blood dripped as she was giving birth to him a sandalwood tree grew, on which could be seen large numbers of pictures of deities and of Tibetan alphabet characters. The mother built the stupa here at the request of her son, who went to live in Tibet. There is a statue of Tsongkhapa in a niche high up in the stupa. Inside, so legend has it, are kept his mother's placenta and some of his personal belongings, and so it is revered by Lamaists as their holy shrine.

Great Hall of the Golden Roof (Dajinwa Si)

The Small Hall of the Golden Roof (1631) is known for its statues and portraits of Buddhist tutelary gods and for its collection of stuffed animals, including a horse which belonged to the 9th Panchen Lama (1883–1937).

Small Hall of the Golden Roof (Xiaojiwna Si)

Originally built in 1606 and later extended, the Hall of the Great Sutra was destroyed by fire in 1913 but rebuilt in 1917.

Hall of the Great Sutra (Dajing Tang)

It is here that the lamas assemble to read the scriptures together or to receive religious instruction. The Hall measures 1981sq.m/21,315sq.ft will hold up to 2000 people. The flat roof of this typically Tibetan edifice rests on 108 square columns encased in priceless tapestries displaying dragon motifs and is decorated with a wheel, the symbol of Buddhist teaching, and with statues of a gazelle and a deer.

The interior is adorned with rolled-up pictures (thangkas), including some appliqué work – a speciality of the monastery. Visitors can also see

In Kumbum Monastery

some typical examples of local crafts – figures carved in butter, painted textiles and relief embroidery.

★Bird Island
(Niao Dao)

Bird Island lies in the western part of Koko Nor (Lake Qinghaihu), some 220km/140 miles from Xining. The large quantities of fish, crabs and aquatic plants provide excellent food for the numerous birds, making the island something of a bird paradise. Between February and March various species of migrating birds from India, South-east Asia, the Mediterranean, the Red Sea and the Caspian Sea join company with the native birds which live on the lake all the year round. The ten or so species of the latter include waterfowl, waders and sparrows. Hunting has been prohibited on the island for a number of years.

Xinjiang   A–G 2–4

Chinese
equivalent

新疆维吾尔族

Autonomous Region
Area: 1,650,000sq.km/637,000sq. miles
Population: 15,550,000. Capital: Ürümqi

Situation

Xinjiang is the largest of China's autonomous regions and provinces and covers one-sixth of the total area of the country. It lies between 73°41' and 96°19'E and 34°29' and 49°20'N, in the north-west of China, on the borders with India, Pakistan, Afghanistan, Tadzhikistan, Kirgiziya and Kazakhstan.

Topography

The main topographical features of Xinjiang are the Junggar Basin (Junggar Pendi) in the north and the Tarim Basin (Tarim Pendi), the great lake

China

Autonomous Region Xinjiang

HEILONGJIANG

JILIN

INNER MONGOLIA (NEIMENGGU)

LIAONING

XINJIANG

©Baedeker

GANSU

INNER MONGOLIA (NEIMENGGU)

BEIJING (PEKING)●

TIANJIN

HEBEI

QINGHAI

NINGXIA

SHANXI

SHANDONG

GANSU

SHAANXI

HENAN

JIANGSU

XIZANG (TIBET)

SICHUAN

HUBEI

ANHUI

SHANGHAI

ZHEJIANG

JIANGXI

HUNAN

GUIZHOU

FUJIAN

YUNNAN

GUANGXI

GUANGDONG

TAIWAN

XIANG GANG (HONGKONG)

AO MEN (MACAO)

HAINAN

The People's Republic of China
Zhonghua Renmin Gongheguo

known as Lop Nur and the Taklamakan Desert in the south. Between these two areas of lowland the eastern Tienshan mountains, ranging from west to east, are 1500km/930 miles in length and 250–300km/150–185 miles wide; the peaks here are between 3000 and 5000m/10,000 and 17,000ft high, and in the west form two main chains separated one from the other by the Ili river. On the south-east flank of the range lie the Hami and Turpan Valleys – the latter is 154m/505ft below sea-level, making it the second lowest place on earth. In the south the predominant features are the Western (7282m/23,900ft) and Central Kunlunshan (7723m/25,347ft) ranges, as well as Mount Altunshan (6161m/20,220ft). In the extreme north Xinjiang forms part of the Mongolian Altaj range.

Climate

The region's remoteness and its great distance from the sea result in an extreme, continental-type, dry climate (more than one-fifth of Xinjiang is desert). In January the average temperatures are −15°C/5°F in the north and −7°C/22·4°F in the Tarim Basin, while in July they are 21°C/70°F in the north and 32°C/90°F in the Turpan Valley.
   Average rainfall is 100–500mm/4–20in. in the north and 25–100mm/1–4in. in the south.

Population

There are a dozen or so different groups of people in the region, the most important being the Uigurs; at one time they formed 75% of the total, but this fell to 45% in 1973 as a result of the mass influx of Chinese after the building of the Lanzhou–Ürümqi railway. Minority peoples include Kazakhs (Kazaks), Kirghiz, Tadzhiks, Uzbeks, Mongols, Tartars, Hui, Russians, Manchurians and Daurs. Most of the population are Moslem.

History

The southern part (East Turkestan) first came under Chinese control in 101 B.C., and the region then became China's major land link with west and south Asia and, in consequence, a matter of permanent dispute between China and its neighbours.
   In the 9th c. the Uigurs settled here, followed by west Mongolian tribes after the Ming period (1368–1644). By the 17th c. the latter had grown in strength so as to constitute a threat to the Manchurian rulers, leading

481

finally to the Junggar Wars (1696–1758). With the pacification of the Jung-gars and the taking of East Turkestan in 1758 the whole of Xinjiang was won and subsequently incorporated into the Chinese empire in the form of a protectorate. Much of it was lost following an uprising by the Islamic Turks in 1862–78, but the Chinese succeeded in re-taking most of it and then absorbed it into China as Xinjiang province. Betwen 1911 and 1941 the region was independent, but in 1949 it finally came under the aegis of the Central Government and in 1955 was designated an Autonomous Region.

There have been constant revolts against Chinese rule, and separatist movements have gained in strength since the collapse of the Soviet Union in the early 1990s.

Economy	The main industries are cotton and silk-processing and comestibles. Handi-crafts, especially carpet-weaving, are well developed.

Xinjiang benefits from rich mineral resources, some of which are now being extracted, namely oil, coal, uranium and iron-ore.

Animal farming with cattle, sheep and horses is now the main industry in the Junggar Basin among the former nomads, mainly Kazakhs and Mon-gols, who now share in "collective" farms. The "oasis industry" plays an important role in the Tarim Basin; at the oases on the northern and south-ern edges of the mountain range wheat, maize, rice, cotton, sugar-beet, apricots, figs and melons are cultivated. The breeding of silkworms is also of importance. |
| Places to visit | See especially entries for Turpan and Kashgar. |

Xuzhou

K 5

Chinese equivalent	徐州市

Province: Juangsu
Altitude: 45m/148ft. Area: 185sq.km/71½sq. miles
Population: 668,000 (conurbation 773,000)

Situation and Communications	Xuzhou, in the north-west of Jiangsu province, lies at 117°12'E and 34°17'N. It is a major transport centre, because China's two most important rail routes, the Beijing–Shanghai and Lianyungang–Ürümqi lines, meet here. There are also air flights to Nanjing and Shanghai.
History	During its long history Xuzhou has proved to be a town of great strategic importance. Since the Xia dynasty (21–16 B.C.) more than 200 wars have been fought here, making the region very interesting from an archaeolog-ical point of view. 2000 years ago Xiang Yu crowned himself king of the Western Chu kingdom and made Xuzhou his capital.

Although it became of less importance politically after his death it main-tained its role as a river port, and in the 15th and 16th c. more than 12,000 ships loaded with corn berthed here every year. In 1604 however, when the Grand Canal closed down, Xuzhou began to decline. In the early 20th c., after the above-mentioned rail routes were opened up, it regained some of its earlier importance. During the latest Civil War (1945–49) one of the three great battles between the Communists and the Kuomintang, in which the latter were defeated, took place in the countryside surrounding Xuzhou. |
| **Sights**
Temple of Xinghua Si | On the east side of the Yunlongshan river, in the south of the town, stands the Temple of Xinghua Si in which visitors can see statues carved out of the rock in the 5th c. |
| Municipal Museum | In the Municipal Museum at 44 Heping Lu wall-paintings from the Han period (206 B.C. to A.D. 220) are on display. Other interesting finds include a bronze lamp and a shroud made from pieces of jade. |

In 1952 the Huaxing Shimu, a tomb from the Eastern Han period (A.D. 25–220) was discovered 14km/9 miles north of the town. Inside it can be seen stone tablets with reliefs which give an insight into the lives of aristocrats of the period.

A sensational find was made in 1984 in a Han period tomb (206 B.C. to A.D. 220), when a terracotta army of more than 3000 figures up to 40cm/16in. tall was unearthed.

The Tablet of the Great Wind, measuring 1·7m/5½ft tall and 1·23m/4ft wide, is displayed in the House of Culture in Peixian – 70km/43½ miles north-west of Xuzhou – the birthplace of Liu Bang, the first emperor of the Han dynasty (206 B.C. to A.D. 220). A poem composed by the emperor was engraved in the stone some 2200 years ago.

At the same place will be found a second stone tablet, 2·23m/7ft 4in. tall and 1·23m/4ft wide, engraved with the same poem but written in a different order. This latter tablet dates from 1306.

Yan'an

延安市

Province: Shaanxi
Altitude: 800–1300m/2626–4267ft
Area: 3556sq.km/1373sq. miles. Population: 220,000

Yan'an is situated on the Yanhe river, on a loess plateau in the north of Shaanxi province, at 109°25′E and 36°38′N. There are rail links with the provincial capital of Xi'an, about 270km/168 miles away.

Yan'an has a history going back 1300 years. However, it was only in the 1930s and 1940s that it became famous as the headquarters of the Red Army and the Communist Party of China.

This pagoda dates from the Ming period (1368–1644) and was restored several times under the Qing (1644–1911). It stands on the top of a hill in the east of Ya'an, on the banks of the Yanhe, and is the town's emblem as well as being the symbol of the Revolution.
  The building is 44m/145ft high and octagonal in plan. There is a beautiful view of the town from here.
  Nearby can be seen a large cast-iron 17th c. bell.

In a small courtyard at the foot of Mount Phoenix (Fenghuangshan) in the north of Ya'an stands the house where Mao Zedong lived from January 1937 to November 1938.

Surroundings

In the village of Wangjia Ping, to the north-west of the town, the public can visit the headquarters of the Military Committee of the Communist Party of China (CPC) which was housed here from 1937 to 1947.

From 1938 to 1940 and again from 1942 to 1943 the offices of the Central Committee of the Communist Party of China (CPC) were located in the village of Yangjia Ling, 3m/2 miles north-west of Ya'an; from 1940 to 1942 and again from 1944 to 1947 they were in Zaoyuan, 10km/6¼ miles north-west of the town. Here visitors can see the offices and the residential quarters of the top Communist party leaders such as Mao Zedong, Zhu De, Zhou Enlai and others.

★Tomb of the Yellow Emperor (Huangdi Ling)

The Tomb of the Yellow Emperor lies some 100km/62 miles south of Ya'an near the town of Huangling at the foot of Mount Qiaoshan.

The mausoleum is 3·6m/11ft 10in. high and 48m/157ft in circumference. In front of it stands a pavilion with a stela, the four characters engraved on which mean "From Mount Quiaoshan he rode to Heaven on a dragon". This reflects the legend which says that the mythical Yellow Emeпror departed this life at the foot of the mountain.

In prehistoric times many different tribes lived in the Huanghe valley, each with its own leader and its own tribal hierarchy. The Yellow Emperor – his real name was Gongsun Xuanyuan – was the chief of one of the strongest tribes. It was actually his successors who gave him the name of "Yellow Emperor", yellow symbolising the soil and the landscape of this region. The legend also explains how the Yellow Emperor promoted agriculture here while his wife showed the womenfolk how to grow mulberry trees and breed silkworms.

Qing Ming Festival

For many centuries, during the Qing Ming Festival which is celebrated in early spring in memory of the departed, the local population has come to Mount Qiaoshan to pay homage at the Tomb of the Yellow Emperor.

Yangzhou   K 5

Chinese equivalent

扬州市

Province: Jiangsu. Altitude: 604m/1982ft. Area: 148km/57sq. miles
Population: 410,000 (conurbation 6,980,000)

Situation and Communications

Yangzhou lies in the central region of Jiangsu province, between the Changjiang river and the Grand Canal, at 119°26'E and 32°27'N. Buses run to the provincial capital Nanjing, about 100km/60 miles to the north.

History

The origins of Yangzhou go back some 2400 years, to the Spring and Autumn period, but it really came into prominence in the 6th c. when the Sui Emperor Yangdi ordered the Grand Canal to be dug. When this project was completed Yangzhou became a major port for foreign trade. Under the Tangs (618–907) the famous Arab missionary Behao Aldin came here to spread the Islamic gospel. During the Yuan period (1271–1368) Marco Polo stayed in the town for a while and even held quite a high position here. In the Ming and Qing periods (1368–1911) the town became prosperous as a result of the salt trade which also attracted considerable patronage. During later years, especially during the reign of Emperor Qianlong (1736–96) Yangzhou grew to become China's second largest political, economic, commercial and cultural centre.

During his tours of inspection through south China the Emperor stayed here five times. In order to gain favour with the "Son of Heaven", as he was known, the local authorities summoned the best cooks from the neighbouring provinces to prepare dishes for him, and thereby established Yangzhou's reputation for high quality cuisine, placing it in the top four regions in China as far as the culinary arts are concerned. It was at that time, too, that the town's school of painting emerged, known for its "Eccentric" style. Yangzhou suffered severely in mid-1800s during Taiping Uprising.

Handicrafts have long had a fine reputation in Yangzhou. These include especially jade-carving and embroidery. Story-telling, too, has remained a traditional art-form right up to the present day.

Sights
Geyuan Garden

Geyuan Garden, in Dongguan Jie Street, dates from the Qing period (1644–1911); some beautiful bamboo groves are its distinguishing feature.

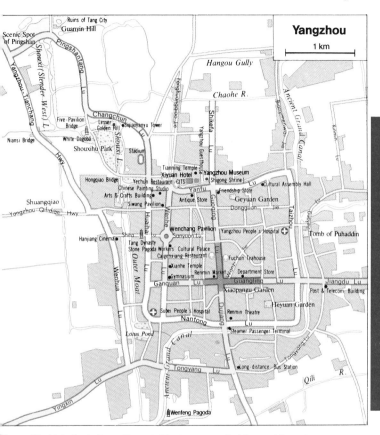

Narrow West Lake lies in the north-west of the town; actually, it is not a lake as such, but rather a section of a stream which was widened first under the Sui (581–619) and then under the Tangs (618–907). It is as beautiful as West Lake in Hangzhou, but smaller and narrower – hence its name. The whole has been made into a public park.

★Narrow
West Lake
(Shouxi Hu)

Of interest to visitors are the Little Mountain of Gold (Xiao Jinshan), surrounded by water, and Angel Square (Diayo Tai), at the foot of the mountain where – according to folk-lore – Emperor Qianlong (reigned 1736–96) used to fish.

Little Mountain
of Gold
Angel Square

West Garden (Xiyuan) was laid out in 1751 in the traditional style.

West Garden

This bridge was originally built of wood and painted red and so was then called "Great Red Bridge". It was replaced by a stone arched bridge in the Qianlong period (1736–96)

Bridge of the
Great Rainbow
(Dahong Qiao)

The White Dagoba, similar to that in Beihai Park in Beijing, also dates from the reign of the Emperor Qianlong (1736–96).

White Dagoba
(Baita)

485

Yangzhou

Bridge of the Five Pavilions (Wuting Qiao)

The Bridge of the Five Pavilions was built in 1757 by salt dealers to welcome the Emperor Qianlong. Five pavilions are ranged along its 55km/180ft length.

Fuzhuang Island

On Fuzhuang Island, reached by a zig-zag bridge, can be seen some pavilions and covered walks.

★ Temple of Heavenly Peace (Tianning Si)

At the foot of the Mountain of the Plum Blossom (Meihua Ling) in the north of the town stands the Temple of Heavenly Peace, built in the Jin period (265–420). Here in 418 a Nepalese monk translated the Buddhist scriptures. In 1757, on the occasion of the visit of Emperor Qianlong, a villa, a garden and an "imperial" mooring berth were built.

Mausoleum of the Sui Emperor Yangdi (Sui Yangdi Ling)

This mausoleum is in Leitang, on the northern outskirts of Yangzhou. The Sui Emperor Yangdi came to Yangzhou in 605, 610, 612 and 618. During his fourth visit to the town he was taken prisoner by some rebel army officers, hanged and buried in a remote grave. In 622 his body was brought here, but it was 1802 before the mausoleum was built.

Xiaopangu Garden

This garden in the south-east part of the town dates from the Qianlong era (1736–96). It is built in the Classical style.

Heyuan Garden

In the south-east of Yangzhou lies the Heyuan Garden, which was purchased and extended by the government official He at the end of the 19th c. The individual buildings are connected by a covered walkway.

Wenfeng Ta Pagoda

Wenfang Ta Pagoda in the south of the town dates from 1582.

Pavilion of the God of Literature (Wenchang Ge)

In the west of Yangzhou can be found the Pavilion of the God of Literature, which goes back to 1585.

Pavilion Looking in Four Directions

The Pavilion Looking in Four Directions, located further north, dates from the year 1559.

Surroundings

★ Temple of Daming Si

The Temple of Daming Si, 4km/2½ miles north-west of Yangzhou, is 1500 years old; however, the present buildings are replacements built in the second half of the 19th c. Before the monk Jianzhen (688–763) went to Japan to spread the Buddhist gospel he lived and worked here for many years. As a result, all Japanese monks attach considerable importance to this temple.

Sumptuous Hall of the Great Hero

In the main temple building, the Sumptuous Hall of the Great Hero (Daxiong Baodian), stand three statues of the Buddha, 18 figures of Luohan and a sculpture of Guanyin.

Jianzhen Memorial Hall

To the east of the main building stands the Jianzhen Memorial Hall, built between 1963–67 with Japanese financial aid. Here can be seen a wooden statue of the monk and a stone tablet bearing an inscription by Guo Moruo (see Famous People).

Hall Level With the Mountains (Pingshan Tang)

The Hall Level With The Mountains, located to the west of the Temple of Daming Si, was built in the middle of the 12th c. by the writer and historian Ouyang Xiu.

Guilin Tang Hall

Near the Ouyang Xiu Memorial Temple (Ouyang Xiu Ci) stands Guilin Tang Hall, built by the poet Su Shi (1037–1101) in memory of his teacher Ouyang Xiu. Paintings and specimens of calligraphy work are exhibited in the building.

Yantai

烟台市

Chinese
equivalent

Province: Shandong
Area: 222sq.km/86sq. miles
Population: 370,000 (conurbation 8,000,000)

Yantai lies in the north-east of Shandong province, at 121°23'E and 37°32'N. It is linked by ship with Shanghai, Qinhuangdao and Dalian, and by rail with Beijing, the provincial capital Jinan, Nanjing and Qingdao.

Situation and
Communications

The town owes its name of Yantai (Terrace of Smoke) to a watch-tower built in the second half of the 14th c, from where smoke signals once gave warning of approaching enemy ships.

History

Sights

On the top of the mountain in the town centre stands a temple, built in the Yuan period (1271–1368) and dedicated to the Jade Emperor.

Mountain of the
Jade Emperor
(Yuhuang Ding)

This small mountain in the north of the town is washed by the sea on three sides. The above-mentioned watch tower was built on top of it in 1398, and a bundle of faggots was lit every time an enemy ship was spotted. Towards the end of the Qing dynasty (1644–1911) a light-house was erected nearby and still operates today.

★ Mountain of the
Terrace of Smoke
(Yantaishan)

Surroundings

The Peninsula of the Magic Mushroom 9km/5½ miles north of the town juts out into the Yellow Sea. Records show that it was visited twice, in 219 and 200 B.C., by the Qin Emperor Shi Huangdi and once by the Han Emperor Wudi.

Peninsula of
the Magic
Mushroom
(Zhifu Dao)

This pavilion on Danya Hill, about 50km/30 miles north-west of Yantai, stands 15m/50ft high and was built in the middle of the 11th c. to commemorate the visits of the above-mentioned emperors.

★ Penglai
Pavilion
(Penglai Ge)

According to tradition, the Eight Immortal Taoists rested on this hill before commencing their long and arduous journey around the world.

Under the canopy on the front of the pavilion hangs a wooden plaque with an inscription made by a famous calligrapher from the Qing period (1644–1911).

Behind the pavilion stand several Taoist buildings, including the Palace of the Three Pure Ones (Sanqing Dian), the Palace of Lü Dongbing (Lu Zu Dian), the Palace of the Queen of Heaven (Tianhou Gong) and the Palace of the Dragon King (Longwang Gong). As well as being of interest from an artistic and architectural point of view, this place will also imbue the visitor with a deep sense of magic and mystery.

Yichang

宜昌市

Chinese
equivalent

Province: Hubei. Area: 195sq.km/75½sq. miles
Population: 280,000 (conurbation 360,000)

| Situation and Communications | Yichang is situated in the west of Hubei province, at the end of the third and last gorge of the Changjiang (Yangtse) river, at 111°12′E and 30°38′N.
There are ships, trains and buses to Yichang from many Chinese towns, as well as flights to Xi'an, Canton, the provincial capital Wuhan and Changsha. |
| History | Yichang has been in existence for 2500 years, and because of its favourable situation has for many years been the political, economic and cultural centre of the western part of Hubei province. |

Surroundings

| ★Gezhou Barrier (Gezhou Ba) | The Gezhou Barrier, 5km/3 miles west of the town, is the first to be built on the Changjiang river and the largest in China. The complex includes a dam, a power station, three sluices and two weirs, one to regulate the water pressure and the other to filter the sand. The dam is 2606m/2860yd long and 70m/230ft high. The power station has 21 generators with an annual output of 13,800,000 megawatts. |
| ★Shennongjia Nature Reserve (Shennongjia Ziran Baohuqu) | This nature reserve, 3250sq.km/1255sq. miles in area, lies near the border with Sichuan province about 150km/93 miles north-west of Yichang. The mountain chain of the same name, with six peaks over 3000m/9846ft, crosses almost the whole of the reserve. The favourable local climate is conducive to the numerous species of plants and animals found here. |
| Lake Dajiuhu | Tigers, leopards, bears and monkeys roam in the countryside around Lake Dajiuhu, 38km/24 miles west of the highest peak.
Many people claim to have seen the "wild man" on the wooded slopes hereabouts, something that scientific expeditions have not so far been able to prove or disprove. |

Yinchuan   I 4

| Chinese equivalent | 银川市 |

Capital of the Autonomous Region of Ningxia
Altitude: 1100m/3610ft. Area: 4487sq.km/1732sq. miles
Population: 384,000 (conurbation 701,000)

| Situation and Communications | Yinchuan lies in the north of the Autonomous Region of Ningxia, at 106°17′E and 38°30′N. Trains run from here to Lanzhou (470km/292 miles) and Beijing (1340km/832 miles). There are also air links with Beijing (about 2 hours), Taiyuan (1½ hours) and Xi'an (1½ hours). |
| History | Yinchuan was founded in the early 11th c. From 1038 to 1227 it served as the capital of the Western Xia kingdom. Under the Yuan, Ming and Qing (from the 13th to the early 20th c.) it was of great political importance to the north-west of China. In 1958, when the Autonomous Region of Ningxia was formed to provide a home for the Hui ethnic group, Yinchuan was made its seat of government.
Today textiles, engineering and chemicals form the basis of the town's industry. Irrigation programmes have made intensive farming possible in the surrounding country. |
| **Sights**

Pavilion of the Jade Emperor | The 22m/72ft high Pavilion of the Jade Emperor in the town centre dates originally from the Ming period (1368–1644), but was rebuilt in 1954. It stands on a terrace of compressed clay covered in bricks and measuring 19m/62ft high, 38m/125ft long and 25m/82ft wide. |

488

The West Pagoda in the south-west of the town forms part of the Temple of Cheng Tian Si and was built in 1050. Both buildings were destroyed in an earthquake in 1738. The pagoda, 64m/210ft high, octagonal in plan and covered with green ceramic tiles, was rebuilt in 1820.

West Pagoda (Xita)

This pagoda, 54m/177ft high and of eleven storeys, stands in a northern suburb of Yinchuan and so is also known locally as the Northern Pagoda (Bei Ta). It was probably built in the early 5th c. but suffered severe damage in two earthquakes in 1712 and 1778. The subsequent restorations have succeeded in restoring it to its former glory.

Treasure pagoda (Haibao Ta)

Cleverly placed niches make the rectangular building look as though it has twelve sides. It differs from other Chinese pagodas in that it has three window openings on all four sides at each floor level, with the centre one projecting forward more than the others. From the upper floors there is a magnificent view of the town, the mountains and the Huanghe river.

The eight imperial mausoleums and more than 70 other tombs from the Western Xia dynasty (1032–1227) are scattered over grounds covering 40sq.km/15½sq. miles, about 30km/19 miles west of Yinchuan.

Surroundings

★Imperial Tombs of the Western Xia (Xixia Huangling)

Each mausoleum is more than 10ha/25 acres in area and comprises external and internal walls, four corner towers, a pavilion, a memorial hall, an altar and an underground burial chamber of compressed soil. One of the imperial tombs was opened up by archaeologists in the 1970s.

Yixing

K 5

宜兴市

Chinese equivalent

Province: Jiangsu
Area: 1640sq.km/633sq. miles. Population: 1,000,000

Yixing lies in the extreme south of Jiangsu province, near its border with Anhui and Zhejiang, to the west of Lake Taihu, at 119°49′E and 31°22′N.

Situation and Communications

There are buses from many towns in all three provinces. It is best to take the bus from Wuxi, 62km/38½ miles north-east of Yixing.

The town is one of the largest and oldest centres of Chinese ceramic production, which is still important today. For the most part everyday articles are made, such as teapots, beakers and flowerpots, frequently decorated with plant and animal patterns.

In Heping Jie Street stands the Residence of the Taiping King, where originally a court official of the Qing dynasty (1644–1911) lived. During the Taiping Uprising (1851–64) one of the leaders chose it as his residence. Today visitors can still see some wall-paintings from that period.

Sights

Residence of the Taiping King

The Pottery Museum exhibits old and new china as well as equipment for making it.

Pottery Museum (Taoci Chenlieguan)

According to legend these caves 20km/12½ miles south of the town were inhabited by Zhang Guolao, an Immortal Taoist from the Tang period (618–907). The cavern goes down 1000m/330ft and contains 72 caves with numerous stalactites and stalagmites.

Surroundings

Mr Zhang's Cave (Zhanggong Dong)

The Cave of the Valley of the Gods, 12km/7½ miles south-west of Mr Zhang's Cave, was discovered by a Tang poet in the 9th c. Numerous visitors from the 10th c. onward have left inscriptions on its walls.

Cave of the Valley of the Gods (Linggu Dong)

★Cave of
Hidden Kindness
(Shanjuan Dong)

The Cave of Hidden Kindness, some 85km/53 miles south-west of Yixing, is divided into four sectors on three different levels. Visitors will walk about 800m/880yd in all. In the upper, spiral-shaped section the temperature is about 23°C/73°F all the year round. At the foot of the caves a waterfall cascades down from a steep rock-face. The cave was probably discovered as early as the 9th c. because a stone was found with an inscription from A.D. 850. Together with the other two caves described above it forms the "Three Wonders of Yixing".

Yueyang   J 6

Chinese
equivalent

岳阳市

Province: Hunan
Area: 22sq.km/8½sq. miles. Population: 230,000

Situation and
Communications

Yueyang is situated in the north of Hunan province, on the north-east bank of Lake Dongtinghu, at 113°08′E and 29°22′N. Trains travel to Yueyang from Wuhan (220km/137 miles south), the provincial capital Changsha (140km/87 miles north), Beijing, Canton and other Chinese cities.

History

The first urban settlement here was over 2000 years ago. In the 6th c., under the Sui, it was known as Yuezhou and was the capital of one of China's largest regions. Today Yueyang's main importance is as a trade centre for timber and cotton.

Sights

★Yueyang Lou
Tower

Yueyang Lou Tower, one of the best-known towers in southern China, stands on the bank of Lake Dongtinghu. Rebuilt in 1045, it replaced a tower built on another site in 716. During the Tang period (618–907) it served as a meeting-place for well-known writers such as Li Bai and Du Fu (see Famous People) and Bai Juyi , who made it famous, as did the literary figure Fan Zhongyan (989–1052) in later years. The three-storey tower is almost 20m/66ft high. It is built without the use of any cross-beams or nails and stands on wooden supports. It comprises four main halls as well as 24 outer and 12 inner rooms; twelve rain spouts point sharply upwards.

Pavilion of the
Three Drunks
(Sanzui Ting)

Three pavilions encircle the Yueyang Tower. In front on the right is the Pavilion of the Three Drunks, dedicated to the Immortal Taoist Lü Dongbin who is said to have got drunk on the tower on three occasions.

Pavilion of the
Magic Plums
(Xianmei Ting)

On the left of the Yueyang Tower stands the Pavilion of the Magic Plums, named after the plum-shaped stone to be found inside it.

Pavilion in
Memory of
Du Fu
(Huaifu Ting)

The third building, the Pavilion in Memory of Du Fu, stands behind the Yueyang Tower and is, as its name implies, dedicated to the poet Du Fu who died in extreme poverty in 770 on a boat anchored on the banks of Lake Dongtinghu.

★Pagoda of
Mrs Ci
(Cishi Ta)

Built in 713–741, this pagoda rises to a height of 39m/128ft in the south-west of the town, on the bank of Lake Dongtinghu. It was named after a Mrs Ci who sold everything she possessed in order to pay for it to be built.

Lake Dongtinghu

Lake Dongtinghu, linked by several canals with the Changjiang river, obtains 40% of its water from the latter and the rest from four other large rivers. In the dry season from October to April, however, water flows from the lake into the Changjiang, so that the lake's water level falls and its area is reduced by almost a third. A boat trip on the lake is not to be missed.

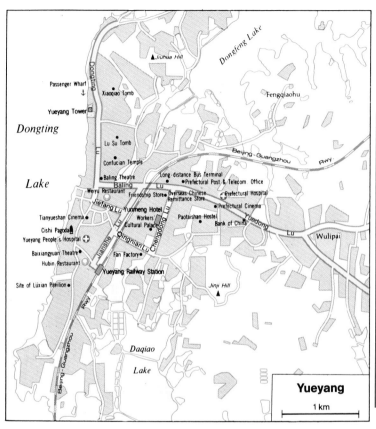

Yueyang

1 km

15km/9½ miles from the town, in Lake Dongtinghu, lies Junshan Island, known for its varied flora, especially the different species of bamboo. The island's tea is also famous.

Surroundings

Junshan Island

Yunnan

G–I 6–7

Chinese equivalent

Province
Area: 394,000sq.km/152,000sq. miles
Population: 37,820,000. Capital: Kunming

Yunnan province lies in south-west China, bordering Myanmar (Burma), Laos and Vietnam, between 97°32' and 106°12'E and 21°08' and 29°15'N.

Situation

The foothills of the Qinghia-Tibet Plateau extend over almost the whole of the province in the form of terraced plateaux 2000 to 3000m/6600 to 9900ft

Topography

491

China

Yunnan Province

The People's Republic of China
Zhonghua Renmin Gongheguo

above sea-level which gradually reduce in height towards the east and south-east. In the north-west the average altitude is 5000m/16,500ft; the highest peak is 6740m/22,120ft. The upper reaches of the Changjiang (Yangtse), Lancangjiang (Mekong), Nuijiang (Nushan/Salween), Yuanjiang and Xijiang rivers have carved out deep valleys through the mountains.

Climate

The differences in topography and altitude within the province have produced varying climatic zones. While extremely raw and cold weather predominates in the north, the climate south of the Tropic of Cancer is dry and hot. The valleys and lake regions, especially the capital Kunming and its surroundings, on the other hand, enjoy a very mild climate all the year round. Temperatures average 22°C/72°F in July and 9°C/48°F in January, and annual rainfall is 1000mm/40in.

Population

About a third of the population of Yunnan belong to national minorities, including the Yi, Bai, Naxi, Hani and Dai. Approximately a half of China's various nationalities live here.

History

Yunnan, which was originally inhabited solely by non-Han peoples, found itself under Chinese dominance in the Qin and Han periods (221 B.C. to A.D. 220), but nevertheless remained substantially independent. The Mongolian Yuan dynasty (1271–1368) then absorbed the region. Separatist movements led to much unrest. In the early 20th c. the French and British tried to expand their empires here. After 1949 the government imposed obligatory industrialisation programmes.

Economy

Because of the rich natural deposits found here mining plays a major part in the economy. The main deposits are tin, followed by copper, coal, iron and phosphorus. 6% of the total area is fertile agricultural land, growing mainly rice but also maize, wheat, yams, coffee, sugar-beet and tobacco.

Places to visit

In addition to the provincial capital of Kunming (see entry), the towns of Dali and Jinghong (see entries) in the Autonomous Region of Xishuangbanna are also worth a visit.

Zhanjiang

湛江

Chinese
equivalent

Province: Guangdong
Area: 12,000sq.km/4630sq. miles. Population: 4,600,000

Zhanjiang lies in the south of Guangdong province, at 10°21'E and 21°16'N. There are buses from the provincial capital Canton and trains from Guilin and Nanning. The town also has a sea-port and ships ply between here and Canton, Haikou and many other south-east Asian harbour towns.

Situation and
Communications

Although still quite a young town Zhanjiang has already experienced many adversities in its short history. In 1898 it was occupied by the French and in 1943 by the Japanese. In 1945 the Chinese again took control.
   In 1984, together with fourteen other harbour towns, it was opened up to international trade.

History

Lake Huguangyan, of volcanic origin and lying 20km/12½ miles south-west of the town, covers an area of 3·6sq.km/1·4sq. miles. Its banks are studded with a number of old monuments and buildings, including the well-known Lengyan Monastery (Lengyan Si) from the Song period (960–1279). Above this temple towers a large rock on which Li Gang (1083–1140) – who occupied a number of important posts under the Song dynasty and was made chancellor – wrote the name of the lake in three Chinese characters.

Surroundings

★Lake
Huguangyan

Zhaoqing

肇庆市

Chinese
equivalent

Province: Guangdong. Area: 197sq.km/76sq. miles
Population: 199,000 (conurbation 5,270,000)

Zhaoqing is situated on the Xijiang river, in the centre of Guangdong province, at 112°25'E and 23°05'N. From the provincial capital of Canton, 110km/68 miles away, there are buses and ships to Zhaoqing.

Situation and
Communications

Zhaoqing is over 2000 years old, and in 1118 was made the capital of an important administrative district. In 1646 the leader of a peasants' uprising used it as his headquarters.

History

The Seven Star Rocks rise up out of Star Lake on the northern edge of the town. The shape of these seven hills, rich in impressive caves, temples and pavilions, resembles the Great Bear (Ursa Major) constellation.
   At the entrance gate there is an inscription by the revolutionary Zhe De. In Stone Chamber Rock (Shishi) lies a cave containing 270 carved stones.

Sights

★Seven Star Rocks
(Qixing Yan)

The Dinghushan massif, 18km/11 miles north-east of Zhaoqing, has been visited by pilgrims for more than 1000 years. It is situated in the middle of some 1200ha/3000 acres of land which has been declared a nature reserve and is home to more than 2000 species of plants and animals. including some very rare and valuable ones such as the Indian antelope, silver pheasant and scaly ant-eater.

Surroundings

★Mount
Dinghushan

On the top of the largest mountain, the 1000m/3300ft high Cockscomb, lies Three-legged Stool Lake (Dinghu). According to legend the Yellow Emperor often came here to show the locals how to make three-legged stools, and that is how the lake got its name.

Cockscomb
(Jilong Feng)

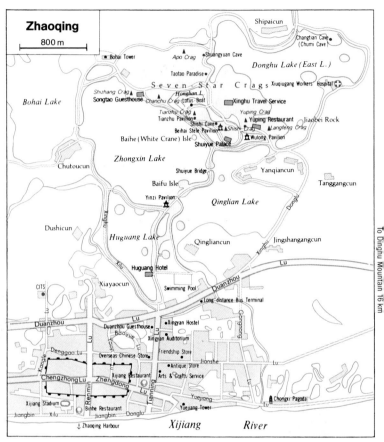

Zhaoqing
800 m

Shipaicun

Bohai Tower
Apo Crag • Shuangyuan Cave
Changtian Cave
(Chumi Cave)

Taotao Paradise
Donghu Lake (East L.)

S e v e n - S t a r   C r a g s   Xiuqiugang Workers' Hospital

Shizhang Crag
Bohai Lake   Songtao Guesthouse   Chanchu Crag Lotus Boat
Hongilian L.
Xinghu Travel Service

Tianzhu Pavilion   Tianzhu Crag
Yuping Crag
Yuping Restaurant • Jiaobei Rock
Shishi Cave   Shishi Crag   Langfeng Crag
Beihai Stele Pavilion
Baihe (White Crane) Isle
Wulong Pavilion
Shuiyue Palace

Zhongxin Lake

Chutoucun
Shuiyue Bridge
Baifu Isle
Yanqiancun
Tanggangcun

Yinzi Pavilion   *Qinglian Lake*

Dushicun   *Huguang Lake*   Qingliancun   Jingshangangcun   Donglu

Huguang Hotel   Xilu   Duanzhou Lu

Xiayaocun   Swimming Pool
Long-distance Bus Terminal

CITS
Duanzhou   Lu
Duanzhou Guesthouse • Xingyan Hostel
Baoyue   Xingyan Auditorium
Denggao lu   Overseas Chinese Store   Friendship Store
Antique Store
Chengzhong Lu   Zhengdong   Xijiang Restaurant   Arts & Crafts Service
Xijiang Stadium   Binhe Restaurant
Jiangbin   Xifu   Jiangbin   Donglu   Yuejiang Tower   Yuejiang   Chongxi Pagoda
Zhaoqing Harbour   *Xijiang   River*

Temple of Qingyun Si	Numerous Buddhist temples are hidden among the dense trees, including the Ming period (1368–1644) Qingyun Si Temple, now a guest house.
It boasts a beautiful bronze bell weighing 500kg/1100lb and a giant iron cauldron in which rice was cooked for 100 people.
Temple of the White Clouds (Baiyun Si)	Some 5km/3 miles south-west of the Qingyun Si Temple will be found the Temple of the White Clouds, dating from the Tang era (618–907).

Zhejiang

K–L 5–6

Chinese equivalent

浙江省

Province
Area: 101,800sq.km/39,300sq. miles
Population: 42,002,000. Capital: Hangzhou

China

The People's Republic of China
Zhonghua Renmin Gongheguo

Zhejiang province lies in eastern China, between 118°01' and 123°08'E and 27°01' and 31°10'N. — Situation

80% of the territory is mountainous and hilly, and 20% plateaux or plains. The highest peak is 1921m/6305ft. — Topography

As the province lies in a subtropical zone the climate is very warm and humid. There are marked seasonal differences. The mean annual temperature lies between 16° and 19°C/61° and 66°F and the annual rainfall is 1850mm/74in approx. — Climate

Zhejiang can trace its history back to the 8th c. B.C.. For a long time it was divided into east and west sectors. The town began to prosper when the Song (960–1279) moved their seat to Hangzhou. This came to an end with the Taiping Uprising (1851–64). — History

The main industries are engineering and chemicals. Only some 20% of the land area is suitable for agriculture; most of this is used for growing rice, corn and maize. Tea and silk is of particular importance. — Economy

The major sights and places of interest will be found in the provincial capital Hangzhou and in Shaoxing, Ningbo, Wenzhou, Jinghua and Jiaxing (see entries). — Places to visit

Zhengzhou · J 5

郑州市

Chinese equivalent

Capital of Henan Province
Altitude: 107m/350ft. Area: 1940sq.km/750sq. miles
Population: 895,000 (conurbation 1,420,000)

To Dengfeng 74 km

Situation and Communications	Zhengzhou lies in the north of Henan province, south of the Huanghe and east of the Songshan rivers, at 113°39′E and 34°43′N.

As the city stands at the junction of China's two major rail routes, the Beijing–Canton and Lianyungang–Ürümqi lines, it is accessible by train from almost any large town in the country. It is also possible to fly here in a few hours from Beijing, Shanghai, Canton, Xi'an and other cities.

History

Zhengzhou is one of China's oldest cities. Archaeological digs have revealed important Neolithic finds and the ruins of a 3500 year-old town wall built in the Shang period (16th–11th c. B.C.). The total length of this wall was more than 7km/4½ miles, it was 9m/30ft high and over 30m/99ft at the base. Zhengzhou expanded considerably under the Western Zhou (11th c.–770 B.C.). It was given its present name in 559 B.C. After the construction of the two above-mentioned railway lines in the early 20th c. Zhengzhou enjoyed rapid economic growth. It played a central role in the 1923 rail strike, the "Strike of February 7th". As well as being the political, cultural and business centre of Henan province it is also an important north Chinese industrial centre (metalworking, machinery).

Sights

★Pagoda in Memory of the Feb. 7th Strike

In 1971 a monument was erected in the city centre to commemorate the General Rail Strike which began on February 7th 1923 and was violently suppressed three days later with much bloodshed. The double pagoda, 63m/207ft high, is polygonal in plan. Documents relating to the events of the time are on display.

The Provincial Museum in the city centre exhibits Neolithic finds, especially those of the Yangshao and Longshan cultures. Further exhibits relating to the history of the Revolution which commenced with the rail strike can also be seen.

Historical Museum of Henan Province (Henansheng Lishi Bowuguan)

The Public Park lies on the banks of the Huanghe, to the west of the Provincial Museum. Its pavilions and covered walkways make it a popular spot with the local inhabitants.

Public Park (Renmin Gongyuan)

Mount Mangshan rises up on the banks of the Huangshe 30km/19 miles north-west of Zhengzhou. Here can be seen a pumping-station built in 1972 which provides the city with water.

From the top of the mountain there is an impressive view of the river.

Surroundings

Mount Mangshan

These two tombs from the Eastern Han period (A.D. 25–220) lie in the village of Dahuting in the Mixian district, 30km/19 miles south-west of Zhengzhou. A governor and his relatives are buried here. The frescos in the tombs show scenes from the lives of the deceased.

Dahuting Han Tombs (Dahuting Hanmu)

More than 3000 years ago Anyang, some 190km/120 miles north of Zheng-zhou, was the capital of the Yin or Shang dynasty. For 273 years it was a major centre of power, but after the fall of the Shang dynasty it also soon went into decline. Ruins of the town near the village of Xiaotun were first excavated in 1899. Many valuable archaeological finds came to light over an area measuring 8km/5 miles from east to west and 3km/2 miles from north to south; these included more than 100,000 carvings and inscriptions on tortoise-shell and ox-bones as well as bronze objects.

★★Remains of the Yin civilisation near Anyang (Anyang Yinxu)

Also near Anyang lie the ruins of the town of Youli, which is known to have existed back in the time of the Zhou (11th c.–771 B.C.). At that time the Zhou King Wenwang often came here to take part in prophecy rituals. Apart from the original terrace all the buildings which have survived were rebuilt in later centuries. Of particular interest is the Stele of the King with its 64 hexagrams which are described in detail in the "Yi Jing", or "Book of Changes". It gives many clues to the prophetic and fortune-telling practices employed in China more than 2100 years ago.

★Remains of the town of Youli (Youli Yizhi)

Zhenjiang

K 5

镇江市

Chinese equivalent

Province: Jiangsu. Area: 215sq.km/83sq. miles
Population: 310,000 (conurbation 2,500,000)

Zhenjiang lies on the south bank of the Changjiang (Yangtse) river, at 119°22′E and 32°14′N, surrounded by the Jiaoshan, Beigushan and Jinshan mountains around which so much in the way of myths and legends and meaningful history has been woven over the centuries. The Beijing–Shanghai–Fuzhou railway line links it with the provincial capital Nanjing (65km/40 miles), Shanghai (238/148 miles) and many other Chinese cities. As Zhenjiang has a large harbour on the Changjiang it can also be reached by ship from Nanjing, Shanghai, Wuhan, Chongqing, etc.

Situation and Communications

Zhenjiang can look back proudly on 2500 years of history. After having been made a military base under the Wu, at the time of the Three Kingdoms (220–280) it became known as Xuzhou and retained that name for several centuries until it was changed to Zhenjiang in the Song period (960–1279). Being so favourably situated at the confluence of the Changjiang and the Grand Canal it soon became a trading centre. Today it is an industrial city.

History

497

Sights

★**Beigushan**	Mount Beigushan, 48m/157ft high and a natural fortress in a strategically favourable location, stands on the south bank of the Changjiang. It was frequently mentioned in the annals of the Three Kingdoms. Sun Quan, the King of the Wu, enticed his rival Liu Bei, King of the Shu, into a trap at the foot of Mount Beigushan by pretending to offer him his sister in marriage.
Temple of the Refreshing Dew (Ganlu Si)	One of the buildings to be found on Mount Beigushan is the Temple of the Refreshing Dew, in which the mother of Sun Quan met with Liu Bei to discuss the above-mentioned marriage. It dates back to the year 265 but over the years it has been destroyed and rebuilt several times.
Tower of the Panorama (Duojing Lou)	Near the Temple of the Refreshing Dew is the Iron Pagoda (Ganlusi Tieta). On the top of the mountain stands the Tower of the Panorama, from which a beautiful view can be enjoyed.
★**Golden Mountain** (Jinshan)	Although Golden Mountain, in the north-west of the city, is only 60m/196ft high it is richly endowed with historical monuments and pretty corners. It derives its name from the gold which was found here in the Tang period (618–907).
Temple of Golden Mountain	The best-known building is the 4th c. Temple Monastery of Golden Mountain (Jinshan Si), where monks still live today.
Cishou Ta Pagoda	The Cishou Ta Pagoda dates from the year 1900, but there is thought to have been a pagoda here back in the Tang era (618–907). A spiral staircase leads up to the individual floors.
Spring No. 1 (Tianxia Diyiquan)	Spring No. 1 on Jinshan's west slope attracts large numbers of visitors.
★**Mr Jiao's Mountain** (Jiaoshan)	This 150m/490ft high mountain rises up out of the Changjiang river. At the time of the Eastern Han (25–220) a certain Jiao Guang sought refuge here – hence its name. On Mount Jiaoshan there are many things to interest the visitor, such as some 300 old stone-carvings and several centuries-old trees including pine, elm and gingko. A stele engraved by the famous calligrapher Wang Xizhi (see Famous People) is housed in its own pavilion.
Temple Monastery of Dinghui Si	The Temple Monastery of Dinghui Si on Mount Jiaoshan, founded in the Eastern Han period (25–230) is also of interest. The present buildings date from the Qing era (1644–1911).
Building of the Breathing River (Xijiang Lou)	On the top of the mountain stands the Building of the Breathing River, which forms part of the Biefeng An temple. On the east side of Mount Jiaoshan can be seen the fortifications which British and Qing troops fought over in the Opium War of 1842.

Zhuhai

Chinese equivalent	珠海

Province: Guangdong. Area: 122sq.km/47sq. miles
Population: 175,000 (conurbation 425,000)

Situation and Communications	Zhuhai lies to the west of the mouth of the Xijiang river, just north of Macau, at 113°29′E and 22°14′N. It is linked by motorway and shipping line with the provincial capital Canton, 140km/87 miles away. Zhuhai's historical town centre embraces 104 small islands which have much to offer in the way of leisure activities and beautiful scenery.

Until the mid-1900s Zhuhai was just a minor township forming part of a larger town. It was 1953 before it became administratively autonomous. In 1979 central government decided to establish a Special Economic Zone here; this meant a freer economic policy and a more flexible form of administration. Since then Zhuhai has enjoyed enormous economic and urban growth.

History

The Beach Park in the east-central part of the town lies in the shadow of Mount Shijingshan. It is also known as Incense Bay because at one time, before going out fishing, fishermen would burn incense here in order to seek the protection of the gods.
   Today the beach with its fine silver sand offers much in the way of modern bathing facilities.

Sights

★Beach Park
(Haibun Gongyuan)

A popular place for outings and excursions is the "Stone Zoo", in the centre of town west of Beach Park. Here visitors can see 22 stone formations shaped like animals, including elephants, rhinos, snakes and various other beasts.

★Excursion venues by the Shijingshan (Shijinshan Luyou Zhongxin)

Zibo

K 4

淄博市

Chinese equivalent

Province: Shandong
Area: 3436sq.km/1327sq. miles. Population: 2,700,000

Zibo lies in the centre of Shandong province, at 118°03′E and 36°45′N. There are trains and buses from Jinan, which is 100km/62 miles away.

Situation and Communications

From the 8th c. B.C. onwards Zibo was the capital of the Qi empire for 630 years. It also became well-known for its traditional ceramics and lacquered works of art. Green glass was first developed in Zibo some 1500 years ago. Under the Tang (618–907) black glazed porcelain from Zibo was a "best seller". In the Song period (960–1279) the local makers of china invented a new technique – they coated the earthenware with a brownish layer of glaze displaying tear-shaped runs. After a long period of decline Zibo's hand-made porcelain enjoyed a revival in the mid-1900s and today it is China's major producer of ceramics.

History

Large numbers of tombs are to be found in the countryside around Zibo, including the Tomb of the Two Kings (Erwang Zong), in which the two Dukes of Qi, Huan (reigned 685–643 B.C.) and Jinggong (reigned 547–490 B.C.), are interred, as well as the Tomb of Guan Zhong (d. 645 B.C.), one of the founders of Legalism.

Surroundings

Tombs

A 30sq.km/11½sq. mile area of the remains of the Qi capital in the Linzi district, north-west of Zibo, has been excavated. Founded 2900 years ago, the city was surrounded by a defensive wall 14,158m/15,570yd (9 miles) long with thirteen gates linked one with the other by made-up roads. The city possessed a perfect sewerage system which also took away the waste water from the bronze and iron-smelting furnaces. In the course of the digs archaeologists also discovered coin mints and workshops in which tools were produced from bones. Some of the finds can be seen in the Archaeological Museum in Zibo's Old Town.

★Remains of the capital of the Qi Kingdom (Qiguo Gucheng)

In the Zichuan district near Zibo stands the house in which Pu Songling (1640–1715) wrote the well-known collection of tales entitled "Curious Stories from the Liao Studio" ("Liaozhai Zhiyi"). He lived here until he was 30, and returned to his native town when he was 71. An exhibition hall provides information on the writer's life and work.

★Dwelling of Pu Songling (Pu Songling Guju)

Practical Information from A to Z

Accommodation

See Hotels, Youth Accommodation

Air Transport

Airports
: The People's Republic has just under a hundred civil airports.

International
: China's major international airport is Beijing's Capital Airport. Besides all the usual facilities this also has an information desk where foreign visitors can enquire about hotels, etc.
  Shanghai's Hongquiao Airport is another hub of international traffic.

Domestic
: A number of the airports which handle domestic flights are listed under airlines.

Connecting Flights
International Flights
: The People's Republic of China links up with the world's air travel network out of Beijing and Shanghai through the routes flown by its national airline Air China, or CAAC, the China Aviation Administration of China as it's also known, Shanghai Airlines and many other international airlines (see Getting to China).

Domestic flights
: Flights out of Beijing also connect with the major cities in China.

Airlines
: Air China, also known as CAAC (Civil Airline Administration of China) and founded in 1988, is the principal carrier of the People's Republic and flies the main domestic routes as well as the international ones (see Getting to China). There are various smaller regional airlines as well which also serve short-haul destinations in neighbouring countries.

Air China abroad
: Air China's overseas offices include those in Australia (Melbourne, Sydney), Canada (Toronto, Vancouver), the United Kingdom (London) and the United States (Los Angeles, San Francisco, New York).

Airlines in China

Air China
: Booking office in Beijing: 15 Chang'an Avenue West;
  tel. (010) 601 77 55

  International reservations: tel. (010) 601 66 67
  Internal flight reservations: tel. (010) 601 33 36
  At Beijing's Capital International Airport: tel. (010) 456 32 20/21
  Bookings can also be made in Beijing through various hotels and in many other Chinese cities such as Shanghai, Hohhot in Inner Mongolia, etc.

China Eastern Airlines
: At Shanghai Hongqiao Airport;
  tel. (021) 255 88 99

China Southern Airlines
: At Guangzhou (Canton) Baiyun Airport;
  tel. (020) 666 13 81

China Northern Airlines
: At Shenyang Dongta Airport;
  tel. (024) 82 25 63

At Shanghai Hongqiao Airport; tel. (021) 255 85 58	Shanghai Airlines
Xiamen; tel. (0592) 62 29 61	Xiamen Airlines
At Chengdu Shuang Liu Airport; tel. (028) 58 14 66	China Southwest Airlines
At Xi'an Xiguan Airport; tel. (029) 438 92	China Northwest Airlines
At Taiyuan Wusu Airport, Taiyuan/Shanxi Prov.; tel. (03 51) 77 56 00	China General Aviation Corp.
At Ürümqi Diwopu Airport; tel. (0991) 33 56 88	Xinjiang Airlines
9 Third Section, Yihuan Road South, Chengdu; tel. (028) 55 11 61	Sichuan Airlines

Foreign airlines in Beijing

Room 210, 2nd floor, SCITE Tower, 22 Jianguomenwai; tel. (010) 512 40 70	British Airways
China World Trade Centre, 1 Jianguomenwai; tel. (010) 500 19 56	Canadian Airlines
Room 101–103, Jianguo Hotel; tel. (010) 500 45 29	Northwest Airlines
5th floor, Beijing Fortune Building, 5 Dongsanhuan Beilu, Chaoyangqu; tel. (010) 500 24 81	Qantas
Room 204, SCITE Tower, 22 Jianguomenwai; tel. (010) 512 88 88	United Airlines

Antiques

Only antiques made since the mid-19th c. may be exported. These must be marked with a red wax seal and be accompanied by a certificate and a written export permit. The state-run Friendship Stores issue these as a matter of course.
Export controls

Until recently only antiques bought in state-run antique stores could be exported. There the prices are set by art experts and the visitor can be sure that they represent the proper value.
Antiques from state-run shops

The authorities have now opened up antique markets, second-hand stores, etc. to private dealers, but they are still only allowed to sell items of a later provenance. If you do buy from them there is no guarantee that you are getting proper value for money nor that an export licence will be granted in due course.
Other stores and markets

In any case be sure to keep the receipt.

See also Business Hours, Customs Regulations, Shopping and Souvenirs.

Bath Houses

Since bathrooms are a rarity in China, even in new buildings, every block of housing traditionally has its public baths. These cost very little by Western standards.
Public baths

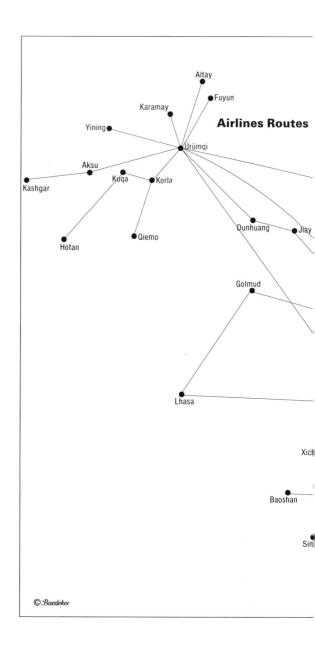

Airlines Routes

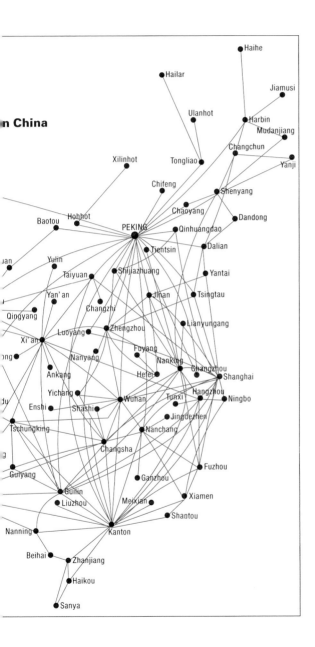

n China

503

Beaches

Xing Hua Yuan
bath house

Xing Hua Yuan bath house in Beijing is much more expensive and consequently especially popular with China's upper echelons. It has a range of jacuzzis, saunas, steam rooms and rest rooms where visitors can relax in aromatic baths and sip tea, coffee or rice wine.

Beaches

China has a number of good beaches for swimming (see below) as well as those along its east coast at Weihai in the north and Tsingtau, Zhoushan, Ningbo and Fuzhou further south.

A word of warning

Swimmers have recently been killed by sharks off Hong Kong's beaches, including Sai Kung; in any case find out about beach conditions from the local CITS (see Information) and take heed of warning flags, etc.

Hainan Island

Hainan Island off the South China mainland is famous for its palm-fringed white sandy beaches, and with its 300 days of sunshine a year, average annual temperature of 22°C/71°F and gentle swell makes a very good place for a holiday by the sea.

In the south of the island a beach of fine sand stretches for 7.2km/4½ miles along Yalongwan Bay, a popular centre for water sports 10km/6 miles out of Sanya, which also has another bathing beach 3km/2 miles to the south-east.

Beidaihe
(Hebei Prov.)

A well-known summer resort, Beidaihe is 15km/9 miles south-west of Qinhuangdao and has a sandy beach over 10km/6 miles long, with a hilly hinterland.

Dalian
(Liaoning Prov.)

Popular beaches around Dalian include Xinghai Gongyuan Park, Laohutan (tiger beach) park and the island of Bangchui (sandy beach).

Shangchuan
Island
(Guangdong Prov.)

Feisha beach, with its fine sand stretching for 11km/7 miles on the eastern edge of the island of Shangchuan, has earnt itself the title of "the Hawaii of the Orient".

Lake Shahu
(Ningxia Prov.)

Lake Shahu, the large (660 ha) lake 56km/35 miles north of Yinchuan, is a favourite place for outings in northwestern China (rowing boats for hire).

Shenzhen
(Guangdong Prov.)

Lake Xili, north of Shenzhen city centre, boasts good swimming and a holiday village.

The tourist centre of Xiaomeisha on Dapeng Bay, 29km/18 miles out of Shenzhen, also has a long beach of fine sand.

Zhuhai
(Guangdong Prov.)

Baiteng Lake Holiday Resort is a recreation area with facilities for water sports plus shopping, etc.

Bicycles (zìxíngchē)

In all large places bicycles – without lights! – can be rented from a number of hotels or cycle shops close to the main sights, and sometimes at rail stations as well. They cost relatively little but usually a deposit (passport) is required.

Shopping quarters in the big towns have supervised cycle parks for which you pay a small charge.

Business Hours

Banks   See Currency

Changing money   See Currency

Bicycles are the most used means of transport in China

Crowds for the buses

Buses

Cinemas	Open until 11.30 or midnight (information from hotel reception or the daily press).
Markets	Find out about dates and times from the local CITS offices (see Information) or from tour guides. Night markets in Beijing: 6–11pm (9pm in winter).
Museums	See entry
Government offices	Offices are usually open Monday to Friday from 8.30/9am to noon and 1.30 to 5.30pm.
Post Offices	See Post and Telecommunications
Restaurants	See entry
Shops	Shops are usually open seven days a week from 9am to 7pm, although many open as early as 8am and close between 6 and 7pm or as late as 8pm. They only remain closed on official holidays (see Festivals and Public Holidays) such as National Day (October 1st) and the Chinese New Year (late January/early February).

Buses

Buses are particularly good for short trips, and in some cases they may be the only form of public transport available. Visitors have a choice between the newer tourist buses or the older single-deckers used by most of the locals – these can get very crowded. At all costs avoid taking a bus during the rush-hour!

Urban and long-distance buses	Buses and trams run on the relatively short distance main road routes in town. Long-distance buses also serve the more outlying areas.
Finding the right bus	Although destinations are only written in Chinese in most cities you will able to find the right bus from its number and route map.
Bus stations	Bus stations (changtuqichezhan) are identified by a three-pronged steering wheel.
Bus tickets	Tickets are sold at the central bus station. If possible buy them the day beforehand; further information can be had from CITS offices (see Information) and hotel reception desks. Fares vary according to destination but are extremely cheap in any case. Unlike trains and boats and planes the fares on buses are usually the same for the foreign tourist as they are for the Chinese.
Departure times	Although the buses seldom leave on time passengers should still be there well beforehand if only to be sure of getting a good seat – avoid the back of the bus which is less comfortable and the front which can be too noisy.
Group travel	Air-conditioned buses are usually available from CITS (see Information) for group travel on sightseeing tours.

Car Rental

See Motoring

Chemists

The medical problems most likely to be encountered in China are colds and digestive upsets because of difficulties in adjusting to the Chinese weather (see When to Go and Facts and Figures, Climate) and over-indulgence in unfamiliar food and drink (see Food and Drink).

As a precaution take any regularly needed medication. There are chemists in every town with a wide range of both Western and Chinese remedies.

Medication

The ancient pharmacy of Hu Qingyu in Hangzhou in Zhejiang province has national monument status as China's only museum of healing herbs. Here displays provide information about the use of Chinese herbs for healing and their international importance in the history of medicine. Visitors can question experts on traditional Chinese medicine and also try out dishes prepared with herbs.
    See also Emergency Services, Health Precautions, Shopping and Souvenirs

Hu Qingyu pharmacy in Hangzhou

Chinese Society and the Visitor

Every visitor to China should definitely familiarise himself or herself beforehand with the many different aspects of this extremely ancient culture in order to gain a better understanding of certain ways of behaviour.

See Information

Leaflets

It goes without saying that travel can sometimes prove frustrating and wearing in a country such as China where contact with foreign tourists is still a relatively new experience in many places.
    Whenever possible just relax and avoid any hassles which might upset you and spoil your enjoyment of the genuine friendliness and hospitality of the true China. With a ready smile, a little tolerance and above all immense patience, your eyes will be opened to the fact that behind the apparent stress and hurly burly of modern life lurks the courtesy and wisdom for which the Chinese are famous.
    Although in the last 10 years China has increasingly opened up to the West and to western influence and its economy has made enormous strides, it is still ruled by customs and traditions which are largely alien to the incoming visitor.
    There are also some things you need to know as a tourist if you are not to embarrass or even anger your Chinese hosts by making them lose face.

Behaviour, traditions and customs

Above all be punctual. Also remember that people in China eat at different times from Westerners and consequently go to the theatre and the cinema at different times (see Business Hours).

Punctuality

The Chinese avoid bodily contact so do not try to shake hands when introduced or touch people when you are talking to them.
    When introducing themselves Chinese give their surname before their first names, so that a Mr Wu Guangwen should be addressed as Mr Wu rather than Mr Guangwen.
    Kissing on both cheeks, which has become a common form of greeting in many western countries, is regarded as overfamiliarity, even between parents and children.

Introductions

Do not bring unduly expensive gifts; they could cause the host to lose face and would have to be refused.

Gifts

Avoid any mention of Taiwan or critical remarks about the Chinese regime; it is better to talk about the differences between China and the West or the progress achieved by the People's Republic; sport is a reliable standby.
    The Chinese are always reluctant to lose face by saying no; if you get an evasive response do not pursue the matter further.

Conversation

It is not always necessary to take off your shoes but you must always remove any headwear.

In temples

507

Chinese Society and the Visitor

Photography	Generally speaking there are few restrictions on photography, although it is always better to seek permission first. This is especially true when taking photographs of people, to guard against giving unintended offence. The Chinese dislike over-familiarity, so avoid for example putting an arm around a Chinese person if being photographed together.
Prostitution	Prostitution is targeted by the authorities as one of the "six bourgeois sins".
Surcharge on foreigners	It is standard practice for foreigners to be charged two or even three times the "domestic" rate for air and rail tickets, hotel accommodation, entrance fees, etc. This does not mean that prices are necessarily unreasonable by western standards, but a degree of watchfulness is required. Any complaint, should the occasion arise, is always best delivered politely and in a friendly manner.

Currency

Official currency (RMB)	China's official currency is the people's money, the renminbi (RMB). This is based on the yuan which is divided into 100 fen or 10 jiao or mao. There are banknotes for 1, 2, 5, 10, 50 and 100 yuan or mao as well as coins and banknotes for 1, 2 and 5 fen.
Foreign Exchange Certificates (FEC)	Foreign tourists before 1993 took their own currency, the Foreign Exchange Certificates (FEC), while the Chinese locals used the renminbi (RMB). Now tourists can acquire RMB from the Bank of China or the Exchange Counter based in tourist hotels.
Import and export of Chinese currency	The import and export of Chinese currency was forbidden until recently but the latest information is that travellers may now take in and bring out up to 6000 yuan – a currency not normally stocked by European banks in any case.
Declaration on entry	It is necessary to complete a declaration form on entry listing any foreign currency or valuables such as jewellery, cameras, etc. which you are bringing in with you. Your copy of this has also to be presented on departure. See also Customs Regulations.
Minimum exchange requirements	China has no minimum exchange regulations for European or North American currencies.
Travellers' cheques, credit cards	Travellers' cheques and international credit cards – but not Eurocheques – are accepted in banks, tourist hotels, Friendship Stores and antique shops.
Changing money	Money can be exchanged in various branches of the Bank of China, Friendship Stores and at the Exchange Counter in tourist hotels at the official rate. Always carry your passport with you.
Banks	Business hours: Mon.–Sat. 8.30am–noon and 1.30–5.30pm Some European banks are represented in Beijing but cannot change money.
Money exchange counters	Money exchange counters in hotels open on holidays as well as through the week, and in some cases stay open until late evening.

Customs Regulations

On arrival	Before entry into China every traveller is handed two forms – a health declaration and an entry card.

Four examples
of Chinese
banknotes

Diplomatic Representation

Forbidden items	It is forbidden to bring in, or take out, any of the following: arms, explosives and ammunition; radio transmitters or receivers; written or otherwise recorded materials that may be deemed state secrets or politically, economically, culturally or morally subversive; drugs, fresh fruit or antiques lacking the proper seal.
On departure	An international airport charge has to be paid before the return flight. You must be able to produce the articles declared on arrival since these may not be exported from China.
Re-entry to EU countries	If you are returning to a member country of the European Union the duty-free allowances for persons over 15 are 500g coffee or 200g powdered coffee and 100g tea or 40g teabags, 50g perfume and 0.25 litre toilet water, and for persons over 17, 1 litre spirits with more than 22% alcohol or 2 litres spirits with less than 22% alcohol or 2 litres sparkling wine and 2 litres table wine and 200 cigarettes or 100 cigarillos or 50 cigars or 250g tobacco.
Re-entry to non-EU countries	For countries outside the European Union the allowances are as follows: Australia 250 cigarettes or 50 cigars or 250g tobacco, 1 litre spirits or 1 litre wine; Canada 200 cigarettes and 50 cigars and 900g tobacco, 1.1 litre spirits or wine; New Zealand 200 cigarettes or 50 cigars or 250g tobacco, 1.1 litre spirits and 4.5 litres wine; South Africa 400 cigarettes and 50 cigars and 250g tobacco, 1 litre spirits and 2 litres wine; USA 200 cigarettes and 100 cigars and a reasonable quantity of tobacco, 1 litre spirits or 1 litre wine.

Diplomatic Representation

Chinese Representation Abroad

Australia	247 Federal Highway, Watson, Canberra, 2600 ACT
Canada	411–415 Andrews Street, Ottawa, Ontario K1N 5H3
New Zealand	2–6 Glenmore Street, Kelburr, Wellington
United Kingdom	31 Portland Place, London W1N 3AG; tel. (0171) 636 5726
USA	Embassy: 2300 Connecticut Avenue NW, Washington DC 20008 Consulates: 3417 Montrose Boulevard, Houston, Texas 77006; 104 South Michigan Avenue, Suite 1200, Chicago, Illinois 60603; 520 12th Avenue, New York, NY 10036

Foreign Representation in China

Australia	Embassy: 15/21 Dongzhimenwai Dajie, Sanlitun Compound, Beijing; tel. (010) 532 23 31 Consulate: 17 Fuxing Xilu, Shanghai; tel. (021) 433 46 04
Canada	10 Sanlitun Lu, Sanlitun Compound, Beijing; tel. (010) 532 30 31
Eire	3 Ritan Donglu, Jianguomenwai Compound, Beijing; tel. (010) 532 26 91
New Zealand	1 Ritan Dong 2–Jie, Jianguomenwai Compound, Beijing; tel. (010) 532 27 31
United Kingdom	Embassy: 11 Guanghua Lu, Jianguomenwai Compound, Beijing; tel. (010) 532 19 61 Consulate: 244 Yongfu Lu, Shanghai; tel. (021) 433 68 80

Embassy: 3 Xiushui Beijie, Jianguomenway Compound, Beijing;
  tel. (010) 532 38 31

Consulates: 2 Xiushui Dongjie, Jianguomenwai Compound, Beijing; 11th
  Floor, Dongfang Hotel, Guangzhou (Canton); 1469 Huahai Zhonglu,
  Shanghai; tel. (021) 433 68 80; Jin Jiang Hotel (office), Chengdu,
  Sichuan; tel. (028) 5 19 12/5 27 91

Electricity

If possible take an international adaptor with you, since in China the right one may not be available.

Before you go
Adaptor

Take a torch and spare batteries since this will come in useful when looking round caves, etc.

Torch

Electricity in China is 220 volts, 50 cycles AC. Sockets are for two or three-pin plugs and often only take American-style plugs with flat metal prongs. Reduced power and total black-outs may sometimes occur.

In China

110 volts, 60 cycles AC

In Taiwan

200/220 volts, 50 cycles AC. Plugs have round prongs.

In Hong Kong

220 volts, 50 cycles AC except in the old city of Macao which has 110 volts.

In Macao

Emergency Services

Police emergency: tel. 110

Police

Beijing Emergency Medical Centre,
West Dajie, Qianmen, Beijing; tel. 120

First Aid

Room 438, Kunlun Hotel,
Beijing; tel. (010) 500 34 19

International
SOS Assistance

9c North Lodge, China World Trade Centre,
Jianguomennei Dajie, Beijing; tel. (010) 505 13 93

Europe
Assistance

Beijing Friendship Hospital,
Yongan Road, Tianqiao, Xuanwu District,
Beijing; tel. (010) 301 44 11

Hospital for
Tropical
Diseases

See also Information, Medical Assistance.

Events

China's many events and local festivals are a good opportunity for getting to know the country and its people. Since the timing of celebrations such as those listed below can vary slightly from year to year you should find out the precise dates beforehand from the CITS (see Information). The names of the provinces are given in the margin in brackets. For the major annual festivals see also Public Holidays and Festivals.

See entry

Public Holidays

Events

Calendar of Principal Events

January/February Harbin (Heilongjiang)	Ice Lantern Festival: fantastic ice sculptures, illuminated at night, ice sports, horse-drawn and motorised sledge rides, cultural events
February Nationwide	Spring Festival/Chinese New Year (see Public Holidays and Festivals): carnivals and fairs with entertainers, arts and crafts, cultural events and special local events
Huangnan (Qinghai)	Buddhist celebrations in Longwu monastery: Tibetan drama and dance, dragon dancing, art exhibition and stalls
Qingdao (Shandong)	Candied fruit fair in the Hayun convent for Buddhist nuns; cultural and folk events
Canton (Guangdong)	Flower market (over 3 miles long) in the street: selling flowers, goldfish, miniature gardens and handicrafts
Many places	Lantern Festival: see Public Holidays and Festivals
Anshun (Guizhou)	Open-air performances on historical themes
Kaili (Guizhou) and Rongshui (Guangxi Auton. Region)	Lusheng Festival: festival of the Miao peoples with folk dance, cockfighting, horse racing, and other sporting and cultural events including contests in playing the lusheng, a kind of panpipes
March Mangshi and Wanding (Yunnan)	Munao song and dance festival of the Jingpo peoples with sword-dances, antiphonal singing and other folk events
March/April Yangzhou (Jiangsu)	Boat Festival: boatmen present opera on board and offer wares for sale
Chengdu (Sichuan)	Flower show lasting 30 to 40 days in Chengdu's Qinyang Gong Palace: also artistic events; many culinary specialities
Wuxi (Jiangsu)	International Winter Cherry Blossom Festival of Culture, including planting of cherry trees
Fengdu (Sichuan)	Ghost Town Fair: evening market and circus, song and dance performances; acrobatic, dragon and lion dances on the streets
April Weifang (Shandong)	International Kite Festival in the "kite capital": exhibition of kites and other craft products, national and international kite-flying contests; 500km/310 mile tour on the theme of folk customs
Suizhou (Hubei)	Festivities commemorating the birthday of Emperor Yan
Shaoxing (Zhejiang)	Calligraphy exhibition and demonstration in the Lanting pavilion, verse recitation, wine-tasting
Suzhou (Jiangsu)	Garden Festival: visits to gardens, garden lantern show and local opera; symposium on the art of garden-making
Xishuangbanna (Yunnan)	Water Festival: see Public Holidays and Festivals
Luoyang (Henan)	Tea Festival with excursions to tea plantations: presentation of different teas, exhibition of period tea ware
Late April Heze (Shandong)	Peony show: over 6 million peonies of many different colours in the flower beds of Chaozhou park (63 ha)

Flower tattoo, lantern show: song and dance by the Han people ("oriental ballet" with a 4000–year old history)	Bengbu (Anhui)
Shanghai Arts Festival (opera, theatre, music, dance, acrobatic contests): performances by national and internationally famous artistes	**May** Shanghai
International Fair of Herbal Medicines: visit to the temple of the Lord of Healing, a pharmaceutical factory and fields for growing therapeutic herbs, sampling dishes with healing properties	Baoding (Hebei)
International Cord Tree Festival: display of blossoms, participation in cultural and sporting events; seafood barbeques and huaihua banquet	Dalian (Liaoning)
Gourmet Festival: various Chinese delicacies on offer as part of a cultural programme	**May–October** Beijing, Tianjin, Shanghai, Canton, Guilin, Chengdu
Dragon Boat Festival: see Public Holidays and Festivals	**June** Many places
Shenzhen and Maoming Lychee Festival: folk song, dance and artistic performances and fashion shows on stage and in the open air as part of the lychee festival	**June/July** Shenzhen and Maoming (Guangdong)
"The Great Wall and Nature" travel month: walks, bike and car trips along the Great Wall of China	**July** from Laolongtou, Shanghaiguan, to Badaling
International Gliding and Sailplane Festival: air show with gliders, sailplanes, hot air balloons, etc.	Jiayuguan (Gansu)
Torch Festival: flaming torch parades, song and dance by minority groups, fireworks, dragon-boat races, bull-fighting, wrestling	In Yunnan and Sichuan provinces
Namadu Fair and Grasslands Festival for tourists: when new grass grows in July and August the Mongols celebrate their Nadamu (i.e. pleasure) festival with events such as wrestling, archery, horse-racing, Mongolian folk-dance and an annual fair.	**July/August** Auton. region of Inner Mongolia
International Beer Festival: including participation by internationally famous brewers with beer tasting, drinking contests and artistic performances	**August** Beijing
Old People Festival: including performances of Korean drum dancing and senior citizens' sports	**Mid-August** Yanbian (Jilin)
Liaoning Peninsula International Festival of Arts and Culture: gala event for local people and visitors from twin cities abroad, with sports and arts events and sightseeing	**Mid/Late Aug.** Shenyang (Liaoning)
Grape Festival: traditional Uigur music, song and dance in the Turpan oasis; camel fair; exhibition of national costume and jewellery of the Xinjiang national minorities, as well as street displays of fruit, melon fair, tastings of grapes and local specialities	Turpan (Xinjiang Auton. Region
Sino-Japanese Folklore Week: festival jointly staged by Beijing and Nagasaki, Aomori and Kitakyushu	**September** Beijing
International mountaineering on the Taishan: a competition takes place every year in which Chinese and foreign climbers take part in scaling the mountain of Taishan (1545m/5071ft, 6293 steps)	Tai'an (Shandong)

513

Principal Tourist Sights in China

:::: Outstanding Sights

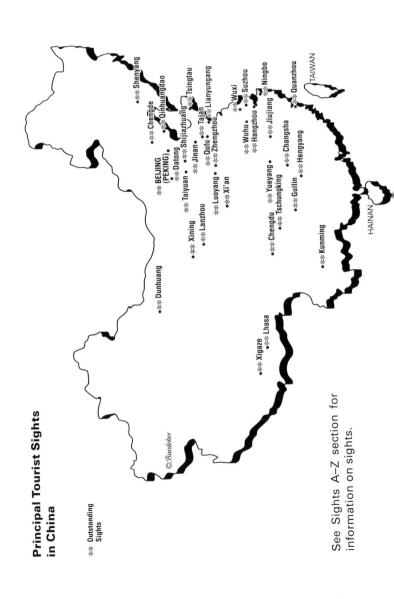

See Sights A–Z section for information on sights.

Shenyang
Chengde
Qinhuangdao
Datong
Shijiazhuang
Tsingtau
Lianyungang
BEIJING (PEKING)
Taiyuan
Jinan
Tajan
Qufu
Zhengzhou
Wuxi
Suzhou
Ningbo
Xining
Lanzhou
Luoyang
Xi'an
Wuhu
Hangzhou
Jiujiang
Quanzhou
Dunhuang
Chengdu
Yueyang
Tschungking
Changsha
Guilin
Hengyang
Kunming
Xigaze
Lhasa
TAIWAN
HAINAN

©Baedeker

Lintong Chinese Pomegranate Festival (near Xi'an): planting of pomegranates, blossom display, sale of pomegranate products and souvenirs; exhibition of Qin dynasty culture	Lintong (Shaanxi)
Moon Festival: see Public Holidays and Festivals	Various regions
Silk festival for tourists: visit to the Silk Museum; displays of silkworm farming, spinning and embroidery	Suzhou (Jiangsu)
International Steam Locomotive Festival: here tourists can see China's oldest steam engines as well as steam locomotives from other periods and countries. Visitors get the chance briefly to be the engine driver, qualifying them for a souvenir and a diploma.	Datong (Shanxi)
International Confucius Festival (26.9.–10.10.): old-style commemorative celebration of Confucius; lecture; study tour around Qufu, birthplace of Confucius	**Sept.–Oct.** Qufu (Shandong)
Chonyang Festival: an opportunity to contemplate nature, climb a hill, drink wine, gaze upon chrysanthemums, fly kites and eat Chongyang cooking	**October** Beijing & Jinan (Shandong)
International Pottery and Porcelain Festival: exhibition of valuable items; archaeological pottery and porcelain study tour	Jingdezhen (Jiangxi)
Chrysanthemum Festival: the whole town is decorated with pots of chrysanthemums	**Oct.–Nov.** Kaifeng (Henan)
Guilin Scenery Festival: cultural events, lanterns, meals on the riverbank, games with balls woven from silk ribbons accompanied by folk song	**November** Liangjiangkou/ Guilin (Guangxi)
Yao National Minority Festival: procession, song and dance contests, wine-tasting, sacrificial rites, gun salutes	Liannan (Guangdong)
Orange Festival (Zhanjiang is China's biggest orange-grower): tours of plantations, talks, exhibitions and other events	**Late November** Zhanjiang and Lianjiang
Dukang Festival: tours of the Dukang distillery and tasting the products	**December** Yichuan district (Henan)
Chaoshan Gourmet Festival: seafood delicacies (lightly seasoned and easily digested)	**Late December** Shantou (Guangdong)
Bell-ringing on December 31st in the temples of Hanshan Si, Dazhong, Jingci and Longhua: during the Tang dynasty (618–907) the bells were struck 108 times on New Year's Eve to drive out the 108 cares of the Old Year; after the final peal firework figures are let off inside and outside the temple	Suzhou (Jiangsu)

Festivals

See Public Holidays and Festivals

Food and Drink

China's famous cuisine differs considerably from region to region, although there tends to be a general distinction made between north and south. Within these two main groups there are five nationally and internationally recognised regional variations, namely, Beijing, Shandong, Shanghai-Zhejiang-Jiangsu, Sichuan and Cantonese.

The visitor should bear these variations in mind and, for example, not ask for Peking Duck in Canton. Chinese cuisine is so specialised because of the availability of local ingredients that the delicacies of one particular region are highly unlikely to be capable of preparation elsewhere. You will also find it helpful to be aware of the local dishes as a way of learning more about China's geography and its history.

Preparation

The ingredients for all these dishes are almost invariably cut into small pieces and then harmoniously combined in terms of their colour, flavour and aroma. The method of cooking is also important: they can be steamed, fried or boiled but usually only briefly in order to retain the crispness and flavour of the vegetables.

The main utensils used for cooking are the wok, now a familiar object in many Western kitchens, the grill and the charcoal-heated pot.

Meals

Most Chinese meals are quite simple. Breakfast in the north is mainly noodles, and in the south boiled rice, supplemented by pickled vegetables and pastry. The other daily meals consist of vegetables, rice, meat or fish, and soup.

Regional Cuisine

Northern China
Beijing and
Shandong

Northern China's two regional cuisines – Beijing and Shandong – characteristically employ simple ingredients but with plenty of warming spices and chilli as you would expect in these colder climes.

Both types of cooking use mainly cereal products from wheat and sorghum such as noodles, small loaves, plain or stuffed and then steamed, and boiled or steamed pastry pouches, often made from rice-flour as well.

Peking is also the home of Imperial cuisine, hallmarked by elaborate presentation and unusual ingredients.

Peking duck

China's capital city is above all renowned for its Peking duck, a dish requiring lengthy and elaborate preparation so that the different parts of a juicy fat duck can be served up in successive courses, starting with the cripy skin and the boned meat of the best pieces served with spring onions, small thin pancakes and a plum sauce, and ending up with a soup made from the rest.

Carp

Shandong specialities include carp from the Huanghe with sweet and sour sauce.

Mongolian hotpot
(shuayangrou)

Mongolian hotpot is a northern Chinese favourite – vegetables, mutton and rice or soya noodles heated up quickly with water in a copper pot and then seasoned with spicy sauces.

**Shanghai-
Zhejiang-
Jiangsu**

The cuisine of Shanghai-Zhejiang-Jiangsu is heavier and more greasy but also tastier and less sharp, with poultry as well as fish and seafood.

The fish or meat is usually cooked in its own juices to retain its original flavour or marinated with herbs and spices to intensify the aroma.

Salt duck is a well known Nanjing speciality, while fish steeped in vinegar is highly prized in Hangzhou.

Cantonese

Cantonese cuisine is the form of Chinese cooking best known in the West, probably because it uses less spice and oil for its vegetable, fish and seafood dishes which lend themselves more to steaming, boiling and frying, making them easier to digest.

Several Cantonese specialities fall into the general category of "diin sum", literally little hearts, including tiny steamed stuffed dumplings, spring rolls (chun kuen) and meat in rice pastry pouches (shiu mai). In China these are never eaten as a main meal but as a lunchtime snack or between meals.

Thousand-year-old eggs (songhua dan) are really only a couple of months old and have been pickled and buried so that when shelled they have the appearance of jade laced with transparent veins.

1000-year-old eggs

The hottest and most highly spiced Chinese cooking is undoubtedly that of Sichuan which makes generous use of garlic and pepper in all its dishes. Smoked duck comes particularly highly recommended.
    Here vegetables are only briefly boiled and sometimes even eaten raw, especially in Yunnan province, home to ethnic minorities like the Thai, Lao and Miao.
    Rice which has been boiled in its own starch until it becomes quite glutinous and sticky is a frequent diet, while mountain fare also includes manioc and tubers.

West and South-west China (Sichuan and Yunnan)

Drink

Tea and water are not often drunk with meals; on festive occasions and particularly when foreign guests are present you will be served non-alcoholic refreshments such as orange lemonade, slightly alcholic drinks like beer or a strong brandy, usually from grain. This comes in a small glass and at banquets the convention is that the Chinese host makes the first toast, when you stand and drink to friendship, downing the whole glass (ganbei, literally dry glass) and the glass is then refilled to the brim. After the first full glass you need only take a sip for any further toasts.

Tea, which is usually served before or after meals, can be green, black, scented, often with jasmine, white and red. It is always made with tea leaves to get the full aroma.
    Green tea which, unlike black tea, is not fermented may come with jasmine flowers and is mainly drunk in the north. Red or "oolong" tea is drunk in the south and always taken without milk, lemon or sugar. Green tea often has the leaves swimming on top and the purest types are longjing and biluochun, while oolong teas are dahongpao and tieguanyin.
    The best sorts of black tea are qihong and yenfeng. White teas include yinzhenbaihao, gongmei and shoumei. If you prefer English-type tea ask for hóng chá (red tea).

Tea

China's Tea Museum is on Hangzhou's West Lake in Zhejiang province. It has extensive tea plantations where you can take part in picking the tea, and several rooms of exhibits where you can find out about tea and tea-making ceremonies and customs as well as joining in some of the ceremonies.

Tea Museum

It is best to avoid coffee which has a stale and bitter taste. Some hotel shops may have imported instant coffee.

Coffee

Besides mineral water (the best known brand is "Laoshan") the sweet soft drinks found everywhere include different kinds of lemonade such as "suānméitāng", made with plums, and fizzy orange juice (juzi shui). The large hotels have tonic, Coca Cola and ginger ale.
    Do not drink the water from the tap. On cruise ships and in hotels flasks of boiled water are provided.

Soft drinks

The beer is very good and comparable with lager and German-style beers, with Qingdao and Beijing the best known brands.

Beer

Wine made from grapes tends to be very sweet, although in places which have large numbers of foreign visitors dryer white wines (baisuan putaojiu) are available. Among the best are Dynasty and those sold under the Great Wall label, which like other names are of a quite acceptable quality but not

Wine

outstanding. Red wine (hongsuan putaojiu) has a rather sweet taste. You can also get more expensive imported wines.

The usual accompaniment to many meals is heated rice wine, which has a high alcohol content. The Chinese prefer Shaoxing, the red wine (shàoxīngjiǔ); the driest is "Jiafan" rice wine.

Spirits

The Chinese produce an enormous range of brandies and other spirits of that type, but since the taste often differs from what Westerners are used to and they have a high alcoholic content you need to treat them with respect. Bailandi, the local brandy, is quite reasonable, and edeke, the Chinese vodka, is good. You would be wise to avoid their versions of whisky, rum and gin. Liqueurs and spirits in the eau de vie range are flavoured with many different ingredients. Maotai schnapps (máotáijiǔ), from Guizhou province, distilled from sorghum, goes down very well and is the usual toast at banquets. Other well-known brandies include Shanxi province's fénjiǔ, also from sorghum, wǔliángyè, the five-grain schnapps from Sichuan province, and zhéyèqīng, made from bamboo leaves.

Glossary of Food and Drink

English	Chinese
Eating Out	
restaurant	fànguǎn
breakfast	zǒafàn
lunch	zhōngfàn
evening meal	wǎnfàn
waiter	fúwùyuān
menu	càidān
toilet	cèsuǒ
bill/check please	qǐng jié zhàng
Soups	tānglèi
lotus seed	liánzitāng
soup (sweet)	
wuntun soup	húntúntāng
noodle soup	tāngmiàn
sweet-sour soup	suānlàtāng
Starters	xiǎochī
cold cuts	lěng pīnpān
spring roll	chūnjuǎn
1000–year-old eggs	pídàn
prawn crackers	xiāpiàn
Fish	yú
fried	zhá
roast	jiān
boiled	shāo
sweet-sour	tángcù
carp	lǐyú
eel	mánlí
flounder	diéyú
salmon	guīyú
sea perch	hǎilú
Seafood	hǎixiān
crab	pángxiè
lobster	lóngxiā
mussels	xiān bèi
prawns	xiāzi
shrimps	dàxiā

English	Chinese
Meat dishes	ròulèi
meatballs	shīzitóu
roast lamb	fěnsī chǎo yángròu
pig's liver	zhūgān
ribs	páigǔ
roast beef with onions	cōngtóu chǎoniúròu
stuffed dumplings	bāozi
sucking pig with noodles	kǎo rǔzhū
sweet-sour pork	gǔlǎoròu
twice-roast pork	huíguōròu
wuntun	jiǎozi
Poultry	jiāqin
Cantonese duck	bǎnyā
coq au vin	zùi jī
crispy chicken/duck	xiāngsūjī (yā)
Peking duck	Běijing tìanyā
Vegetables	sùcài
asparagus	lúsǔn
aubergines	qiézi
bamboo shoots	zhúsǔn
beans	dòu
carrots	húluóbo
Chinese cabbage	báicài
Chinese lettuce	wōsǔn
cucumber	huángguā
lotus root	ǒu
mushrooms	mógu
peas	wāndòu
potatoes	tǔdòu
soya beans	huángdòu
soya sprouts	dòuyá
spinach	bōcài
sweetcorn	yùmǐ
tomatoes	xīhóngshì
noodles	miàntiáo
rice	mǐfàn
Desserts	tiánshí
almond jelly	xìngrén dòufu
icecream	bīngqílin
sugar-glazed apples	bāsī pínggguó
eight-spice rice	bābǎofàn
(rice pudding	
with lotus seeds,	
melon seeds,	
dates and fruit)	
Fruit, Nuts	shuǐguǒ, gānguǒ
apple	pínggguǒ
banana	xiāngjiāo
cherry	yīngtáo
Chinese gooseberry	yángtáo
date	zǎozi
lemon	níngmeng
grape	pútao
hazelnut	zhēnzi
lychee	lìzhī
orange	chénzi

519

English	Chinese
peach	táozi
peanut	huāshēngmǐ
pear	lízi
pineapple	bōluó
plum	lǐzi
strawberry	cǎoméi
sweet chestnut	lìzi
Drinks	yǐnláo
beer	píjiǔ
coffee	kāfēi
lemonade	qìshuǐ
milk	niúnǎi
mineral water	kuàngquánshuǐ
tea	chá (shuǐ)
wine	pǔtaojiǔ
white wine	bái pǔtaojiǔ
red wine	hóng pǔtaojiǔ
Bread	miànbāo
biscuit	dàn'gāo
dough stick (fried in oil)	yóutiáo
sesame roll	shāobing
butter	huángyóu
honey	fēngmì
jam	guǒjiàng
Egg	jīdàn
hard	lǎode
soft	nènde
scrambled	châodàn
fried	jiāndàn
Spices	tiànshí
aniseed	húixiāng
chilli	làjiāo
curry	gālí
garlic	suàn
ginger	jiāng
pepper	hújiāo
salt	yán
sesame oil	xiāngyóu
soya sauce	jiàngyóu
sugar	táng
vinegar	cù

Getting to China

By air

Most of China's international flights pass through its airports at Beijing and Shanghai (see Air Transport) but although there are also direct flights to and from many other Asian and Western destinations the cheapest and most popular entry point for a large number of North Americans and Europeans is Hong Kong, with its air, rail, road and sea links to the mainland.

There are regular flights to Beijing and Shanghai by Air China (CAAC) in conjunction with several European airlines from a number of Europe's capital cities including London. British Airways and Cathay Pacific are among the airlines flying out of London to Hong Kong.

For travellers from North America direct flights to China include those from Vancouver in Canada and the West Coast of the USA, while some airlines operate flights via Tokyo and Hong Kong.

Coming from Australia and New Zealand there are scheduled flights into Beijing and Shanghai, stopping off at Tokyo, Manila or Hong Kong, from Melbourne, Sydney and Auckland by airlines such as Air New Zealand and Cathay Pacific, as well as the weekly flight by CAAC to Beijing from Sydney and Melbourne.

The main route into China by rail, other than flying into Hong Kong and then taking the train, is to go from Europe by the Trans-Siberian Railway. Information about travelling this route from Berlin via Moscow and Irkutsk to Beijing can be obtained from CITS offices (see Information) and travel agents. You can chose between the shorter route via Ulan Bator in Mongolia, arriving in Beijing on the ninth day, or go the longer way round, arriving a day later, via Harbin in Manchuria. If you decide to go by Mongolia you can also include a stopover in Ulan Bator, while the Manchurian route allows you to break your journey at Lake Baikal. Intourist, the Russian State travel agency, can arrange the necessary transit visas, but allow at least six weeks for processing. Seats get booked up well in advance in the summer season, so make your arrangements in plenty of time. Intourist also offers independent travellers a route from Moscow to Urumqi on the trail of the Silk Road via Tashkent and Alma Ata or just via Alma Ata.

By rail
Trans-Siberian
railway

If you want to read about the journey in more detail get the "Trans-Siberian Rail Guide" by Robert Strauss or the "Trans-Siberian Handbook" by Bryn Thomas.

The opening of the transcontinental rail link between Asia and Europe in 1992 has made it possible to travel the 10,900km/6778 miles from Rotterdam in the Netherlands to Lianyungang on China's Yellow Sea by rail all the way. The opening of the Channel Tunnel in 1994 will even mean that for the

Trans-
continental
connections

The Trans-Siberian Railway by Lake Baikal

first time ever it will be possible to travel by train direct from London to China.

The rail route from Rotterdam is 8000km/5000 miles shorter than going by sea, and takes in Berlin, Warsaw, Minsk, Moscow, Alma Ata, Urumqi, Lanzhou, Xi'an and Zhengshou en route to Lianyungang, although as yet there is no through train. For further information check with local travel agents or the international bureau in Rotterdam (tel. Netherlands (10) 411 71 00).

By sea
Cruises

Various cruises call in at Shanghai and Ningbo, Dalian and Tianjin, as well as Hong Kong and Taiwan's Keelung. For further information contact travel agencies which specialise in cruises.

Ferries and
cargo boats

Cargo boats, some of which take passengers, run regularly between European ports and the port of Hong Kong. Ferries and hovercraft also operate regular services from Hong Kong and Macau to Shanghai, Canton, Shantou, Xiamen, Haikou, Sanya and Wuzhou, and there are also services from Shanghai to South Korea and Japan.

Tour Operators

Most travellers to China go as part of a group tour, and a number of travel agents offer tours of China, many with specialist interests ranging from horseback riding in Mongolia to birdwatching on the roof of the world in Tibet and beach holidays on Hainan Island. For further information consult your local travel agent or read the travel pages of the national press.

Health Precautions

The changes in climate and time zones and the unfamiliar food and drink can all combine to upset your metabolism when travelling in China so you would be well advised to take any necessary precautions beforehand and get a medical checkup before you go, especially if you plan on visiting Tibet. Avoid undue physical exertion and staying out in the sun for long periods at the start of your trip; wear some form of headgear as well. Make it a basic rule to avoid raw food, and shellfish, fruit which is unpeeled, icecream, drinks chilled with icecubes and other unbottled drinks. Mineral water is safe for drinking but ordinary water should be boiled for five to ten minutes. Cleanliness is the best protection against falling sick, so wash your hands frequently, rinsing them and changing the water, and take your own lavatory paper with you. Consult a doctor immediately if insect bites swell up badly or are surrounded by a red strip.

Medical kit

You will find it much more important to carry your own medical kit with you than you would do in Europe or North America. Seek the advice of your GP or physician, and obviously take along sufficient quantities of any medication that you take regularly. Because of China's strict rules about the use of drugs – the same as in the other Asian countries – you will need to carry a doctor's certificate if your medication involves the use of narcotics.

Your travelling medical kit should include a thermometer, scissors, tweezers, cotton wool, a couple of bandages, sticking plasters, medicated gauze, antiseptic cream, painkillers, something for constipation and diarrhoea, travel sickness pills, cardiac stimulants, suncream and insect repellent.

Vaccinations

The only compulsory vaccinations for China are for cholera, smallpox and yellow fever if you are coming from an infected area. However, you should in any case consult your doctor or local travel clinic about precautions against malaria, which can occur all year round in parts of the country below 1500m/4900ft, and vaccination against tetanus, hepatitis B, typhoid, Japanse encephalitis and polio is strongly recommended. Since conditions can change very suddenly you would be well advised to check on the latest situation before leaving, either through your doctor, travel clinic, travel agent, official tourist office (see Information) or Institute for Tropical Diseases.

One way of avoiding catching a cold is to be prepared for sudden changes in temperature as a result of moving from high outdoor temperatures into the much cooler air-conditioned atmosphere of a restaurant, hotel room or coach. Make sure you have an additional layer of warm clothing ready such as a pullover or a jacket and if possible only have the air conditioning on in your room when you are not in it.

Avoiding colds

There are a number of books and other publications which give much more detailed information on the general subject of travel health. These include a leaflet published by the World Health Organisation (WHO Distribution and Sales Service, CH 1211 Geneva 27, Switzerland; tel. (022) 791 21 11) and books such as "Staying Healthy in Asia, Africa and Latin America". Information can also be obtained from the London School of Hygiene and Tropical Medicine, Kippel Street, London WC1, tel. (0171) 636 8636.

Publications on travel health

Hotels

China currently has more than 320,000 rooms in over 2100 hotels, about half of which fall within the star system of international classification.

Hotels in the cities most popular with tourists are up to international standards but although the facilities in the top hotels are often very good, complete with air conditioning, telephones, satellite TV, swimming pool, bar, business centre, laundry service, etc., the service can still fall short of expectations. You must not drink the water from the tap in China, so it is standard hotel practice to supply guests with flasks of boiled hot water and china teacups with teabags or small tins of green tea in their room.

Standards

Some hotels impose an additional, often exhorbitant, surcharge on foreigners, while others may accept only Chinese guests.

Rates

An effort is made in the starred luxury hotels to provide a variety of entertainment in the evening, and the big hotels have discos and bars.

Evening entertainment

The hotels for foreign visitors listed below in alphabetical order are from various categories providing accommodation to suit individual requirements, with the starred luxury hotels offering exceptional comfort. The Chinese pronunciation follows the name of the hotel in brackets.
  Since most Chinese towns and cities can now be reached by international direct dialling the area codes in brackets are given below the place names in the margin. The international code for China is 86 and when dialling from abroad the first zero of the area code is omitted.

List of hotels

Anshan Hotel (Anshan Jiudian), 121 Nan Shengli Lu, Tiedong; tel. 207 17/279 33
Shengli Hotel (Shengli Fandian), Shengli Square (Guanchang); tel. 254 58

Anshan (0412)

Baotou Guest House (Baotou Binguan), Kungqu Gangtie Dajie; tel. 266 12

Baotou (0471)

Luxury hotels:
★Beijing Hotel (Beijing Fandian), 33 Dong Chang'an Jie, 910 r.; tel. 513 77 66, Fax. 513 77 03
  Very large, centrally situated hotel of considerable history, somewhat in need of renovation; new luxury wing; famous banqueting halls used at one time for state receptions
★Capital Hotel (Shoudu Binguan), 3 Qianmen Dong Dajie, 296 r.; tel. 512 99 88, fax. 512 03 09
  Conveniently located between the station and Tian'anmen Square; business centre, variety of restaurants, sauna, swimming pool, tennis courts, billiards, bowling; garden

Beijing (Peking) (010)

★ China World, 1 Jianguomenwai Dajie, 740 r.; tel. 505 22 66, fax. 505 31 67
In the World Trade Center; business centre; sauna, swimming pool,
gymnasium; 15 restaurants and bars

★ Great Wall Sheraton Hotel (Beijing Changcheng Fandian), 6A Dongsanhuan Bei Lu, 1007 r.; tel. 500 55 66, fax. 500 33 98
Renowned, sizeable, luxury hotel situated in the east of the city; several
restaurants, gymnasium, swimming pool, mini-golf, discothèque;
extensive gardens with traditional as well as modern features

★ Hilton, 1 Dongfang Lu, Dongsanhuan Beilu, 350 r.; tel. 466 22 88,
fax. 465 30 52
Not far from the Lufthansa Center; good standard of cuisine, including
Beijing's only Cajun restaurant

★ Holiday Inn Crown Plaza (Jiari Yiyuan Jiudian), 48 Wangfujing, 385 r.;
tel. 513 33 88
Pleasant, extremely well-appointed and spacious inner city hotel;
modern art gallery; occasional concerts

★ Jianguo Hotel (Jianguo Fandian), 5 Jianguomenwai Dajie, 399 r.;
tel. 500 22 33, fax. 500 28 71
A welcoming atmosphere and high standard of service make this a
particularly popular hotel; a favourite rendezvous even among people
staying elsewhere

★ Kempinski Hotel, Beijing Lufthansa Center, 50 Liangmaqiao Lu, 540 r.;
tel. 465 33 88, fax. 465 33 66
At the centre of an office, shopping and hotel complex; a fine building
architecturally: modern, elegant and unmarred by any hint of preten-
siousness; superlative cuisine

★ Palace Hotel (Wangfu Fandian), 8 Jinyu Hutong, Wangfujing, 578 r.;
tel. 512 88 99, fax. 512 90 50
Large and very grand hotel in the city centre, with a lovely view extending
as far as the Imperial Palace; wide choice of restaurants, entertainment
(discothèque, ballroom) and sport (swimming pool, billiards,
gymnasium)

★ Peace Hotel, 3 Jinyu Hutong, 495 r.; tel. 512 88 33, fax. 512 68 63
Centrally situated and well-appointed, with sauna, swimming pool and
discothèque

★ Shangri-La Hotel (Beijing Xianggelila Fandian), 29 Zizhuyuan Lu, Haidianqu; tel. 841 22 11
Stylish hotel on the western edge of the city, elegant and comfortable;
3 restaurants; business centre, gymnasium, swimming pool; live music

★ Traders, 1 Jianguomenwai Dajie, 298 r.; tel. 505 22 77, fax. 505 08 18
Expertly managed hotel belonging to the Shangri-La group; near the
World Trade Center

Other hotels:
Bamboo Garden Hotel (Beijing Zhuyuan Binguan), 24 Xiaoshiqiao Hutong,
Jiugulou Dajie, 39 r.; tel. 403 29 29
A gem among Beijing hotels; small, with leaf-shaded, red-lacquered
pergolas adorning its classical Chinese garden
Beijing Airport Mövenpick Radisson Hotel (Beijing Guodu Da Fandian),
Xiao Tianzhu Village, Shunyi County; tel. 900 02 86
Exhibition Centre Hotel (Beijing Zhanlanguan Binguan), 135 Xizhimenwai
Dajie; tel. 831 66 33
Large, well-designed, middle-of-the-range hotel in a very quiet location
near the old Exhibition Centre
Guanghua, 38 Dongsanhuan Beilu, 100 r.; tel. 501 88 66, fax. 501 65 16
Smallish hotel not far from the World Trade Center offering good value
for money; Chinese breakfast only
Guoan, Dong Daqiao, 128 r.; tel. 500 77 00, fax. 500 45 68
Well-appointed medium category hotel in a distinctive red building
Huadu Hotel (Huada Fandian), 8 Xinyuan Nan Lu, Chaoyangqu, 250 r.;
tel. 500 11 66
Very comfortable, older-style hotel offering good value for money

Hui Zhong Hotel Beijing (Hui Zhong Fandian), 120 Zhushuikou Xi Dajie;
  tel. 301 22 55
International Hotel (Beijing Guoji Fandian), 9 Jianguomennei Dajie, 1049 r.;
  tel. 512 66 88, fax. 512 99 72
  Huge hotel handily placed as regards transport, near the station; revolv-
  ing restaurant on the 25th floor with a view unmatched by any other
  restaurant in the city
Jimen Hotel (Jimen Fandian), Huangtingzi, Xueyuan Lu, Haidianhu;
  tel. 201 22 11
Jingfeng Hotel (Jingfeng Fandian), 71 Fengtai Lu; tel. 37 24 11
Jinlang, 75 Chongwenmennei Dajie, 408 r.; tel. 513 22 88, fax. 513 68 09
  Another very comfortable hotel, part of the Meridian group; situated
  near the station
Kunlun Hotel (Kunlun Fandian), 2 Xinyuan Nan Lu, Chaoyangqu;
  tel. 500 33 88
Liang Ma Hotel & Apartments (Liang Ma Jiudian, Liang Ma Gongyu),
  8 Dongsanhuan Bei Lu, Chaoyangqu; tel. 500 59 53
Luyuan Hotel (Luyuan Binguan), 101 Weizikang, Liulitun; tel. 500 42 33
Minzu Hotel (Minzu Fandian), 51 Fuxingmennei Dajie; tel. 601 44 66
Overseas Chinese Mansion (Huaqiao Dasha), 2 Wangfujing Dajie;
  tel. 55 88 51
Park Hotel Beijing (Beijing Baile Jiudian), 36 Puhuangyu Lu; tel. 721 22 33
Novotel Beijing, 88 Dengshikou, 310 r.; tel. 513 90 88, fax. 513 90 88
  Central and extremely comfortable; good value
Olympic Hotel (Oulinpike Fandian), 52 Baishiqiao Lu, Haidianqu, 338 r.;
  tel. 831 66 88
  A pleasant hotel; glazed atrium with trees; two restaurants and business
  centre
Qianmen Hotel (Qianmen Fandian), 175 Yongan Lu; tel. 301 66 88,
  fax. 301 38 83
  Medium-sized hotel in the south-east of the city; all the usual modern
  amenities, good standard of service and other facilities; adjacent to the
  Liyuan Theatre (Beijing opera nightly)
Ritan Hotel (Ritan Binguan), 1 Ritan Lu, Jianguomenwai; tel. 512 55 88
Summer Palace Hotel (Yiheyuan Fandian), inside the Summer Palace;
  tel. 258 12 00
Taiwan Hotel (Taiwan Fandian), 5–15 Jinyu Hutong, Wangfujing Bei;
  tel. 513 66 88
Taoran Hotel (Taoran Binguan), Taoranting Park, Taiping Jie, Xuanwuqu;
  tel. 33 70 43
Temple of Heaven (Haoyuan Binguan), A 9 Tiantan Donglu, 100 r.;
  tel. 701 44 99, fax. 511 27 19
  A very reasonably priced hotel with small, pleasant garden; quiet cul-de-
  sac location
Tiantan Sports Hotel (Tiantan Tiyu Binguan), 10 Tiyuguan Lu, Chong-
  wenqu; tel. 75 28 31
Xin Dadu Hotel (Xin Dadu Fandian), 21 Chegongzhuang Dajie, Xichengqu;
  tel. 831 99 88
Xinqiao Hotel (Xinqiao Fandian Youxian Gongsi), 2 Dongjiaomin Xiang,
  Dongchengqu; tel. 55 77 31
Xiyuan Hotel (Xiyuan Fandian), Erligou, Xijiao; tel. 831 33 88
Xizhimen Hotel (Beijing Xizhimen Fandian), 14 Cixiansi, Xiwai; tel. 802 11 55
Yanjing Hotel Beijing (Beijing Yanjing Fandian), 19 Fuxingmenwai Dajie;
  tel. 86 75 47
Yanxiang Hotel (Yanxiang Fandian), 2A Jiangtai Lu, Dongzhimenwai;
  tel. 500 66 66
Yongan Apartment Hotel (Beijing Shi Yongan Gongyu), 5A Zaoying Lu,
  Dongsanhuan Bei; tel. 501 11 88
Zhaolong Hotel Beijing (Beijing Zhalong Fandian), 2 Gongti Bei Lu,
  Chaoyangqu; tel. 500 22 99
Zijin Guest House (Zijin Binguan), Chongwenmen Xi Dajie; tel. 54 92 15
Ziyu Hotel (Ziyu Fandian), 5 Huayuancun, Xisanhuan Bei Lu; tel. 89 01 91

Hotels

Luxury hotels:

★China Hotel (Zhongguo Da Jiudian), Liuhua Lu; tel. 666 68 88, fax. 667 70 14

Large hotel on the edge of Yuexiu Park; good shopping facilities; popular snack bar inside the hotel open night and day

★Garden Hotel (Huayuan Jiudian), 368 Huanshi Dong Lu; tel. 333 89 89, fax. 335 04 17

Set amidst lush greenery some distance from the city centre; some sports facilities

★Guangdong International, 339 Huanshi Dong Lu; tel. 331 18 88, fax. 331 66 66

★Holiday Inn Centre (Guangzhou Wenhua Jiria Jiudian), 28 Guangming Lu, Overseas Chinese Village, Huanshi Dong; tel. 76 69 99

★White Swan Hotel (Bai Tian'e Binguan), 1 Nan Jie, Shamian; tel. 88 69 68, fax. 886 11 88

One of the best hotels in China, or even the world; famous for the waterfall in the foyer

Other hotels:

Aiqun Hotel (Aiqun Da Jiudian), 113 Yanjiang Xi Lu; tel. 66 14 45

Baiyun Hotel (Baiyun Binguan), 367 Huanshi Dong Lu; tel. 33 39 98

Guangzhou Hotel (Guangzhou Binguan), Haizhu Square (Guangchang); tel. 33 81 68

Hotel Landmark Canton (Huaxia Da Jiudian), 2 Qiaoguang Lu, Overseas Chinese Building; tel. 35 59 88

Kowloon Hotel (Guangzhou Jiulong Jiudian), 10 Guanyuan Xi Lu; tel. 66 89 88

Kuanquan Villa (Kuanquan Bieshu), Sanyuanli; tel. 66 13 34

Liuhua Guest House (Liuhua Binguan), 194 Huanshi Xi Lu; tel. 66 88 00

Nanfang Mansion (Nanfang Dasha), Xidi Er Malu; tel. 88 81 33

Nanhu Hotel (Guangdong Nanhu Binguan), Tonghe, Shahe; tel. 70 67 06

New Asia Hotel (Xin Ya Da Jiudian), 10–12 Renmin Nan Lu; tel. 88 47 22

New Mainland Hotel (Xin Dadi Binguan), 70 Zhanqian Lu; tel. 67 86 38

Novotel Jiang Nan (Guangzhou Nuofute Jiang Nan Da Jiudian), 348 Jiang-nan Dadao Zhong; tel. 41 88 88

Ocean Hotel (Yuangyang Binguan), 412 Huanshi Dong Lu; tel. 76 59 88

Overseas Chinese Hotel (Guangzhou Huaqiao Jiudian), 63 Zhanqian Lu; tel. 66 34 88

Pearl Island Hotel (Zhudao Binguan), 443 Yanjiang Dong Lu; tel. 75 07 25

Plum Flowers Hotel (Meihua Yuanlin Binguan), Meihuayuan, Shahe; tel. 70 56 00

Shahe Hotel (Shahe Da Fandian), 318 Xianlie Dong Lu, Shahe; tel. 70 59 98

Shamian Binguan, 52 Shamian Nanjie; tel. 888 81 24, fax. 886 10 68

Small hotel with well-run restaurant

Victory Hotel (Guangdong Shengli Binguan), Shamian Island, 53 Beijie; tel. 886 26 22–89 (old building 886 26 13), fax. 886 10 62 (old building 886 24 13)

Solid, quiet hotel in what was once the old concessionary district; good restaurant; rooms in the old building represent the best value

Xinhua Hotel (Xinhua Da Jiudian), 2–6 Renmin Nan Lu; tel. 88 97 88

Xinqiao Hotel (Guangdong Sheng Xinqiao Jiudian), 40 Zhongshan Er Lu; tel. 77 62 44

Yangcheng International Hotel (Yangcheng Guoji Jiudian), 96 Xianlie Zhong Lu; tel. 75 88 88

Yanjiang Hotel (Yanjiang Ludian), 277 Xanjiang Er Lu; tel. 33 32 02

Yuhua Mansion (Yuhua Dasha), 320 Huanshi Dong Lu; tel. 33 78 99

Yunshan Hotel (Yunshan Da Jiudian), 8 Yunhe Bei Jie, Xianlie Zhong Lu; tel. 76 52 59

Changbaishan Guest House (Changbaishan Binguan), 12 Xinmin Dajie; tel. 88 35 51

Changchun Guest House (Changchun Fandian), 128 Changchun Lu;
  tel. 267 71
Changchun Hotel (Changchun Binguan), 10 Xinhua Lu; tel. 82 26 61
Chunyi Guest House (Chunyi Binguan), 2 Sidalin Dajie; tel. 384 95
Nanhu Guest House (Nanhu Binguan), Nanhu Park (Gongyuan); tel. 535 71

Changsha Hotel (Changsha Fandian), 116 Wuyi Xi Lu; tel. 250 29   **Changsha**
Huatian Great Hotel (Huatian Da Jiudian), 16 Jiefang Dong Lu; tel. 428 88   (0731)
Hunan Guest House (Hunan Binguan), 9 Yingbin Lu; tel. 263 31
Lotus Guest House (Furong Binguan), Wuyi Dong Lu; tel. 40 18 88
  Large hotel near the station
Xiangjiang Hotel (Xiangjiang Binguan), 2 Zhongshan Lu; tel. 40 88 88,
  fax. 44 82 85
  Changsha's best hotel, centrally situated; some multi-bedded rooms
  available reasonably priced

Changzhou Hotel (Changzhou Fandian), Dong Dajie; tel. 237 37   **Changzhou** (0519)

Chengde Hotel (Chengde Fandian), 33 Nanying Xi Dajie; tel. 25 51   **Chengde**
Mongolian Yurt Holiday Village (closed in winter), East Gate; tel. 22 22 69 (0314)
  Accommodation in yurts in the grounds of the Imperial Palace
Yunshan Hotel (Yunshan Fandian), 6 Nanyuan Donglu; tel. 22 61 71,
  fax. 22 45 51
  Comfortable modern tourist hotel

Chengdu Hotel (Chengdu Fandian), Dongfeng Lu; tel. 44 33 12   **Chengdu**
Jinjiang Hotel (Jinjiang Binguan), 36 Renmin Nanlu Erduan; tel. 558 22 22, (028)
  fax. 558 23 48
  Has seen better days; central position on the river
Minshan Hotel (Minshan Fandian), 17 Erduan, 2 Renmin Nan Lu;
  tel. 58 33 33
Tibet Hotel (Xizang Fandian), 10 Renmin Bei Lu; tel. 33 40 01
  Renovated hotel near the railway station in one of the best parts of
  Chengdu

Chung King Hotel (Chongqing Binguan), 41–43 Xinhua Lu; tel. 34 93 01, **Chongqing**
  fax. 34 30 85   (0811)
  Well-run city centre hotel
Holiday Inn Yangtze (Chongqing Yangzijiang Jiari Fandian), 15 Nanping
  Beilu; tel. 20 33 80, fax. 20 08 84
  First-class hotel on the Changjiang
People's Hotel (Renmin Binguan), 175 Renmin Lu; tel. 35 14 21, fax. 35 13 85
  Vast, mock-Classical hotel built in 1953

Number Two Guest House (Di Er Zhaodai Suo), Huguo Lu   **Dali**
  Central location

Bangchui Island Hotel (Bangchuidao Binguan), 1 Bangchuidao; tel. 23 51 31 **Dalian**
Dalian Guest House (Dalian Binguan), 4 Zhongshan Square (Guangchang);   (0411)
  tel. 23 31 11
Dalian Hotel (Dalian Fandian), 6 Shanghai Lu; tel. 231 71
Dalian International Hotel (Dalian Guoji Jiudian), 9 Sidalin Lu, Zhong-
  shanqu; tel. 23 82 38
Friendship Hotel (Youyi Binguan), 137 Sidalin Lu; tel. 23 41 21
Furama Hotel (Dalian Fulihua Da Jiudian), 74 Sidalin Lu; tel. 23 08 88
Holiday Inn (Dalian Jiuzhou Jiari Jiudian), 128 Shengli Square, Zhong-
  shanqu; tel. 80 88 88
Nanshan Hotel (Dalian Nanshan Binguan), 56 Fenglin Jie, Zhongshanqu;
  tel. 23 87 51

Dadong Guest House (Dadong Binguan), 8 Yingbin Xi Lu; tel. 334 81   **Datong**
Yungang Hotel (Yungang Fandian), 21 Yingbin Dong Lu; tel. 52 16 01,   (0352)
  fax. 52 49 27
  Very comfortable with air-conditioned rooms

Hotels

Dunhuang
(09473)

Dunhuang Hotel (Dunhuang Binguan), Dong Dajie; tel. 224 15
in the town; decent modern facilities
Mingshan Hotel (Mingshan Fandian), Dingzi Nan Lu; tel. 22 94

Foshan
(0757)

Foshan Hotel (Foshan Binguan), 75 Fengjiang Nan Lu; tel. 28 79 23
Golden City Hotel (Jin Cheng Da Jiudian), 48 Fengjiang Nan Lu; tel. 22 72 24
Overseas Chinese Building (Foshan Huaqiao Dasha), 14 Zumiao Lu;
tel. 22 38 28
Xuangong Hotel (Xuangong Jiudian), Zumiao Lu; tel. 28 56 22
Zhujiang Hotel (Zhujiang Da Jiudian), Chenren Lu; tel. 28 75 12

Fushun
(0413)

Fushun Hotel (Fushun Binguan), Yongan Square (Guangchang); tel. 231 71
Hubian Hotel (Hubian Binguan), Xintai Jie; tel. 213 05

Fuzhou
(0591)

Donghu Hotel (Donghu Binguan), 44 Dong Da Lu; tel. 55 77 55
Foreign Trade Center Hotel (Waimao Zhongxin Jiudian), Wusi Lu;
tel. 55 01 54
Fuzhou Overseas Chinese Hotel (Fuzhou Huaqiao Dasha), Wusi Lu;
tel. 55 76 03
Haishan Hotel (Haishan Binguan), Wusi Lu; tel. 55 77 66/53 45 28
Hot Spring Hotel (Wen Quan Dasha), 218 Wusi Lu Zhong Duan; tel. 85 18 18,
fax. 83 51 50
Built over a hot spring from whence comes the hot water piped to rooms
Lakeside Hotel (Xihu Da Jiudian), 1 Hubin Lu; tel. 53 98 88, fax. 53 65 85
First-class hotel on West Lake
West Lake Guest House (Xihu Binguan), 150 Qianjin Bei Lu;
tel. 55 60 38/55 77 55
Yushan Guest House, Gutian Lu; tel. 55 16 68
Beautiful location immediately below the White Pagoda

Guilin
(0773)

Luxury hotels:
★Guishan Hotel (Guishan Da Jiudian), Chuanshan Lu; tel. 44 33 88,
fax. 44 48 51
Situated on an arm of the Lijiang river
★Holiday Inn (Guilin Jiari Binguan), 14 Ronghu Nan Lu; tel. 22 39 50,
fax. 22 21 01
In the town centre, beside Ronghu Lake
★Osmanthus Hotel (Dangui Da Jiudian), 451 Zhongshan Nan Lu;
tel. 33 43 00
★Sheraton Hotel (Guilin Wenhua Da Jiudian), Binjiang Nan Lu;
tel. 22 55 88, fax. 44 48 51
Every comfort; central location on the embankment

Other hotels:
Garden Hotel (Guilin Huayuan Jiudian), Yanjiang Lu; tel. 44 24 11–2
Garland Hotel (Kaiyue Jiudian), 86 Zhongshan Nan Lu; tel. 33 25 10–1
Guilin Hotel (Guilin Fandian), 25 Zhongshan Zhong Lu; tel. 22 22 49
Guilin Pine Garden Resort (Guilin Songyuan Dujiacun), 9 Lijang Lu;
tel. 44 23 11
Hotel Universal (Guilin Huanqiu Da Jiudian), 1 Jiefang Dong Lu;
tel. 22 82 28
Jiashan Hotel (Jiashan Fandian), Lishai Xi Lu; tel. 22 29 86
Lijiang Hotel (Lijiang Fandian), 1 Shanhu Bei Lu; tel. 22 28 81
Novotel Sight-Seeing (Guilin Nuofute Jiudian), 20 Lijiang Lu; tel. 44 24 88
Pine Garden Holiday Resort (Guilin Songyuan Dujiacun), Yangguling, San-
lidian; tel. 44 23 11
Riverside Resort (Guilin Liyuan Binguan), Anjiazhou; tel. 22 49 73
Ronghu Hotel (Ronghu Fandian), 17 Ronghu Bei Lu; tel. 22 38 11
Taihe Hotel (Taihe Fandian), 427 Zhongshan Nan Lu; tel. 33 55 04
Tailien Hotel (Tailian Jiudian), 102 Zhongshan Zhong Lu; tel. 22 28 88
Xiyuan Hotel (Xiyuan Fandian), 17 Nanxiang, Jiangjun Lu; tel. 33 38 53

Guiyang Plaza Hotel, 2 Yan'an Donglu; tel. 62 58 88, fax. 62 92 76

Guiyang
(0851)

Guizhou Park Hotel (Guizhou Fandian), 66 Beijing Lu; tel. 62 38 88, fax. 62 43 97

Jinqiao Hotel (Jinqiao Fandian), 34 Rujin Lu; tel. 52 53 10

Haikou Hotel (Haikou Binguan), 4 Haifu Da Dao; tel. 72 66

Haikou
(0750)

Haikou International Financial Center (Haikou Gouji Jinrong Dasha), 33 Datong Lu; tel. 730 88

★ Haikou Tower Hotel (Haikou Taihua Jiudian), Binhai Da Dao; tel. 77 29 90

Nantian, Haikou Jichang Xilu; tel. 77 48 88

Handan Guest House (Handan Binguan), Zhonghua Bei Dajie; tel. 231 68

Handan (0310)

Luxury hotels:

Hangzhou
(Hangchow)
(0571)

★ Dragon Hotel (Huanglong Fandian), Shuguang Lu; tel. 55 44 88

★ Shangri-La Hotel (Hangzhou Xianggelila Fandian), 78 Beishan Lu; tel. and fax. 707 79 51

First-class hotel at the northern end of the Sudi Causeway

Other hotels:

Friendship Hotel (Hangzhou Youhao Fandian), 53 Pinghai Lu; tel. 77 78 88, fax. 77 38 42

Middling comfort; central location

Huagang Hotel (Huagang Fandian), 4 Xishan Lu; tel. 707 13 24

Quiet, situated between tea plantations and the lake, a little way from the city centre

Huajiashan Hotel (Huajiashan Binguan), 12 Faxiang Xiang, Santaishan, Xihuqu; tel. 77 12 24

International Chinese Hotel or Hangzhou Overseas Chinese Hotel (Huaqiao Fandian), 15 Hubin Lu; tel. 77 44 01

International Mansion (Hangzhou Guoji Dasha), 157 Tiyuchang Lu; tel. 55 62 24

Jiangcheng Hotel (Hangzhou Jiancheng Fandian), 893 Jiangcheng Lu; tel. 77 28 24

Jinlou Hotel (Jinlou Fandian), 706 Jiangcheng Lu; tel. 21 11 55

Liuying Guest House (Liuying Binguan), 6 Qingboqiao Hexia; tel. 211 29

Wanghu Hotel (Wanghu Binguan), 2 Huancheng Xi Lu; tel. 707 10 24

Comfortable hotel in a central location on the lakeside promenade

Xi Hu State Hotel (Xi Hu Guo Binguan), 7 Xishan Lu; tel. 77 68 89

Xinqiao Hotel (Hangzhou Xinqiao Fandian), 176 Jiefang Lu; tel. 77 66 88

Xinxin Hotel (Xinxin Fandian), 58 Beishan Lu; tel. 77 71 01

Yanan Hotel (Yanan Fandian), 236 Yanan Lu; tel. 55 36 01

Zhejiang Guest House (Zhejiang Binguan), 68 Santaishan Lu, Xihuqu; tel. 77 79 88

China Harbin Modern Hotel (Maxuaner Binguan), 129 Zhongyang Dajie, Daoliqu; tel. 41 58 45

Harbin
(0451)

Garden Hamlet (Huayuan Cun Binguan), 10 Custom House (Haiguan), Jie, Nangangqu; tel. 357 81

Heilongjiang Northern Building (Heilongjiang Sheng Beifang Dasha), 105 Huayuan Jie, Nangangqu; tel. 330 61/330 81

International Hotel (Gouji Fandian), 124 Dazhi Jie; tel. 364 14 41, fax. 362 56 51

Centrally situated, very comfortable

Peace Hotel (Heping Cun Binguan), 109 Zhongshan Lu; tel. 22 01 01

Swan Hotel (Tian'e Fandian), 73 Zhongshan Lu; tel. 22 02 01

Daoxianglou Guest House (Daoxianglou Binguan), 253 Jinzhai Lu; tel. 25 25 48

Hefei
(0551)

Jianghuai Hotel (Jianghuai Fandian), 68 Changjiang Lu; tel. 722 21

Luyang Hotel (Luyang Fandian), Shushan Lu; tel. 33 11 33

Hotels

Hengyang
(0734)
Hengyang Guest House (Hengyang Binguan), in the street opposite the station

Hohhot
(0471)
Hohhot Guest House (Huhehaote Binguan), Yingbin Lu; tel. 262 70
Inner Mongolia Guest House (Nei Menggu Binguan), Wulan Chabu Xi Lu; tel. 262 41
Xincheng Guest House (Xincheng Binguan), Hulun Bei Er Nan Lu; tel. 257 54
Zhaojun Hotel (Zhaojun Da Jiudian), 11 Xinhua Dajie; tel. 66 22 11

Huai'an
Huai'an Hotel (Huai'an Binguan), 2 Youyi Lu; tel. 27 57

Huzhou (0572)
Huzhou Hotel (Huzhou Fandian), 23 Hongqi Lu; tel. 233 64

Jilin
(0432)
Dongguan Guest House (Donguan Binguan), 4 Jiangguan Lu; tel. 235 56
Jiangcheng Hotel (Jiangcheng Binguan), 4 Jiangguan Lu; tel. 277 21
Tinhe Travel Mansion (Tinhe Luyou Dasha), 175 Songjiang Lu; tel. 417 80
Xiguan Guest House (Xiguan Binguan), 155 Songjiang Lu; tel. 471 41

Jinan
(0531)
Haidai Guest House (Haidai Binguan), Jing Er Lu; tel. 221 97
Jinan Hotel (Jinan Fandian), 240 Jing San Lu; tel. 389 81
Nanjiao Hotel (Nanjiao Binguan), 2 Maanshan Lu; tel. 61 39 50–1
Qilu Hotel (Qilu Binguan), Qianfoshan Lu; tel. 479 61
Shandong Hotel (Shandong Binguan), Jing Yi Wei San Lu; tel. 200 41

Jindezhen
(0798)
Jindezhen Guest House (Jindezhen Binguan), 60 Fengjing Lu; tel. 49 27
Jindezhen Hotel (Jindezhen Fandian), Zhushan Lu; tel. 40 29

Jinggangshan
Grand Hotel Jinggangshan (Jinggangshan Dasha), Cipingzhen; tel. 332
Jinggangshan Guest House (Jinggangshan Binguan), Cipingzhen; tel. 272
Jinggangshan Hotel (Jinggangshan Fandian), Cipingzhen; tel. 328

Jinhong
Banna Hotel (Banna Binguan), near the bus station

Jinhua (0579)
Jinhua Hotel (Jinhua Fandian), 117 Zhongshan Lu; tel. 227 52

Jiujiang (0595)
Nanhu Guest House (Nanhu Binguan), 28 Nanhu Lu; tel. 22 72

Jiuquan (0937)
Jiuquan Hotel (Jiuquan Fandian), 2 Cangmen Jie; tel. 25 60

Kaifeng
(0378)
Dongjing Hotel (Dongjing Da Fandian), 14 Yingbin Lu; tel. 310 75
Kaifeng Hotel (Kaifeng Binguan), 64 Ziyou Lu Zhong Duan; tel. 229 86

Kashgar
Kashgar Guest House (Kashi Binguan), east of the town centre; tel. 23 67
Seman Hotel (Seman Fandian), in a side-street off Renmin Xi Lu; tel. 21 29
    Hotel of reasonable standard occupying a former Russian consulate
Tian Nan Hotel (Tian Nan Fandian), Renmin Dong Lu

Kunming
(0871)
Beijing Hotel (Beijing Fandian), 53-4 Xinxiangyung Jie, Panlonqu; tel. 232 14
Golden Dragon Hotel (Jinlong Fandian), 575 Beijing Lu; tel. 313 30 15, fax. 313 10 82
Jade Lake Hotel (Cuihu Binguan), 6 Cuihu Nan Lu; tel. 515 57 88, fax. 515 32 86
    Lovely location by Cuihu Park
Kunhu Hotel (Kunhu Fandian), 44 Beijing Lu; tel. 313 37 37
Kunming Hotel (Kunming Fandian), 145 Dongfeng Dong Lu; tel. 316 21 71, fax. 316 37 84
    Comfortable first-class hotel, renovated
Yunnan Hotel (Yunnan Fandian), 83 Dongfeng Xi Lu; tel. 255 33

Friendship Hotel (Youyi Fandian), 14 Xijin Xi Lu, Qilihequ; tel. 330 51
Jincheng Hotel (Jincheng Binguan), 363 Tianshu Lu; tel. 279 31
Lanzhou Hotel (Lanzhou Fandian), 204 Donggang Xi Lu; tel. 221 31
People's Hotel (Renmin Fandian), 225 Zhangye Lu; tel. 277 11–8

Lanzhou (Lanchow) (0931)

Holiday Inn (Lasa Fandian or Lasa Jiari Jiudian), 1 Minzu Lu; tel. 322 21,
fax. 357 96
   The Tibetan capital's best hotel
Lhasa Guest House No. 1 (Lasa Di Yi Zhaodai Suo); tel. 234 11
Tibet Hotel (Xizang Fandian), Beijing Xilu; tel. 249 66
Xizang Guest House No. 1 (Xizang Di Yi Zhaodai Suo); tel. 221 84
Xizang Guest House No. 2 (Xizang Di Er Zhaodai Suo); tel. 221 85

Lhasa (0891)

Longhai Hotel (Longhai Fandian), 11 Hailian Zhong Lu, Xinpu; tel. 527 59
Shenzhou Hotel (Shenzhou Fandian), 1 Beiyingzuishan, Xugou; tel. 230 80
Yuntai Hotel (Yuntai Binguan), Yunshan Lu, Xinpu; tel. 541 01

Lianyungang (0518)

Liujiang Hotel (Liujiang Fandian), 72 Gongyuan Lu; tel. 250 21
Liuzhou Hotel (Liuzhou Fandian), 1 Youyi Lu; tel. 249 21
Longcheng Hotel (Longcheng Fandian), 48 Jiefang Bei Lu; tel. 241 64

Liuzhou (0772)

Luoyang Friendship Guest House (Luoyang Shi Youyi Binguan), 6 Xiyuan
Lu; tel. 41 27 92, fax. 41 38 08
   Well-run older-style hotel in the west of the city; very comfortable
Peony Hotel (Mudan Da Jiudian), 15 Zhongzhou Xi Lu; tel. 41 36 99,
fax. 41 36 68
   New, centrally located

Luoyang (0379)

Hubin Hotel (Hubin Fandian), Jiefang Lu; tel. 28 39
Yushanhu Hotel (Yushanhu Fandian), Hu Nan Lu; tel. 32 53

Ma'anshan (0555)

Hongdu Hotel (Hongdu Fandian), Baiyi Lu; Jiangxi Guest House (Jiangxi
Binguan), 56 Baiyi Da Dao; tel. 678 91–8
Jiangxi Hotel (Jiangxi Fandian), 54 Baiyi Da Dao; tel. 22 24 12
Nanchang Hotel (Nanchang Fandian), 2 Zhanqian Lu; tel. 635 95
Qingshanshu Hotel (Qingshanshu Binguan), 31 Fuzhou Lu; tel. 22 11 62

Nanchang (0791)

Dingshan Hotel (Dingshan Binguan), 90 Chahaer Lu; tel. 80 59 31
Jing Du Hotel (Jing Du Da Jiudian), Xinjiekou; tel. 40 80 00
Jingling Hotel (Jingling Fandian), Xinjiekou Square (Guangchang);
tel. 74 28 88
Nanjing Hotel (Nanjing Fandian), 259 Zhongshan Bei Lu; tel. 63 41 21,
fax. 31 69 98
People's Hotel (Renmin Fandian), 591 Taiping Nan Lu; tel. 62 37 79
Shengli Hotel (Shengli Fandian), 75 Zhongshan Lu; tel. 64 81 81
Shuangmenlou Hotel (Shuangmenlou Binguan), 185 Huju Bei Lu;
tel. 80 59 61

Nanjing (Nanking) (025)

Mingyuan Hotel (Mingyuan Fandian), 38 Xinmin Lu; tel. 289 23
Nanning Hotel (Nanning Fandian), Minsheng Lu; tel. 239 71
Xiyuan Hotel (Xiyuan Fandian), 38 Jiangnan Lu; tel. 299 23
Yongzhou Hotel (Yongzhou Fandian), 59 Xinmin Lu; tel. 283 23

Nanning (0771)

Nantong Hotel (Nantong Da Fandian), 43 Qingnian Dong Lu; tel. 51 89 89
Tian Nan Hotel (Tian Nan Da Jiudian), 76 Renmin Xi Lu; tel. 51 81 51

Nantong (0513)

Asia Garden Hotel (Yazhou Huayuan Binguan), Mayuan Lu; tel. 668 88
Ningbo Hotel (Ningbo Fandian), 65 Mayuan Lu; tel. 663 34
Overseas Chinese Hotel (Ningbo Huaqiao Fandian), 130 Liuting Jie;
tel. 631 75

Ningbo (0574)

See Beijing

Peking

Hotels

Qingdao
(0532)

Friendship Hotel (Youyi Binguan), 12 Xinjiang Lu; tel. 22 32 31
Huanghai Hotel (Huanghai Fandian), 75 Yanan Yi Lu; tel. 27 02 15
Huiquan Dynasty Hotel (Huiquan Wangchao Da Jiudian), 9 Nanhai Lu;
tel. 27 92 79
Overseas Chinese Hotel (Huaqiao Fandian), 72 Hunan Lu; tel. 27 07 55
Qingdao Hotel (Qingdao Fandian), 53 Zhongshan Lu; tel. 27 90 68
Stone Cliffs Beach Hotel (Qingdao Shifeng Binguan), Shilaoren Tourism
Development District; tel. 59 78 88
Zhanqiao Hotel (Qingdao Zhanqiao Binguan), 31 Taiping Lu; tel. 287 05 02,
fax. 287 09 36
Small but good quality hotel situated on the promenade; lovely view
over the sea

Qinhuangdao
(0335)

Qinhuangdao Cindic Hotel (Qinhuangdao Xinyi Da Jiudian), Yingbin Lu;
tel. 33 22 43

Quanzhou
(0595)

Overseas Chinese Mansion (Huaqiao Dasha), Baiyuan Qingchi Lu;
tel. 22 21 92, fax. 22 33 11
Rooms in a range of price categories
Quanzhou Golden Fountain Hotel (Jinquan Jiudian), Baiyuan Lu; tel. 243 88

Qufu
(05473)

Confucius Mansion Hotel (Kong Fu Fandian), 1 Donghuamen Daije;
tel. 41 23 74
Historic guest house in part of the Confucius family residence
Queli Hotel (Queli Fandian), 1 Queli Jie; tel. 41 13 00
Combines comfort with culture; classical Chinese music in corridors and
theatre

Sanya
(0899)

South China Hotel (Huazhonguan Dajiudian) Dadonghai; tel. 21 38 88,
fax. 21 20 21

Shanghai
(021)

Luxury hotels:
★Garden Hotel (Huayuan Fandian), 58 Maoming Nan Lu; tel. 433 11 11,
fax. 433 88 66
Shanghai's best hotel, next to the Hilton
★Hilton International (Jingan Xierdun Jiudian), 250 Huashan Lu;
tel. 248 00 00, fax. 248 38 48
Boasts the most expensive rooms in the city; swimming pool, tennis
courts, 5 restaurants
★Holiday Inn Yin Xing (Yinxing Jiari Jiudian), 172 Xinhua Lu; tel. 259 53 12
★Jinjiang Tower (Xin Jinjiang Da Fandian), 161 Changle Lu; tel. 433 44 88
★Nikko Longbai Hotel (Rihang Longbai Fandian), 2451 Hongqiao Lu;
tel. 259 36 36
★Rainbow Hotel (Hongqiao Binguan), 2000 Yan'an Xi Lu; tel. 275 33 88
★Shangri-La International Hotels and Resorts (Xianggelila Guoji Fandian),
1376 Nanjing Xi Lu; tel. 279 88 88
★Sheraton Hua Ting Hotel (Hua Ting Binguan), 1200 Caoxi Bei Lu;
tel. 439 60 00
★Yangtze New World Hotel (Shanghai Yangzijiang Da Jiudian), 2099
Yan'an Xi Lu; tel. 275 00 00

Other hotels:
Changyang Hotel (Changyang Luguan), 1800 Changyang Lu; tel. 543 48 90
Cherry Holiday Villa (Yinghua Dujiacun), 77 Nonggong Lu; tel. 275 83 50
City Hotel (Chengshi Jiudian), 5–7 Shaanxi Nan Lu; tel. 255 11 33
Cypress Hotel (Longbai Fandian), 2419 Hongqiao Lu; tel. 432 93 88
Dahua Guest House (Dahua Binguan), 914 Yanan Xi Lu; tel. 251 25 12
Dong Hu Hotel (Donghu Binguan), 167 Xinle Lu; tel. 437 00 50
Galaxy Hotel (Yinhe Fandian), 888 Zhongshan Xi Lu; tel. 259 46 85
Hotel Equatorial (Guido Guoji Da Fandian), 65 Yanan Xi Lu; tel. 258 17 79
Huaqiao Hotel (Huqiao Fandian), 104 Nanjing Xi Lu; tel. 327 62 26

Hyland Hotel (Shanghai Hailun Binguan), 493–521 Nanjing Dong Lu;
  tel. 327 49 33
Jinjiang Hotel (Jinjiang Fandian), 59 Maoming Nan Lu; tel. 258 25 82
Jinshajiang Hotel (Jinshajiang Da Jiudian), 801 Jinshajiang Lu;
  tel. 254 60 00
New Asia Hotel (Xin Ya Da Jandian), 422 Tiantong Lu; tel. 324 22 10
Nanjing Fandian, 200 Shanxi Nanlu; tel. 322 14 55, fax. 320 65 20
  Clean, well-appointed hotel centrally located among the city's night
  spots; good value for money
New Garden Hotel (Xin Yuan Binguan), 1900 Hongqiao Lu; tel. 432 99 00
Ocean Hotel (Yuanyang Binguan), 1171 Dong Da Ming Lu; tel. 545 88 88,
  fax. 545 89 93
  First-class hotel, congenial atmosphere; revolving roof restaurant (the
  "Revolving 28")
Peace Hotel (Heping Fandian), 20 Nanjing Dong Lu; tel. 321 12 44,
  fax. 329 03 00
  Fine view over the harbour
Rui Jin, 118 Ruijin Erlu; tel. 472 52 22, fax. 473 22 77
  Quietly situated together with several guest houses in a city centre park;
  again good value for money
Shanghai International Airport Hotel (Shanghai Guoji Jichang Binguan),
  2550 Hongqiao Lu; tel. 251 88 66
Shanghai International Club Co Ltd (Shanghai Guoji Julebu Youxian
  Gongsi), 65 Yanan Xi Lu; tel. 258 17 70
Shanghai Mansion (Shanghai Dasha), 20 Bei Suzhou Lu; tel. 324 62 60,
  fax. 326 97 78
  Expensive Art Déco-style hotel built in the 1930s; outstanding views over
  the city from many of its windows
West Garden Hotel (Shanghai Xiyuan Fandian), 2384 Hongqiao Lu;
  tel. 432 91 73
Westin Taiping Hotel (Shanghai Weisiting Taiping Yang Da Jiudian), 5
  Zunyi Nan Lu; tel. 275 88 88
Xianxia Hotel (Xianxia Binguan), 555 Shiucheng Lu, Changningqu;
  tel. 259 94 00
Xijiao Guest House (Xijiao Binguan), 1921 Hongqiao Lu; tel. 433 66 43
Xingguo Guest House (Xingguo Binguan), 72 Xingguo Lu; tel. 437 45 03
Yunfong Guest House (Yunfeng Binguan), 1665 Hongqiao Lu; tel. 432 89 00

Friendship Hotel (Youyi Binguan), 7 Wai Malu; tel. 27 44 26   **Shantou**
Longhu Hotel (Longhu Binguan), Yingbin Lu. Shantou SEZ; tel. 26 07 06   (0754)
Overseas Chinese Hotel (Huqiao Fandian), Shanzhang Lu
Shantou International Hotel (Shantou Guoji Da Jiudian), Jinsha Zhong Lu;
  tel. 25 12 12
Swatow Peninsula Hotel (Zhongtai Hezuo Qiye Shedao Binguan), Jinsha
  Dong Lu Tou; tel. 23 46 36
Xinxing Hotel (Xinxing Binguan), 21 Xinxing Lu; tel. 27 58 19

Chaoyang Guest House (Chaoyang Luguan), Jiefang Bei Lu; tel. 329 30   **Shaoxing**
Overseas Chinese Hotel (Huaqiao Fandian), 91–5 Shangda Lu; tel. 323 23   (0575)
Shaoxing Hotel (Shaoxing Fandian), 9 Huanshan Lu; tel. 358 81

Chengjing Hotel (Chengjing Fandian), 6 Zhongyang Lu San Duan, Shen-   **Shenyang**
  hequ; tel. 44 30 71   (024)
Dongbei Hotel (Dongbei Fandian), 1 Qi Li San Duan Taiyuan Jie;
  tel. 73 42 55
Friendship Hotel (Youyi Binguan), 1 Huanghe Bei Dajie, Huangguqu;
  tel. 46 65 81–5
Liaoning Hotel (Liaoning Binguan), 97 Zongshan Lu; tel. 383 91 04,
  fax. 383 91 03
Liaoning Mansion (Liaoning Dasha), 105 Huanghe Nan Dajie;
  tel. 46 25 46

Hotels

Phoenix Hotel (Fenghuang Fandian), 109 Huanghe Nan Dajie; tel. 680 58 58, fax. 680 72 07
  The city's foremost hotel, situated on the edge of Beiling Park
Shanhao Guest House (Sanhao Lushe), Sanhao Jie; tel. 482 29 24
Shenyang Hotel (Shenyang Fandian), 2 Zhonghua Lu Yi Duan; tel. 333 91
Youyuan Hotel (Youyuan Fandian), 4 Er Duan Taishan Lu; tel. 605 86

Shenzhen
(0755)

Luxury hotel:
★Shangri-La Hotel Shenzhen, Jianshe Lu; tel. 223 98 78
  The best hotel in Shenzhen; non-smoking rooms; revolving restaurant with views of the city and Hong Kong New Territories

Other hotels:
Airlines Hotel (Huangkong Da Jiudian), 130 Shennan Dong Lu; tel. 23 80 66
Asia Hotel (Shenzhen Shi Yazhou Da Jiudian), Jianshe Lu; tel. 23 80 66
Bamboo Garden Hotel (Zhuyuan Binguan), Dongmen Bei Lu; tel. 22 29 34
Bay Hotel (Shenzhen Wan Da Jiudian), Overseas Chinese Town; tel. 77 01 11/77 88 20
Century Plaza (Xindu Judian), Jianshe Lu; tel. 22 08 88
Changan Hotel (Changan Dasha), Wenjin Lukou, Shennan Dong Dao; tel. 25 25 11–2
Chin Loong Wan Hotel (Qinlongwan Binguan), Kangle Lu, Shekou; tel. 69 19 18
Continental Hotel (Shenzhen Zhouji Jiudian), Shangbu Bei Lu; tel. 26 38 38
East Lake Hotel (Donghu Binguan), Shenzhen Reservoir; tel. 22 27 27–8
Forum Hotel (Fulin Da Jiudian), 67 Heping Lu; tel. 25 25 69–73
Golden Lustre Hotel (Jinbi Jiudian), 59 Chunfeng Lu, Wenjindu; tel. 25 26 40
Grand Skylight Hotel (Gelan Yuntian Da Jiudian), 68 Shennan Zhong Lu; tel. 36 36 98
Guangxin Hotel (Guangxin Jiudian), East Ming International Commercial Building, Renmin Nan Lu; tel. 23 89 45
Honey Lake Country Club (Shenzhen Xiangmihu Dujiacun), Shennan Zhong Lu, Xi Duan; tel. 74 50 61
Hongyan Hotel (Hongyan Da Jiudian), Lianhua Building, Renmin Nan Lu; tel. 25 42 28
Huadeng Hotel (Huadeng Binguan), 17 Yanhe Dong Lu; tel. 22 30 28
King Wu Hotel (Jinghu Da Jiudian), 66 Renmin Nan Lu; tel. 22 66 66
Nanhai Hotel (Nanhai Jiudian), Shekou Industrial Zone; tel. 69 28 88
Nanshan Hotel (Nanshan Binguan), Minhua Lu, Shekou; tel. 69 13 64
New Garden Hotel (Xinyuan Da Jiudian), 6 Xinyuan Lu; tel. 22 63 33
Oriental Regent Hotel (Jing Du Jiudian), Financial Centre Building, Hongling Nan Lu; tel. 24 70 00
Shenzhen Hotel (Shenzhen Jiudian), 156 Shennan Dong Lu; tel. 25 35 83
Shenzhen International Hotel (Shenzhen Yayuan Binguan), 1 Dongmen Bei Lu; tel. 22 27 63
Shenzhen Overseas Chinese Centre (Shenzhen Huaqiao Fuwu Zhongxin), 140 Shennan Dong Lu; tel. 23 80 60
Shiyan Lake Hot Spring Holiday Country Hotel (Shiyanhu Wenquan Dujiacun Jiudian), Gomgmingqu, Boan County; tel. 22 44 71–2
Xihu Hotel (Xihu Binguan), Baoan Lu East Side; tel. 23 66 55
Xili Lake Holiday Resort Village (Xilihu Dijiacun), Nantou; tel. 66 00 22

Shijiazhuang
(0311)

Hebei Guest House (Hebei Binguan), 23 Yucai Jie; tel. 61 59 61
Shijiazhuang Guest House (Shijiazhuang Fandian), Qingyuan Jie; tel. 499 86

Suzhou
(Soochow)
(0512)

Bamboo Grove Hotel (Suzhou Zhuhui Fandian), Zhuhui Lu; tel. 22 56 01, fax. 20 87 78
  Suzhou's best; modern "garden-style" hotel built around a courtyard
Gusu Hotel (Gusu Fandian), 5 Xianwang Lu, Shiquan Jie; tel. 22 51 27
Lexiang Hotel (Lexiang Fandian), 18 Dajing Xiang, Renmin Lu; tel. 22 28 90
  Central, good value
Nanlin Hotel (Nanlin Fandian), 20 Guxiufang; tel. 22 46 41, fax. 23 10 28

Royal Grand Hotel (Suyuan Fandian), Renmin Nan Lu; tel. 72 16 21
Suzhou Hotel (Suzhou Fandian), 115 Shiquan Jie; tel. 22 46 46, fax. 77 10 15
   Comfortable hotel in the Old City; with a garden

Mount Tai Summit Hotel (Daiding Binguan), Taishan Dingfeng; tel. 38 86   **Tai'an**
Taishan Grand Hotel (Taishan Da Jiudian), 27 Daizong Dajie; tel. 72 23   (0538)
Taishan Guest House (Taishan Binguan), Hongmen Lu; tel. 22 32 59
   Hotel of good standard ideally situated at the foot of Mount Taishan

Bingzhou Hotel (Bingzhou Fandian), 32 Yingze Dajie; tel. 44 21 11   **Taiyuan**
Shanxi Grand Hotel (Shanxi Da Jiudian), Yingze Dajie/Xinjiang Nanlu;   (0351)
   tel. 404 39 01, fax. 404 35 25
   Central location
Yingze Guest House (Yingze Binguan), 51 Yingze Dajie; tel. 44 32 11

Luxury hotels: **Tianjin**
★ Crystal Palace Hotel Tianjin (Tianjin Shujing Gong Fandian), 28 Youyi Lu,   (022)
   Hexiqu; tel. 31 05 67
★ Hyatt Tianjin Hotel (Tianjin Kaiyue Fandian), 219 Jiefang Bei Lu;
   tel. 331 88 88, fax. 331 00 21
★ Sheraton Hotel (Tianjin Xilaideng Da Jiudian), Zijinshan Lu, Hexiqu;
   tel. 34 33 88
★ The First Hotel (Tianjin Di Yi Fandian), 158 Jiefiang Lu; tel. 31 07 07

Other hotels:
Astor Hotel (Lishunde Da Fandian), 33 Taierzhuang Lu, 223 r.; tel. 331 16 88,
   fax. 331 62 82
   Long-established hotel (1863) in which many prominent people have
   stayed
Dongfang Hotel (Dongfang Fandian), Heping Lu, Hepingqu; tel. 31 39 45
Friendship Hotel Tianjin (Youyi Binguan), 94 Nanjing Lu; tel. 31 03 72–3
Geneva Hotel (Jinlihua Da Jiudian), 30 Youyi Lu, Hexiqu; tel. 34 22 22
Grand Hotel (Tianjin Binguan), Youyi Lu; tel. 31 90 00
Hebei Hotel (Tianjin Hebei Fandian), Zhongshan Bei Lu, Hebeiqu;
   tel. 26 51 15
International Hotel (Guoji Fandian), Liaoning Lu, Hepingqu; tel. 70 01 68
Jindong Hotel (Jindong Fandian), 99 Liuwei Lu, Hedongqu; tel. 41 19 74
Park Hotel (Tianjin Leyuan Binguan), 1 Leyuan Hu, Hexiqu; tel. 28 59 82
Qishilin Hotel (Tianjin Qishilin Jiudian), Zhejiang Lu, Hepingqu;
   tel. 31 38 54
Victory Hotel (Tianjin Shengli Binguan), 11 Jintang Gong Lu, Tangguqu;
   tel. 98 58 33

Oasis Hotel (Lüzhou Binguan), 43 Qingnian Lu; tel. 223 65   **Turpan**
   Air-conditioned luxury in the newer part; cheap multi-bedded rooms in
   the old wing
Turpan Hotel (Tulufan Binguan), near the long-distance coach station;
   tel. 29 07

Friendship Guest House (Youyi Binguan), Yanan Lu; tel. 239 91   **Ürümqi**
Holiday Inn, 168 Xin Hua Bei Lu; tel. 21 87 88, fax. 21 74 22   (0991)
   New international hotel near the bazaar
Overseas Chinese Hotel (Huaqiao Fandian), 51 Xinhua Nan Lu; tel. 244 06
World Plaza Hotel (Shijie Fandian), Beijing Lu; tel. 378 89
Xinjiang Guest House (Xinjiang Binguan), 53 Xinhua Bei Lu; tel. 796 06

Weifang Hotel (Weifang Binguan), Shengli Dajie; tel. 28 91   **Weifang**
Yuanfei Hotel (Yuanfei Da Jiudian), Shengli Dajie; tel. 29 81   (0536)

Overseas Chinese Hotel (Huaqiao Fandian), 17 Xinhe Jie; tel. 22 39 11   **Wenzhou**
Wenzhou Dongou Dasha, Wangjiang Dong Lu; tel. 22 79 00   (0577)

Hotels

Xin Ou Hotel (Wenzhou Shi Xin Ou Fandian), 33 Yangongdiangang; tel. 22 48 74

Wuhan
(027)

Binjiang Hotel (Binjiang Fandian), 2 Shanhaiguan Lu, Hankou; tel. 211 51
Jianghan Hotel (Jianghan Fandian), 245 Shengli Jie, Hankou; tel. 21 16 00, fax. 21 43 42
    Renovated 1914 building in French colonial style; situated between the main railway station and the Changjiang
Qingchuan, Xima Changjie, Hanyang; tel. 44 66 88, fax. 56 49 64
    Delightful position on the Changjiang
Victory Hotel (Shengli Fandian), 11 Siwei Lu; tel. 225 31
Wuhan Hotel (Wuhan Fandian), 332 Jiefang Dadao, Hankou; tel. 35 66 11
Yangtze Hotel (Changjiang Da Jiudian), 529 Jiefang Dadao, Hankou; tel. 56 28 28, fax. 55 41 10
    New hotel with good standard of amenities located at the southern end of Zhongshan Park; comfortable rooms

Wuhu
(0553)

Eshan Guest House (Eshan Binguan), 3 Gengxing Lu; tel. 839 20
Tieshan Guest House (Tieshan Binguan), Tieshan; tel. 845 30
Wuhu Hotel (Wuhu Binguan), Renmin Lu; tel. 830 60

Wuxi
(0510)

Hubin Hotel (Hubin Fandian), Liyuan; tel. 66 88 12
Jinyuan Guest House (Jinyuan Binguan), Jinyuan; tel. 22 29 34
Liangxi Hotel (Liangxi Fandian), 147 Shantang Nan Lu, Zhonshan Lu; tel. 22 68 12
Milido Hotel (Milidu Da Jiudian), 2 Liangxi Lu; tel. 66 56 65
Taihu Hotel (Taihu Fandian), Meiyuan; tel. 66 79 01/66 83 98
Wuxi Grand Hotel (Wuxi Da Fandian), 1 Liangqing Lu; tel. 66 67 89

Wuzhou

He Bin Hotel (He Bin Fandian), Nan Huan Lu (beyond the bridge)
Yuan Jiang Hotel (Yuan Jiang Fandian), Xijiang Yi Lu

Xiamen
(0592)

East Ocean Hotel, 1 Zongshan Lu; tel. 22 11 11, fax. 23 32 64
Gulangyu Guest House, 25 Huangyan Lu; tel. 23 18 56
    Old but renovated complex at the heart of Gulang Island
Holiday Inn Harbourview, 12/8 Zhenhai Lu; tel. 22 33 33, fax. 23 66 66
    Extremely comfortable hotel centrally situated in the Old City
Jinbao Hotel (Xiamen Jinbao Jiudian), 124 Dongdu Lu; tel. 468 88
Lujiang Hotel (Lujiang Binguan), 54 Lujiang Dao; tel. 22 29 22, fax. 22 46 44
    Somewhat noisy location close to the ferry terminal; rooftop bar with good views of the harbour
★Mandarin Hotel (Xiamen Yuehua Jiudian), Huli, Waishang Zhutuoqu; tel. 62 33 33, fax. 62 14 31
    Comfortable hotel in leafy surroundings on a hill; 22 adjoining villas
Seaview Garden Tourist Village (Guanhai Yuan Luyoucun), 8 Tianwei Lu, Gulangyu Island; tel. 269 51–9
Xiamen Hotel (Xiamen Binguan), 16 Huyuan Lu; tel. 222 85

Xi'an
(029)

Luxury hotels:
★Dynasty Hotel (Taidu Jiudian), 55 Huacheng Xi Lu Bei Duan; tel. 71 27 18
★Garden Hotel (Tanghua Binguan), 4 Dongyanyin Lu; tel. 526 11 11, fax. 526 19 98
    Near the Pagoda of the Great Wild Goose; hotel built as a joint venture with the Japanese; imitation Tang architecture, comfortable rooms
★Holiday Inn (Xian Shenzhou Jiari Jiudian), 8 Huancheng Dong Lu, Nan Duan; tel. 33 42 20/33 38 88
★Hyatt Xi'an (Afang Gong Kaiyue Fandian), 158 Dong Dajie; tel. 71 20 20
★Jianguo Hotel (Jianguo Fandian), 20 Jinhua Nan Lu; tel. 33 88 88
New World Dynasty Xi'an Hotel (Gudu Da Jiudian), 48 Lianhu Lu; tel. 71 68 68/288 70
★People's Hotel, 319 Dong Xin Jie; tel. 71 51 11
★Shangri-La Golden Flower Hotel (Jinhua Fandian), 8 Changle Xi Lu; tel. 33 29 81

★Sheraton Hotel (Xian Xilaideng Da Jiudian), 12 Fenghao Lu, Xijiao; tel. 74 18 88

Other hotels:
Bell Tower Hotel (Zhonglou Fandian); tel. 727 92 00, fax. 721 87 67
  Medium-priced hotel in a central position; views of the Bell Tower; spacious rooms
Hawaii Hotel (Xian Xiachengyi Fandian), 54 Youyi Dong Lu; tel. 71 12 88
Jiefang Hotel (Jiefang Fandian), 321 Jiefang Lu; tel. 721 29 27, fax. 721 26 17
  Inexpensive, near the station
New World Hotel (Xin Shijie Jiudian), 5 Nan Dajie; tel. 71 99 88
Renmin Hotel (Renmin Dasha), 319 Dongxin Dajie; tel. 71 51 11
Scarlet Bird Hotel (Zhuqiao Fandian), 26 Xiaozhai Xi Lu; tel. 533 11
Tangcheng Hotel (Tangcheng Binguan), 3 Lingyuan Lu Nanduan; tel. 75 57 11, fax. 75 10 41
  Comfortable and reasonably priced
Xi'an Hotel (Xi'an Binguan), 26 Changan Lu Bei Duan; tel. 75 57 11, fax. 75 10 41
Xiaozhai Hotel (Xiaozhai Fandian), 3 Changan Lu; tel. 526 90

Friendship Hotel (Youyi Binguan), Hongguang Lu Zhong Duan; tel. 38 50   **Xiangfan**
White Crane Hotel (Baihe Binguan), Fangcheng Huochezhan (station);   (0710)
tel. 39 07
Xiangfang Hotel (Xiangfang Fandian), Dingzhong Jie; tel. 32 85

Xigaze Hotel (Xigaze Fandian), 13 Jiejang Lu; tel. 25 19   **Xigaze**
  Xigaze's first hotel catering for foreigners; on the outskirts near the bus station

Xining Guest House (Xining Binguan), 215 Qiyi Lu; tel. 427 01   **Xining**
Xining Hotel (Xining Fandian), 93 Jianguo Lu; tel. 779 91   (0971)

South Suburb Guest House (Nanjiao Binguan), 55 Heping Lu; tel. 223 71   **Xuzhou** (0516)

Yan'an Guest House (Yan'an Binguan), 56 Beiguan Dajie; tel. 31 22   **Yan'an** (0911)

Xiyuan Hotel (Xiyuan Fandian), 1 Fengle Shang Jie; tel. 226 11–496   **Yangzhou**
Yangzhou Hotel (Yangzhou Fandian), 5 Fengle Shang Jie; tel. 426 11–452   (0514)

Overseas Chinese Hotel (Huaqiao Binguan), 15 Huanshan Lu; tel. 224 31   **Yantai**
Zhifu Hotel ((Zhifu Fandian), Dongjiao; tel. 224 31/248 41   (0535)

Taohualing Hotel (Taohualing Fandian), 29 Yunji Lu; tel. 238 12   **Yichang**
Three Gorges Hotel (Sanxia Fandian), Yanjiang Da Dao; tel. 232 25   (0717)

Helanshan Hotel (Helanshan Fandian), 1 Shoufang Lu; tel. 773 02   **Yinchuan**
Luzhou Hotel (Luzhou Fandian), Jiefang Jie; tel. 48 08   (0951)
Xinhua Hotel (Xinhua Fandian), Xinhua Dong Dajie; tel. 220 89
Yinchuan Hotel (Yinchuan Fandian), 91 Jiefang Xi Jie; tel. 226 15

Yixing Guest House (Yixing Binguan), Chezhan Lu; tel. 25 31   **Yixing**
Yixing Hotel (Yixing Fandian), Renmin Nan Lu; tel. 29 25

Yueyang, 26 Dongting Bei Lu; tel. 22 30 11   **Yueyang**
  Beautifully situated right by the lake   (0730)
Yunmeng Guest House (Yunmeng Binguan), 25 Chengdong Lu; tel. 22 11 15
  Pleasant, reasonably priced hotel serving good food

Chikan Hotel (Chikan Binguan), 2 Yuejin Lu; tel. 33 71 16   **Zhanjiang**
Haibin Hotel (Haibin Binguan), 32 Haibin Er Lu; tel. 22 35 55   (0759)
Xiashan Hotel (Xiashan Binguan), Jiefang Da Dao; tel. 22 31 51
Zhanjiang Friendship Hotel (Zhanjiang Shi Youyi Binguan), 39 Xiashan Renmin Da Dao; tel. 22 23 55

Information

Zhaoqing (0758)	Furong Hotel (Furong Binguan), Kangle Bei Lu; tel. 255 12 Overseas Chinese Mansion (Huaqiao Dasha), Tianning Bei Lu Songtao Hotel (Songtao Binguan), Qixingyan Fenjingqu; tel. 22 44 12
Zhengzhou (0371)	Friendship Hotel (Youyi Binguan), Jinshui Da Dao Xintongqiao; tel. 233 88 Henan Guest House (Henan Binguan), 26 Jinshui Lu; tel. 222 16 International Hotel (Henan Sheng Guoji Fandian), 114 Huanghe Lu; tel. 33 64 83 Regent Plaza Hotel, 113 Jinshui Da Dao; tel. 542 55
Zhenjiang (0511)	Jinjiang Hotel (Jinjiang Fandian), 111 Jiefang Lu; tel. 22 28 42–6 Jinshan Hotel (Jinshan Fandian), 1 Jinshan Xi Lu; tel. 23 29 71 Yiquan Hotel (Yiquan Binguan), 1 Yiquan Lu; tel. 23 40 61 Zhenjian Jing-Kou Hotel (Zhenjiang Jingkou Fandian), 407 Zhongshan Dong Lu; tel. 22 48 66

Zhuhai
(0756)
	Bihai Hotel (Bihai Jiudian), Bihai Lu, Xiangzhouqu; tel. 22 20 75
	Fenghuang Hotel (Fenghuang Fandian), 135 Fenghuang Lu, Xiangzhouqu;
	   tel. 22 24 23
	Gongbei Palace (Gongbei Binguan), Shiuwan Lu, Gongbeiqu; tel. 88 68 33
	Shijinshan Hotel (Shijinshan Zhuang), 1 Jinshan Lu; tel. 33 35 11
	Yunhai Hotel (Yunhai Da Jiudian), Jiuzhou Da Dao; tel. 33 30 73–6
	Zhong Lu Hotel (Zhong Lu Jiudian), Haibin Nan Lu; tel. 33 32 77
	Zhuhai Holiday Resort Hotel (Zhuhai Dujiacun Jiudian), Shihua Shan,
	   Zhuhai; tel. 33 20 38
	Zhuhai Resort (Zhuhai Binguan), Jingshan Lu, Jida; tel. 33 37 18
	Zhuhai SEZ Gongbei Hotel (Zhuhai Jingji Tequ Gongbei Jiudian),
	   36 Lianghua Lu, Gongbei; tel. 88 52 60

Zibo (0533)	Zibo Guest House (Zibo Binguan), Zhongxin Lu, Bei Shou, Zhangdianqu; tel. 22 53 41

Information

Australia	China National Tourist Office, Floor 19, 44 Market Street, Sydney, New South Wales 2000; tel. (2) 299 4057
United Kingdom	China Tourist Office, 4 Glentworth Street, London NW1; tel. (0171) 935 9427/9787
U.S.A.	China National Tourist Office, 350 Fifth Avenue, Suite 6413, New York, NY 10118; tel. (212) 760 9700, fax. (212) 760 8809 China International Travel Service Inc., 60 East 42nd Street, Suite 3126, New York, NY 10165; tel. (212) 867 0271

In China

CITS (Guoji Luxingshe)	The China International Travel Service (CITS, or Guoji Luxingshe in Chinese, Luxingshe for short) is the official organisation that deals with foreign tourists in China. It has offices in all the main cities and resorts and makes travel arrangements as well as providing information. The area codes for the following phone numbers are shown in brackets but not all places can be reached by direct dialling as yet.
Head Office **in Beijing**	China International Travel Service (CITS), 103 Fuxingmen Nei Ave., 100800 Beijing, People's Republic of China; tel. (010) 601 11 22 For other offices in Beijing see under the entry for Beijing below.
Anshan	CITS, 121 Shengli Lu; tel. (0412) 244 03

CITS, Baotou Binguan, Kunqu Gangtje Dajie; tel. (0471) 246 15   Baotou

International CITS office, 28 Jianguomenwai Dajie; tel. (010) 515 88 44/   Beijing
   515 25 04 (also available here, information and tickets for international   (Peking)
   rail services)
CITS Beijing, 2 Qianmendong; tel. (010) 512 22 11
CITS station office, Hotel Chongwenmen; tel. (010) 55 48 66
CITS office for independent travellers, Hotel Chongwenmen;
   tel. (010) 75 52 72
   There is also an information desk at Beijing Airport where foreign tourists can get information on hotels, etc.
   Beijing also has a 24-hour English-language information hotline;
tel. (010) 513 08 28

International CITS office, 179 Huanshi Lu; tel. (020) 667 72 71, fax. 667 80 48   Canton
Local CITS Office, 4 Qiaoguang Lu; tel. (020) 66 11 12   (Guangzhou)

CITS, Xinmin Dajie; tel. (0431) 88 24 01 and 88 50 69   Changchun
Chunyi Guest House, 2 Sidalin Lu; tel. (0431) 387 72

CITS, Wuyi Donglu Jie; tel. (0731) 262 62 and 222 50   Changsha

CITS, 75 Yanling Xi Lu; tel. (0519) 60 04 81   Changzhou
101 Dong Dajie; tel. (0519) 248 86

CITS, Yunashan Hotel, 6 Nanyuan Dong Lu; tel. (0314) 22 68 27   Chengde
11 Zonghua Lu; tel. (0314) 34 01 and 34 54

China West Expedition Travel, Zongbei Xiaoqu, Zhuyuan Block 11/1;   Chengdu
tel. (028) 555 13 44, fax. 555 62 37

CITS, Renmin Hotel, 175 Renmin Lu; tel. (0811) 35 12 48   Chongqing

CITS, 1 Changtong Jie, Xiganqu; tel. (0411) 33 57 95 and 33 79 56   Dalian
56 Fengling Lu; tel. (0411) 357 95 and 251 03

CITS, 21 Yingbin Dong Lu; tel. (0352) 522 65   Datong

CITS, Dingzi Lu Nanmen; tel. (09473) 224 92   Dunhuang

CITS, 75 Fenjiang Nan Lu; tel. (0757) 22 33 38 and 28 79 23   Foshan

CITS, Fushun Hotel, Yongan Square (Guangchang); tel. (0413) 228 07   Fushun

International CITS office, 44 Dongda Lu; tel. (0591) 55 55 06   Fuzhou
Local CITS office, 4 Wusi Lu; tel. (0591) 55 63 04

CITS, 14 Ronghu Beilu; tel. (0773) 22 69 36   Guilin
Guilin also has an English-language information hotline;
   tel. (0773) 22 65 33

CITS, Jinqiao Hotel, Ruijin Lu; tel. (0851) 52 42 66   Guiyang
11 Yan'an Zhonghlu; tel. (0851) 52 30 95

CITS, 17 Datong Lu; tel. (0898) 77 26 52   Haikou

CITS, Zhonghua Bei Dajie; tel. (0310) 239 21   Handan

CITS, 1 Shihan Lu; tel. (0571) 515 28 88   Hangzhou

CITS, Tian'e Hotel, 73 Zhongshan Lu; tel. (0451) 262 26 55   Harbin

Information

Hefei	CITS, 68 Changjiang Lu; tel (0551) 618 90
Hohhot	CITS, Hohhot Guest House, Yingbing Lu; tel. (0471) 262 41 Nei Menggu Guest House, Wulachabulu; tel. (0471) 244 94
Jilin	CITS, Xiguan Guest House, 661 Songjiang Lu; 155 Chuangjing Lu; tel. (0432) 277 21
Jinan	CITS, 26 Jing Shi Lu; tel. (0531) 61 58 58 Jinan Hotel, 240 Jing San Lu; tel. (0531) 353 51
Jingdezhen	CITS, 8 Lianhuatang; tel. (0798) 29 39/22 93
Jinggangshan	CITS, Jinggangshan Guest House, Cipingzhen; tel. 504
Jinhong	CITS, Banna Hotel; tel. 27 08
Jiujiang	CITS, Nanhu Hotel, 28 Nanhu Lu; tel. (0595) 22 33 90
Kaifeng	CITS, Kaifeng Hotel, 64 Ziyou Lu; tel. (0378) 237 37
Kashgar	CITS, Xingshuxuan (administration office); tel. 31 56
Kunming	CITS, 218 Huancheng Nan Lu; tel. (0871) 313 28 95 Kunming Hotel, Dongfeng Dong Lu; tel. (0871) 272 59 Golden Dragon Hotel, 575 Beijing Lu; tel. (0871) 330 15/331 04
Lanzhou	CITS, 361 Tianshui Lu; tel. (0931) 261 81/496 21 Nanchang Lu; tel. 261 37
Lhasa	Tibet Tourist Corporation, 208 Beijing Xilu; tel. (0891) 263 15
Liuzhou	CITS, Liuzhou Hotel, 1 Youyi Lu; tel. (0772) 256 69
Luoyang	CITS, Friendship Guest House, 6 Xiyuan Lu; tel. (0379) 41 37 01
Ma'anshan	CITS, Hu Nan Lu; tel. (0555) 29 44
Nanchang	CITS, Jiangxi Guest House, 64 Bayi Da Dao; tel. (0791) 22 66 81
Nanjing (Nanking)	CITS, 18 Zhongshan Bei Lu; tel. (025) 330 28 61
Nanning	CITS, Mingyuan Hotel, 40 Xinmin Lu; tel. (0771) 220 42
Nantong	CITS, Qingnian Dong Lu; tel. (0513) 71 57
Ningbo	CITS, 65 Mayuan Lu; tel. (0574) 686 90/663 34
Peking	See Beijing
Qingdao	CITS, Huiquan Wangchao Da Hotel, 9 Nanhai Lu; tel. (0532) 286 15 13
Qinhuangdao	CITS, tel. (0335) 342 69
Quanzhou	CITS, Huaqiao Dasha Hotel, Baiyuanqingchi Xilu; tel. (0595) 22 21 92, fax. 22 33 11
Qufu	CITS, Hotel Xingtan Binguan, Xueguan Lu; tel. (05473) 41 24 91
Shanghai	CITS, Guangming Bldg., 2 Jinling Xilu; tel. (021) 321 72 00
Shantou	CITS, Peninsula Hotel, 1/F Jinsha Lu; tel (0754) 23 52 26/23 56 23

CITS, 20 Fushan Xi Lu; tel. (0575) 332 52	Shaoxing
CITS, 1/F Stadium Bldg., 3 Gongyuan Lu; tel. 23 25	Shashi
CITS, 113 Huanghe Nan Dajie; tel. (024) 680 87 72	Shenyang
CITS, 2 Chuanbu Jie, Heping Lu; tel. (0755) 557 79 70 Shenzhen Overseas Chinese Center, 140 Shennan Dong Lu	Shenzhen
CITS, Shijiazhuang Guest House, Qingyuan Jie; tel. (0311) 447 66	Shijiazhuang
CITS, Suzhou Hotel, 115 Shiquan Jie; tel. (0512) 22 30 63 Nanlin Hotel, 20 Gunxiufang, Shiquan Jie; tel. (0512) 22 46 41	Suzhou
CITS, Taishan Guest House, Hongmen Lu; tel. (0538) 22 32 59	Tai'an
CITS, Yingze Guest House, 51 Yingze Dajie; tel. (0351) 44 11 55	Taiyuan
CITS, 22 Youyi Lu, Hexiqu; tel. (022) 335 83 49 242 Heping Lu; tel. (022) 212 24/258 88	Tianjin
CITS, Lüzhou Hotel, 47 Qingnian Lu; tel. 227 68	Turpan
CITS, Renmin Square (Guangchang); tel. (0991) 257 94 72 Heping Lu; tel. (0991) 257 94 Huaqiao Hotel, 51 Xinhua Nan Lu; tel. (0991) 244 06	Ürümqi
CITS, 131 Huangcheng Dong Lu; tel. (0577) 22 74 81/22 98 57	Wenzhou
Hubei Overseas Tourist Corporation, 48 Jianghan Yilu; tel. (027) 21 21 29, fax. 21 18 91	Wuhan
CITS, 7 Xingsheng Lu; tel. (0510) 22 68 12 53 Chezhan Lu; tel. (0510) 22 36 13	Wuxi
CITS, Beihuan Lu; tel. 41 97	Wuzhou
CITS, 15–16/F Zhenxing Bldg., Hubin Bei Lu; tel. (0592) 55 75 85 Overseas Chinese Building; 70/74 Xinhua Lu; tel. (0592) 256 02 and 256 17	Xiamen
CITS, 32 Chang'an Lu; tel. (029) 526 20 66	Xi'an
CITS, Changzheng Lu; tel. (0710) 28 80/28 73	Xiangfan
CITS, Xining Guest House, 215 Qiyi Lu; tel. (0971) 239 01–700	Xining
CITS, 106 Chengnei Dajie; tel. (0911) 27 49/25 89 Yan'an Guest House, 55 Beiguan Dajie; tel. (0911) 24 04	Yan'an
CITS, 1 Fengle Shang Jie; tel. (0514) 419 25	Yangzhou
CITS, 10 Shuntai Lu; tel. (0535) 256 26	Yantai
CITS, Three Gorges Hotel, Yanjiang Da Dao; tel. (0717) 232 25	Yichang
CITS, 150 Jiefang Xi Jie; tel. (0951) 337 20/221 31	Yinchuan
CITS, Renmin Nan Lu; tel. 25 59	Yixing
CITS, Yunmeng Guest House, 25 Chengdong Lu; tel. (0730) 22 11 15	Yueyang
CITS, Renda Palace, 5th floor, Xiashan; tel. (0759) 236 88	Zhanjiang

Zhaoqing	CITS, Kangle Bei Lu; tel. (0758) 227 58
Zhengzhou	CITS, 15 Jinshui Lu; tel. (0371) 55 20 72/320 70/253 96 Henan Sheng Guoji Hotel, 114 Jinshui Da Dao Dong Dua
Zhenjiang	CITS, 25 Jiankang Lu; tel. (0511) 22 25 38/23 32 87
Zhuhai	CITS, Aomen Shajiadulaijiabai Bai Jie 6A; tel. (0756) 566 62–13 4 Shuiwan Lu, Gongbei; tel. (0756) 88 57 77
Zibo	CITS, Zhongxin Lu Bei Shou, Zhangdianqu; tel. (0533) 22 53 41
Complaints hotline	Over 40 of the places most visited by tourists in China have a complaints hotline which visitors with a problem can ring and get a response in English. A list of the numbers is obtainable from Chinese Tourist Offices. They include Beijing (010) 513 08 28; Shanghai (012) 439 06 30; Tianjin (022) 31 88 14; Jiangsu Province (025) 30 12 21; Zhejiang Province (0571) 55 66 31; Guangdong Province (020) 67 74 22; Shaanxi Province (029) 71 14 80; Gansu Province (0931) 268 60, and Guilin (0773) 22 65 33.
Taiwan	Tourism Bureau, Republic of China, P.O. Box 1490, Taipei; tel. (02) 721 85 41
Hong Kong	CITS (Luxingshe International) Hong Kong, 6th Floor, Tower II, South Seas Centre, 75 Mody Road, Tsim Sha Tsui East, Kowloon, Hong Kong; tel. 732 58 88
Information about Hong Kong in Hong Kong	Hong Kong Tourist Association, 35th floor, Jardine House, 1 Connaught Place, Central Hong Kong; tel. 801 71 11 Information hotline (in several languages): 801 71 77 Offices also in the Buffer Hall at the International Airport (for arriving passengers only) and at the Star Ferry Concourse, Kowloon.
in Australia	Hong Kong Tourist Association, Bligh House, 4–6 Bligh Street, Sydney, NSW; tel. (2) 232 24 22
in New Zealand	Hong Kong Tourist Association, 29–31 Shortland Street, P.O. Box 2120, Auckland; tel. (9) 79 86 42
in the United Kingdom	Hong Kong Tourist Association, 14–16 Cockspur Street, London SW1Y 5DP; tel. (0171) 930 47 75 Macao Tourist Information Centre, London; tel. (0171) 224 3390
in the United States	Hong Kong Tourist Association, 339 North Michigan Avenue, Chicago, IL 60601; tel. (312) 782 38 72
	Hong Kong Tourist Association, 548 Fifth Avenue, New York, NY 10036; tel. (212) 947 5008
Macau	Macau Government Tourist Office (MGTO), 1 Travessa do Paiva, Macao; tel. 772 18 and 56 11 67

Insurance

General	Visitors to China are strongly advised to ensure that they have adequate holiday insurance, including loss or damage to luggage, loss of currency and jewellery.
	Tourist offices and travel agents are usually able to obtain travel insurance on behalf of customers. Package tours generally include an element of insurance in the total price, but it is sensible to ensure that the proposed cover is adequate.
Health	See Medical Assistance

Language

Spoken Chinese breaks down into a number of dialects with a basic difference between those of the north and the south. There are eight main dialects in total with many sub-dialects which differ so much that speakers of one dialect cannot understand what is said by speakers of another. As a general rule southern dialects are older and longer-established than those of the north.

Dialects

In addition to the different dialects China's numerous national minorities also have many of their own idioms.

Minority idioms

The official national language known as guoyu or putonghua has been developed from Mandarin, as it is known in the west, which is the dialect spoken around Beijing. This is the language taught in schools and used in all official circles and now employed throughout the country as a *lingua franca* to get round the problem of the different dialects. Thus children who do not come from Beijing can speak putonghua in addition to their own regional language.

Official language

Meaning is given to spoken Chinese by the use of four different tones – indicated in this guide by accents on the letters in question – which impart meaning to each syllable according to its pitch or tonal inflection. For example, the word "ma" has four different meanings depending on the tone in which it is spoken. "mā", with a high, flat tone, is "mother", "má" with a rising tone is "hemp", "mǎ" with a falling-rising tone is "horse", and "mà" with a falling tone is "to scold or swear".

Tonal inflection

Written Chinese largely bears no relation to the regional variations of the spoken language and uses pictographs rather than letters. The traditional characters have been considerably simplified, reducing the number of official pictographs from around 50,000 to between three and four thousand. In this respect the written language in China differs considerably from that used in Hong Kong, Taiwan and overseas which still make general use of the traditional written forms.

Written Chinese

Romanisation, the transliteration of Chinese words into the Roman alphabet, tries to get as close as possible to the phonetic pronunciation of Chinese. Various systems have been used in the past and those who want to acquaint themselves with China's more significant literature should at least know something of the two most important, namely Wade-Giles and Pinyin.

Romanisation

Tourists will particularly need to have some grasp of how to speak Pinyin which since 1979 has been the only official system. This will enable them to have at least a passable pronunciation. The names of stations, streets and stores appear in Pinyin as well as the Chinese characters, which usually take precedence.

Pinyin

In Pinyin most letters are pronounced as in English except for c, q and x. The list below provides some idea of the general rules for pronunciation.

Pronunciation according to the Pinyin method

Pinyin	Pronunciation
a	a as in "father"
ao	ow as in "cow"
b	as English
c	ts as in "its"
ch	as English but with the tongue curved back
d	as English
e	ur as in "blur" except after i, u, ü, y when e as in "egg"

Pinyin	Pronunciation
ei	like ei as in "rein"
er	as in "her"
f	as English
g	always hard as in "go"
h	ch as in "loch"
i	like ee in "beet" but after c, ch, r, s, sh, z or zh oo as in "book"
ian	as in "yen"
iao	iaow as in "miaow"
ie	as "yeah" in English
j	as English
k	as English
l	as English
m	as English
n	as English
o	as o in "or"
ong	ung as in German
ou	ow as in "low"
p	as English
q	ch as in "children"
r	as English
s	as English
sh	as English but with the tongue curved back
t	as English
u	as in "flute"
ui	like "way"
w	as English
x	sh as in "shine"
y	as English
z	ds as "lids"
zh	j as in jungle but with the tongue curled back

Foreign languages

Few Chinese speak foreign languages although many are familiar with English from school and television, and tour guides will specialise in at least one other language. Taxi drivers, on the other hand, are unlikely to know any English and the best course is, if possible, to have written instructions in Chinese telling them where you want to go (see Taxis).

If travelling on business carry visiting cards printed in English and Chinese.

Numerals

English	Chinese
0	líng
1	yī
2	èr (liǎng)
3	sān
4	sì
5	wǔ
6	liù
7	qī
8	bā
9	jiǔ
10	shì
11	shíyī
12	shíèr
13	shísān
14	shísì
15	shíwǔ
16	shíliù
17	shíqī
18	shíbā
19	shíjiǔ

English	Chinese
20	èrshí
21	èrshíyī
22	èrshíèr
30	sānshí
40	sìshí
50	wǔshí
60	liùshí
70	qīshí
80	bāshí
90	jiǔshí
100	yībǎi
101	yībǎilíngyī
200	èrbǎi
1000	yīqiān

Finger counting from one to ten

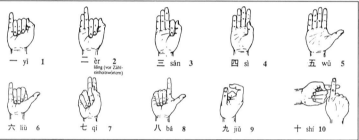

一 yī 1   二 èr 2 liǎng (vor Zähleinholtswörtern)   三 sān 3   四 sì 4   五 wǔ 5

六 liù 6   七 qī 7   八 bā 8   九 jiǔ 9   十 shí 10

To make ordinal numbers (first, second, third, etc.) add the prefix "dí": thus, fourth = dí sì.

Ordinal numbers

English	Chinese	
1 mm	háo-mǐ	Weights and measures
1cm	lí-mǐ	
1km	gōng-lǐ	
½	bān	
¼	sì-fēn-zhī-yī	
1 litre	gōng-shēng	
1 kg	gōng-jīn	

do you speak	nǐ shuō	Useful phrases
. . . English	yīng wén ma	
I don't understand	wǒ tīng bù dǒng	
yes, it is so	shì	
no, not so	bú shì	
no thanks	bùyào xièxie	
thank you	xièxie-buxiè	
many thanks	fēicháng gǎnxiè	
please	qǐng	
I'm sorry	duìbùqi	
it doesn't matter	méi guānxi	
hello	nín hǎo	
good day		
good evening	wǎnshàng hào	
good night	wǎn ān	
goodbye	zai jiàn	
Mr.	. . . xiānsheng	
Mrs.	. . . nǚshì	

Language

English	Chinese
Miss	xiǎojiě
(after the name)	
yesterday	zuótiān
today	jīntiān
tomorrow	míngtiān
where is?	. . . zài nǎr?
where is the	Lūxíngshè zài nǎr?
Luxingshe office?	
airport	fēi-jī-chǎng
avenue	dà-mā-lù
botanical garden	zhí-wù-yuán
bus	gōng-gòng qì-chē
centre (of town)	nèi-chéng
consulate	zǒng-lǐng-shì-guǎn
embassy	dà-shǐ-guǎn
gate	mén
hospital	yī yuàn
island	dǎo
lake	hú
library	tú-shū-guǎn
market	shì-chǎng
monument	jì-niàn-bēi
mosque	qhīng-zhēn-sì
mountain	shān
mountains	shān-mài
museum	bó-wùguǎn
pagoda	tǎ
palace	gōng-diàn
police	jǐng-chà
port	gǎng-kǒu
river	hé
shopping centre	gòu wù zhōng-xīn
station	huǒ-chē-zhàn
(bus) stop	zhàn
street	lù/jiē
taxi	chū-zū-chē
temple	miào-yǔ
underground	dí-tiě
valley	shān-gǔ
zoo	dòng-wù-yuan
when?	shé-me shí-hou
when is . . .	shé-me shí-hou
. . . open?	kāi mén?
. . . closed?	shé-me shí-hou
	kāi guān?
the post office	yóujú
the bank	yínháng
exchange bureau)	(duìhuànchù)
where is the . . . hotel?	. . . bīnguǎn zài nǎr?
I'd like	wǒ xiǎng yáo yìjiān
. . . a single room	. . . dānrén fáng
. . . a double room	. . . shuāngrén fáng
with bath	yǒu yùshì
the key please!	qīng nǐ gei wǒ yàoshi!
WC (gents)	nán-cèsuǒ
WC (ladies)	nǚ-cèsuǒ
doctor	yīshēng
left	zuǒbian
right	yòubian
straight on	wàng qián zǒu

English	Chinese	
English	**Chinese**	
here	zhèr	
there	nàr	
how much is it?	duōshǎo qián?	
restaurant	cāntīng	
breakfast	zǎofàn	
lunch	zhōngfàn	
evening meal	wǎnfàn	
I'm hungry	wǒ è le	
I'm thirsty	wǒ kě le	
the bill/check please	qǐng suánzhàng	
See Food and Drink		Eating Out
entrance	rùkǒu	Signs
exit	chūkǒu	
Ladies	nǚ	
Gents	nán	
ticket office	shòupiàochù	
closed	xiūxi	
bus stop	chēzhàn	
way in	shàngchē	
way out	xiáché	
waiting room	xiūxi shì	
no smoking	bù zhǔn xīyān	
emergency exit	tàipíngmén	
watch out!	xiǎoxīn	
danger!	wēixiǎn	
January	yī-yuè	Months
February	èr-yuè	
March	san-yuè	
April	sì-yuè	
May	wu-yuè	
June	liù-yuè	
July	qī-yuè	
August	bā-yuè	
September	jiǔ-yuè	
October	shí-yuè	
November	shí-yí-yuè	
December	shí-èr-yuè	
Monday	xīngqīyī	Days of the week
Tuesday	xīngqīèr	
Wednesday	xīngqīsān	
Thursday	xīngqīsì	
Friday	xīngqīwǔ	
Saturday	xīngqīliu	
Sunday	xīngqītiān or xīngqīrì	
See entry		Public holidays and festivals
post office	yóujú	At the post office
letterbox	yóutōng or xínxiāng	
stamps	yóupiào	
this letter by . . .	Zhèfēng xìn jì . . .	
. . . airmail	hángkōngde	
. . . express mail	tèkuàide	
. . . registered post	guàhàode	
I should like to send a	Wǒ yào dǎ	
telegram	diànbao	
telex	diànchuàn	

547

	English	Chinese
	I should like a	Wǒ yào dǎ
	long-distance call	yíge chángtú
	to . . .	diànhuà yù

Chinese answer the phone by saying "wéi" (hello).

Place names
Although some Chinese words – especially place names – have entered the western vocabulary you can not rely on the western forms being understood throughout China.

Chinese
phrasebooks
A number of Chinese phrasebooks are available from bookshops, usually published by companies specialising in travel guides.

Maps

In addition to the map of China which is part of this guide you may well find it useful to take other maps with you. The selection that follows includes the Map of the People's Republic of China published in Beijing by the Cartographic Publishing House. This is also available in China along with detailed local maps of the tourist highspots.

1:9000 000
National Tourism Administration Beijing, Tourist Map of China

1:6000 000
Bartholomew, China & Mongolia (World Travel Map) including maps of Beijing, Canton and Shanghai, plus Hong Kong

1:5400 000
K+G, Hildebrand's Map 46: China

1:5000 000
K+F, 1258 roadmap of China, also covering Mongolia, Japan, North and South Korea

1:4000 000
Map of the People's Republic of China (Zhongguo Renmin Gongheguo Ditu), by Cartographic Publishing House, Beijing, in pinyin and Chinese script
RV, World Maps, China (in Chinese and international script)

1:1500 000
Nelles, China Map 1 (north-east), Map 2 (north), Map 3 (centre), Map 4 (south)

Medical Assistance

**Before
leaving home**
China's extremes of altitude and of heat and cold (see Facts and Figures, Climate, and When to Go) can cause the kind of heart and respiratory problems that make it highly advisable to get a checkup from your doctor before leaving home, especially if you are planning a visit to Tibet or doing any form of trekking.

Up-to-date
information
You should get up-to-date information well before you leave from your travel clinic or some similar organisation (see Health Precautions) on what vaccinations, etc. are recommended or required.

Health Insurance
You would be well advised to take out some form of separate travellers' health insurance to cover such emergencies as being flown home for treatment, since this can prove very expensive.

In China
For minor ailments you can get medication from chemists and pharmacies if you have nothing suitable with you (see Health Precautions, Medical Kit). For more serious illness you should consult your tourist guide, the local CITS office or the desk clerk at your hotel. They will be able to arrange for you to see a doctor or direct you to a hospital (yī yuan) with a special section for foreign patients where you can make yourself understood in English.

Some of the larger tourist hotels also have their own medical facility with a nurse and sometimes a doctor in attendance.

The following three hospitals have medical clinics which specialise in treating foreigners: | Hospitals

Capital Hospital Clinic for Foreigners (Shoudu Yiyan), Dongda Bei Dajie,
   Beijing; tel. (010) 55 37 31
Canton No. 1 People's Hospital, 602 Renmin Bei Lu,
   Canton; tel. (020) 33 30 90
Shanghai No. 1 People's Hospital, 190 Suzhou Bei Lu,
   Shanghai; tel. (021) 24 01 00

Foreign patients are required to pay treatment costs immediately. Although doctor's visits and medication are relatively cheap, a stay in hospital is expensive. Keep your receipts to claim on insurance when you return home. | Treatment costs

See also Chemists, Emergency Services, Health Precautions

Motoring

The Chinese road network has been considerably expanded in recent years, with a number of major roadbuilding projects still under way. | **Roads**

China has very few motorways, most of which are still in construction. Although there are plenty of trunk roads and minor roads these are mostly unmetalled and only about half are passable all year round. | Motorways

Getting behind the wheel yourself in China as a foreign visitor is so fraught with problems as to be virtually out of the question. Besides having to contend with fuel shortages, an inability to read Chinese place names and roadsigns, and difficulties in making yourself understood outside the big towns, you will find renting a car on your own almost impossible. You will also require a special permit to visit areas open to foreigners (see Open Cities). On the other hand it is possible to arrange for chauffeur-driven cars to go sightseeing, and shorter trips can be made by taxi. | Independent road travel

None of the internationally well-known car hire firms such as AVIS, Budget, Europcar or Hertz are currently represented in China. | Car Rental

See also Bicycles, Public Transport, Rickshaws, Taxis

Traffic travels on the right in China and Taiwan and on the left in Hong Kong and Macau. | **Rules of the Road**

The speed limit is usually 50–60km.p.h./31–37m.p.h. in built-up areas, 60–70km.p.h./37–43m.p.h. elsewhere, and 100–120km.p.h./62–75m.p.h. on motorways. | Speed limits

Mountaineering and Trekking

Within its vast confines China boasts several of the world's highest mountains, most notably in the autonomous regions of Tibet and Xinjiang and the provinces of Sichuan and Qinghai.

Anyone interested in mountaineering or trekking in China should contact the Chinese Mountaineering Association or the China International Travel Service (CITS, see Information). Both organisations can supply information about expeditions and also issue any permits required. | Organisations to contact

Museums

Organisations providing information about Tibet include:
Tibet Mountaineering Sports Commission, Linguo South Road,
Lhasa; tel. (0891) 229 81

Himalayas

Mount Everest

At 8846m/29,033ft the highest mountain on Earth, Mount Everest (Zhumu-luangma Feng in Chinese, Chomolungma, or Mother Goddess, in Tibetan), surrounded by other towering peaks in the "autonomous region" of Tibet on the border with Nepal, must surely be the greatest lure for any moun-taineer visiting China. There are three different routes up its northern face: the north-east ridge, the west ridge or the north wall.

Xixabangma

Xixabangma, north-west of Mount Everest, is another of the world's great 8000m mountains, at 8012m/26,295ft, and known as the peak shrouded in secrets, because of the many crevasses and precipices concealed under its deep snow and changeable weather conditions that hamper any ascent.

Pamirs
Kongur,
Kongur Tiubie
Tagh

Kongur (7719m/25,334ft) and Kongur Tiubie Tagh (7595m/24,927ft) are among the mightiest peaks of the Pamir ranges in the west of China. The summit of Kongur is so steep it has so far remained unconquered by any climber.

Muztagata

Muztagata (7546m/24,766ft), also in the Pamirs, with its many glaciers and comparatively gentler slopes, is the mountain that lends itself best to skiing.

Siguniang

The southern flank of Siguniang (6250m/20,513ft), also in Tibet, is covered by a large glacier up to a height of 4000m/13,128ft. The remaining sides are steep and rocky.

Tanshan

Bogda Feng

The best way to enjoy the wonderful natural spectacle of Tianchi, the Lake of Heaven (1900m/6236ft), is to make the climb between June and Septem-ber of Bogda Feng (5445m/17,870ft), the mightiest peak in the Tianshan massif in the Autonomous Region of Xinjiang.

**Hengduan
Mountains**

Gonggashan

Majestic Gonggashan (7556m/24,800ft), surrounded by 20 sister peaks in Szechuan Province's Hengduan Mountains, is characterised by steep pre-cipices and numerous icefields.
    Watch out for avalanches!

Museums

The principal museums in the People's Republic of China, as well as Taiwan, Hong Kong and Macao, are covered in the A to Z section under the headings for where they are located.

Opening times,
admission

For opening times and admission charges you should check with your tour guide or at the CITS offices listed in the Information section.

Newspapers and Periodicals

Chinese
newspapers and
periodicals

The English-language official newspaper "China Daily" reports throughout the week on events in China and abroad, and also has the TV programmes and a "What's On in Beijing". Its weekly publications include "Beijing Weekend" and "Shanghai Star" and there are other official periodicals such as "Beijing Review" and "China Pictorial".

Foreign
newspapers and
magazines

The news stands of the international hotels in China's main cities sell several leading foreign newspapers and magazines such as the "Interna-tional Herald Tribune" as well as the "South China Morning Post" and the "Asian Wall Street Journal" published in Hong Kong.

Open Cities

The number of towns and cities in China open to foreign visitors is increasing all the time, and currently stands at over 888.

As a rule all that is needed to visit China's open areas is a valid visa (see Travel Documents), and the same applies to travel to these open places within China by rail, air or bus.

Special permit

If however you do decide to travel there by car independently – and some of the many reasons for not attempting this are listed under Motoring – you will also require a special permit for sightseeing in the open cities.

If you want to visit closed areas you require an Alien Travel Permit (Luxing Zheng) which has to be obtained from the Public Security Bureau. No special permit of this kind is required for the places covered in this guide since they all fall within the "open" category.

Alien
Travel Permit

Opening Times

See Business Hours

Photography

See Chinese Society and the Visitor, also Golden Rules, page 574

Post

Direction générale des postes
du Ministère des postes et télécommunications
Case Postale
100804 Beijing, People's Republic of China

Information

Post offices are open daily, except on public holidays (see entry), from 8am to 6pm.

Opening Hours

Stamps can only be bought from post offices or sub-offices in some hotels.

Stamps

Letterboxes are usually dark green. Posting mail in letterboxes with a yellow top will ensure that it arrives more quickly.

Letterboxes

Overseas:
Airmail letters to Europe take up to a week and cost 2 yuan. Postcards are 1.60 yuan.

Postal rates

Within China:
Letters sent surface mail cost 10 fen within the same city and 20 fen to destinations elsewhere. Airmail inside the country costs 30 fen. There is also an express service for mail within China.

The rate for small packets depends on the weight and whether they are sent by air or surface mail.

The larger tourist hotels have their own post offices where you can send letters, telegrams and small packets both within China and overseas. Many have fax and telex facilities as well.

Post offices
in hotels

Public Holidays and Festivals

Since Chinese society has for centuries revolved around farming its calendar for thousands of years depended more on the phases of the moon than the sun. Because the twelve lunar months only cover 354 days – 11 and a quarter days fewer than the solar calendar – extra months used to be added at regular intervals. The Gregorian Calendar introduced in 1912 determines the dates of the political and international public holidays but the timing of the traditional popular festivals continues to be governed by the old farming calendar and consequently they have no fixed dates.

Official Public Holidays (Gregorian calendar)

January 1st	New Year's Day (yuán-dàn)
March 8th	International Women's Day
May 1st	Labour Day (wǔyī)
May 4th	Youth Day (commemorating May 4th 1919)
June 1st	Children's Day
July 1st	Chinese Communist Party Founding Day (July 1st 1927)
August 1st	Founding Day of the People's Liberation Army (August 1st 1927)
October 1st	National Day: founding of the People's Republic of China (October 1st 1949)

Traditional Festivals (lunar calendar)

Chinese people everywhere still celebrate their traditional festivals according to the old lunar calendar.

Spring Festival
(chūn jié)

The lunar New Year is ushered in by the Spring Festival, China's most important family holiday. This usually lasts for at least three days and the time off study or work is used by most Chinese to visit family in their home town.

This Chinese New Year according to the lunar calendar usually falls between the end of January and mid-February and is the occasion for much celebration within the family circle. All preparations must be complete by the eve of the festival, homes spring cleaned, new clothes bought and debts settled. At midnight fireworks and firecrackers are let off to welcome the New Year, and in the days that follow friends and relations visit one another and exchange presents and greetings. Grand festive meals are prepared in people's homes and these have to last until the end of the festivities since the days should be given over to pleasure and relaxation. Dragon and lion-dancing carries on in the streets and brightly coloured pictures, usually of the two house-gods Qin Qiong and Yu Chigong, festoon doorways and houses are draped with red banners inscribed with new year's greetings made specially for the occasion.

During the festival most services come to a halt and the number of people travelling makes getting about the country very difficult.

Lantern Festival
(yuánxiāo jié)
1994: 24.2

The Lantern Festival, which used to signal the end of the New Year celebrations, is celebrated on the 15th day of the first lunar month, but is not a public holiday. It owes its origins to the tradition, still carried on today, of having a wonderful display of lanterns on this day. In north-western China lanterns are made from snow and ice which are truly spectacular when lit from within (see Events). The speciality eaten at this time, from which the festival gets its Chinese name "yuán-xiao", is delicious riceballs stuffed with sugar and nuts.

Dragon Boat Festival
(duánwǔjié)

The Dragon Boat Festival heralding the arrival of summer is celebrated on the fifth day of the fifth lunar month, around the end of May, and again is not a public holiday. It is dedicated to the dragon, symbolising the bringer of rain to whom the farmers turn for help at times of drought; the dragon is also supposed to drive out the evil spirits from the river in which the revered statesman and poet Qu Yuan was drowned long ago by those who plotted against him, since when Qu has been venerated by the Chinese people as a figure symbolising human dignity and honour. Dragon boat races are staged every year to commemorate this event, which is accompanied by the eating of "zongzi", sweet rice cakes wrapped in bamboo leaves.

The Moon Festival, also known as the mid-autumn festival, is always celebrated in various parts of the country on the 15th day of the eighth month of lunar calendar and is a time when family gatherings eat "moon cakes", with rich fillings of ground sesame and lotus seeds or dates.

Moon Festival (mid-autumn festival; chóng-yáng-jié)

In Wuxi in Jiangsu Province the inhabitants admire the reflection of the full moon in Lake Taihu and enjoy all kinds of entertainments, while local specialities are served on board pleasure boats and there are firework displays.

The festival honouring ancestors, the day of purity and light, usually falls in early April. People in the rural areas traditionally sweep the graves of their ancestors, making them offerings of food and drink and burning paper creations.

Festival of the ancestors (quingming)

There are many other popular festivals based on the ancient legends that have been handed down from generation to generation. These and the other major festivals are covered in greater detail in the section on Events.

Other popular festivals

China's many national minorities have retained their own original traditions and festivals.

Festivals of the national minorities

These too are based on the lunar calendar.

Every year around the middle of April (usually between the 13th and 15th) the Dai peoples in the autonomous district of Xishuangbanna in Yunnan Province hold the water festival to wash away the dirt, sorrows and demons of the old year. During the three days of festivities they hold dragon boat races and a market. Everyone gets splashed with water, a ritual that even foreign visitors cannot escape; in fact, the wetter you get, the better luck you will have in the coming year.

Water festival

The Tibetans celebrate their bathing festival in seven clear starlit nights between late summer and early autumn. They stage games and bathe in the river.

Bathing festival

See also Events

Public Transport (local)

China has a good local public transport network.

Bicycles are one of China's main means of transport (see entry).

Bicycles

See entry

Rickshaws

See entry

Taxis

See Taxis

Minibuses

Buses and trams run for short distances over the main routes in the cities (see also Buses). They are usually overcrowded, very slow and to be avoided at all costs during the rush hour. Fares are based on distance.

Buses, trams

Beijing and Shanghai have their own underground railway systems, and another metro is under construction in Canton. These subway trains are faster and much less crowded than the other forms of local transport and signs at the stations are written in Pinyin as well as Chinese; the name of

Metros in Beijing, Canton and Shanghai

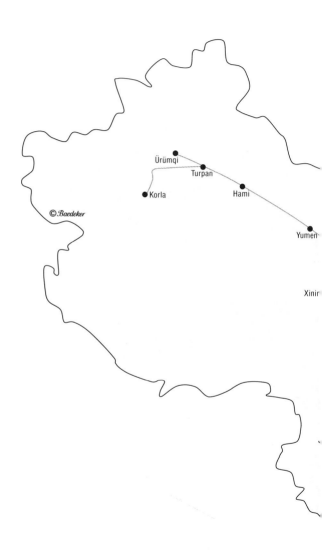

Ürümqi

Turpan

Korla

Hami

Yumen

Xinir

©Baedeker

the next station will be announced over the loudspeaker. There is just the one fare irrespective of distance.

See also Trains, Air Transport, Shipping

Radio and Television

Radio Beijing, Domestic Scene

Radio Beijing Domestic Scene is a programme for foreigners in Beijing which broadcasts news, sport and weather, as well as reporting on various aspects of China. It goes out in English on 1251 kHz medium wave from 1 to 3pm and 11pm to midnight and between 4 and 6am, and on FM on 91.55 MHz (for further information call 801 31 35 in Beijing).

Television

China's state-run television CCTV (China Central Television) transmits a number of news and weather reports in English, and some of the big hotels have satellite TV which can pick up English-language broadcasts such as those by CNN.

Railways

A journey by train is one of those unique experiences that no visitor to China should miss. The slow pace will give you as a foreigner a real chance to absorb the scenery and to get to know the people. There are special trains for tourists between the main cities open to tourism, and overseas groups can ask for additional carriages to be attached.

Rail network

China's rail network covers every part of the country except Tibet. The first line to be electrified was the western section of the Baocheng line which connects Shaanxi Province with south-western China and crosses the Longhai line running through the province.

Trains

Chinese trains usually run to time and there are express and special express trains, for which you pay a supplement, as well as the slower regular services – the lower the train number the faster the train. Air-conditioned trains run between Beijing and Shanghai and between Canton and Hong Kong.

Dining cars

Most express trains have dining cars where the Chinese food is usually preferable to other dishes. Dining car attendants bring round flasks of hot water and will sell you small packets of green tea.

Seats and sleepers

Instead of different classes the carriages have different kinds of seats and sleepers. "Ruanzuo" are soft seats, and carriages with these are more comfortable and less crowded than those with "yingzuo" or hard seats, although these are worth trying for shorter trips. "Ruanwo" are soft sleepers, with four bunks in an enclosed compartment. These can be booked with the sleeping-car attendant, if still available, and are twice as expensive as "yingwo" or hard sleepers, doorless compartments with six bunks in three tiers.

Soft seats and soft sleepers are usually the province of foreigners and high-ranking party officials and army officers who can afford the greater comfort, cleanliness and privacy. If you want to make closer contact with ordinary Chinese people then opt for hard seats and hard sleepers since this is what the vast majority of the population use.

Tickets

Tickets should definitely be bought several days in advance. Reservations can be made and tickets bought at CITS offices or you can get them from the normal station ticket counters – be prepared to push and do not expect to have to apologise – and from special Chinese Railways ticket offices for foreigners at the larger rail stations as well as ticket offices in the centre of town. Prices vary according to train speed and the kind of seat or sleeper, but in any case foreigners have to pay much more for their tickets than the Chinese.

Tel. (010) 512 89 31

Beijing station infoline

Railway timetables are published in English and Chinese. The English version can be bought in Hong Kong and at the ticket office for foreigners in Beijing.

Railway timetable

Beijing–Shanghai: 17 hrs; Beijing–Hangzhou 28 hrs; Beijing–Harbin 17 hrs; Beijing–Qiqihar 17 hrs; Beijing–Hohhot 14 hrs; Beijing–Tianjin 2 hrs; Beijing–Jilin 22hrs
Canton–Beijing 35 hrs; Canton–Shijiazhuang 32 hrs; Canton–Zhengzhou 30 hrs; Canton–Wuhan 22 hrs; Canton–Wuchang 21 hrs; Canton–Shanghai 32 hrs; Canton–Hangzhou 36 hrs; Canton–Fuzhou 35 hrs; Canton–Guilin 18 hrs; Canton–Liuzhou 22 hrs; Canton–Nanning 26 hrs; Canton–Xi'an 43 hrs; Canton–Changsha 14 hrs
Shanghai–Qingdao 24 hrs; Shanghai–Nanjing 4 to 5 hrs; Shanghai–Hangzhou 3 hrs
Xi'an–Xining 21 hrs; Xi'an–Ürümqi 62 hrs

Journey times

Passengers making the rail journey from Hong Kong to Beijing currently have to change trains at Canton but it is planned to have a direct rail link in place covering the 2200km/1367 miles between the two cities by 1996.

Beijing–Hong Kong

The luxury tourist train the Silk Road Express, with air-conditioned coaches, sleeping cars and dining car serving Chinese and European food, runs at irregular intervals on the over 3000km/1864 mile stretch between Xi'an and Alataw Shankou. Information can be obtained from the rail travel office in Lanzhou. For further information about rail travel such as the Trans-Siberian railway see Getting to China.

Silk Road Express

Restaurants

The following list gives the most acclaimed restaurants but not those in the major hotels (see Hotels). These are usually also very good and serve international, Far Eastern and European food as well as China's various regional specialities.

The opening times of the State-run restaurants reflect the rhythm of life in China, opening up as early as 5.30am and closing at about 7 or 8pm with a break between 9 and 10.30 in the morning and again between 1 and 4.30 in the afternoon. Other places keep to the usual international opening hours. The popular hot food stalls are open virtually round the clock.
    Around street markets you will find vendors selling all kinds of delicacies.

Opening times

See also Food and Drink, Tipping

Area codes for the places listed below are given in the margin in brackets.

Peking Duck:
Beijing Kaoya Dian, Tuanjie Hu Beikou; tel. 507 30 12
    Friendly restaurant with many foreigners among its regular customers; excellent duck and a superb selection of other dishes
★Quanjude Kaoya Dian, 32 Qianmen Dajie; tel. 511 24 18
    Beijing's best Peking duck restaurant; great atmosphere and lavish preparation of the duck over a wood fire; Imperial menu of 168 courses served (six meals over three days)

Beijing (Peking) (010)

557

Cuisine of the Imperial Court:

★Fangshan Restaurant, Beihai Gongyuan Park; tel. 401 18 89/401 18 79

The best known restaurant in China, situated in a former Imperial summer residence on the edge of the North Lake; authentic palace cuisine presented with truly remarkable skill; the taste of the dishes however may not always appeal today; when making a reservation – essential in the evening – a price limit is agreed and the kitchen creates a menu accordingly; parties only, minimum of eight persons; quite reasonably priced lunches are also served

Tingliguan, Summer Palace; tel. 258 16 08

With its lovely setting, classical architecture and well-chosen menu – a culinary cross-section of dishes from the various regions of China but with the focus firmly on Imperial cuisine – this restaurant in the "Pavilion for Listening to Orioles" is particularly popular with foreigners; caters principally for groups (the independent customer must expect a lengthy wait, even supposing a place can be obtained at all)

Cantonese:

Dasanyuan Restaurant, 50 Jingshan Xi Jie; tel, 401 81 83

Specialities: tortoise and snake meat, Dongjiang chicken, sucking pig; reasonably priced dim sum breakfast

Summer Palace, China World Hotel, 1 Jianguomenwai Dajie;
tel. 505 22 66–34

Beijing's leading Cantonese restaurant, Chinese cuisine at its very best

Windows on the World, CITIC Bldg., 19 Jianguomenwai Dajie;
tel. 500 22 55/500 28 28

Another favourite among foreigners; music, splendid view, excellent food and faultless service; choice of Cantonese starters (dim sum) followed by Peking duck highly recommended

Muslim:

Hongbinlou Restaurant (Hongbinlou Fanzhang) 82, Xi Chang'an Jie;
tel. 603 84 60

Long-established restaurant, refurbished; renowned for its lamb dishes, Mongolian hotpot, seafood and Peking duck, the latter excellent value

Sichuan:

★Sichuan Restaurant (Sichuan Fandian), 51 Xi Rongxian Hutong;
tel. 65 63 48

Beijing's best known Sichuan restaurant; classical Peking architecture, all the rooms (apart from those in the new wing) being off what were once residential courtyards; simple fare in the front rooms, in the rear rooms the service and furnishings are better, the prices higher and there are more foreigners; the smoked duck, hot bean quark dishes and braised aubergines are especially to be recommended

Ritan Fanzhuang, south-west corner of Ritan Park; tel. 500 49 84

Large restaurant in buildings of traditional design set around a pretty courtyard (al fresco service in summer); parties of 20 to 30 catered for in lavishly and imaginatively decorated private rooms; reasonably priced lunches in café adjoining

Sichuan Donhua, Guangqumenwai; tel. 771 26 72

Smaller parties well catered for; ideal also for larger groups, with meals served in stylishly decorated rooms on the first floor; such heights of epicurean pleasure are seldom found at this price

Sichuan Hometown, Jianguomenwai Yong'an Xili; tel. 502 24 91

Typical private restaurant: plain, wholesome food, foreign customers, good value; al fresco service under the trees in summer

Yuen Tai, Hotel Great Wall Sheraton, Donghuan Bei Lu;
tel. 500 55 66/500 21 62

Excellent restaurant, fine vista; classical Chinese musical evenings (very atmospheric)

Tang:
Tang Cuisine, 4 Yong'an Lu; tel. 301 21 98
   Choose between Tang cooking – everything from camel hoof soup to "drunk under the blossom" – or delicious stuffed pastry pouches; the ground floor represents good value

Hunan:
Makai Canting, 33 Di'anmenwai Dajie; tel. 404 48 89
   Spicy-hot sweet and spicy-hot sour sauces are typical of Hunan cooking (dog meat dishes even more so); view of the Drum Tower from the upper floor

Manchu:
Sunflower Village Food Street, 51 Wanquanhe Lu; tel. 256 29 67
   Courtyard rooms in several of which customers are seated on kangs (traditional heated sleeping platforms); tasty country food – plenty of maize, some unusual ingredients e.g. silkworms, and herbs served as a vegetable

Vegetarian:
Gongdelin Restaurant (Gongdelin Sucai Guan), 158 Qianmen Dajie;
   tel. 702 08 67
   Beijing's oldest and most celebrated vegetarian restaurant; best food on the upper floor

Foreign:
Justine's, Jianguo Hotel, 5 Jianguomenwai; tel. 500 22 33/500 80 39
   French restaurant; fine cuisine and pleasant ambience; has long been the first choice among Beijing's expatriate Europeans – a fact reflected in the prices
Kyotaru, Capital Hotel, 3 Qiamendong Dajie; tel. 512 99 88/512 77 77
   Japanese restaurant; highly thought of by Beijing's foreign community – not only the Japanese – on account of the excellence of the food and delightful atmosphere; the lunchtime teishoku (platter) is relatively affordable
La Fleur, China World Hotel, 1 Jaingguomenwai Dajie;
   tel. 505 22 66/505 66 97
   Popular French restaurant in the China World Hotel; exquisite food in elegant surroundings; expensive in the evenings, more reasonable at midday
Metro Cafe, 6 Gonggrentiyuchang Xilu; tel. 5691 78 18
   Small Italian restaurant; informal atmosphere and good food, including home-made pasta and truly delicious tiramisu
Shan Fu, Deshengmenxi Dajie, Huitong; tel. 618 03 62
   Unusually situated on a man-made hill beside Lake Jishuitan; discreet, modern interior; excellent Korean cooking, also Chinese dishes and Mongolian hotpot
Symphonie, Kempinski Hotel, 50 Liangmaqiao Lu; tel. 465 33 88/465 41 56
   European and international delicacies to a background of violin and harp music; specialises in everything expensive e.g. caviar

Banxi Jiujia, 151 Longjin Xi Lu; tel. 881 57 18
   Canton's largest, most famous and most imposing restaurant (20 different outlets) built out into Lake Liwan; classical surroundings in park; many regular customers; especially tasty dim sum served in the mornings

Canton (Guangzhou) (020)

Beiyuan Jiujia, 202 Xiao Bei Lu; tel. 333 00 87
Datong Jiujia, 63 Yanjiang Yi Lu; tel. 888 89 88
   Multi-storey restaurant with river view
Guangzhou Jiujia, 2 Wenchang Nan Lu; tel. 888 38 88
Nanyuan Jiujia, 142 Qianjin Lu; tel. 444 92 11
Shewang Man Haixian Jiulou, 41 Jianglan Lu; tel. 888 44 98
   Snake meat restaurant

Restaurants

Tsai-Ken-Hsiang Vegetarian Restaurant (Caigenxiang Shiguan), 167 Zhongshan Liu Lu; tel. 88 68 35
Good, varied vegetarian cooking

Chengdu
(028)

Chen Mapo Doufu, Jiefang Lu Erduan; tel. 333 16 36
Has served traditional hot doufu for more than 100 years
Longchaoshu, Chunxi Lu Nandian; tel. 662 69 47
Very reasonably priced snacks (ground floor) and live classical music (second floor)
Shufengyuan, 153 Dong Dajie; tel. 662 76 28
Beautiful old Chinese décor and the finest Sichuan cooking
Zhong Shuijiao, 7 Tidu Jie; tel. 667 34 02
Established 1893; delicious hongyoujiao (pastry pouches) and other reasonably priced snacks

Fuzhou
(0591)

Juchunyuan, 130 Bayiqi Bei Lu; tel. 55 30 38
Fotianqiang stew made from, among other things, sharks fins, doves eggs and various kinds of fish, is said to have originated here; traces its history back to 1877

Hangzhou
(Hangchow)
(0571)

Louwailou Restaurant (Louwailou Jiujia), 30 Waixihu, Gushan Island; tel. 702 54 63
Established 1849; beautiful lake view

Kunming
(0871)

Guaqiao Mixian Guan, Nantong Jie
"Over the Bridge Noodles" served in a strong broth, one of the region's best-known specialities, can be enjoyed here

Nanjing
(Nanking)
(025)

Capital Recreation Club, Hunan Lu/Gaoyunling
New restaurant with live classical music

Shanghai
(021)

Canglangting Restaurant (Canglangting Dianxin Dian), 9 Chongqing Nan Lu; tel. 328 38 76
Meilongzhen Restaurant (Meilongzhen Jiujia), No. 22, 1081 Nanjing Xi Lu; tel. 253 53 53
Always busy, three-storeyed restaurant in the city centre, famous since 1938 for its Sichuan cooking with touches of Shanghai
Meiweizhai Restaurant (Meiweizhai), 600 Fuzhou Lu; tel. 322 17 05
Meixin Restaurant (Meixin Fandian), 314 Shaanxi Nan Lu; tel. 437 39 91
Old Shanghai Restaurant (Shanghai Lao Fandian), 242 Fuyou Lu
Country-style restaurant in the Old City, established 1862; serves reasonably priced snacks
Xinhualou Restaurant (Xinhualou), 343 Fuzhou Lu; tel. 328 27 47
Yanyulou Restaurant (Yanyulou), 755 Nanjing Dong Lu; tel. 322 32 98
Yangzhou Restaurant, 308 Nanjing Dong Lu; tel. 322 28 73
Specialises in mild Yangzhou cooking

Shantou
(0754)

Shantou Diet Service Co. (Shantou Shi Yinshi Fuwu Gongsi), 16 Nei Malu; tel. 27 51 91

Shenyang
(024)

Laobian Dumpling Restaurant (Laobian Jiaozi Guan), Shifu Da Lu; tel. 44 79 41/44 79 46

Shenzhen
(0755)

Friendship Fast Restaurant (Youyi Kuai Canting), 206 Catering Services Co., 156 Shennan Dong Lu; tel. 25 41 70/25 41 73
Huayuan Seafood Restaurant (Huayuan Haixian Jiujia), 68 Renmin Nan Lu; tel. 23 98 13
Shanzhenlou Restaurant (Shanzhenlou Jiujia), 141 Jiefang Lu; tel. 22 83 81/22 37 60
Jincheng Lounge Folk Song Restaurant (Jincheng Jiulang Minge Canting), G/F Blk 1 Jincheng Bldg., 1 Shennan Dong Lu; tel. 22 04 83/90 18 88
Xilingmen Restaurant (Xilingmen Jiujia), 32 Dongmen Zhong Lu; tel. 22 31 84

Songhelou Restaurant (Songhelou Caiguan), 141 Guanqian Jie; **Suzhou**
  tel. 22 79 28 **(Soochow)**
    The Emperor of China himself enjoyed the speciality of the house – sweet **(0512)**
and sour Mandarin fish – here in 1737
Xinjufeng Restaurant (Xinjufeng Caiguan), 615 Renmin Lu; tel. 77 37 94

Chuansu Restaurant (Chuansu Caiguan), 189 Changchun Dao, Hepingqu; **Tianjin**
  tel. 70 51 42 **(022)**
Dengyinglou Restaurant (Dengyinglou Fandian), 94 Binjiang Dao,
  Hepingqu; tel. 70 20 70/70 20 71
Goubouli Baozipu, 77 Shandong Lu
  Goubouli pastry pouches, a Tianjin speciality, originated here
Tianjin Roast Duck Restaurant (Tianjin Kaoya Dian), 146 Liaoning Lu;
  tel. 70 26 60
Yanchunlou Restaurant (Yanchunlou Fanzhuang), 46 Rongji Jie, Hepingqu;
  tel. 75 27 61
Yuelaihai Restaurant (Yuelaihai Canting), 59 Nanjing Lu; tel. 3 90 91
  Popular restaurant serving good Cantonese food

Furong Restaurant (Furong Jiulou), 1041 Zhongshan Dadao, Hankou; **Wuhan**
  tel. 2 17 96 **(027)**
Laotongcheng Restaurant (Laotongcheng Jiulou), 1 Dazhi Lu, Hankou;
  tel. 21 18 43
  Old-established restaurant; doufu with three ingredients a speciality
Sihimei, 898 Zhongshan Dadao, Hankou; tel. 21 18 43
  Good snacks and light meals

China Restaurant (Zhongguo Fandian), Tongyun Lu **Wuxi**
Jiangnan Restaurant (Jiangnan Fandian), 435 Zhongshan Lu **(0510)**

Defachang, at the Bell Tower **Xi'an**
  Specialises in every variety of stuffed pastry pouches, also mijiu rice **(029)**
wine; mouth-watering menus on the upper floor (individual customers
welcome as well as groups)
Xi'an Restaurant (Xi'an Fandian), 289 Dong Dajie; tel. 2 20 37
Wuji Restaurant (Wuji Fandian), 381 Dong Dajie; tel. 2 38 42

Gongbei Maxim's Restaurant (Gongbei Meixin Canting), 6 Lianhua Lu; **Zhuhai**
  tel. 88 52 09/88 52 11 **(0756)**

Rickshaws

Nowadays rickshaws (sānlúnchē) are more strictly speaking "pedicabs"
with passengers in covered seats pulled along by someone pedalling a
bicycle rather than running between the shafts.
   If you're not in too much of a hurry pedicabs are a good way to go
sightseeing but agree on the fare beforehand if you want to avoid an
argument at the other end.
   All rickshaw are numbered and carry a licence plate showing their number. A quicker way of getting about is by motorised rickshaw, with a
motorbike engine powering an enclosed three-wheeler and sometimes
with carrying platforms at the back.

River Boats

See Shipping

Security

See Insurance

Shipping and River Boats

Coastal shipping

There are many shipping services which ply the busy lanes between the main ports on China's east coast.

From Shanghai they run north to places such as Qingdao, Yantai, Tianjin and Dalian, and south to Ningbo, Wenzhou, Fuzhou, Xiamen, Shantou and Canton as well as Taiwan and Hong Kong. From Canton you can cross by boat to the island of Hainan (see Beaches).

Ferries and hovercraft on regular services run out of Hong Kong to destinations which include Shantou, Zhanjiang, Shanmei and Rongqi on the south China coast.

Inland boating

On the Li River

One of the highlights of a visit to China is the 83km/52 mile boat trip on the Li River from Guilin to Yangzhuo. The tourist boats travel through lovely karst scenery, passing the many fantastically shaped peaks, some of them wreathed in cloud, arising from a shimmering grey and green fairytale landscape dotted with fishing villages, paddy fields and the occasional grazing water buffalo, while as evening falls you can watch the captive cormorants diving for fish from the lamplit bamboo rafts drifting past.

On the Yangtze (Changjiang)

China's greatest river, the Yangtze (Changjiang) and at over 6000km/3728 miles the world's third longest, rises in Tibet and flows into the Yellow Sea just north of Shanghai. Chongqing in Sichuan Province is the starting point for regular cargo and passenger riverboat services down to Wuhan and on to Shanghai, although the trips outlined below could change with the completion of the hydro-power project announced in 1992. This will involve the construction of a 600km/373 mile long reservoir between Chongqing and Yichang and a 185m/610ft dam at Sandouping near Yichang, so check with CITS beforehand for the latest situation.

Three Gorges

The most exciting and impressive trip on the Yangtze is the cruise between Baidicheng (White King Town) and the Nanjin Pass through the legendary San Xia, the river's Three Gorges (Qutang Xia, Wu Xia and Xiling Xia), now even more awesome as they have been made steeper, with the possibility of a detour in smaller boats into the gorges of its tributary the Daninghe. Once through the gorges the river broadens out and its banks are lined with orange groves and tea plantations as the river journey carries on through Wuhan to Nanjing and eventually Shanghai. You can travel either on the normal passenger boats used by the Chinese, which are usually quite crowded and have second, third, fourth and fifth class accommodation, but no first class, or join a package tour on one of the dozen or so luxury chartered cruise ships for foreigners. These have all the facilities of a hotel, including restaurant, bar, swimming pool, shop and laundry service, and the five-day trip allows for sightseeing visits on shore.

On the Huangpu

A good way to see Shanghai from the water is to make the trip round the harbour on the Huangpu River.

On Lake Taihu and the Grand Canal

Another popular boat trip is on Lake Taihu, one of China's largest freshwater lakes with many islands, gardens, pagodas and lookout points, and Da Yunhe, the Grand (or Imperial) Canal, the longest canal in use and the world's first. This links Hangzhou, 160km/99 miles south-west of Shanghai, with Beijing and takes you past fertile fields and under centuries-old bridges. The journey from Wuxi to Suzhou, "Venice of the East" and famous for its canals and gardens, takes four hours.

Sightseeing boats also ply the waters of Hangzhou's West Lake.

On the West Lake (Xi Hu)

A trip on the Yellow River, the Huanghe, "mother of the Chinese nation", from the Sanmenxia dam to Ruicheng 120km/75 miles distant, affords magnificent views of this great river from which you can see into deep gorges and look out over placid lakes on either side. It is possible to travel by hovercraft to the foot of Mangshan mountain.

On the Yellow River (Huanghe)

Old-fashioned bamboo rafts and rowing boats take visitors on the winding waters of the Jiuqu as it snakes through the scenery of northern Fujian's Wuyishan mountains, with their many bizarre rock formations towering over the river.

On the Jiuqu

Riverboats also travel on the Xijiang from Canton to Wuzhou.

On the Xijiang

Further details and bookings can be had from the CITS (see Information) or other travel agents who specialise in China travel; tickets can also be bought locally at the shipping company offices.

Information, bookings

A boat ticket is three times more expensive for foreigners than for the Chinese.

Ticket prices

See Getting to China

Cruises, Cargo boats

Shopping and Souvenirs

China's economic reforms and open door policy have laid the foundations for greater market freedom and growing privatisation in the past few years. There are still the state-run shops and department stores but these face increasing competition from the many small businesses that have sprung up free from the constraints of central control.

The best place to get local arts and crafts and other typical Chinese products are the state-run Friendship Stores (youyi shangdian) found in all the major cities. The main store in Beijing and its branches in Shanghai and Canton offer a particularly wide variety of items ranging from silk, porcelain, tea, and traditional Chinese remedies to furniture and carpets, as well as foodstuffs and consumer goods imported from the West.

Friendship Stores

The Arts and Crafts department stores specialise in offering for sale the work of local craftspeople.

Arts and Crafts Stores

The small hotel shops carry more or less everything a foreign tourist is likely to need.

Hotel shops

It is still possible to purchase genuine antiques in some cities (see Antiques).

Antique shops

A great many shops specialise in particular items such as tea, calligraphy and artists' materials, paper-cuts, and products typical of the place or the region such as articles from bamboo or woven straw.

Speciality shops

See entry

Business Hours

Shopping in China's major cities

The big shopping streets provide the best choice, but you should also take a look at what the stores in the smaller side streets have to offer.

Shopping and Souvenirs

The main shops in the big cities listed below give some indication of the different tastes and requirements they cater for as well as the typical products of their particular region.

Beijing (Peking)

China's capital offers a broad range of goods for sale, from the particularly well-stocked Friendship Store at 21 Jianguomenwai Dajie to the busy shopping streets of Chang'an Jie, Wangfujing, Xidan and Dongdan and Underground City, a former air-raid shelter full of many small shops. The best silk is to be found near Qianmen (the Front Gate) at 5 Dazhalan Huton and in the department store north of the Temple of Heaven; Dazhalan Hutong also has Tongrentang at no. 24, famous for centuries for its herbal medicines. For furniture try Dongsi Bei or Nan Dajie. Lovers of the Beijing Opera and their magnificent costumes should make their way to the Arts and Crafts Store Trust Company in Chongwenmennei.

Liulichang, the street south-west of Qianmen, holds several shops specialising in antiques and objets d'art. For household goods of all kinds and presents, including cloisonné enamelwares, a Beijing speciality, try the various Arts and Crafts Stores and the Marco Polo Shop at 10 Jianguomenwai Dajie.

Other very popular stores include the Beijing branch of the Japanese Yaohan chain, selling international wares on several floors, and the Friendship Store in the Beijing Lufthansa Center in the north-east of the city.

Canton (Guangzhou)

The cosmopolitan city of Canton has an enormous market where you can buy just about anything, including foreign goods, and which is particularly famous for its oddities. In any event try to get to the Qingping market in Qingping Lu which sells an amazing quantity of products such as bonzai trees, very fine ones but relatively inexpensive.

Canton's main shopping streets are Bijing Lu, Zongshan Lu and Jiefang Lu; the Friendship Store, one of China's best, is at 368 Huanshi Dong Lu. For antiques look for the Guangdong Antique Store at 575 Hongshu Bei Lu in the Bright Filial Piety Temple complex (Guangxiao Si) and the Guangdong Antique Shop at 170 Wende Bei Lu. Finally, there is also the Jiangnan Product Store at 399 Zhongshan Lu, where you can buy articles of bamboo and woven straw, and the shop inside the White Swan Hotel at 1 Nan Jie Shamian which has a big selection of arts and crafts.

Chengdu

Chengdu is famous for its brocade and has many little markets selling painted fans and artworks on silk, including those on Chunxi Lu, the main shopping street, which also has a shop for musical instruments, the famous apothecary Deretang at no. 22, and the Friendship Store. The Exhibition Hall (Zhanlanguan Menshibu) in Renmin Lu has many kinds of traditional arts and crafts for sale. The very well-stocked Sichuan Antique Store north of Chunxi Lu in the Shaocheng Lukou, Shudu Dadao. is the place to find antiques.

Dali

Typical local products of Dali, north-west of Kunming, include the marble for which it is famous, batiks hand-made by the region's ethnic minorities but also mass-produced locally, and Tibetan-style goods sold on the streets. It is worth paying a visit to the market at Shapin, not far from Dali, where the traders from the surrounding district assemble on Mondays to sell their colourful wares.

Guilin

Guilin, which has developed into a major centre for Chinese and foreign tourism, has nothing special in the shopping line but you may find it worthwhile taking a look around the Guilin Antique Store at 79 Zhongshan Zhong Lu and the neighbouring quarter.

Hangzhou

The silk painted parasols and Longjing Cha tea for which Hangzhou is famous make it a good place for a shopping expedition. The most interesting shops are the Friendship Store at 18 Hubin Lu, the Zhejiang Antique Store at 22 Huancheng Xi Lu and the Arts and Crafts Stores on Huancheng Lu and Zhongshan Zhonglu, where you can buy scissors, another well-known product of the city, and a great variety of traditional Chinese medicines.

Harbin is undoubtedly the country's main centre for Chinese furs and skins. These can be bought in the Fur Product Shop on Zhongyang Lu as well as in the Friendship Store at 93 Dong Dazhi.

Harbin

Famed for centuries for its high-quality porcelain which was sent abroad as well as supplying the Imperial Court, Jingdezhen today still makes porcelain and other ceramics. The porcelain museum on Fengling Lu documents the development of this very Chinese art and you can buy all kinds of modern china wares at the Jingdezhen People's Porcelain Factory (54 Fengling Lu; tel. 44 98) and in the Jingdezhen Porcelain Friendship Store (13 Zushan Lu; tel. 22 31).

Jingdezhen

On the far north-western border of China Kashgar, with its largely Muslim Uigur minority population, is renowned for its Central Asian bazaars. The biggest one, around Id Kah Square, is a colourful jumble of stalls selling the locally made headwear (embroidered skullcaps and furlined hats), ornate knives and fleecy boots at very reasonable prices.

Kashgar

You would expect Kunming as the capital of Yunnan province with its many minorities to have plenty of interesting and original wares for sale, but the city's shops rate quite poorly on this score. The Friendship Store is at 99 Dongfeng Lu and there are other shops around here selling local crafts but it is better to look around for some of the lovely embroidery on Jinbi Lu or do a deal with the women from the minorities who sell their bags and other colourful embroidered articles near the Kunming Hotel. The pharmacy on Zhengyi Lu has a vast range of original Chinese medicines.

Kunming

For the visitor stopping off in the Tibetan capital it is worth going to Baijiao Jie which is a focal point for local people here on pilgrimages, and it is possible to buy typical local products such as religious items, earrings, Tibetan boots, etc.

Lhasa

See Beijing

Peking

A shop not far from Qufu's Confucius Mansions (Kong Fu) sells craft wares and some interesting antiques.

Qufu

Much of the business life of Shanghai, China's most densely populated city, goes on in the famous street of Nanjing Lu, always thronged with people, leading west from the Bund (Zongshan Lu) for a couple of miles to the former French Concession. There are also good places to shop on the streets running parallel and across, such as Sichuan Lu or further south Jinling Lu and Huaihai Lu, which lie on the northern edge of the old town, the Yuyuan, itself crammed full of little shops. 118 Nanjing Dong Lu is worth recommending for its musical instruments, and the Caitongde pharmacy, behind the façade of no. 320, specialises in Chinese medicines. The Friendship Store on the Bund carries just about every kind of typically Chinese wares, including magnificent silks, handicrafts and works of art. Occasionally really fine pieces can be found in the antique shops at 694 Nanjing Xilu and 194/226 Guandong Lu.

Shanghai

Suzhou certainly deserves its reputation as China's leading silk producer, and the quarter around Guangian Lu is full of silk stores and workshops, where exquisite hand embroidery as well as silk by the yard is sold. The finest pieces can be seen at the Suzhou Embroidery Research Institute at 292 Jingde Lu (tel. 22 24 60 and 22 24 15). Renmin Lu holds the Suzhou Antique Store and the Arts and Crafts Store, while the Friendship Store is on Guanqian Jie.

Suzhou

Tianjin is famous for its kites, carpets and clay figurines. Most of the kites are made in a factory in Beijing but in Tianjin itself they can be bought in the Arts and Crafts Factory on Huanghe Dao, Nankaiqu. Carpets are on sale in

Tianjin

Number Three Carpet Factory at Hexi in the southern part of the city (tel. 817 12), which is also the location of a workshop making the clay figurines, available from 270 Machang Dao and the art gallery on Jiefang Lu.

Weifang

The little city of Weifang in Shandong Province is famous for kite-making and producing the posters used for the Chinese New Year festival. A kite museum established there a few years ago is a very good place to buy kites and to watch the people at work making them.

Wuxi

Like Suzhou and Hangzhou, Wuxi is one of China's major silk-producing centres. If you intend to buy silk, make your way to the shops around Dongfanghong Guanchang Square, and especially the Arts and Crafts Store at 192 Renmin Lu and the Friendship Store at 8 Zongshan Lu where you can also buy another local specialty, brightly painted clay figurines.

Xi'an

In Xi'an, the historic capital of the Middle Kingdom, as well as innumerable copies of the warriors of the famous terracotta army, available in every conceivable shape and size, there are also on sale lovely silk scrolls and the characteristic three-coloured porcelain of the Tang dynasty. The best places for shopping are the Arts and Crafts Stores on Nanxin Jie, Nan Dajie and Dong Dajie.

See also Antiques, Business Hours

Social Customs

See Chinese Society and the Visitor

Souvenirs

See Shopping and Souvenirs

Sport

National sports

By far the most popular sport in China is table tennis. Chinese players have dominated the world table tennis scene for many years, and foreign players nowadays often come to China to learn the finer points of the game. Other sports such as gymnastics, athletics, badminton, swimming, basketball and volleyball also have their followings, and football is fast gaining ground as a game in which women as well as men are already starting to excel.

Martial arts

There is a long tradition of the martial arts in China, where they take more than a hundred different forms. Dating back to several centuries B.C. and originally developed for self-defence, in the course of time these have become techniques for physical and spiritual relaxation.

Recent years have seen a growing interest abroad in the martial arts of Gongfu (kungfu as it used to be called, wushu in Chinese) and Shaolin, the form of unarmed combat developed by the monks of Shaolin Monastery. Younger people in particular prefer physical training in the more aggressive forms of this kind of sport, performed at high speed with jump kicks and lightning blows and using fists, fingers, and feet.

Gongfu and Taiji (shadow boxing) entail the exercise of mental as well as physical faculties with a view to strengthening the muscles and improving breathing and bodily tone, although Gongfu also uses weapons such as swords, staves, etc. and calls for greater speed of reaction and considerable agility.

In the early morning the Chinese streetscene includes people of all ages, on their own or in groups, preparing for their day's work with jogging, keepfit exercises or slow motion shadow boxing – performing the gently flowing arm and leg movements of Taijiquan, or Taiji as it's called in the West. This is regarded not as a sporting activity but as a form of exercise requiring inner peace and concentration which brings mind and body into one harmonious whole.

Shadow boxing (Taijiquan)

Aerobics are also popular, often to tape recorded music.

Aerobics

The number of sporting activities for foreign visitors to China is expanding, including trekking (see Mountain Trekking) in Tibet or other largely untouched mountain regions such as those of Guilin, hiking in Hong Kong and the New Territories, windsurfing and para-gliding in Guangdong, and skiing in the north-east of the country. Golf is still relatively undeveloped.

Sport for foreign visitors

Many Chinese cities put on courses where foreigners can learn or perfect their knowledge of the various martial arts.

A training camp has been set up near the Shaolin Monastery for Shaolin martial arts and here visitors can watch demonstrations of Shaolin and the hard form of Qigong.

Visitors can play tennis, billiards and table tennis in Beijing at the International Club on Ritanlu, west of the Friendship Store.

Sporting facilities in Beijing

Hotel Kempinski (see Hotels) has a fitness centre with a pool, sauna and solarium, and squash and tennis courts. There is also a 9–hole golf course next door.

Hotel Kempinski

The Olympic Village north of the city centre, 20km/12 miles west of Capital International Airport, was built in 1990 for the 11th Asian Games and has a hotel, apartment block, offices and shopping centre as well as all the sporting facilities. These include a football stadium, badminton and volleyball arena, international tennis centre, baseball and softball stadium, hockey stadium, indoor swimming pool, handball arena (Northern Suburbs' Arena) and a table tennis hall (Beijing Workers' Arena).

Olympic Village

Taxis

There are plenty of taxis in the major cities – over 120,000 in all – and these can be hired for longer trips as well as shorter journeys.

There are taxi ranks at airports, bus and rail stations and in front of Friendship Stores and tourist hotels as well as at the major places for sightseeing.

Ranks

Taxis can be booked at hotel reception desks or hailed in the street. You need to make allowance in the fare for the time spent waiting for the taxi to arrive.

Booking taxis

You would be well advised to take with you the name of your destination and your hotel written, or preferably printed, in Chinese script to show to your taxi driver. In Beijing for example the best course is to carry a map of the city in both English and Chinese with where you want to go marked by a cross.

Instructions to taxi drivers

If there is any doubt as to whether a taxi will be available to take you back from your destination you should ask the taxi to wait for you.

All taxis are equipped with meters. Fares are based on the comfort and type of the vehicle as well as on distance.

Fares

Telephone

Minibuses
One alternative to taxis are the minibuses which run on certain routes in the bigger cities or to nearby tourist sites. These can be more expensive, especially for foreigners, who are expected to haggle, but are relatively problem-free.

Other taxi services
In some places taxi services are replaced by rickshaws in the form of cycle-drawn or motorised pedicabs (see Rickshaws).

See also Public Transport

Telephone

You can make phone calls abroad in most of the large city hotels. Waiting times are not too long and the lines are usually quite good.
It is not always possible to dial direct to places within China even when a dialling code is given.

International dialling codes
China from abroad: dial the international code followed by 86 then the area code without the first 0 followed by the number required.

From China: 00 followed by the country code (Australia 61, Canada 1, Eire 353, New Zealand 64, South Africa 27, United Kingdom 44, United States 1).

Hong Kong from abroad: 852; from Hong Kong 001
Macao from abroad: 853; from Macao 001
Taiwan from abroad: 886; from Taiwan 002

Cardphones
Phonecards with values of 20, 50 or 100 yuan are available for use in cardphones.

Enquiries for China
In Beijing: tel. 114

International enquiries
In Beijing: tel. 116

Speaking clock
In Beijing: tel. 117

Time

Beijing time
The whole of China operates on Beijing Time which is Greenwich Mean Time plus eight hours.

Summer time
Summer time (GMT + nine hours) from mid April to mid September has been in force for some time, but there are indications that it may shortly be discontinued.

Tipping

Tipping is officially not allowed but it is becoming increasingly common in places which have been opened up to tourism, so use your discretion.
A more acceptable practice, especially in the smaller provincial cities, is to give some small gift such as stamps, books or photos as a souvenir of your home country.

Travel Documents

Visitors to China must have a valid passport, with at least six months before expiry after leaving China, and a visa. This can be obtained via a travel agent or direct from the Chinese embassy or consulate in your own country (see Diplomatic Representation). A passport photograph is required, as well as the fee and application form.

If you want to extend your visa you should apply to the local police at the Public Security Bureau.

Anyone travelling on, for example, the Trans-Siberian railway from Berlin to Moscow and Mongolia then on to Beijing (see Getting to China), will also require a visa (and three passport photographs) for the former Soviet Union; transit through Mongolia does not require a visa but you will need photographs (e.g. two for a stopover in Mongolia).

If you are visiting Hong Kong you can get a visa for China on supplying two passport photographs from the Travellers Hostel (Block A, 16th floor, Chungking Mansions, Tsimshatsui, Kowloon, Hong Kong; tel. 368 77 10/ 723 30 06), Guangdong (H.K.) Tours Company Ltd. (6 & 7F Guangdong Tours Building, 9–15 Yee Wo Street, Causeway Bay, Hong Kong; tel. 839 34 33) or the Visa Office of the Ministry of Foreign Affairs of the People's Republic of China (Lower Block, 5th floor, 26 Harbour Road, Wanchai, Hong Kong; tel. 827 95 69).

If you need the visa on the same day it will cost more.

Anyone wanting to go to Hainan Island can apply for a visa on arrival at Haikou Airport.

Animals may not be brought into China. | Pets

Trekking

See Mountain Trekking

When to Go

Because China is such a vast country it has a variety of different climate zones. The north and north-west have a dry continental climate while the weather in the centre and the south tends to be tropical, humid and rainy.

This means that temperatures can differ between north and south at the same time of year by as much as 20 degrees Centigrade.

Kunming in Yunnan Province has no summer at all and goes straight from spring into autumn. Canton and Nanning in the far south have no winter or spring but go immediately from autumn into summer. | Peculiarities of the south

The best times to visit China are spring and autumn when temperatures are quite even and the climate is moderate almost everywhere. | Spring and Autumn

Summer, from May to September, is very hot, and that applies roughly to the country as a whole; the weather is hot and humid with a little rain in both north and south, but southern China also gets the monsoon from June to August.

The winter climate in the centre and the south is usually relatively mild and never drops below freezing point, unlike the north and north-west which have clear skies, icy winds and mostly snow to follow. | Winter

The hot summer months call for light clothing and protection against the sun (sunglasses, etc.). In the south-west rainwear is needed and an umbrella to cope with the frequent downpours. | **Clothing**

Youth Accommodation

	January	February	March	April	May	June	July	August	September	October	November	December
Chengdu	5.6	7.6	12.1	17.0	21.1	23.7	25.8	25.1	21.4	16.7	12.0	7.3
Dalian	−5.3	−3.5	1.8	8.9	15.5	19.3	22.9	24.1	20.0	13.8	5.6	−1.5
Datong	−11.8	−7.9	−0.1	8.2	15.4	19.8	21.8	20.1	14.3	7.4	−1.7	−9.1
Fuzhou	10.4	101.6	13.4	18.1	22.2	25.3	28.7	28.2	26.0	21.6	17.8	13.
Guilin	8.0	9.0	13.1	18.4	223.1	26.2	28.3	27.8	25.8	20.7	15.2	10.1
Harbin	−19.7	−15.4	−5.1	6.1	14.3	20.0	22.7	21.4	14.3	5.9	−5.8	−15.5
Kanton	13.4	14.2	17.7	21.8	25.7	27.2	28.3	28.2	27.0	23.8	19.7	15.2
Kunming	7.8	9.8	13.2	16.7	19.3	19.5	19.9	19.2	17.6	15.0	11.5	8.3
Lanzhou	−7.3	−2.5	5.3	11.7	16.7	20.5	22.4	21.0	15.9	9.4	1.6	−5.7
Nanking	1.9	3.0	8.4	14.7	20.0	24.5	28.2	27.9	22.9	16.9	10.7	4.5
Peking	−4.7	−2.3	4.4	13.2	20.2	24.2	26.0	24.6	19.5	12.5	4.0	−2.8
Shanghai	3.3	4.6	8.3	13.8	18.8	23.2	27.9	27.8	23.8	17.9	23.5	6.2
Shenyang	−12.7	−8.6	−0.3	9.1	17.0	21.4	24.6	23.7	17.2	9.6	−0.3	−8.7
Tsingtau	−2.6	−0.5	4.6	10.9	16.7	20.9	24.7	25.4	20.5	14.3	7.4	0.5
Ürümqui	−10.6	−9.8	−3.8	2.7	8.4	12.9	14.7	13.5	8.6	1.9	−5.5	−8.7
Wuhan	2.8	5.0	10.0	16.0	21.3	25.8	29.0	28.5	23.6	17.5	11.2	5.3
Xiamen	12.6	12.5	14.9	19.0	23.2	26.0	28.3	28.3	27.0	23.2	19.7	15.2
Xi'an	−1.3	2.1	8.0	14.0	19.2	25.3	26.7	25.4	19.4	13.6	6.5	0.6

In winter the visitor will need very warm clothing in northern China for both day and night to keep out the wind and the cold. Elsewhere medium-weight clothes and an umbrella should suffice.

In spring and autumn be sure to take sweaters, jackets and possibly some form of rainwear.

Good footwear is essential at any time of year.

Laundry
Since hotels and the Yangtze cruise ships have a laundry service which will usually return your washing within 24 hours (laundry bags in your room/cabin) you need not take more with you than is absolutely necessary.

Weather
See Facts and Figures, Climate

Youth Accommodation

Information
In China
CYTS Tours Corporation, 23B Dong Ziao Min Xiang, Beijing; tel. (010) 51 27 70

In Hong Kong
Hong Kong Youth Hostels Association, Room 225–226, Block 19, Shek Kip Mei Estate, Shamshuipo, Kowloon, Hong Kong; tel. 788 16 38

In Taiwan
Chinese Taipei Youth Hostel Association, 12F–14, 50 Chung Hsiao W. Rd., Sec. 1, Taipei; tel. (02) 331 83 66

Kang Wen Culture & Education Foundation, Suite 502, 142 Chung Shiao E. Rd., Sec. 4, Taipei; tel. (02) 775 11 38

Federal Transportation Co., 8F, 61 Nanking East Rd., Sec. 3, Taipei; tel 507 81 33

Index

Accommodation 500
Agriculture 56
Air Transport 500
Airlines 500
Airports 500
  Connecting Flights 500
Amoy 458
Anhui 120
Anshan 121
  Surroundings 121
Antiques 501
Architecture 93
Art and Culture 84

Baotou 123
Bath Houses 501
Beaches 504
Behaviour, traditions and
  customs 507
Beidaihe 361
Beijing · Peking 124
  Further City Centre Sights
    135
  Further Sights in the
    Beijing area 154
  Imperial Palace
    (Gugong) 131
  Key sights in the City
    Centre 129
  Shopping Centre
    (Shangye Qu) 144
  Sights outside the City
    Centre 137
  Summer Palace
    (Yiyeyuan) 147
  Surroundings of
    Beijing 146
  Western Mountains 151
Bicycles 504
Buses 506
Business Hours 504

Calendar of Principal
  Events 512
Calligraphy 89
Canton · Guangzhou 159
  Sights 160
  Surroundings 167
Car Rental 506
Celebrations 103
Changbaishan Nature
  Reserve (Changbaishan
  Ziran Baohuqu) 287
Changchun 167
  Surroundings 168

Changjiang · Yangtse
  River 169
  Witches Gorge 172
Changsha 173
  Surroundings 176
Changzhou 176
  Sights 177
Chemists 506
Chengde 179
Chengdu 182
  Sights 183
  Surroundings 187
China From A to Z 120
China in Quotations 108
Chinese Deities 47
Chinese Representation
  Abroad 510
Chinese Society and the
  Visitor 507
Chinghai 359
Chongqing 191
  Sights 194
  Surroundings 195
Climate 22
Communications 59
Currency 508
Customs Regulations 508

Dali 196
  Sights 197
  Surroundings 197
Dalian 199
  Sights 202
  Surroundings 203
Datong 204
  Sights 205
  Further Sights 208
  Surroundings 206
Diplomatic
  Representation 510
Dragon's Gate Grottoes
  325
Drink 517
Dunhuang 209
  Other Sights 213
  Surroundings 210

East Lake 448
Economic situation 55
Economy 54
Education and Science 40
Electricity 511
Emergency Services 511
Environmental problems 33
Events 511

Facts and Figures 9
Famous People 74
Festivals 515
Flora and Fauna 30
Food 104
Food and Drink 515
Foreign Representation in
  China 510
Foshan 214
  Sights 215
Fujian 215
Fushun 216
  Surroundings 217
Fuzhou 218
  Sights 219
  Surroundings 220

Gansu 221
  Sights 222
General Information 9
Getting to China 520
Giant Panda 34
Glossary of Food and
  Drink 518
Golden Rules for Travel in
  China 574
Great Wall 223
Guangdong 225
Guangxi 226
Guangzhou 159
Guilin 228
  Sights 231
  Surroundings 233
Guiyang 233
  Sights and
    surroundings 235
Guizhou 236

Haikou 237
  Sights and
    surroundings 237
Hainan 238
Handan 239
  Sights and
    surroundings 240
Hangzhou 240
  Other Sights 246
  Surroundings 248
  West Lake 241
Harbin 249
  Sights 250
  Surroundings 252
Health Precautions 522
Hebei 253
Hefei 254
  Sights 255

Index

Heilongjiang 256
Henan 257
Hengyang 258
  Surroundings 259
History 61
Hohhot 259
  Sights 260
  Surroundings 261
Hong Kong 263
  Happy Valley 271
  Hong Kong Island 268
  Kowloon 272
  Mong Kok 273
  New Territories 273
  Sha Tin 273
  The islands of Lantau,
    Chek Lap Kok, Cheung
    Chau and Peng
    Chau 275
  Victoria 269
  Wan Chai 270
Hotels 523
Huai'an 276
  Sights and
    surroundings 276
Hubei 276
Hunan 278
Huzhou 279

Imperial Dynasties and
  Capitals 66
Industry 57
Information 538
Inner Mongolia 279
Insurance 542

Jiangsu 282
Jiangxi 283
Jiaxing 284
  Surroundings 285
Jilin 285, 286
  Sights and
    surroundings 286
Ji'nan 290
  Surroundings 291
Jingdezhen 292
  Surroundings 293
Jinggangshan 293
  Surroundings 294
Jinghong 294
  Surroundings 295
Jinhua 295
  Sights and
    surroundings 296
Jiujiang 296
  Sights and
    surroundings 298
Jiuquan 300

Kaifeng 301
  Sights 302

Kashgar 304
  Sights and
    surroundings 308
Kumbum Monastery 478
Kunming 308
  Sights 309
  Surroundings 310

Lake Dianchi 310
Lake Dongtinghu 490
Lake Taihu 455
Lakes and rivers 19
Lanzhou 315
  Sights and
    surroundings 316
Leshan 189
Lhasa 317
  Sights 318
  Surroundings 319
Lianyungang 320
Liaoning 321
Lijiang River 233
Literature 98
Liuzhou 323
  Surroundings 324
Lunan Stone Forest 314
Luoyang 324
  Sights 325
  Surroundings 325
  Other places of interest in
    the surrounding
    area 327
Lüshun (Port Arthur) 203

Ma'anshan 329
Macau 330
  Macau Peninsula 333
  Taipa and Coloane 336
Maotai 336
  Sights 337
Maps 548
Medical Assistance 548
Mogao Ku Caves 210
Motoring 549
Mount Dinghushan 493
Mount Emeishan 189
Mount Everest 478
Mount Hengshan 209, 259
Mount Hongshan 448
Mount Huashan 472
Mount Lishan 468
Mount Lushan 298
Mount Panshan 432
Mount Taishan 407
Mount Wudangshan 474
Mount Wutaishan 427
Mount Wuyishan 220
Mountain of the Nine
  Blossoms 450
Mountaineering and
  Trekking 549
Museums 550

Nanchang 337
Nanjing · Nanking 340
  Surroundings 346
Nanning 346
  Sights and
    surroundings 347
Nantong 347
  Sights and
    surroundings 351
Newspapers and
  Periodicals 550
Ningbo 351
Ningxia 353
Nishan Mountain 368

Official Public Holidays 552
Open Cities 551
Opening Times 551
Opera 102

Painting 84
Photography 551
Pool of Black Dragon 312
Population 36
Post 551
Pottery 90
Practical Information from
  A to Z 500
Public Holidays and
  Festivals 552
Public Transport (local) 553

Qingdao 354
  Sights 355
  Surroundings 358
Qinghai 359
Qinhuangdao 360
  Sights 361
Quanzhou 362
  Sights 362
  Surroundings 364
Qufu 365
  Sights 365
  Surroundings 368

Radio and Television 556
Railways 556
Regional Cuisine 516
Religion and Philosophy 42
Religious teachings 43
Restaurants 557
Rickshaws 561
River Boats 562

Sanya 370
Security 562
Shaanxi 371
Shandong 373
Shanghai 374
  Sights 375
  Surroundings 380

Shantou 383
Shanxi 383
Shaolin Monastery 328
Shaoxing 384
    Sights and
        surroundings 385
Shashi 386
    Sights 386
    Surroundings 387
Shenyang 387
    Sights 390
    Surroundings 391
Shenzhen 392
Shigatse 475
Shijiazhuang 393
    Sights and
        surroundings 394
Shipping and River
    Boats 562
Shopping and
    Souvenirs 563
Shopping in China's major
    cities 562
Silk Road 117
Sichuan 397
Social Customs 566
Songshan Mountain 328
Souvenirs 566
Sport 566
State and Administration
    49
Suggested Routes 110
    1. From Beijing to Hohhot
        via Taiyuan and
        Datong 110
    2. From Beijing to Qufu
        via Tianjin, Jinan and
        Tai'an (Taishan) 112
    3. From Beijing to Xi'an
        via Anyang, Zhengzhou,
        Songshan, Kaifeng and
        Luoyang 112
    4. From Chengdu to
        Wuhan via Emei (and
        the Emeishan) and
        Chongqing (through the
        Changjiang gorge) 113
    5. From Nanjing to
        Shanghai via the Grand
        Canal, Wuxi, Suzhou
        and Hangzhou 114
    6. From Beijing to
        Qingdao via Shenyang
        (Mukden), Changchun,
        Harbin, Dalian (Port
        Arthur) and Yantai 115

    7. From Canton to
        Kunming via Guilin and
        beyond into the
        Autonomous Region of
        Xishuangbanna 116
    8. Tibet 116
    Along the Silk Road from
        Lanzhou to Kashgar via
        Dunhuang, Turpan and
        Ürümqi 117
Suzhou 398
    Further Sights 402
    Surroundings 403
    The Gardens 399

Table Etiquette 105
Tai'an 404
Taipei 413
    Close surroundings 416
    More distant
        surroundings 417
    Other places to visit 418
Taiwan 408
Taiwanese Islands of
    Penghu, Lan Yu and Lu
    Tao 423
Taiyuan 423
    Sights and
        surroundings 425
Taxis 567
Telephone 568
Three Gorges of Changjiang
    River 170
Tianjin 428
    Sights 429
    Surroundings 432
Tibet · Xijang 432
Time 568
Tipping 568
Topography 11
Traditional Festivals 552
Travel Documents 569
Trekking 569
Turpan 437
    Sights and
        surroundings 438

Ürümqi 439
    Sights and
        surroundings 442

Weifang 442
Weihai 443
Wenzhou 443
    Sights and
        surroundings 444

When to Go 569
Wuhan 444
    Sights 445
    Surroundings 449
Wuhu 450
Wuxi 454
    Sights and
        surroundings 455

Xiamen 458
    Sights 459
Xi'an 461
    Other Places of Interest in
        the surroundings 471
    Sights 464
    Surroundings 467
    Terracotta Army 469
Xiangfan 473
    Surroundings 474
Xigaze · Shigatse 475
    Surroundings 476
Xining 478
Xinjiang 480
Xuzhou 482
    Surroundings 483

Yan'an 483
Yangzhou 484
    Surroundings 486
Yantai 487
Yellow Mountain 451
Yichang 487
    Surroundings 488
Yinchuan 488
    Surroundings 489
Yixing 489
    Surroundings 489
Youth Accommodation 570
Yueyang 490
    Surroundings 491
Yungang Shiku Caves 206
Yunnan 491

Zhanjiang 493
Zhaoqing 493
Zhejiang 494
Zhengzhou 495
    Sights 496
    Surroundings 497
Zhenjiang 497
    Sights 498
Zhuhai 498
    Sights 499
Zibo 499

Golden Rules for Travel in China

- Never go out without your *Baedeker*.

- Keep luggage to a minimum.
  Only take clothes that are practical and hardwearing.

- Double your amount of spending money to be on the safe side.

- Carry a well-stocked medical kit. Check on weather conditions and current health requirements as well as potential health hazards before you leave.

- Do not carry drugs under any circumstances.
  You could end up in prison or even facing the death penalty.

- Carry all films, whether exposed or not, in your hand luggage.
  Whatever you are told to the contrary, the effects of scanning your luggage with X-rays can damage film.

- Allow plenty of time to cater for last-minute surprises.
  Making a scene will not help, so be patient.

- Never drink water from the tap; always use boiled water from the flasks provided to clean your teeth.
  Do not eat raw food, fresh fruit or any form of ice.

- Remember that China is not actively seeking tourists but accepts them because they bring in much needed currency.

- Make sure you always have a supply of small change in the local money as well as some hard currency in small amounts. This will avoid having to change a large sum unnecessarily.

- Avoid being cheated by agreeing on the taxi or rickshaw fare before you set out.

- If you have to cancel a flight do so well before it is due to leave; otherwise you risk being unable to claim a refund.

- Remember you are a guest in someone else's country, so respect the feelings of your Chinese hosts. Avoid bodily contact, do not take photographs of them without their permission, and wait for them to make the first move.

- Do not wear immodest or provocative clothing.
  Before you enter any holy places take note of what the local people around you are doing. This often means taking off your shoes.

- If you are travelling on business it is especially useful to have visiting cards printed in both Latin script and Chinese characters.

- Take a torch and some spare batteries.

Principal Sights of Tourist Interest

★★	Page	★★	Page
Beijing	124	Ningbo	351
Changsha	173	Qingdao	354
Chengde	179	Qinhuangdao	360
Chengdu	182	Quanzhou	362
Chongqing	191	Qufu	365
Datong	204	Shenyang	387
Dunhuang	209	Shijiazhuang	393
Guilin	228	Suzhou	398
Hangzhou	240	Tai'an	404
Hengyang	258	Taiwan	408
Hong Kong	263	Taiyuan	423
Ji'nan	290	Wuhu	450
Jiujiang	296	Wuxi	454
Kunming	308	Xi'an	461
Lanzhou	315	Xigaze	475
Lhasa	317	Xining	478
Lianyungang	320	Yueyang	490
Luoyang	324	Zhengzhou	495

★	Page	★	Page
Baotou	123	Nanjing	340
Canton	159	Nanning	346
Changchun	167	Nantong	347
Changzhou	176	Sanya	370
Dali	196	Shanghai	374
Dalian	199	Shantou	383
Foshan	214	Shaoxing	384
Fushun	216	Shashi	386
Fuzhou	218	Shenzhen	392
Guiyang	233	Tianjin	428
Haikou	237	Turpan	437
Handan	239	Ürümqi	439
Harbin	249	Weifang	442
Hefei	254	Weihai	443
Hohhot	259	Wenzhou	443
Huai'an	276	Wuhan	444
Huzhou	279	Xiamen	458
Jiaxing	284	Xiangfan	473
Jilin	285	Xuzhou	482
Jingdezhen	292	Yangzhou	484
Jinghong	294	Yantai	487
Jinhua	295	Yichang	487
Juquan	300	Yinchuan	488
Kaifeng	301	Yixing	489
Kashgar	304	Zhanjiang	493
Luizhou	323	Zhaoqing	493
Ma'anshan	329	Zhenjiang	497
Macau	330	Zhuhai	498
Nanchang	337	Zibo	499

Note: The above list includes only the more important places of touristic interest in China which are worth seeing either for themselves or for other attractions in the vicinity. There are a great number of other sights which are designated by one or two asterisks within the text of each entry.

Imprint

161 illustrations, 137 maps, plans and drawings, 1 large map at end of book

Original text "Cina" in Italian (authors: Marina Basso, Renzo Cavalieri, Alberto Farina, Yuan Huaqing, Laura Orsenigo) from the series "Guide De Agostini-Baedeker" (Istituto Geografico De Agostini, Novara)

German translation: Dr Susanna Kolb

Additional text: Vera Beck (Practical Information from A to Z); Prof. Dr Wolfgang Hassenpflug (climate); Manfred Strobel (natural regions)

Editorial work (German edition): Carmen Galenschovski

Editorial work (English language edition): Margaret Court, Crispin Warren

General direction (German edition): Dr Peter Baumgarten, Baedeker Stuttgart; (English edition): Alec Court

Cartography: Istituto Geografico De Agostini, Novara; Gert Oberländer, Munich; Ingenierbüro für Kartographie Harms, Erlenbach bei Kandel/Pfalz; Archiv für Flaggenkunde Ralf Stelter, Hattingen

Source of Illustrations: Air China (1); Archivio Istituto Geografico De Agostini (103); Bulloz (2); Direcção dos Serviços de Turismo, Macau (1); Gstaltmayr (2); Lade (6); Interchange (4); Janicke (1); Lonati (1); Lotti (1); Müller Kai Ulrich (30); Paireault (1); Schuster (5); Staatliche Museen zu Berlin-Preussicher Kulturbesitz (1); Ullstein Bilderdienst (2)

English translation: David Cocking, Brenda Ferris, Paul Fletcher, Jennifer Wagner, Crispin Warren

Revised text: Wendy Bell

2nd English edition 1996

© Baedeker Stuttgart
Original German edition 1996

© 1996 Jarrold and Sons Limited
English language edition worldwide

© 1996 The Automobile Association
United Kingdom and Ireland

Published in the United States by:
Macmillan Travel
A Simon & Schuster Macmillan Company
1633 Broadway
New York, NY 10019–6785

Macmillan is a registered trademark of Macmillan, Inc.

Distributed in the United Kingdom by the Publishing Division of the Automobile Association, Fanum House, Basingstoke, Hampshire RG21 2EA

Licensed user:
Mairs Geographischer Verlag GmbH & Co.,
Ostfildern-Kemnat bei Stuttgart

Printed in Italy by G. Canale & C.S.p.A – Borgaro T.se –Turin

ISBN 0–02–861365–1 USA and Canada
      0 7495 1397 7 UK